Western Civilization

A Concise History

COMBINED EDITION

From Early Societies
to the Present

Western Civilization

A Concise History

COMBINED EDITION

From Early Societies
to the Present

Glenn Blackburn

Clinch Valley College of the University of Virginia

St. Martin's Press
New York

To the many colleagues
and students
at Clinch Valley College
of the University of Virginia
who helped make this work possible.

Senior editor: Don Reisman
Development editor: Bruce Glassman
Project editor: Elise Bauman
Production supervisor: Alan Fischer
Text design: Leon Bolognese & Associates, Inc.
Graphics: G&H Soho, Inc., Dolores Bego
Photo researcher: Tara Dooley
Cover design: Jeanette Jacobs Design
Cover photo: Lithograph of a printing press. England, 19th century.

Library of Congress Catalog Card Number: 89-63885

Manufactured in the United States of America.
54321
fedcba

For information, write:
St. Martin's Press, Inc.
175 Fifth Avenue
New York, NY 10010

ISBN: 0-312-04239-6

ACKNOWLEDGMENTS

Page 200, from *The Complete Poems of Thomas Hardy,* edited by James Gibson (New
York: Macmillan, 1978).
Page 478, reprinted with permission of Macmillan Publishing Company from *The Poems
of W. B. Yeats: A New Edition,* edited by Richard J. Finneran. Copyright 1924 by Macmillan Publishing Company, renewed 1952 by Bertha Georgie Yeats.
Page 497, *W. H. Auden, Collected Poems,* edited by Edward Mendelson. Copyright 1940
and renewed 1968 by W. H. Auden. Reprinted by permission of Random House, Inc.

Preface

In *Western Civilization: A Concise History*, I attempt to present the text in ways that are appealing and useful to both instructors and students. First, I strive to tell the story of Western Civilization *concisely*. Second, I integrate many themes into Western history that allow examination of Western Civilization in a global context. Third, analyses of Western technology appear throughout the text in an effort to demonstrate its powerful influence on the course of Western history. Finally, I emphasize the impact of religious beliefs and philosophical ideas on both Western and "non-Western" history.

A concise text can be valuable to both instructors and students because it presents the major themes and basic facts of Western history without overwhelming the student. Highly detailed texts often tempt students to perceive the study of history as an exercise in memorization of data, whereas a concise text encourages students to concentrate on the most important themes and facts. To be more precise, a concise text allows instructors to teach Western history in one semester or one quarter, since the major themes of that history are crisply presented. For two-semester courses (using either the two-volume edition or the combined edition), a concise text is short enough to allow instructors the opportunity to develop other assignments for students—supplementary readings from other sources or library work, for example—while using the text as the core reading.

Integration of non-Western influences on Western history allows discussion of several important topics, such as the beliefs and impact of the major world religions and an understanding of the various technologies that the West has adopted from other civilizations. Another significant question, why the West eventually became wealthier and more powerful than other societies and civilizations, is analyzed in some detail in Chapter 14.

The influence of technology on Western history is demonstrated both in the primary text and, more specifically, in the **Technology boxes** that are included in most chapters. These special illustrated sections contain discussions of new technologies that became important in a particular period and integrate the prevailing attitudes that encouraged the interest in, and the development of, technology. Examples of technologies discussed include the development of irrigation, the Indian (Arabic) numeral system, new types of plows, the windmill, gunpowder, the printing press, the log cabin, the railroad, the steam engine, and modern military weapons.

The study of religious beliefs and philosophical ideas is intrinsically important to the text, for it is through religion and philosophy that humans define and express their understanding of their world. The text frequently turns to discussion of religious and philosophical trends throughout history because these themes often reveal the most fundamental desires and goals of people.

In addition, *Western Civilization: A Concise History* includes **timelines** that serve to introduce each chapter, numerous **maps** and **illustrations,** and an *Instructor's Manual.*

ACKNOWLEDGMENTS

In preparing the manuscript, I received assistance and encouragement from many people and institutions. I learned a great deal during my twenty years of teaching, from my students and colleagues at Clinch Valley College of the University of Virginia, and particularly from the members of the Department of History and Philosophy: Stanley Willis, E. L. Henson, William F. Maxwell, David Rouse, and Robert Dise. The library staffs of Clinch Valley College and Wake Forest University were especially helpful, as was Professor George Munro of Virginia Commonwealth University. Always resourceful were the able people at St. Martin's Press, including Don Reisman, Bruce Glassman, and Elise Bauman. I am also grateful to those colleagues who reviewed the various drafts of this manuscript and offered me their valuable insights in shaping the text: Douglas D. Alder, Dixie College; Erving E. Beauregard, University of Dayton; Gerald P. Bodet, University of New Orleans; Werner Braatz, University of Wisconsin, Oshkosh; Edward A. Cole, Grand Valley State College; Patrick Foley, Tarrant County Junior College; Richard M. Golden, Clemson University; Louise E. Hoffman, Penn State University, Harrisburg; Jerry A. Pattengale, Azusa Pacific University; William C. Reynolds, Mercer County Community College; Barry Rothaus, University of Northern Colorado; Thomas Turley, Santa Clara University; and Charles W. Webber, Wheaton College.

Finally, my wife, Jere, and my mother, Margaret Blackburn, were very supportive and patient during the years in which I was writing this text. I thank them both.

Glenn Blackburn
Wise, Virginia

To the Student

Cynics sometimes say that history is "one damn thing after another," the implication being that history is just a chronicle of facts. But history is much more than a series of facts. Most historians try to present facts as part of an interpretation in which events fit together in an overall pattern. In this way, historians seek to make sense of the past, to find some coherence in historical events.

This book emphasizes the impact of science and technology on Western Civilization. Science—the attempt to understand the natural world—and technology—the development of tools to manipulate the natural world for human use—have been developed by many societies and civilizations but have been particularly prominent in Western Civilization. This prominence is well illustrated by two mythical stories. One is the story of Prometheus, a deity in ancient Greek mythology who stole fire, a symbol of creativity, from the gods and gave it to humans. In doing this, Prometheus became a symbol embodying the human ability to create. The second is the story of a sixteenth-century German astrologer named Faust, who according to legend sold his soul to the devil in exchange for forbidden knowledge. Thus, both Faust and Prometheus symbolize the human quest for knowledge and power as well as the human willingness to suffer in order to attain knowledge. Historians and others sometimes refer to Western Civilization as "Promethean" or "Faustian," meaning that the West was particularly driven to use science and technology to understand and manipulate nature for human purposes.

The first eleven chapters of this book (Vol. 1 of the two-volume edition) tell the story of Western Civilization from our prehistoric ancestors to the seventeenth century A.D. The Western desire to understand nature began in prehistoric times, but it first became clearly defined by the ancient Hebrews and ancient Greeks. The Hebrews created a unique religion (the source of Christianity, in particular) in which God was considered to be *transcendent*, a spirit separate from nature. This notion of a transcendent God implied that nature is an inanimate thing that could and should be used by humans. The Greeks contributed the idea that the universe is a rational place governed by orderly laws that are comprehensible to humans. These two concepts—the Hebrew idea of a transcendent God and the Greek idea of a rational universe—eventually became the theoretical underpinning of what we call modern science.

The Hebrew-Greek influence was passed on to the Romans who, in turn, passed it on to the Germans—people who settled in Europe and were the ancestors of modern Europeans and many North Americans. During the early Middle Ages (A.D. 500–1000), the Germanic peoples created a powerful technological tradition. They developed new farming techniques, windmills, and watermills as sources of nonhuman energy. Certainly peoples in other places also developed new tools and technologies, but by the end of the Middle Ages it was the Europeans who were particularly innovative.

Chapters 12 through 22 of this book (Vol. 2 of the two-volume edition) cover the period from the seventeenth century to the present. During this time, science and technology began to support each other. Science in the form of astronomy, for example, helped create the knowledge and navigational expertise that allowed European sailors to find the sea routes to North and South America and to Asia. Technology in the form of telescopes helped astronomers to peer into the heavens and in the process initiate a scientific revolution. By the eighteenth century, science and technology, in addition to certain political and social developments, helped to produce an industrial revolution. The Industrial Revolution, a new way of producing goods, slowly made Western Civilization wealthier and more powerful than any other civilization on earth. In the nineteenth century, Western Civilization dominated the world. By the twentieth century, that domination began to dissipate, as many Western nations became embroiled in wars that weakened European power. Furthermore, the use of technology began to have many undesirable consequences, such as the despoliation of the environment.

It should already be obvious, from the preceding paragraphs, that science and technology are central elements in the story of Western Civilization. Certainly, other things—political developments, intellectual and artistic achievements, the lives of the common people—are also important, and they are studied in this book as well. But particular emphasis is given to the role of science and technology, for that role is a unique aspect of Western history.

Contents

List of Maps

Western Civilization

A Concise History

COMBINED EDITION

From Early Societies
to the Present

1

The Beginning of the Human Story to 800 B.C.

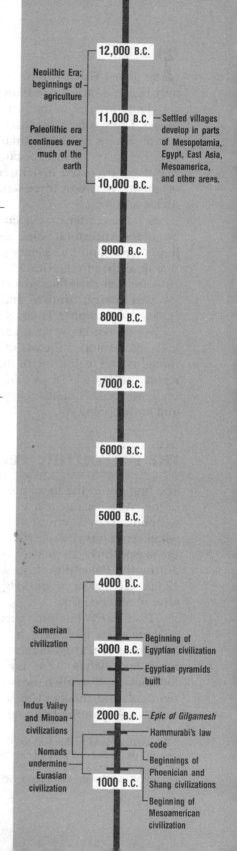

12,000 B.C.

Neolithic Era; beginnings of agriculture

11,000 B.C. — Settled villages develop in parts of Mesopotamia, Egypt, East Asia, Mesoamerica, and other areas.

Paleolithic era continues over much of the earth

10,000 B.C.

9000 B.C.

8000 B.C.

7000 B.C.

6000 B.C.

5000 B.C.

4000 B.C.

Sumerian civilization

Beginning of
3000 B.C. Egyptian civilization

Egyptian pyramids built

Indus Valley and Minoan civilizations

2000 B.C. — *Epic of Gilgamesh*

Hammurabi's law code

Nomads undermine Eurasian civilization

Beginnings of Phoenician and
1000 B.C. Shang civilizations

Beginning of Mesoamerican civilization

The planet Earth is four to five billion years old, but the human story only began a little more than one million years ago. A million years is a very long time, of course, but it is only a small part of the history of our planet. There was no precise moment at which humans first appeared, for our ancestors evolved human characteristics slowly (such as standing upright) and gradually "became" human. The drama of becoming human may have occurred first in east Africa, but it is possible that humans originated in two or three separate places across the wide tropical belt in Africa and Asia.

Scholars differ on the question of whether life was easy or hard for our oldest ancestors. Some argue that early humans "worked" only a few hours a day and had plenty of leisure time, that life was somewhat like that described in the Garden of Eden story in the Old Testament. Others contend that early humans endured a violent struggle for survival, that life was "nasty, brutish, and short" in the words of the seventeenth-century philosopher Thomas Hobbes.

We do not know what early humans thought about their lives. They had not developed the art of writing and could not communicate their thoughts and feelings with the written word to people of later ages. As a result, our knowledge of early history is fragmentary and inexact, based on fossil records painstakingly gathered and analyzed by archaeologists and anthropologists.

THE PALEOLITHIC ERA

The first era in the human story is known as the *Paleolithic Era* or "Old Stone" Age because early humans used chipped stones for tools and weapons. They survived at first by gathering food and scavenging for whatever plants or animals could be eaten raw. Most people died before the age of thirty, so they produced relatively few children. Consequently, during the Paleolithic Era, which lasted over a million years, down to 12,000–10,000 B.C.),* probably no more than half a million humans were alive at any one time.

That early humans survived at all was due in part to certain advantageous biological traits. They had large, well-developed brains and, therefore, great mental capacity. They could walk upright, so their arms and hands were not brawny instruments used primarily for locomotion. Instead, hands became nimble tools capable of grasping and manipulating things. The brain and the hands gradually became co-workers—what the brain could conceive (a stone turned into a tool, for

---

*The method used in this text for dating years is based on a Christian system that centers around the presumed date of the birth of Jesus Christ. Those years before his birth are designated as B.C. ("before Christ"); those years after Christ's birth are designated as A.D. (from the Latin *anno Domini,* or "in the year of the Lord").

example) the hands could make. Another biological advantage was a special kind of vision: the eyes of early humans were capable of seeing in color and in three dimensions. Humans also had a well-developed larynx, which made them capable of developing speech and language.

These biological traits were typical of all humans, regardless of differences in body appearance or skin color. Racial differentiation occurred as humans developed genetic differences and adapted to different environments around the world. (Differences in skin color, for example, evolved to protect the skin against different intensities of sunlight. Since sunlight intensity is greatest in tropical areas, darker skin colors evolved to protect the body by filtering out some of the sun's rays. Lighter skin colors prevailed in colder climates where sun rays are less intense.) Eventually, different racial groups became associated with particular parts of the world—the Caucasoid in Europe and the Middle East, the Negroid in sub-Saharan Africa, the Australoid in Australia and Southeast Asia, and the Mongoloid in East Asia and the Americas.

In addition to biological advantages, early humans survived because of their ability to adapt culturally. One important aspect of this cultural adaptation was social cooperation. Early humans lived together in groups, or tribes, which protected them from danger and enabled them to gather food more efficiently. These tribal groups were composed of several dozen interrelated people and were egalitarian in nature, with men and women working together and participating in making important decisions. The tribes were also nomadic, constantly on the move in search of food.

Another aspect that made these tribes culturally adaptive was their development of language. No one knows exactly when or how language evolved, but the development of linguistic ability during Paleolithic times greatly expanded human capacities. For example, language allowed small groups of men to cooperate in hunting large animals, thus enabling them to become hunters as well as gatherers.

Hunting brought a degree of specialization to Paleolithic society. Mature men tended to concentrate on the hunt, while women stayed at the camp to care for the children, to collect berries and wild fruits, and to keep the home fires burning. Some scholars believe that the development of hunting may have destroyed Paleolithic egalitarianism by leading to male dominance over women. Others argue that, since hunting was only occasionally successful, women remained equal to men because they were the more reliable providers of food.

Human Thought and Religion during the Paleolithic Era

The development of language was one of the most important episodes of the Paleolithic Era, not only because it made hunting easier but also

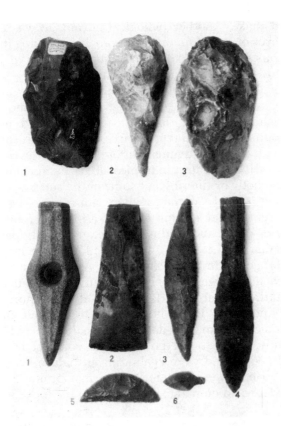

Paleolithic and Neolithic Tools   The ability to make tools was one of the most distinctive traits of early humans. Paleolithic tools *(top)* were made by striking flakes off a small stone to give it an edge. Neolithic tools *(bottom),* more finely ground or polished stones, were used in farming communities. (American Museum of Natural History)

because it revealed the fundamental source of human strength—the ability to think. Words, after all, are simply sounds that express externally the concepts or feelings we have inside ourselves. Early humans were "thinkers," seeking to understand the world in which they lived. In particular, they sought to understand the sources of important natural events, such as rain, heat, and sunlight.

Paleolithic religion was *animistic,* meaning that early humans believed that all natural objects had souls or spirits within them. With no source of knowledge but their own experiences, early humans tended to compare everything to themselves. They knew that they were alive and also that nature was full of life, that plants grew, rivers flowed, and animals searched for food. From this they concluded that all things in the world were to some degree alike and shared a common existence. Thus they attributed their own inner feelings or "souls" to other things in the world. Just as a person did something because he wanted to, so the river flowed because it wanted to and the cloud gave rain because it wanted to.

For early humans, nature and humanity were not separate; rather, they were together a reality akin to human life. Since nature was alive, any natural event was seen as a form of intentional action (the river wanted to flow) and any accounting of a natural event was told in the form of a story or myth. The myths of early humans described dramatic actions and explained events in nature. A typical myth, for example, would explain the creation of the world by comparing it to human birth. A primeval couple—the earth and sky—would be portrayed as parents of all that exists. Myths explained such things as how the world originated, who controlled it, and how the world operated. Thus, early humans were engaged in an early form of *cosmology*, a study of the structure and nature of the universe.

The early human's animistic conception of nature gradually developed into a religion of *polytheism*—a belief in many gods—in which the sun, the rain, the soil, and other things important to humans were deified (worshipped as gods). These gods, or spirits, were not considered omnipotent; rather, each had power only in a particular sphere. Thus the rain-god controlled rain and the sun-god controlled the sun. Further, the gods were presumed to have power only in the area occupied by a tribal group, for different tribes had different gods.

Early humans believed that they could influence these gods of nature. Assuming that anything that affects a person is real, ancient peoples made no distinction between what we call subjective processes—dreams and ideas, for example—and external realities. They assumed that what was in the mind was just as real as any physical reality. Thus, they came to believe that by acting out what was in the mind they could influence the course of natural events. When they wanted rain, they acted out this idea through a rain dance, communicating their wishes to the rain-god. Often, these rituals seemed to provide the desired consequences. The ritual to encourage the return of warm weather, usually performed at the end of a cold winter, for example, appeared, rather consistently, to cause spring weather to soon follow. After this happened for several years, it became an accepted fact that the ritual had to be performed to help ensure the coming of spring. Early humans were not foolish enough to think that they alone controlled the forces of nature. They knew that some other force controlled the sequence of the seasons and that their rituals alone did not produce the arrival of spring. Correct performance of the rituals, they believed, was only one of the factors necessary to produce the desired result.

Obviously, the commonly held beliefs and religion of our ancient ancestors were different from those of the modern day. In fact, it is easy to contrast primitive animistic thought with modern scientific thought and imply that Paleolithic humans were ignorant and childish. But this limited view denigrates our ancestors. Given the extent of their knowledge and experiences, animistic religion was a logical and reasonable response to the world in which they lived. After all, if one assumes that nature is alive in the same way as humans, then it is reasonable to conclude that natural objects have spirits or gods within them. Paleolithic religion reveals that people were capable of thinking logically, reasoning coherently from one thought to another.

The Last Millennia of the Paleolithic Era

The Paleolithic Era was the longest period in human history. During this time tribes migrated over much of the earth. They crossed into the Americas by way of a land bridge from Asia to present-day Alaska. They learned how to make tools, how to speak, how to live together in social groups, how to dance and create music (in rituals), and how to draw (cave art). Most of this learning occurred slowly over thousands of years, but near the end of the Paleolithic Era human development advanced rapidly.

Between 30,000 and 10,000 B.C., a people we call the Cro-Magnon inhabited much of the earth. The Cro-Magnon ate better than their predecessors, in large part because they invented a spearthrower that made hunting more fruitful. As a result, the Cro-Magnon were better nourished and their numbers multiplied. They were also artists of considerable skill, drawing animals on cave walls and decorating some of their dwelling places with tiny statuettes. The Cro-Magnon people were more intelligent and skilled than their ancestors, and were, in a sense, at the pinnacle of Paleolithic achievement.

THE NEOLITHIC ERA

For thousands of years humans lived as nomads, constantly moving to follow the animal herds and to find new sources of food. This nomadic way of life began to change between 12,000–10,000 B.C., the beginnings of the *Neolithic Era* or the "New Stone" Age. The primary characteristics of the Neolithic Era were the creation of more sophisticated tools formed by grinding and polishing stones, the discovery of agriculture, and the transformation of growing numbers of people from hunters into peasant farmers.

Why did the Neolithic revolution occur? One reason was overpopulation in some areas that encouraged searching for new sources of food. Another was a gradually warming climate that made farming more rewarding. The most recent ice ages ended around 10,000 B.C., and the glaciers that melted in North America and Eurasia left more land available for farming. But the change from hunting to farming was a slow process, occurring at different times in different places. In hunting societies, where women usually stayed at the camp while men were on

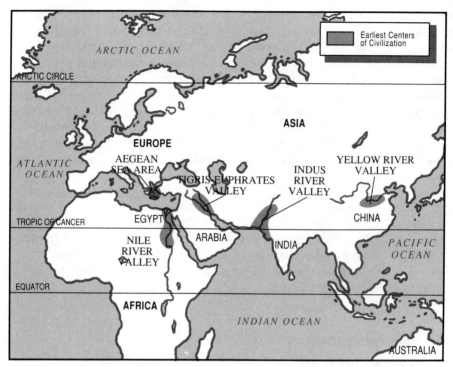

Figure 1.1   The First Civilizations, 3500–1500 B.C.

the hunt, it was probably women who invented agriculture by learning that wild plants could be domesticated and cultivated. As women started to grow small crops, men began to remain at home in order to expand the fields and do the heavy work of plowing and harvesting. Gradually, over dozens of generations, the men in a particular area became farmers instead of hunters, sedentary dwellers instead of nomads.

The discovery of agriculture occurred independently in several areas of the world. It happened first around 12,000–10,000 B.C. in the western end of Asia—between the eastern end of the Mediterranean Sea and the deserts of Central Asia—where some people learned how to grow wheat and barley. By 7000 B.C., yams and rice were being grown in East and Southeast Asia, and beans, potatoes, and corn were cultivated in Mesoamerica (central America and Peru). It wasn't until 2000 B.C., however, that crops were cultivated in sub-Saharan Africa. Agricultural gains were slow there partly because debilitating diseases such as yellow fever and malaria hindered human development, and partly because the drying up of the Sahara desert restricted African communication with the rest of the world.

Life changed dramatically for those who settled in farming villages. Most farmers were less free than hunters, in the sense that they could not move about as they pleased but had to remain near their land. Also, in contrast to hunting societies which had little social structure, farming villages were often tightly organized so as to ensure cooperation. A small group of elders usually controlled the important decision making—such as how to plant and how to parcel out land. Farmers lost a certain degree of freedom but gained a slightly improved standard of living. Their food supply from crops was more regular and secure than in the hunting days, and they could build permanent homes. In their homes, they could accumulate items to make life more comfortable: rough pieces of furniture, more tools and cooking utensils, and pottery for cooking and storing grain and beer.

Permanent homes and the accumulation of goods brought some problems, though. Permanent homes meant that human and animal wastes were collected in one area, making diseases and epidemics common in Neolithic villages. Accumulation of goods and food tempted nearby nomads to steal. Organized warfare originated in Neolithic times, as the nomads raided the villages and the villagers formed or supported military forces for protection.

Neolithic Religion

The Neolithic Era also witnessed modified religious beliefs and practices. The primary concern of farmers was ensuring the fertility of the soil. Since they perceived a connection between human fertility and soil fertility, the primary deity in Neolithic religion was usually an earth goddess that symbolized fertility, and the primary rituals were sexual in nature. Some modern scholars contend that the superiority of the feminine principle in Neolithic religion indicates that some Neolithic societies were matriarchal (governed by women); others refute this idea because it has not been proven.

The most common Neolithic religious myth told of a mother goddess who was impregnated each year by a masculine god of vegetation or rain, thereby ensuring the renewed fertility of the soil. The masculine god, which disappeared or died during the winter, was revived in the spring to be reunited with the mother goddess. The farmers often reenacted this separation and reunion of the gods in symbolic dramas, including sexual acts of various kinds performed by sexually active young people. Here was the origin of many sexually oriented rituals in early societies— orgies, sacred prostitution, and the emasculation of men who were to be priests to the goddess. The farmers believed that correct performance of the rituals, as well as their own labor and adequate rainfall, was essential to producing good crops. Thus, those who participated in the rituals were honored.

The Impact of Neolithic Society

The farming way of life gradually came to dominate most human societies during the New Stone Age, as all but a few hunting tribes slowly disappeared. The farming life-style was one of unchanging conservatism; farmers lived in accordance with the enduring rhythms of nature, planting and harvesting the same way at the same time every year. Whatever political, social, or intellectual changes occurred in Neolithic societies were usually accomplished by small, privileged, groups— elites—who lived off the agricultural surplus produced by farmers. This kind of social organization, in which small elite groups controlled large masses of villagers, continued to dominate most human societies until the eighteenth or nineteenth century A.D. At this time, political revolution and industrialization in Europe led to the creation of industrial societies.

THE DEVELOPMENT OF CIVILIZATION

During the fourth millennium (4000 to 3000) B.C., two village societies in areas dominated by river valleys—Mesopotamia and Egypt—evolved into *civilizations*. Other civilizations, also centered in river valleys, developed later in the Indus valley (modern Pakistan), China, Mesoamerica, and around the eastern end of the Mediterranean.

The development of civilization brought a more complex way of life, including the formation of an elaborate political structure. The political leaders of the time were usually priests thought to have influence with the gods. Gradually, the chief priest became recognized as a "king" with political powers. Civilization also meant the growth of cities, the elaboration of formal laws and a system of taxation, the creation of the art of writing, the development of economic specialization, the division of people into social classes based on their economic and political status, the organization of permanent military forces for protection, and the encouragement of the arts and large-scale architecture. Not all of these characteristics were present in every early civilization—writing, for example, had not yet developed in parts of Mesoamerica.

The term *civilization* implies a value judgment, the connotation being that "civilized" peoples are more advanced and somehow superior to noncivilized peoples. In some respects, civilized life was an improvement, for life in farming villages was often harsh (because of crop failure and famine) and dangerous (because of attacks by nomadic robbers). But whether the rise of civilization marked an overall advance or decline in human fortunes remains an interesting question. On the positive side, the early civilizations provided law and order and protection from nomad attacks. They also provided greater economic security, since they were better able than villages to accumulate and store agricultural surpluses as a hedge against famine. Furthermore, economic and artistic opportunities were more abundant in cities, so life for some was more stimulating and colorful. However, early civilizations also introduced large-scale slavery and warfare to the world. Many formerly free farmers were enslaved to support the needs of the governing classes, while others remained technically free but oppressed by heavy taxes. Women lost the equal status they had enjoyed in many Paleolithic and Neolithic societies, for most early civilizations prevented women from participating in public life and relegated them to the home. At the same time, the scope of warfare was enlarged, because early civilizations often sought to conquer more land and because small societies were tempting targets for nomad invaders. Furthermore, more extensive social organization allowed for the creation of larger fighting forces.

"Civilization" was a mixed blessing for those involved, but modern historians regard it as the great breakthrough that triggered the development of written records. These records enable us to know a great deal more about the past and have, in particular, taught us more about the early civilizations of the third and fourth millennia than about Paleolithic and Neolithic societies. One of the first questions that written records help to clarify is: What caused the rise of civilizations?

The answer seems to be that civilization arose from an interaction of several factors, all of them results of human creativity. Population increases required greater agricultural production, so farming societies in some river valleys began to construct irrigation systems to improve soil fertility. Governments gradually evolved to organize the labor forces necessary to enlarge and maintain the irrigation systems. Another factor that contributed to the rise of civilization was new technology. In particular, the plow—originally just a sapling with a sharp point—and the wheeled cart slowly made agriculture more productive, and helped to produce a surplus that could be taxed and used to support an upper class of governing officials. A third element in the creation of civilization was growth of trade, caused in part by the invention of the sail. It was much easier and more efficient to transport goods by water than by pack animals on land, and the resulting increase in commerce created wealth that could be used to construct cities and support governments. Commerce also encouraged interchange of ideas and technologies between different societies and thus facilitated the spread of civilization. Finally, a fourth factor that advanced civilization was the invention of bronze, which was used to fashion weapons for the armies that were formed to protect the new civilizations. These factors, developed slowly over several centuries, reinforced one another and encouraged many farming societies to evolve into civilizations. This evolutionary process occurred first in Mesopotamia.

TECHNOLOGY
The Paradox of Technological Advance

The creation of civilization resulted in part from the development of several new technologies, the most fundamental being irrigation. Little rainfall occurred in Mesopotamia, for example, but irrigation from the Tigris and Euphrates rivers brought moisture and soil-enriching silt to the nearby lands. Irrigation created problems, however. A major problem was caused by silt, which kept clogging up the irrigation canals. To battle this, gangs of slaves had to be continually employed in clearing the canals.

Civilization lasted in Mesopotamia as long as the canals could be kept relatively free of silt, but after several thousand years of irrigating, the canals were so clogged that large-scale civilization gradually disappeared from the area and the desert sands slowly covered the ruins of old cities. The creation of civilization is, therefore, an early example of how technology can lead to great human achievement but also despoil the natural environment, in many ways cancelling out the gains of the same achievement.

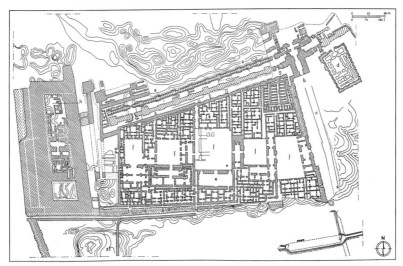

Plan of the Southern Fortress at Babylon, alongside the Euphrates River   *The layout is typical of early cities in Mesopotamia. City walls and a fortress* (left) *protected the royal palace, the temples, and the residences of the most powerful people. Outside the city were the farmlands, irrigation canals, and huts of farmers. (The Granger Collection)*

Mesopotamian Civilizations

Mesopotamia means "between two rivers," and it carries that name because it is the land between the Tigris and Euphrates rivers, which both flow into the Persian Gulf. For centuries Mesopotamia had been a site of human settlement, since it contained fertile land and was in the middle of a huge plains area that nomads regularly crossed. By the fourth millennium B.C., the farming villages in the area came under the domination of a people known as the *Sumerians* (named after their city, Sumer). The Sumerians probably came from present-day Iran or southern Russia to conquer the native Mesopotamian peoples, and the first civilization arose out of the political and social interchange between these conquerors and their new subjects.

Sumerian civilization evolved slowly as a result of many of the economic factors previously mentioned: the need to organize people to build irrigation systems and growing urbanization and trade. The leaders of this "civilizing" effort were probably the Sumerian priests, who were thought to represent divine will. Consequently, the first government was a *theocracy*—government by the gods or by representatives of the gods. This early priest-run government gradually turned into a *monarchy*, and by the late fourth millennium kings embodied divine power and were governing Sumer. The first fully developed civilization was in place.

The Sumerians were never able to form a fully centralized government. Their civilization consisted of a collection of semi-independent city-states scattered around Mesopotamia. These city-states, each dominated by a monarch, had populations of less than fifty thousand and contained masses of peasant huts centered around a few large religious shrines and royal palaces. (Peasants were farmers of low social status.) Outside the city walls were the fields where the peasants grew beans, peas, dates, and especially barley, which they ate as bread and drank as beer. Most of the fields were temple lands, believed to be owned by the gods, so the peasants were considered to be serfs or servants of the gods. In reality, they were controlled by the priests.

The Sumerians were extraordinarily creative. They were the first to accomplish the political breakthrough of forming a government based on laws and administration rather than on kinship ties. They also developed a mathematical system to keep commercial accounts and used early astronomical data to keep a calendar. The Sumerians invented a writing system to record government actions and to glorify human deeds and beliefs in literature. Writing was done in the cuneiform system (*cuneus* means wedge), in which symbols composed of various combinations of wedge shapes represented different objects or ideas. They built the first schools in an effort to pass these skills on to later generations. They also held the first political congress, around 3000 B.C. On that occasion, a monarch called some of the upper-class citizens to an assembly to

Winged Lion   From an Assyrian royal palace of the ninth century B.C., this statue of
a winged lion represents the Assyrians' admiration of masculine military prowess
and suggests a sense of power and sternness. (Metropolitan Museum of Art, NY)

consider a question of war and peace, thus marking a first in the history
of political representation.

Despite their creativity, though, the Sumerians were not an optimistic people. The Tigris and Euphrates rivers often flooded at irregular

intervals and destroyed their crops. The Mesopotamian climate was harsh, with extreme heat and dust storms from the desert in the summer months and extreme cold from the northern mountains in the winter. Occasionally, torrential rains turned the entire area into a mud sea. It was during these times that the Sumerians developed a strong sense of human weakness and frailty and tended to assume that the gods were cruel and capricious.

The Sumerians conceived of their gods as being human-like in form but immortal and with superhuman qualities. The gods personified the various powers of nature and, since nature was harsh, the gods were believed to be harsh. For example, the god Enlil represented the essence of storms, as is expressed in the following ancient verse.

> Enlil called the storm.
>   The people mourn.
> Exhilarating winds he took from the land.
>   The people mourn.
> Good winds he took away from Sumer.
>   The people mourn.
> He summoned evil winds.
>   The people mourn.[1]

Even though they were cruel, the gods were the source of life. The god Enki personified the power of water that was the source of life in the desert. His actions are celebrated in the following words.

> To clear the pure mouths of the Tigris and Euphrates, to make
>   verdure plentiful,
> Make dense the clouds, grant water in abundance to all
>   ploughlands,
> To make corn lift its head in furrows and to make pasture
>   abundant in the desert,
> To make young saplings in plantations and in orchards sprout.[2]

The gods had absolute control over the universe and human beings. (The world as the Sumerians knew it was quite small, extending only from modern Armenia in the north to the Persian Gulf in the south and from Iran in the east to the Mediterranean in the west.) The Sumerians believed that they were servants to the gods in life and at death descended to a dark, shadowy world of spirits. They sometimes wished wistfully that life could be better. Like other peoples, they had a myth about a Golden Age in their past.

> Once upon a time, there was no snake, there was no scorpion,
> There was no hyena, there was no lion,

There was no wild dog, no wolf,
There was no fear, no terror,
Man had no rival.³

But they knew better than to expect a Golden Age in reality, particularly in an area so susceptible to bad weather and nomad attacks from without.

It was probably nomad invasions that eventually destroyed the Sumerians. Late in the third millennium B.C., the Akkadians, led by their great king Sargon I, conquered all of southern Mesopotamia. The Akkadian Empire lasted from approximately 2360 to 2180 B.C., when it was destroyed by another wave of invaders. Soon thereafter, a people known as the Babylonians established a new empire in Mesopotamia that lasted about four hundred years.

The Babylonian Empire produced at least one great monarch, Hammurabi, who ruled from 1792 to 1750 B.C. Hammurabi's reign revealed a new human awareness—that people were more than just the playthings of the gods, as the Sumerians had believed. The instrument of this new awareness was Hammurabi's law code, which implied that people were entitled to justice as a right rather than as a favor from the gods. Previously, justice was conceived as being whatever the gods deemed it to be. Although Hammurabi's code still portrayed laws as being received from the gods, it was based on the principle of "an eye for an eye, and a tooth for a tooth." The code defined justice as a system of standardized rules that provided a degree of fair treatment to people. Fairness, of course, was most readily available to the upper classes; slaves were always punished more harshly than nobles, and women were regarded as legally inferior to men, although widows had certain specified rights.

Another Mesopotamian example of the increased awareness humans had of themselves as independent of the gods is illustrated in the *Epic of Gilgamesh*. An *epic* is a long poem usually about great heroes in a peoples' past. Epics were often memorized, recomposed, and recited orally by bards for several generations before they were written down. The *Epic of Gilgamesh*, originating in Sumerian culture, was written in its final form sometime around 2000 B.C. The story of a heroic human figure, Gilgamesh, and his adventures, the poem is unlike others of its time because it does not focus on the gods. Rather, it focuses on emotional and spiritual questions important to people, such as the need for friendship, the love of adventure, and the fear of death.

The *Epic of Gilgamesh* is one of the last great creations of the first wave of civilization in Mesopotamia. Sumerian culture was the basis of Mesopotamian life for more than a thousand years (including the times of the Akkadian and Babylonian empires), but it died out during the first half of the second millennium B.C. The first Babylonian Empire also died when, around 1595 B.C., another wave of invaders—the Kassites— overran Mesopotamia.

Egyptian Civilization

Ancient Egypt was dominated by the Nile River. Unlike the unpredictable rivers in Mesopotamia, the Nile flooded at regular intervals and brought soil-enriching silt to the land alongside the river. Thus was created in the midst of a desert a green belt of fertile land from five to twelve miles wide, the demarcation between the two being so sharp that in some places a person could stand with one foot in the desert and the other on cultivated soil. It is no wonder that the Egyptians sang hymns to the river: "Hail to Thee, O Nile, that gushest forth from the earth and comest to nourish Egypt."[4]

Peasant villages existed along the Nile through much of the Neolithic Era. Beginning around 3100 B.C., these villages were gradually united into a centralized state by the first pharaohs, or kings. The impetus for centralization was much the same as in Mesopotamia: the need for an irrigation system, population pressures, and new technologies. The pharaohs who led the centralization effort probably evolved out of either the priestly caste or the merchant class, both of which were natural sources of leadership in farming societies. As creators of a new way of life, the pharaohs were thought to embody the divine gift of creation and thus were assumed to be gods. More precisely, they were thought to be gods descended to earth in human form.

The unification of the peasant villages occurred gradually between 3100 and 2700 B.C., during what historians call the Protodynastic stage of Egyptian history. During the next five hundred years, down to about 2160 B.C., Egypt enjoyed a long period of stability and prosperity known as the Old Kingdom. During the era of the Old Kingdom, the Egyptians developed a unique perspective on life. The Egyptian world was dominated by regularities—the Nile flooding at the same times every year, the sun (rarely interrupted by rainfall) rising and setting every day, and the deserts protecting Egypt from sudden changes brought by foreign interference or invasion. Thus, the Egyptian worldview stressed stability, the assumption being that life was generally good and the goal of life was to be tranquil and in harmony with nature and the gods. Unlike the pessimistic view of the Mesopotamians, the cheerful Egyptians sang happy, optimistic songs:

> The Earth-god has implanted his beauty in every body.
> The Creator has done this with his two hands as balm to his heart.
> The channels are filled with water anew
> And the land is flooded with his love.[5]

Compared to other peoples of their time, the Egyptians lived relatively well. Most favored among them was the pharaoh, but it was his duty to see that the entire land was favored. As a god, a pharaoh was expected to ensure that crops were good and Egypt was protected from invaders. However, the pharaohs did little actual governing, leaving the day-to-day decisions to a large bureaucracy staffed by the upper classes. Upper-class people were often educated and well-off materially, living in large houses that sometimes had rudimentary bathrooms and were constructed to be naturally cool in summer and warm in winter. The great majority of Egyptians were peasants or slaves who toiled in the fields. The peasants lived in crude huts with their animals and endured a hard life, but they were no worse off than peasants elsewhere and their rural life-style was slow and tranquil. Although some slaves were allowed to rent and cultivate land, most were required to work on large construction projects, such as the pyramids.

Life expectancy through most of ancient Egypt was around thirty-six years, about the average for other civilizations of that epoch. And life, though short, was relatively good for many, since Egypt had great resources. The land produced wheat, figs, grapes, melons, lettuces, beans, and peas. Wine and beer were common, and there were herds of sheep, pigs, and goats.

Many Egyptians loved life and came to believe they could extend its pleasures after death. At first, only the pharaoh was believed to live eternally, but gradually the promise of eternal life was thought to be available to more and more people. This belief in eternity led to construction of the great pyramids, the most famous monuments in ancient Egypt. The pyramids were tombs for pharaohs, built early in the Old Kingdom. Politically they were construction projects for which the pharaohs organized peasant and slave labor and thus asserted their authority. Spiritually, the construction of the pyramids was a way for peasants to serve the gods, in this case by building resting places for the divine pharaohs before they ascended to eternity.

The pyramids reveal an Egyptian confidence in human power: they represent an attempt to overcome nature by overcoming death. The historian James Breasted once said:

> The Great Pyramid of Gizeh is thus a document in the history of the human mind. It clearly discloses man's sense of sovereign power in his triumph over material forces. . . . The pharaoh's engineer was achieving the conquest of immortality by sheer command of material forces.[6]

Another example of the Egyptian sense of human power is the sphinxes, colossal statues of a human head on an animal body. According to the nineteenth-century philosopher G. W. F. Hegel, the sphinxes express an

Pyramids at Giza, Egypt   The Egyptian pyramids were built as tombs for the pharaohs. The pyramids represent the human desire for power over nature and immortality. They also represent the power of people to control others, for thousands of
farmers and slaves were forced to work for many years to build these enormous
structures. (Trans World Airlines)

awareness of the human world emerging out of the natural, animalistic
world. The Egyptian affinity for gigantic architecture is thus comparable
to the creation of the *Epic of Gilgamesh* in Mesopotamia. Both the
Egyptians and the Mesopotamians were celebrating human creativity, a
creativity that they knew enabled them to build a new way of life—
civilization.

The era of the Old Kingdom in Egypt declined in the middle of the
twenty-second century B.C. Local rulers weakened the centralizing power
of the pharaohs, and for nearly fifty years Egypt endured a period of
political instability and economic decline. In about 2135 B.C., central
authority was restored and the Middle Kingdom began, lasting about
three hundred years. In 1786 B.C. another period of chaos ensued, when
Egypt was invaded by Asians whom the Egyptians called "Hyksos." For
the first time, Egypt was burdened by external intervention, and it was
more than a century before the Egyptians drove the intruders out.
Around 1575 B.C., the New Kingdom was established by a succession of
pharaohs, and it lasted nearly five hundred years (until c. 1087 B.C.). That
kingdom was followed by the Late Period, which extended from 1087 to
332 B.C., when Alexander the Great conquered Egypt.

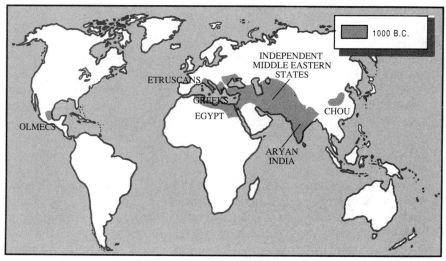

Figure 1.2 World Civilizations, 1000 B.C.

Egyptian attitudes changed dramatically during the New Kingdom and the Late Period. The confident, optimistic days of the Old Kingdom were gone. The pyramids were already regarded as ancient monuments to be visited by sightseers. The Egyptians now constantly feared foreign attack, first from the Hyksos, then in succession from the Hittites, the so-called "Sea Peoples," the Libyans, and the Assyrians. Fear led them to stress the need for national security rather than individual happiness. It also led them to regard humans as helplessly dependent on the gods and unable to control their own destiny. With this loss of confidence, the Egyptians became a superstitious people, turning for solace to oracles, horoscopes, and magical spells.

The most impressive feature of ancient Egyptian civilization is its endurance. By the first millennium B.C., it was already an ancient civilization that fascinated other peoples with its architectural marvels. Its energy and creativity were gone, however, and Egypt was a somnolent land of toiling peasants and slaves and a small, indolent upper class.

OTHER EARLY CIVILIZATIONS

Indus Valley

Early civilizations developed in several other areas of the world. Some of these civilizations were stimulated by contact with the Mesopotamians or the Egyptians whereas others evolved independently. The Indus valley civilization (located in modern Pakistan) originated around 2500 B.C.

and lasted for nearly a thousand years. Because Indus writing has not yet been deciphered, little is known about Indus civilization. It was similar to Mesopotamian and Egyptian civilizations in that it centered around a river valley where irrigation systems were organized to increase agricultural production. It carried on some commerce with the Mesopotamians through the Persian Gulf and was a thriving society for a time. Eventually, it collapsed due to invasions by external enemies and the silting up of the irrigation system.

Minoan

In the eastern Mediterranean on the Greek island of Crete, a civilization known as Minoan emerged sometime between 2500 and 2000 B.C. It lasted until about 1400 B.C., when it was destroyed either by foreign attack or by some kind of natural disaster. This early Greek civilization was probably stimulated by contact with the Egyptians, and the Minoans quickly became a powerful, creative people. In particular, they were great engineers and architects, constructing paved streets, aqueducts, and sewer systems. The Minoans were also enterprising sailors, dominating the eastern Mediterranean between 1600 and 1400 B.C. During that time they colonized much of Greece and their culture became one of the bases of later Greek civilization.

One interesting aspect of Minoan civilization is that women appear to have been much more powerful than their counterparts in other civilizations, sometimes participating in political decisions and usually controlling religious rituals. Minoan religion, like Neolithic religion, centered on mother goddesses who symbolized fertility. Also interesting is the particular reverence that the Minoans extended to bulls. In one religious performance, young men seized the horns of a charging bull and leaped over its back. (Modern Spanish bullfighting may be descended from this ancient ritual.) Bulls were also celebrated in legend. One legend told of a Minotaur, a monster with the body of a man and the head of a bull; the Minotaur inhabited the center of a labyrinth from which no one could escape until a young hero left a trail of thread to follow back after he had killed the monster. A final note about the Minoans is the gaiety and gracefulness expressed in the art displayed on pottery and wall paintings. This art suggests that the Minoans enjoyed and appreciated life on this earth.

Phoenician

Close to the Minoans (in present-day Lebanon), a people known as the Phoenicians organized a civilization during the second millennium B.C. Originally farmers who practiced a brutal religion that included human sacrifices, the Phoenicians became sailors and merchants of the entire

Minoan Snake Goddess Only three inches in height, this statuette symbolizes several aspects of Minoan culture: the importance of females in Minoan religion and society; the association of snakes with the divine (snakes were considered friendly creatures that protected Minoans from other, harmful creatures); and the style of dress for upper-class Minoan women. The Minoans were a fun-loving people who encouraged open sexuality, and women sometimes dressed so as to expose their bare breasts in public. (Museum of Fine Arts, Boston)

Mediterranean region from 1000 to 500 B.C. Some even sailed into the Atlantic Ocean, a risky venture at that time.

The Phoenicians gradually established colonies around the shores of the Mediterranean, and as they did so they proliferated the use of one of their greatest discoveries—the alphabet. The Phoenician alphabet, probably derived from the ideas of other peoples as well as their own, was one of the Phoenicians' greatest achievements and an important breakthrough in human history, providing a much simpler form of writing than the earlier picture-writing system of cuneiform (see the Technology Box in Chapter 2).

Shang

On the other end of the Eurasian landmass, the Shang civilization arose in the Yellow River area of northern China around 1500 B.C. The Shang were nomads who may have had some contact with the peoples of Mesopotamia or the Indus valley and, thus, were exposed to some civilized arts—such as writing and the wheel—when they conquered peasant villages along the Yellow River. But Shang civilization was not wholly derivative. It was unique in its emphasis on rice cultivation, its manufacture of fine silk cloth, and its development of ancestor worship in its religion.

The Shang dynasty disappeared around 1000 B.C., when the Chou dynasty assumed power. However, agricultural prosperity continued around the Yellow River and Chinese civilization retained many of the features introduced by the Shang, such as ancestor worship and silk manufacturing.

Mesoamerican

Unlike the Indus, Minoan, Phoenician, and Shang civilizations, which were stimulated partly through contact with older civilizations, Mesoamerica (Middle America) was an elaborate civilization that developed independently around 1200 B.C. During that time, a people known as the Olmecs lived in present-day Mexico, and they created the foundation for what would later become Mesoamerican civilization. The Olmecs established an agricultural society based on peasant slavery, an authoritarian political structure, and a fertility-based religion, all of which remained basic components of the Mesoamerican heritage. By 300 B.C. in southern Mexico, Mayan civilization evolved out of what the Olmecs had created. The Mayans were eventually succeeded by the Toltec (800–1200 A.D.) and Aztec (1200–1520 A.D.) civilizations. The Aztecs were still flourishing when the Spanish came to the New World in the sixteenth century A.D.

Another early American civilization emerged around 1100 A.D. in present-day Peru. This was the Inca Empire which at its height extended from the mountains of Peru down the Pacific coast into present-day Chile. The Incas were farmers who developed engineering skills to hold their empire together. An elaborate road and bridge system facilitated transportation and communication within their empire, and some Inca cities were so elaborately planned and constructed (often out of rock) that they still inspire awe in the twentieth century. The Inca Empire lasted until the Spanish came to the Americas and conquered it in 1532–33.

THE DECLINE OF THE EARLY CIVILIZATIONS

During the second millennium B.C., many ancient civilizations either collapsed or just barely survived as a result of nomad warriors who surged across Eurasia and attacked everything in their way. The nomads were in search of food and were probably threatened by famine. Two new developments gave the nomads a military advantage over their civilized opponents. One was the domestication of the horse, which the nomads attached to war chariots. The other was iron, used to forge weapons more powerful than those previously made. Thus, the second millennium B.C. marks the beginning of what historians call the Iron Age.

There were two waves of nomad attacks. The first occurred from 1700 to 1500 B.C. As noted earlier, the Kassites, a Semitic tribe from the deserts, conquered Mesopotamia. In addition, the Hyksos invaded Egypt, and other nomads destroyed the Indus civilization. The second wave of nomad attacks followed soon after and lasted until 1100 B.C. An obscure group of nomads known only as the "Sea Peoples" threatened Egypt and may have destroyed Minoan civilization as well. Farther east, Mongols (from Mongolia, an area north of China) destroyed the Shang dynasty in China. As a result of these nomad attacks, most ancient civilizations were either gravely weakened or disappeared altogether. In many areas, population declined and organized society was reduced to localized farming units.

The lands around the eastern end of the Mediterranean began to recover sometime after 900 B.C. Iron, first worked by the Hittites of Asia Minor (modern Turkey), became a source of improved farm implements. The development of the Phoenician alphabet further stimulated economic activity. Although small kingdoms gradually arose (such as the Hebrew state of Israel), most of them were soon conquered by a series of large empires centered in Mesopotamia. The first of these was the Assyrian Empire, which lasted from the mid-eighth century to 612 B.C. The Assyrians established peace and orderly government for their subjects, but they had a reputation for extreme cruelty. One Assyrian king, Ashurbanipal, boasted that after defeating an enemy army he ". . . caught the survivors and impaled them on stakes in front of their towns."[7]

The Assyrians were defeated by a new Babylonian Empire established by a people known as the Chaldeans, but that empire lasted only a few decades. The most famous of the Chaldean rulers was Nebuchadnezzar (reigned 604–562 B.C.), builder of the legendary Hanging Gardens, an elaborate roof garden constructed for a Persian concubine who was tired of the flat Mesopotamian landscape. In 550 B.C., Babylon was conquered by the Persians, the most successful empire-builders of that time. The Persian Empire, which lasted about two hundred years (until 333 B.C.), extended from the Iranian plateau eastward almost to India and westward to Greece and Egypt. The Persians, more tolerant than the Assyrians and Babylonians, allowed their subjects to retain their own local governments and religious traditions. It was for this reason that the Persians gained a reputation for fair, honest government.

CONCLUSION

By the first millennium B.C., ancient peoples had developed various ways of living. The Paleolithic hunters of nomadic tribes wandered in search of animals to kill in some parts of the world. Neolithic farmers lived in small villages in other areas. And large-scale civilizations existed in a few places. Common to all these different ways of life was the belief, shared by almost all people, in some form of animistic religion. Animistic beliefs would begin to change, however, with the spiritual and intellectual transformation that occurred in several parts of the world during the first millennium B.C. This transformation is the subject of the following chapter.

THINGS YOU SHOULD KNOW

The biological and cultural advantages of humans
Paleolithic thought and religion
Cro-Magnon people
Neolithic thought and religion
Characteristics and significance of "civilization"
Sumerians
Irrigation technology in ancient Mesopotamia
Hammurabi
Epic of Gilgamesh

Ancient Egyptian civilization
Significance of the pyramids
Indus valley civilization
Minoan civilization
Phoenician civilization
Shang civilization
Mesoamerican civilization
Why many of the early civilizations were undermined in the second millennium B.C.

SUGGESTED READINGS

Two good introductions to the development of prehistoric humans are Robert J. Braidwood, *Prehistoric Man* (Chicago: Scott Foresman, 1957) and Richard Leakey and Roger Lewin, *Origins* (New York: 1977). On the Sumerian and Egyptian civilizations, see Samuel N. Kramer, *History Begins at Sumer* (New York: Univ. of Pennsylvania Press, 1956) and Cyril Aldred, *The Egyptians* (New York: Praeger, 1961). An old but still valuable analysis of the thoughts and beliefs of early humans is H. A. Frankfort, John A. Wilson, and Thorkild Jacobsen, *Before Philosophy: The Intellectual Adventure of Ancient Man* (Baltimore: Penguin, 1946). For an introduction to the status of women in ancient societies as well as in later ages, see Elizabeth Fox-Genovese and Susan Mosher Stuard (eds.), *Restoring Women to History: Materials for Western Civilization I* (Bloomington: Univ. of Indiana Press, 1983). Also important is Frances Dahlberg (ed.), *Woman the Gatherer* (Yale: Yale Univ. Press, 1981). A good examination of how early civilizations (and later ones as well) used and often destroyed agricultural land is Vernon Gill Carter and Tom Dale, *Topsoil and Civilization* (Norman, Okla.: Univ. of Oklahoma Press, 1974). Arthur Ferrill analyzes the early history of warfare in *The Origins of War* (New York: Thames and Hudson, 1985).

NOTES

[1]Quoted in Thorkild Jacobsen, "Mesopotamia," in *Before Philosophy: The Intellectual Adventure of Ancient Man,* rev. ed. H. A. Frankfort et al. (New York: Penguin, 1959), p. 154.

[2]Ibid., p. 161.

[3]Ibid., p. 255.

[4]Quoted in Sabatino Moscati, *The Face of the Ancient Orient* (New York: Anchor, 1960), p. 101.

[5]Quoted in Cyril Aldred, *The Egyptians* (New York: Praeger 1961), p. 139.

[6]James Breasted, quoted in John A. Wilson, "Egypt," in *Before Philosophy: The Intellectual Adventure of Ancient Man,* rev. ed. H. A. Frankfort et al. (New York: Penguin, 1959), p. 105.

2

A Spiritual and Intellectual Transformation, 800 to 200 B.C.

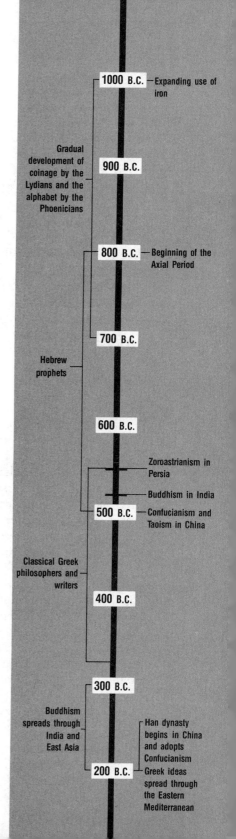

1000 B.C. — Expanding use of iron

Gradual development of coinage by the Lydians and the alphabet by the Phoenicians

900 B.C.

800 B.C. — Beginning of the Axial Period

Hebrew prophets

700 B.C.

600 B.C.

Zoroastrianism in Persia

Buddhism in India

500 B.C. — Confucianism and Taoism in China

Classical Greek philosophers and writers

400 B.C.

300 B.C.

Buddhism spreads through India and East Asia

Han dynasty begins in China and adopts Confucianism

Greek ideas spread through the Eastern Mediterranean

200 B.C.

In *The Origin and Goal of History,* the German philosopher Karl Jaspers defines the time span of 800–200 B.C. as the *Axial Period* of world history. This period is, according to Jaspers, the axis—the central point around which world history revolves—because a spiritual and intellectual transformation occurred in several parts of the world during this time.[1] In China, two new religions appeared—Confucianism (founded by Confucius) and Taoism (founded by Lao-tzu). In India, the Buddha created Buddhism, a new religion with roots grounded in the older Indian religion of Hinduism. In Persia, Zoroaster taught another new religion that became known as Zoroastrianism. In Israel, the Hebrew prophets changed the ancient Hebrew religion into the fully developed religion of Judaism, the ancestor of Christianity and Islam. And, in Greece, a succession of intellectual figures created what is referred to as rational thought and philosophy.

GENERAL CHARACTERISTICS OF THE AXIAL PERIOD

The great teachers of the Axial Period transformed the spiritual and intellectual world and were, therefore, far more influential than any military conqueror or political leader. Except for some Taoist teachers, they all repudiated the polytheistic religions that deified nature and sought instead a more universal, more spiritual conception of the divine. In the process, they helped to create most of the modern world's major religions. Most Axial teachers also repudiated the magic and ritual associated with the polytheistic religions, and the new moral codes that they introduced defined many of the ideals and rules that have motivated people ever since. The historian Herbert J. Muller believes that the Axial Period is "the most extraordinary creative era in man's history between the rise of civilization and the rise of modern science."[2]

The spiritual revolution of the Axial Period was limited to five areas—China, India, Persia, Israel, and Greece—and at first involved only small minorities within them. Many people in other parts of the world were not affected; the few people who remained food gatherers and hunters continued to follow Paleolithic religious practices, and the peasants, representing the majority of the world's population, continued to follow agricultural religions based primarily on analogies between human and soil fertility. The adherents of these old religious practices may have been happy with their way of life, but they would not play the leading roles on the stage of world history. Those roles would be filled by the Axial peoples, those who experienced the spiritual breakthrough of the Axial period.

Causes of the Axial Revolution

Why some peoples and not others participated in the Axial revolution remains a mystery. It is difficult if not impossible to determine the ultimate source of spiritual and intellectual creativity. It is significant, though, that the five Axial areas were in or near regions where one or more of the early civilizations developed. The Chinese religions emerged in areas close to where Shang civilization had existed, Buddhism flourished in areas near the old sites of Indus civilization, Zoroastrianism developed in an area of Persia close to the old center of Mesopotamian civilization, and both the Hebrews and Greeks lived in close proximity to Mesopotamian and Egyptian civilizations. The old civilizations had disappeared or were declining by the time of the Axial Period and they did not share in the spiritual revolution. However, they contributed to it by passing on their knowledge and ideas to the Axial peoples. Furthermore, the end of the old civilizations produced a political and spiritual crisis in the first millennium B.C. The old beliefs and ideas were questioned, leading to a search for the new. This search was a major stimulus of the spiritual revolution.

Another cause of the Axial revolution was technological development, which fostered social as well as spiritual change. The growing availability of iron, a cheap metal used to produce better plows, tools, and weapons, resulted in a growing agricultural prosperity and became the economic base for cities where spiritual, intellectual, and political debate could be pursued. The invention of coinage, developed in the eastern Mediterranean area by the Lydians (who lived in Anatolia or present-day Turkey) also encouraged the Axial revolution. Before coinage, bars of metal were used for monetary exchange. The bars were bulky and difficult to transport over long distances. They also represented only large monetary values, making trade among local merchants and farmers difficult. The development of coinage alleviated these difficulties, stimulated trade over wider areas, and even encouraged exchange of ideas among trading peoples. Finally, there was the important invention of the Phoenician alphabet, which affected primarily those people in the eastern Mediterranean. The alphabet allowed more people to become literate and, therefore, better able to study and discuss spiritual and intellectual issues.

The various causes of the Axial revolution affected each of the five Axial areas in a different way. Although Zoroastrianism influenced Judaism and Buddhism influenced the Chinese religions, for the most part the five areas had little contact with each other and developed independently.

CHINA

The first Chinese civilization—the Shang—was overthrown around 1000 B.C., by a new group of rulers known as the Chou. The Chou dynasty governed most of China for over two centuries, but invading nomads in the eighth century B.C. forced the Chou to move eastward. Now known as the Eastern Chou, the same dynasty ruled eastern parts of China until the fifth century B.C. In reality, however, Chou control was precarious. Through much of the first millennium B.C., local princes ignored the Chou emperors and fought each other in local wars, while nomads occasionally invaded and conquered parts of China. This political upheaval was short-lived, though, and Chinese social structure changed very little.

Chinese society was conservative, stable, and hierarchical, in part because of the nature of the agricultural system. The main crop was rice, which requires a great deal of water. Consequently, large irrigation systems and water conservancy projects had to be built and maintained, and these public works were managed by strong, local governments that enforced social cooperation and social order. In theory, every person regardless of wealth had an assigned place in the social hierarchy; in practice, though, Chinese rural life was dominated by a landowning elite.

The hierarchical social structure was intertwined with a worldview that stressed "quiet" virtues, such as living in harmony with nature and accepting one's position in life. The Chinese traditionally interpreted everything in ecological terms, in the sense that all things in nature and human society were considered parts of one interconnected reality and, therefore, people were expected to live harmoniously within the whole.

Confucianism

The great Chinese teacher Confucius (c. 551–479 B.C.), was born into a world of social stability interrupted periodically by political upheaval. He was a wandering intellectual who spent much of his life as a school-teacher and tutor to princes. After his death, his students collected his words and ideas into a book known as the *Analects*.

The goal of Confucius's teachings was to show people how to live in a harmonious social order. Thus, he was a conservative, speaking for the traditional Chinese worldview. He was also a humanist, teaching a "this-world" religion that focused on humanity rather than on gods. Confucius rarely mentioned gods or any other kind of supernatural realm, and he opposed magical practices derived from the Shang civilization, like the sacrifice of young women to the gods of the Yellow River. Confucius used the word *heaven* not to refer to someplace beyond the earth but to refer to a spiritual and moral order that he regarded as immanent in everyday life.

TECHNOLOGY
The Alphabet

Most early civilizations used some form of picture-writing: the Mesopotamians developed the cuneiform system, the Egyptians created a system known as hieroglyphics, and the Chinese evolved their own type of writing in symbols. Since at least several hundred symbols, often several thousand, were needed to express an entire language in writing, only a few professional scribes had the time and training to be literate. In most early civilizations, these scribes controlled the means of communication.

In contrast, the Phoenician alphabet formed words out of only twenty-two consonants, leaving the reader to add vowel sounds. The Greeks improved the Phoenician system by adding five vowel signs. Later the Romans and still later the Europeans evolved alphabetic systems based on the Greek model.

The alphabetic system made it easier for people to become literate and gain access to knowledge. Certainly, most poor people remained illiterate, and many parts of the world—China, for example—retained their picture-writing systems for many centuries. But the alphabetic system gradually came to dominate the Mediterranean area that gave birth to Western Civilization. Since education is one of the prerequisites for technological development, the creation of the alphabet was one of the major steps in the history of Western technology.

Egyptian Hieroglyphics *This funerary papyrus from the eleventh century b.c. is an example of hieroglyphic writing, which required a greater number of more complicated symbols to communicate than does the alphabet system. (Metropolitan Museum of Art, NY)*

Confucius (551–479 B.C.)
A 1734 ink rubbing that
portrays the traditional
conception of Chinese philosopher K'ung Ch'iu,
known as Confucius. Dedi-
cated to a life of government reform and teaching,
Confucius became the
most revered person in
Chinese history. His teachings on ethics, happiness,
and family have provided
the cornerstone for much
Chinese thought through
the ages. (The Granger
Collection)

Confucius taught that a person must cultivate his inner self in order
to learn how to live in harmony with the spiritual and moral order of the
world. In practice, self-cultivation meant studying the ancient Chinese
classics, including *The Classic of History* (also known as *The Book of
Documents*) and *The Classic of Change* (also known as *I Ching*). By so
doing, a person could deepen his self-awareness, develop his understanding of the "good" and the "beautiful," and gradually become a "good
man." By studying the classics, a person would learn that "goodness"
meant performing one's assigned duties in life. The first duty was within
the family, for being a good man required being a good son. According to
Confucius:

> Filial piety is the root of all virtue, and the stem out of which grows
> all moral teaching. It commences with the service of parents; it
> proceeds to the service of the ruler. . . .[3]

Having become a good son and later a good father, the good man, as
Confucius asserted, should strive further to become a good citizen. In
practice, this meant serving the state. Confucius believed that harmony

within the state was produced by the same virtues that brought harmony within the family—self-awareness and diligence in performing duties.

At its best, Confucianism taught the Chinese to cultivate those moral and aesthetic qualities that are most distinctively human, so its practice was more conscious of the human spirit than were the traditional animistic religions. At its weakest, however, Confucianism emphasized harmony and duty to such a degree that it tended to undermine the spirit of adventure and experimentation. It also tended to limit the highest human goal—the sustained cultivation of human character—to an elite few. It clearly favored men and the leisured upper classes, who had the time and energy to study the ancient classics.

Taoism

Taoism, another Chinese religion created during the Axial Period, was founded by the renowned figure Lao-tzu, who lived at about the same time as Confucius. Whereas Confucianism stressed living in harmony within society, Taoism emphasized living in harmony with nature. The Taoist conception of nature was philosophical rather than scientific. The Taoists did not seek to understand how nature operated but to comprehend the underlying order and meaning of nature. They were mystics who often withdrew from society so they could meditate on the *Tao*, or "the Way." *Tao* was the rational principle found in nature, the basic order of the universe. Sometimes this order was expressed in the terms *yin* and *yang*. The yin-yang concept held that everything in the universe could be explained in terms of contrasting pairs (female–male, weak–strong, cold–hot).

For Taoists, the good life consisted of identifying themselves with the order of nature. In practice, this meant living a simple life by limiting desires and disregarding the artificial rules and customs of organized society. Lao-tzu described the Taoist conception of utopia as follows:

> There are no books; the people have no use for any form of record save knotted ropes. They relish the simplest form of food, have no desire for fine clothing, take pleasure in their rustic tasks, are content to remain in their home. The next village might be so close that one could hear the cocks crowing in it, the dogs barking, but the people would grow old and die without ever having been there.[4]

Taoism was first followed by a few self-disciplined mystics but gradually became popular among ordinary Chinese. When it was adopted by the lower classes, Taoism came to include belief in several supernatural deities and forces and even in witchcraft. Thus, the popularized version of Taoism did not repudiate polytheism, as did most of the other religions of the Axial Period.

The Impact of Religion on Chinese History

Both Confucianism and Taoism envisioned the attainment of harmony as the supreme goal of life; the Confucians stressed social harmony and the Taoists stressed harmony with nature. This common goal meant that Chinese religions were not "exclusive" but that a person could follow several religious traditions. For example, a Chinese individual might be married in a Buddhist ceremony (after that Indian religion came to China in the first century A.D.), adopt a Taoist attitude of calmness when facing adversity, and adhere to Confucian practices in family and social life.

Chinese religion discouraged interest in science and the actual workings of nature. Certainly, China produced notable scientists and a scientific tradition over the centuries, but the study of science never became a dominant force in Chinese society. The Confucians were primarily concerned with human society and had little interest in nature, while the Taoists wanted only to live in a kind of mystic harmony with nature and made no attempt to investigate it by any scientific means.

In terms of China's political history, Confucianism had a great influence. Around 202 B.C., the Han dynasty imposed political order on most of China and established a centralized empire that lasted until A.D. 220. (The Han Empire flourished at the same time as the late Roman Republic and the early Roman Empire.) The Han rulers adopted Confucianism as the official state religion, using it to impose ideological unity in China. The Han required, for instance, civil service exams (and, hence, access to government employment) to be based on knowledge of the Confucian classics. This practice became a tradition, and for much of the next two thousand years Chinese bureaucrats were trained in Confucian teachings. The Confucians welcomed this practice, believing that their teachings would humanize politics by training government officials to behave humanely. In reality, though, Chinese rulers usually used Confucianism as a means of training docile, conservative bureaucrats who would loyally serve royal purposes.

The religious and cultural influences of Confucianism eventually extended beyond China to Korea, Japan, and other East Asian societies. As we will see later in the chapter, Buddhism (after it came to China) also spread into those smaller Asian countries. Thus, Chinese and Indian philosophies permeated all of East Asia.

INDIA

After the decline of Indus civilization during the second millennium B.C., India remained politically chaotic and divided into separate kingdoms for most of the next thousand years. Political disunity did not, however, prevent the growth of cultural and religious unity throughout much of the Indian subcontinent. For example, several intellectual figures wrote the *Vedas,* a collection of religious and philosophical poems that expressed the religious beliefs held by many Indians. Others produced the *Upanishads,* another series of philosophical poems. From these sources Indians derived a worldview that stressed tolerance and the need to understand differing points of view.

The Indians tended to assume that all religions attempt to understand the same divine reality but through different perspectives. This attitude is supported by an old Indian parable about several blind men and an elephant. One blind man feels the elephant's trunk and says it is a snake, another feels a leg and calls it a tree, and a third feels the tail and calls it a rope. The point, of course, is that each man "saw" only a part of the elephant and not the entire reality.[5]

Hinduism

The Indians derived from their ancient scriptures a system of beliefs known as Hinduism. Hinduism distinguished sharply between ultimate reality and the material reality of this world. Ultimate reality is the *Brahman* (or "world-soul"), the undefinable spiritual reality that underlies and transcends the material world. It is like an ocean on which the material reality floats. The material world is just an "appearance," a manifestation of the basic reality, and as such it is an inferior, essentially meaningless form of existence. For the Hindu, the goal of life is to achieve *moksha* ("release") from this world and sink back into the ocean of divine reality. Most people cannot achieve this goal, however. They are enticed by worldly desires (such as the desire for wealth or fame) that have the *karma* ("consequence") of tying them to this world. So, when they die they are reborn into this world in accordance with the laws of *karma.* Those who lived by the rules appropriate to their place in society might attain rebirth to a higher status, whereas those who were cruel or unjust might be reborn as a wild beast. Only those who are able to give up worldly desires can attain release from the endless cycle of rebirths and return to divine reality.

Obviously, Hindu beliefs were closely intertwined with a hierarchical social structure that prescribed for each person a well-defined social status. In fact, a caste system was probably brought to India by Aryan invaders, who imposed the system on the native Indians they conquered. (The Aryans were Indo-European nomads, who conquered much of Iran and northern India during the late second millennium B.C. and early first millennium B.C. It may have been the Aryans who destroyed the Indus civilization.)

A *caste* was a social group into which a person was born and from which there was virtually no escape. A person spent his or her entire life in a caste, performing the occupations and living by the rules appropriate to that caste. Originally, there were three upper castes, populated mostly by the Aryans: the priests *(Brahmins)*, the warrior rulers *(Kshatriya)*, and the merchants *(Vaisya)*. These castes were sharply distinguished from the two lower castes, which contained most of the Indian natives conquered by the Aryans: the laboring caste *(Sudra)* and the "untouchables" *(pariahs)*. The untouchables were considered "polluted" because they were descended from backward tribes and because their occupations involved "dirty" work, such as the taking of animal life (butchers and fishermen, for example).

Hinduism and the caste system clearly complemented each other. According to Hindu teachings, a person was born into a caste in accordance with the *karma* achieved in a previous existence. Furthermore, depending on whether people adhered to the rules of their caste, they would after death be reborn into a higher or lower caste. A higher rebirth was very desirable, since Hindus believed that only members of the Brahmin caste could attain *moksha*, release from this world.

Buddhism

Many Indians resented the Brahminic assertion that only they could achieve *moksha*. As a result, Buddhism took hold in the sixth century B.C. as a more egalitarian religion, teaching that "release" was available to everyone. At the time, the Ganges River valley in northern India was enjoying a wave of prosperity. The use of iron to make farm implements and the domestication of the horse produced agricultural growth and led to the expansion of cities where commerce thrived. Prosperous commercial and farming classes emerged, which in turn supported the rise of Buddhism that taught that *moksha* was available to them as well as to Brahmins.

Buddhism was founded by Siddārtha Gautama Sakyamuni (c. 563–483 B.C.), a minor Indian prince who eventually acquired the name "Buddha" or "the enlightened one." As a young man, he renounced his wealth, left his home and family, and began to travel around India in search of spiritual enlightenment. Having found it, he then began to teach others. His religion was completely humanistic—he did not teach about gods but focused solely on people's ability to achieve a form of salvation through their own efforts.

According to the Buddha, human life is characterized by pain, sorrow, and meaninglessness. It is meaningless because people cannot attain any kind of salvation from ordinary ways of living; it is full of pain and sorrow because people constantly experience physical and emotional pain. The ultimate cause of all this evil is human desire, because desire for things (such as wealth or fame) creates a kind of restless striving for more that leaves people constantly anxious and frustrated. Thus, without those desires people could free themselves of the sources of anxiety and

Buddha (563–483 B.C.)
From the second or third
century A.D., this statue of
the Buddha was created at
a time when he was
thought of as a god.
Siddhārtha Gautama,
known as the Buddha, was
the founder of Buddhism,
a belief system that advo-
cates meditation, austerity,
and a rejection of material
things as a means of at-
taining spiritual happiness.
(Seattle Art Museum)

pain. In the Buddha's words, "The fire of life must be put out. For
everything in the world is on fire with the fire of desire, the fire of hate,
and the fire of illusion."[6] One could escape desire through detachment, by
renouncing all passions and ambitions. A person could do this by
following the "Eightfold Noble Path"—right beliefs, aspirations, speech,
conduct, living, efforts, thoughts, and contemplation. By following this
path, a person could attain *nirvana,* a state of being in which desire and
hate are extinguished and life (on earth, not in heaven) is detached,
enlightened, filled with compassion and love for others.

Jainism

Originating in the sixth century B.C., Jainism was similar to Hinduism
and Buddhism in its teachings that the chief goal for humans was release
from earthly life. Jainism was unique, however, in its emphasis on
nonviolence, extending to a refusal to kill even the smallest creature.
Nonviolence became a fundamental belief of many Indians. A notable
example of Jainist influence is the life and teachings of Mohandas

Gandhi, the great Indian political leader who used a philosophy of nonviolence during the Indian struggle for independence from Britain during the twentieth century A.D.

The Spread of Buddhism

The number of Buddhist adherents remained relatively small during the first decades after the founding of the new religion, largely because Buddhist teachings were so demanding that only a few ascetics who withdrew from everyday life could hope to follow them. Buddhism began to expand when Mahayana ("Great Vehicle [of salvation]") Buddhism evolved out of the Buddha's original teachings. Mahayana Buddhism was developed by those Buddhists who wanted to make the new religion available and comprehensible to ordinary people. In so doing, the Mahayana teachers gradually began to portray the Buddha as a god—an object of religious devotion—rather than as just a teacher. Soon, likenesses of the Buddha, who never claimed to be a god, began to appear in much Indian art and architecture.

By the third century B.C., Buddhism had spread over much of India. At that time most of India was ruled by the Mauryan Empire, which lasted from 321 to 181 B.C. The most famous Mauryan ruler, Aśoka (274–237 B.C.), converted to Buddhism. He encouraged Buddhists to send out missionaries, and over the next few centuries Buddhism spread to China, Korea, and Japan. Although it thrived for a time, after A.D. 700 Buddhism began to decline. In India it all but disappeared, as it was either reabsorbed into Hinduism or replaced by Islam, which was then spreading to India from the west. Outside of India, it survived as a significant force in China, Japan, and Southeast Asia.

The Impact of Religion on Indian History

The reabsorption of Buddhism into Hinduism was easy in India. Those two traditions, as well as Jainism, shared a common worldview that earthly life was ultimately unimportant and was something to be escaped. That attitude had certain implications. One was a tendency for Indians to accept the realities of earthly life and not to be overly concerned about political, social, or economic change. Certainly, Indian history includes many individual political figures who sought to accomplish political change, and many merchants who sought to amass wealth. But these figures rarely dominated Indian society because Indian religion taught Indians to accept the caste system, not to seek social reform or material wealth. Another implication of seeing earthly life as unimportant was the assumption that physical nature is of little significance, so there was little reason to explore and understand the workings of the natural world. Religion was not the only force inhibiting the growth of Indian science, but it was a powerful one.

The strength of Indian religion was its ability to teach people how to achieve spiritual and emotional contentment. Its weakness was its indifference to social change and the development of science.

PERSIA

Zoroastrianism

The Persians, who had lived quietly on the Iranian plateau for centuries, created a powerful empire in the middle of the sixth century B.C. (see the last section of Chapter 1). They also developed a new religion— Zoroastrianism—that was named after its chief prophet, Zoroaster (sometimes called Zarathustra). Zoroaster taught that the universe is controlled by two divine forces, one good and the other evil. The god of light and justice—Ahura-Mazda—was believed to wage eternal combat with, and seek victory over, Ahriman, the god of darkness and evil. Humans, according to Zoroaster, could choose sides. They could support Ahura-Mazda by following the appropriate rules of moral goodness. In this case, they would be rewarded with entry into paradise (a Persian word) after death. However, if they ignored the moral commandments and supported the god of darkness, then they were believed to be condemned to eternal damnation.

Zoroastrianism captured the allegiance of the Persian upper classes and gradually eliminated some of the superstitions and magical rites practiced by ordinary Persians. It became the dominant religion in Persia only in the first centuries A.D., but after A.D. 700 it was supplanted by Islam (see Chapter 6). From that time on, only a handful of adherents in India continued to follow Zoroaster's teachings.

Even though Zoroastrianism did not survive as an independent force, some scholars believe that it endured through its impact on Judaism and Christianity. As we will see in Chapter 3, the ancient Hebrews were ruled by the Persians for a time (the sixth and fifth centuries B.C.) and probably adapted some of Zoroaster's teachings into their faith. Specifically, they probably absorbed the concepts of paradise and hell. The ancient Hebrews had only vague concepts of an afterlife at first, but under Zoroastrian influence they began to believe in a clearly defined heaven for the virtuous and a hell for those who were evil. These beliefs they later passed on to Christianity.

THE HEBREWS AND THE GREEKS

The Hebrews and the Greeks were the spiritual and intellectual cofounders of Western Civilization and, therefore, are studied in greater detail in Chapters 3 and 4. At this point a brief summary of the Hebrew and Greek

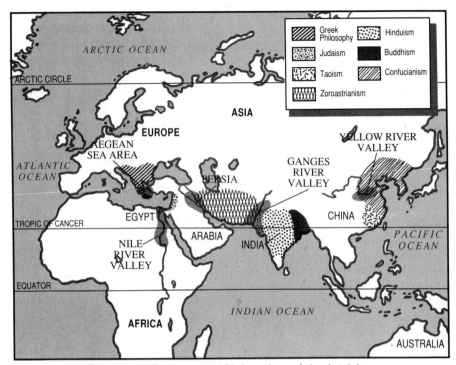

Figure 2.1 Religions and Philosophies of the Axial Age

spiritual breakthroughs of the Axial Period is needed, so that these breakthroughs may be compared with those of China, India, and Persia.

Judaism

The Hebrews were a semi-nomadic people who eventually settled in Israel, along the eastern shore of the Mediterranean. Over a thousand years or more, they developed a religion—Judaism—that is the original source of both Christianity and Islam.

Hebrew religion was different from polytheistic religions in a number of ways:

1. It was monotheistic, repudiating the chaotic variety of polytheism (gods scattered throughout nature) and eventually insisting that only one God created and ruled the entire universe. Actually, Hebrew monotheism evolved slowly over the centuries. The Hebrews originally conceived of their god as ruler only of Hebrews and made no attempt to deny the existence of other gods for other peoples. Not until the rise of the Hebrew prophets during the eighth to sixth centuries B.C. did the Hebrews begin to become pure monotheists, followers of only one God.

2. The Hebrews conceived of their god as transcendent, separate from, and superior to, the material world. God revealed himself through historical events, not in nature as the adherents of animistic religions believed. God was pure spirit and nature in the Hebrew conception was a separate earthly reality, created by God. This separation of God from nature would have far-reaching implications, some of which are discussed in the final section of this chapter.

3. The Hebrews also believed that God demanded moral behavior rather than the performance of rituals from humans. They gradually developed a moral code that was relatively humane and included demands for social justice for the poor and oppressed. In addition, they opposed the rituals—fertility rites or human sacrifices, for example—associated with the polytheistic religions.

Greek Thought

The Greeks lived around the Aegean Sea and were the cultural heirs of Minoan civilization. They accomplished a spiritual breakthrough that was more intellectual and philosophical than religious. A number of Greek intellectuals sought to use the reasoning abilities of the human mind to understand the world in which they lived. As a result, during the eighth to sixth centuries B.C., they began to define rational thought ("rational" in the sense of using the human mind to think logically from one point to another). These intellectuals came to think of the world as a *cosmos* ("world order"), an orderly whole that operated according to laws that humans could discover and understand. They repudiated the polytheistic assumption that the world was a chaotic place where different gods controlled different things. The philosophical concept of an orderly nature governed by laws was accompanied by the development of a political concept of human society as also governed by law. Hence, the Greeks created what would later be termed "constitutional government," government by laws agreed upon by rational people rather than government by monarchical decrees. This new conception of human government and society was elucidated by a number of brilliant Greek poets, philosophers, dramatists, and artists.

Even though the Hebrews and the Greeks lived within a few hundred miles of each other, they had virtually no contact during the Axial Period. Their spiritual breakthroughs occurred independently, but their ideas would eventually meet and joint to form the spiritual basis of Western Civilization.

THE SIGNIFICANCE OF THE AXIAL PERIOD

Fundamental changes in human thought occurred during the Axial Period. People began to distinguish more sharply between a spiritual reality and the natural, material world in which they lived. The polytheistic worldview held that two realities existed—a divine and a material—but it assumed that the two were inextricably intertwined and explained them in similar terms. Gods were portrayed as looking and acting much like humans and they were thought to work through ordinary natural events such as rainstorms or the growing of crops. In contrast, many of the Axial Period thinkers emphasized a sharp divide between the natural world and a much deeper or higher spiritual reality. The Hebrews, for example, portrayed God as radically superior to nature, and the Buddha conceived of *nirvana* as a detachment and spiritual separation from the material world. Karl Jaspers refers to this change in thought as "spiritualization," a growing human awareness of a spiritual realm above or behind the natural realm.[7] Another historian, Benjamin Schwartz, calls it a "strain toward transcendence," a search for a reality that surpasses the material world.[8] Whatever the terminology, the Axial thinkers usually conceived of the change in one of two ways: as a supreme supernatural being (such as the Hebrew god or the Zoroastrian Ahura-Mazda) or a supernatural order (such as the Greek conception of a lawful *cosmos* or the Taoist search for the fundamental way of nature).

People also began to think in universal terms during the Axial Period, in contrast to the earlier tribalistic or regionalistic notions about gods. The Axial leaders professed teachings that were universally applicable to all people. The Buddha taught that release from the material world was possible for all, not just the Brahmin priesthood. The Confucians believed that a harmonious life was possible for all who cultivated the appropriate virtues. The Hebrews believed that God ruled the entire universe, and the Greeks contended that the laws of the *cosmos* applied everywhere. In practice, the universalistic implications of these teachings were limited. The Hebrew God was originally revealed only to the Hebrews, and the Hindu conception of rising through the caste system in successive reincarnations made sense only in a society where a caste system existed. Nevertheless, the Axial thinkers thought in more universal terms than did those of earlier religious traditions and, therefore, developed systems of belief that could be adopted by entire civilizations. This is why the Axial Period witnessed the birth of several "world" religions. World religions did not literally encompass the entire world, but they were shared throughout an entire civilization (such as Confucianism in China or Hinduism in India) and they often had at least some appeal to those living outside the civilization.

In the Axial Period, people became more self-conscious, more aware of themselves as independent beings. Previously, most people thought of themselves as parts of nature intertwined with natural processes. The Axial thinkers defined humans as somewhat spiritual creatures, distinct from the natural world. The Confucians, for example, stressed harmony within and between people and society; they said almost nothing about a person's relationship with nature. The Taoists talked about harmony with nature, but they were referring to a philosophical understanding of an underlying natural reality, not to the visible natural world. The Hebrews thought of humans as spiritual beings created in the divine image. The Greeks contended that humans were rational beings superior to nature and thus uniquely qualified to govern themselves. The effect of these teachings of the Axial Period was to proclaim a kind of human freedom and spiritual independence from nature. With this new-found freedom went responsibility. Polytheistic religions demanded of humans only that they perform the appropriate rituals at the appropriate time. The religions of the Axial Period taught that humans had to obey the moral standards imposed by whichever god or conception of the good life they followed. Confucians had to adhere to ways of behavior that produced harmony, Buddhists to the Eightfold Noble Path, Hebrews to God's commandments. Humans were in the process of becoming moral creatures governed by moral canons.

The spiritual transformation of the Axial Period destroyed a simpler world and produced spiritual uncertainty for many people. During the long millennia when animistic religions prevailed, most humans shared the same basic assumptions, the same mentality. With the Axial Period came a deep spiritual chasm between the spiritual leaders—such as the Buddha or the Hebrew prophets—and many ordinary people. The spiritual leaders taught new ways of understanding the world, ways that were so complex and profound that many ordinary people preferred to continue the traditional polytheistic practices that were familiar and more comforting. Ordinary people, after all, had a great deal to lose. The nature religions made people feel like they were a part of nature and at home in the world. This comfortable feeling of unity with nature began to disappear during the Axial Period; many people regretted the loss, and for that reason various aspects of the nature religions continued to be a part of popular beliefs for centuries to come.

CONCLUSION

Western Civilization is unique. That uniqueness originated during the Axial Period. Looking back at world history since the Axial Period, we can see first, as previously mentioned, that many peoples were unaffected by the Axial breakthroughs and continued to practice animistic religions. We can also see that the great Asian civilizations became dominated by religions that stressed harmony; for Hindus and Buddhists, it was harmony with the universe; for Confucians, it was social harmony; and for Taoists, it was harmony with nature. Thus, Asian religions encouraged people to cooperate rather than compete, to be agreeable rather than aggressive. Certainly, religious distinctions cannot account for all of the differences among civilizations, but it is significant that Western Civilization, in contrast to other societies and civilizations, developed a worldview that honored human assertiveness and aggressiveness. This worldview originated with the Hebrews and the Greeks.

From the Hebrews, Western Civilization inherited its dominant form of religion—the belief in one God who is the sole ruler of the universe but who cares about people and expects humane moral behavior from them. This religion contained distinctive attitudes toward both nature and human history. With respect to nature, the Hebrews de-spiritualized the natural world by believing that God is separate from and superior to nature. (The implications of this belief are explored in Chapter 3.) From this belief Western Civilization eventually derived the view that, since nature is inanimate, humans can dominate it and use it with impunity. Thus, Hebrew beliefs helped create the spiritual underpinning for that Western technology that sought successfully to understand and use the forces of nature. With respect to human history, the Hebrews believed that God revealed himself to humans through historical events (the Exodus, for example, which is also discussed in Chapter 3). They concluded that what happened in history was meaningful and purposive, in the sense that God was leading them forward toward some great goal. (This is the origin of the "linear" conception of history—that history advances like a line. Most ancient peoples other than the Hebrews tended to accept a cyclical view of history; that is, that historical events repeat themselves in endless cycles.) From this Hebrew conception of history, Western Civilization evolved the broad assumption that God wanted people to participate actively in the political, social, and economic affairs of this world and not retreat passively into a life of spiritual contentment. In sum, then, Hebrew religion encouraged Western people to be assertive, both in exploring and using nature and in being involved in worldly affairs.

From the Greeks, Western Civilization inherited the idea of *law*. The Greek belief that nature is governed by law is one of the philosophical foundations of Western science. Science assumes that nature can be understood because natural events occur, not randomly, but in regular patterns in accordance with natural laws. The Greek idea of law also led to the development of constitutional government (government by laws). Thus, the Greeks also encouraged Western people to be assertive; they taught that humans were intelligent, noble beings capable both of understanding the workings of nature and governing themselves.

The story of Western Civilization begins around the eastern end of the Mediterranean Sea with first the Hebrews and then the Greeks. It continues with the Romans, who brought Hebraic and Greek ideas together.

THINGS YOU SHOULD KNOW

The Axial Period
Some causes of the Axial revolution
The significance of the Phoenician
    alphabet
Confucianism
Taoism
The impact of religion on Chinese
    history
Hinduism

Caste system
Buddhism
Jainism
The impact of religion on Indian
    history
Zoroastrianism
Judaism
Greek thought
The significance of the Axial Period

SUGGESTED READINGS

Karl Jaspers, *The Origin and Goal of History* (New Haven: Yale Univ. Press, 1953) is the basic work on the Axial Period, but it is somewhat difficult to read. Much more accessible and an excellent introduction to some of the world's religions and philosophies is Abraham Kaplan, *The New World of Philosophy* (New York: Random House, 1961). More specific works include W. Norman Brown, *Man in the Universe: Some Continuities in Indian Thought* (Berkeley: Univ. of California Press, 1970) and R. C. Zaehner, *Hinduism* (New York: Oxford Univ. Press, 1966) on Indian thought, and Benjamin I. Schwartz, *The World of Thought in Ancient China* (Cambridge, Mass.: Harvard Univ. Press, 1985) on Chinese thought.

Particularly interesting on the relationship between Western and Asian civilizations is Joseph Needham, *Within the Four Seas: The Dialogue of East and West* (Toronto: Univ. of Toronto Press, 1969). The dynamism of Western Civilization is perceptively explored by Lynn White, Jr., *Machina ex Deo: Essays in the Dynamism of Western Culture* (Boston: MIT Press, 1968) and *Medieval Religion and Technology* (Berkeley: Univ. of California Press, 1978).

NOTES

[1]Karl Jaspers, *The Origin and Goal of History* (New Haven: Yale Univ. Press, 1953), pp. 1–6.

[2]Herbert J. Muller, *Freedom in the Ancient World* (London: Secker & Warburg, 1961), p. 107.

[3]Quoted in Abraham Kaplan, *The New World of Philosophy* (New York: Random House, 1961), p. 284.

[4]Quoted in Benjamin I. Schwartz, "Transcendence in Ancient China," *Daedalus* (Vol. 104, no. 2, Spring 1975): p. 66.

[5]Kaplan, p. 209.

[6]Ibid., p. 252.

[7]Jaspers, *The Origin and Goal of History*, p. 3.

[8]Benjamin I. Schwartz, "The Age of Transcendence," *Daedalus* (Vol. 104, no. 2, Spring 1975): pp. 2–3.

3

The Hebrews:
2000 to 100 B.C.

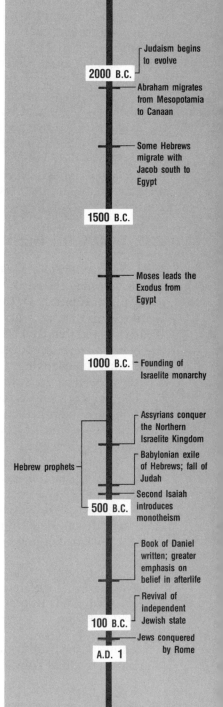

Judaism begins to evolve

2000 B.C.

Abraham migrates from Mesopotamia to Canaan

Some Hebrews migrate with Jacob south to Egypt

1500 B.C.

Moses leads the Exodus from Egypt

1000 B.C. — Founding of Israelite monarchy

Assyrians conquer the Northern Israelite Kingdom

Hebrew prophets —

Babylonian exile of Hebrews; fall of Judah

Second Isaiah introduces monotheism

500 B.C.

Book of Daniel written; greater emphasis on belief in afterlife

Revival of independent Jewish state

100 B.C.

Jews conquered by Rome

A.D. 1

Between 2000 and 100 B.C., Hebrews gradually evolved the religion that became known as Judaism. Judaism was distinct in two ways: (1) it was *monotheistic* (belief in one God) rather than polytheistic, and (2) it stipulated that God expected moral behavior from people rather than the performance of magical rituals. The evolution of Judaism proceeded in three stages. In its first stage, the Hebrew religion was a form of *monolatry*, meaning that Hebrews worshipped one God but did not deny the existence of other people's gods. In its second stage, the religion became monotheistic, as the prophets insisted that God was a universal deity who ruled all peoples. In its third stage of development, Judaism placed new emphasis on certain beliefs, such as the promise of eternal life after death and the expectation of the future coming of a Messiah.

THE BOOK OF GENESIS

According to the Hebrew Old Testament, "In the beginning God created the heavens and the earth" (Genesis 1:1).* This one sentence announced a spiritual revolution. By saying that God "created" the earth, the Hebrew writer (whose name is unknown to us) was proclaiming that only one God exists and that God is distinct from nature. The Hebrews repudiated the belief in several gods existing within nature. They also saw God as masculine, thus denying the existence of mother goddesses symbolizing fertility as well as the sexual rituals that had accompanied this belief.

The Book of Genesis also contains some striking passages about the creation of human beings. It refers to the first man as "Adam," but in Hebrew "Adam" means "the man," so the Genesis writer was referring to humankind in a general sense. From Adam, God took a rib and made it into a "woman" named Eve, a companion for man. But being a secondary creation, Eve was considered inferior to Adam. (This religious view of sexual inequality was common among most ancient peoples.) Adam and Eve were portrayed as living in the Garden of Eden, but their sense of human pride got them into trouble. God told them not to eat of the "tree of the knowledge of good and evil," but when Eve

> saw that the tree was good for food, and that it was a delight to the eyes, and that the tree was to be desired to make one wise, she took of its fruit and ate; and she also gave some to her husband, and he ate. (Genesis 3:6)

The eating of the fruit from the tree of knowledge was an act of rebellion, a grasping for total knowledge that only God can possess. Humans were

*Unless otherwise noted, all quotations from the Old Testament are taken from the Revised Standard Version.

thus portrayed as assertive and even arrogant, a view significantly different from conceptions of humanity in Asian religions. So God said, "Behold, the man has become like one of us, knowing good and evil; and now, lest he put forth his hand and take also of the tree of life, and eat, and live for ever," he must be banished from the Garden of Eden (Genesis 3: 22–23). People had come to know good and evil and were therefore "like" God, but God refused to let them eat of the tree of life, become immortal, and "be" God.

The first chapters of Genesis tell an entrancing story about the relationships between God and nature and between God and humans. The story reflects the ideas and beliefs held by most Hebrew people, for the Book of Genesis was compiled from a number of documents written by different authors. What is important about Genesis is not the facts, but what the facts represented to Hebrews and later to other peoples. (It makes little difference, for example, whether the Creation occurred in six twenty-four-hour days or in six eons.) The underlying message of Genesis is simple: there is one God who is the creator of all things, this God is a concrete personality who has a special relationship with humans rather than with nature, but humans are independent of God and free to choose between good and evil.

Although the underlying message of Genesis may be simple, the quest to understand that message was a complex one for Hebrews. Hebrew monotheism evolved gradually over more than a thousand years, so the story of the Hebrews is also the story of the spiritual awakening of a people.

THE ORIGINS OF HEBREW RELIGION

Abraham

Little is known of the origins of the people we call Hebrews. They were probably a seminomadic Semitic tribe who lived as sheepherders and craftspeople in and around Mesopotamia. Their story as we know it begins with Abraham, who sometime early in the second millennium B.C. had a religious experience that induced him to leave Mesopotamia. Abraham and his family migrated westward to the land then called Canaan, near the southeastern end of the Mediterranean Sea.

Abraham and his descendants (Isaac, Jacob, and so on) were the patriarchs, or fathers, of the Hebrew people. Yet, in a sense, the real father was the divine spirit that the Hebrews worshipped, for Hebrew identity came from their adherence to a unique religion, not from living in a certain area or from building a particular governmental structure. Their religion focused on the worship of one God, whose original name we do not know but who was later called the "God of Abraham." Modern scholars often use the word *Yahweh*—derived from the Hebrew sacred letters *YHWH*—to refer to the God of the early Hebrews. Yahweh insisted that Abraham and his descendants worship only him; in return, Yahweh would protect and aid the Hebrews in various ways. But Yahweh did not deny the existence of other gods for other peoples. Exodus, for example, poses the question, "Who is like unto thee, O Lord, among the gods?" (15:11). Thus, early Hebrew religion was a form of monolatry; eventually, though, it would develop monotheistic ideas.

Hebrew patriarchs believed that God was more concerned with human moral behavior than with rituals. In Genesis, God is depicted as angry about human moral blindness: "The Lord saw that the wickedness of man was great in the earth, and that every imagination of the thoughts of his heart was only evil continually" (6:5). Although the Hebrews were as bloodthirsty as any other people in their wars, they came to believe that they should behave more humanely in their dealings with each other. Thus, Hebrew religion had no sexual orgies or human sacrifices, though it did have animal sacrifices. A unique feature of the religion was a kind of questioning spirit, a willingness by the patriarchs to argue with God to ensure that justice was done. For instance, when God said that he was going to destroy Sodom because of the wickedness of its citizens, Abraham objected and God agreed to spare Sodom if there were at least ten righteous men in the city. In the end Sodom was destroyed because ten righteous men could not be found, but the important point is that Abraham was able to negotiate with God and to insist that he be fair and just.

Although some Hebrews remained in and around Canaan indefinitely, Abraham's grandson, Jacob, led others south to Egypt, probably in search of better farming possibilities. This occurred at about the same time the Hyksos from Asia invaded and conquered Egypt (sometime between 1700 and 1500 B.C.). Hebrews remained in Egypt for several centuries. However, as the Egyptians tried to reestablish national unity after driving out the Hyksos, they began to insist that Hebrews give up their religion and worship Egyptian gods instead. If the Hebrews had agreed to do so, they probably would have ceased to be a separate people and gradually would have integrated with the Egyptian people. But sometime around 1300 B.C., the Hebrews rebelled against the Egyptians under the leadership of Moses, forcing their way out of Egypt in what would become known as the Exodus. Ever since, the Exodus has been considered by Hebrews a great historical event, for it was God who led them out of Egypt in order to protect them. Also significant about the Exodus is that God was portrayed as supporting rebellion against a monarch. Thus it inspired among Hebrews a strong dislike of political despotism, especially political authority that purports to replace divine authority.

The Consequences of the Book of Genesis

What is the relationship between an ancient religious document such as the Book of Genesis and modern technology? Some scholars argue that the Hebrew conceptions of God, nature, and humans created a religious and philosophical orientation that encouraged Western people to develop technologies that could explore and use nature. Although all peoples have developed technologies and used nature to some extent, Western Civilization has been much more aggressive than have other civilizations in its use of technology. The question is, then, what accounts for this aggressiveness?

One important element in the Hebrew religious and philosophical orientation is its de-spiritualization of nature. By believing that God is distinct from nature, the Hebrews were implying that nature is inanimate, empty of gods and spirits. Over the centuries, this idea gradually persuaded many Western people to view nature as a reality that could be used to their advantage. Thus, people were free to develop tools and techniques for exploring nature in any way they saw fit.

The Hebrews also considered human beings to be exalted creatures, entitled to help rule and use the earth. God is quoted as saying, "Let us make man in our image, after our likeness; and let them have dominion over the fish of the sea, and over the birds of the air, and over the cattle, and over all the earth" (Genesis 1:26). The sense of human superiority is also expressed in Genesis 2:19: "So out of the ground the Lord God formed every beast of the field and every bird of the air, and brought them to the man to see what he would call them; and whatever the man called every living creature, that was its name." When Genesis says that God lets "man" name the animals, he is implying that humans are participants in the Creation as a kind of subsidiary partner of God.

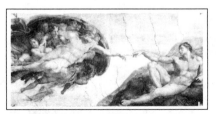

The Creation of Man *The story of the Creation was painted by the Renaissance artist and sculptor Michelangelo on the ceiling of the Sistine Chapel (see Chapter 10). Here, God reaches out to give life to humans, Michelangelo portrays God as distinct from his creation and the earthly world; humans are portrayed as creatures of great worth, created in the divine image. (The Granger Collection)*

Moses

Little is known with certainty about Moses. We know that he was a decisive figure in Hebrew history and that he lived sometime between 1350 and 1250 B.C. We also know that he was a political leader who guided the Hebrews out of Egypt into the Sinai desert, where they wandered for several decades waiting for divine guidance from Yahweh to return to the "Promised Land" (Canaan). Moses was also a religious teacher, who reinvigorated the covenant between God and the Hebrews that had originally been made with Abraham. In particular, Moses received from God the Ten Commandments, a set of moral codes that governed the behavior of Hebrews.

The religion that Moses taught was in the same tradition as that followed by Abraham. Although Yahweh did not deny the existence of other gods, he insisted that Hebrews worship only him. Yahweh was clearly different from other gods in several respects. As a spiritual deity, he could not be identified with any one place and would not tolerate "graven images" of himself. Yahweh also had a special relationship with Hebrews, one that was embodied in a covenant by which he promised to protect Hebrews if they obeyed his commandments. The covenant was unique in several ways. For one thing, it was based on free moral choice on both sides. Most other peoples of the time believed that they had no choice but to worship the gods of their particular areas. The Hebrews were not bound in this way, as they were free to choose to worship Yahweh, and Yahweh was similarly free to leave the Hebrews if they did not obey his commandments. Also unique about the covenant was its moral content, most notably the Ten Commandments (see Exodus 20:1–17). Thus obeying Yahweh meant adhering to certain moral standards. Yet another unique element of the covenant was its assumption of equality. The covenant applied equally to all Hebrew people, not just to priests, tribal leaders, or the upper classes.

THE ESTABLISHMENT OF A HEBREW STATE

Canaan was populated primarily by the polytheistic Canaanites, but during the decades before and after 1200 B.C., Hebrews gradually invaded the land. This invasion was in part a series of battles to defeat and conquer the Canaanites and in part a gradual and peaceful infiltration into Canaan. Sometime after 1200 B.C., twelve Hebrew tribes formed a sacred confederation among the people of Yahweh. This confederation was called *Israel*, and Hebrews were subsequently known as *Israelites*.

The sacred confederation lasted from around 1200 to 1020 B.C. During that time, Israel was united only by the covenant with Yahweh and had no central governnment or capital city. It was endangered,

Moses Michelangelo's statue of Moses (c. 1515–1516) portrays the ancient Hebrew leader as a powerful, majestic figure, holding the tablets containing the Ten Commandments. (The Granger Collection)

however, when the Philistines began to occupy Israelite land. The Philistines were a militarily powerful people who lived to the west of the Hebrews, on the shores of the Mediterranean. They were probably related to the Phoenicians, who lived north of the Israelites.

Unlike the historical records of most other ancient peoples, which contain few accounts of clearly defined individual personalities, the account of the Israelite resistance to the Philistines contains several memorable and distinct human personalities. Samson, for example, is a heroic figure known for his great strength, allegedly having killed a thousand Philistines with the jawbone of an ass. Samson, of course, was undone by Delilah, a beautiful Philistine woman who by enchanting him was able to cut off his hair and thus destroy the source of his strength. David, another folklore hero of the Israelite resistance, is said to have destroyed the Philistine giant, Goliath, in an epic battle. Goliath was armed with a spear while David fought with a slingshot, a highly developed weapon at that time.

To defend themselves against the Philistines, the Israelites instituted a monarchical government sometime around 1020 B.C. The first king was Saul, a man who was periodically seized by spiritual frenzies and thus presumed to have been anointed by Yahweh. After Saul came David, who eventually ended the Philistine threat and organized a central government in the capital city of Jerusalem. The Israelites thought of David as a model king; indeed, Jesus would later be identified as a descendant of David. David was succeeded by Solomon, a powerful ruler who acquired a reputation for being wise. Solomon conquered additional territory for Israel and increased its prosperity by developing extensive commercial ties with other states and rulers (including possibly the Queen of Sheba in Africa). He also used some of this wealth to build the temple at Jerusalem, which became the center of Yahweh worship.

During the reigns of David and Solomon, much of the Old Testament was written. An extraordinary body of literature, the Old Testament was inspired in various ways by Israel's religious spirit. Some of it took the form of devotional poetry:

> As the hart panteth after the water brooks,
> So panteth my soul after thee, O God.
> My soul thirsteth for God, for the living God:
> When shall I come and appear before God?
>
> Psalms 42:1–2

Some of it inquired about what constitutes a good life. The following passage declares the meaninglessness of material possessions:

> Vanity and vanities, saith the Preacher;
> Vanity of vanities, all is vanity.
> What profit hath man of all his labor,
> Wherein he laboureth under the sun?
> One generation goeth, and another generation cometh,
> And the earth abideth for ever.
> The sun also ariseth and the sun goeth down,
> And hasteth to his place where he ariseth.
>
> Ecclesiastes 1:2–5

Yet other parts of the Old Testament were written as lyrical poetry. The following passage expresses the passionate love of a young shepherd and shepherdess (or, in a more religious interpretation, the love of God for Israel):

> The voice of my beloved! behold he cometh,
> Leaping upon the mountains, skipping upon the hills. . . .
> My beloved spake, and said unto me:
> Rise up, my love, my fair one, and come away;

David Michelangelo's statue of the Israelite King David presents him as a heroic figure full of youthful vitality. (B. Glassman)

For lo, the winter is past,
The rain is come and gone;
The flowers appear upon the earth,
The time of the pruning is come.

                                        Song of Songs 2:8–12

These words express well the exuberance felt by many Israelites in the days of David and Solomon. But this exuberance was soon overshadowed by political quarrels within the Israelite kingdom. Although some Israelites had always opposed the establishment of the monarchy, the voices of protest grew louder during Solomon's reign. Solomon was an enormously wealthy and sometimes despotic ruler who had seven hundred wives and three hundred concubines. To support his entourage and continue his construction projects, he imported slaves from Phoenicia (present-day Lebanon) and imposed labor requirements on lower-class Israelites. Solomon's policies resulted in a sharp division between the classes—poverty and sometimes slavery for the lower classes and wealth and power for the upper classes.

Soon after Solomon's death (c. 922 B.C.), a rebellion erupted as his empire disintegrated into two weak states—the Northern Kingdom of Israel (sometimes called Samaria) and the Southern Kingdom of Judah. The two kingdoms lived side by side for a time, until the Northern Kingdom was destroyed by the Assyrians in 721 B.C. and Judah was conquered by the Babylonians in 597 B.C. In both events, many Israelites were either killed or carried off into exile to become slaves.

In addition to these political calamities, the Israelites faced religious problems as well. These problems originated when the Israelites first settled in Canaan. Canaanite religion was polytheistic and focused on soil fertility and good crops. Like the religions of many other ancient peoples, the Canaanites believed in the analogy of human fertility and that of the soil, and they practiced the rituals common to this belief—sexual orgies, sacred prostitution, and sometimes even human sacrifice. As the Israelites settled among and often intermarried with the Canaanites, they began to absorb some of the Canaanite religious practices. Yahweh worship gradually became intermingled with Canaanite religion, and Yahweh was sometimes identified with Baal, the Canaanite god of storms and vegetation.

The Israelite tradition was thus changed in two major ways. One was political and economic in nature: the Israelites lost their equality in political and economic status when under their monarchy they became divided into the rich or the poor. The other major change in Israelite tradition was religious, propelled by the intermingling of Israelite and Canaanite beliefs and practices. These changes, in turn, led to the prophetic movement, in which the prophets protested against what they saw as religious corruption and social injustice in Israelite society. As we will see, the prophetic movement transformed Israelite religion during the eighth to sixth centuries B.C.

THE PROPHETIC MOVEMENT

The word *prophet* is broadly defined as "one who is called." More specifically, it refers to one who is called by God to transmit God's messages. Prophets had long been a part of Hebrew history, serving as advisers to Israelite kings. It wasn't until the ninth century B.C., however, that some prophets began to criticize the behavior of monarchs. The ninth-century prophets were mostly ecstatic visionaries, whereas those of the eighth century B.C. began to write and preach in more reasoned and literary terms. Indeed, their pronouncements constitute large parts of the

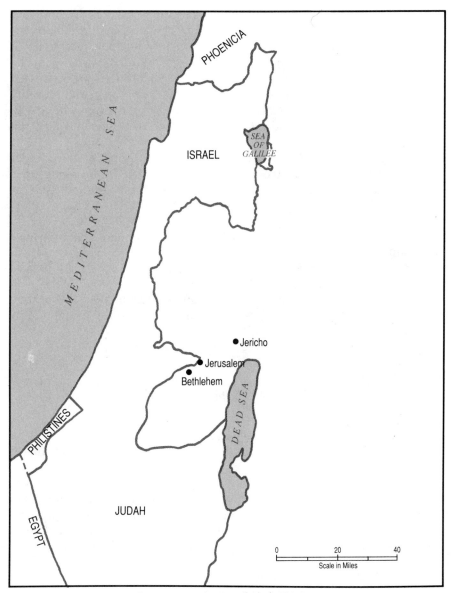

Figure 3.1   Ancient Israel, 800 B.C.

Old Testament. It is not known precisely who put the prophetic books in written form. Probably the sayings of the prophets were passed on orally for a time and then written down.

The prophets of the eighth century B.C. came from the lower classes and hence were not highly respected. They were often provocative and even insulting in their criticisms of Israelite society. As a result, they were usually disliked and sometimes punished. The prophet Jeremiah, for example, was flogged several times by order of various monarchs of Judah who were angered by his prophecies that Judah would soon be destroyed. Yet the prophets were great religious teachers who stressed above all monotheism and morality. Although monotheism and morality had long been implicit in Hebrew religion, the prophets were the first to teach explicitly that one God rules all people and demands morality, not rituals, from them.

The first of the eighth century prophets was Amos, a sheepherder who around 750 B.C. burst onto the Israelite scene by breaking up a religious service that included fertility rites. Amos quoted God as denouncing the rituals:

> Even though you offer me your burnt offerings and cereal offerings,
> I will not accept them.
>
> Amos 5:22

Amos told the Israelites that God wanted justice for the poor rather than rituals, and that people would be judged according to the moral quality of their lives:

> Seek good, and not evil,
>   that you may live;
> and so the Lord, the God of hosts, will be with you,
>   as you have said.
> Hate evil, and love good,
>   and establish justice in the gate.
>
> Amos 5:14–15

"Establish justice in the gate" meant helping the poor and oppressed who often congregated around city gates. Amos warned the Israelite upper classes that God would punish them if they continued to seek personal wealth and ignore the needs of the lower classes. One of Amos's successors, Hosea, described God's punishment in graphic terms:

> They shall fall by the sword,
> Their infants shall be dashed in pieces,
> And their pregnant women ripped open.
>
> Hosea 14:2

Hosea's prediction was realized as small kingdoms were crushed by larger empires and the Northern Kingdom of Israel was conquered by the Assyrians in 721 B.C. More interesting, though, was that the prophets viewed the Assyrian conquest as a carrying out of God's purposes. According to traditional religious thought, God was assumed to protect

Hebrews from all enemies; his failure to do so would reveal his inferiority to the Assyrian gods. Refusing this traditional assumption, the prophets preached that the Assyrians were instruments of God used to punish the Israelites for their sins. In effect, the prophets portrayed God as ruler of both Assyrians and Israelites, thus marking a major step in the development of monotheistic religion. The Assyrian conquest was for the Israelites a political disaster but it was also a spiritual breakthrough.

Still more political calamities ensued. The Southern Kingdom of Judah was destroyed by the Babylonians early in the sixth century B.C., and most of its surviving population was taken into exile in Babylon. At this time, Israelites were increasingly known as Jews, a name derived from Judah. Unlike their counterparts from the Northern Kingdom, the Judean exiles were able to survive as an identifiable community and were able to continue worshipping in their traditional faith.

The experience of exile raised a fundamental spiritual issue: if God is responsible for everything that happens, then why does he allow the good to suffer and the wicked to prosper? This question is confronted in the Book of Job, a long series of poems about a good man who suffers greatly and who wonders what he has done to deserve such suffering. God responds by telling Job that humans will never understand divine ways and must simply accept their fate. The broader message, of course, is that a monotheistic God is so transcendent, so far beyond human comprehension, that his ways cannot be understood.

Babylon was conquered by the Persian Empire in 539 B.C. The Persians were more benevolent than the Babylonians and allowed many Jewish exiles to return home. This good fortune was celebrated by the last of the great prophets, the Second Isaiah. His real name is unknown, but he is called the Second Isaiah because he wrote the last parts of the Book of Isaiah. Ironically, this poet is regarded as one of the greatest writers and spiritual leaders of all time. He was an explicit monotheist and the first prophet to state unequivocally that there is only one God:

> I am the first and I am the last;
>   besides me there is no God.
>
> Isaiah 44:6

Although some early prophets hinted at the concept of monotheism, the Second Isaiah was the first to make its true meaning clear. Jews responded to monotheism by asking the question: If only one God exists, why do only Jews know him? The Second Isaiah explained that Jews were designated by God to suffer for the sins of others and thereby to transmit the divine message to all people. Suffering then, was a sign of the love of God and a means through which people could attain purification and redemption. This concept of the "suffering servant" is described by the Second Isaiah in the following words:

He is despised and rejected of men;
A man of sorrows, and acquainted with grief. . . .
He was wounded for our transgressions,
He was bruised for our iniquities. . . .
With his stripes we are healed. . . .
The Lord hath laid on him the iniquity of us all.

Isaiah 53:3, 5–6

The prophetic movement ended sometime late in the sixth century B.C. Although led by a relatively small number of people, the movement had a tremendous impact on Jewish religion. The prophets universalized Jewish religion by teaching that God ruled the entire universe. They also universalized morality in the sense that they spread the idea of equality among all people in the eyes of God. The prophets were not political revolutionaries, nor did they attempt to overturn the established political order. But their demands for social justice place them among the first social reformers in Western history.

JUDAISM AFTER THE PROPHETS

The people of Judah kept the Hebrew tradition alive; thus their religion came to be known as *Judaism*. Judaism bound the Jewish people together by giving them an identity even though they no longer constituted a politically independent nation. The Jewish people were controlled by the Persians until the second half of the fourth century B.C., when they were absorbed into Alexander the Great's empire (see Chapter 4). After a brief period of Judean independence (142–63 B.C.), they were conquered by the Roman Empire in 63 B.C.

Judaism continued to evolve during the last five centuries B.C. Among the most important developments were new beliefs about the afterlife, which had previously been a minor concern of Judaism (since the Jews assumed that God would reward them in this life by protecting them from enemies). However, encouraged by the political calamities that continued to befall them as well as some Zoroastrian influence (see Chapter 2), Jews began to contend that God's rewards and punishments would be given to them after death. Thus they began to teach that in this life people had to choose between following God, the source of goodness and righteousness, or following Satan, the embodiment of evil. Further, bodily resurrection would occur in the afterlife followed by a divine judgment, at which time the pious would achieve immortality in heaven and the wicked would be damned to eternal hell.

Particularly significant to the development of these ideas about the afterlife was the Book of Daniel, written sometime during the second century B.C. Daniel is apocalyptic—that is, it makes predictions about the ultimate destiny of the world—and much of it is written in allegorical, obscure language. In particular, the Book of Daniel was highly influential in teaching about the "last things"—the resurrection of the dead and the final reign of God.

Another development in Judaism was a belief in the coming of a *Messiah*, meaning one who is "anointed" by God. Some Jews believed that God would send a political Messiah to restore their political independence; others assumed that the Messiah would be a spiritual leader unconcerned with politics. In either case, the belief in a Messiah gave Judaism a sense of expectation, a sense of waiting for some great event. This sense of expectation would later contribute to the rise of Christianity, since the followers of Jesus believed that he was the awaited Messiah.

CONCLUSION

The spiritual journey of the Jewish people had several major impacts on the history of Western Civilization:

1. From it emerged, directly or indirectly, three major religions— Judaism itself, which remained the religion of many Jews; Christianity, which developed out of Judaism in the first century A.D.; and Islam, inspired in part by Judaism in the seventh century A.D.

2. As noted earlier, the Jewish conception of a monotheistic God superior to nature had the effect of de-spiritualizing nature. Since nature was no longer regarded as having spirits, Western people eventually came to believe that they could investigate and use nature to their advantage. Over the centuries, the de-spiritualization of nature encouraged the development of Western science and technology.

3. The Jewish belief that humanity is God's greatest creation helped create a strong sense of pride among Western people. It also supported the idea of freedom, in that people were portrayed as being able to choose between good and evil. Ultimately, Western people came to believe that they could accomplish great things, and this tendency helped make Western Civilization a dynamic and aggressive force in world history.

4. The Jewish belief that God cares for all people helped create a sense of moral responsibility. According to the historian Harry Orlinsky, the prophets taught that "justice was for the weak as well as the strong, . . . that one could not serve God at the same time that he mistreated his fellow man."[1] In Leviticus is the admonition: "And you shall love your neighbor as yourself" (19:18). Jewish moral precepts were far more humane than those of other ancient peoples; indeed, they would ultimately become the source of the most noble, ethical teachings in Western Civilization.

5. The Jewish conception of history was unique. Most other ancient peoples took the fatalistic view that history repeats itself in ever-recurring cycles (see Chapter 2). This cyclical view assumes that every society proceeds through a predetermined sequence of

events—birth, maturity, and inevitable death. The Jews, however, looked forward to a future golden age—the final judgment of God and the entry of the pious into paradise. The effect was to portray history as developing in a linear fashion, as progressing toward a goal. This idea of progress became a fundamental assumption in Western history. Eventually, the Judeo-Christian belief in spiritual progress was modified to include material progress, the presumption that life on earth can be made continually better.

6. Ironically, even though the Jews are cofounders of Western Civilization, they have been persecuted by other Western peoples over the centuries. Christians, for instance, have often perceived Jews as religious and racial enemies, the result being periodic outbursts of anti-Semitism and sometimes the torturing and killing of Jews. The ultimate example of anti-Semitism is the twentieth-century Holocaust, the murdering of more than six million Jews by German Nazis and their collaborators during World War II.

THINGS YOU SHOULD KNOW

Early Hebrew religion
Abraham
Moses
Genesis and Western technology
The Israelite monarchy (1000–900
    B.C.)
The prophetic movement

Amos
Job
The Second Isaiah
Judaism after the prophets
Daniel
Messiah
The significance of Judaism

SUGGESTED READINGS

The Old Testament is, of course, the fundamental source on the spiritual journey of the Jewish people. The stories contained in the Old Testament—such as the life of Moses or the liaison of Samson and Delilah—are not always historically reliable, but they have inspired the writing of many literary works and musical compositions over the centuries.

A good modern analysis of the Old Testament is Dane R. Gordon, *The Old Testament: A Beginning Survey* (Englewood Cliffs, N.J.: Prentice-Hall, 1985). Three good histories of ancient Israel are John Bright, *A History of Israel* (Philadelphia: Westminster Press, 1976); Harry M. Orlinsky, *Ancient Israel*, 2nd ed. (Ithaca, N.Y.: Cornell Univ. Press, 1960); and G. W. Anderson, *The History and Religion of Israel* (New York: Oxford Univ. Press, 1966).

NOTE

[1] Harry M. Orlinsky, *Ancient Israel*, 2nd ed. (Ithaca, N.Y.: Cornell Univ. Press, 1960), p. 144.

4

The Greeks: 1200 to 30 B.C.

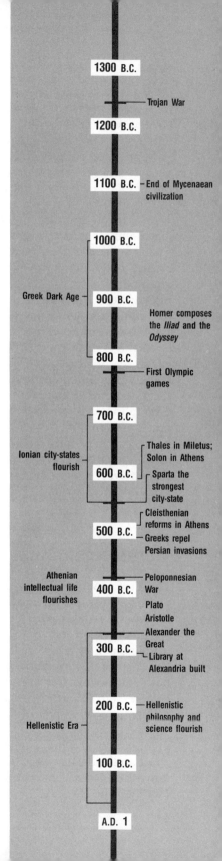

1300 B.C.	
	— Trojan War
1200 B.C.	
1100 B.C.	– End of Mycenaean civilization
1000 B.C.	
Greek Dark Age — **900** B.C.	Homer composes the *Iliad* and the *Odyssey*
— **800** B.C.	
	— First Olympic games
700 B.C.	
Ionian city-states flourish — **600** B.C.	┌ Thales in Miletus; Solon in Athens ┌ Sparta the strongest city-state
500 B.C.	┘ Cleisthenian reforms in Athens — Greeks repel Persian invasions
Athenian intellectual life flourishes — **400** B.C.	— Peloponnesian War, Plato, Aristotle
300 B.C.	— Alexander the Great └ Library at Alexandria built
200 B.C.	— Hellenistic philosophy and science flourish
Hellenistic Era — **100** B.C.	
A.D. 1	

We live round the sea like frogs around a pond," wrote the philosopher Plato of himself and his fellow Greeks. The heart of ancient Greece was the Aegean Sea, with its European and Asiatic coasts on either side and many islands in the middle. There, in that small world, grew an extraordinary civilization founded by one of the most fascinating peoples who ever lived. In terms of material wealth and military power, ancient Greece was not impressive, but in the realm of the human spirit the Greeks were magnificent. In many ways, they "discovered" the human "mind" through their philosophy and rational thought ("rational" meaning the intellectual power of humans to think logically and coherently). The Greeks also developed politics, in that they were the first people to create governments in which decisions are the product of public debate among free citizens. The creations of rational thought and politics were interrelated, since both philosophy and political debate drew on the reasoning powers of the mind.

We do not know with certainty when or how Greek civilization began. Even the Greeks knew little of their origins. Their legends contain only vague references to two older civilizations: the Minoan and the Mycenaean. Minoan civilization flourished on the Greek island of Crete until the middle of the second millennium B.C. (see Chapter 1). Mycenaean civilization was composed of Greek-speaking people who dominated much of mainland Greece from about 2000 to 1100 B.C. The Mycenaeans were a harsh people, predatory warriors who used their military strength to full advantage. They are most famous for their participation in the Trojan War, waged against the city of Troy on the Asiatic coast. The Trojan War of around 1200 B.C. marks the beginning of Greek history as we know it.

THE HOMERIC AGE

The Trojan War is immortalized in the *Iliad* and the *Odyssey*, two epic poems probably written by Homer in the eighth or ninth century B.C. For later Greeks these poems were virtually a "bible" that contained both a religious system and a moral code by which people lived. Homer was thus a religious and moral teacher who more than anyone else formed the Greek spirit. But we know little else about him or even if he indeed wrote both epic poems. Most scholars agree that Homer lived sometime during the so-called Dark Age (1100–800 B.C.), the time after Mycenaean civilization collapsed due to civil wars and attacks by the Dorian peoples who settled in southern Greece. According to Greek legend, Homer was a "blind poet" who wandered through the Greek part of the Asiatic coastland and earned his living by "singing" stories that had been handed down from past generations. In written form, these stories became the *Iliad* and the *Odyssey*.

The *Iliad* and the *Odyssey* portray a brutal world in which success and winning were attained at any cost. The battle scenes described in the poems tell of heads being cut off and bowels gushing out of wounded warriors. The historian Frank Frost describes Homeric warriors as "crude supermen breaking other people's heads, destroying cities, and in general crashing through life with the maximum noise and inconvenience to others."[1]

However, the epic poems are not only vivid accounts of war; for Greeks they were a form of moral and religious instruction. Achilles, the hero of the *Iliad*, is described as "godlike"; he personified for Greeks the brave, courageous warrior who sought everlasting fame through the performance of great deeds. Achilles was a symbol of the model warrior, and later Greeks would honor and imitate him. Similarly, the *Odyssey* is a story about the hero Odysseus, a middle-aged warrior who wandered into all sorts of adventures during his ten-year-long journey back to Greece after the Trojan War. Odysseus is characterized in the poem as wise and curious, traits that later Greeks would admire and seek to emulate.

The attitudes exemplified by Achilles and Odysseus in the Homeric sagas formed what historian C. M. Bowra calls the Greek "heroic outlook."[2] This outlook embodied a strong sense of human worth and thus encouraged Greeks to perform great deeds and to seek honor and fame. The Greeks called it *arete*, meaning "excellence" in the sense that a person should strive to surpass all others in the society. The Greeks' admiration for excellence and greatness was the primary source of their creativity. However, it also imparted a ruthless character to Greek life. Since the goal of life was to surpass all others, the effect was to glorify the superiority of the strong and to degrade those who were considered physically weaker, including women.

The heroic outlook was embodied in Greek religion as well. The Greeks followed a polytheistic religion taught to them by both Homer and Hesiod (the latter poet wrote the *Theogony*, or "genealogy of the gods," sometime during the eighth century B.C.). The most prominent Greek gods were the Olympians, so named because they were reputed to live on Mt. Olympus. These gods usually represented either natural forces (such as Zeus, who controlled the sky) or human forces (such as Aphrodite, who symbolized beauty and the power of attraction between people). Other Greek gods included Poseidon, god of the sea; Hades, god of the underworld; Apollo, god of light and intelligence; Dionysus, god of the vine; Ares, god of war; and Hera, wife of Zeus and goddess of motherhood. The Greeks usually portrayed their gods as constantly fighting, partying, and fornicating. Zeus, for example, the chief Greek god, was notorious for his love affairs and his violent temper. In one story, Zeus ate his first wife just before she gave birth, because he was afraid the child would eventually dethrone him. But having second

The Laocoön Group This marble statue, a good example of Hellenistic art, is a Roman copy of a work done by Agesander, Polydorus, and Athenodorus from the island of Rhodes in the second century B.C. It portrays the priest Laocoön and his two sons, who according to Greek legend were strangled by sea serpents for offending the gods. (Vatican Museum, Rome)

thoughts about the child, Zeus had his own head cleaved open with an axe so that the child—Athena—was born fully grown from Zeus's head.

Although the stories of the Greek gods may seem strange to us, for the Greeks they contained an underlying message. The gods behaved and looked like humans, although they were more powerful than humans—superhuman, higher forms of humanity—and, unlike humans, they could expect to live eternally. A Greek saying expressed this idea well: "What are men? Mortal gods. What are gods? Immortal men."[3] The Greeks were so impressed by human potential that they could not imagine anything higher.

Thus, Greek morality and religion celebrated human greatness. In the early periods of their history, the Greeks stressed the individual's pursuit of fame and glory. Beginning in the sixth and fifth century B.C., however, the Greeks began to emphasize participation in a communal greatness.

IONIA AND THE DISCOVERY OF THE "MIND"

The Greek Dark Age ended early in the eighth century B.C., and a new period of Greek history began (one that historians know much more about). The Greeks themselves dated this new period from 776 B.C., the year of the first Olympic games. Olympia was an old site used for religious festivals honoring Zeus, and the games—a celebration of human strength and power—were one way of paying homage to the humanlike gods. The competitions were all-male affairs that eventually included foot races, chariot races, javelin throws, boxing, wrestling, and many other athletic contests.

Politically, there was no unified "Greece," for the Greeks were divided into several hundred independent communities. The mountainous terrain contributed to this political disunity, since the people of each valley or plateau tended to guard their independence jealously. Each community was known as a *polis* (the origin of the English word *political*) or "city-state." Physically, a *polis* consisted of a city and the surrounding farmland, the entire area often being no more than twenty to forty miles across in any direction. Spiritually, it was a closely knit community bound together by worship of a patron god or goddess. Most of the Greek city-states were small, poor farming areas that had little impact on history. Others, however, became prosperous and powerful merchant cities with populations of three to four hundred thousand.

In the seventh and sixth centuries B.C., the most vigorous Greek city-states were in Ionia, a region on the Asiatic coast in present-day Turkey. It was here that a spiritual and intellectual revolution began— the creation of rational thought. This revolution marks the beginning of a transition in human thought as people began to use "reason"—the intellectual powers of the human mind—rather than mythology to explain natural and human events.

Why did an intellectual revolution occur in Ionian Greece? It occurred partly because the Ionians were open to new ideas and new ways. They lived in a frontier area far from the Greek mainland and, therefore, tended to disregard the old customs and to be skeptical about traditional religion. Furthermore, the Ionian cities were large commercial centers that conducted trade all over the eastern Mediterranean. As a result, the Ionians were stimulated by contacts with the older Egyptian and Persian civilizations. Most influential, though, was the Ionians' idea of *law*—that both nature and human society should be governed by regularities. We do not know with certainty how the Ionians came to develop this concept. One possibility is that it grew out of the Homeric conception of fate; that is, fate controls human destiny in much the same way as laws control nature and society.

The Ionian intellectual revolution was intimately connected with a political revolution. The Ionian cities were dominated by a merchant class that developed written law codes by which it governed. Although written laws were not new to the world, the Ionian laws were the first to express the political will of citizens. Previously, decrees expressed the will of some higher authority, such as a king or a small group of nobles. This is not to say that all Ionian citizens were permitted to express their political views, for women, slaves, and usually the lower classes were excluded. But this was the first time in Western history that people were governed by written rules that at least some ordinary citizens had helped fashion. Political decisions were increasingly made as a result of some public debate, encouraging citizens to learn how to think, reason, and persuade one another. Thus, the habit of reasoned argument developed in the political life of some Ionian cities, and the same habit was carried over into the intellectual realm.

Thales and Other Ionians

Thales of Miletus, born around 625 B.C., was the most prominent figure in the Ionian intellectual revolution. Later Greeks considered him one of the seven "wise men" and frequently recounted stories about him. One typical story about an absentminded intellectual told of Thales falling head over heels into a well because he was gazing at the stars and forgot to watch where he was going.

Thales is regarded as the first Western philosopher, primarily because of his contention that water is the basic reality in the universe. He probably was not saying that everything comes from water; rather, he was trying to account for life in the universe by portraying water as the fundamental sustaining principle of life. Thales's contention was unique in several respects. Perhaps most significant is the fact that he attempted to explain life by analogy to a natural substance—water—instead of to a god of water. Thales viewed nature as a thing not as a realm full of spirits. His view marks an important change in Western scientific thought. Another significant thesis in Thales's theory is that all living things are derived from one fundamental reality. He was assuming, therefore, that there is a fundamental order that underlies the diversity of life. This was another important change in Western thought, the beginning of the idea that nature is governed by law. Perhaps most significant, though, is the fact that Thales based his argument not on myths or some other authority, but solely on his own ability to think and reason. In effect, he was saying that "I" think all things are made of water, not the "gods" or the "ancient authorities." For the first time in Western history, a man was appealing to human reason, the rational mind, as the arbiter of truth.

Thales was not a lone original genius; he was a part, perhaps the most important part, of a long tradition of curiosity and inquisitiveness that flourished in Ionian Greece. Lyric poetry, for example, had been created long before Thales's time. Through it Ionians like Sappho and Archilochus expressed their personal feelings, even erotic desires, thereby displaying the individual human voice. Sappho, one of the few women to make a mark on Greek history, established a finishing school for young women on the island of Lesbos (hence the English word *lesbian*), and often wrote love poems to other women. An example is a poem written to

Aphrodite, the goddess of love: "Ornate-throned immortal Aphrodite,/ wile-weaving daughter of Zeus, I entreat you:/do not overpower my heart, mistress, with ache and anguish,/but come here." Archilochus was even more exuberant in proclaiming his desires. Speaking of his girlfriend, he wrote that he wanted "to fall upon her busy paunch and thrust belly against belly, thighs against thighs." After being reproached for running away from a losing military clash, he said: "One of the Saians is rejoicing in the shield/which I left reluctantly by a bush. . . ./But I saved myself. What does that shield matter to me?/It can go to hell! I'll get another one some day just as good."[4]

After Thales came a long succession of "wise men," who became known as "philosophers" (*philosophy* means "love of wisdom"). They included Anaxagoras, Anaximenes, Pythagoras, Heraclitus, and Empedocles. Some of these philosophers applied the idea of law to the entire universe and thereby created the concept of a *cosmos* ("world order"), the assumption that the universe is governed by one fundamental force and can be understood by the human mind. Other philosophers applied the powers of human reason in different ways. *History* was born in Ionia; the first known historians—Cadmus and Hecataeus—were from Miletus. Their writings did not survive, but most scholars agree that they were the first to apply the critical, rational approach to the study of human affairs and human history.

Despite their intellectual creativity, the Ionians did not endure long. During the second half of the sixth century B.C., they were threatened by the rising power of the Persian Empire. Most of the Ionian cities were soon conquered or destroyed by the Persians, marking the end of the Ionian period. The center of Greek life then shifted from Asiatic Ionia to the Greek mainland.

SPARTA

On the Greek mainland, Sparta was the most powerful and prestigious city-state during the sixth century B.C. It was also unique in one respect, for the Spartans had organized themselves into a tightly disciplined military state. The Spartans believed that the law code that defined their way of life had been established by Lycurgus, a quasi-legendary figure who may have lived in the eighth century B.C.

Located on the Peloponnesus peninsula in the southernmost part of the Greek mainland, Sparta was one of the most fertile agricultural areas in all of Greece. But the rich land was not alone sufficient to support Sparta's growing population; thus, sometime during the eighth or seventh century B.C., the Spartans conquered neighboring lands and enslaved those who lived there. These state-owned slaves, called *helots*, did all of the farm work necessary to supply the citizens with food.

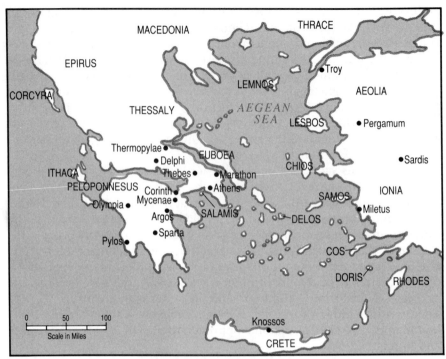

Figure 4.1   Ancient Greece

By the sixth century B.C., the helots outnumbered the Spartan citizens by approximately ten to one, and the Spartans constantly feared the possibility of slave revolt. One such revolt occurred between 650 and 620 B.C.

To protect themselves against slave revolt, the Spartans became a nation of soldiers. They left farm work to the *helots* and business and commerce to another class of noncitizens—the *perioeci*. Only male Spartans were citizens, and they spent their entire lives in the army. All male children were examined at birth by a council of elders for deformities or other signs of weakness. Those deemed weak or deformed were taken to a local mountainous area and left to die. Those who passed this first test would remain at home until the age of seven, at which time they were sent to a military barracks and trained for military service. These young boys were taught to suffer pain without complaining, to obey their elders without questioning, and to eat sparingly (the basic Spartan food was an unappetizing wheat porridge). The military training period lasted until the young men turned twenty. At this time, Spartans entered the army and continued to serve there until the age of sixty or until death.

Even though Spartan males spent most of their lives in the military, they were still expected to marry and to produce male children. Celibacy, in fact, was a crime in Spartan society. According to one Greek story, if male Spartans reached adulthood without being married, they might be pushed into a dark room containing an equal number of women and left to choose their wives in the darkness. The role of married Spartan women was crucial. Since Spartan men were nearly always in the army and away from home, the women had the primary responsibility of raising the children and supervising the household. The household work, however, was done by slaves. In general, Spartan women had greater freedom and were better educated than women in other Greek city-states.

In effect, everyone who lived in Sparta was a slave of some sort. Spartan men, although considered free citizens and the governors of the state, were actually enslaved to the military system. Spartan women had no choice but to perform their assigned roles—marrying and raising children. The helots lived under a perpetual reign of terror: a secret police watched them constantly and killed any who were even suspected of causing trouble. Once a year, the Spartans proclaimed a state of siege during which any citizen could kill any helot with impunity.

Such a way of life might seem extraordinarily unappealing. Other Greeks greatly admired the Spartans but refused to imitate them. The Athenians quipped that the Spartans were willing to die for their city because they had no reason to live. Nevertheless, most Spartans were probably content with their situation, for they were known to be enormously proud and protective of their city. During the sixth and fifth centuries B.C., Sparta had the most powerful army in Greece and was a recognized leader among the city-states.

In the end, however, the Spartan way of life produced the seeds of its own destruction. Obsessed with a military-based life-style, the Spartans became notoriously narrowminded and unable to adapt to change. In the fourth century B.C., Spartan's power as a city-state began to decline and many of the helots were freed. Sparta never flourished again.

ATHENS

Athens is the best known of the Greek city-states, both because it created a *democratic* form of government and because the new democracy helped stimulate several generations of intellectual and artistic genius. *Democracy* is here defined as government by citizens, meaning the free men of Athens. Athenian democracy was much more limited than the twentieth-century perspective, since only free males had political rights and foreign residents, women, and slaves—the bulk of the Athenian population—did not. Nevertheless, Athens defined for the first time the concept of democracy and was more open and democratic than most other societies of its time.

Political Evolution

Why did Athens, rather than some other city or nation, create the first democratic government? One reason may be its close relationship with the Ionian city of Miletus, where public debate and reasoned argument emerged during the seventh to sixth centuries B.C. Another reason may be the Phoenician alphabet, which enabled many Athenians and other Greeks to become literate. Yet another reason may be that Athens was a sufficiently wealthy commercial city to support a large citizenry. Finally, Athens produced creative political leaders at crucial times in its history.

Creative leadership was needed in Athens to respond to a social and economic crisis. Like Sparta and other parts of the Greek world, Athens became overpopulated by the seventh century B.C., and the result was a land shortage. (Unlike Sparta, though, Athens did not respond to this problem by installing a military system of government.) Many Athenian farmers were in debt and were sold into slavery to pay off their debts. This situation not only produced considerable social turmoil among the farmers but also threatened to weaken or destroy the Athenian army. Since the Athenian army included citizens who were farmers, Athens could not afford to allow too many citizens to become slaves.

The Athenian government was at this time an aristocracy, in which a few noble families dominated the life of the city. Around 594 B.C., the nobles, fearful that the economic crisis would lead to social revolution, designated a man named Solon to resolve the situation. Fortunately for Athens, Solon was a political genius who had gained the confidence of both the nobility and the indebted lower classes. He immediately established a number of social reforms, including a prohibition on selling debtors into slavery, a program for buying freedom for those already enslaved for debts, and a procedure for allowing some limited political participation by the lower classes. According to Greek legend, Solon insisted that the Athenians agree to maintain these measures for at least ten years and then set off on a tour of the world.

Solon's reforms, which guaranteed the freedom of lower-class citizens, were the first major step toward the creation of democracy. Although social turmoil continued in Athens for a while—the lower classes clamored for a redistribution of land and the noble families struggled among themselves for control of the government—it came to an end when the government appointed another reform-minded states-man, Cleisthenes, to overhaul the entire Athenian political structure. Cleisthenes came to power around 508 B.C., and with popular support he formulated a democratic constitution for Athens. The Cleisthenian reforms consisted of four major elements:

1. Athens was divided into a number of local units called *demes* (hence the word *democracy*), from which representatives were

The Parthenon (built between 447 and 432 B.C.)   Towering above Athens, the Parthenon, a temple to the goddess Athena, was built on a high mountain known as the Acropolis. The great structure could be seen for miles and also symbolized the Athenians' pride in their city. (B. Glassman)

elected by the free men—the citizens—to a Council, or *Boulê*, of five hundred members. The Council carried out the daily business of the city, and many citizens participated since membership was limited to two years.

2. The public assembly, a legislative body that could debate and approve or reject all major governmental decisions, was open to all citizens. The assembly became the heart of Athenian democracy and its meetings were often boisterous affairs, with speakers being applauded, jeered, and even shouted down.

3. A board of ten generals was elected each year to lead the city in times of war. Since a general could be reelected indefinitely, the board became a center of strong leadership.

4. A unique custom known as *ostracism* was designed to prevent a powerful leader from becoming a tyrant. Each year a ballot could be held, if it was felt necessary, and whoever received the largest number of votes was banished from the city for ten years.

The Cleisthenian reforms guaranteed citizen participation in government. However, only adult males were considered citizens, and they numbered only about 42,000 out of a total Athenian population of

400,000. Excluded from political participation were women and slaves, the latter representing about half of Athenian population.

The Position of Women and Slaves

Athenian women were not permitted to vote, make contracts, conduct business involving large sums of money, or serve as witnesses in legal cases. A woman was always under the authority of a man. Before marriage, a woman's father controlled her, and after marriage, her husband assumed control. Athenian women spent most of their lives secluded at home; their roles in society were to work in the household and to produce future Athenian citizens. It is difficult to describe much more than this with great accuracy, since Athenian women were uneducated and therefore left few writings that tell of their thoughts and feelings. One interesting point, though, is that the great Athenian dramatists often portrayed strong female characters, usually of noble birth. This suggests that there may have been some assertive, independent women in Athens.

The Athenian practice of subordinating women had several side effects. One was the acceptance of homosexuality. Many Athenian men believed that love between men was natural, and some suggested that, since men were superior to women, homosexual love was superior to heterosexual love. Another manifestation of female subordination was the acceptance of widespread prostitution. So many female slaves became prostitutes that in many Greek cities the young males knew prostitutes better than women who remained at home. Athens, in particular, had a great variety of prostitutes. Most were ordinary prostitutes, known as *pornai* (hence the modern word *pornography*), who sometimes wore sandals that had nails on the soles spelling "Follow Me!" in the mud of the street. The higher-class prostitutes, called *hetairai*, were usually well-educated and attractive women who had managed to accumulate some money. In one sense, the hetairai were the most "liberated" women in Athens, since they were the only females allowed to mix freely in male company. Their freedom was limited, however, in that neither they nor their children could ever become citizens. Some of the hetairai became famous among the Athenians. Lais of Corinth, for example, was so renowned that many Greeks claimed she was the greatest conqueror they had ever known.

Athenian males considered their various sexual practices nonexclusive. Most believed that the same man could love his wife heterosexually, love a male friend homosexually, and also have sexual relations with prostitutes.

The other subjugated people in Athens were, of course, the slaves. The Greeks accepted slavery as natural. Most slaves were captured in warfare, and since war was thought to be natural, slavery was as well.

Legally, slaves were just pieces of property, but some were treated reasonably well. A housemaid or a field hand on a small farm might have become virtually one of the family. Many slaves who were skilled craftsmen worked alongside free citizens, and an enterprising slave might have saved enough money to rent his own home and even eventually buy his freedom. Other slaves, however, were treated harshly. Girl and boy slaves were often sexually abused, and many adult slaves died from hard labor in the silver mines at Athens. One of the anomalies of the Greek experience is that as the Athenians were evolving a democratic constitution they were also operating a slave market from which tax revenues were a major source of income for the democratic state. (Much the same can be said about the early history of the United States.)

The Persian Threat

Despite the fact that Athenian democracy was so limited, Athens was still closer to being a self-governing community than any other society of the time. But the new democracy soon faced a severe threat. The mainland Greeks, especially the Athenians, had helped the Ionian Greeks in their fight against the Persians. Thus, to exact revenge and also to continue their imperial expansion, the Persians invaded Greece in 490 B.C. Many Greek city-states surrendered to what appeared to be the overwhelming might of the great Persian Empire from the east, but Athens and a few others successfully defeated the Persian invasion at the battle of Marathon (490 B.C.). In the aftermath, a professional runner named Pheidippides allegedly ran the first "marathon" race by carrying the message of Athenian victory from Marathon back to Athens. According to the story, Pheidippides was so exhausted by his exertions that he ran into the city, announced the victory, and fell over dead.

The Persian threat continued, however, and in 480 B.C. the Persians invaded again. This time they won a hard-fought battle at Thermopylae, but were defeated at the naval battle of Salamis. This was the last major attempt by the Persian Empire to subjugate the Greeks.

Intellectual and Artistic Creativity

By the end of the year 480 B.C., the Athenians could look back on a remarkable thirty-year period in which they had not only created a democratic government but also had taken the lead in twice defeating the mighty Persian Empire. These achievements naturally produced great pride and self-confidence, and for the next sixty to eighty years Athens was at its peak. During that time, politicians and citizens debated momentous political issues in the assembly, dramatists debated questions of justice in their plays, philosophers argued about how humans

Woman Vase From the fifth century B.C., this vase portrays a young Greek woman in typical ancient Greek dress. The lyre, a stringed musical instrument, was often played while reciting poetry. (Metropolitan Museum of Art, NY)

could attain greater knowledge, historians told stories about the great events of the past and present, and artists and sculptors sought to capture the essence of beauty in their work. In short, for a few brief decades Athens became the center of a "prolonged conversation." This conversation focused on the questions that Athenians regarded as most important—how to live well, how to create a just society, how to create beauty in an often brutal and ugly world. The Athenians never regarded economic matters as the only important thing in life. Rather, they often preferred to devote their energies to a consideration of how to use what wealth they had to live a good life.

One of the most brilliant voices in the Athenian conversation was that of the dramatist Aeschylus (525–456 B.C.). Drama was one of the Greeks' favorite art forms. Dramatic productions attracted large audiences; they were not only a form of public entertainment but also a means of moral and religious education for the Greek community. Tragic dramas, in particular, were educational, often communicating to their audiences the Greek conception of life. The tragedians taught that humans are great and noble but not perfect; even the greatest suffer from a "flaw" that will eventually destroy them. Aeschylus presented this view in a series of plays that focused on the character Prometheus. Prometheus, though a god, was also a symbol of humanity because he stole fire from the gods and gave it to humans, who used the gift to build civilization. Thus, Prometheus represented both the greatness and weakness of humanity. Zeus, the chief god, punished Prometheus's rebellion by having him chained to a rock, where each day an eagle ate his liver, which then grew back at night so that it could be eaten again the next day. Zeus also punished humankind by sending to earth a young woman named Pandora, who brought with her a box that, when opened, released numerous evils into the world. The introduction of evil into the world was associated with female figures in both the Greek tradition—Pandora—and the Hebrew tradition—Eve. Aeschylus thus used a myth to teach the Athenians about great moral issues.

Sophocles (496–406 B.C.), the second of the great tragic dramatists, composed in *Antigone*, a long meditation on what happens when one moral good conflicts with another. Antigone was required by traditional family obligations to bury her dead brother, but the king of her city opposed a proper burial for her brother because he had perished in rebelling against the city. The king argued that obedience to the law was a moral good that outweighed Antigone's family obligations. When Antigone insisted on following the laws of her conscience as opposed to the laws of her city, she was executed.

At the same time that Sophocles was writing, Herodotus (490–425 B.C.) was reciting his histories in the Athenian marketplace (the *agora*). Often called the "father of history," Herodotus said that he wanted to ensure that the great deeds of the past would be remembered. Thus he told the story of the Persian Wars, in which he portrayed Athens as a hero defending Greek freedom against Persian tyranny. His story, in written form, is the first great historical work of Western culture.

These and other creative activities quickly turned Athens into an intellectual and artistic center. From all over Greece came a number of men called *Sophists* ("wise men"), who offered to educate young men in the art of politics. The Sophistic declaration that "man is the measure of all things" was an affirmation of human ability, particularly the ability of people to govern themselves. The education that the Sophists provided was an education in how to persuade an audience, how to speak well in the citizen's assembly. The subjects they taught—grammar (how to write), rhetoric (how to speak), dialectic (how to think)—became the core of what would later be called "liberal arts education." The Sophists' reputation eventually suffered, however, partly because they insisted on being paid for their services at a time when most teachers were independently wealthy nobles. The Sophists also lost credibility because other philosophers (principally Plato) accused them of being cynical relativists who cared only about winning arguments and not about truth.

Athenian Society

It would be inaccurate to say that Athens became a pristine paradise in which great and noble people did great and noble things, for all its creative vitality occurred in a poverty-stricken, even squalid society. In terms of such basic things as housing, dress, and food, the ordinary Athenian was quite poor. His house was small, without plumbing or heating. His dress was a woolen blanket, designed to be wrapped around his body, and a pair of shoes, both made to last a lifetime. The typical Athenian diet consisted of coarse bread, cheese, some vegetables, watered-down wine, and occasionally some meat. Garbage and sewage were thrown in the streets until washed away by the rain. The streets were narrow and dirty, and in the hot, dry summers must have given off an extraordinary stench.

Obviously, economic wealth was greatly limited in Athenian society. Many Athenians were poor farmers, eking out a living on a small plot of land. In the city, most Athenian men worked as merchants or craftsmen in small shops, while women remained at home. The result of this poverty in Athens and most other Greek city-states was that the Greeks were unable to provide for all of the children they produced. Consequently, the Greeks exposed unwanted children, particularly females. It was not uncommon in a Greek city to see an infant left alone to die on the streets or in some other place. These infants usually either died of exposure or were taken and reared by slave dealers.

To understand Athenian society, we must, in the words of historian Alfred Zimmern, "learn how to be civilized without being comfortable."[5] The Athenians, in spite of, and perhaps because of, their primitive living conditions, sought to civilize and beautify their city. On the Acropolis, the mountain in the middle of the city, they built the Parthenon between 447 and 432 B.C., a temple to the goddess Athena. The Parthenon is considered one of the most beautiful of all the Greek architectural creations. (The most lavish Greek buildings were often temples, usually in the form of rectangles with the roof supported by rows of columns.)

The Parthenon and other buildings on the Acropolis were embellished by sculptures created by numerous artists. Greek art was representational, meaning that the artist sought to copy or imitate some aspect of the natural world—the human body, for example. (Partly because of Greek influence, the representational approach to art dominated Western history for much of the next two thousand years.)

Athenians and other Greek sculptors wanted, in particular, to represent the human body. Some of the most notable examples are the statues of Zeus and Athena by Phidias, the *Discus Thrower* by Myron, and the *Aphrodite of Cnidus* by Praxiteles.

The Peloponnesian War

Athens's greatest age began to decline during the last third of the fifth century B.C. A major reason for the Athenian decline was the Peloponnesian War (431–404 B.C.); the underlying cause of the war was fear of Athens by other Greeks. After the Persian invasions of 480 B.C., Athens had organized the Delian League, a military alliance of Greek cities designed to ward off future Persian threats. Over the years that followed, the Delian League came to be more like an Athenian empire than a military alliance, as Athens dominated the other cities and collected taxes from them. The Athenians became enormously proud of their city, and their great political leader Pericles (governed 460–430 B.C.) sought to make Athens the "school of Hellas," a shining example of democracy and beauty to the other Greek cities. But the other cities, led by Sparta, saw Athenian pride as arrogance and began to resist Athens's expanding influence. Thus the war broke out in 431 B.C.

The Peloponnesian War was a full-scale Greek civil war—Athens and its allies against Sparta and its allies—that lasted twenty-seven years. In military terms, it was a relatively small affair. Fighting was sporadic and scattered; the largest battle of the first ten years involved only seven thousand Athenian soldiers against a similar number from the city-state of Boeotia. But the war gradually brutalized and undermined Greek society. A plague struck Athens and killed about a quarter of its population. Both Sparta and Athens began to execute prisoners, and in some cases entire cities were destroyed by fire or famine.

The pace of the Peloponnesian War was slow, so the Athenian political and intellectual conversation continued. In fact, the war provided much of its subject matter. Euripides (485–406 B.C.), the most radical of the great tragic dramatists, condemned warfare and slavery in *The Trojan Women*. Thucydides (460–403 B.C.), one of the greatest historians of all time, wrote his history of the Peloponnesian War while in exile from Athens. For him, the city of Athens was a tragic hero, proud and great but "flawed." In effect, Thucydides was celebrating Athenian spiritual and political greatness, even though he knew his native city was losing the war.

The man who cheered Athens through the dark hours of the Peloponnesian War was Aristophanes (450–385 B.C.), the greatest of the comic dramatists. Comedy began in bawdy revels and became an integral part of the Greek theater. The Greeks knew that humans could be obscene, ridiculous, and absurd as well as heroic and great. Aristophanes used this comic tradition to oppose and mock those who encouraged the war. In *Lysistrata*, for example, he portrays a general strike of Athenian women who refuse to sleep with their husbands until the men agree to stop the fighting. The drama is both a satire on the stupidity of men and a plea for peace. It is also a hilarious farce, in that the women are so oversexed that they can barely stay away from their husbands and the men are so sex-starved that they cannot concentrate on the peacemaking process.

The Peloponnesian War ended with the defeat of Athens in 404 B.C., though military conflicts continued to erupt for another sixty or seventy years. The war gravely weakened all of the Greek city-states. Athens, occupied by Sparta for a few years after the war, managed to rebuild and maintain its democratic government for another century and a half. Its greatest days were over, though, as the Athenian population steadily declined and its economic strength slowly dissipated. Only in the field of philosophy did Athens remain a leader in the fourth century B.C.

The Great Philosophers

Socrates   Socrates (469–399 B.C.) was the greatest Athenian philosopher of the late fifth century B.C. A village "character," he was an obese and unattractive man who spent his days roaming the streets of Athens and arguing ethics and politics with young men. Forceful and argumentative, Socrates often browbeat his opponents. The nineteenth-century German philosopher G. W. F. Hegel once labeled Socrates the "patron saint of moral twaddle." At his best, though, Socrates taught people to think. His teachings were recorded (by his student Plato) in dialogue form, thereby displaying the intellectual activity of discussion and the search for truth. Socrates believed that the good life meant a continual quest for knowledge, that knowledge produced good moral conduct, and that good conduct led to happy, good citizens. He may have been right, but his questioning, irreverent attitude enabled his enemies to portray him as a subversive influence. He was brought to court on charges of corrupting the youth and being "impious" toward the gods. He was convicted and forced to drink poison. Socrates' revenge on his enemies, of course, was that his death created an enduring image of himself as a brave philosopher who died for his beliefs.

Plato   The philosophical tradition was carried on by Socrates' student Plato (427–347 B.C.), considered one of the most influential philosophers in Western history. Plato traveled about the Mediterranean for a while before returning to Athens, where he founded an educational institution called the *Academy*. There he taught and wrote such works as *The Republic*, in which is examined the nature of human knowledge and the ideal of a perfect society. Many of Plato's works are written in dialogue form, thus emphasizing that knowledge is the product of debate and intellectual conflict.

As a philosopher, Plato was an idealist; that is, one who believes that truth and reality are spiritual. He argued that the material world in which humans live cannot be ultimate reality because things in the material world are always changing (people grow older, for example) and ultimate, perfect reality would by definition never change. Thus Plato concluded that truth had to be sought in a spiritual realm where perfection exists. The idea of perfect justice, for example, exists in a spiritual realm, and earthly forms of justice are imperfect copies of the perfect justice. In *The Republic,* Plato uses the analogy of men chained in a cave. Because the chained men (symbolically representing humanity) faced the inside of the cave, they could only see and know whatever shadows appeared on the cave walls. Thus real knowledge is available only to those few—philosophers—who can free themselves from the chains and go outside the cave to see reality in the bright sunlight.

Plato's search for perfection led him to prescribe what an ideal society would be like. His ideal was nondemocratic, reflecting his pessimism about Athens in the aftermath of the Peloponnesian War. Plato contended that a perfect society would be one where justice dominates. Justice requires that each person do what he or she is best suited to do. Some people are more suited to farming or to carrying on business, so they should be in a producing class. Others more strong and courageous are best suited to defending the society, so they should be in a warrior class. Still others—the rational and intelligent—should rule, these being in Plato's words the "philosopher-kings."

Aristotle   After Plato came Athens's last great philosopher—Aristotle (384–322 B.C.). A prolific writer who collected and organized information on such diverse subjects as biology, logic, politics, ethics, and metaphysics, Aristotle's approach to the search for knowledge was different from Plato's. Whereas Plato followed the deductive method—reasoning from general principles to the particular fact—Aristotle used the inductive method—studying and reasoning from specific facts to form a basis for defining general principles. For example, to determine the true meaning of justice, Plato would say that we would have to begin with some standard through which we could identify particular forms of justice. Aristotle, however, would say that we would have to study a variety of particular examples of justice before we could generalize or establish a universal standard.

Aristotle's writings are a massive summary of Greek knowledge. He defined the discipline of logic, and the information he collected on plants and animals provided the basis for much Western scientific thought over the next fifteen hundred years. Aristotle's political writings became a

basis for political thought as well, for he and his assistants collected over
150 constitutions from Greek city-states. In so doing, he contended that
there are only a few forms of government—government by an individual,
government by a few, and government by the many. Each of these three
types could, according to Aristotle, be good or bad. If an individual rules
well, then government is a monarchy; if not, it is a tyranny. If the few rule
well, government is an aristocracy (rule by the best); if not, it is an
oligarchy or plutocracy (rule by the rich). If the many rule well, the result
is government by laws (constitutional government); if not, the result is
democracy (defined as government by the mob). Like Plato, Aristotle
feared democratic rule.

THE HELLENISTIC ERA

The Greeks believed they were descended from an ancient ancestor
named Hellen; thus they called themselves *Hellenes* and their country
Hellas. Modern historians use the term *Hellenistic* to describe the last
phase of ancient Greek history, spanning from the time of Alexander the
Great to the final Roman conquest of the Greek-speaking world around
30 B.C. During this period of about three hundred years, Greek thought
and culture spread throughout the eastern Mediterranean.

The Hellenistic Age began with Alexander the Great or slightly before
with his father, Philip of Macedon. Philip built Macedonia, the mountainous area north of Greece proper, into a powerful kingdom, and in 338
B.C. his armies conquered the Greek city-states. Two years later, Philip
was killed by an assassin and was succeeded by Alexander. Over the next
thirteen years (336–323 B.C.), the new Macedonian ruler would become
Alexander the Great, one of the most triumphant military conquerors of
all time. By the end of his life, Alexander commanded a vast empire that
extended southward to Egypt and eastward all the way to India. We do
not know with certainty what Alexander's goals were as a ruler. Some
historians believe that he was simply a great military leader who knew
well how to fight and conquer. Others see Alexander as what he claimed
to be, an apostle of Greek culture who used Greek language and
institutions to unify a cosmopolitan empire. Once, for example, Alexander sought to encourage the mixture of peoples by presiding over a
mass wedding, in which several thousand of his Greek soldiers married a
similar number of Persian women.

Alexander died in 323 B.C. Almost immediately, his empire fell apart
as his generals fought among themselves and eventually divided the
empire into three separate kingdoms—the Antigonid kingdom on the
Greek mainland, the Seleucid in the Near East, and the Ptolemaic in
Egypt. These Hellenistic monarchies ruled large areas for their own
profit, using Greeks and Macedonians to staff their armies and bureaucracies. Thus, Greeks became the dominant upper class throughout

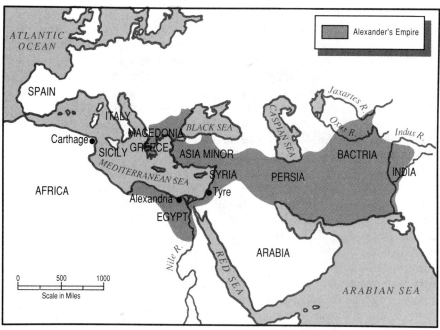

Figure 4.2 The Empire of Alexander the Great, 323 B.C.

much of the eastern Mediterranean and controlled huge masses of native farmers, many of whom were enslaved.

The Hellenistic world was in many ways a chaotic, brutal place, where powerful men competed for wealth and influence and many people lived in poverty. Hellenistic cities were often larger than the old Greek city-states and usually contained large slum areas inhabited by rootless people searching for some well-being and security in their lives. It was no accident later on that Christianity, which offered hope to the struggling masses, would grow rapidly in this harsh environment.

Hellenistic Creativity

Hellenistic intellectual life was vibrant. It gave birth to two new schools of philosophy that sought to instruct people on how to attain individual happiness in a chaotic world and that had considerable impact on the Hellenistic upper classes and later on the Roman aristocracy. One was *Epicureanism,* named after its founder Epicurus (371–270 B.C.) Believing that the gods have nothing to do with humans, Epicurus told people not to fear divine forces or punishment in an afterlife but to seek happiness on earth. For Epicurus, happiness meant withdrawing from the material world into a life of contemplation, but his philosophy was misinterpreted by many to mean "enjoy yourself" and "eat, drink, and be merry."

The other philosophy to emerge from Hellenistic culture was *Stoicism,* founded by Zeno of Citium around 300 B.C. The Stoics envisioned the universe as controlled by a divine force. Thus, people were taught to accept their role in life without questioning it. Self-control and the ability to accept one's fate were considered great virtues. Another implication of Stoicism was a general notion of equality. Since it was presumed that one god controls all people, then it followed that they are equal in some fundamental sense. The Stoics never went so far as to consider freeing the slaves or establishing political equality, but their idea of equality, or what they called "brotherhood," would be influential in later ages.

Hellenistic culture also produced a creative proliferation in science, mathematics, and technology—much of it centering in Alexandria, Egypt. The Ptolemaic rulers of Egypt (323–30 B.C.) built a large library and museum called the "House of the Muses" at Alexandria around 300 B.C. The library eventually gathered over half a million manuscripts and the museum became a scholarly research complex that included laboratories, astronomical observatories, private study areas, and lecture halls. For several hundred years—from the third century B.C. to the fourth century A.D.—Alexandria was a vibrant center of scientific research. The well-known mathematician Euclid wrote *Elements of Geometry,* and Archimedes did much research in higher mathematics. Herophilus studied anatomy, traced much of the human nervous system, and continued the medical tradition begun by Hippocrates (460–377 B.C.), the "Father of medicine." The geographer Erastosthenes calculated the circumference of the earth, while the astronomer Aristarchus theorized that the earth revolves around the sun. (His view, however, did not prevail; in the second century A.D., the astronomer Ptolemy convinced most scholars that the earth was the center of the universe. Ptolemy's view dominated until the sixteenth century A.D., when Copernicus revived Aristarchus's conception of the universe.)

Alexandria was thus the site of the greatest achievements in Western science and mathematics before modern times. Unfortunately, much of the knowledge that was accumulated in Alexandria during this time was lost when, in the fourth century A.D., Christians destroyed the museum because they thought it was a center of pagan learning. The knowledge that did survive became the foundation for further research by later scientists.

CONCLUSION

The scientific enterprise at Alexandria was the last creative surge of the ancient Greeks. Creativity had enabled the Greeks to define the concept of democracy, to develop the habit of rational thought in philosophy, and to

Roman Roads

Romans governed successfully in part because they provided many material advantages for the peoples of the empire. Roman engineers constructed large baths, theaters, aqueducts, and roads. The baths and theaters were centers of entertainment, and the aqueducts brought water from rivers to cities. The water was used for drinking, for irrigating crops, for the baths, and for ornamental fountains.

Perhaps most impressive, though, was the Roman road system. Over the centuries, the Romans built about fifty thousand miles of road to connect the various parts of their empire. The roads were adapted to local climates and weather conditions. In marshy areas, for example, the roads were made of staked-down timbers on which layers of gravel and stone were placed. In areas with solid ground, the road foundations consisted of layers of gravel and clay, with stones placed on top. In addition, milestones were placed at the appropriate points along the roads to assist the traveler, and in some areas small roadside hotels were provided.

The Roman road system was far more advanced than that of other ancient peoples. In some areas, Roman roads were better constructed than anything else that would be built until the nineteenth and twentieth centuries A.D. Some Roman roads are still in use today.

Via Appia ("The Appian Way")   *The Appian Way was one of the first major roads built by the Romans, stretching over three hundred miles from Rome to southeastern Italy. In this nineteenth-century depiction, a section of the Appian Way near Rome has tombs and monuments on both sides. (The Granger Collection)*

do a great deal of important scientific and mathematical work. By the
first century B.C., the days of political and intellectual brilliance were
over, although the memories remained. The Olympic games continued
until 393 A.D., and Athens retained its role as an educational center for
several centuries. These and other monuments served to remind Romans
and later peoples of the days when the Greeks taught humans to be proud
of their physical and intellectual gifts. The words of the ancient Greek
poet Pindar (518–438 B.C.) capture the essence of the Greek spirit:

> A changeable creature, such is man; a shadow in a dream.
> Yet when god-given splendour visits him
> A bright radiance plays over him, and how sweet is life![6]

THINGS YOU SHOULD KNOW

Homer
The heroic outlook
Olympic games
The Greek city-state (polis)
Why an intellectual revolution began
    in Ionian Greece
Thales
Sappho and Archilochus
Sparta
Solon
Cleisthenes
Women and slaves in ancient Sparta
    and Athens
Aeschylus

Sophocles
The Sophists
Athenian society
The Peloponnesian War
Thucydides
Aristophanes
Socrates
Plato
Aristotle
Alexander the Great
The Hellenistic Era
Epicureanism
Stoicism
Science and technology in the Hel-
    lenistic Era

SUGGESTED READINGS

Two good introductions to Greek history are Chester G. Starr, *The Ancient Greeks*
(New York: Oxford Univ. Press, 1971) and Frank Frost, *Greek Society* (Lexington,
Mass.: D.C. Heath, 1980). A valuable but complex study of Greek thought is C. M.
Bowra, *The Greek Experience* (New York: New American Lib./Mentor, 1959). On
the details of social and economic history, see John Scarborough, *Facets of
Hellenic Life* (Boston: Houghton Mifflin, 1976). Sarah B. Pomeroy, *Goddesses,
Whores, Wives, and Slaves* (New York: Schocken, 1976) is an excellent analysis of
the position of women in Greek society. A good survey of the Hellenistic Era is
Michael Grant, *From Alexander to Cleopatra: The Hellenistic World* (New York:
Scribner, 1982).

    For more specific subjects, see Alfred Zimmern, *The Greek Commonwealth*
(New York: Modern Library, 1911), an old but still insightful history of the
political evolution of Athens; and John Herman Randall, Jr., *Plato: Dramatist of*

the Life of Reason (New York: Columbia Univ. Press, 1970), a lively introduction to one of the most influential philosophers in Western history. Finally, a modern historical novel that catches the flavor of ancient Greece is Mary Renault, *The Last of the Wine* (New York: Vintage, 1975).

NOTES

[1]Frank J. Frost, *Greek Society,* 2nd ed. (Lexington, Mass.: D. C. Heath, 1980), p. 14.

[2]C. M. Bowra, *The Greek Experience* (New York: New American Library/Mentor, 1957), pp. 32–33.

[3]Quoted in John Scarborough, *Facets of Hellenic Life* (Boston: Houghton Mifflin, 1976), p. 145.

[4]Quoted in Frost, *Greek Society,* p. 31.

[5]Alfred Zimmern, *The Greek Commonwealth* (New York: Modern Library, 1911), p. 217.

[6]Pindar, "Pythian Ode VIII" (ll. 95–97), quoted in Chester G. Starr, *The Ancient Greeks* (New York: Oxford Univ. Press, 1971), p. 211.

5

Rome and the Birth of Christianity, 800 B.C. to A.D. 400

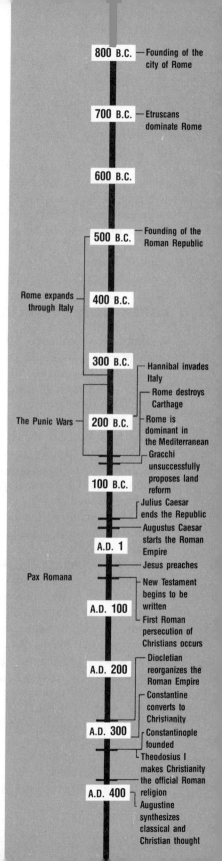

800 B.C. — Founding of the city of Rome

700 B.C. — Etruscans dominate Rome

600 B.C.

500 B.C. — Founding of the Roman Republic

Rome expands through Italy — 400 B.C.

300 B.C. — Hannibal invades Italy
— Rome destroys Carthage

The Punic Wars — 200 B.C. — Rome is dominant in the Mediterranean
— Gracchi unsuccessfully proposes land reform

100 B.C.
— Julius Caesar ends the Republic
— Augustus Caesar starts the Roman Empire

A.D. 1
— Jesus preaches

Pax Romana
— New Testament begins to be written

A.D. 100 — First Roman persecution of Christians occurs

A.D. 200 — Diocletian reorganizes the Roman Empire
— Constantine converts to Christianity

A.D. 300 — Constantinople founded
— Theodosius I makes Christianity the official Roman religion

A.D. 400 — Augustine synthesizes classical and Christian thought

The phrase "Eternal Rome" was sometimes inscribed on ancient Roman coins. Rome, of course, was not forever lasting, but it endured so long that it seemed immortal to many people of the ancient world. Roman history extended well over a thousand years, and during that time the Mediterranean world was slowly united by two forces. The first was the Romans themselves, who conquered a vast empire and ruled the entire Mediterranean basin for several centuries. The Roman Empire eventually began to disintegrate, however, and as it did, a second unifying force emerged. This was Christianity, a new religion that by the end of Roman history won the adherence of most Mediterranean peoples and thus created a spiritual unity that replaced the disappearing political unity of Rome.

EARLY ROMAN HISTORY

We know few real facts about early Roman history. The Romans were descendants of a people known as the Latins, who settled alongside the Tiber River in central Italy sometime around 800 B.C. The agricultural village established by the Latins marks the founding of the city of Rome. For two or three centuries, the Latins remained simple farmers living between two more civilized neighbors—the Greeks, who had colonized southern Italy, and the Etruscans to the north. The Etruscans, who probably came to Italy from Asia Minor (present-day Turkey) around 850 B.C., were a wealthy and powerful people who at some uncertain point gained control of Rome. In 509 B.C., however, the Romans launched a war of independence, driving the Etruscans out and establishing a republican form of government. Nevertheless, Etruscan influence had a significant impact on several aspects of Roman life, including religion, politics, literature, architecture, military techniques, and the tradition of staging gladiatorial combats. In particular, the Roman Senate was based on Etruscan precedent, and the Romans received the alphabet from the Etruscans, who had received it from the Greeks.

These facts explain in general terms some of the events of early Roman history, but they do not convey the thoughts and beliefs of the Roman people. When the Romans talked about the early days of their city, they recited legends that told of how they were descended from heroes and how their city was destined for greatness. One such legend was told by the Roman poet Virgil (70–19 B.C.) in his great epic poem *The Aeneid*. It tells the story of Aeneas, a Trojan warrior who escaped from Troy at the end of the war with the Greeks (see Chapter 4) and migrated to Italy to father a new line of warrior heroes. Among his descendants were twin brothers, Romulus and Remus, and it was Romulus whom the Romans believed founded their city in 753 B.C. Another Roman legend tells the story of Horatius. As an invading army was approaching a bridge that led to Rome, Horatius held off the invaders single-handedly while his comrades destroyed the bridge behind him. One version of this story says that Horatius then swam across the river, whereas another version says he died heroically.[1]

The Roman belief in a heroic past was reflected in Roman religion, which was a religion of patriotism. Unlike the Greeks, the early Romans did not believe in personalized deities or gods; rather, they believed that events in this world were controlled by divine spirits or forces that could be only vaguely understood by humans. These forces had to be placated by sacrifices and offerings of various kinds, so that they would bring good fortune to Rome. Thus, the essence of early Roman religion lay not in an emotional religious experience with a personal god or in a search for eternal salvation, but in the dutiful performance of rituals designed to gain divine favor for Rome.

Early Roman history thus stressed political developments far more than intellectual or spiritual ideas; indeed, Roman creativity was often manifested in politics and government. The Romans gradually built a massive international empire held together by the rule of international law and an expanded concept of citizenship. But Roman creativity was also expressed in architecture and engineering: the Romans built roads, aqueducts, baths, and theaters in many places.

THE ROMAN REPUBLIC

The Roman Republic was established in 509 B.C. It had a republican form of government in which all governing officials were elected by the upper classes. This was inspired in large part by the recently overthrown Etruscan tyranny, causing Romans to distrust strong, centralized governments. The republican system of government prevented any one individual from dominating Rome, so for several centuries the city was governed by many upper-class Romans who held power for short periods of time. (A unique feature of Roman history was that Rome was built by an entire people and not by a great individual conqueror like Alexander the Great.)

At first, the government was controlled solely by the upper classes, called the *patricians.* Three hundred or so patricians were members of a *Senate* that held legislative powers and was the ultimate source of authority. In addition, the patricians elected each year two *consuls* to share the executive power, with the stipulation that no one consul could be reelected.

As time passed, the lower classes—called the *plebeians*—began to demand political rights for themselves. The plebeians wanted to end the practice of debt slavery, the custom of people selling themselves into slavery in order to pay off their debts. (As noted in Chapter 4, this same

A Roman Aqueduct   The Romans were great builders, and some of their most impressive constructions were the aqueducts that brought water to cities. The water was pumped from mountain lakes or streams to an aqueduct, high enough to allow for a gradual drop in elevation so the water could flow downhill and be sent several miles to nearby cities. The aqueduct shown here was built about two thousand years ago and still exists today. (Italian Tourist Office)

issue led to political change in sixth-century B.C. Athens.) The plebeians also demanded political rights because they supplied most of the manpower for the army and felt they should have some voice in political decisions.

From the fifth to the third centuries B.C., the patricians and plebeians gradually compromised their political differences and a series of measures allowed broader political rights to the plebeians. A *Tribal Assembly* was created as a forum for plebeians to debate political issues. The office of *tribune* was established to protect plebeian rights, and eventually it won the power to *veto* ("forbid") legislation considered harmful to plebeians. Plebeians also gradually became eligible for election to the consulship, and finally, in 287 B.C., the Hortensian Law stipulated that decrees of the Tribal Assembly were the basic laws of government. In theory, the Hortensian Law made Rome a democratic state in which the will of the people was supreme, but in practice the patricians continued to dominate the consulship and Senate and thereby control Roman politics. Still, Rome had broadened the political participation of plebeians without undergoing a civil war or revolution, an accomplishment that few other cities in the ancient world could match. (The Roman political system was so impressive that many later peoples imitated Roman practices. The United States Constitution, for example, includes Roman conceptions of the Senate, the veto, and the principle of separation of powers.)

Internal political transformation in Rome was accompanied by external expansion. Like most other ancient peoples, the Romans had to fight small wars every summer to protect their lands from aggressors. Among the first Roman enemies were the Etruscans and the Gauls, the latter a tribe of Celtic peoples who lived in northern Italy and raided farming areas in central Italy. The Romans particularly disliked the Gauls, who sometimes stormed into battle stark naked while screaming curses and swinging large slashing swords.

The Conquest of Italy

The Romans slowly gained a reputation as defenders of Italy against the Gauls and so began to offer protection to those local cities that would give allegiance to Rome. Between 509 and 275 B.C., Rome continued to dominate more and more cities until it finally controlled most of central and southern Italy. In the process, Romans began to believe that they were natural leaders destined to conquer other peoples and other lands, and eventually they became some of the most successful imperialists of all time. Why were the Romans able to build and maintain such a large republic for centuries?

One reason for the longevity of Rome was its military strength. Roman armies were not invincible, but they rarely conceded defeat and usually maintained an offensive until victory was attained. (One example of strict Roman military discipline was the practice of *decimation,* whereby a unit that displayed cowardice in battle was condemned to have every tenth man executed.) Furthermore, Roman armies received great rewards from military success: for the common soldier, fame and prestige; for the generals, a celebratory parade or "triumph," through Rome.

Another reason for Rome's preeminence was its ability to gain and retain the loyalty of conquered subjects who appreciated relatively benevolent Roman rule. The Romans, like most other ancient peoples, were often brutal in war, but after the battle they were more tolerant and relatively good-natured people. From the Italian cities that they conquered, the Romans expected an annual contribution of soldiers to their armies but no taxes. In return, the Italians received protection as well as the freedom to govern their own local affairs. Some upper-class Italians were even granted Roman citizenship rights. Overall, it was a good bargain for the Italians, and the result was a growing allegiance to Rome.

The Punic Wars

By 275 B.C., Rome governed a population of more than one million Italians, a large number for that day. Also by this time, the Romans were coming into contact with another rising imperial power, the city of Carthage on the North African coast. The Romans and the Carthaginians soon came to regard each other as enemies, largely because both were expanding into southern Italy. The eventual result of this territorial conflict was the Punic Wars (so-named because the Romans called the Carthaginians the *Poeni*, meaning descendants of the Phoenicians).

The Punic Wars were a succession of three wars separated by two periods of truce. Together they lasted from 264 to 146 B.C. The First Punic War (264–241 B.C.) led to the Roman conquest of Sicily and Sardinia. In the Second Punic War (218–201 B.C.), the great Carthaginian general Hannibal invaded and ravaged Italy but eventually conceded victory to Rome. In 201 B.C., Rome gained control of Spain from Carthage. The Third Punic War (149–146 B.C.) was deliberately provoked by Rome and ended with the destruction of Carthage. The Romans killed all Carthaginian men and sold the women and children into slavery.

While defeating Carthage, the Romans were also expanding into the lands that the successors of Alexander the Great ruled. Between 200 and 146 B.C., Rome assumed control of Greece, Macedonia, and other eastern countries, largely to prevent other possible conquerors from taking them. By 146 B.C., Rome was the dominant military power in the Mediterranean.

HOW THE ROMAN CONQUESTS CHANGED ROME

The Roman conquests and the expansion of Rome brought about several changes and problems. Growing contact with other peoples made Rome more cosmopolitan, more open to new ideas and customs. Greek culture, in particular, strongly influenced Roman thought and art. The Romans began to identify the Greek gods with the impersonal divine forces that they had traditionally worshipped (the Greek Zeus, for example, became the Roman Jupiter), and so Roman religion was conceived of in more personal terms. The Romans also learned the philosophy of Stoicism from the Greeks, which would become highly influential by the time of the Roman Empire.

Although the Roman Republic had expanded considerably, the Romans were unwilling or unable to build an effective administrative system to govern the areas they had conquered. Usually, influential

The Colosseum at Rome   The Colosseum is the most famous Roman amphitheater.
Constructed in the first century A.D. for gladiatorial shows, it was a marvel of design
and engineering and could seat about 45,000 people. (B. Glassman)

patricians were sent to govern a province for a year or so, but many of
them used their power to enrich themselves by raising taxes and
accepting bribes. One result was the gradual corruption of traditional
Roman honesty and integrity; another was an increasing resentment of
Romans by the peoples they conquered. In the fifth and fourth centuries
B.C., the Romans governed their conquered subjects with fairness and
decency. As Rome continued to expand during the third to the first
centuries B.C., however, the Romans governed their colonies with less
honesty and they became more despotic. The earlier tradition of good
imperial government was restored only after Augustus Caesar became
the first Roman emperor late in the first century B.C.

Social divisions also deepened within Rome during this time. In the
early days of the Roman Republic, patricians and plebeians had similar
standards of living. By the second century B.C., however, many plebeians
were losing their farmland because they were spending so much time
fighting in wars and could not maintain their farms. These plebeians
gradually migrated to the city of Rome in search of work. However,
employment was often unavailable, so the government had to provide
free food and entertainment to pacify this new urban proletariat. Many
patricians, on the other hand, were becoming rich from the spoils of
Roman expansion and began living luxuriously. They often bought the

land lost by the plebeians, combined a number of small farms into one large plantation, and imported slaves to work their new estates. This, of course, created the threat of slave revolt.

The Roman army gradually became an independent force in the society. By the late second century B.C., army commanders began to offer long-term enlistments to unemployed plebeians and to promise recruits a share in the booty captured in war. Thus, what had originally been a citizen-based army motivated primarily by patriotism slowly became a professional army (somewhat separate from the body of citizens) motivated by desires for personal wealth.

A CENTURY OF TURMOIL AND THE END OF THE REPUBLIC

By the middle of the second century B.C., a power struggle began to disrupt Roman politics. On one side were the *Optimates,* the conservative patricians who wanted the Senate to govern Rome in the traditional manner. On the other side were the *Populares,* political leaders (many of them also patricians) who sought to mobilize popular support to break the power of the Senate and institute political and social reforms.

The first great *Popularis* was Tiberius Gracchus, a tribune who in 133 B.C. tried to launch a reform program that would give land to unemployed plebeians, but he was murdered by assassins financed by patricians. Ten years later, Gaius Gracchus, brother of Tiberius, was also murdered after he too proposed land reform. The fundamental problem was that behind the issue of land reform lay the basic issue of who should control Rome: the Senate representing the traditionalists, or a popular tribune with public support? The murders of the Gracchi meant that the Senate would retain power for a time, but they inaugurated a century of political violence in Rome.

The *Optimates* soon confronted other problems. By the end of the second century B.C., Gaius Marius, a general and a popular hero, became the most powerful man in Rome. Angered by patrician arrogance, Marius had many of his opponents murdered. A Greek historian named Appian described how Marius's men "killed remorselessly and severed the necks of men already dead, and they paraded these horrors before the public eye, either to inspire fear and terror, or for a godless spectacle."[2] Another difficulty faced by the *Optimates* was the revolt of many Italian towns against Rome in 90–88 B.C. The rebels were angered by Rome's unwillingness to allow them to share in the economic benefits of the expansion, and Rome had to pacify the rebels by granting citizenship rights to all free males in Italy.

By the middle of the first century B.C., Rome was engulfed by political factions. Speaking for the *Optimates* was Cicero, a famous lawyer and

Figure 5.1   The Expansion of Rome, 264 B.C.–A.D. 120

orator. Cicero was one of Rome's greatest prose writers, producing essays and speeches that defended liberty and republicanism. He knew that the *Optimates* were often greedy and selfish, but he argued that only the Senate could protect Rome from the dangers of military rule.

Cicero's greatest enemy was Julius Caesar, an able general who was popular with the *Populares*. In 60 B.C., Caesar, together with another general named Pompey and a financier named Crassus, formed a political alliance known as the *First Triumvirate*. But Crassus died soon thereafter, and Pompey for a variety of reasons began to support Cicero and the Senate. Civil war broke out in Rome in 49 B.C. Caesar led his armies from Gaul into Italy, eventually defeated Pompey, who was later killed, and became dictator of Rome from 49 to 44 B.C. Thus, Caesar destroyed the republican government that had been decaying for a century or more. Although the Senate still existed, its power was taken away.

Caesar ruled Rome for only five years. In 44 B.C., he was assassinated by senators claiming to be defenders of liberty. Once again, a power struggle erupted in Rome. The senators were incapable of governing

Rome and many of them, including Cicero, were soon killed. In 43 B.C., the Second Triumvirate was formed. It included Mark Antony (one of Caesar's lieutenants), an obscure general named Lepidus, and Octavian, Caesar's grandnephew and heir. Lepidus was soon forced out of the Triumvirate, so Mark Antony governed the eastern provinces and Octavian took control of the western provinces. Antony, however, soon became the lover and political ally of Cleopatra (69–30 B.C.), the queen of Egypt. (Cleopatra was the last of the Ptolemaic rulers of Egypt and was determined to become a powerful political figure in the Mediterranean world. Toward that end, she used her mind and body to entrance Julius Caesar and then Mark Antony.) Octavian gradually came to distrust Antony and Cleopatra, and the distrust grew into open conflict. In 31 B.C., Octavian's navy defeated Antony and Cleopatra's ships off the Greek coast at Actium, and soon thereafter Antony and Cleopatra committed suicide.

THE ROMAN EMPIRE

Augustus, the First Emperor

Following a century of political chaos and civil war, Octavian assumed full control of the Roman state. He quickly modified the governmental structure, transforming Rome from a republic governed by the upper classes into an empire in which one man—an emperor—directed an authoritarian regime. Although republican institutions survived and the Senate continued to meet, Octavian held absolute power. He was *imperator* (origin of the word *emperor*), meaning "commander of the armies," as well as *princeps* (origin of the word *prince*), meaning "first citizen." To signify his new exalted status, Octavian changed his name to Augustus (meaning "revered") Caesar.

Augustus ruled Rome from 31 B.C. to A.D. 14 and was in many ways an excellent emperor. He brought stability to the Roman Empire and began the process of building an administrative system that would govern the provinces fairly and honestly. He inaugurated the *Pax Romana* ("Roman Peace"), the period from 31 B.C. to A.D. 180, when most of the Mediterranean world enjoyed prolonged peace and prosperity. He also helped sponsor a literary renaissance in Rome. In *The Aeneid*, Virgil proclaimed that Rome was destined to rule the world; he defined the Roman ideal in the following words:

> Remember Roman,
> To rule the people under law, to establish
> The way of peace, to battle down the haughty,
> To spare the meek.[3]

Bust of Julius Caesar
(c. 100–44 B.C.) Among
Rome's greatest political
and military leaders, Julius
Caesar conquered Gaul
(present-day France) and
then destroyed the republican government in Rome.
The name "Caesar" came
to mean "emperor" (for example, the modern Ger-
man word for emperor,
kaiser, is derived from the
word *caesar*). (New York
Public Library)

Another poet, Horace (65–8 B.C.), wrote lyric poems, some of which were
patriotic odes to Roman splendor. Ovid (43 B.C.–A.D. 17), however, wrote
erotic poems in his *The Art of Love* that so offended Augustus, who
wanted to strengthen the family as an institution, that the poet was
banished from Rome.

Ovid's fate illustrates another side of the new political system in
Rome, for Augustus sometimes used secret police to stifle intellectual
dissent and to punish anyone who opposed him. Eventually, the
authoritarian system established by Augustus would sow the seeds of its
own destruction, particularly because it eliminated political and intellectual debate and thereby undermined the creativity that helps any society
to thrive.

The Grandeur and Degradation of Roman Society

Before continuing a chronological account of Roman politics, we need to know something about Roman society. As we will see, life in the Roman Empire was both grand and brutal.

By the time of Augustus Caesar, the Roman Empire covered the entire Mediterranean basin and contained nearly one hundred million people from diverse cultural and linguistic backgrounds. Many of these people lived in a relatively cosmopolitan environment, in coastal towns where sea transport encouraged travel and commerce. Aristocrats usually traveled frequently, many going to Greece to study philosophy or to visit the tourist attractions at Athens and Olympia. Yet other people lived in inland areas in a more isolated, provincial atmosphere. Land transport was very difficult and expensive for these people, so they rarely traveled. They obtained most of the material goods they needed from the surrounding countryside.

Why were the Romans able to govern such a diverse mixture of peoples and societies so successfully for several centuries? One obvious reason was their military power, but less obvious was the Roman tradition of tolerance and open-mindedness. Compared to other peoples of the ancient world, the Romans were more willing to allow people to live their lives as they saw fit (provided, of course, that they remained loyal to Rome). One example of this tolerance is the Roman attitude toward women. Upper-class women, for example, attended banquets and actively helped their husbands conduct business and political affairs. Although they had no political rights, in daily affairs they could come and go largely as they pleased.

The Roman tradition of tolerance extended to imperial governance, as the Romans tended to allow conquered peoples to live in accordance with their own customs and religion. At their best, the Romans developed *humanitas,* an attitude of respect for others regardless of their race or nationality. In practice, this concept was implemented to form a body of international law to govern all peoples equitably.

The development of Roman law began around 450 B.C., when in its first phase the Twelve Tables—a listing of the then-existing laws—were written. By around 200 B.C., Roman jurists began to modify these laws to reflect the need to govern a growing empire. In this regard, the Romans did two significant things: (1) they universalized their laws so they could be applied to a variety of peoples; and (2) they conceived of law as something made by people, not god-given, and thus were able to understand law as something that can be analyzed, used, and interpreted by people. In the second phase of Roman law, from 200 B.C. to A.D. 250—the classical period—the laws were internationalized and came to be based on principles of fairness and equity. These principles would be handed down to later ages. A third phase of Roman law occurred as the

TECHNOLOGY
Hellenistic Inventions

The Hellenistic Era produced a number of intriguing technological developments. Pytheas of Massalia (present-day Marseilles), for example, was an enterprising navigator and one of the greatest explorers of ancient times. Late in the fourth century B.C., he refined several navigational instruments, advanced the art of mapmaking, and undertook a long voyage on the Atlantic and up around England. Few people of his time believed his account of the journey, entitled *On the Ocean*.

Alexandria was the center of technological innovations. Some homes in the city had devices that opened doors and inventions that washed clothes by delivering soap and water as needed. A few temples even had water-sprinkler systems to protect against fire. Several inventors built important labor-saving devices. Hero designed a siphon, a force pump, and even a small steam engine. The mathematician Archimedes developed a screw pump used to lift water.

By the last century B.C., Greek science and technology indeed possessed the knowledge needed to initiate an industrial revolution. Of course, such a revolution did not occur until much later in Western history, but scholars have long debated why the Greeks failed to use their knowledge to its full potential. One theory is that slave labor was less expensive than machine-powered labor, so the Greeks had no economic incentive to encourage machine construction. Whatever the reason, it would take another two thousand years before the Industrial Revolution would become a reality in the Western world.

Device for Opening Temple Doors. *Hero of Alexandria, who lived in the first century A.D., understood how to produce steam power. One of his inventions opened temple doors: a sacrificial fire heated the air in a sphere; as the heated air expanded, it forced water into a receptacle that sunk under the weight of the water, which pulled cords that opened the temple doors. All but the fire was hidden so the doors appeared to open by magic. (The Granger Collection)*

laws were codified in large legal collections. This phase lasted until the sixth century A.D., when Justinian—discussed in Chapter 6—directed the codification of all Roman laws.

Despite Rome's great achievements, life for many in the Roman Empire was brutal. The poor always lived precariously. The rural poor survived by constant toil on the land, and they had little access to the attractions in the cities. The urban poor often lived in large, wooden tenement buildings that were vulnerable to fire, had no toilet facilities, and provided little heating. And the poor in Rome were always threatened by the possibility of unemployment, since slaves did most of the unskilled work. Wealthy Romans used slaves to perform household chores, to run errands, and to work on their farms. Some Romans owned slaves as an investment, hiring them out to others for a fee. Although some slaves were treated reasonably well, at times being accepted as virtual members of the family and eventually being granted their freedom, most slaves were treated brutally and were forced to work in mines or on farms until their death.

The brutality of Roman society was most strikingly manifested in the gladiatorial contests. The Roman government often provided so-called circuses, a form of entertainment for urban crowds, particularly the unemployed. These games were held in Rome at a huge arena called the *Colosseum*. At first, they involved trained gladiators who fought each other to the death while the large audience cheered. But as time went on, the spectators demanded novel events. Thus the gladiatorial contests came to feature such things as dwarfs fighting women, animals (crocodiles, giraffes, and elephants) fighting each other or men (often Christians), and even dramas in which the leading actor was murdered. That the crowds enjoyed and even exulted in such violence is in stark contrast to the civilized attitudes of tolerance and respect for law that the Romans exhibited in other areas of life.

First-Century Emperors

When Augustus transformed the Roman Republic into the Roman Empire, enormous tension erupted among the Roman aristocracy and continued for nearly a century. With all power concentrated in the hands of one man—the emperor—many aristocrats related to the ruling family sought to influence or even assassinate the emperor in order to attain power for themselves. The emperors, in turn, felt forced to imprison or murder suspected rivals. So, Roman imperial government in the century after Augustus was conducted in an atmosphere of suspicion and murderous intrigue.

The Julio–Claudian emperors—Tiberius, Caligula, Claudius, and Nero—ruled Rome from A.D. 14 to A.D. 68. They were all in some indirect way related to the family of Augustus Caesar (Augustus had no direct heirs). Several of them ruled effectively for a time, but fear of assassination led Tiberius, Caligula, and Nero to execute entire aristocratic families. The historian Tacitus tells of a frightened young woman being led to her execution, saying: "What have I done? Where are you taking me? I won't do it again."[4] The emperors had reason to be just as afraid as the young woman; Caligula and Nero were killed by their own guards, and Claudius was poisoned by his wife.

After Nero died in A.D. 68, a brief power struggle ensued until Vespasian became the first of three emperors of the Flavian dynasty, which ruled from A.D. 69 to A.D. 96. Vespasian's two sons—Titus and Domitian—were the other two. Vespasian was a strong ruler, in part because he was an Italian provincial and the first emperor to come from outside the city of Rome. The Roman Empire was beginning to use the talents of people outside the traditional aristocracy.

The Five Good Emperors

When the Flavian dynasty ended in A.D. 96, the Senate appointed Nerva to the throne. Nerva immediately established what would become an important reform in the method of choosing an emperor. During the first century A.D., Rome had no established way of selecting a successor to a dead emperor, and the result was often political instability. To correct this problem, Nerva instituted a reform by which an emperor could adopt his successor (someone he thought would be a good emperor). This practice of adoption led to a series of able rulers often referred to as the *Five Good Emperors*—Nerva, Trajan, Hadrian, Antoninus Pius, and Marcus Aurelius.

The period of the Five Good Emperors (A.D. 96–180) was a time of prosperity and improved standards of living for many Romans. The emperors were honest, hardworking men who provided peace, law and order, and capable government for their subjects. The Mediterranean prospered like never before in Roman history. The city of Rome had a population of nearly one million, and in the provinces were dozens of other cities, most of them dotted with baths, gymnasiums, and theaters. Even the life-style of the poor had improved as a result of welfare programs instituted by the imperial government, providing such things as food for children. The government also issued decrees that to some degree protected slaves against harsh treatment by their owners.

However, the prosperity of the Roman Empire in the second century A.D. was based on a weak foundation. The emperors, though effective rulers, held such absolute power that few others had the opportunity to make decisions. Imperial government slowly sapped the life out of the empire. Local governments gradually declined into insignificance, and political and intellectual discussion largely disappeared. Many individuals became fatalistic, as is attested to by a popular tombstone epitaph of those days: "I was not, I was, I am no more, I care not."[5]

Chaos in the Third Century

By the third century A.D., the Roman Empire was facing economic and political problems as well. Its economic production stagnated and its population declined, perhaps due to a plague. Furthermore, the empire was threatened by external foes, a revived Persian Empire in the east and Germanic barbarians from the north. The need for national defense meant that the Roman army became more powerful, intervening in politics and appointing and deposing emperors. Between 235 and 285 A.D., there were twenty-six emperors, many of them assassinated by rival army factions. Nevertheless, the empire endured through the chaos of the third century. That most Romans believed that their empire would survive indefinitely was not unreasonable, for in A.D.. 248 they celebrated the one-thousand-year anniversary of the founding of the city of Rome.

THE ORIGINS AND GROWTH OF CHRISTIANITY

During the first centuries of the Roman Empire, a new religion—Christianity—was gaining acceptance in an obscure Roman province. The Romans conquered an area inhabited by the Jewish people in the first century B.C. and renamed it *Palestine*. Palestine was a land where spiritual and religious questions preoccupied many people. Prophets and preachers wandered about the area, spreading their messages to those who would listen. Most Jews still adhered to the old Hebrew faith, the belief in one God who expects moral behavior from humans.

The Teachings of Jesus

Jesus of Nazareth was born in Palestine sometime between 6 and 4 B.C. (Logically, the birth date of Jesus should be the year 1. However, when the sixth-century A.D. monk Dionysius Exiguus invented the B.C.–A.D. system of dating, he miscalculated the years, leaving the Western calendar with some anomalies.)

Little is known about Jesus' early days, but he is said to be descended from the house of David, the great Israelite king. Furthermore, Jesus was taught the main tenets of the Jewish religious heritage. Sometime around A.D. 28 or 29, he was baptized by the preacher, John the Baptist. (Baptism—the immersion in or sprinkling of the body with water—symbolizes purification.) Jesus then began his own ministry.

According to the four Gospels of the New Testament—Matthew,

Mark, Luke, and John—Jesus healed people, exorcised demons, and preached the imminent coming of the Kingdom of God. The healings and exorcisms were, according to Jesus, signs that the rule of God had begun. The blessings of this reign of God were available to everyone, for Jesus taught an egalitarian message in which the poor were just as blessed (if not more so) as the rich and powerful. In Luke, Jesus is quoted as saying: "Blessed are you poor, for yours is the kingdom of God. Blessed are you that hunger now, for you shall be satisfied. Blessed are you that weep now, for you shall laugh" (6:20–21).* Significantly, many of Jesus' first followers were simple people—fishermen, peasants, and even prostitutes. And the morality he taught these people was one of love and gentleness toward all: "You shall love the Lord your God with all your heart, and with all your soul, and with all your mind. . . . You shall love your neighbor as yourself" (Matthew 22:37–39).

Jesus clearly believed that he had a special relationship with God, though modern scholars disagree on the precise nature of that relationship. Some scholars contend that Jesus regarded himself as the Son of God, while others point out that he usually referred to himself as the "Son of Man," a somewhat vaguer phrase. More important, though, is that the established authorities—Jewish leaders and the local Roman rulers—believed that Jesus was claiming to be the Messiah who would lead the Jews against their enemies. Consequently, when Jesus went to Jerusalem sometime in the early 30s A.D., he was condemned by the Romans as a revolutionary and crucified. (Crucifixion—the nailing of a person on a cross—was a fairly common Roman form of execution.)

Jesus' Followers

When the leaders of earlier movements were killed, the followers of those movements usually disappeared. Jesus' followers, however, came to believe that Jesus had in some sense been resurrected—raised from the dead—and that fellowship with him was still possible. The belief in the Resurrection thus had the effect of resurrecting the Christian movement.

Jesus' followers were originally known as the *Galileans* because of their association with the area around the Sea of Galilee. At first, the Galileans believed that their movement was a part of the broader Jewish religion and recognized the Jerusalem church—headed by James, supposedly the brother of Jesus—as the center of the movement. Gradually, however, the Galileans began to preach to non-Jews, or so-called *Gentiles*, and to travel to distant areas to spread their message. The Apostle Peter, for example, went as far as Rome; others traveled to Greece, Mesopotamia, and possibly Arabia. In the city of Antioch, just up the coast from Palestine, the Apostle Paul began to preach that Jesus'

*All quotations from the New Testament are taken from the Revised Standard Version.

Jesus Christ Holding the Orb   The orb is a symbol of the earth surmounted by a
cross. Here the artist, whose name is unknown, uses the orb to portray Jesus as the
spiritual ruler of the earth. (Pierpont Morgan Library)

teachings were for all people, not just Jews. Paul was of Jewish heritage
and at one time had been a persecutor of the Galileans, but he was
converted and had a major impact on shaping the new religion. Under his
influence, Jesus' followers began to call themselves *Christians,* since they

believed that Jesus was the Christ, the Savior, and to think of themselves as adherents of a new religion, *Christianity*. The belief that the Galileans were a part of Judaism died with the destruction of the Jerusalem church in A.D. 70. A Jewish revolt against Rome had erupted in A.D. 67, and the Romans destroyed the city of Jerusalem and most of the Jewish Galileans in A.D. 70.

The Christian Message

As Christianity slowly grew, it developed its sacred writings and teachings. The four Gospels of the New Testament were written down sometime during the second half of the first century A.D. These accounts of Jesus' teachings and life were not written down at first, because his followers expected the end of the world to come soon. When that expectation proved false, the Gospels were transmitted from memory and oral recitation to parchment. Many other parts of the New Testament are letters written by Paul to early Christian churches around the middle of the first century A.D.

From the sacred writings of the New Testament, Christian preachers and missionaries gradually evolved the message that they wanted to transmit to nonbelievers. This message was simple: a Christian had to have faith in God and in Jesus as the Son of God. Even though all people sinned, in the sense of being separate from God, God loved them and expected them to love him and their fellow humans. Because God loved people, he allowed his Son to become human and die a horrible death. The death of Christ was a divine sacrifice that made amends for human sin. Thus, it was possible for all who believed to be forgiven for their sins, to be saved, and to attain eternal life. Soon, the early Christians taught, the Second Coming of Christ would take place, at which time the righteous would ascend into heaven and the wicked would be condemned to hell. As the years passed and it became apparent that the Second Coming would not occur immediately, this last teaching was modified to say that Christ would return at some unspecified time in the future.

The Christian message appealed to many people in the Roman Empire for a number of reasons. One reason was the promise of salvation to those who believed. Another was the message of a loving God, which was particularly appealing in a brutal age. A third reason was the growing belief that Christian exorcists could cast demons out of people, a clear sign that they were recipients of divine power.

Christian Institutions

Another aspect of the growth of Christianity was the evolution of a permanent institutional structure primarily during the first and second centuries A.D. Local Christian communities developed a sacramental system to give spiritual support to members. The two most important sacraments were *baptism,* presumed to purify and admit the recipient into the Christian community, and a celebration of the *Lord's Supper* (later known as the *Eucharist*), Jesus' last meal with his disciples.

In addition, a hierarchical church organization began to develop. The first Christian communities were informal groups directed by elders, later known as *priests.* When several communities emerged in one city or area, an official known as a *bishop* ("overseer") was appointed or elected to guide all Christians in that area. Then, as Christians sought to unify over a still larger area, the large cities—Alexandria, Antioch, and Rome—began to appoint *archbishops* to supervise the Christian communities of an entire province. Thus, over the course of two or three centuries, a church organization emerged: priests guided the local congregations, bishops directed the priests and congregations in certain areas, and archbishops supervised hundreds of bishops and priests.

The final part of the church hierarchy appeared when the bishops of Rome began to argue that they should have precedence over all other bishops, because Peter—Jesus' leading disciple—was the founder of the church at Rome. By the fifth century A.D., the bishop of Rome was increasingly called the *Pope,* meaning "father of the church."

Christianity In the Early Roman Empire

The growth of Christianity gained the attention of the Roman government. Although the Romans were usually tolerant of different religions, they feared Christians in particular for several reasons. One reason was the Christian insistence on meeting in secret, which appeared subversive to the Romans. Another reason was the Christian refusal to worship the Roman emperor, an act that to the Christians was idolatry but to the Romans was simply a sign of allegiance to Rome. Further, the Romans accused the Christians of being atheists because they questioned the existence of the traditional pagan gods.

As a result of the Romans' fear of Christians, some emperors tried to destroy Christianity through intimidation. The first imperial persecution of Christians took place in A.D. 64; others occurred sporadically over the next two and half centuries. Christians were sometimes crucified, sometimes torn to death by wild animals in the gladiatorial games, and sometimes simply murdered. Ironically, the Roman persecution of Christians increased the popularity of Christianity. Most Christians believed that dying for their faith would guarantee them salvation, so many perished willingly. Further, the spiritual strength and conviction of these Christian martyrs impressed many non-Christians as well.

By the end of the third century A.D., however, Christians were still a small minority within the Roman Empire. Many people continued to worship the traditional pagan deities, with the sun god being particularly popular (*Sunday* was a "divine" day for many). Others turned to religions that, like Christianity, promised human salvation. Mithraism, for example, told of the god Mithras, who ascended to heaven from where he offered redemption to the faithful. Thus, Christianity was at this point only one of several competing religions.

THE POLITICAL TRANSFORMATION OF THE ROMAN EMPIRE

The political structure of the Roman Empire changed fundamentally in the late third and early fourth centuries A.D. One change was the growing militarization of the empire, accompanied by an increase in the power of the emperor. Another fundamental change was the Christianization of the Roman Empire, as Christianity won a political victory over other religions of the time and became the official religion of Rome.

Militarization

Beginning around A.D. 260, a succession of Roman emperors implemented a military revolution designed to make the army more effective in fighting the Persians in the east and the Germanic tribes in the north. Military commands were no longer given to senatorial aristocrats but to professional soldiers. The new commanders instituted tighter discipline and new military tactics, which enabled the Roman armies to defeat the foreign foes. The long-range effects of the military revolution were to turn the military into a major source of political talent and to allow army leaders to replace aristocrats in the governing councils of the empire.

Centralization of Power

Additional changes occurred when Diocletian became emperor in A.D. 285. He launched a thorough reorganization of the imperial administration, designed to restabilize the empire after the political instability and economic stagnation it faced in the third century. Politically, he turned the Roman Empire into an autocracy, in which the central government was in complete control. Diocletian was known as "Lord and God" and held absolute power. He used his power in particular to persecute Christians throughout the empire. Diocletian's economic reforms included making occupations hereditary; for example, the sons of peasants had to remain peasants. His purpose here was to stabilize economic production by forcing people to remain at their assigned tasks.

Through his reforms, Diocletian transformed the Roman Empire into an armed camp governed by an absolute monarch. The reforms worked throughout much of the fourth century A.D., a time of stability and prosperity in Rome. At the same time, though, basic Roman institutions were being undermined. In the western half of the Roman Empire, Diocletian's economic reforms hindered commerce and thereby weakened the economic foundation of the cities—the heart of Roman society. Also in the west, Germans from northern Europe (see Chapter 6) were being recruited into the Roman army to fight other Germans, who were pushing against the Roman frontiers in the north.

Christianization

The Christianization of the Roman Empire advanced rapidly after the emperor Constantine was converted in A.D. 312. In A.D. 313 the new convert issued the Edict of Milan that decreed governmental toleration of Christianity. Thereafter, the number of converts grew steadily—many hoped that conversion would gain them favor with the government and others were impressed by the popular belief that Christians could perform miracles. One story of the time told of a pagan prophet who challenged a bishop to a debate, but was struck dumb and died before she could utter what Christians called her "blasphemies."

Constantine also built a new capital for the empire. In A.D. 330, Constantinople was founded on the site of the ancient Greek village of Byzantium. Its location—on a peninsula commanding the sea route between the Black Sea and the Mediterranean—enabled Constantinople to become the principal city and capital of the eastern half of the Roman Empire. More important to Constantine was the fact that the new city was a Christian capital, distinct from the old pagan capital of Rome.

By the late fourth century A.D., Christianity was becoming the dominant religion within the Roman Empire and Christians were actively trying to destroy paganism. Those who had once been the persecuted now became the persecutors, as Christian mobs ransacked pagan temples and intimidated pagans into converting to Christianity. Religious feelings were so strong that at times they caused riots in which people had their eyes torn out or tongues cut off.

The final political victory of Christianity over paganism came in A.D. 380, when the emperor Theodosius I decreed Christianity to be the official state religion and thereby transformed Rome from a pagan empire into a Christian one. Theodosius I was also significant in that he was the last emperor to govern the entire empire effectively. At his death, his two sons divided control of the empire and the two halves were never again united. Thus, the reign of Theodosius I (A.D. 379–395) marked both the end of the old pagan Rome that ruled the entire Mediterranean basin and the beginning of a new Christian world still being born (discussed in Chapters 6 and 7).

THE SPIRITUAL TRANSFORMATION OF THE ROMAN EMPIRE

Christianity became the state religion of Rome in large part because of a spiritual transformation that was occurring among the people of the Roman Empire. Pagan, classical thought was slowly giving way to Christianity, and the transition produced the most profound intellectual debate since the great days of Athens in the fifth century B.C.

On one side of the debate were the Hellenes, those who still adhered to the ancient ways of learning that had originated in Greece a thousand years earlier. The Hellenes defended human reason as the primary vehicle for discovering truth, and in the universities they studied the ancient Greek philosophers. They argued that the best life for humans lay in the *polis,* a city where intelligent, free people could debate political issues and try to create the good life on this earth. The Hellenes were at this time recopying the texts of the Greek philosophers for use by later generations.

On the other side of the debate were the Christians, who were defining an alternative way of life. One aspect of this new way of life was the movement known as *monasticism,* which began with an extraordinary man named Anthony of Egypt. Anthony took literally Jesus' admonition to "sell all you have and give to the poor and follow me." In A.D. 269, Anthony moved into the Egyptian desert to live as a hermit, believing that solitude would enable him to pray and worship God without distraction. His example stirred others to do the same, and within a century the monastic movement spread to Syria. There Simeon the Stylite allegedly squatted on top of a fifty-foot column for forty years, so that, like Anthony, he could concentrate on meditating and worshiping God. Anthony and Simeon had many imitators, some of whom embarrassed other Christians by engaging in such extreme actions as starving themselves to death to demonstrate contempt for their bodies. So, church leaders gradually began to organize these people into monasteries, communities where monks lived by an iron discipline that focused on constant prayer and meditation. Gradually, a number of monastic orders for women were established as well. By the late fourth century A.D., dozens of monasteries existed in Egypt, and the monastic movement was growing rapidly. Over the next several centuries, monasticism would be one of the most vital institutions within Christianity.

Another aspect of the new Christian way of life was the attempt by Christian theologians to define precisely what Christianity meant. The greatest of these theologians was Augustine (A.D. 354–430), who for over three decades was bishop of Hippo in northern Africa (present-day Algeria). Northern Africa had long been one of the more prosperous areas of the Roman Empire. Africa produced large quantities of grain, and some cities, such as Alexandria in Egypt, were centers of intellectual life. By the third and fourth centuries A.D., Africa was the home of many important Christian theologians and teachers.

Augustine wrote two books that had a decisive impact on Christian thought. *Confessions* is an autobiographical examination of his own search for spiritual truth. In it Augustine focuses on himself as an individual personality, marking a new kind of thinking that stressed the importance of the individual. According to the traditional classical thought, a person was part of a community and the community was more important than any one individual. In contrast, Christianity argued that every person has an individual soul, and so each individual is valuable in the eyes of God. This belief was manifested in Christian condemnations of ancient practices that were cruel and harsh to individuals—such as fatal exposure for deformed infants and the practice of gladiatorial contests.

Augustine's other great work is the *City of God,* an assault on classical philosophical thought. In it Augustine argues that all humans live in one of two spiritual worlds, the City of Man or the City of God. According to Augustine, Romans who lived in the spiritual City of Man saw the good life as something that could be defined in terms of political and economic well-being, and believed that human reason alone could discover truth. In short, the City of Man placed its ultimate confidence in people. Those who lived in the spiritual City of God saw reason and faith as essential to the attainment of truth, and professed to put the service of God before the service of people. Only in this way could people overcome the pride and greed for material possessions that characterized the City of Man. Augustine contrasts the two cities in the following words:

> That which animates secular society is the love of self to the point of contempt for God; that which animates divine society is the love of God to the point of contempt for self. The one prides itself on itself; the pride of the other is in the Lord; the one seeks for glory from men, the other counts its consciousness of God as its greatest glory.[6]

Augustine, educated in ancient classical thought, did not repudiate it entirely. He only insisted that classical thought was incomplete and that faith in God had to be added to confidence in human reason. Thus, Augustine defined a new synthesis of human experience, a Christian synthesis that combined the Greek faith in reason with the Jewish and Christian faith in God. This new synthesis and its resulting tensions would dominate the Western world in the succeeding centuries.

CONCLUSION

Roman history spans over a thousand years. During those years, the Romans conquered and ruled one of the largest empires ever assembled, and made enduring achievements in the areas of law and government. Furthermore, the Roman Empire was the site of a major spiritual transformation in Western Civilization, as Christianity gradually became the dominant religion of Western peoples.

The decline of Roman power from the third to the sixth centuries A.D. marked the end of a major phase of Western history. The events of ancient history centered around the Mediterranean Sea, but as we will see in Chapters 6 and 7, the center of Western Civilization after Rome shifted to Western Europe.

THINGS YOU SHOULD KNOW

Virgil and *The Aeneid*
The governmental structure of the
    early Roman Republic
The Punic Wars
How the Roman conquests changed
    Rome
The Gracchi
Cicero
Julius Caesar
The Roman Empire
Octavian (Augustus Caesar)
Roman law
Roman roads and other technologies
Gladiatorial contests
The Julio-Claudian Emperors
The Flavian Dynasty

The Five Good Emperors
Jesus of Nazareth
The Galileans
The Apostle Paul
Early Christian teachings
The organization of the early Chris-
    tian church
Roman persecution of the Christians
The growth of Christianity
The political and spiritual transfor-
    mation of the Roman Empire
Diocletian
Constantine
Theodosius I
monasticism
Augustine

SUGGESTED READINGS

Two good introductions to the history of Rome are Finley Hooper, *Roman Realities* (Detroit: Wayne State Univ. Press, 1979), and L. P. Wilkinson, *The Roman Experience* (New York: Knopf, 1974). Geza Alfoldy, *The Social History of Rome* (Baltimore: Johns Hopkins Univ. Press, 1988) is a good account of the details of social history. For the Roman Empire, see Chester G. Starr, *Civilization and the Caesars: The Intellectual Revolution in the Roman Empire* (New York: Norton, 1965). Robert Graves, *I, Claudius* (New York: Random 1989) is an historical novel that captures the atmosphere of intrigue and fear that surrounded the first Roman emperors.

On the early history of Christianity, see Martin Marty, *A Short History of Christianity* (New York: New American Library, 1959), and Ramsay MacMullen, *Christianizing the Roman Empire* (New Haven: Yale Univ. Press, 1984). Edward Gibbon, *The Decline and Fall of the Roman Empire* (New York: Penguin, 1983) was written in the late eighteenth century but remains a masterpiece of historical literature. An excellent modern analysis of the decline of Rome and the rise of Christianity is Peter Brown, *The World of Late Antiquity*, A.D. *150–750* (New York: Harcourt Brace Jovanovich, 1971). Finally, a high-level but rewarding work on the intellectual struggle between Christian and classical thought is Charles Norris Cochrane, *Christianity and Classical Culture* 2nd ed. (New York: Oxford Univ. Press, 1957).

NOTES

[1]Quoted in Finley Hooper, *Roman Realities* (Detroit: Wayne State Univ. Press, 1979), p. 37.

[2]Ibid., p. 204.

[3]Quoted in Chester G. Starr, *Civilization and the Caesars: The Intellectual Revolution in the Roman Empire* (New York: Norton, 1965), p. 181.

[4]Quoted in Hooper, *Roman Realities*, p. 368.

[5]Quoted in L. P. Wilkinson, *The Roman Experience* (New York: Knopf, 1974), p. 193.

[6]Quoted in Charles Norris Cochrane, *Christianity and Classical Culture*, 2nd ed. (New York: Oxford Univ. Press, 1957), p. 489.

6

The Great Migrations, Byzantine Civilization, and Islamic Civilization, A.D. 400 to 700

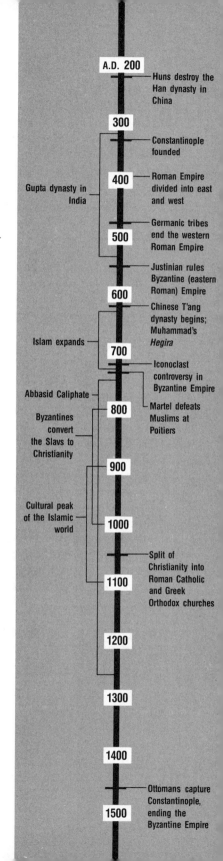

A.D. 200 — Huns destroy the Han dynasty in China

300 — Constantinople founded

400 — Roman Empire divided into east and west

Gupta dynasty in India

500 — Germanic tribes end the western Roman Empire

— Justinian rules Byzantine (eastern Roman) Empire

600 — Chinese T'ang dynasty begins; Muhammad's *Hegira*

Islam expands

700 — Iconoclast controversy in Byzantine Empire

Abbasid Caliphate — Martel defeats Muslims at Poitiers

800

Byzantines convert the Slavs to Christianity

900

1000

Cultural peak of the Islamic world

— Split of Christianity into Roman Catholic and Greek Orthodox churches

1100

1200

1300

1400

— Ottomans capture Constantinople, ending the Byzantine Empire

1500

$\mathbf{I}$n *The Decline and Fall of the Roman Empire,* the eighteenth-century historian Edward Gibbon created an enduring image of the Roman Empire declining, falling, and disappearing. The image is somewhat exaggerated, for Rome neither fell suddenly nor disappeared completely. Rather, it slowly disintegrated and in its place emerged three new cultural realms that inherited much from the Greco-Roman-Christian past. In the western parts of the empire, the imperial government was gradually overwhelmed by Germanic peoples and replaced by a Western Christian society that eventually became the basis for Western European Civilization. In the east, centered in Constantinople, an eastern Roman Empire (later known as the Byzantine Empire) endured for another thousand years after the western half of Rome disappeared. In the seventh century A.D., the Arabic peoples created a new religion—Islam— and surged out of the Arabian peninsula to expand over much of what had been the southern part of the Roman Empire and to seize some territory from the Byzantine Empire.

The transformation of the Mediterranean world from one united Roman Empire into three distinct cultural realms occurred roughly between A.D. 400 and 700 and involved a vast movement of peoples. Various Germanic tribes—for example, the Goths, Franks, Vandals, Lombards, Angles, and Saxons—migrated from northern Europe into Italy, France, Spain, and North Africa. The Slavs, who first appeared in northeastern Europe (or present-day Poland), spread over much of eastern Europe. The Huns, an Asiatic people from somewhere near Mongolia, invaded parts of Europe but eventually left and soon disappeared from Western history. The Avars, another Asiatic people, moved into southern Russia and part of eastern Europe, but they too eventually disappeared. Finally, the Arabs, a Semitic people from southern Arabia, spread into some eastern Mediterranean lands and across North Africa. These various migrations were a part of a vast movement of peoples across much of the Eurasian landmass that affected not only Rome but other civilized areas as well.

CIVILIZATION AND NOMAD INVADERS ACROSS EURASIA

Four civilized areas stretched across central Eurasia: Rome, Persia, India, and China. In the third to fourth centuries A.D., each of these civilizations was internally weak. One source of their weakness was political fragmentation, as central governments were increasingly unable to maintain control of their vast realms. Another source of weakness was technological stagnation, particularly in agriculture where continued use of inefficient tools and techniques restricted productivity. Internal weakness left the civilized areas of central Eurasia vulnerable to external attack by nomad invaders. Thus, between A.D. 200 and 600, several waves of nomads swept across Eurasia. Many of the nomads came from Mongolia, peoples known in China as the *Juan-juan* and in Europe as the Huns. The origin of the Huns is somewhat obscure, as are the reasons they invaded Eurasia at this time. Historians know with certainty only that the Huns were nomads and skilled horsemen who probably moved through Eurasia in search of food and pasture for their animals.

The first encounter between the Huns and the civilized world occurred in China. The Han dynasty (202 B.C.–A.D. 222) ruled a stable and prosperous China for several centuries, but its power declined after A.D. 100 and the ensuing disorder bore many similarities to events of the same period in the Roman Empire (as we will see later in this chapter). The central government in China slowly lost power to local warlords, who used their new strength to assert greater control over the peasantry. Although the long-suffering peasants sometimes rebelled against the warlords, many of them lost their farms and some were forced to sell their children into slavery to survive. The Han dynasty collapsed in A.D. 222, and over the next two or three centuries China was plagued by civil wars among the warlords and invasions by the Huns. China was more resilient than Rome, however, for late in the sixth century the Sui dynasty drove most of the nomads out and restored a central government. The Sui were soon succeeded by the T'ang dynasty (A.D. 618–907), which sustained a long period of stable government in China.

While China was suffering social disorder and war, India was thriving both politically and culturally. In the fourth century A.D., the Gupta dynasty (A.D. 320–535) imposed political unity in northern India. The Gupta period quickly became one of the greatest cultural eras in Indian history. During this time, the Indians developed one of the greatest human creations—a new and improved numerical system (see the Technology box on page 119). Indian creativity was also expressed in literature, as writers produced dramas and romantic poetry and transcribed the epic poems that had earlier been transmitted orally. Two new forms of entertainment—chess and animal fables—were also developed in India at this time. Indian art and culture began to expand throughout eastern Asia, primarily through the efforts of Buddhist missionaries who were seeking converts. As a result, Buddhism and Indian culture became a cultural bond not only for Indians but for many Chinese, Koreans, Japanese, and Indonesians as well. This great age of Indian culture began to decline, however, when the Gupta dynasty was undermined by Hun invaders in the mid-sixth century A.D. The Huns were unable to establish a centralized government, so India became politically fragmented. It remained culturally united, however, through Hinduism and adherence to the caste system.

Nomads also attacked but were unable to defeat a revived Persian Empire. After A.D. 226, the Sassanian (from *sasan*, the Persian word for commander) monarchs formed what was known as Sassanian Persia, a deliberate imitation of the ancient Persian Empire of the sixth to fourth centuries B.C. Although Sassanian Persia was strong enough to repel Hunnish and other invaders, it was finally defeated by the Muslims in the seventh century A.D.

Consequences of the Nomad Invasions

The Huns eventually moved into Europe and helped precipitate the fall of Rome, a sequence of events that is examined later in the chapter. We first need to examine the nomad invasions in terms of their religious and political effects and their role in the destruction of three empires—the Han in China, the Gupta in India, and the western half of the Roman Empire. We also need to consider why only two civilized areas— Sassanian Persia and the eastern Roman Empire—were able to resist the nomad invasions.

One important effect of the invasions was the expansion of world religions. Many people sought spiritual consolation in this age of war and chaos. Christianity spread throughout most of the Mediterranean and into Ethiopia as well. Zoroastrianism was revived by the Sassanian monarchs in Persia. Islam emerged in the Arabian peninsula during the seventh century A.D., and eventually supplanted Zoroastrianism in Persia and Christianity in most of North Africa. (Since Zoroastrianism had few adherents outside of Persia, it ceased to be a significant religion after Islam gained wide acceptance in the Sassanian Empire.) In addition, Buddhism was carried throughout Asia by Indian missionaries and became a major influence in Korea, Japan, Southeast Asia, and parts of China. Interestingly, though, Buddhism gradually lost influence within India as a revived Hinduism became the religious tie among most Indians. Buddhism also lost influence in China. Although it had spread into China after the collapse of the Han dynasty in A.D. 222, the Sui and T'ang dynasties sponsored a revival of Confucianism during the late sixth and seventh centuries A.D. Confucianism again became the dominant religion in China, with Buddhism having only marginal influence.

Three major developments thus occurred across much of Eurasia between A.D. 400 and 700. First, the old centers of civilization—Rome, Persia, India, and China—were either destroyed or fundamentally transformed because of internal weakness and external attacks. China and India were able to recover and rebuild fairly quickly, but the collapse of the western half of the Roman Empire meant that a new civilization would be formed in Western Europe. Second, religious revival gradually brought new spiritual values and attitudes to civilized peoples. The religious influence of the Axial Period (see Chapter 2) spread rapidly during this time, as an increasing number of people were turning away from polytheistic and nature religions and developing loyalties to more

TECHNOLOGY
A Better System of Numbers

A modern numeral—6,789
The Roman numeral for 6,789—VMDCCLXXXIX
Performing addition of roman numerals and arabic numerals:

Roman Numerals	Arabic Numerals
CCLXVI	266
MDCCCVII	1807
DCL	650
MLXXX	1080
MMMDCCCIII	3803

Using Roman numerals, the problem is difficult if not impossible to solve.

O ver history, different peoples have used different systems for writing and calculating numerals. Prior to the Gupta dynasty in India, most peoples used cumbersome numeral systems that were difficult to manipulate. The Romans, for example, used letters to designate numerals.

The Indians developed a new numerical system that used only nine digits (1 to 9) and a special sign—the zero—that enabled the nine digits to be continually reused. The zero was the key to the development of a positional system of numeration. By putting a numeral in a position to the left of where it had been, it then designated a higher power, ten or a hundred (or more) times as great as the original. Thus the number 1 with a zero added to it became the number 10, with two zeroes it became 100, and so on. The zero was first used in ancient Babylon and passed from there into India. Between the third and eighth centuries A.D., the Indians gradually adopted the zero and made it a part of their new numerical system. The system was eventually passed on to the Arabs and then to the Europeans late in the tenth century A.D. The Europeans referred to the nine digits as arabic numerals, as we still do today. However, it is more accurate to call it the Hindu-Arabic numeral system since the Indians developed it.

The Hindu-Arabic system of numbers is much less complex than the old roman numeral system. The Europeans slowly adopted the Hindu-Arabic system, and it eventually became the mathematical system used in modern science and technology.

universal and transcendental religions. Third, civilized institutions and skills were spreading into uncivilized areas. Japan, Korea, and Southeast Asia came under the influence of both China and India. The Arabs came into contact with more civilized peoples when Islam expanded, and the Germanic peoples were civilized in part through their conversion to Christianity. (It is interesting to note that civilization was also spreading in the Americas at this time with the development of the Mayan and the Incan civilizations.)

THE GERMANIC PEOPLES
AND THE END OF ROME IN THE WEST

The Germanic peoples lived in a number of independent tribes, but they were interrelated and spoke variants of a common Germanic language. They were simple agricultural people who had not developed city life, had little written language, and no "civilized" political, educational, or legal systems. Their politics consisted of allegiance to a king or chieftain; their laws were simply customs and traditions handed down from past generations.

The Germanic tribes originated somewhere around present-day western Russia or Scandinavia. In about 500 B.C., they began to move south in search of better land and a warmer climate. By the second and first centuries B.C., many Germanic tribes were in central Europe where further movement was naturally blocked by the Rhine and Danube rivers—the northern frontiers of the Roman Empire. For the next several centuries, Romans and Germans coexisted peacefully, with some commerce being conducted across the rivers and some Germans moving into the empire as slaves or soldiers in the Roman army. But by the late fourth century A.D., two factors persuaded the Germanic tribes to push their way into the Roman Empire. One was the division and weakening of the imperial government after the death of the Emperor Theodosius in A.D. 395 (see Chapter 5), which encouraged the Germanic peoples to take over Roman farmland. The other was a fear of the Huns, whose movement toward Europe caused the Germanic tribes to seek protection within the Roman Empire.

The Visigoths were the first Germanic tribe to move into the boundaries of the Roman Empire. They were admitted peacefully in A.D. 376. However, various quarrels over where the Visigoths should live led to the battle of Adrianople in 378, in which the Visigoths defeated a large Roman army. That Roman defeat left the Danube frontier unprotected, causing many peoples, including the Huns, to drive into the empire. In A.D. 406, the Roman government brought in troops from the Rhine in an attempt to control the situation, but this left the Rhine frontier unprotected. Thus, during much of the fifth century, Germans and Huns moved back and forth through the empire. Some of the movements were violent: the Visigoths sacked Rome in A.D. 410; the Huns attacked Italy before eventually being driven off; and the Vandals terrorized Spain and North Africa (thereby inspiring the word *vandalize*). Other movements were relatively peaceful, for most of the Germanic tribes wanted only to settle on good farmland and enjoy the benefits of Roman government.

The Germanic invasions were primarily a result of the migration of immigrants seeking a better life. They did not intend to destroy the Roman government. But their migrations weakened Rome's political and military institutions, severed its communication and transportation ties, and undermined its educational and legal structures. Controlling and civilizing the immigrants was more than the weakened Roman Empire could manage. A symbolic event occurred in A.D. 476, when a Germanic general deposed the last official Roman emperor in the west, a young boy ironically named Romulus Augustulus.

Western Europe after the Fall of Rome

Even after A.D. 476, the Roman emperor in Constantinople still claimed to govern the entire empire, but that claim had no substance. The west was now controlled by the Germanic tribes, and some of their chieftains tried to build kingdoms and rule the mixed populations of Romans and Germans. In Britain, the Angles, Saxons, and Jutes each formed small kingdoms; later the name "Angleland" would be transformed into "England." In Gaul, the Franks built "Frankland," later shortened into "France." The Visigoths organized a kingdom in Spain, the Ostrogoths in Italy, and the Vandals in North Africa. But most of these kingdoms survived only briefly, since the Germanic tribes did not possess the governing and administrative skills necessary to sustain large political structures. What had been the western half of the Roman Empire slowly collapsed into chaos and confusion.

We do not know with certainty what happened to ordinary people in these chaotic times. Some wealthy landowners were probably able to withdraw to their estates and build fortress-like villas for protection. Others probably joined monasteries to seek spiritual consolation. The poor either worked on the estates or took to the mountains and survived by robbery. The situation varied in different areas; in some places absolute confusion reigned while in others a semblance of Roman civilization remained. Historian Peter Brown describes the atmosphere of this time as follows:

> A Roman senator could write as if he still lived in the days of Augustus, and wake up, as many did at the end of the fifth century A.D., to realize that there was no longer a Roman emperor in Italy. Again, a Christian bishop might welcome the disasters of the

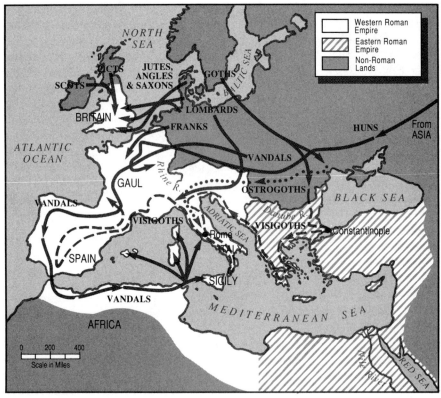

Figure 6.1 Barbarian Invasions and the Division
of the Roman Empire

barbarian invasions, as if they had turned men irrevocably from
earthly civilization to the Heavenly Jerusalem, yet he will do this in a
Latin or a Greek unselfconsciously modelled on the ancient classics:
and he will betray attitudes to the universe, prejudices and patterns of
behavior that mark him out as a man still firmly rooted in eight
hundred years of Mediterranean life.[1]

Roman attitudes toward the Germanic invaders varied. Some Romans spoke well of their attempts to maintain effective government, as in
this description of Theodoric, an Ostrogothic king of Italy:

He so governed two races at the same time, Romans and Goths, . . .
that by the Romans he was called a Trajan or a Valentinian, whose
times he took as a model; and by the Goths . . . he was judged to be
in all respects their best king.[2]

Other Romans described the barbarians as dirty, violent, and drunken: "Happy the nose that cannot smell a barbarian." Gregory of Tours described the cruelty of one Germanic tribe—the Thuringians—as follows:

> The Thuringians murdered the hostages in all sorts of different ways. . . . They hung our young men up to die in the trees by the muscles of their thighs. They put more than two hundred of our young women to death in the most barbarous way: they tied their arms round the necks of their horses, stampeded these animals in all directions by prodding them with goads, and so tore the girls to pieces; or else they stretched them out over the ruts of the roads, attached their arms and legs to the ground with stakes, and then drove heavily-laden carts over them again and again, until their bones were all broken and their bodies could be thrown out for the dogs and birds to feed on.[3]

Underlying the cruelty and chaos was the fact that the period from A.D. 400 to 700 was, more than most, an age of transition. The historian C. Warren Hollister calls it a "twilight" age—in the sense that there is twilight at sundown when something old is disappearing and twilight at dawn when something new is being born.[4] The old was the crumbling western half of the Roman Empire. The city of Rome ultimately declined to the point where its population numbered only seventeen thousand and its Forum—the old political center of Rome—was a cow pasture. The new was the Germanic and increasingly Christian West (as we will see more clearly in the next chapter).

The transition from Roman to Germanic Europe was a significant event in the history of Western Civilization. The Roman Empire had grown stagnant and despotic, and the arrival of the Germanic tribes brought a surge of fresh energy to Western Europe. Some Germanic traditions, however, were harsh by modern standards. One such tradition was trial by ordeal: a person was considered innocent if he held a red-hot bar and the burn wound healed; he was guilty if the wound did not heal. Other Germanic customs were more positive, such as the belief that royal power could never be absolute since laws were derived from the customs of the people that could not be abridged by anyone. This belief was one source of the eventual development of the principle of government by law later on. Whether harsh or positive, Germanic ideas and traditions reinvigorated Western Europe and over several centuries helped create a new civilization there.

The Germanic invasions caused the western half of Rome to fall, but the eastern half of the Roman Empire lasted for another thousand years.

THE EASTERN ROMAN, OR BYZANTINE, EMPIRE

The history of the eastern Roman Empire began when Constantine founded Constantinople in A.D. 330. The new city quickly became the center of an empire that was both Roman and Christian and that continued to thrive while western Rome was collapsing.

The eastern empire endured for several reasons. One reason was that the strategic location of Constantinople helped to block the barbarian invasions and turn the invaders westward. A second reason for its success was that the east had a stronger economic base than the west, with more productive agriculture, particularly in Egypt, and more commercial activity in the cities. A third factor in survival was that the east had deeper cultural roots than the west; the easterners often thought of themselves as "Greeks" and heirs to a civilization over a thousand years old.

During the fifth century A.D., the emperors in Constantinople did not fully comprehend the extent of the troubles in the west, for their economy was thriving and their cities were full of merchants working and philosophers teaching. When they realized that the west was disintegrating, they began to hope of reconquering the west from the Germanic tribes and restoring the Roman Empire.

Justinian

The foremost advocate of this plan was Justinian, eastern Roman emperor from A.D. 527 to 565. Aided by the advice and encouragement of his wife, the Empress Theodora, Justinian hoped to rebuild a unified Roman Empire. Much of his reign was taken up by wars, in which his armies briefly reconquered Italy, parts of North Africa, and parts of Spain. These reconquests did not endure, however, and those areas soon fell back into Germanic hands.

More successful was Justinian's effort to restore the spiritual and intellectual foundations of imperial rule. Constantinople was at this time one of the most prosperous and productive cities in the world. There, among others, was Procopius of Caesarea, who saw himself as the spiritual heir of Herodotus and Thucydides and wrote a history of the wars fought to reconquer western Rome. Also at this time a number of jurists acting on the emperor's direction, compiled and codified all existing Roman law. The *Codex Justinianus* preserved the Roman legal tradition for later ages. Justinian personally contributed to the lively atmosphere of Constantinople by directing a massive public building program. The most famous construction project in his program was the Church of Sancta Sophia ("Holy Wisdom"). The church was among the largest buildings of the time—250 feet by 220 feet—and was dominated by a dome of 107 feet in diameter. When Justinian saw the church completed, he exclaimed; "Glory to God who has judged me worthy of accomplishing such a work as this! O Solomon, I have outdone thee!"[5]

Justinian's failure to reconquer the west marks the end of the old Roman Empire and the beginning of a new Christian empire. The people of the east continued to call themselves Romans and the intellectuals continued to study the Greek classics. But the spiritual essence of the east was no longer Roman or Greek but Christian. As a result, historians refer to the eastern Roman Empire after Justinian as the *Byzantine Empire,* because Constantinople was built on the site of the ancient village of Byzantium.

Byzantine Christianity

Byzantine Christianity, somewhat different from the Christianity that developed in Western Europe, affected every aspect of life in the eastern empire. In politics, the Byzantine emperors were regarded as being chosen by God, and so their powers were thought to be divine. A ruler was called the "equal to the Apostles," the "God-resembling Emperor," and a "god on earth." In practice, this meant that the Byzantines adhered to a political doctrine adapted from the Persians. This doctrine was called *caesaropapism* (*caesar* means "emperor" or "head of state"; *papism* means "pope" or "head of church"), and it held that the emperor was an autocrat who controlled both state and church. Although they exercised absolute power, Byzantine emperors were still often overthrown. The common belief was that God could withdraw divine favor from an emperor at any time. Thus an emperor who was assassinated or succumbed to a rebellion was assumed to have lost divine protection. The effect of this theory was to create a murderous competition for control of the imperial throne. During the thousand-year history of the Byzantine Empire, sixty-five emperors were forced out of power and over forty of them died as a result. Only thirty-nine Byzantine emperors died peacefully of natural causes.

Byzantine Christianity stressed the transcendence and omnipotence of God, an attitude that assumed a deep chasm separated the world of God from the world of humanity. Byzantine Christians tended to be mystics, relatively uninterested in the earthly world and whose major goal was to bridge the chasm and attain spiritual reunion with God. One device thought to help in achieving spiritual reunion was the *icon*, a statue (of Jesus or one of the apostles, for example) or some other physical representation of the divine. An icon was believed to be a point of contact between the human and divine worlds.

One effect of the Byzantine religious attitude was to de-emphasize the rational powers of the human mind, for the Byzantines believed that reason and logic were incapable of penetrating the divine mysteries and so were relatively unimportant. Another effect was to encourage Byzan-

Byzantine Empress Theodora Wife of the emperor Justinian, Theodora was one of
the most powerful women of ancient times. In this mosaic from the sixth century
A.D., the artist portrays her in lavish robes and jewelry and with several attendants.
Mosaics were a popular Byzantine art form. (Metropolitan Museum of Art, NY)

tine monks to be almost exclusively concerned with the care of their own
souls. Compared to their counterparts in Western Europe, Byzantine
monks were relatively unconcerned with the spiritual welfare of the
larger community and uninterested in reasoning and thinking about
religious doctrine. A third effect of Byzantine religion was to encourage
development of a new kind of art. Most classical Greek and Roman art
had been naturalistic. In the sixth century, however, the Byzantines
began to develop an abstract art in which human figures were portrayed
with large, piercing eyes and in a flattened form without any sense of
three-dimensional space. The purpose of this art form was to lead people

to the transcendent by picturing humans as seekers after spiritual peace rather than as participants in a realistic, physical world.

External and Internal Conflict

The Byzantines' obsession with spiritual peace and reunion with God may have been influenced by the conflict and chaos that characterized their world. The Byzantine Empire was constantly threatened by invaders from two directions. From the north, a succession of nomadic invaders attacked the empire regularly; first the Huns, then the Avars, and finally the Slavs. From the southeast, the original threat was from Sassanian Persia, but the Byzantine Emperor Heraclius (A.D. 610–641) managed to subdue the Persians after a long series of wars. In the process, however, both the Byzantines and the Persians were gravely weakened and left vulnerable to the rising power of Islam. The Arabs burst out of the desert in the mid-seventh century A.D., destroying the Persian Empire and taking Palestine, Syria, and Egypt from the Byzantine Empire. The Byzantine losses seriously undermined the empire, since Egypt was a major source of grain, Syria the culmination point of trade routes across Asia, and Palestine the location of major religious shrines. Arab attacks continued for years and included several sieges of Constantinople. It was not until A.D. 863 that the Byzantines were able to defeat the Arabs decisively and diminish the Arab threat for a time.

During the late seventh and eighth centuries A.D., the territorial possessions of the Byzantine Empire were reduced to Asia Minor, some parts of the Balkan peninsula, and a few areas in Italy captured during Justinian's rule. Most of Spain and Italy was lost to Germanic invaders, much of the Balkans to the Slavs, and much of the eastern Mediterranean to the Arabs. As a result, the Byzantine Empire became increasingly militarized, since the main concern of the imperial government was national defense. Large numbers of peasants were conscripted into armies and stationed permanently along the frontiers. Also during this time arose a religious controversy known as *iconoclasm* ("breaking of icons"). Many Byzantines believed that the long succession of military defeats was a punishment from God brought on by some kind of theological error. In the A.D. 720s, the Emperor Leo proclaimed that the error had to do with icons, for in his view they were an attempt to represent the spiritual in physical form and thus constituted idolatry. Over the next several decades, the government forced the destruction of numerous statues, paintings, and other forms of religious art. But many monks were icon worshippers, so the controversy became a power struggle between emperors—who sought the destruction of icons—and monks—who demanded continuation of the iconic tradition. The struggle was often violent and many monks were exiled or even killed.

Eventually, the emperors asserted their control over the monks and the church. In the mid-ninth century A.D., however, some forms of icon worship were allowed.

The End of the Byzantine Empire

For a time during the ninth century Byzantine power was revived. In A.D. 867, Basil I came to the throne and founded the Macedonian dynasty that ruled for nearly two centuries. Under the Macedonians, the Byzantine Empire recaptured some land in Asia and the Balkans. (The fighting in the Balkans was often brutal. In A.D. 1014, the Byzantines captured a Bulgarian army of fifteen thousand and blinded their prisoners, allowing each hundredth man to keep one eye so to guide the rest back to Bulgaria.) Byzantine influence also expanded to the Russian state of Kiev, which was converted to Christianity in A.D. 989.

Contacts between the Byzantines and the Slavic peoples were increasing. The Slavs—the ancestors of the Russians, the Poles, the Czechs, the Slovaks, and the Bulgars—originated in northeastern Europe and moved into eastern Europe and the Balkan peninsula at about the same time the Germanic tribes were invading Western Europe. During the ninth to eleventh centuries A.D., various Slavic peoples established states in Bulgaria, Moravia, and Poland. Many of the Slavs were gradually Christianized by the Byzantines, although the Poles and many Czechs adopted Roman Catholic Christianity. But expansion in the east was counterbalanced by loss of Byzantine influence in the west. In the eleventh century, the empire lost its last possessions in Italy. Moreover, in 1054, a split occurred between western and eastern Christianity, caused largely by the Byzantine refusal to recognize the Roman pope as the supreme leader of all Christians.

Christianity was thus divided, with the Roman Catholic Church dominating Western Europe and the Greek Orthodox Church centered in Constantinople claiming the loyalty of Greeks and most of the Slavic world. The religious split was the most prominent aspect of a larger cultural split, for Byzantines and western Europeans were increasingly perceiving each other as religious, political, and military rivals. This rivalry intensified during the Crusades of the eleventh to thirteenth centuries (discussed in greater detail in Chapter 8). The Crusades were a response to the capture of Palestine late in the eleventh century by the Seljuk Turks (central Asian nomads who converted to Islam). Both Byzantine and western European Christians agreed that the Holy Land (Palestine) had to be restored to Christian control, and for two hundred years Crusader armies fought, unsuccessfully, to retake the area. At first, the Byzantines and the Europeans cooperated against the common enemy, but the Europeans soon turned on their allies largely because the church split of 1054 made them regard the Byzantines as heretics. In 1204, a European Crusader army attacked and captured Constantinople, an event that marks the beginning of the end of the Byzantine Empire. The Byzantines later managed to retake their capital, but the empire was gravely weakened. Then, in the fourteenth century, there appeared a new enemy: the Ottoman Turks. Over several decades, the Ottomans conquered Byzantine territory and, in 1453, took Constantinople, thereby bringing the Byzantine Empire to an end.

The Byzantine Empire was destroyed because it was caught between two rising powers—the Muslim Turks from the east and the European Christians from the west. With its destruction, the last remnant of the old Roman Empire disappeared. But during its thousand-year history, the Byzantine Empire made a number of significant contributions to human history. Among the most important contributions in terms of the history of Western Civilization was the Byzantines' preservation of much of the Greco-Roman cultural heritage, passing it on to both the Arabs and the western Europeans. The Byzantines also brought much of the Slavic world within the realm of Christian culture and civilization. And, by continually fighting off Asian and Arabic invaders, they unintentionally helped to protect Western Europe and thereby made it easier for Europeans to build the foundations of a new civilization.

ISLAM

The rise of the religion of Islam was significant in several respects. It marked the creation of a new world religion during a time when major religious changes were taking place, especially the change from the old animistic religions in the Mediterranean to monotheism (Judaism, Christianity, and Islam). It also marked the emergence of the Arabic peoples as an influential force in world history. And, the rise of Islam was the last phase in the transformation of the Roman unification of the Mediterranean into three new cultural and religious realms.

Islam originated in Arabia. For centuries Arabia played only a peripheral role in the great events occurring throughout Eurasia, since it lacked both the population base and the political unity necessary to be influential. It was primarily important as a transit area, through which passed caravans carrying goods between Asia and the Mediterranean. Agriculture was common only in the Yemen, the southern part of the Arabian peninsula. Most of Arabia consisted of waterless deserts and steppes, punctuated only by an occasional oasis. Small communities existed around each oasis, but much of the population were members of Bedouin tribes that wandered the deserts. Most Arabs practiced some form of polytheistic nature religion.

Muhammad

The traditional Arabic world was transformed largely by one man—Muhammad. Born sometime after A.D. 570, Muhammad became a trader and merchant in the small caravan town of Mecca. Mecca was one of the few Arabic areas that had much contact with the non-Arabic world, and as a result Muhammad became familiar with the Jewish and Christian religious traditions. At about the age of forty, Muhammad experienced a religious conversion and felt called by Allah (the Arabic word for "God") to preach to the Meccans. Many Meccan businesspeople disliked Muhammad's preaching, both because he opposed traditional Arabic religion and because his preaching disrupted their business. As a result, in A.D. 622, he was forced to flee from Mecca to Yathrib (later named Medina), where he had a few supporters. This flight, known to Muslims as the *Hegira* ("flight" or "exodus"), was a turning point in Muhammad's career, and eventually the year 622 was designated as the first year of the Muslim calendar. From then on Muhammad's powerful personality and his appeal of monotheism, which was more coherent than traditional polytheism, induced many Arabs to convert to Islam. When Muhammad died in A.D. 632, Islam was the dominant Arabic religion.

According to Muhammad, Islam was the last and greatest revelation from God, the culmination of an ancient religious tradition that began with the Hebrew patriarch, Abraham. (Thus Islam was the latest manifestation of an Axial Period religion.) God called Abraham to follow him, and Judaism eventually evolved from that call. Christianity developed later, after God called Jesus, who Muhammad regarded as a prophet but not the Son of God. Since neither Jews nor Christians had properly followed God's commands, God called his last and greatest prophet—Muhammad—to found Islam, the supreme embodiment of the divine revelation.

The Islamic Faith

Like Judaism and Christianity, Islam is a faith in one God who judges people, eventually sending the righteous to paradise and the wicked to hell. But there are differences in the attitude toward humans. Judaism and Christianity often portray humans as relatively strong-willed creatures prone to rebel (sin) against God. Islam, however, regards humans as weak and ignorant, needing guidance from God on how to live and what to believe. The word *Islam* means "submission to God," and a *Muslim* is "one who submits." Through submission the believer is directed to worship God through performance of the Five Pillars of Islam: (1) accepting the confession of faith that states "there is no God but Allah, and Muhammad is his prophet"; (2) praying five times a day at appointed times; (3) giving alms to the poor; (4) fasting from daybreak to sunset

Muhammad A line engraving showing an artist's conception of Muhammad, Arab prophet and founder of Islam. (The Granger Collection)

during the holy month of Ramadan; and (5) making a pilgrimage to Mecca at least once in a lifetime.

Further guidance for the believer is contained in the *Koran,* the Islamic holy book compiled by Muhammad's followers. The Koran is a collection of the revelations that God made to Muhammad and is regarded by most Muslims as the literal words of God. Every Muslim is expected as an act of worship to memorize and recite some of the Koran. Here is one example of a commonly memorized passage:

> In the name of God, the Merciful, the Compassionate: Praise belongs to God, Lord of all Being; the Merciful, the Compassionate; Master of Judgment Day. Thee we serve, on Thee we call for help. Guide us in the straight path, the path of those whom Thou art bounteous to, not those whom anger falls on, nor those who go astray.[6]

Another source of authority for Islamic followers is the *hadith,* a collection of the teachings of Muhammad compiled after his death.

No official priesthood exists in Islam, so any Muslim can perform the rituals. However, those known as *imans* or *ayatollahs* are recognized as spiritual leaders. Also, there is an informal group of religious scholars or

Suleymaneye Mosque, Istanbul (16th century A.D.)   Muslims built numerous mosques as sites for public religious worship. The mosques are characterized by domed roofs and minarets, high slender towers from which the call to prayer was chanted at the appointed times of the day. (Turkish Tourist Office)

clergy called the *ulema,* whose role is to explain the teachings contained in the Koran and hadith. The ulema are expected to explain and transmit Muhammad's teachings, not to think or give their own opinions. (An ulema said once, "Piss on my opinion.")[7] The teachings in the Koran and hadith guide all aspects of Muslim life, including what Muslims can eat, how they can dress, punishments for crimes, relations between the sexes, and so on. Some of the teachings encourage toleration and love toward others. Muhammad taught, for example, that "the Arab is not superior to the non-Arab; the non-Arab is not superior to the Arab. You are all sons of Adam, and Adam was made of earth."[8] Other teachings, however, express an attitude of intolerance. Women are regarded as inferior to men in Muslim societies. They have no identity outside the family and are always under the control of a male. (In the twentieth century, some Muslim women began to assert their independence from male control.) The subjugation of women eventually led to the required practice of wearing a veil over their faces when in public, the idea being that no male outside the family should see the face of a mature woman. Another example of intolerance is the Muslim belief (here similar to Christian belief) that only they know the truth of God and that this truth applies to everyone. This belief justified the practice of holy war (*jihad*), by which Muslims sought to conquer non-Muslim societies.

Islam Expands

Holy wars dominated Arab history in the decades after Muhammad's death. *Caliphs* (or "successors") were selected to act as both political and religious leaders, and they led a series of conquests. In A.D. 636, the Arabs took Syria and Palestine from the Byzantine Empire. In 637, they conquered the Sassanian Persian Empire, and in 640–641 seized Egypt from the Byzantines. Thus, within five years the Arabs overran much of what had been the eastern half of the Roman Empire and in the process destroyed most of the influence of Greco-Roman culture in the east (much like the Germanic tribes destroyed it in the west). The Arabs were successful in part because the Byzantine and Persian empires had weakened in fighting each other and in part because religious zeal and overpopulation in Arabia impelled the Arabs to expand.

To govern the new acquisitions, the Caliph Muawiya founded the Umayyad dynasty in A.D. 661. Under the Umayyads, the Arab capital was Damascus and the government was a monarchy supported by a military aristocracy who dominated the conquered peoples. Military expansion continued, as Arab armies pushed eastward all the way to India. In the west they drove across North Africa; in A.D. 711 they launched an invasion of Spain and were quickly victorious. The growth of Arab power was soon halted, however. In A.D. 717–718, the Byzantines defeated the Arab siege of Constantinople, thereby ensuring the survival of their empire. In 733, the Frankish warlord Charles Martel defeated an Arab army at Poitiers (known today as Tours) in southern France, so further Arab expansion into Western Europe was blocked. Most of Europe remained independent of the Muslim world. But by the early eighth century A.D., the Muslim world included Spain, all of North Africa, Syria and Palestine, Arabia, Persia, Afghanistan, and parts of India.

Despite this expansion, the power of the Umayyad Caliphate was gradually undermined by two forces. One was feuds among the Arabs. The vast majority of Arabs were *Sunni*, or orthodox, Muslims, but they were opposed by a minority that became known as *Shiite* Muslims. The Shiites were originally a political faction that claimed the Umayyads had usurped power from Muhammad's cousin, Ali, and his descendants. However, they soon became a source of both political and religious opposition to the Sunni majority. The other force that undermined the power of the Umayyads was Islam itself, for all Muslims—Arab and non-Arab—were considered equal. Consequently, the Arab population was quickly outnumbered by non-Arab converts to Islam. These converts,

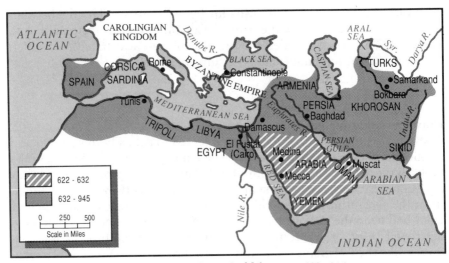

Figure 6.2   The Spread of Islam, A.D. 622–945

many of whom were urban merchants and artisans, disliked the militarism of the Arab aristocracy and wanted a new, more stable social order in which trade and agriculture would be more important than war. The tensions created by these two forces led to the Abbasid revolution of A.D. 747–750, which replaced the Umayyad dynasty with a new Abbasid Caliphate.

With the Abbasid revolution, the nature of the Muslim world changed. It was no longer controlled only by Arabs, for the Abbasids treated all Muslims equally and used Islam rather than Arab ethnic unity as the binding force of their empire. The capital was moved to Baghdad, where the caliphs became autocrats who called themselves the "Shadow of God upon Earth" and claimed that God gave them the power to rule. The caliphs governed through a bureaucracy, chosen by merit from both Arabs and non-Arabs.

Islamic Society and Culture

The Abbasid Caliphate lasted from A.D. 750 to 1258. During most of that period the Islamic Empire was both powerful and prosperous, since it was at the center of both north–south and east–west trade routes. Furs from Scandinavia came to Baghdad, as did gold and slaves from Africa. Silks and spices came from India and China, some of which were transported on to north Africa and Spain. Also from India came the new nine-digit numerical system that later became known in Europe as arabic numerals. In addition, scientific knowledge was exchanged with China. The following account tells of an Arab physician who passed his

knowledge of an ancient Greek scientist named Galen to a Chinese scholar:

> A Chinese scholar came to my house and remained in the town about a year. In five months he learnt to speak and write Arabic. When he decided to return to his country, he said to me a month or so beforehand, "I am about to leave. I would be glad if someone would dictate to me the sixteen books of Galen before I go." . . . So together with one of my students we read Galen to him as fast as we could, but he wrote still faster.[9]

The cultural and intellectual life of the Islamic world reached its height during the tenth to twelfth centuries A.D. Contact with China and India as well as knowledge of the Greek philosophical and scientific heritage stimulated an explosion of Islamic talent and creativity. Avicenna, an eleventh-century philosopher and physician, wrote *The Canon of Medicine*, which became a basic source of medical knowledge both in the Islamic world and later in Europe. Averroes, a twelfth-century philosopher, composed commentaries on Plato and Aristotle, which helped revive interest in Greek philosophy in Europe. And, in the eleventh century, the astronomer Al-Biruni postulated the revolutionary theory that the earth revolves around the sun, an idea that nobody at the time accepted. Many other innovations were also developed. Eye surgery was performed in several of the larger cities, and glass-making became a major industry. Windmills were common in some rural areas, and in some places, a sweet, cool drink known as sherbet was available.

Islamic art also flourished, emphasizing the depiction of natural forms because Islam prohibited the display of human forms in art. The most notable Islamic style was known as *arabesque*. Arabesque is a highly ornamental art form that stresses elaborate designs, infinite patterns, and graceful flourishes. The style is so intricate and complex as to suggest a source of inspiration beyond the natural world. One example is the Topkapi Palace at Constantinople, the interior of which is decorated with so many representations of flowers and trees that it resembles a flower garden. Another is the Alhambra Palace in Granada, Spain, in which virtually all interior surface areas are covered with vivid colors and geometric designs.

The political unity of the Islamic world began to weaken in the ninth and tenth centuries A.D. Local governments in Egypt, North Africa, and Spain asserted independence from the central government in Baghdad. Then, in the late eleventh century, a growing spirit of religious conservatism began to stifle the creative impulses of Islamic learning and scholarship. In 1258, the Mongols, a nomadic people from Mongolia in northern China, captured Baghdad and ended the Abbasid Caliphate. After that, the Islamic world remained important in many ways, and

Islam continued to expand in Asia. The great days of political power and intellectual creativity, however, were over.

CONCLUSION

The centuries between A.D. 400 and 700 were a chaotic time around the Mediterranean Sea, but by shortly after 700 three cultural areas were clearly demarcated: the Germanic in Western Europe, the Byzantine, and the Muslim. The Muslims dominated the southern and eastern Mediterranean, but their defeat at Constantinople in A.D. 717–718 ensured the independence of the Byzantine Empire, and their loss at Poitiers (Tours) in A.D. 733 guaranteed the autonomy of Western Europe. One of the ironies of the time was that these three cultures were very much alike but continually hostile to one another. They shared a monotheistic religion inherited from the Hebrews and together cultivated the Greco-Roman cultural heritage. Yet, despite—or perhaps because of—their similarities, the three fought one another during the seventh to eighth centuries and would fight again later in the Crusades (see Chapter 8).

Finally, it is significant that after A.D. 700 the Mediterranean Sea was no longer a major center of civilization. The Byzantine Empire was in the northeastern Mediterranean, the center of the Islamic world shifted eastward toward Persia, and the center of Western Christian culture shifted northward into the heart of Europe. It was there in Europe that a dynamic new civilization would develop—our focus in the following chapters.

THINGS YOU SHOULD KNOW

Constantinople
The Huns
The Han dynasty in China
Hindu-Arabic numeral system
Gupta Age in India
The Germanic tribes
Justinian
Byzantine Christianity
Iconoclasm

The Slavs
Muhammad
Basic teachings of Islam
Expansion of Islam
Umayyad dynasty
Abbasid Caliphate
Islamic philosophy, art, and
  medicine

SUGGESTED READINGS

Edward Gibbon, *The Decline and Fall of the Roman Empire* (Baltimore: Penguin, 1983) is the classic work on the decline of Rome. C. Warren Hollister, *Medieval Europe: A Short History* (New York: McGraw, 1982) and William R. Cook and

Ronald B. Herzman, *The Medieval World View: An Introduction* (New York: Oxford Univ. Press, 1983) contain good discussions of the Germanic migrations into the Roman Empire. Two good introductions to the Byzantine Empire are Robert Browning, *The Byzantine Empire* (New York: Scribner's, 1980) and D. A. Miller, *The Byzantine Tradition* (New York: Harper & Row, 1966). A more detailed work, on the wife of the Emperor Justinian, is Antony Bridge, *Theodora: Portrait in a Byzantine Landscape* (Chicago: Academy Chi. Pubs., 1984). On Islam, Marshall G. S. Hodgson, *The Venture of Islam*, vol. 1: *The Classical Age of Islam* (Chicago: Univ. of Chicago Press, 1974) is excellent. A good biography of Muhammad is W. Montgomery Watt, *Muhammad: Prophet and Statesman* (New York: Oxford Univ. Press, 1974). Also important are Bernard Lewis, *The Arabs in History* (New York: Harper & Row, 1966) and R. M. Savory (ed.), *Introduction to Islamic Civilization* (Cambridge, Engl.: Cambridge Univ. Press, 1976).

NOTES

[1]Peter Brown, *The World of Late Antiquity*, A.D. *150–750* (New York: Harcourt, 1971), p. 8.

[2]Quoted in William R. Cook and Ronald B. Herzman, *The Medieval World View: An Introduction* (New York: Oxford Univ. Press, 1983), pp. 128–29.

[3]*Ibid.*, pp. 127–28.

[4]C. Warren Hollister, "Twilight in the West," Lynn White, Jr.(ed.), *The Transformation of the Roman World: Gibbon's Problem After Two Centuries* (Berkeley: Univ. of California Press, 1966), p. 179.

[5]Quoted in Robert Browning, *The Byzantine Empire* (New York: Scribner's, 1980), pp. 39–40.

[6]Quoted in Marshall G. S. Hodgson, *The Venture of Islam*, vol. 1, *The Classical Age of Islam* (Chicago: Univ. of Chicago Press, 1974), p. 185.

[7]Quoted in Michael Cook, "The Emergence of Islamic Civilization," in *The Origins and Diversity of Axial Age Civilizations*, ed. S. N. Eisenstadt (Albany: State Univ. of New York Press, 1986), p. 482.

[8]Quoted in Joseph Needham, *Within the Four Seas: The Dialogue of East and West* (Toronto: Univ. of Toronto Press, 1969), p. 208.

[9]Quoted in L. S. Stavrianos, *A Global History: The Human Heritage*, 3rd ed. (Englewood Cliffs, N.J.: Prentice-Hall, 1983), pp. 124, 126.

7

The Early Middle Ages: A Dynamic Frontier, 500 to 1000

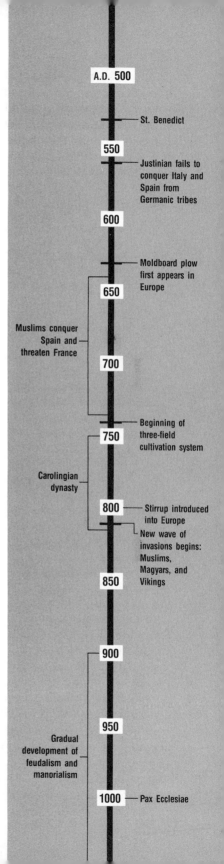

A.D. 500

St. Benedict

550

Justinian fails to conquer Italy and Spain from Germanic tribes

600

Moldboard plow first appears in Europe

650

Muslims conquer Spain and threaten France

700

Beginning of three-field cultivation system

750

Carolingian dynasty

800

Stirrup introduced into Europe

New wave of invasions begins: Muslims, Magyars, and Vikings

850

900

950

Gradual development of feudalism and manorialism

1000 — Pax Ecclesiae

European history from roughly A.D. 500 to 1400–1500 is traditionally designated as the *Middle Ages,* or the *medieval* period, because it came between ancient history and modern history. The traditional term for the early Middle Ages is the *Dark Ages,* since it was a time of decline in comparison with the highly developed civilizations of the ancient world. In many respects, the so-called Dark Ages were a bad time; most governmental structures disappeared, educational and social institutions collapsed, and economic conditions were harsh. Historian Georges Duby describes early medieval Europe this way:

> A mere handful of men—unending emptiness stretching so far west, north, and east that it covers everything . . . clearings here and there, wrested from the forest but still only half-tamed; within this food-producing area . . . huts of stone, mud, or branches, clustered in hamlets surrounded by thorn hedges and a belt of gardens; . . . sparsely scattered towns, the mere whitened skeletons of Roman cities invaded by rural nature, streets in ruins . . . , fortifications haphazardly repaired, stone structures dating back to the Roman Empire that have been turned into churches or strongholds.[1]

Despite the harsh living conditions of the early Middle Ages, it is somewhat of a misnomer to refer to this period as the Dark Ages. Western Europe at this time was more like a dynamic frontier in two senses: (1) it was a relatively underpopulated area, much of it untamed by human settlement; and (2) this was a time of great creativity, when a new civilization—Western European Civilization—was being born. As the historian L. S. Stavrianos remarks, "It was an age of birth as well as of death, and to concentrate on the latter is to miss the dynamism and significance of a seminal phase of human history."[2]

THE SIXTH TO EIGHTH CENTURIES

Western Europe was buffeted by successive waves of migrations and invasions between the sixth and eighth centuries. The various Germanic tribes fought one another sporadically for control of land. The Byzantine Empire under the rule of Justinian tried to reconquer Italy and Spain in the sixth century. Arab armies subdued Spain and threatened France in the eighth century. Constant violence and warfare changed the way people lived. Travel and communications were difficult, so political and economic life became concentrated on the local level. Long-distance commerce all but vanished. Architecture was modified, as the wealthy sought protection by building their homes like fortresses with thick walls and small windows. The poor sought help from the wealthy, but, as usual, they suffered the most. Archaeological finds from this time commonly include skeletons and bones deformed by malnutrition.

A few educated people realized the significance of the disappearance of Roman civilization. Pope Gregory the Great wrote in the late sixth century, "For where is the Senate? Where is the People? The bones are all dissolved, the flesh is consumed, all the pomp of the dignities of this world is gone. The whole mass is boiled away."[3] A few scholars tried to preserve the Greco-Roman cultural heritage. Cassiodorus (480–575), for example, helped Christianize the Ostrogoths in Italy and transcribed several ancient manuscripts to ensure their survival. Boethius (c. 480–524) wrote the *Consolation of Philosophy,* one of the last ancient works to look to pre-Christian philosophy for spiritual truth and comfort.

Preserving the Greco-Roman heritage was important, for it became one of the elements from which Western European Civilization would be formed. The other two elements important to Western European Civilization were the spiritual and moral tradition of Christianity and the political and cultural tradition of the Germanic peoples who now populated most of Europe. These three elements were first brought together by monks and nuns—people who withdrew from ordinary society to devote their lives to God—who more than anyone else converted the Germans to Christianity and also preserved the Greco-Roman heritage for later ages.

CONTRIBUTIONS OF MONKS AND NUNS

In 597, Pope Gregory the Great sent a mission of monks to England to convert the Angles and Saxons, who practiced animistic religions, to Christianity. His mission found that a movement of Irish monks had already developed in western Scotland, Ireland, and Wales. According to legend, many Irish had been converted to Christianity by St. Patrick in the mid-fifth century. The Irish monks were unique in that they followed a tradition of pilgrimage and voluntary exile from their native land, going wherever God called them to go. One story, for example, tells of three monks ". . . who stole away from Ireland in a boat without any oars because they would live in a state of pilgrimage for the love of God, they recked not where."[4]

During the seventh and eighth centuries, Irish monks migrated throughout much of Western Europe, establishing dozens of monasteries and converting large numbers of German peasants to Christianity. The monks were joined by thousands of nuns, many of whom built large convents that controlled great amounts of land. Hilda of Whitby, for example, founded and governed several large monasteries in England in the seventh century, and Herlinda of Eika (Belgium) became known in the eighth century as a skillful copier of manuscripts. For both women and men in the early Middle Ages, the monastic life offered a sanctuary for those who were especially devout and provided a center of activity for those who were especially ambitious.

The Benedictine Rule

As monasticism spread, it gradually became organized according to the *Rule* of St. Benedict of Nursia (480–543). Benedict was an extraordinary individual who, like many others of his time, felt an intense antagonism between the temptations of the flesh and the pious, spiritual life he wanted to live. The following medieval account tells of how he overcame a temptation:

> For the evil spirit brought back before the mind's eye a certain woman whom he had once seen. So intensely did the Tempter inflame his mind by the sight of that woman that he could hardly control his passion. . . . Then suddenly God graciously looked upon him and he returned to himself . . . he stripped off his garments and flung himself naked upon stinging thorns and burning nettles. He rolled about there for a long time, and came out with his whole body wounded by them. So through the wound of his skin he drew out from his body the wound of the mind by changing the lust to pain.[5]

Benedict's spiritual struggles led him to found a monastery at Monte Cassino, Italy. There he developed a set of regulations to govern himself and his fellow monks. This *Rule* quickly came to dominate the lives of most monks and nuns in Western Europe.

Although the Benedictine *Rule* may seem overly demanding to us, to early medieval people it was considered moderate and reasonable. Benedict stipulated that the monk or nun had to take vows of poverty and chastity, giving up all private property and sexual gratification. Those who took the vows were expected to devote their lives to the service of God and to achieve salvation. Their daily schedule was strictly regulated—the first prayer service was held around 2:30 A.M. and followed by seven more scattered throughout the day until the last one at 7 P.M. In addition to the prayer services, there were periods set aside for reading and study and for agricultural labor to produce the food needed. This routine was followed daily, except in extraordinary circumstances.

Benedictine monasticism was different from that in other parts of the world. Buddhist monasticism, for example, denied the value of manual labor, and Buddhist monks lived by charity rather than by their own work. Byzantine monasticism stressed mysticism, and the monks lived in isolation from the rest of the world and denigrated human reason. Both were unlike the Benedictines, who read books, farmed, and performed charitable and educational activities for local peasants. In comparison with the Buddhists and the Byzantines, Benedictine monks were more practical and more interested in worldly affairs. This worldly orientation had a significant impact on at least three aspects of Western Civilization: (1) Western conceptions of time, (2) Western attitudes toward education and learning, and (3) Western beliefs about the value of manual labor.

St. Benedict　A fifteenth-century drawing of St. Benedict giving instructions to two monks. St. Benedict, who established many of the rules that now govern monks around the world, founded twelve monasteries in Italy that eventually became the centers of European monasticism. (Pierpont Morgan Library)

In the ancient world, time was a vague concept. People lived by the rhythms of nature, rising at sunrise and going to sleep at sundown. They were not concerned with the "time of day" as we are today. Although medieval peasants also lived by the rhythms of nature, the Benedictines and some other Christians were interested in time measurement. According to Benedict, "Idleness is the enemy of the soul," and so he established an elaborate schedule to absorb the energies of monks and nuns. Punctuality was important in this schedule, for lateness might make it necessary to shorten a prayer service. The importance of being on time was expressed by the English monk, Bede: "I know that the angels are present at the canonical hours, and what if they do not find me among the brethren when they assemble? Will they not say, where is Bede? Why does he not attend the appointed devotions with his brethren?"[6] This Benedictine concern with punctuality and schedules would slowly help to develop a growing Western consciousness of time. The late Middle Ages would see the invention of the mechanical clock (the importance of which is discussed in Chapter 8).

The Benedictines also exhibited a new attitude toward education, for they believed that reading and copying books was a form of worship. Cassiodorus said once:

> Oh, blessed the perseverance, laudable the industry which preaches to men with the hand, starts tongues with the fingers, gives an unspoken salvation to mortals and against the iniquitous deceits of the Devil fights with pen and ink. For Satan receives as many wounds as the scribe copies words of the Lord.[7]

Monks and nuns respected books and in many cases organized monastic schools for the local population. Their interest in education was a decisive departure in Western history, for the Benedictines were the first organized group to do both intellectual and manual labor. In the ancient world, the two forms of labor were divided socially, with intellectual labor reserved for the educated upper classes and manual labor assigned to slaves and the lower classes. The monks helped to weaken the social barrier between the intellectual and the manual and thus helped create in Western history a respect for learning that was both theoretical and practical. This new attitude would eventually lead to modern science, in that it encouraged early scientists' interest in pure scientific thought and in practical experimentation.

The ancient world generally associated manual labor with slaves and viewed it as degrading. That monks and nuns gardened and did other work with their hands began to impart a new dignity to the performance of manual labor. Christianity developed more of a mixed attitude. In Genesis, for example, labor is portrayed as a punishment for sin—"by the sweat of thy face shalt thou eat bread" (Genesis 3:19). But the Apostle Paul supported the value of work—"if any would not work, neither should he eat" (2 Thessalonians 3:10). Benedict stated that "to labor is to pray" and stipulated that monks should work regularly. The Benedictines did not regard manual labor as good in itself; rather, it was a form of penitence for sin and a remedy for the idleness that could invite temptations from the devil. Nevertheless, since monks and nuns were the most admired people in the early Middle Ages, their work had the effect of slowly raising the social and spiritual prestige of labor, even though the upper classes continued to shun manual labor. Other factors also contributed, most notably the reality that in a frontier society manual labor was necessary for survival.

The Benedictines were the first in Western history to place a spiritual value on work. This attitude later helped to produce the Western belief that work (in the sense of practical, productive activity) is both socially useful and spiritually important.

THE PEASANTS CREATE AN AGRICULTURAL REVOLUTION

At the same time that the Benedictines were dignifying manual labor, the peasants—who still did most of that work—were creating the first of several European agricultural revolutions. This revolution would eventually enable Europe to be more productive than ancient Rome or Greece had ever been. The ancient Roman and Greek economies were based on slave labor, which did not foster technological creativity and thus caused economic production to remain at a low level, leaving most people to live in poverty. Medieval society, however, encouraged creativity and thus developed several technological innovations that increased agricultural productivity and provided a foundation for a better economy.

The medieval agricultural revolution was carried out by large numbers of ordinary peasants whose names we do not know; it was, in a sense, a democratic revolution. The peasants adapted farming techniques to local conditions all over Europe and, in the process, slowly learned better ways of doing things. The first agricultural breakthrough was a new moldboard plow (see the Technology box).

The moldboard plow changed the lives of peasants in several ways. Since the plow required several oxen for its operation and few peasants had more than one or two oxen, they had to pool their animals and work together. This led to a communal farming system, in which the peasants of a community worked in one large field with each being entitled to a certain share of the produce. In addition, cattle were allowed to graze on another large field that was left fallow for the next year's planting, so their droppings fertilized the soil. In some places, manure piles became recognized as a sign of wealth.

Another agricultural breakthrough was the substitution of a three-field system for the earlier two-field one. In the sixth and seventh centuries, most peasant villages divided their land in half, with one field being cultivated each year and the other lying fallow so that soil nutrients could be naturally replenished. But increased manure from animals so enriched the soil that in the eighth century some peasants north of the Alps moved to a three-field system. By dividing land into thirds and cultivating one field in autumn and another in spring, these peasants increased the amount of land farmed each year from one-half to two-thirds. The result, of course, was increased productivity.

The horse was the focus of other agricultural innovations in the ninth century. The Romans had been unable to use the horse with their scratch plow, since the harness was simply a lasso placed around the neck that choked the animal when it pulled anything heavy. They used either oxen or slaves to pull the plows, both of which were slow and inefficient. Two inventions in early medieval times—the shoulder harness and the horseshoe—enabled peasants to use the horse, faster and cheaper than the ox, to operate the moldboard plow in Europe. The shoulder harness was probably developed in central Asia and brought to Europe in the ninth century. It allowed animals to pull greater weights. The horseshoe, which appeared in Europe by the ninth century, protected the horse's hooves from breaking or wearing down.

The life-style of the peasant gradually improved as a result of this agricultural revolution. The most basic improvement was an increase in the amount of food grown. Another was the opportunity for peasants to live in larger communities. A horse could move faster than an ox, so peasants could live further from their fields and congregate in villages of several hundred people rather than in small hamlets. The village offered greater safety, access to a church, and in some cases the availability of water-powered grain mills (the mills are discussed in the Chapter 8 Technology box).

Why were European peasants more willing and able than their ancient counterparts to invent or develop so many new agricultural technologies? There are at least five interrelated answers to this question.

1. Medieval peasants were more free than ancient peasants. While most ancient peasants were actually slaves under the control of their owners, medieval peasants were either free citizens or serfs (farm workers controlled by an upper-class authority) and were often able to make their own decisions about how to farm.
2. Medieval peasants lived on a frontier and had to be creative in order to survive. They thus had to develop new tools to meet new conditions, such as the moldboard plow discussed in the Technology box.
3. The peasants, most of whom were of Germanic descent, inherited a tradition of developing innovations to cope with the cold climate of northern Europe. Over the centuries, the Germans either invented or adopted from other peoples the chimney and the easily heated compact house, trousers and sleeves, and the ski.
4. The successive waves of invasions of Europe—by the Germans, Byzantines, Arabs, Slavs, and so on—destroyed most of the old customs and habits derived from Roman civilization. Thus, Europeans had to begin anew.
5. Christianity's conception of nature gradually encouraged Europeans to exploit the natural world more aggressively. As discussed in Chapter 3, the Judaeo-Christian perception of God as transcendent and separate from nature encouraged the idea that nature is spiritless or inanimate. The early Germans did not share this conception, since they perceived nature as full of divinity and spirit. As they became Christianized, however, the Germans slowly modified their conceptions of religion and nature. Peasants, for example, began to pray to Christian saints rather than to spirits in

TECHNOLOGY
The Moldboard Plow

The Romans and other ancient peoples had used a scratch plow that simply had a blade to split the soil. The scratch plow barely broke the surface of the soil, although it was adequate for the thin soil of Mediterranean lands. The wet, thick soil of the northern parts of Europe required a heavier, more efficient tool—the moldboard plow. We do not know with certainty the precise origin of the moldboard plow, but it was probably developed sometime in the sixth century A.D. by the Slavic peoples of eastern Europe. The moldboard plow appeared in parts of France and northern Italy in the seventh century, in Germany by the eighth century, and in England by the ninth century.

The real innovation was in the way the plow cut the soil. A knife, at the front of the frame, cut the soil vertically to make it easier for the "share" behind it to split the soil horizontally down to the grass-roots. Behind the share was the moldboard, a curved board diagonal to the frame, which lifted the cut sod and threw it to the side. Wheels on the front allowed the relatively large plow to be moved more easily.

The two most important advantages of the moldboard plow were (1) its effectiveness in the wet soils of northern and Western Europe and (2) its ability to cut deeply into more nutrient-rich soil. The result was an increase in agricultural production for many medieval peasants.

The Moldboard Plow   *In this drawing (c. 1340), English peasants are using the moldboard plow. The knife in the front of the plow cut the soil, the share behind it and parallel to the ground split the soil, and the long moldboard turned over the soil. (The Granger Collection)*

nature. Over several centuries, peasants gradually came to perceive nature as spiritless and to believe that they could use nature without fear of retribution from any gods or spirits. This change in perspective occurred slowly and haltingly. Furthermore, it was not a complete break with the past, for peasants had always used nature to some extent. Nevertheless, European peasants were evolving a more aggressive attitude toward nature, and one reason for that was their different conception of the natural world. The question of why Byzantine Christianity did not also create a more aggressive attitude toward nature is an interesting one. One possible reason may be that Byzantine Christianity was more contemplative and less action oriented than Western Christianity. The Byzantine Christians taught, for example, that sin largely results from theological error, whereas Western Christians tended to think of sin as wrong action. Our example reveals a fundamental difference: Byzantine Christianity evolved a relatively passive attitude toward many earthly things including nature, whereas Western Christianity was more aggressive in its attitude toward nature and other earthly things.

Taken as a whole, the medieval agricultural revolution was one of the most significant developments in the history of Western Civilization. Its short-term effects were to expand the food supply and allow populations to grow and cities to develop, thereby providing the foundation for the creativity of the High Middle Ages (discussed in Chapter 8). It also helped to eliminate slavery in Western Europe, since the growing use of animal-powered plows reduced the need for human labor. The long-term effect of the agricultural revolution stands out even more clearly, for it displayed the technological creativity that is a fundamental characteristic of Western history.

It is important to remember that this very significant revolution was carried out by people who by twentieth-century standards were ignorant and superstitious. Medieval peasants were capable both of thinking clearly enough to develop new technologies and of believing things that later ages would regard as wildly improbable. For example, a popular story of early medieval times tells of a bishop who drove away a serpent dragon that was terrorizing the population of Paris. Another story tells of a young man who married a beautiful stranger that turned out to be a dragon. To drive off the evil spirit, the young man sprinkled holy water on his wife, who promptly jumped over their house, screamed, and vanished into thin air. The peasants were regarded with contempt by their economic and social superiors. In medieval literature, they are portrayed at best as nameless creatures who did the manual labor, at worst as barely human monsters who lived in dark forests and frightened those who traveled. The peasants were innovators unrecognized in their own time.

THE CAROLINGIAN EMPIRE

The emergence of the Carolingian dynasty brought a brief period of political stability to the early Middle Ages. It is named after its greatest ruler, Charlemagne, or Charles the Great (from the Latin *Carolus* meaning "Charles"). The greatest years of the Carolingian dynasty extended from 751 to 814, and at its height it governed much of Western Europe, including today's France, Belgium, the Netherlands, the western half of Germany, and northern Italy.

The Carolingian empire was largely agrarian—there were a few towns such as Aachen and Lyons—an empire without cities and held together by rulers who were regularly on the move and fighting to maintain their power. Its origins can be traced to the late fifth century, when the Franks conquered Roman Gaul, which then became known as Frankland and later as France. But the empire developed only in the eighth century when a series of Frankish warlords asserted control. First was Charles Martel, whose armies defeated the Arabs at Poitiers (Tours) in 733, and thus helped prevent a Muslim conquest of Europe. Then came his son, Pepin the Short (751–768), who strengthened his power by forging an alliance with the pope. It was Pepin's son, Charles (768–814), who became Charlemagne, the greatest of the Carolingian rulers.

Charlemagne was in many ways a barbarian warrior. He was a tall, potbellied man who enjoyed the pleasures of the flesh and spent much of his life on military campaigns. But Charlemagne was also a Christian who built churches and provided financial support to monasteries. Indeed, he believed that his struggles were done in the name of Christianity:

> For it is our task, with the aid of divine goodness, to defend the holy church of Christ everywhere from the attacks of pagans without and to strengthen it within through the knowledge of the Catholic faith. . . . With God, our leader and benefactor, the Christian people may always and everywhere be victorious over the enemies of his Holy Name, and the name of Our Lord Jesus Christ be proclaimed throughout the world.[8]

Charlemagne was also interested in scholarly and artistic activities. These interests resulted in what modern scholars call the Carolingian Renaissance. Even though his own writing skills were poor, the emperor established a palace school at his capital, Aachen, to which several dozen scholars from all over Europe came to settle. Under the guidance of the school's leader, Alcuin of York, many ancient manuscripts were copied and some artistic works were created. The Carolingian Renaissance ended soon after Charlemagne died in 814, but it was influential in later cultural developments in Europe.

Crowning of Charlemagne In A.D. 800 on Christmas Day, Pope Leo III crowned Charlemagne emperor of Rome. (Pierpont Morgan Library)

A significant event occurred on Christmas day in the year 800: Charlemagne was crowned emperor by the pope in Rome. His coronation designated Charlemagne as both a successor to the Roman emperors and as the political leader of Catholic Christendom. It also signified a growing sense of European independence from the Byzantine Empire. Byzantium had long claimed to be the only Christian and Roman empire, but now there was a rival claimant.

The Carolingian dynasty was the first political manifestation of a new civilization that some were already calling "European." (The word *Europe* comes from the Greek *Eurōpē*, meaning "land of the setting sun.") A surge of energy was sweeping through Europe. Peasants were clearing land to expand the area available for agriculture. A change in thought was developing, as demonstrated by the illustrations used on calendars: instead of passive, allegorical characters who represented a saint or something similar, by the year 800 calendars began to show a concrete person actively engaged in some kind of labor. These new "labors of the months," as they were called, indicated a more realistic concern with work and the practical problems of the everyday world.

The Carolingian period also saw a change in the position of women. The Germanic tribes had usually treated women as property always under the control of men. But by the ninth century, some married women were acquiring a degree of economic independence. A new custom required that just before marriage a groom give his bride a gift, usually land, which was hers to control. Furthermore, some women were able to share in the inheritance of land and other property.

The Carolingian surge of energy lasted only briefly, for the dynasty disintegrated soon after Charlemagne's death. In 843, his grandsons concluded the Treaty of Verdun that divided the empire into three parts: Louis the German received what is today known as western Germany, Charles the Bald got most of what is present-day France, and Lothair got a "middle kingdom" between the other two, which is today northern Italy and the French and German lands that center on the Rhine River. Charlemagne's grandsons thus helped initiate the process by which Europe became divided into national states, since the Treaty of Verdun marked the beginning of France and Germany and of a middle area over which the two nations would fight for the next one thousand years.

ANOTHER WAVE OF INVASIONS

One reason for the collapse of the Carolingian dynasty was a wave of invasions that afflicted Europe in the ninth and tenth centuries. In the south, Muslim pirates known as Saracens raided Mediterranean villages and drove up rivers in southern France. In the east, Magyars (Hungarians) invaded Germany and northern Italy. In the north and west, Vikings (Norsemen, or Northmen from Scandinavia) attacked the British Isles, the lands around the Baltic and North Seas, and France. The result was a breakdown of political and social order in Europe and the devastation of many towns, churches, and monasteries. It was not unusual for peasants to flee their homes and wander the countryside in search of food and shelter. Also common was the sight of monks leaving monasteries about to be attacked and carrying only some food and a few precious possessions.

The Vikings

Of all the invaders, the Vikings had the greatest impact on Western Civilization. A maritime people with the best ships and navigational skills of their time, the Vikings became raiders and conquerors in part because overpopulation in Scandinavia pushed them out of their homeland and in part because they lived in a war-oriented society that honored military

Figure 7.1 Charlemagne's Empire and Invasions
by the Vikings, Magyars, and Muslims, A.D. 800–950

virtues and lived by attacking others. Their attacks were usually vicious
and highly destructive.

The first recorded Viking attack occurred in 793, at the monastery of
Lindisfarne in England. Over the next century, the Vikings conquered
much of England, raided and settled in large parts of the French coast,
sent an occasional expedition into the Mediterranean, and invaded
Russia. Their most spectacular achievement was a drive across the North
Atlantic. The Vikings established small colonies in Iceland and Greenland
and eventually reached North America. In 986, a Viking named Bjarni
Herjolfsson was blown off course in the North Atlantic and ended up in
Labrador. He stayed only briefly, but a few years later Leif Eriksson led
a small Viking band that tried unsuccessfully to settle on the Canadian
coast.

The Viking explorations in the North Atlantic were unsuccessful.
They lacked the organizational skills necessary to sustain large coloniz-
ing ventures and were operating in a harsh Arctic environment that was
becoming harsher due to climatic change. One account of the survivors of

A Viking Invasion   This illustration depicts an invasion of England by Danish Vikings in the ninth century A.D. As shown, typical Viking sea vessels were curved both front and back and were powered by many people with long wooden oars. (Pierpont Morgan Library)

a Viking shipwreck tells of how they saved themselves by hiking over miles of ice floes and glaciers. The Vikings were more successful in Europe. By the eleventh century, they dominated trade in Norway, Denmark, and England, and they populated much of Ireland, the French area of Normandy (named for the Northmen), and parts of northern Russia.

The Viking destructiveness was slowly tamed as they were gradually Christianized and absorbed into European populations. In the process, the Vikings imparted a new vigor to Europe. They opened up new trade routes and taught Europeans the arts of navigation that would be used later to explore the world. The age of the Vikings was the beginning of a long history of European expansion, as we will see in later chapters.

FEUDALISM AND MANORIALISM

When the Viking, Muslim, and Magyar invasions subsided in the tenth century, the Europeans began to restore some measure of social order and economic prosperity. The legal and governmental system known today as *feudalism* was a major part of that restoration of order. (The word *feudalism*, invented by modern historians, was derived from the Latin *foedum*, meaning "fief.") Feudalism originated in part as a Germanic tradition of free fighting men who swore to fight for their chieftain. In addition, feudalism characterized the old Roman patron–client relationship in which clients gave their land to more powerful patrons in exchange for protection from marauders and the right to continue using the land.

Feudalism was based on an economic system called *manorialism,* which will be discussed shortly. In the manorial system, unfree laborers known as serfs farmed under the direction of a lord.

The Feudal Relationships

The roots of feudalism lay in the chaos of the seventh and eighth centuries, when powerful nobles offered protection to less powerful nobles who, in exchange, agreed to join the military retinue of their protectors. Then, in the late eighth century, a military innovation—the stirrup—led to the practice of powerful nobles granting landed estates to the members of their retinues. Traditionally, European warriors (and the Greek and Roman warriors before them) fought on foot because a mounted warrior without a stirrup could be easily dislodged and destroyed. The stirrup, developed by central Asian nomads, came into Europe in the eighth century. It enabled the rider to bind himself to the horse. Consequently, the nobility became mounted, armored knights rather than foot soldiers, and they also needed landed estates to finance their horses, armor, and weapons.

By the tenth century, these traditional practices began to coalesce into an elaborate feudal structure. The powerful noble was a *lord* who occupied a position of authority on earth similar to that of the Lord in heaven. Those in his retinue were his *vassals*. Vassals usually owed their lords at least three things: (1) *homage*, or loyalty; (2) *aid*, which meant certain specified financial support as well as military service in the lord's army for a certain number of days each year; and (3) *advice*, or consultation with the lord about whatever public matters needed to be discussed. In return, the vassal received from the lord's army protection against bandits or foreign invaders. He also received a *fief*, a means of financial support, usually in the form of an estate with peasants to cultivate the land.

Feudalism was initially a localized arrangement by which the nobles in an area organized small armies to protect their land. As time passed, the feudal structure expanded and became more complex. Through a process known as *subinfeudation*, many vassals gave parts of their fiefs to other people, who then became their vassals. Thus, it was possible for a given person to be both a lord and a vassal, a lord to the vassal below him and a vassal to the more powerful lord above him. In some places, subinfeudation created an elaborate feudal hierarchy covering a large area, with several levels of lords and vassals owing various forms of allegiance to one another. Another complicating factor developed when some land-hungry vassals began to acquire fiefs from two or more lords (see the accompanying diagram). Since a vassal with two lords could not be loyal to both if his two lords competed or fought with each other, it became necessary for the vassal to declare that one lord was his *liege*, or first lord.

THE FEUDAL STRUCTURE

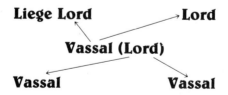

Feudalism dominated much of Europe from the tenth to the thirteenth centuries. It was most prevalent in France, western Germany, and northern Italy (the heart of the old Carolingian empire), but feudal institutions also spread in varying degrees to England, parts of Spain, the Slavic lands of eastern Europe, and even to the kingdom of Jerusalem established for a time by the Crusaders. In all cases, feudalism affected legal and governmental practices. European monarchs trying to consolidate their power often forced the greatest nobles in their kingdom to swear feudal loyalty to their king. Thus, feudal oaths were a means of enforcing royal power and thereby building the national kingdoms of Europe (see Chapter 8). But feudalism did more to limit than to expand monarchical power. Under the feudal system, a monarch was always subject to feudal law (the conditions of the feudal contract) and so could not do just as he pleased. For example, the great nobles of a kingdom were often able to insist that their king could not increase taxes without their consent (an early form of "no taxation without representation"), since feudal contracts stipulated that vassals had to agree to any increase in financial payments to their lord. Another example was the feudal stipulation that vassals give advice to their lord. In some places, the obligation of the vassal to give advice was gradually transformed into the right of the vassal to advise and the obligation of the king to listen. In England, this vassal right was one of the factors leading to the emergence of the English parliament (see Chapter 8).

Vassals also had a recognized right of resistance to monarchs who broke feudal laws and customs. This right of resistance, which limited the power of monarchs, eventually helped create constitutionalism (government by laws) and representative government in Western Civilization. Other civilizations (the Islamic and Chinese, for example) that did not develop a principle of rightful resistance to governmental authority also did not evolve any significant forms of representative government.

Feudalism was not often a matter of high legal principle, however. The feudal structure applied only to the nobility—the wealthier 10 to 15 percent of the population. These nobles were a rough, rowdy group accustomed to fighting, carousing, and intimidating those less powerful. Historian C. Warren Hollister describes a typical knight of this period as "a rough-hewn warrior; his armor was simple, his horse was tough, his castle was a crude wooden tower atop an earthen mound, and his lady fair was any available wench."[9] Fighting and feuding among knights was often destructive, in many cases causing damage to churches, monasteries, and peasant's crops. In the tenth and eleventh centuries, the church tried to impose some order and discipline on knights. One way of doing this was to encourage knights to go on crusades to fight for the church in distant lands. Another was to try to establish peace in Europe. In the tenth century, the church pronounced the Peace of God, a measure that condemned all those who destroyed church property or attacked the poor. In the eleventh century, the church added the Truce of God, which attempted to limit knightly fighting to certain days and seasons of the year. Known collectively as the *Pax Ecclesiae* ("Peace of the Church"), these two edicts represented a religious attempt to limit warfare. The *Pax*

Ecclesiae was only partially successful but was significant in that it attempted to establish international peace in a turbulent world.

Serfdom and Manorialism

Feudalism had little direct impact on the 80 to 85 percent of the population who worked the land. Some medieval peasants were free to till their own soil, but most were *serfs*. *Serfdom* (from the Latin *servi* meaning "slave") originated late in the third century when the Roman Emperor Diocletian decreed that peasants had to remain on their land and continue farming it. Gradually, many peasants lost their freedom and came under the control of their owners.

Serfs worked within a form of agricultural organization known today as *manorialism*. The manor, or large estate, was a community of peasant-serfs who worked together under the authority of a lord (a member of the upper classes). The land of a manor was usually divided into several large fields, some belonging to the serfs and others to the lord. Within the serf fields (one for a winter crop, one for a spring crop, one to lie fallow), each serf household had one or more strips of land to farm and use for its own benefit. The produce of the lord's fields belonged to the lord, but the serfs were required to work his fields as well as their own. In addition to the cultivated land was a certain amount of common land (such as woods and pastures) available for use by everyone in the community. Also on large manors were buildings of varying sizes, including the lord's manorhouse, the peasants' huts, a blacksmith's barn, a chapel, and a mill to grind grain. The manor was similar in appearance to a small village, designed to be self-sufficient and, if necessary, cut off from the rest of the world.

Most serfs led a hard, laborious life. They were bound to their land, unable to sell or leave it. They had to perform a specified amount of labor for their lord, and they could not marry or otherwise change their manner of living without the lord's permission. But serfs were not slaves. They could not be bought or sold like slaves, and they had a right to a share of the manor's land and the produce derived from it. By the eleventh century, slavery had largely disappeared from Europe in part because Christian teachings stressed God's love for everyone (thus gradually undermining the attitudes that caused people to enslave others) and in part because the agricultural revolution produced a rising prosperity that made slavery unnecessary.

CONCLUSION

Despite the chaos of the early Middle Ages, it was one of the most creative epochs in Western history. Benedictine monks and nuns began to change

Western conceptions of time, education, and manual labor. Peasants began to use many new agricultural technologies that helped produce an agricultural revolution. The Carolingian dynasty marked the first political manifestation of a new European civilization. And, after the decline of the Carolingians, the growth of feudalism laid the foundation for a new legal and political order in Europe. These developments prepared the way for a fully developed medieval European civilization of the High Middle Ages—our focus in the following chapter.

THINGS YOU SHOULD KNOW

The Benedictine *Rule* and its signifi-
    cance
The moldboard plow
The three-field system
The shoulder harness and the horse-
    shoe
Why the European peasants were so
    inventive
The Carolingian dynasty

Charlemagne
The Viking, Muslim, and Magyar in-
    vasions
The stirrup
Feudalism and its significance
Pax Ecclesiae
Serfdom
Manorialism

SUGGESTED READINGS

Francis Oakley, *The Medieval Experience: Foundations of Western Cultural Singularity* (New York: Scribner's, 1974) is an excellent survey of medieval history that stresses medieval contributions to Western cultural uniqueness. Christopher Dawson, *The Making of Europe* (New York: World, 1956) is a scholarly argument that the early Middle Ages were not a "Dark Age" but a creative epoch when European civilization was born. Good studies of more specific topics include Pierre Riche, *Daily Life in the World of Charlemagne* (Philadelphia: Univ. of Pennsylvania Press, 1978) and Johannes Bronsted, *The Vikings* (London: Harmondsworth, 1960).

Jacques Le Goff, *Time, Work, and Culture in the Middle Ages*, trans. Arthur Goldhammer (Chicago: Univ. of Chicago Press, 1980) includes important studies of time and work in the Middle Ages. Lynn White, Jr., has written several perceptive essays on technology and the connection between religion and technology in the Middle Ages that are collected in *Machina ex Deo: Essays in the Dynamism of Western Culture* (Boston: MIT, 1968), *Medieval Religion and Technology* (Berkeley: Univ. of California, 1978), and *Medieval Technology and Social Change* (New York: Oxford Univ. Press, 1962). Also good on medieval economic life is Georges Duby, *Rural Economy and Country Life in the Medieval West* (Columbia, S.C.: Univ. of South Carolina Press, 1968).

NOTES

[1]Georges Duby, *The Age of the Cathedrals: Art and Society, 980–1420,* trans. Eleanor Levieux and Barbara Thompson (Chicago: Univ. of Chicago Press, 1981), p. 3.

[2]L. S. Stavrianos, *The Promise of the Coming Dark Age* (San Francisco: W. H. Freeman, 1976), p. 2.

[3]Quoted in Christopher Dawson, *The Making of Europe* (New York: World, 1956), p. 171.

[4]Ibid., p. 177.

[5]Quoted in William R. Cook and Ronald B. Herzman, *The Medieval World View: An Introduction* (New York: Oxford Univ. Press, 1983), p. 171.

[6]Quoted in Richard Barber, *The Penguin Guide to Medieval Europe* (New York: Penguin, 1984). p. 126.

[7]Quoted in Francis Oakley, *The Medieval Experience: Foundations of Western Cultural Singularity* (New York: Scribner's, 1974), p. 143.

[8]Quoted in Cook and Herzman, *Medieval World View,* pp. 181–82.

[9]C. Warren Hollister, *Medieval Europe: A Short History* (New York: John Wiley & Sons, 1964), p. 136.

8

The High Middle Ages, 1000 to 1300

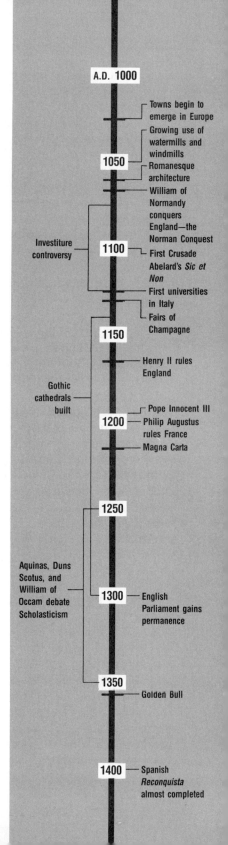

A.D. 1000

Towns begin to emerge in Europe

Growing use of watermills and windmills

1050

Romanesque architecture

William of Normandy conquers England—the Norman Conquest

Investiture controversy

1100

First Crusade

Abelard's *Sic et Non*

First universities in Italy

Fairs of Champagne

1150

Henry II rules England

Gothic cathedrals built

Pope Innocent III

1200

Philip Augustus rules France

Magna Carta

1250

Aquinas, Duns Scotus, and William of Occam debate Scholasticism

1300

English Parliament gains permanence

1350

Golden Bull

1400

Spanish *Reconquista* almost completed

Early eleventh-century Europe was divided into five cultural areas. (1) In the north, Scandinavia and much of England were dominated by the Viking warriors and were just starting to be Christianized. (2) In eastern Europe, from the Black Sea to the Baltic, the Slavic peoples were being Christianized by the Byzantines. (3) In the southeast, Byzantine civilization prevailed in the Balkans, around the Aegean Sea, and in a few Italian trading cities. (4) In the southwest, Spain was a thriving outpost of Islamic civilization. (5) Only in the middle of Europe—the old heartland of the Carolingian dynasty—did Western Christian culture dominate.

Western Christian culture would eventually expand to cover most of Europe, but in A.D. 1000 it was backward and barbaric in comparison with the Byzantine, Islamic, Indian, and Chinese civilizations. A tenth-century Arab geographer described the Western Europeans with contempt:

> their bodies are large, their natures gross, their manners harsh, their understanding dull, and their tongues heavy . . . their religious beliefs lack solidarity . . . those of them who are farthest to the north are the most subject to stupidity, grossness, and brutishness.[1]

But these Europeans would soon become one of the most aggressive, innovative people in history. During the eleventh through the thirteenth centuries, they developed an energetic economic system, built new political structures, created new social, artistic, and educational concepts, and began to influence other regions. This period of creativity and expansion is known today as the *High Middle Ages*, so to distinguish it from the early Middle Ages. The High Middle Ages began with and sustained a surge of economic growth, and its achievements were greater than those of the early Middle Ages.

TOWNS, TECHNOLOGY, AND TRADE

The initial stimulus for economic growth during the High Middle Ages was the agricultural revolution of the seventh to tenth centuries. As agricultural productivity increased, populations grew. Between A.D. 1000 and 1300, the English population expanded from 2 to 5 million people, the French from 5 to 15 million, the German from 3 to 12 million, and the Italian from 5 to 10 million. Furthermore, agricultural surpluses stimulated short-distance commerce as the inhabitants of one region traded for products available in other nearby regions. To facilitate this trade, towns with a merchant class began to emerge.

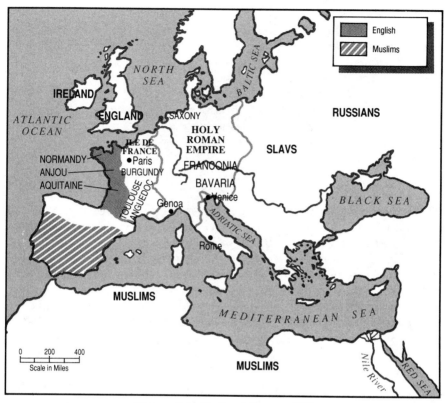

Figure 8.1 Medieval Europe, 1200

Towns

Most of the early medieval towns were clustered in northern France, the Low Countries (present-day Belgium and the Netherlands), and in northern Italy. Usually they were located on a crossroads, where two or more trading routes met, or alongside a river to take advantage of shipping traffic. The early towns were small, crowded areas of a few thousand people, often hidden behind walls and ramparts for protection. Inside the town walls, life was often chaotic and boisterous. A covered marketplace housed merchants selling meat, bread, cheeses, game, hay, wood, and so on. But often the markets overflowed with peddlars parading their wares through the streets and fishwives carrying their merchandise in baskets on their heads. Prostitution usually flourished in the marketplace, as tradeswomen and peasants' daughters sought to earn money.

These boisterous early towns were new to European life, for they were independent of the feudal hierarchy that dominated most of medieval politics and social life. The early towns usually had to pay feudal dues to a local lord, but they could make and enforce their own laws and collect their own taxes. Thus, many towns were bastions of local self-government, free to develop new political and social institutions and new ways of life. The towns developed a new type of economy, one that used currency and that gradually replaced the barter economy of the early Middle Ages. The towns also produced a new social class—a middle class of business people and merchants that was socially and economically below the feudal nobility but above the peasantry.

Technology

The early towns gradually became the centers of a small-scale industrial revolution, systematically using machinery to increase productivity. Some machines were borrowed from other parts of the world. The Persians, for example, were the original inventors of the windmill, and the Chinese the original creators of the canal lock gate, rotary fan, and wheelbarrow. Although the Europeans also invented some new devices, more important was their willingness and ability to use machines like the water mill and windmill on a large scale (see the Technology box). The widespread use of machines affected many aspects of European life, including dress and housing. The button was invented in the thirteenth century by someone who wanted tighter clothes to keep out the winter cold. Housing construction also changed to protect people from the weather. Fireplaces and chimneys were developed and used by some in early medieval Europe, but they became common in the eleventh and twelfth centuries (see the Technology box in Chapter 9).

The idea of creating new mechanical devices fascinated many medieval Europeans. The eleventh-century monk Eilmer of Malmesbury is considered a forerunner of modern aviation. He built a glider, took off in it from the top of Malmesbury Abbey, flew about six hundred feet, crashed, and broke both his legs because he forgot to put "a tail on the rear end."[2] Another example is Philip the Good, Duke of Burgundy in the fifteenth century and a practical joker who used machines to startle unwary visitors to his chateau:

> In the entrance, there are eight conduits for wetting women from below and three conduits which, when people stop in front of them, cover them with flour. When someone tries to open a certain window, a figure appears, sprays the person with water, and shuts the window.[3]

Eilmer of Malmesbury was particularly significant in that he was both a monk and an inventor, a man of God and a man of technology. Religion and technology were closely intertwined in the High Middle Ages, as

TECHNOLOGY
The Water Mill and Windmill

During the High Middle Ages, thousands of water mills—mills powered by river-driven waterwheels—were operated in northwestern Europe. The water mills provided a new source of energy that stimulated production and trade.

The Romans had used water mills on a small scale, but the availability of slaves in the ancient world undermined a strong commitment to labor-saving machinery. Also, the scarcity of rivers flowing year-round in the dry Mediterranean area limited the value of water mills. The northern Europeans faced neither of these difficulties, for slavery had all but disappeared and there were many rivers in northern Europe.

The first water mills used a rotary movement of millstones to grind corn and wheat. Gradually, the Europeans began to use a camshaft, which produced a reciprocal motion like that of a smith with a hammer. With the addition of the cam the mills could crush metal and perform various tasks in the cloth-making industry. Water mills were also used to power bellows at ironworks, to propel mechanical saws, and to pump water from mines.

Other mills were developed as well. Windmills began to appear in the twelfth century and were most often used in water-drainage projects. Tidal mills were constructed in some coastal areas.

A Windmill *In the foreground are peasants cutting hay. In the background to the right is a small town; and to the left is a windmill probably used for grinding corn or wheat. (Pierpont Morgan Library)*

many of the inventors and users of medieval technology were monks and priests. Technological advance was encouraged by the Christian teaching that nature should be used for human benefit. Historian Lynn White, Jr. describes the religious significance of medieval technology:

> The labor-saving power-machines of the later Middle Ages were produced by the implicit theological assumption of the infinite worth of even the most degraded human personality, by an instinctive repugnance towards subjecting any man to a monotonous drudgery which seems less than human in that it requires the exercise neither of intelligence nor of choice. . . . The chief glory of the later Middle Ages was not its cathedrals or its epics or its scholasticism [The medieval philosophy that attempted to make faith and human reason compatible]: it was the building for the first time in history of a complex civilization which rested not on the backs of sweating slaves or coolies but primarily on non-human power.[4]

Technology improved the lives of many in the lower classes, though it also had some less desirable side effects. With the emergence of a new working class came harsh treatment by employers. Workers were valued by only their output, so those who couldn't produce enough were often discarded into the ranks of the unemployed. Although serfs also lived a harsh life, unlike the workers they could expect to live their lives on the manor in which they were born. Furthermore, the upper classes were usually contemptuous of those who performed manual labor. One story tells of a vegetarian abbot who, unconcerned with the feelings of the masons whom he employed, threw away a pig they had killed and planned to eat. In addition, technology led to abuse of the natural environment. Millions of acres of forests were destroyed for the timber. By the thirteenth century, wood was so scarce in some areas that poor families could not afford wooden coffins for their dead relatives. At the same time, London was suffering from atmospheric pollution caused by burning coal.

Trade

The technological revolution stimulated the medieval economy and revived long-distance trade. By the eleventh and twelfth centuries, northern Italy and northern Europe dominated medieval commerce. In northern Italy, cities like Venice and Genoa organized trade across the Mediterranean and grew steadily wealthier. To facilitate trade, these cities developed (or borrowed from the Arabs) several business innovations, most notably banking and credit institutions and accounting methods to keep track of large sums of money. In northern Europe, specifically in the area of the Low Countries (the Flemish towns) and north Germany, over seventy towns organized the Hanseatic League, a

Village Street This drawing shows a typical village street, including a village gate in the background, a cobble-stoned road, and houses packed tightly together. In order to get as many buildings as possible inside the city walls for protection, the buildings in a village were constructed in clusters. (Pierpont Morgan Library)

miller to grind grain, a smith to make and repair farm implements, an innkeeper, a parish priest, and perhaps a few local "gentlemen" who owned large farms but hired others to work the land. In appearance, the village was a collection of huts centered around a church building and a cemetery. Outside the inhabited area were the fields—some pastures, a few orchards, a pond perhaps for fishing, and, most important, the cultivated land. The main crops were cereals—oats, wheat, and barley—that fed both people and livestock. Small livestock were more numerous than large, since they were easier to support. A peasant might own several pigs, chickens, and ducks, but only one or two horses or cows.

Each village was expected to be self-sufficient, to produce everything it needed. There was usually a lot of activity on local rural roads—peddlars going to local fairs, herdsmen driving sheep or cattle to local markets, pilgrims walking to religious shrines. But long-distance travel was difficult, so most villages were isolated from the rest of the world. This isolation made peasants suspicious of strangers and discouraged attitudes other than those dominated by local custom and the farming way of life. Routine was the norm, unless a calamity struck. Sons and daughters lived as their parents did before them, often cultivating the same fields and living in the same huts. The nineteenth-century English poet and novelist Thomas Hardy describes well the spirit of peasant life:

> Only a man harrowing clods
>   In a slow silent walk
> With an old horse that stumbles and nods
>   Half asleep as they stalk.
>
> Only thin smoke without flame
>   From the heaps of couch-grass;
> Yet this will go onward the same
>   Though dynasties pass.[3]

In many villages, local noble families were usually comparatively well-off, and peasants were expected to respect and submit to them. One parish church, for example, expected peasants to follow this rule: "When the Lord or Lady de Bretennières or their family are entering or leaving the church, all the inhabitants and parishioners of the said place shall keep silence and make their respects."[4] The most unfortunate peasants were the landless. They were usually desperately poor and survived only by hiring out their labor or by begging.

Customs and Attitudes

The majority of European peasants had a little land and a few animals; their goal in life was to wrest a living from the land and then pass the property on to the next generation. The peasant family was more than a personal or sexual relationship; it was also an economic partnership in which property was considered more important than sentiment or physical attraction between husband and wife. Two French proverbs indicate this importance: "Love may do much, but money more" and "Never trust a nice arse or a starry sky."[5]

Marriage customs usually allowed peasant women to choose their husbands. Many peasant women waited until their mid-twenties to choose a partner. One reason for this was that chronic malnutrition delayed their reaching puberty before their late-teens. Another reason was that delayed marriages resulted in fewer children and thus kept family sizes down. (In some parts of the world, peasants tried to have as many children as possible so as to have more people to help in the fields. Many Western European peasants, however, preferred to keep family size down so that more land and wealth could be passed on to each member of the next generation.) After marriage, the wife and children worked alongside the husband, sometimes laboring in the fields but more often spinning cloth or doing other household chores. If the husband died before the wife, the widow was sometimes left in an unfortunate situation. Peasant women had few legal rights, and inheritances passed through the male line, so a widow was dependent on the good will of her children. If the children refused to support her, she was forced to live alone, and it was not uncommon for single women to be suspected of witchcraft.

Peasant life did have some positive aspects. Most villages held numerous festivities throughout the year to celebrate church holidays, saints' days, and special events like weddings. The church was the social center of the community, a place not only for religious services but also for meeting neighbors, exchanging gossip, and discussing business. It might also serve other purposes, such as a place to store grain or a fortress to which villagers could retreat for protection.

Virtually all European peasants considered themselves Christians. They usually attended church services on Sunday, occasionally went on short pilgrimages, and tried to bury their dead in consecrated ground. But most peasants knew little about the formal theological doctrines of Christianity. Many distrusted the priests and bishops, who often lived more comfortably than peasants. One peasant said, for example, that "priests want us under their thumb, just to keep us quiet." He also asserted that Masses for the dead were pointless: "What are you doing giving alms in memory of these few ashes?"[6] His skepticism resulted in his being burned at the stake. Another peasant blamed God for poor harvests: "Old man God is too old, he does not know what he is doing anymore. He spoils everything. Our vineyards and our pear orchards are lost. We'll have to make another God."[7] Although most peasants were not so outspoken, historians agree that a considerable number of peasants did not submit meekly to religious authorities. Peasants were Christian, but their beliefs were not necessarily orthodox and their attitudes were not always respectful.

Some peasants either left voluntarily or were forced out of the tightly knit village community. (Leaving voluntarily was, of course, not an option for serfs.) The more adventuresome joined a king's army or found work on a merchant sailing vessel. Those considered troublemakers were often driven away and left to survive by begging, banditry, smuggling, or piracy. For women, a respectable route out of the village was to find work as a domestic servant in a nearby city. The wealthier nobility employed dozens of cooks and maids; in some cities, domestic servants constituted 10–20 percent of the population. Another respected female occupation was that of wet nurse. Abandoned children and the illegitimate offspring of upper-class men were often cared for by wet nurses, who thus performed an essential social service. A less respectable but common means of survival for women was prostitution. Virtually every city contained large numbers of prostitutes, many of them peasant women who had come to the city in search of work. A popular saying in southern France illustrates this point: "On the bridge at Avignon you are always certain to encounter two monks, two asses, and two whores."[8]

TIMES OF FAMINE

Our discussion has thus far focused on peasant life in normal times, when harvests were reasonably good and external threats such as army attacks were absent. But not all times were normal. Famine and plague constantly threatened the peasants' existence, and when these calamities struck, peasants quickly became desperate and miserable.

Famines were usually regional phenomena, occurring whenever two or more bad harvest years followed successively in one particular area. Famine led to malnutrition, which, in turn, led to epidemics like cholera and the bubonic plague as well as smallpox, typhoid fever, and diphtheria. The devastation of famine and disease occurred at different times in different places, but virtually every area of Europe endured them sporadically for centuries. For example, famine afflicted the region of Languedoc (southern France) for twenty years between 1302 and 1348. Four bad harvest years occurred from 1302 to 1305, and then in 1310 torrential rains produced several more crop failures. The years 1322 and 1329 were also bad, and the poor had to survive on raw herbs through the winter of 1332. In 1348, the Black Death (bubonic plague) swept through Europe, decimating the population in what one historian calls the "holocaust of the undernourished."[9] At a religious community in Montpellier, only 7 out of 140 friars survived the plague. The depopulation of Languedoc was so severe that forests and wild game reappeared on abandoned farmland.

The following account reveals on a more personal level how crop failures drove up the price of bread and destroyed what had been a reasonably fortunate family:

> There was a family in Beauvais in the year 1693 named Cocu: Jean Cocu, weaver of serges, and his wife with three daughters, all four spinning wool for him, since the youngest daughter was already nine years old. The family earned 108 sols a week, but they ate 70 pounds of bread between them. With bread up to 0.5 sol a pound, their livelihood was secure. With bread at one sol a pound, it began to get difficult. With bread at 2 sols, then at 3.2, 3.3, and 3.4—as it was in 1649, in 1652, in 1662, in 1694, in 1710—it was misery.
>
> They went without; they pawned their things; they began to eat unwholesome food, bran bread, cooked nettles, mouldy cereals, entrails of animals picked up outside the slaughter-houses. . . . The family was registered at the Office of the Poor in December 1693. In March 1694, the youngest daughter died; in May the eldest daughter

The Black Death In a fifteenth-century written account of a Catholic religious service known as the *Office of the Dead*, the illustration shows a goldsmith, a victim of the bubonic plague, being carried off by Death. The first outbreak of bubonic plague lasted from 1347–1351 and killed nearly a third of Europe's population. (Pierpont Morgan Library)

and the father. All that remained was a widow and an orphan. Because of the price of bread.[10]

Another poignant account simply quotes from the 1623 death register of Greystoke (England):

27th March: A poor hungerstarved beggar child, Dorothy, daughter of Henry Patteson, Miller.

19th May: At night James Irwin, a poor beggar stripling born upon the borders of England. He died in Johnby in great misery.

11th September: Leonard, son of Anthony Cowlman, of Johnby, late deceased, which child died for want of food and maintenance to live.

12th September: Jaine, wife of Anthony Cowlman, late deceased, which woman died in Edward Dawson's barn of Greystoke, for want of maintenance.

27th September: John, son of John Lancaster, late of Greystoke, a waller by trade, which child died for want of food and means.

4th October: Agnes, wife of John Lancaster, late of Greystoke, a waller by his trade, which woman died for want of means to live.[11]

When famine struck, many peasants left their homes in search of food. They often wandered to cities to beg, but they were usually met with hostility and punished by the authorities. One eyewitness account describes the punishment of peasant beggars in Languedoc in the famine year of 1595:

> They imprison them, they nail them down by their outstretched arms and hands; others force their mouths open and inflate them until they burst, hanging them by the feet. Oh, poor peasants. Be consoled in your misery. Help us to bear the cross of Our Lord.[12]

PEASANT REBELLIONS

Peasants rarely had any political power or influence. In addition, the upper classes expected peasants to bear their burdens without complaint. German nobles likened peasants to dumb beasts: "A peasant is just like an ox, only he has no horns."[13] Rebellion and war were the only means by which peasants could vent their rage and express their opposition to the forces that dominated them.

Peasant rebellions usually were not revolutionary attempts to overthrow the existing social order. Most peasants were conservative, and their rebellions were aimed at correcting some specific abuse of traditional peasant rights. The most common peasant grievance was increased taxation. In most areas, the upper classes paid little if any taxes and the peasantry assumed most of the tax burden. Peasant resistance to both state and church taxation was chronic, as indicated in the following conversation among peasants in a village square:

> "We're going to have to pay the bishop's tax on new born lambs," says one of five peasants sitting under the elm tree in the village square in the year 1320.
> "Don't let's pay anything," answers another. "Let us rather find one hundred *livres* to pay two men to kill the bishop."
> "I'll willingly pay my share," replies a third man. "Money could not be better spent."[14]

Some peasant outbursts were actual wars in which well-organized peasant armies were able to sustain long military campaigns. These wars were usually defensive struggles waged to protect peasants' land from predatory princes and aristocrats. They occurred during the thirteenth and fourteenth centuries in northern Germany and Switzerland, where peasants who controlled their own land were able to form peasant republics. The legend of William Tell grew out of the Swiss peasant wars.

More common than wars, though, were badly organized relatively spontaneous peasant rebellions that usually lasted only briefly. These rebellions were numerous and occurred throughout Europe. In Aquitaine (southern France), for example, there were nearly five hundred peasant insurrections between 1590 and 1715. Roughly two hundred rebellions occurred in Germany between 1301 and 1550. In all of Europe between 1300 and 1800, tens of thousands of peasant outbursts occurred. The most famous of these rebellions include the Jacquerie around Paris in 1358, the Peasants' Revolt of 1381 in England, and the German Peasants' War of 1525.

The Jacquerie derived its name from a French nickname—Jacques—for peasants. In 1358, peasants around Paris rebelled against increased taxes imposed by the government to support the Hundred Years' War fought between France and England (see Chapter 10). The rebels plundered several noble estates and killed a few people. The nobility reacted with vengeance, executing over twenty thousand people, including some children, priests, and monks.

The Hundred Years' War also caused turmoil in England, as the political instability and increased taxation produced by the war helped precipitate the Peasants' Revolt of 1381, inspired in part by Biblical ideals. For several years before 1381, an itinerant preacher named John Ball traveled through northern English villages proclaiming that all men were equal and that church lands should be given to peasants. A popular rhyme was associated with Ball:

When Adam delved, and Eve span,
Who was then a gentleman?[15]

In 1381, an army of peasants, inspired by Ball and led by Wat Tyler, marched into London, burned some houses, and forced the king to agree to reforms. The peasants beheaded one of their enemies, the archbishop of Canterbury, and then played football with his severed head. But the king's forces quickly recovered, dispersed the peasants, and executed Ball and Tyler. English folklore still remembers the two peasant leaders as spokesmen for the lower classes.

The German Peasants' War of 1525 was caused in part by the religious upheavals of the Reformation in which Protestant churches in some parts of Europe split from the Catholic church (see Chapter 11). German peasants, in addition to their usual grievances against the upper classes, began to believe that scriptural teachings sanctioned rebellion against oppression. Thus peasants rose in revolt. But, just as in England and France, the upper classes destroyed the rebellion and killed over 75,000 peasants in the process.

As these three examples indicate, most peasant rebellions were quickly crushed. Yet peasant rage continued to explode sporadically, and the aristocracy and urban classes lived in constant fear of peasant reprisals. This fear was often depicted in artwork created for or by the upper classes. Many paintings of the time portray peasants as brutish, dirty, drunken people usually engaged in fighting or rioting.

CHANGES IN PEASANT LIFE

Peasant life was not the same at all times in all places. Indeed, there was both variety and similarity among the European peasantry. For instance, while most peasants lived in tightly knit villages, some peasants lived in isolation on separate homesteads such as in mountainous areas. Mountain peasants tended to engage more in cattle grazing than in farming, and the need to guide cattle to distant pastures meant that they had to live near the pastures rather than in the villages.

Other differences in peasant life resulted from economic and social changes that developed over long periods of time. The most important of these changes were in the peasant standard of living, the decline of the medieval manorial system in Western Europe, and the expansion of serfdom in eastern Europe.

Peasant Standard of Living

The peasant standard of living varied greatly, depending on the general condition of the European economy. From 1150 to 1300, Europe enjoyed sustained agricultural prosperity and population growth, so most Europeans were relatively well-off. Gradually, though, population expansion outstripped food supplies, causing famines, plagues (the Black Death), population declines, and agricultural depression from 1300 to about 1450. A slow recovery began in the mid-fifteenth century, and some agricultural prosperity and population growth occurred between 1450 and 1600. After this came another depression, as both food production and population remained the same from about 1600 to 1750. At this point began a long agricultural boom and rapid population growth that continued into the twentieth century (See Table 9.1.) The basic economic "law" of preindustrial Europe was that food production was sharply limited by inferior farming technologies, so famines and hard times resulted whenever population expanded beyond the available food supplies. Only with the agricultural and industrial revolutions of the eighteenth and nineteenth centuries did Europe break through the old

TABLE 9.1 VARIATIONS IN THE GENERAL CONDITION OF THE EUROPEAN ECONOMY, 1150–1950

1150–1300	General prosperity
1300–1450	Economic depression
1450–1600	Some renewed prosperity
1600–1750	Economic depression
1750–1950	Continued economic growth

A Farmyard A drawing of a typical peasant farmyard, with small but well-constructed buildings. However, many peasant dwellings were more crude and less comfortable than portrayed here. (Pierpont Morgan Library)

limits on food production and create the conditions for a continually improving standard of living.

The Manorial System Declines in Western Europe

The decline of the manorial system in Western Europe began during the hard economic years between 1300 and 1450. Previously, most Western European peasants were serfs, unfree laborers who worked for and obeyed a lord in exchange for protection and access to some land. But the population decline of 1300–1450 created a severe labor shortage, and peasants were thus able to demand better working conditions, a reduction in the labor services they owed, and even some wages for work performed. Gradually, a growing number of serfs either bought or were given their freedom and became peasants who owned or rented land. This change in the legal status of serfs occurred at different times in different places. In northern France and the Low Countries (Belgium and the Netherlands), for example, serfdom largely disappeared by the sixteenth century. Other, more economically backward areas—southern

Spain, southern Italy, Ireland, the Highlands of Scotland—retained serfdom until well into the eighteenth century. In these areas, the landowning classes were so conservative that they fought any attempt to modify the practice of serfdom.

When serfs became free peasants, their lives were fundamentally transformed. They could now make contracts, buy or sell land, and borrow money from a moneylender. In short, their destiny was in their hands, for their well-being depended on their ability to manage property and income. Some peasants prospered in their new freedom. Others, however, lost more than they gained. They lost first the economic and psychic security provided on a manor that was guided and protected by an able lord. Then, some free peasants lost access to land because of a change in land organization known as the *enclosure movement*. Medieval manors usually divided land into three cultivated fields and common land—one field was for a fall crop, another for a spring crop, and the third lay fallow (see Chapter 7). Farming was communal, as each villager controlled several plots of land scattered among the three fields and also used the common land for grazing cattle and gathering nuts and berries. The enclosure movement sought to combine the landowners' cultivated land and their share of the common land into one united area, thus "enclosing" the land into one large farm. The reality was that the large landowners usually initiated the request that legal authorities grant permission to enclose in a given area. They, unlike illiterate serfs, had the legal documentation and political power to claim most of the land for themselves whenever a village was subjected to the enclosure process. One result was that some landowners acquired increasingly larger, privately owned farms, on which they could graze large herds of cattle or raise cash crops. Enclosure was one source of the new concept of *private property*. Another result was that many peasants lost their land and many peasant villages simply disappeared. One peasant complaint said bitterly that the large landowners "leave no grounde for tillage, thei enclose al into pastures, thei throw downe houses, thei plucke downe towns, and leave nothing standynge, but only the churche to be made a shepehowse."[16]

The enclosure movement began in England during the mid-fourteenth century. First one village and then another was enclosed, so that gradually over a four-hundred-year period (1350–1750) much of English farmland passed into the hands of large landowners. A similar process began in other countries in the sixteenth and seventeenth centuries. In some parts of Italy, Spain, and Germany, large landowners began to annex common lands, drive many peasants off the land, and create larger farms for themselves.

Serfdom Expands in Eastern Europe

A very different process occurred in eastern Europe. Whereas in the west many serfs became free peasants, in the east, particularly in Poland and

Russia, many formerly free peasants were forced into serfdom during the fifteenth and sixteenth centuries. One reason for this difference between the west and east lay in political factors. In Western European countries, monarchs often used financial help from the urban business classes to assert their authority over the nobility (see Chapter 10) and put an end to serfdom. The monarchs were not consciously trying to help the serfs; rather, they were seeking to weaken the nobility by decreasing their control over the peasantry and to strengthen themselves by forcing free peasants to pay taxes directly into royal purses. In Poland the nobility remained more powerful than the monarchs, and in Russia the monarchs received their strongest political support from the nobility. The result was that eastern nobles were more influential than their counterparts in the west and thus free to force serfdom on the peasants.

Another reason for the divergence between east and west was the gradual evolution of *capitalism* in Western Europe. Capitalism encouraged the development of a monetary economy. The availability of coinage made it easier to transform the lord-serf relationship based on labor services into a noble-free peasant relationship based on a peasant's paying cash to buy or rent land.

The living conditions of eastern European serfs varied greatly. Some serfs were little different from slaves, being completely controlled and sometimes physically abused by their lords. Others were relatively well-off, particularly those who were protected by good lords and had steady access to some land. But all serfs were unfree, subject to the will of their owners. The only difference between a serf and a slave was that the law recognized the serf as a human being with some legal rights (sometimes only the dubious right of paying taxes), while the slave was considered property.

By the seventeenth century, significant variations existed in the legal and economic status of European peasants. In the east, most peasants were enserfed. In the west, most peasants were free. However, in some Western countries like England, the free peasants were losing their land and sinking deeper into poverty; in others like France, large numbers of small peasant farms survived and an independent peasantry endured for centuries. Despite these variations, most peasants shared a life of poverty, a closeness to the land, and subjection to the relatively wealthy landed class—the aristocracy.

THE ARISTOCRACY

The word *aristocracy* means "rule by the best," specifically rule by a small, privileged group presumed to be best qualified to govern. For over a thousand years—from the early Middle Ages to the beginning of the twentieth century—European nations were governed by aristocracies of various kinds. Monarchs were usually the actual rulers, but they were in a sense the greatest of the aristocrats. Furthermore, monarchs governed through the aristocratic elite, since aristocrats usually served as royal advisors and often assumed the responsibility of implementing royal decisions on the local level.

The European aristocracies were a varied group. Some aristocrats claimed to be descended from the knights of the Middle Ages and professed to be able to trace their lineage back over the centuries. Others, particularly in commercial areas like Holland, were descended from urban merchants who were wealthy enough to buy a noble title. The common denominator among almost all types of aristocrats was ownership of land, since land was a source of both wealth and prestige. Actually, some aristocrats were quite poor, owning only small tracts of land and living little better than the peasants around them. But a few in each country controlled vast areas, usually divided into small farms rented by tenants. These few great landowners were the "real aristocracy," the less than 1 percent of the population that held most political and economic power. (The one exception is Poland, where nearly 10 percent of the population was aristocratic.) The most powerful aristocrats usually numbered only a few thousand in each country, but they seemed to be everywhere. The Duke of Norfolk (England), for example, at one time owned ten residences, including castles in four different areas and an enormous townhouse in London.

Aristocrats used a variety of means to distinguish themselves and to assert their superiority over the rest of the population. One was the display of wealth—wearing fine clothes, maintaining great residences, and employing large numbers of servants. Another was the use of violence to intimidate people. Aristocrats were trained to use both sword and pistol, so upper-class violence was a customary part of everyday life. An extreme example of this violence is the case of Lord Rich, who directed twenty-five retainers to attack a man in broad daylight while he stood yelling "Cut off his legs" and "Kill him!"[17]

Most aristocrats were acutely aware of their social rank and status. Their prestige and power resulted in part from the appearance of superiority, so appearances mattered. Who bowed first to whom was important, as was who sat where at dinner parties. An elaborate system of rules governed the relationships among the various ranks within the aristocracy. One episode, although ludicrous to twentieth-century readers, illustrates the importance attached to rules of etiquette. In this episode, a fifteen-year-old duchess became socially superior to her mother because she married a powerful duke. The young duchess was outraged and threw a fit when both leaves of a door were opened for her mother to enter a room, because her mother as an inferior was entitled to have only half the door opened for her.

For the wealthiest aristocrats, life was filled with good things and good times. Compare with the earlier analysis of peasant ways of life the following description of a young nobleman of the late Middle Ages who attended the university at Montpellier (France):

> He had a room on the first floor, paintings on the wall, a gilded easy chair to study in. . . . The distractions multiplied; suppers of partridge, drinking bouts of muscatel and hippocras, masked balls. . . . [He] watched the nobles, their plumed mounts adorned with multicolored panoplies, tilting at the ring; the defenses of academic theses that invariably drew a crowd; the fine autopsies; the popular spectacle of criminals being tortured or executed in public in the presence of young girls and entire families. Innocent gaiety, cruel pleasures, money, sadism, luxury.[18]

Only a few lived so luxuriously, but even they lacked many things. Heating was scarce, so aristocratic residences were cold and drafty. Toilet facilities, even in the richest palaces, were never more than narrow passageways with holes in the floor. Food was often available in great quantities, but aristocrats, like peasants, ate a monotonous diet—the same breads and meats every day. Although the upper classes ate meat regularly, the meat had to be heavily salted in order to preserve it, and so large amounts of wine and beer were consumed to quench the thirst produced by the salt. The lack of certain technologies—central heating, indoor plumbing, refrigeration—meant that in many ways aristocrats lived little better than peasants. Of course, most twentieth-century Americans and Europeans live much more comfortably than the aristocrats of preindustrial Europe.

THE CULTURE OF THE CITY

Life in the city was significantly different from life in the countryside. The cities were more crowded. Most of them had populations of 20,000–30,000, but a few like Paris and Naples contained more than 200,000 by the sixteenth century. Many citizens of cities were more free than peasants in the countryside, since cities were basically independent political entities that governed themselves. The cities derived their income from business and commerce rather than from land, and in many cases the people of the cities were wealthier than those of the surrounding countryside. Finally, the people of the cities were more inclined than peasants and aristocrats to welcome social change and economic growth. In describing life in the cities, we focus on four groups (1) the bourgeoisie, (2) the artisans, (3) women, and (4) the poor.

The word *bourgeoisie* means "townsmen" (from the French *bourg*, meaning "town"). More precisely, the term was used in preindustrial Europe to refer to a member of a commune, since the bourgeoisie was the

The Chimney

Material comfort slowly began to increase, particularly for the wealthy, with the development of the chimney. During the early Middle Ages, buildings were heated by a fire in a central hearth. The smoke simply went out through a hole in the roof. The central-hearth approach was very inefficient in producing heat, and gradually people began to understand the physics of updraft and downdraft, which enables the fire both to keep going and to carry away smoke. As a result, the first well-developed chimney stacks to vent smoke out of the building appeared in the eleventh and twelfth centuries.

As time passed, improved chimney construction allowed placement of several fireplaces throughout a building. Thus, people could live and sleep in separate rooms, and some privacy was created, at least for the rich. Previously, everyone— parents, children, servants—had lived, eaten, and slept in one large room where the central fire was located. The new privacy fostered a growing sense of individuality, a sense of being apart from the group. Belief in the importance of privacy and of individualism would slowly become a major influence in European political and social history, though some in the Middle Ages disliked the general decline in communal association. William Langland in the *Vision of Piers the Plowman* (written in three versions between 1362 and 1387) lamented the fact that rich and poor no longer lived together in the great hall:

> Woe is in the hall each day of the week.
> There the lord and lady like not to sit.
> Now every rich man eats by himself
> In a private parlor to be rid of poor men,
> Or in a chamber with a chimney,
> And leaves the great hall.[19]

The Chimney   *A middle-class man and boy warm their hands by the fire, while another man and woman prepare for a meal. (Pierpont Morgan Library)*

dominant voice in the communal city governments. They were the merchants and businesspeople who controlled the cities. Their social status lay somewhere between the aristocracy and the peasantry, so they were sometimes termed a *middle* group or class.

The distinctive feature of the bourgeoisie was that they derived their livelihood from business and commerce, from manipulating money rather than cultivating land. Some of them eventually became quite wealthy. This account describes the home of a rich merchant in the sixteenth century:

> A circular staircase leads to seven rooms in the upper stories; there is a reception hall, a kitchen, an attic, and a cellar. . . . His strongbox is filled with money. He owns gold rings, precious stones, jaspar, bracelets. . . . There are dozens of chairs, stools and footstools, and banks and benches, all of walnut, the rich man's wood.[20]

A few of the bourgeoisie became wealthier than all but the greatest aristocrats. Their wealth enabled them to buy titles of nobility and to marry their children into the aristocracy. It also enabled them to acquire the education and expertise that made them valuable to monarchs as advisors and administrators. In short, the wealthiest of bourgeoisie gradually began to compete with the aristocracy for positions of political power and social prestige.

The artisans were craftspeople who used tools to make things like clothing, shoes, and jewelry. Most of them worked in small workshops and marketed their wares through a local merchant. Their wages were usually inadequate and their standard of living far lower than that of the bourgeoisie. Some artisans—the "journeymen"—had to travel from city to city to learn and practice their craft. To protect their employment and wages, artisans usually organized *guilds,* associations of all those engaged in a particular craft. Thus, in each city there might be a clothier's guild, a jeweler's guild, and the like. The purpose of the guilds was to guarantee stable employment and wages, a policy that seemed desirable to artisans who feared unemployment more than anything else. So, the guilds were licensed to control entry into a craft, thus ensuring that a city had only as many craftspeople as were needed. They also controlled pricing in an attempt to guarantee that the artisans received a fair price for their products. Finally, the guilds sought to provide certain social services for their members, such as charity for the needy and some education for the children. What they did not do, and never desired to do, was to foster economic competition.

Urban women, like peasant women, were not equal to men and were excluded from universities and professions like law and medicine. But some urban women had opportunities unavailable to their counterparts in the countryside. The wife of a well-to-do bourgeois had to manage a

The Hunt of the Unicorn   Many Europeans believed in the existence of imaginary creatures. This fifteenth-century painting shows the unicorn, a mythical horse with one long horn. (Metropolitan Museum of Art, NY)

large household of family and servants and thus had access to some wealth and power. Furthermore, many cities established municipal schools through which middle-class girls and boys could acquire some education. Lower-class women were less well-off. Particularly vulnerable were unmarried servant women, who worked from dawn to dusk and ate table scraps in the hope of saving enough dowry money to attract a husband. That hope was sometimes destroyed when the master of the house seduced and impregnated the woman and then drove her out into the streets to join the ranks of the poor.

The poor—those who were chronically unemployed and lived in abject poverty—constituted 10 to 20 percent of most urban populations. Usually the poor were classified into two categories: (1) *paupers*, local poor who were considered deserving of some charity; or (2) *beggars*, who wandered into a city from other areas and were driven out as quickly as possible. The presence of large numbers of paupers and beggars had undesirable consequences for a city. Babies abandoned by the poor were common, and large cities employed a number of people to pick up abandoned children every morning and transport them to orphanages. The adult poor might live and die in a crowded poorhouse. Every day in a large city a number of pathetic funeral processions carried the dead from the poorhouse to unmarked graves in the pauper's cemetery.

CRIME, PUNISHMENT, AND DEATH

Crime was always present in both the countryside and the city. Peasants stole from other peasants. Politicians and businesspeople engaged in fraud, bribery, and even assassination. The poor often tried to survive by stealing.

Greatly feared were the hordes of vagrants who moved from place to place and stole or extorted what they could. These hordes often included those who were unwilling or unable to find a place in stable society: orphans, cripples, defrocked priests, war victims, ex-soldiers, discharged servant-girls, and the like. The more enterprising hordes turned to banditry, and a few became folk heroes famed for daring exploits. One Spanish robber was said to be "the most courteous bandit . . . never did he dishonor or touch churches, and God aided him."[21] Less resourceful vagrants lived as best they could until they died of malnutrition or were executed by the authorities.

Governments sought to control crime by decreeing harsh punishments. Relatively minor crimes were punished by physical disfigurement—the chopping off of a hand or an ear, for example. Major crimes—murder, treason, heresy, witchcraft, robbery of a significant amount—were punished by execution. Those convicted of religious crimes such as heresy were burned at the stake; others guilty of secular crimes were hanged or beheaded. Executions were usually public, the theory being that public torturings and executions would deter others from a life of crime. Yet many spectators enjoyed the spectacles—one town went so far as to buy a convicted thief so that the citizens could watch him being drawn and quartered (his body forcibly spread out and then hacked into four pieces). Executions were a form of entertainment in which the crowds participated. Once, in Brussels, a young murderer addressed his spectators just before his execution and "so softened their hearts that every one burst into tears and his death was commended as the finest that was ever seen."[22] On another occasion, in Paris, the criminal, a nobleman, was berated:

> At the moment when he is going to be executed, the great treasurer of the regent appears on the scene and vents his hatred against him; he climbs the ladder behind him, shouting insults, beats him with a stick, and gives the hangman a thrashing for exhorting the victim to think of his salvation. The hangman grows nervous and bungles his work; the cord snaps, the wretched criminal falls on the ground, breaks a leg and some ribs, and in this condition has to climb the ladder again.[23]

Why did so many people flock to executions? One reason may be that people in traditional Europe were so accustomed to death that they were often callous about it. The severed heads of executed criminals were sometimes kept on display for weeks. The church, both Catholic and Protestant, used torture and burnings to suppress enemies. The poor and the weak were usually treated harshly. Little attention was paid to the children who regularly died of malnutrition or disease. The great essayist Montaigne commented: "I lost two or three children as nurslings not without regret but without great grief."[24] Montaigne was not a cruel man, but he lived in an age when brutality and death were common and life was easily lost.

CONCLUSION

An analysis of social history from 1200 to 1700 reveals two major themes. The first is that even in the best of times most Europeans were impoverished, constantly threatened by possible famine and disease. The second is that some factors—the growth of trade, the gradual emergence of the bourgeoisie and capitalism—were slowly laying a foundation for a rising standard of living in Europe.

THINGS YOU SHOULD KNOW

The material conditions of peasant life

Peasant villages

Peasant customs and attitudes

Times of famine and plague

The Jacquerie

The Peasants' Revolt of 1381 in England

The German Peasants' War of 1525

The decline of the manorial system in Western Europe

The expansion of serfdom in eastern
   Europe
The enclosure movement
European aristocracies
The bourgeoisie

The artisans
The position of women, both in the
   countryside and the cities
The poor in the cities
Crime and punishment by execution

SUGGESTED READINGS

An excellent introduction to the study of peasant life is Natalie Zemon Davis, *The Return of Martin Guerre* (Cambridge, Mass.: Harvard Univ. Press, 1983), the true story of a peasant who disappeared from his native village and returned years later to expose the imposter who had assumed his identity. A more traditional but still excellent survey of European social history before the Industrial Revolution is Carlo M. Cipolla, *Before the Industrial Revolution: European Society and Economy, 1000–1700*, 2nd ed. (New York: Norton, 1980). Another very readable survey with much information on specific people and places is George Huppert, *After the Black Death: A Social History of Early Modern Europe* (Bloomington: Indiana Univ. Press, 1986). On the material condition of everyday life in preindustrial Europe, see Fernand Braudel, *Civilization and Capitalism, 15th– 18th Century*, vol. 1: *The Structures of Everyday Life: The Limits of the Possible*, trans. Sîan Reynolds (New York: Harper & Row, 1979). For the history of agriculture, see B. H. Slicher van Bath, *The Agrarian History of Western Europe*, A.D. *500–1850*, trans. Olive Ordish (London: Edward Arnold, 1963). Two excellent works that focus on Languedoc (France) and England, respectively, are Emmanuel LeRoy Ladurie, *The Peasants of Languedoc*, trans. John Day (Urbana: Univ. of Illinois Press, 1974), and Peter Laslett, *The World We Have Lost*, 2nd ed. (New York: Scribner's, 1971). Johan Huizinga, *The Waning of the Middle Ages* (New York: Doubleday, 1969) provides a revealing analysis of the pessimism that engulfed much of Europe near the end of the Middle Ages. Finally, Rosalind and Christopher Brooke, *Popular Religion in the Middle Ages* (London: Thames Hudson, 1984) is a good source on the religion of the common people.

NOTES

[1]B. H. Slicher van Bath, *The Agrarian History of Western Europe*, A.D. *500–1850*, trans. Olive Ordish (London: Edward Arnold, 1963), p. 3.

[2]Quoted in Michel Mollat, *The Poor in the Middle Ages: An Essay in Social History*, trans. Arthur Goldhammer (New Haven: Yale Univ. Press, 1986), p. 70.

[3]Quoted in Jerome Blum, *The European Peasantry from the Fifteenth to the Nineteenth Century* (Washington, D.C.: American Historical Association, 1960), p. 22.

[4]Quoted in Marc Bloch, *French Rural History: An Essay on Its Basic Characteristics*, trans. Janet Sondheimer (Berkeley: University of California Press, 1966), p. 149.

[5]Natalie Zemon Davis, *The Return of Martin Guerre* (Cambridge, Mass.: Harvard Univ. Press, 1983), p. 1.

[6]Quoted in George Huppert, *After the Black Death: A Social History of Early Modern Europe* (Bloomington: Indiana Univ. Press, 1986), pp. 136, 138.

[7]Ibid., p. 154.

[8]Quoted in Emmanuel LeRoy Ladurie, *The Peasants of Lanquedoc,* trans. John Day (Urbana: Univ. of Illinois Press, 1974), p. 112.

[9]Ibid., pp. 13–14.

[10]Quoted in Peter Laslett, *The World We Have Lost,* 2nd ed. (New York: Scribner's, 1971), pp. 118–19.

[11]Ibid., pp. 121–122.

[12]Quoted in LeRoy Ladurie, *The Peasants,* p. 199.

[13]Quoted in Slicher van Bath, *Agrarian History,* p. 189.

[14]Quoted in Huppert, *Black Death,* pp. 56–57.

[15]Quoted in Slicher van Bath, *Agrarian History,* p. 192.

[16]Ibid., pp. 165–66.

[17]Quoted in Huppert, *Black Death,* p. 58.

[18]LeRoy Ladurie, *The Peasants,* pp. 152–53.

[19]Quoted in Lynn White, Jr., "Technology Assessment from the Stance of a Medieval Historian," in *Medieval Religion and Technology* (Berkeley: Univ. of California Press, 1978), p. 271.

[20]LeRoy Ladurie, *The Peasants,* p. 155.

[21]Quoted in Huppert, *Black Death,* p. 109.

[22]Quoted in Johan Huizinga, *The Waning of the Middle Ages* (New York: Doubleday, 1969), p. 11.

[23]Ibid., p. 25.

[24]Quoted in Carlo M. Cipolla, *Before the Industrial Revolution: European Society and Economy, 1000–1700,* 2nd ed. (New York: Norton, 1980), p. 156.

10

The Renaissance and the European Discovery of the Americas, 1300 to 1600

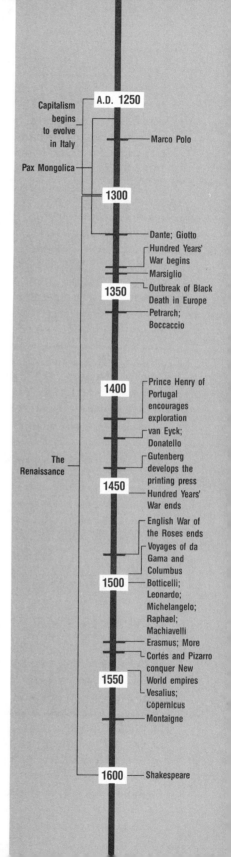

Capitalism begins to evolve in Italy

Pax Mongolica

The Renaissance

A.D. 1250

— Marco Polo

1300

— Dante; Giotto
— Hundred Years' War begins
— Marsiglio
— Outbreak of Black Death in Europe
— Petrarch; Boccaccio

1350

1400

— Prince Henry of Portugal encourages exploration
— van Eyck; Donatello
— Gutenberg develops the printing press

1450

— Hundred Years' War ends
— English War of the Roses ends
— Voyages of da Gama and Columbus

1500

— Botticelli; Leonardo; Michelangelo; Raphael; Machiavelli
— Erasmus; More
— Cortés and Pizarro conquer New World empires

1550

— Vesalius; Copernicus
— Montaigne

1600

— Shakespeare

The period from 1300 to 1600 was a time of both decline and rebirth. The early part of the period was one of the most devastating times in European history. Crop failures and famines, the plague known as the Black Death, and several prolonged wars brought misery and death to large numbers of European people. Population declined precipitously. Many people were convinced that the end of the world was near. Fear of death and hell was pervasive. Artwork sometimes portrayed skeletons doing death dances and tombstones were occasionally decorated with the image of a naked corpse crawling with worms.

Yet, in the midst of great hardship and death, Europeans were creating and discovering anew. The *Pax Mongolica*—the peaceful era administered by the Mongols across much of Eurasia—allowed some Europeans to travel to China and develop trade there. That trade encouraged the growth of *capitalism* in Italy and later in other areas. Italy was also the original home of the intellectual and cultural revival known as the *Renaissance*, which eventually spread to northern Europe. Portugal and Spain were the initiators of a European drive into the world's oceans, finding both a sea route to Asia and two continents previously unknown to Europeans—North and South America. This was an age of discovery. Some of the discoverers were merchants developing new business techniques, others were artists creating new art forms, and still others were adventurers exploring unknown parts of the globe.

FAMINE, PLAGUE, AND WAR

Much of Europe was relatively prosperous during the High Middle Ages because increased crop production supported its growing population. By the late thirteenth century, however, population growth began to outstrip food supplies, and the inevitable results were famine, malnutrition, and death for many Europeans. Population continued to decline as Europe was struck with two more calamities—plague and war—over a two-hundred-year period.

The Black Death

The famines that occurred throughout Europe made people more vulnerable to disease and particularly to the *Black Death*, which struck in 1347. Known today as the bubonic plague, the Black Death was a disease in which the afflicted person suffered high fever, large buboes or swellings in the groin and armpits, and death within two or three days. The plague spread across much of Eurasia in the fourteenth century and was carried to Europe by rats living in ships. (The rats spread rapidly in Europe, in part because many Europeans thought cats—the natural enemies of rats—were agents of the devil and killed them.) It spread through Europe quickly, intensified by the unsanitary conditions of the

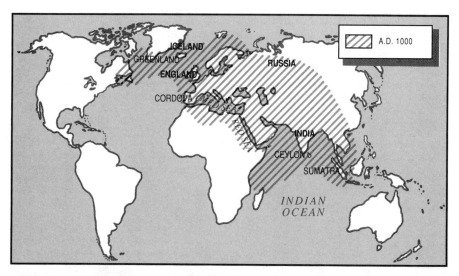

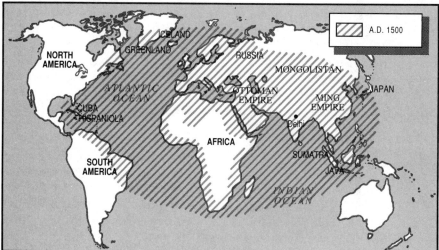

Figure 10.1 The Known World, 1000–1500

time and the general vulnerability of a population already weakened by famine and malnutrition.

Since the real source of the plague was not known at the time, most Europeans interpreted it as a divine punishment and called the buboes "God's tokens." The result was growing fear and despair. In the *Decameron*, the Renaissance writer Giovanni Boccaccio (1313–1375) describes the consequences of the Black Death:

> many died daily or nightly in the public streets; of many others, who died at home, the departure was hardly observed by their neighbors,

until the stench of their putrefying bodies carried the tidings . . . one and the same bier carried two or three corpses at once . . . one bier sufficing for husband and wife, two or three brothers, father and son . . . nor, for all their number, were there obsequies honored by either tears, or lights, or crowds of mourners; rather it was to come to this, that a dead man was then of no more account than a dead goat would be today.[1]

The Black Death killed nearly a third of Europe's population between 1348 and 1351. Although it then became dormant for a time, there were several more outbreaks of the plague over the next four hundred years. It was not until the eighteenth century that the disease was finally eliminated from most of Europe.

The Hundred Years' War

It was as if the Four Horsemen of the Apocalypse were galloping across Europe, for famine and plague were accompanied by war. (In the New Testament Book of Revelation, the Four Horsemen of the Apocalypse— Famine, War, Pestilence, and Death—personify the evils of the world.) In the fourteenth and fifteenth centuries, there were Mongol attacks on Hungary and Poland, incessant conflicts among the city-states of northern Italy, and the continuing battles of the Christian reconquest of Spain. But the most devastating war was the *Hundred Years' War* (1337–1453) centered in France.

The Hundred Years' War was precipitated by three primary factors: (1) a dispute over the succession to the French throne, which was claimed by both English and French monarchs; (2) a dispute over the boundaries of some lands in France owned by the English king; and (3) the English nobility's desire to capture some rich land in France. These factors led to a series of intermittent conflicts, known collectively as the Hundred Years' War. The war was particularly terrible for France, not only because many French died in the fighting but also because the armies often burned entire towns and destroyed the crops needed to feed the population. For a time the English won most of the major battles, but they were disadvantaged by being in a foreign land far from home. The French also had the good fortune to find in their midst a heroine—Joan of Arc—who became their inspiration and rallying point in the war.

The French ultimately drove the English out and in the process gained control of the rich province of Aquitaine (southwestern France). Aquitaine had belonged to the English crown since the twelfth century (see Chapter 8), but with the end of the Hundred Years' War it became a permanent part of France. One result was the establishment of most of France's national boundaries along lines that would last for many centuries; in short, France was now largely unified. Another was that

The Four Horsemen of the Apocalypse This drawing, from a woodcut by the German artist Albrecht Dürer (1471–1528), portrays Famine, War, Pestilence, and Death galloping across Europe in the fourteenth and fifteenth centuries. (Museum of Fine Arts, Boston)

England was left an essentially island kingdom with no significant territories on the continent. In the future, the English would seek to gain territory, not on the continent, but in other worlds across the oceans.

The War of the Roses

The English endured another calamity, as the turmoil of the Hundred Years' War helped produce a civil war in England. The *War of the Roses* (1455–1485)—so named because each side adopted a different colored rose as its symbol—was a struggle between two noble families, the Lancasters and the Yorks, for control of the English throne. The war was filled with brutality, murder, and treachery, with much of the English nobility being destroyed. Not until 1485 did a strong monarch—Henry VII—restore peace and stability in England. A century later, William Shakespeare would use the War of the Roses as the subject of many of his historical dramas.

Reactions to the Calamities

The combination of famines, plague, and wars produced feelings of despair, hysteria, and anger among many Europeans. One reaction to the chaos of the times was peasant revolt, such as the Jacquerie and the English Peasants' Revolt discussed in Chapter 9. Another reaction was the practice of flagellation, by which some especially pious people whipped themselves as penance for the sins that they believed had caused the plague. A third reaction by some people was the feeling that humanity had been abandoned by God and so had no choice but to seek happiness on earth. This attitude helped precipitate the Renaissance. A contrasting reaction led to a revival of the mystic tradition, as some sought consolation in a direct spiritual experience with God. One noted mystic was Meister Eckhart of Germany (1260–1327); another was Catherine of Siena (1347–1380), who once saw a vision in which "Christ appeared clothed in a pure white garment . . . and he smiled at the young girl and there issued from him, as from the sun, a ray which was directed at her."[2] In their desire for a more personal and individual relationship with God, the mystics were expressing the attitudes that would help initiate the Reformations of the sixteenth century.

PAX MONGOLICA AND THE GROWTH OF CAPITALISM IN ITALY

While Europe was enduring the torments of famine, plague, and war, momentous events were occurring across Eurasia. The Mongols, a group of east Asian nomadic tribes, were building an enormous empire after they were united by their great leader, Genghis Khan (reigned 1206–1227). Genghis Khan was one of the greatest military conquerors in history, and during his lifetime he extended Mongol power across much of central Asia. After his death, his successors increased Mongol influence by leading armies northward into Russia and westward into Germany and Poland. By the mid-thirteenth century, the Mongol Empire stretched from the Pacific Ocean through much of China all the way west to the Black Sea and from the Baltic Sea and Siberia in the north to the Persian Gulf in the south.

The Mongols were tolerant, able rulers, who allowed most of their subjects to live in peace. By the time of Kublai Khan, who ruled the Mongol Empire from 1260 to 1294, a Pax Mongolica (Mongolian peace) prevailed across most of Eurasia. It lasted several decades—until the Mongol Empire splintered into several Mongol states—and fostered both cultural interaction and trade. One example of such exchange is the astronomical observatory in Persia, where Chinese astronomers compared notes with Arab scientists from Spain.

European Trade with the East

The Mongolian trade routes connected Europe with a prosperous and creative China. During the Sung dynasty (960–1279), the Chinese built a thriving commercial economy that engaged in trade and shipping throughout the entire Indian Ocean area. In addition, by the end of the tenth century, they had developed several new inventions—the compass, gunpowder, and the printing press—that would eventually be transported to Europe. But it was spices and silks that first attracted European traders to China. These products were so eagerly sought by the European upper classes that eventually ambitious Europeans would invade and dominate much of Asia in order to get them.

In *Science and Civilization in China,* the historian Joseph Needham points out the irony of the Pax Mongolica—that this time of peace and toleration stimulated the European desire for Asian products and thereby encouraged the later European conquest of Asia: "No nomad horseman, watching from his shaggy red pony a quiet caravan amble by, could have imagined that it was the distant forerunner of conquerors more merciless than the four hounds of Temujin."[3] (Temujin was the original name of Genghis Khan, and the four hounds symbolize the powerful military forces of the Mongol conqueror.)

The first Europeans to profit from trade with Asia were from northern Italy. Several north Italian cities—Venice, Milan, Florence, Pisa—first enriched themselves during the Crusades, when they supplied ships to crusading armies and developed trading networks in the eastern Mediterranean. By the thirteenth century, they were the main contacts in the Asian–European trading system. A noteworthy example of Italian enterprise is the Venetian merchant Marco Polo, who in the 1270s traveled across Asia to the court of Kublai Khan. Polo lived and worked there for nearly twenty years before returning to Venice with his vast knowledge of and experience in Asia.

Capitalism

Long-distance commerce between Europe and Asia hastened the development of a new economic mentality in Europe—*capitalism.* Although capitalism has its roots in late medieval cities, it wasn't until the twelfth to the thirteenth centuries that the word *capital* was first used in northern Italy to mean the accumulated wealth of a person or company that was then invested to produce more wealth. (The terms *capitalist* and *capitalism* did not appear until much later.)

The essence of the new idea of capitalism was a more aggressive and more calculating attitude toward business and commerce. Those who used capital were consciously seeking economic gain—to make profits rather than just live day to day as the feudal nobility and the peasantry usually did. They calculated their monetary resources, assessed business opportunities, and then invested in whatever projects seemed most likely to produce wealth. Since most investments were risky endeavors at that time, merchants had to be willing to gamble.

The north Italian cities adapted several new methods of operation to aid business and commerce and the creation of wealth. One was double-entry bookkeeping, borrowed from the Arabs, which enabled businesspeople to maintain accurate records of profits and losses. Another was banking, which allowed wealthy merchants to make more money by lending at interest to others. The new banks also offered a substitute for monetary exchange—a bill of exchange or a "check." The bill of exchange made it easier to exchange large sums of money over long distances, since bulky sacks of coins didn't have to be transported. Also during this time was the gradual evolution of a new type of business firm, the joint-stock company, in which capital could be raised by selling shares in the firm to the public.

THE RENAISSANCE

The term *Renaissance* (meaning "rebirth") is used to refer to an era of intellectual and artistic creativity that began in Italy during the four-teenth century and gradually spread northward to France, the Low Countries, and England. What produced this outburst of creativity? The people of the time believed that the Renaissance was stimulated by the rediscovery of ancient Greek and Roman writings. They argued that the ideas contained in the classics caused a rebirth of intellectual life. This is partially true, since some ancient writings were recovered and did create great intellectual excitement during this time. But the argument is overstated, for intellectual life was not "dead" during the Middle Ages and so could not have been "reborn" in the fourteenth century. It is more accurate to say that the Renaissance was stimulated by a fundamental transition in European society and thought. European society was gradually becoming more urbanized (see Chapter 9), and Renaissance creativity was in many ways a response to the new urban culture. The people of the Renaissance gradually defined a new attitude toward life that was more humanistic (in terms of its focus on life on earth) than the scholasticism of the Middle Ages. This new attitude was congenial to many of the merchants and artisans in the thriving cities.

Italy during the Renaissance

The Renaissance is considered to have begun in Italy early in the fourteenth century and continued there until the mid-sixteenth century. Renaissance Italy was a tumultuous place. External foes—the Ottoman

The Printing Press

The invention of the printing press was particularly important in spreading Renaissance ideas. Its invention was made possible by two new techniques. One was the use of flexible paper, which was more supple than parchment and could be used with machinery. Paper was probably developed first in China, but by the thirteenth century, linen paper was being produced in Europe. The other new technique important to the invention of the printing press was movable type, in which letters of the alphabet were fashioned on separate pieces of metal that could be arranged to form words and then reused. Movable type may have been invented by the German printer Johan Gutenberg (1398–1468) in the 1440s, and he is usually regarded as the designer of the first modern printing press. Prior to Gutenberg, printers had used the woodblock method, in which entire pages of text were carved into blocks of wood and then imprinted on paper.

The printing press had a revolutionary impact on Europe and eventually on the world. Gradually, printers were able to produce books that were sufficiently inexpensive to be bought by large numbers of people. The result was to "democratize" knowledge by making it available to more people. In particular, the expanding amount of printed material encouraged literacy, scholarly research and publication, and education, as more people attended schools and universities.

The Gutenberg Press
An 1869 engraving of Johan Gutenberg examining the first page produced by his new printing press. (The Granger Collection)

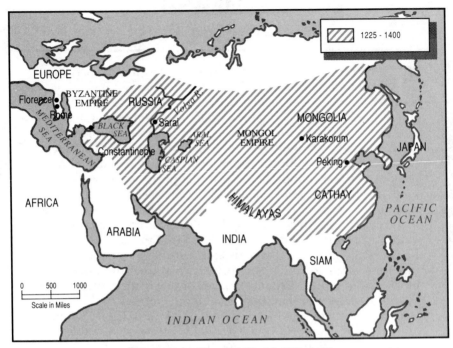

Figure 10.2 The Old World, 1225–1400

Turks, Barbary pirates from North Africa, and the French—periodically attacked the Italian peninsula. Furthermore, Italy itself was disunited, since there was no central Italian state. In southern Italy, there was a conservative kingdom centered on the city of Naples; in central Italy, there were Papal states controlled by the Catholic church; and in northern Italy, there were several small duchies as well as city-states dominated by merchants.

It was the north Italian city-states—Florence, Venice, Milan—that were the first centers of Renaissance thought and art. These cities were controlled by a merchant upper class that often used violence to dominate the governments. Each city was controlled by one or more merchant families, a notable example being the Medici family that led Florence during much of the fifteenth century. Renaissance Italy was a class-ridden place in which women had little influence on the great art and literature of the time and the lower classes were excluded from most everything except their obligation to pay taxes, some of which supported artistic projects.

The Italian Renaissance began with a gradual reorientation of thought, one that placed less emphasis on eternal life and more emphasis on life on earth. Even so, the majority of Renaissance people were still devout Christians who felt certain that their ideas and beliefs were just as pious as the ideas and beliefs of medieval thinkers. The nature of Renaissance thought is revealed in the writings of four Italians of the late thirteenth and early fourteenth centuries: Dante, Petrarch, Boccaccio, and Marsiglio.

Dante Dante Alighieri (1265–1321), author of the *Divine Comedy*, is often regarded as the last great literary representative of medieval culture. The *Divine Comedy* is a poetic representation of a journey through hell, purgatory, and paradise. In this imaginary tour, Dante speaks with the souls of both the damned and the saved, and in the process creates images of what it is like to be in hell or heaven. The subject of the *Divine Comedy* is typically medieval, in that it expresses an obsession with the afterlife. Dante's writing style is also medieval, for the *Divine Comedy* is an allegory (a story in which the actions are symbolic of something else) describing the Christian's pilgrimage from darkness to light, or from sin to blessedness. Yet, as distinctly medieval as he was, Dante was also a forerunner of the Renaissance. He wrote in Italian, the everyday language of the northern Italian people, rather than in Latin, the traditional language of medieval intellectuals.

Petrarch More clearly oriented to the new age of the Renaissance was the poet and essayist Francesco Petrarca (1304–1374), usually regarded as the first Renaissance humanist. Petrarch's poems and essays helped initiate the enthusiasm for the ancient Greek and Roman classics. He explored old libraries in search of long-forgotten ancient manuscripts and then used them as models for his own writing. For Petrarch, the ancient manuscripts were much more than old pieces of paper; they were sources of wisdom. He believed that they taught a new and stimulating way of life, one that stressed human happiness and human accomplishments on earth.

Boccaccio and Marsiglio Some of the implications of that new way of life were developed by Giovanni Boccaccio (1313–1375) and Marsiglio of Padua (c. 1275–1343). Boccaccio wrote the *Decameron,* a collection of stories purportedly told by a group of young people who had gone into rural exile to escape the Black Death. The stories satirize priests, monks, and other "respectable" people and are often raucously humorous. One, for example, tells of a virile young man who satisfies sexually an entire convent of sex-starved nuns. The *Decameron* is significant in terms of the Renaissance because it expresses a love of life, of the beauty and joy to be found in this world.

Marsiglio of Padua was a political thinker whose *Defensor Pacis* marks a radical break from the medieval assumption that the church should be directly involved in political affairs. Marsiglio argued that the church should concern itself only with spiritual matters and leave politics to the secular state. He argued further that within the secular state the people should be the ultimate source of authority. In his words, "the legislator, or the primary and efficient cause of the law, is the people or the whole body of the citizens, or the weightier part thereof, through its election or will expressed by words in the general assembly of citizens."[4] Although Marsiglio's ideas were far too radical to have much influence in the fourteenth century, they presaged Machiavelli's theory of a secular state and would have great influence in the sixteenth and later centuries.

Other Renaissance Humanists   Petrarch, Boccaccio, and Marsiglio were early Renaissance humanists, in that they put people at the center of intellectual inquiry and looked to the ancient classics for inspiration. Other humanists established the classics as the basis of educational programs for the upper classes in Italian cities. One example is the Platonic Academy founded in Florence by Cosimo de Medici, head of the prominent family that dominated Florence. At the Platonic Academy, the scholar Marsilio Ficino fostered neo-Platonism, reviving the Platonic contention that human knowledge is based on knowledge of spiritual concepts. Ficino believed that the study of Platonism was the best way to teach political and ethical ideals to Florentines. One of Ficino's disciples, Pico della Mirandola, wrote the "Oration on the Dignity of Man"; another, Gianozzo Manetti, wrote the book *On the Dignity and Excellence of Man*. The phrase *the dignity of man* was popular in fifteenth-century Florence, for it not only expressed the Renaissance humanists' faith in the freedom and power of people, but it was also considered to be a Christian idea.

Giotto, Donatello, Ghiberti, and Botticelli   The close relationship between humanism and Christianity was portrayed by early Renaissance artists. Art became more realistic and naturalistic than the symbolic religious art of the Middle Ages, and Christianity provided much of the subject matter for artists. Giotto di Bondone (1266–1337), for example, painted the New Testament story of Mary and Jesus, but he portrayed human figures in a much more naturalistic, full-bodied fashion than had medieval artists who pictured humans as flat figures.

Another example is the statue of *David* produced by Donatello (1386–1466), the first great Renaissance sculptor. Although David is an Old Testament folk hero, Donatello used the humanistic perspective to present him in a new light. The statue was the first freestanding nude sculpted since ancient times, and its realistic portrayal of the human body celebrates humanity.

Lorenzo Ghiberti (1378–1455), also a sculptor, received a commission from a secular organization—the Guild of Cloth Merchants—to cast two bronze doors for the Baptistery of the cathedral at Florence. The

The Madonna of the Magnificat (1483) by *Sandro Botticelli* The Renaissance painter Botticelli depicts the Virgin Mary and Jesus naturalistically, unlike medieval artists who tended to portray humans as flat figures. (Firenze Museum)

two doors, on which Ghiberti worked for nearly forty years, depict the Old Testament story of Abraham's sacrifice of Isaac in such realistic terms that Michelangelo later called them the "Doors of Paradise."

Not all Renaissance art was religiously inspired, though. The painter Sandro Botticelli (1444–1510), for instance, used classical mythology as the subject for his *The Birth of Venus,* one of the greatest works of the Renaissance era.

The Renaissance fascination with art and beauty had an unintended but significant influence on manual labor. Many art patrons were merchants and businesspeople who admired and mixed easily with sculptors and painters. As they became familiar with the workings of artists' workshops, they gained a new respect for the labor that went on within them. The result was an appreciation of the manual labor that went into the artistic creation of something beautiful. Thus, the association of manual labor with beauty helped to elevate the status of those who worked with their hands.

Savonarola Not everyone in Italy was enraptured by Renaissance humanism. In the late fifteenth century, a Dominican friar named Girolamo Savonarola (1452–1498) persuaded the people of Florence that the Renaissance was an anti-Christian, upper-class movement. He gained control of Florence for a time and directed a program of Christian repentance that included the destruction of humanist books and paintings in gigantic bonfires. Savonarola was so uncompromising, however, that he had many enemies and was eventually executed as a heretic.

Leonardo, Michelangelo, and Raphael   Despite the brief influence of Savonarola, the last flowering of the Italian Renaissance occurred during the latter decades of the fifteenth century and the early decades of the sixteenth. This was the time of Leonardo da Vinci (1452–1519), Michelangelo Buonarotti (1475–1564), Raphael (1483–1520), and Niccolo Machiavelli (1469–1527).

Leonardo da Vinci was so versatile that it is difficult to identify him with any one field of endeavor. He was a military engineer and inventor who often supported himself by working for rulers in northern Italy. He was also an anatomist who was fascinated by the human body and spent many hours dissecting cadavers. His most enduring fame resulted from his artistic work. His *Mona Lisa* is still considered one of the greatest portraits ever created, and his *The Last Supper* immortalizes the last meal shared by Jesus and his disciples.

Both Michelangelo and Raphael did their greatest work in Rome. A succession of popes began to rebuild and rebeautify many of the church buildings in the old imperial city. Pope Sixtus IV (1471–1484) built the Sistine Chapel in the Vatican Palace (the papal headquarters), and Pope Julius II (1503–1513) commissioned the construction of a new St. Peter's Basilica to serve as the centerpiece of Western Christendom. Julius called Michelangelo and Raphael to Rome. Michelangelo, a painter, sculptor, and architect, carried out several artistic and architectural projects, including planning the future St. Peter's. His most renowned achievement was the decoration of the walls and ceiling of the Sistine Chapel. (See Chapter 3 for three examples of Michelangelo's work.) On the ceiling, he painted what art historian Kenneth Clark calls "a poem on the subject of creation":

> Man, with a body of unprecedented splendour, is reclining on the ground in the pose of all those river gods and wine gods of the ancient world who belonged to the earth and did not aspire to leave it. He stretches out his hand so that it almost touches the hand of God and an electric charge seems to pass between their fingers. Out of this glorious physical specimen God has created a human soul.[5]

Two decades later, Michelangelo painted the Last Judgment on one of the walls of the Sistine Chapel. The artist thus told the entire story of humanity—from beginning to end.

At the same time that Michelangelo was painting the Creation, Raphael was decorating the papal apartments. There he painted the *School of Athens*, which illustrates the Greek influence on the Renaissance. Raphael portrayed Plato, Aristotle, and the other ancient philosophers seeking to understand and interpret the world.

Machiavelli   The Renaissance ended in Italy during the sixteenth century, in part because Italian political and economic power was

The Virgin and Child with St. Anne (c. 1502) by Leonardo da Vinci In this painting, Leonardo shows the Virgin Mary and Jesus in the company of St. Anne. Leonardo's brilliant style, which focused on the beauty of the human form, captured the essence of the Renaissance in Europe. (Musée National du Louvre)

declining. The discovery of the Americas and the development of Atlantic sea routes by Portugal and Spain gradually undermined the Mediterranean commerce that was the source of Italian wealth. Furthermore, early sixteenth-century Italy became an international battlefield where Spain, France, and others fought for influence. The resulting chaos weakened Italy, but it also stimulated Niccolo Machiavelli to write *The Prince*, one of the most important political treatises of European history.

Machiavelli, like Marsiglio before him, developed a theory of the secular state distinct from the church and Christian ideology. He argued that a ruler should not be bound by traditional moral precepts and should do whatever is necessary to preserve the power and independence of the state:

how we live is so far removed from how we ought to live, that he who abandons what is done for what ought to be done, will rather learn to bring about his own ruin than his preservation. . . . Therefore it is necessary for a prince, who wishes to maintain himself, to learn how not to do good, and to use this knowledge and not use it, according to the necessity of the case.[6]

Machiavelli became most famous for advocating that rulers ignore moral standards (hence the word *machiavellian* came to mean "ruthlessness"). However, more significant was his theoretical basis for a new politics, by which European monarchs would concentrate their attention on expansion of state power.

The Northern Renaissance

The ideas of Renaissance Italy spread to parts of northern Europe during the fifteenth and sixteenth centuries. The greatest artist of the northern Renaissance, Jan van Eyck (1390–1441), came from the urbanized, commercial areas of the Low Countries (present-day Belgium and the Netherlands). Van Eyck was a painter and a realist. His work celebrates humanity in a realistic sense rather than in a religious or philosophical sense. In a portrait of his wife, for example, van Eyck portrayed her not as a glamorous or brilliant figure but as she was—an ordinary person in ordinary clothes.

Also from the Low Countries was Desiderius Erasmus (1466–1536), though he was actually an international man who lived and traveled throughout much of Western Europe. Erasmus was the most renowned learned man of his time and often gave advice to popes and kings. One source of his fame was his *Praise of Folly*, a satire of what he considered the stupidities of his world—wars, political maneuverings, and the like. Erasmus also studied and wrote theological treatises, for he considered himself a Christian humanist—one who combines Christian teachings with an appreciation of human abilities.

Another Christian humanist of the northern Renaissance was Sir Thomas More (1478–1535), an English statesman whose *Utopia* describes an ideal society. (Depictions of ideal worlds have since been called "utopias" or "utopian.") In *Utopia,* More portrays a world in which everyone has enough to eat and a decent place to live, because society is organized so that all material goods are shared equally. Since everyone has what they need, there is no crime and no war. Obviously, such a place does not exist, but More was using an ideal to criticize the realities of poverty and crime in England. In many ways, More was arguing against progress, particularly against the kind of progress in which enclosure movements, for example, destroyed the livelihood of many peasants. He was saying, in effect, that life could be better, and that Christian and humanist teachings about the dignity of the individual should be taken more seriously.

Some northern Renaissance humanists were more skeptical than More and Erasmus. The Frenchman Michel de Montaigne (1533–1592) expressed his ideas in a new form of writing—the personal essay. His *Essays* analyze a number of fundamental human problems—such as education, superstition, marriage, and death—and characterize Mon-

The Marriage of Giovanni Arnolfini by Jan van Eyck—Van Eyck painted realistic portraits of ordinary people, in this instance a businessman and his wife. (National Gallery)

taigne as a tolerant, thoughtful, and even wise man who had little confidence in human nature.

Another skeptic was William Shakespeare (1564–1616), by far the greatest poet and dramatist in the history of the English language. Many of Shakespeare's dramas deal with how great issues affect the individual. His characters struggle for political power, meditate on the meaning of life, agonize over moral questions, regret the growing influence of money and capitalism. The twentieth-century poet T. S. Eliot called Shakespeare a poet of chaos, in the sense that the great dramatist reflected and expressed the doubts and uncertainties that characterized his age. These doubts sometimes drove him to complete skepticism:

> To-morrow, and to-morrow, and to-morrow,
> Creeps in this petty pace from day to day,
> To the last syllable of recorded time;
> And all our yesterdays have lighted fools
> The way to dusty death. Out, out, brief candle!
> Life's but a walking shadow, a poor player,
> That struts and frets his hour upon the stage,
> And then is heard no more. It is a tale
> Told by an idiot, full of sound and fury,
> Signifying nothing.
>
> (*Macbeth*, act V, scene v)

Shakespeare's greatness rests in part on his ability to be the supreme poet of his time, a poet who expressed the ambivalence—both the confidence and the pessimism—felt by so many people. In *Hamlet*, the title character defines the Renaissance belief in the dignity of the individual:

> What a piece of work is a man, how noble in reason, how infinite in faculties, in form and moving, how express and admirable in action, how like an angel in apprehension, how like a god! The beauty of the world! The paragon of animals!
>
> (*Hamlet*, act II, scene ii)

But Hamlet's soliloquy ends in disillusionment: "And yet to me what is this quintessence of dust? Man delights not me—nor women neither."

Science and Magic during the Renaissance

During Renaissance times, a number of people studied nature, and some of them practiced various forms of magic. The sixteenth-century French astrologer Nostradamus, for example, sought to predict the future through study of heavenly bodies. (Astrology is a pseudo-science that purports to study the influence of heavenly bodies on human affairs and

William Shakespeare (1564–1616) A nineteenth-century engraving of the English poet and dramatist. Shakespeare is considered by many to be the greatest writer of all time. All together, more than thirty-six major plays are attributed to him as well as many sonnets. (The Granger Collection)

to foretell earthly events by the positions of heavenly bodies.) Paracelsus, a sixteenth-century German chemist and alchemist, tried to use secret methods to transmute base metals into gold. (Alchemy was popular during the Renaissance, since it promised to reveal how to create gold as well as how to prolong life.) There also was the sixteenth-century German alchemist and astrologer who became known in history as Dr. Faust. Exactly who Dr. Faust was is uncertain, but according to European legends he sold his soul to the devil in exchange for forbidden knowledge. As a personification of the willingness to pay any price to learn the unknown, Dr. Faust was celebrated in some European literature and his name was symbolic of the drive for power and knowledge in Western Civilization.

The study of nature also led in the direction of modern science. Renaissance humanists rediscovered or received from the Arabs a number of Greek scientific writings and thus helped increase the fund of scientific knowledge. Furthermore, the business classes of northern Italy supported those scientific studies that promised to lead to greater use of natural resources. It was, therefore, no coincidence that several major works in the history of science were produced during the Renaissance. In 1543, Andreas Vesalius published *On the Fabric of the Human Body*, a detailed work that originated modern anatomical studies. In the same year, Nicolaus Copernicus posited a heliocentric (sun-centered) conception of the universe in *On the Revolutions of the Celestial Bodies*. Copernicus's work eventually revolutionized the study of astronomy and helped launch a scientific revolution. In the late sixteenth and seventeenth centuries, Tycho Braehe, Johannes Kepler, Galileo Galilei, and others gathered the scientific data needed to prove that the Copernican conception of the universe was right.

THE CONQUEST OF THE OCEANS BY PORTUGAL AND SPAIN

During the fifteenth century, European explorers began to lead sailing expeditions far out into the Atlantic Ocean. Some pushed into the South Atlantic and eventually found a sea route around Africa to the Indian Ocean and Asia. Others drove westward across the Atlantic and unexpectedly found the continents that would become known as North and South America. These explorers in a sense conquered the oceans, such that the waters gradually became a vast highway for European commerce and exploration.

The Europeans pushed out into the oceans because they wanted to acquire gold and slaves from Africa and to find a new route to the east—to Cathay (China) and the Spice Islands (present-day Indonesia). For a thousand years, an overland trading system had brought Asian luxury goods to Europe—Chinese and Persian silks, Indian cottons, emeralds from India and rubies from Burma, and various kinds of spices, food preservatives, perfumes, and drugs. The luxury trade peaked during the Pax Mongolica but then began to decline with the erosion of Mongolian power. In addition, the fall of the Byzantine Empire in 1453 left the Muslims in control of eastern Mediterranean lands and the trade routes to the east. Thus, the Europeans hoped to bypass the difficulties associated with the overland trade routes by finding a new sea route to Asia. The potential rewards were enormous, for at times a merchant could ship six cargoes from Asia to Europe, lose five, and still make a profit when the sixth was sold.

The Europeans had not only the desire but also the ability to conquer the oceans. They had, most importantly, an aggressive attitude, fed both by the Renaissance impulse to seek new knowledge and by the Reformation enthusiasm for gaining new converts to Christianity (the Reformation is discussed in Chapter 11.) They also had several new technologies in the areas of navigational equipment, ship construction, and armaments (see the Technology box). The first to use these technologies to travel the oceans were the Portuguese and the Spanish.

The Portuguese Voyages

Portugal began the conquest of the oceans. The Portuguese had several advantages: (1) geographically, they were ideally situated to drive either out into the Atlantic or down the coast of Africa; (2) they knew the benefits and perils of long-distance trade because of their economic contacts with Muslim Africa; (3) they had a stable government during the fifteenth century, at a time when other European states—England, France, Spain—were plagued with internal conflict; and (4) they had Prince Henry the Navigator (1394–1460), a member of the royal family who encouraged and sponsored oceanic voyages.

Prince Henry organized a sailor's school where the latest navigational and shipbuilding techniques were taught. He also launched the first voyage of discovery in 1416. Henry never went on any of the voyages, but his voyagers soon found their way to the Azores and, by 1444, were down the African coast as far as Cape Verde. Portugal began to receive sugar from the Azores and gold and black slaves from Africa. The Portuguese voyages continued after Henry's death. Sailors crossed the equator in 1471, found the mouth of the Congo River in 1482, and reached the southern tip of Africa in 1487. Vasco da Gama established a sea route to Asia in 1498, when he sailed around Africa into the Indian Ocean and to India.

During the sixteenth century, the Portuguese dominated the seas across much of Asia. They sailed into Goa (India), Hormuz (the Persian Gulf), Macao and Canton (China), Nagasaki (Japan), and Malacca

(Indonesia) and brought rich cargoes back to Europe. But the Portuguese did not have enough sailors and resources to maintain their dominant position for long. In 1580, the Spanish ruling dynasty, after inheriting rights to the Portuguese throne, seized control of Portugal. By the end of the sixteenth century, the Dutch were expanding into Asia and taking over many of the best trade routes. The Portuguese finally regained their independence from Spain in the mid-seventeenth century, but by then their empire was enmeshed in a slow, lingering decline.

The Spanish Discoveries

The Portuguese explorations inspired others, especially the Spanish, to search for another sea route to Asia. (Though the Portuguese tried to prevent others from following them around Africa by refusing to share their hard-earned geographical and navigational knowledge.)

The man who led the Spanish quest was a Genoese sea captain, Christopher Columbus (1451–1506). Columbus, like most educated people of his time, believed that the earth was round and that it was thus possible to get to Asia by sailing west. In 1492, the Spanish monarchs Ferdinand and Isabella commissioned Columbus to undertake a westward voyage. They provided him with a letter of introduction to the Great Khan of China and an interpreter who spoke Arabic. When Columbus found some islands after a journey of several months, he thought he was sailing between Cipangu (Japan) and Cathay (China). He was actually among the Caribbean Islands, but even after several more voyages he still half-believed that the islands were somewhere off the coast of Asia.

A succession of other explorers quickly followed Columbus. The Spanish took control of Hispaniola (modern Haiti and the Dominican Republic) before 1500, Jamaica in 1511, Cuba in 1511–1514, and moved into Panama in 1519. The Portuguese commander Pedro Alvarez Cabral accidentally found the coast of Brazil in 1500, when he strayed off course on his way around Africa. Amerigo Vespucci made two voyages in 1499 and 1501, respectively, during which he mapped much of the Atlantic coast of South America. Since his mapping finally convinced Europeans that they had found a "New World," his name in the form of "America" became attached first to the southern continent and later to the northern as well.

Yet, for a time, the Spanish continued to think of America as nothing more than a barrier between Europe and Asia. In 1519, they sent Ferdinand Magellan to find a way around South America. Magellan's fleet returned to Spain in 1522, after circumnavigating the entire globe. The dangers faced by these and other early explorers are illustrated by what happened to Magellan's fleet. Magellan was killed in the Philippines during a small battle with natives. As for his crew, only fifteen survived to

TECHNOLOGY
Improvements in Navigation

During the early Middle Ages, the ships that sailed the Mediterranean were propelled either by oars or by the old Roman square sail. Early ships lacked the freedom to sail any place at any time, since the square sail forced them to go only in the same direction as the prevailing winds. This situation changed in the late Middle Ages with the development of the *lateen sail.* The lateen, a triangular-shaped sail fitted to a mast and a movable boom, could catch the wind from any direction and thus allow sailors to leave port at any time. The Europeans got the lateen from the Arabs, who either invented it themselves or received it from the Chinese.

A number of other developments in navigation were also occurring in the late Middle Ages. Shipbuilders along the Atlantic and North Sea coasts were learning how to construct strong ships that could withstand oceanic weather. They were producing new instruments—an improved astrolabe and the quadrant—to measure the altitude of heavenly bodies and thus give sailors more accurate ways of calculating their positions on the seas. The magnetic compass, invented in China probably in the eleventh century, appeared in Europe by the late twelfth century. Also from China came knowledge of gunpowder, which the Europeans began to use in cannons. (See Chapter 11 for a detailed discussion of the importance of gunpowder.)

By the late fifteenth century, the Portuguese, Spanish, and others were using a new ship called the *caravel* that could withstand harsh oceanic weather, catch the wind from any direction, and carry cannon. The caravel allowed the Europeans to overpower navies in all other parts of the world.

The Lateen Sail   *This drawing illustrates the versatility of the lateen sail. The sail was attached to a boom, which could move around the mast and was fastened to the flooring of the ship. (The Granger Collection)*

return to Spain and most of the others died of scurvy during the voyage. Scurvy, a deficiency disease caused by a lack of vitamin C and clean water, sometimes turned ships on long voyages into floating cemeteries. The English later eliminated the disease by having their sailors eat citrus fruits, particularly limes; hence, English sailors were often called "limeys."

The Spanish in the Americas

The Spanish, of course, were not the first people to come to America. Thousands of years earlier Asian peoples had come to the Americas probably via a land bridge from northeastern Siberia to Alaska. The Europeans called these native Americans *Indians*, because they first thought they had found Asia and sometimes referred to Asia as India. Some of the native Americans had built large civilizations (see Chapter 1). The first Indians encountered by the Spanish were the Aztecs of central Mexico. One Spaniard, seeing the Aztec capital for the first time, was greatly impressed by what he observed:

> With such wonderful sights to gaze on we did not know what to say, or if this was real that we saw before our eyes. On the land side there were great cities, and on the lake many more. The lake was crowded with canoes. At intervals along the causeway there were many bridges, and before us was the great city of Mexico.[7]

In 1519, Hernando Cortés (1485–1546) led an expedition of six hundred troops into Mexico. Cortés was a complex man, driven both by the desire to perform great deeds and by the wish to Christianize the heathen. His small army defeated the much more numerous Aztecs by 1521, in part because the Spanish had firearms and horses, while the Aztecs had neither; in part because the Spanish allied with other native Americans who hated the Aztecs; and in part because the Aztec ruler Montezuma at first welcomed the arrival of Cortés as the return of the god Quetzalcoatl.

Other Spanish *conquistadores* (conquerors) pushed further into the two continents. In the south, Francisco Pizarro conquered the Incas in Peru during the 1530s. Pedro de Mendoza founded the city of Buenos Aires in 1536. In the north, the coasts of lower California were explored, and Acapulco soon became a port from which Spanish ships sailed to Asia. Hernando de Soto led an expedition from Florida west to the Mississippi in 1539, and in 1541 Francisco Vásquez Coronado marched into the great prairies west of the Mississippi and found large herds of buffalo, which he called "cows." Other nations began to emulate the Spanish. The French, for example, directed Jacques Cartier to find a northwest passage to Asia, but he ended up exploring much of the Canadian coast.

By 1540, the Spanish held a large empire centered in Central America with its capital at Mexico City. The Spanish conquerors expected the native Americans to work for them just as peasants worked for their masters in Spain. Usually, this meant laboring on farms or in mines. Forced labor killed many native Americans, while many more died from smallpox or typhus. These diseases were previously unknown in the Americas, so the native Americans had no immunity to them when the Spanish carried them across the ocean. The native American population of Mexico dropped from about twenty-seven million in 1519 to around one million in 1600, and in Peru the native American population fell during the same period from seven million to less than two million. The Spanish destruction of the native Americans was not completely deliberate, but it was nonetheless devastating.

The Spanish received many things—good and bad—from their new empire. They brought back to Europe syphilis, a disease that would plague many Europeans for centuries. They also brought many products—gold, silver, sugar, the potato—that temporarily made Spain a wealthy nation. The Spanish were unable, however, to use their imperial wealth to build a strong, competitive economy that could sustain Spanish power. Too many wars consumed the wealth from the Americas (as we will see in Chapter 11). Too many people refused to learn business and technical skills, since the Spanish nobility thought of labor as demeaning and the educated preferred to seek employment in government or church bureaucracies rather than in business. The result was a chronically weak economic base. Although the Spanish were able to retain their overseas empire, their political and economic strength began to dissipate in the seventeenth century.

Indeed, both exploring nations—Portugal and Spain—were unable to sustain their power for very long. Yet they had inaugurated a new era in history—one in which the full geographical contours of the globe would become known and Europe would dominate much of the world.

CONCLUSION

The period from 1300 to 1600 was a time of great change in Europe. Europeans lived through the gradual weakening of the old medieval order, the beginning of a transition from a rural to an urban way of life, the creation of new forms of art and literature, and the expansion of European power into overseas areas. They also lived through a religious upheaval, the Reformation, in the sixteenth century—our focus in the next chapter.

THINGS YOU SHOULD KNOW

Famines in Europe	Machiavelli
The Black Death	The Northern Renaissance
Hundred Years' War	van Eyck
War of the Roses	Erasmus
Pax Mongolica	More
Capitalism	Montaigne
The printing press	Shakespeare
The Renaissance in Italy	Nostradamus
Dante	Paracelsus
Petrarch	Dr. Faust
Boccaccio	Vesalius
Marsiglio	Copernicus
Giotto	The lateen sail
Donatello	Prince Henry the Navigator
Ghiberti	da Gama
Botticelli	Columbus
Savonarola	Vespucci
Leonardo da Vinci	Magellan
Michelangelo	Cortés
Raphael	

SUGGESTED READINGS

A good introduction to late medieval pessimism is Johan Huizinga, *The Waning of the Middle Ages* (New York: Doubleday, 1969). One cause of that pessimism was the Black Death, for which see William H. McNeill, *Plagues and Peoples* (New York: Doubleday, 1977) and Robert S. Gottfried, *The Black Death: Natural and Human Disaster in Medieval Europe* (New York: Free Press, 1985). Fernand Braudel, *The Wheels of Commerce*, vol. 2: *Civilization and Capitalism, 15th–18th Century*, trans. Siân Reynolds (New York: Harper & Row, 1986) is useful on the growth of capitalism. The classic work on the Italian Renaissance, written in the mid-nineteenth century, is Jacob Burckhardt, *The Civilization of the Renaissance in Italy* (New York: Modern Library, 1954). It is still worth reading. Other good works on the Renaissance include Wallace K. Ferguson, *The Renaissance* (New York: Henry Holt, 1940) and Denys Hay, *The Italian Renaissance in its Historical Background* (Cambridge, Eng.: Cambridge Univ. Press, 1977). Two good surveys of European expansion and exploration are J. H. Parry, *The Age of Reconnaissance: Discovery, Exploration and Settlement, 1450 to 1650* (New York: Praeger, 1963) and G. V. Scammell, *The World Encompassed: The First European Maritime Empires, c. 800–1650* (Berkeley: Univ. of California Press, 1981).

NOTES

[1]Quoted in Jean Gimpel, *The Medieval Machine: The Industrial Revolution of the Middle Ages* (New York: Penguin, 1976), p. 209.

[2]Quoted in Donald J. Wilcox, *In Search of God and Self: Renaissance and Reformation Thought* (Prospect Heights, Ill.: Waveland Press, 1975), p. 241.

[3]Joseph Needham, *Science and Civilization in China*, vol. 1: *Introductory Orientations* (Cambridge, Eng.: Cambridge Univ. Press, 1954), p. 189.

[4]Quoted in George Holmes, *Europe: Hierarchy and Revolt, 1320–1450* (New York: Harper Torchbooks, 1975), p. 146.

[5]Kenneth Clark, *Civilisation* (New York: Harper & Row, 1969), p. 129.

[6]Quoted in Wilcox, *In Search of God*, p. 165.

[7]Quoted in C. C. Lamberg-Karlovsky and Jeremy A. Sabloff, *Ancient Civilizations: The Near East and Mesoamerica* (Menlo Park, Calif.: Benjamin Cummings, 1979), p. 305.

11

The Reformations and Subsequent Conflicts, 1500 to 1715

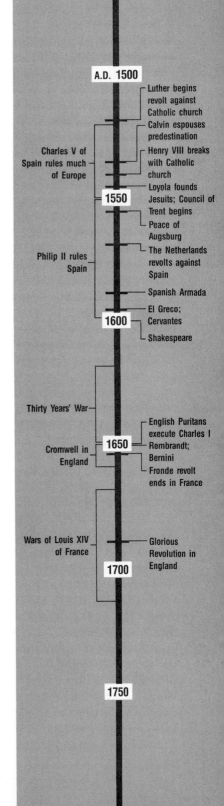

A.D. 1500

Luther begins revolt against Catholic church

Calvin espouses predestination

Charles V of Spain rules much of Europe

Henry VIII breaks with Catholic church

Loyola founds Jesuits; Council of Trent begins

1550

Peace of Augsburg

Philip II rules Spain

The Netherlands revolts against Spain

Spanish Armada

El Greco; Cervantes

1600

Shakespeare

Thirty Years' War

English Puritans execute Charles I

Cromwell in England

1650

Rembrandt; Bernini

Fronde revolt ends in France

Wars of Louis XIV of France

Glorious Revolution in England

1700

1750

During the sixteenth and seventeenth centuries, much of Western and central Europe was dominated by two interconnected developments. One was the *Reformation,* a complex upheaval that included both the *Protestant Reformation,* in which many Christians left the Roman Catholic church to establish independent churches, and the *Catholic Reformation,* in which the Catholic church sought to reform and rejuvenate itself. The other was the gradual emergence in Spain, France, and England of strong monarchical states, in which monarchs increasingly dominated the politics of their countries.

The Reformations and the emergence of strong monarchical states were connected in various ways. Sometimes monarchs used the religious struggles of the Reformation to increase their political power. At other times, religious leaders used monarchical armies to support their religious causes. At still other times, aristocrats in various areas used the religious conflicts to oppose the growth of monarchical power, which usually undermined the power of the aristocracy.

One result of the religious and political struggles was war. There were civil wars within countries as well as international conflicts. Most significant were the Spanish wars with various countries, particularly the Netherlands; the Thirty Years' War in the Germanies; the long English civil war in the seventeenth century; and the wars of the French monarch, Louis XIV.

THE PROTESTANT AND CATHOLIC REFORMATIONS

Several underlying factors helped produce the Reformations that split the Catholic church. First, resurgence of religious belief and emotions encouraged many Europeans to take their religious loyalties more seriously and to refuse compromise with those who disagreed with them. Second, a growing emphasis on individualism impelled many Christians to reject the organizational discipline of the Catholic church. Third, the constant traveling of people engaged in commerce helped break down traditional loyalties to the Catholic church. Finally, the growth of literacy, aided by the printing press, and the rise of universities helped create ways of learning and thinking that were often independent of traditional religious institutions.

Divisions within Christianity had begun well before the sixteenth century. The first division was the Greek Orthodox-Roman Catholic split of 1054. Then, in the late Middle Ages, there was a political split within Roman Catholicism. French monarchs acquired strong influence over the papacy for a time and, from 1305 to 1378, the popes resided in Avignon (present-day France) rather than in Rome. This was the so-called Babylonian Captivity of the papacy, named after the Babylonian defeat of the Hebrews during Old Testament times. Then followed the Great Schism (1378–1417), during which one line of popes continued to live in Avignon while another was established in Rome. The Avignon papacy eventually disappeared, leaving only the popes in Rome. But while the Schism lasted, Europe witnessed two successions of popes, each denouncing and excommunicating the other. The Schism created many dilemmas for the ordinary believer. According to Catholic doctrine, only legitimate priests can administer the sacraments—baptism and the eucharist, for example—through which Christians receive divine grace. With the Schism, it was difficult for Christians to know which priests to approach in order to receive the sacraments.

Another problem for the medieval church was the growth of several heretical movements, such as the Hussite rebellion in Bohemia (present-day Czechoslovakia). Early in the fifteenth century, John Hus initiated a religious reform designed to free the Bohemian church from papal control. Hus was burned at the stake, but Bohemian anger against the papacy and against the German kings of Bohemia kept the rebellion alive for a time. The church and the German rulers finally had to organize a crusade to regain control of the area.

Still another difficulty for the church was a growing anticlericalism among many ordinary people. One reason was a slowly emerging sense of nationalism in some areas, which fostered resentment of papal money-raising activities that took wealth from all over Europe to Rome. Another was the amount of land and other resources already owned by the church. By the late fifteenth century, the church owned almost 25 percent of the land in England and 20 percent in Sweden. Land-hungry peasants often perceived the clergy as parasites who accumulated land and lived off the labor of others. One peasant ridiculed the vows of poverty and chastity taken by clergy: "They go to the houses of rich, young, and beautiful women. They take their money and, if they consent, they sleep carnally with them, putting on appearances of humility the while." A young shepherd had an equally low opinion of monks: "Instead of saving the souls of the dead and sending them to Heaven, they gorge themselves at banquets, after funerals. . . . They are wicked wolves! They would like to devour us all, dead or alive."[1]

Martin Luther and the Reformation in Germany

Certainly not everyone in Europe was anticlerical or antipapacy, but there was enough opposition to the church to spark protest. The spark came from a German friar, Martin Luther (1483–1546), and signals the beginning of the Protestant movement. As a young man, Luther was obsessed by a fear of God as a stern judge who condemned most people to perdition. In his anxiety, he joined a monastery in an effort to find spiritual satisfaction and peace. During his years as a monk, Luther

Martin Luther A 1529 portrait of the Protestant reformer Martin Luther, by Lucas Cranach the Elder (1472–1553). (The Granger Collection)

constantly pondered the phrase "the righteousness of God" and gradually came to believe that salvation was possible for humans only because God imparted righteousness to them. The Biblical passage that inspired Luther is from the Book of Romans—"The just shall live by faith"— meaning people cannot earn salvation by their own efforts but only through God. The implication was that the center of the Christian experience is an individual's personal relationship with God through which God grants righteousness to the person. The institutional church, though, was not that important.

Luther's views might have led him into a conflict with the church under any circumstances, but the actual conflict began over the relatively minor issue of the sale of *indulgences*. Indulgences were monetary payments to the church by means of which, the church said, people could reduce the penalties (but not the guilt) for their sins. In 1517, a German indulgence seller named Johann Tetzel began to preach, wrongly, that indulgences would remove a sinner's guilt as well as his penalty. Luther immediately protested Tetzel's errors and, according to tradition, posted "Ninety-five Theses" (a challenge to a debate) on the door of a church in Wittenberg, Germany. His protest was quickly supported by many Germans who resented the church's wealth and power. Luther was emboldened, and by 1518 he was attacking the church on a number of issues, including the claim that the pope had final authority to interpret the scriptures. As a result, he was soon excommunicated by the pope and outlawed by the German emperor.

Originally, Luther did not intend to split from the Roman Catholic church, but several factors soon encouraged him to start what became the *Lutheran* church. One was his growing conviction that the Roman Catholic church was so overly organized and wealthy that it hindered the individual Christian in his or her quest for a personal relationship with God. Another factor was the support he received from evangelical preachers in Germany, who carried Luther's message to ordinary people. In addition, Luther was supported by many German princes, in part for religious reasons and in part for the opportunity to expropriate church property and wealth. Some of the princes also saw Luther's revolt as an opportunity to enhance their political power in the areas they governed. They supported Luther against the German Emperor Charles V, who sought to increase his power over the princes and was supporting the Catholic church against Luther. (The princes stood for decentralized politics in Germany so they would control their own small areas, while the emperor stood for centralized power in imperial hands.)

During the 1520s and 1530s, Germany was embroiled in constant religious and political conflict. Luther encouraged the revolt against Rome by preaching, writing hymns, interpreting the Bible, and training missionaries. Evangelical preachers carried the revolt into many German cities, where Lutheran churches were often established. Religious wars between Lutherans and Catholics erupted several times. The German Peasants' War of 1525, caused both by religious emotions and the peasant complaints, exploded and was savagely repressed by the princes, who had Luther's support.

The eventual result was that much of north Germany became Lutheran while south Germany remained predominantly Catholic. Then, in 1555, the Peace of Augsburg formulated a truce that allowed each German prince to establish which church he wanted in his realm. The Peace of Augsburg both recognized Lutheranism as permanent and contributed to the religious and political fragmentation of Germany.

The Peace of Augsburg recognized only Lutherans and Catholics; it did not tolerate the other sects that emerged in Germany during Luther's revolt. One new sect was the *literalists*, who sought to live by the exact words of the Bible. A particularly notorious literalist got so carried away that he imitated the prophet Isaiah in throwing off his clothes and running through the streets to look for a sign from God. More numerous were the *Anabaptists*. Anabaptism was an evangelical movement that flourished primarily among poor townspeople and peasants. It had no central organization, but its defining characteristic was a belief that baptism should occur only when a person reaches adulthood. Both

Figure 11.1   The Religious Division of Europe, 1517–1648

Lutherans and Catholics regarded the Anabaptists and other sects as
radicals who should be persecuted and destroyed. Many of the persecuted eventually migrated to North America.

John Calvin and the Reformation in Switzerland

The *Protestant* movement (which "protested" against and split from
Catholicism) spread to Switzerland in the 1520s. Huldrych Zwingli
(1484–1531) established a reformed church in Zurich, but more significant was the work of John Calvin in Geneva.

Calvin (1509–1564) was a Frenchman who wrote *The Institutes of the
Christian Religion* in 1536. His belief in the absolute power of God led
him to espouse a doctrine of *predestination,* which stipulated that God
has foreordained the ultimate destiny of all people. Those who are chosen
for salvation are the elect, and, according to Calvin, they should live
rigorously disciplined lives in conformity with God's laws. The logic and

clarity of Calvin's writings were so persuasive that in 1541 he was invited to Geneva to lead a Protestant reform. Under his guidance, the Genevans established a theocracy, a government dominated by ministers and churches. The government promulgated numerous regulations to control behavior: card playing and dancing were prohibited, children were strictly disciplined to obey their parents, and everyone was expected to attend church services regularly. A number of people were executed for heresy, blasphemy, or adultery.

John Calvin may seem to have been a harsh, demanding figure who took all the fun out of life. It is important to remember, though, that most Genevans accepted his leadership willingly, because they too believed that a morally disciplined life was a sign of their salvation. Others outside of Geneva also followed Calvin's leadership. Switzerland, being in the middle of Europe, was ideally positioned to spread the Reformation, and Geneva became a haven where religious exiles could learn from Calvin and then carry his message back to their home countries. As a result, *Calvinism* rather than Lutheranism took root in the Netherlands, France (the Huguenots), Scotland (the Presbyterians), and England (the Puritans).

The Reformation in England

In England, religious change was caused by a combination of religious and political factors. Many English wanted religious reform for the same reasons as people elsewhere, but the issue that precipitated a split with the Catholic church was Henry VIII's marital problems.

Henry VIII (reigned 1509–1547) was obsessed with wanting a son to succeed him. He believed that a secure succession would prevent the kinds of conflicts that had plagued England in the preceding century (such as the War of the Roses). But he and the queen, Catherine of Aragon, were unable to produce a son. By the 1520s, Henry was convinced that their marriage was invalid because of Catherine's earlier marriage to Henry's deceased elder brother. So, Henry requested that the pope grant an annulment of his marriage to Catherine. The pope refused and later excommunicated Henry when he married Anne Boleyn in 1533. In his rage, Henry appealed to the English Parliament, which in 1534 passed the Act of Supremacy that made the monarch the head of the English church and stipulated that the English owed no allegiance to the Roman pope. This political action was supported by many English for religious reasons; they were already anti-Rome and wanted religious reform.

Henry soon had Anne Boleyn beheaded because of her alleged plotting against him. His desire for a son drove him to marry again, and his third wife, Jane Seymour, gave birth to a boy. (After Jane Seymour died, Henry married three more times.) It is ironic that what Henry

From his paternal grandfather,
Maximilian of Austria

From his paternal grandmother,
Mary of Burgundy

From his maternal grandfather,
Ferdinand of Aragón

From his maternal grandmother,
Isabella of Castile

NORTH SEA

BALTIC SEA

ATLANTIC
OCEAN

NETHERLANDS

AUSTRIA

BLACK SEA

ADRIATIC SEA

ARAGÓN

CASTILE

SARDINIA   NAPLES

SICILY

MEDITERRANEAN SEA

0   200   400

Scale in Miles

Nile River

RED SEA

Figure 11.2   Lands Ruled by Charles V, 1514

wanted most, a strong successor, turned out to be, not his son, who died
after a brief reign, but the daughter he had by Anne Boleyn. She became
Queen Elizabeth I (reigned 1558–1603) one of the greatest rulers in
English history.

The Catholic Reformation

During the early years of the Protestant Reformation, the Catholic church
was too confused and disorganized to respond effectively to the
Protestant challenge. Gradually, however, the Catholics launched a
reform of their own—the *Catholic Reformation* (sometimes called the
Counter-Reformation).

The Catholic Reformation began with individuals seeking a closer
relationship with God, particularly in Spain, one of the most loyal
Catholic nations. St. Teresa of Avila (1515–1582) was a mystic who
reinstituted monastic discipline in the Carmelite convents in Spain. (The

Carmelites were a mendicant order originally founded in the twelfth century.) St. John of the Cross (1542–1591) was a follower of St. Teresa's, and he helped reform the Carmelite monasteries in Spain.

The most prominent of the Spanish reformers was Ignatius Loyola. Loyola (1491–1556) was a boisterous soldier as a young man and became intensely religious only after being seriously wounded. He began to practice spiritual exercises—various forms of meditation and contemplation—and to teach the spirituality so prevalent in his day: "Love ought to manifest itself in deeds rather than in words."[2] Loyola gradually acquired some followers, and in 1540 the pope designated his group as a new religious order—the Company of Jesus, or *Jesuits*. The Jesuits were committed missionaries. Some became scholars and founded schools and colleges; others went to the New World and even to China to convert non-Christians. Thus, the Jesuits were instrumental in reviving Catholicism.

The Catholic Reformation also included a variety of measures more directly intended to block the spread of Protestantism. One was the *Index*, a list of books (mostly Protestant writings) that Catholics were forbidden to read. Another was the Inquisition, a church court created during the Middle Ages, which the Catholics used to identify and punish heretics. In addition, the Catholic response to Protestantism included the calling of a church council. The Council of Trent met off and on for eighteen years (1545–1563) and had two primary goals: (1) to institute reforms to strengthen the church internally and (2) to respond to Protestantism on a doctrinal level. The Council clarified Catholic thought in a number of areas, including the matter of indulgences that had initially precipitated the Protestant revolt. It also established a better training system for priests, required stricter discipline with regard to the behavior and morality of clergy, and prohibited the practice of a bishop's holding more than one bishopric. Basically, the Council of Trent refused any compromise with Protestantism, but it clarified Catholic doctrines and made church organization more efficient. Thus, it helped prepare the Catholic church for the future.

Art during the Reformation

The heightened religious feelings of the Reformation era helped inspire several great artists. Some of these were Hans Holbein, Pieter Brueghel, and Peter Paul Rubens. Two of the most influential were Rembrandt van Rijn (1606–1669) and Giovanni Lorenzo Bernini (1598–1680).

Rembrandt was a Dutch Protestant, a devout man who read the Bible regularly. He painted both secular and religious subjects. His *Supper at Emmaus*, for example, portrays Jesus breaking bread with his disciples. The clearest evidence of Rembrandt's concern with religion and spirituality is the overwhelming use of drab colors like browns and dark reds in his work. He did not want his paintings to be so spectacular that they blinded viewers to the inner meaning of his art.

Bernini was an Italian sculptor, painter, and architect as well as a loyal Catholic. In fact, his most famous work was done at St. Peter's Basilica in Rome. It is the massive place of worship next to the papal residence. Michelangelo had designed the dome for St. Peter's, and Bernini added to Michelangelo's work. He built, on the inside, a large and elaborate bronze canopy above the central altar. On the outside, Bernini built two enormous colonnades that enclose a piazza in front of the Basilica. The piazza quickly became a gathering place for pilgrims and visitors coming to visit the Basilica and seek an audience with the pope.

Consequences of the Reformation

Some of the most important consequences of the Reformation era were the following:

1. Europe was split along religious lines. Much of northern Europe—northern Germany, the Scandinavian countries, Switzerland, parts of France, the Netherlands, England, and Scotland— became Protestant. Most of southern Europe—Spain, Italy, southern Germany, most of France, and Poland—remained Catholic.
2. The religious divisions led to numerous wars caused by both religious and political factors. During the sixteenth and seventeenth centuries, Protestants and Catholics fought each other and both persecuted the smaller religious sects. This had the further consequence of encouraging persecuted religious minorities to escape by emigrating to the Americas at the same time that, slowly, a desire grew for religious toleration, since most Protestants and Catholics eventually tired of trying to destroy each other.
3. Some old institutions and customs were abolished in Protestant areas; monasteries were disbanded and Protestant clergy were allowed to marry.
4. The phenomenon of witch-hunting was encouraged. Heightened religious tensions, added to the general chaos of the age, led in the sixteenth and seventeenth centuries to many women being accused of witchcraft. Europeans had believed in witches for a long time, but until the fourteenth century few people were actually identified as witches. After that, a growing number of single women who lived alone were accused of heresy, of worshipping the devil, or of bewitching people. Once an entire convent of nuns began to mew and purr like cats, and a woman was charged with casting a spell over them. By the sixteenth century, witchcraft trials were common in some parts of Europe. The bishop of Bamberg (Germany) had six hundred alleged witches burned in a

single year, and in Savoy (Italy) eight hundred were executed in one batch. In Salem, Massachusetts, twenty witches were killed in 1692. During the sixteenth and seventeenth centuries, more women were killed for witchcraft than for all other crimes combined. The exact number of women executed is unknown, but it was probably in the range of 60,000 to 80,000.

5. In some Protestant areas, the religious revolt helped increase the power of monarchs. Protestants no longer owed allegiance to an international institution—the papacy—and thus could be encouraged to focus their political loyalties on their kings or queens. Furthermore, Protestant monarchs often used religious reform as an excuse to confiscate property from the Catholic church.

THE EMERGENCE OF STRONG MONARCHICAL STATES

During the late Middle Ages, some European monarchs began to organize large states (see Chapter 8), but in most areas real political power continued to rest in the hands of the local feudal nobility. By the sixteenth century, monarchs in England, France, and Spain were building on the work of their predecessors, destroying the power of the local nobility and forming genuinely centralized kingdoms. England, after the chaos of the War of the Roses, experienced a succession of powerful monarchs—Henry VII (1485–1509), Henry VIII (1509–1547), and Elizabeth I (1558–1603). France, after driving out the English during the Hundred Years' War, received strong leadership from Louis XI (1461–1483) and Francis I (1515–1547). Spain was finally united in 1492 by Ferdinand (1479–1516) and Isabella (1474–1504), who were followed by Charles V (1519–1556) and Philip II (1556–1598).

The monarchs of England, France, and Spain used primarily four methods to strengthen their power. (1) They began to monopolize the use of force. Traditionally, the nobility was the backbone of royal armies, the result being that nobles had military training and power that could be used to enhance their political and social positions. By the sixteenth century, monarchs were hiring mercenaries to aid armies that used cannons and rifles. Thus, the new weapons made the armies more powerful and the paid mercenaries gave the monarch more control over military forces. (2) Monarchs began to build bureaucracies in which permanent officials collected taxes and applied royal law throughout the kingdom. Originally, these bureaucracies were small, but they gradually expanded and extended the power of centralized, royal government. (3) Monarchs began to justify their power in various ways. One way was through the theory of the divine right of kings, which held that rulers received their power from God. Monarchs also staged elaborate court ceremonials and public tours that were designed to build in the eyes of the populace an image of royal grandeur and majesty. (4) Finally, the monarchs sought to instill some cultural unity in their kingdoms by encouraging similarity of opinion among the members of the upper classes. In practice, this meant religious uniformity. Protestant monarchs tried to insist that all the leading members of society be Protestant, while Catholic monarchs demanded loyalty to Catholicism from their upper classes.

The emergence of large monarchical states in England, France, and Spain affected European history in several ways but two are most important. First, England and France in particular encouraged economic development and the growth of capitalism. This occurred in part because the governments were major customers for some products and in part because they provided the social stability and peace that allowed merchants to expand business and commerce. Second, England, France, and Spain fostered European expansion across the oceans. The monarchs wanted to increase their power and prestige and had the financial resources to sponsor oceanic voyages.

EUROPEAN WARS OF THE SIXTEENTH AND SEVENTEENTH CENTURIES

Many military conflicts occurred in Europe during the sixteenth and seventeenth centuries. Their causes were varied and intermixed. The religious hostilities between Protestants and Catholics contributed, as did the dynastic struggles over who would inherit the thrones in some countries. Another cause was the continuing struggle between monarchs, who sought to centralize political power, and nobles, who sought to decentralize power into their own hands. Further, some monarchs wanted to conquer more territory.

Spain and the Netherlands

Spain was in many ways the most powerful nation in Europe during the sixteenth century. Spanish *conquistadores* were gradually conquering a vast empire in the Americas, and the colonies were sending gold and silver back to Spain. Within Europe, the Holy Roman Emperor Charles V (reigned 1519–1556) ruled Spain as well as an extraordinary range of other territories. Charles was a member of the Hapsburg family, which had gradually acquired power in much of Europe. From his mother, the daughter of Ferdinand and Isabella of Spain, Charles inherited the throne of Spain (where he was known as Charles I). From his father, he inherited the territories of Burgundy (eastern France) and the Netherlands (present-day Holland and Belgium). And, from his paternal grandfather, the Holy Roman Emperor Maximilian I, he inherited the throne of

TECHNOLOGY
Weaponry

One reason for the political success of the European monarchs was the growing use of gunpowder and cannons. The Chinese discovered and used gunpowder as early as the eleventh century, but they never took the decisive step of inventing the cannon. The gunpowder discovery was passed on to the Arabs, and the Europeans probably learned about gunpowder from the Arabs in Spain. Early cannons were long wooden tubes. Stones inside the tube were propelled by a gunpowder explosion. Europeans first used cannons as siege guns in Spain during the thirteenth century. By the fourteenth century, the first portable rifles were in use in Europe.

The sixteenth century was the first great age of gunpowder in Europe. Cannons were mounted on wheels and thus became more mobile. Rifles were improved by the invention of the matchlock. The earliest rifles were just iron tubes in which the gunpowder had to be lit by hand, but the matchlock, operated by a trigger, made ignition of gunpowder easier and quicker.

Military forces armed with cannons and rifles were obviously much stronger than those equipped only with pikes and the weapons carried by soldiers on horseback. In particular, cannon fire could penetrate the walls of a noble's castle, so the availability of cannon weakened the power base of the nobility and thus strengthened the authority of many monarchs.

Cannons *A 1575 wood engraving of early cannons, which were mounted on mobile carriages. (The Granger Collection)*

Austria as well as the imperial throne of Germany. (Germany was politically divided—see Chapter 8—with real political power in the hands of the princes of the individual German states. However, there was a Holy Roman Empire to which the German states belonged, and the Holy Roman emperor exercised a nominal leadership in the Germanies.)

Ruling much of Europe as well as the Americas may have been more of a curse than a blessing to Charles V, for he spent much of his life planning and fighting wars. He fought the Ottoman Turks, who were asserting power in the Mediterranean, and he continually competed with France for control of Italy. (The Spanish-French wars in Italy helped destroy the economic prosperity that supported the Italian Renaissance.) Furthermore, as a loyal Catholic, Charles was embroiled for years in the religious wars in Germany and lived to see Catholicism lose much of its power and influence. Weary of his struggles, Charles abdicated his thrones in 1555 and 1556. His brother, Ferdinand I, received the Austrian and Holy Roman thrones, and his son, Philip II, became king of Spain and the overseas empire as well as ruler of Burgundy and the Netherlands.

Philip II (reigned 1556–1598) was also involved in several military conflicts. In France, Protestants and Catholics were struggling for power, and Philip's Spain intervened on the Catholic side. On the seas, the English and Dutch were attacking Spanish convoys from the Americas. Philip sent the Spanish Armada, a naval expedition, to punish the English in 1588, but it was defeated by a combination of English resistance and bad weather. Philip's longest struggle was with the Netherlands. In 1568, the Netherlands rebelled against Spanish rule. The rebellion was in part a war for political independence and in part a religious fight between the Protestant Dutch and the Catholic Spanish. The southern provinces of the Netherlands (present-day Belgium) eventually made peace with Spain, but the northern provinces (present-day Netherlands) continued fighting until they won independence in 1609. The Spanish later tried to reconquer them, but Dutch freedom was finally confirmed in 1648. (As in many other wars of the time, the fighting forced many people to leave their homes and migrate to other areas, as both Protestants and Catholics tried to escape the focus of the other side.)

Gaining independence stimulated Dutch energy and creativity, and the seventeenth century was a great age in Dutch history. The painter Rembrandt (1606–1669) was doing his greatest work then. The jurist Hugo Grotius (1583–1645) wrote an influential exposition of international law. Dutch scientists and artisans made important discoveries in the fields of human anatomy and optics. And, for a time, the leading Dutch city of Amsterdam was the world center of capitalism. The first stock exchange was created there, its function being to raise capital for large-scale enterprises. The largest banks and the largest collection of merchant vessels were also in Amsterdam. Dutch ships carried cargoes

The Resurrection of Jesus, (c. 1596–1600) by *El Greco*   The Spanish painter El Greco (1541– 1614) was originally from Greece; his birth name was Kyriakos Theotocopoulos. El Greco's style was gritty and dark. It repre- sented a movement away from painting Jesus and other subjects as "glowing" and "perfect look- ing." (Gallery del Prado)

throughout the Baltic Sea as well as to and from Asia and the Americas. In the mid-seventeenth century, the Dutch seemed to be everywhere—in Russia building iron-smelting plants, in China buying silk, in Brazil organizing sugar plantations, in North America establishing New Am- sterdam (now New York City). They were, for a time, the wealthiest people in Europe.

If the war of independence brought prosperity and power to the Dutch, it was for the Spanish one more step in a story of decline. As noted in Chapter 10, too many wars drained Spanish wealth and energy, and Spain was unable to build a permanently strong economy. Consequently, seventeenth-century Spain slowly lost power and wealth. At the same time, however, the Spanish enjoyed a cultural flowering. The artist El Greco (1541–1614) painted primarily religious subjects and expressed the spirit of the Catholic Reformation. The dramatist Lope de Vega (1562–1635) produced hundreds of plays and poems and helped found modern drama. And, Miguel de Cervantes (1547–1616) wrote *Don Quixote,* a masterpiece of world literature. In one sense, *Don Quixote* is a satire on the chivalric romances that appealed to many Spanish; in another sense, it is an inspiring examination of human idealism.

The Thirty Years' War in the Germanies

In the first half of the seventeenth century, the Germanies became enmeshed in a terrible struggle known as the *Thirty Years' War* (1618–1648). It was a conflict in which political and religious disputes were intermixed. As noted earlier, the Germanies were politically divided, with an emperor exercising nominal leadership over the whole but with real political power resting in the individual states. The Germanies were also religiously divided, with the north German states being predominantly Protestant and the south German states predominantly Catholic. The Thirty Years' War originated in a struggle between Protestant princes, defending both their religion and their political power, and the Catholic emperor, fighting to increase his imperial control over the Germanies and also to strengthen his church. As other nations intervened in the struggle, the conflict widened and became more intense. For the people of Germany, the war was a hideous nightmare. Many were killed, and some towns suffered so much destruction that they disappeared. When the fighting finally ended in 1648 with the Peace of Westphalia, the political decentralization of the Germanies was reaffirmed, and an exhausted German people began a slow recovery from the horrors of a long civil war.

Because several great powers intervened in the German struggle, the Thirty Years' War had a wide-ranging impact on European politics. France, for example, gained valuable parcels of land from the Peace of Westphalia. The small duchy of Brandenburg (northern Germany) captured some territories within Germany and began to grow and evolve into the state of Prussia (northeastern Europe, along the Baltic coast). Sweden tried to take several north German ports and thereby become the greatest power in the Baltic Sea area, but Swedish ambitions were finally contained by other nations. Muscovy (Russia) was also beginning to assert its power, while Poland was starting a long decline.

The English Civil War and the Glorious Revolution

The English civil war lasted through most of the seventeenth century. It was precipitated in part by a dispute between the English monarchs and Parliament. Because the expenses of armies and armaments were rapidly increasing, English monarchs continually tried to increase their tax revenues, often without the consent of Parliament. Many members of Parliament, particularly those representing the merchant class, interpreted the monarchical actions as attempts to impose tyranny on England.

Another cause of the English civil war was a religious quarrel between the monarchs, who headed the established Anglican church, and the Puritans, followers of Calvinism who wanted to "purify" Anglicanism. The Puritans objected in particular to the elaborate religious ceremonials and the complex administrative apparatus of the Anglican church, as they seemed similar to Roman Catholic practices. The Puritans favored simpler forms of religious worship that included a doctrine of spiritual equality in which believers could read and interpret the Bible themselves. To conservative Anglicans, the Puritan doctrine sounded like an invitation to religious chaos. The philosopher Thomas Hobbes wrote sarcastically: "Every man, nay, every boy and wench that could read English thought they spoke with God Almighty, and understood what he said."[3]

Serious disputes began during the reign of James I (1603–1625) and continued through the years of his son, Charles I (1625–1649). Both monarchs tried to increase taxes and impose Anglican church rules on all English, and neither was willing to compromise. The parliamentary opponents of taxation and the Puritan opponents of Anglicanism gradually became merged in a common front against monarchical policies. By the 1640s, the quarrel was increasingly tense and blunt, and fighting broke out in 1642.

On one side were the forces loyal to Charles I, sometimes called the *Cavaliers;* on the other was the parliamentary army led by the Puritan Oliver Cromwell, its members often called *Roundheads* (because their short hair marked them as socially inferior to the nobility). The parliamentary-Puritan army had an emotional advantage in that the Puritans were convinced they represented God's cause. Several years of fierce fighting led to the final defeat of the Cavaliers in 1646. (Not all Englishpeople knew or cared about what was happening. One farmer, told to get out of the way of a battle between royalist and parliamentary forces, did not know that "them two had fallen out."[4])

In 1649, Charles I was placed on trial and then executed by the Puritan-dominated Parliament, an extraordinary event in an age when monarchs were presumed to be God's representatives on earth. From 1649 to 1660, a Puritan republic first led by Oliver Cromwell (he died in

1658) governed England, but it gradually lost popularity. One reason was a war with the Dutch, which led to higher taxes in England and the disruption of English commerce. Another was that the Puritans tried to impose their strict moral precepts on the English. The Puritans prohibited gambling, profanity, and sometimes the playing of games. In one instance, a certain John Bishop was called to court for having "wilfully and in a violent and boisterous manner run to and fro" while kicking a football.[5]

After Cromwell's death in 1658, leading aristocrats invited Charles, son of Charles I, to become king. Charles II (reigned 1660–1685) ruled fairly effectively for a time, but his successor James II (reigned 1685–1688) resumed the uncompromising tax and religious policies of his predecessors. By 1688, James had little if any public support, and parliamentary leaders were able to force him out of the country in an essentially bloodless coup. Parliament then invited William and Mary of the Netherlands to become king and queen of England. Both were Protestants, and Mary was James II's daughter. This event became celebrated as the *Glorious Revolution* because in exchange for the throne William and Mary agreed to accept a Bill of Rights that limited the powers of the monarchy and guaranteed that monarchs would govern only with the consent of Parliament. The Glorious Revolution thus marked the end of the long English conflict. It was a victory for the upper classes, who being represented in Parliament would rule England in cooperation with the monarchs. The lower classes were not represented before or after the Glorious Revolution. During the 1640s, there had been some radical groups—the Levellers and the Diggers—who espoused egalitarian, democratic ideas, but they were suppressed by the Puritans.

These political and religious events in England stimulated a great deal of thought that influenced not only England but much of Western Europe and the future United States as well. In 1651, Thomas Hobbes wrote *Leviathan*, a defense of absolutist government that would continue to be read for centuries. (*Absolutism* refers to a type of government in which one person or group holds all power.) The theories of the Levellers and the Diggers had some impact on the founders of the United States. John Milton, the great poet of the Puritan cause, created *Paradise Lost* (1667), a prolonged meditation on the nature of divine justice and the sinfulness of humanity. And, John Locke, the philosophical defender of the Glorious Revolution, began to define what would later be known as *liberalism*.

The Wars of Louis XIV

France, like many other countries, endured civil strife during the sixteenth and seventeenth centuries. In the sixteenth century, Catholics and Protestants (often called *Huguenots* in France) fought so much that the stability of the French state was threatened. In the seventeenth century, a series of rebellions known as the *Fronde* (1649–1653) shook the country. The Fronde was launched by numerous aristocrats and townspeople who wanted to decentralize political power to the local level. French monarchs, however, were able to quash the rebellions and continue to centralize power in their own hands.

When Louis XIV (reigned 1643–1715) ascended the French throne, France began to assert its power on the international level even more forcefully than before. Louis saw himself as an absolute monarch, whose power was unrestricted in France. He sought, among other things, to control French industries and overseas trade and to enhance French culture by patronizing artists such as the dramatist Molière (1622–1673). But Louis's greatest passion was *la gloire*, "military glory," in order to enhance his and France's reputation. The result was a series of wars in which Louis sought to gain more territory for France. The War of Devolution (1667–1668) enabled Louis to annex part of the Spanish Netherlands (present-day Belgium). In the Dutch War (1672–1678), Louis sought to destroy Protestantism in the Netherlands (present-day Holland). He did not achieve that goal but did gain some more territory for France. The War of the League of Augsburg (1689–1697) resulted in some small annexations of German territory by France. Finally, the War of the Spanish Succession (1702–1713) was an unsuccessful attempt by Louis to ensure that one of his grandsons would inherit the Spanish throne. None of these wars was particularly deadly or involved large numbers of military forces, but together they did absorb much of France's wealth and therefore helped to weaken the French economy. Louis did acquire some small areas of land, but various coalitions of European powers always fought against him and prevented him from making large territorial gains. When Louis died in 1715, after several decades of warfare, France had relatively little to show for his ambitions.

CONCLUSION

Western Civilization experienced fundamental changes during the sixteenth and seventeenth centuries. The Reformation produced religious divisions that contributed to numerous wars. These wars were so destructive that they gradually produced among many people a desire for religious toleration in order to stop the killing. Another major change was the growth of monarchical power in some countries, as monarchs increased the authority of their centralized governments.

Also present in the sixteenth and seventeenth centuries were developments in capitalism, science, and overseas expansion that would become more significant in following centuries. As capitalism developed, it gradually produced more wealth and power for Europeans. Modern science gave people a deeper understanding of nature. And the expansion of European power overseas in the Americas and Asia would continue.

At the beginning of the eighteenth century, Western Civilization was still centered in Europe and continued to be dynamic and aggressive. That dynamism would be accentuated during the next three centuries.

THINGS YOU SHOULD KNOW

The Babylonian Captivity of the papacy and the Great Schism
The Protestant Reformation
Luther
Peace of Augsburg
Literalists
Anabaptists
Calvin and predestination
Henry VIII
The Catholic Reformation
Loyola
Council of Trent
Rembrandt

Bernini
Consequences of the Reformation era
Significance of new weaponry
Charles V
Philip II
Cervantes
Thirty Years' War
English civil war
Cromwell
Glorious Revolution
Louis XIV

SUGGESTED READINGS

Two good introductions to the Reformation era are Lewis W. Spitz, *The Protestant Reformation, 1517–1559* (New York: Harper & Row, 1986) and A. G. Dickens, *Reformation and Society in the Sixteenth Century* (New York: Harcourt Brace, 1966). On Martin Luther, see James Atkinson, *Martin Luther and the Birth of Protestantism* (Louisville, Ky.: Westminster/John Knox Press, 1981). Richard L. DeMolen (ed.), *Leaders of the Reformation* (Cranbury, N.J.: Susquehanna Univ. Press, 1984) offers good essays on Zwingli, Calvin, Loyola, and Cromwell.

A good text on the wars of the sixteenth and seventeenth centuries is Richard S. Dunn, *The Age of Religious Wars, 1559–1689* (New York: Norton, 1979). More specific works include Cicely V. Wedgwood, *The Thirty Years' War* (London: Routledge, Chapman, & Hall, 1981), which is very readable, and Christopher Hill, *The Century of Revolution, 1603–1714* (New York: Norton, 1961), a major interpretation of the English civil war emphasizing the radical groups that emerged in seventeenth-century England.

NOTES

[1]Quoted in George Huppert, *After the Black Death: A Social History of Early Modern Europe* (Bloomington: Indiana Univ. Press, 1986), p. 143.

[2]Quoted in John C. Olin, "The Catholic Reformation," in *The Meaning of the Renaissance and Reformation,* ed. Richard L. DeMolen (Boston: Houghton Mifflin, 1974), p. 274.

[3]Quoted in Christopher Hill, *The Century of Revolution, 1603–1714* (New York: Norton, 1961), p. 173.

[4]Quoted in Christopher Hibbert, *The English: A Social History* (New York: Norton, 1987), p. 254.

[5]Ibid., p. 260.

12

Early Modern Europe, 1600 to 1770: An Intellectual and Spiritual Revolution

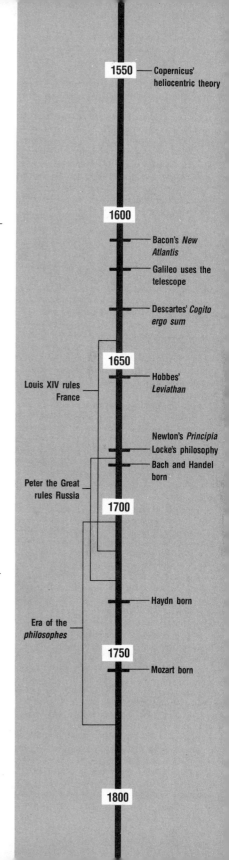

1550 — Copernicus' heliocentric theory

1600

— Bacon's *New Atlantis*

— Galileo uses the telescope

— Descartes' *Cogito ergo sum*

1650

— Hobbes' *Leviathan*

Louis XIV rules France

Newton's *Principia*
— Locke's philosophy
— Bach and Handel born

Peter the Great rules Russia

1700

— Haydn born

Era of the *philosophes*

1750

— Mozart born

1800

The contemporary historian Franklin L. Baumer refers to the seventeenth century as the beginning of the modern period in Western Civilization because it was at this time that European thought became recognizably distinct from ancient or medieval thought.[1] Prior to the seventeenth century, most European intellectuals looked to the past; they sought spiritual guidance, for example, from traditional sources like Christian teachings or ancient Greek philosophy. The new modern intellectuals, however, looked more to the present and the future. They sought to gain knowledge, not through tradition, but through the study of nature and the use of human reasoning abilities. By reorienting thought, they began an intellectual and spiritual revolution so fundamental that it ultimately transformed Western Civilization.

One element of this transformation was the gradual emergence of modern science. Philosophers developed new ways of thinking about nature while scientists discovered new facts about nature. Another element of the transformation was the Enlightenment, an intellectual movement that defined and taught new political and cultural ideas in an attempt to "enlighten" European societies. These new ideas gradually came to challenge the prestige and influence of Christian teachings and to secularize Western thought.

The intellectual revolution was accomplished by a small number of people. Most Europeans were unaware of the revolution, and their lives were affected primarily by the usual sorts of political events (wars and struggles for political power) and economic realities (the need for food, clothing, and shelter) that characterized everyday life.

THE SCIENTIFIC REVOLUTION

If *science* is defined as the systematic study and analysis of nature, then scientific thought has existed for centuries in various parts of the world. Early Chinese scientists studied nature, as did the ancient Greeks and Romans and the medieval Europeans. But the early forms of science were different from modern science in important ways. Early science was usually thought of as a philosophical discipline. The scientist thought about nature and tried to understand it in a theoretical sense. In medieval Europe, for example, nature was presumed to be a revelation from God and the purpose of studying nature was to understand the meaning of the revelation.

By contrast, the modern science created in Europe during the sixteenth to eighteenth centuries had four important characteristics.

1. It was experimental in that it stressed the use of tests or experiments to prove or disprove theories about events in nature.

2. It was an empirical-based science, relying on observations of nature rather than on preconceived ideas. The Europeans, unlike other peoples, had developed a number of instruments, such as the microscope and telescope, that allowed nature to be observed more easily and accurately.
3. It was mechanical, in that scientists saw nature as an inanimate mechanism or machine.
4. It was utilitarian, in that scientists hoped to use their knowledge of nature to accomplish practical, useful things (such as using wind currents for windmills).

The utilitarian aspect of modern science was especially important. During ancient and medieval times, science and technology were the concerns of two different social groups. Scientists, those who thought about nature, were usually people from the upper classes who had the education and time to think and study. People who worked with technology, those who invented practical devices, were usually manual laborers from the lower classes. As a result of this class division, science and technology had little to do with one another. However, during the fourteenth to eighteenth centuries, as the new cities broke down some of the traditional social barriers and encouraged the growth of literacy, it became easier for scientists and workers to cooperate and work together. Gradually, the study of science began to provide a theoretical underpinning for technology and to suggest areas where technological developments might occur.

Another important point is that the new science was an international movement. The great scientists came from several countries and communicated with one another through an international language—Latin—inherited from the Catholic church.

Why did the Scientific Revolution originate in Europe at this time? Historians have long pondered this complex question without a definitive answer. However, there were at least four contributing factors to the rise of the new science:

1. Freedom of thought was relatively vigorous in Europe because the variety of nations and cities prevented any one political unit from imposing conformity on everyone.
2. Europeans' contact with other peoples (such as Muslims) stimulated their curiosity and provided important knowledge, particularly in the areas of astronomy and mathematics.
3. The Greek philosophical heritage and its teaching that the world is a rational and orderly cosmos taught European intellectuals to think of nature as a rational reality that could be understood by human reason.
4. Christianity taught that the world is God's creation and thus should be studied with care. Late medieval theologians like

Anatomy Ths drawing by the anatomist
Andreas Vesalius (1514–1564) presents the
human figure in skeletal form. It expresses
the rationalistic, scientific conception of
life that grew in influence in the seventeenth and eighteenth centuries.

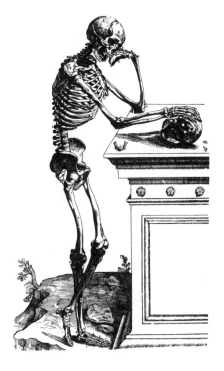

William of Occam reoriented Christian thought so as to encourage
the empirical study of nature.

Astronomy

Astronomy was a traditionally important area of study, because knowledge of the stars allowed early scientists to establish calendars (and fix
the dates of religious events like Easter) and enabled sailors to navigate
the oceans. Thus, it is not surprising that the Scientific Revolution began
in the field of astronomy.

For centuries the early astronomers followed the teachings of
Ptolemy, an ancient Greek scientist who worked in Alexandria, Egypt,
during the second century A.D. Ptolemy stipulated that the earth is at the
center of the universe and that the sun, moon, other planets, and stars are
attached to a number of transparent rings that revolve in circles around
the earth. Out beyond the last ring is heaven, the realm of God. Thus,
Ptolemy's system attempted to explain not only how the universe
operates but also the location of heaven. The system also usually worked
in practice; sailors, for example, navigated accurately on the basis of
Ptolemaic assumptions.

Copernicus Eventually, astronomers learned, through more accurate observation of heavenly bodies, that the Ptolemaic system was flawed; that planets and stars continually appeared where they should not be according to Ptolemy. In the sixteenth century, the Polish mathematician and astronomer Nicolaus Copernicus (1473–1543) set out to correct the Ptolemaic system. In his *On the Revolutions of the Heavenly Spheres*, published in 1543, Copernicus argued that the earth, rather than being stationary, revolves around the sun. He proposed, in effect, to replace the geocentric (earth-centered) view of the universe with a heliocentric (sun-centered) view.

Brahe, Kepler, and Galileo Copernicus's proposal had profound implications, since it challenged the traditional human conception of the universe and the location of heaven. Growing scientific evidence slowly increased support for the Copernican view. The Danish astronomer Tycho Brahe (1546–1601), although an opponent of the Copernican thesis for most of his life, compiled elaborate tables of astronomical observations that eventually helped to prove the heliocentric hypothesis. Johannes Kepler (1571–1630), a German mathematician, used Copernican assumptions to demonstrate that planets move in elliptical orbits rather than in circles. And, the Italian astronomer Galileo Galilei (1564–1642) was the first to use the newly developed telescope to peer into the skies. With this new device, Galileo found stars, mountains and valleys on the moon, and moons orbiting Jupiter—all of which had been unseen before.

Galileo was by far the most notorious scientist of his day. He was outspoken about the inadequacies of the Ptolemaic system. Furthermore, as an Italian he was physically close to Rome, where the hierarchy of the Catholic church resisted the assaults on Ptolemaic teachings. In a famous episode, Galileo was summoned before a church court where he was condemned and forced to recant his opinions. He was treated leniently in that he was not burned as a heretic, but the church gained the reputation of being antiscientific.

The church was not alone in its unease about the new science. Many intellectuals were also confused by the new scientific findings. The English poet John Donne wrote:

> And new philosophy calls all in doubt;
> The element of fire is quite put out;
> The sun is lost, and th' earth, and no man's wit
> Can well direct him to look for it.[2]

Not only did the new scientific views seem radical and strange to many educated people, but they also discredited the old scientific truths. As a

Galileo   Galileo was the first to use a telescope to better see the heavenly bodies, thereby helping to prove correct the Copernican conception of the universe. (The New York Public Library Picture Collection)

result, some became skeptical of the human ability to ever again know the truth.

A New Way of Thinking

Descartes   René Descartes (1596–1650), often regarded as the first modern philosopher, proposed a new method for attaining knowledge and truth. In his *Discourse on Method*, Descartes argued against the traditional sources of knowledge—Christian dogmas and ancient philosophy—claiming they were vague speculations that often proved false. Instead, he argued that human reason is the only reliable basis for knowledge. The *Discourse* begins with the assertion, "I think, therefore I am." The meaning of this statement is that one must think through and doubt everything in order to distinguish the true from the false; but if one doubts everything then the only certainty left is that someone is doubting; therefore, the act of doubting proves the existence of the human mind and establishes the first principle of a new basis for knowledge. Descartes's reasoning was in his time a declaration of independence for the rational, thinking individual. No longer did philosophers or scientists have to rely on traditional sources of knowledge; they could now think for themselves and discover truths by themselves.

Descartes's argument provided a philosophical foundation for modern science. It also helped to popularize the mechanical view of nature, for Descartes contended that nature is inanimate matter that operates like an elaborate machine. Further, he argued that human beings are different from nature, in that they have an immortal soul created by God.

Bacon Another characteristic of the Scientific Revolution was its emphasis on practicality. According to the English philosopher Francis Bacon (1561–1626), the goal of science should be the "relief of man's estate." Scientists should seek not only to understand nature but also to use their understanding to make human life better (for example, knowledge of the human body could be used to cure diseases). Bacon's proposal shows how scientific thought changed—from a "science of understanding to a science of power," a science in which practical technologies would enable people to use the powers of nature.[3]

In the *New Atlantis*, Bacon envisions a future earthly paradise where science would allow people to live longer, happier lives. This vision captured the imagination of many in the urban commercial classes of the seventeenth century, and it gradually became a fundamental justification for modern science. Over the next two to three centuries, the Baconian creed—that science should foster technology—would help to encourage the growth of modern technology.

God as Clockmaker

Newton The English mathematician and physicist Isaac Newton (1642–1727) was the last great figure of the early modern Scientific Revolution. Newton confronted a fundamental issue left unresolved by earlier scientists: If the earth and other heavenly bodies are revolving around the sun, what makes them move in an orderly rather than a chaotic manner? That is, what keeps a moving earth from flying off into outer space?

In the *Principia Mathematica,* Newton formulated the law of grav-ity—that "mutual attraction" holds planets in their orbits and pulls earthly objects toward the earth rather than away from it. He thus explained how the entire universe operates. According to Newton, the earth is part of a larger physical system, and the law of gravity applies both to heavenly and to earthly bodies. His theories were so impressive and seemed to bring together all the elements of the new physics that they came to be known as the Newtonian synthesis, which replaced the discredited Ptolemaic synthesis.

That Newton and others saw God as a clockmaker demonstrates an important point. Most early modern scientists and philosophers were devout Christians, who thought that the new science strengthened Christian beliefs by leading people to a deeper understanding of God. Bacon, for example, believed that using science to improve human life was part of a divine plan, and Newton wrote religious treatises in his later years. However, one long-term effect of the Scientific Revolution was to encourage people to interpret the world in mechanical rather than spiritual terms. The new science was quickly popularized by a number of amateur scientists in Europe and the Americas, and many of these popularizers argued that religion was just a mass of superstitions and that science held the only keys to truth and knowledge.

A CENTURY OF POLITICAL STABILITY

During the first sixty years of the seventeenth century, Europe endured a number of major wars. The war for Dutch independence from Spain continued until around mid-century. The Thirty Years' War (1618–1648) devastated much of Germany. An English constitutional conflict that included civil war during the 1640s lasted until 1688, when the Glorious Revolution reduced the power of English monarchs and gave Parliament a greater voice in English politics. The Swedes, the Poles, and the Russians struggled for control of eastern Europe, and that struggle continued into the eighteenth century.

After 1660, however, Europe began to enjoy a century of relative calm, political stability, and, in some areas, economic growth. There were some conflicts, such as the various wars by which Louis XIV sought to gain more territory for France and the Seven Years' War (1756–1763). But these conflicts were not large enough to undermine the general stability during the late seventeenth century and the first two-thirds of the eighteenth century.

Evidence of stability and growth was the emergence of very large cities. By the late eighteenth century, London held a population of over 800,000, Paris somewhat less, and Naples about half a million. Amster-dam, Madrid, and Vienna were growing as well. These growing cities

TECHNOLOGY
The Clock and the Clockwork Universe

Newton and others used the metaphor of a clock to explain the new physics to the educated public. Nature was characterized as a simple machine operating according to regular laws, in the same way that a clock regularly counts off the hours and days. The presumption was that a great clockmaker—God—wound the world up and started it running.

By the seventeenth century, the mechanical clock was increasingly prominent in Western Civilization. The ancient world had used sundials and water clocks, but clouds and darkness interfered with the former and the latter were impractical in northern Europe because they froze in winter. The first European mechanical clocks appeared in the thirteenth century in medieval cities, and by the late fourteenth century some cities had clock towers that used chimes to strike the hours. By the sixteenth century, small household clocks and wristwatches began to appear in England and the Netherlands.

Before the invention of the mechanical clock, most people organized their days according to the rhythms of nature. They began the day at sunrise, ended it at sundown, and never knew or cared precisely what time it was. The mechanical clock allowed and even encouraged people, particularly those living in cities, to organize their days more punctually. Thus, businesspeople sought to impose an orderly, timed routine on their employees, and many workers came to see the clock as a tyrannical force controlling their lives (see Chapter 15).

Town Clock   *Above a city gate in Bern, Switzerland, is a clock that signals the hours for townspeople. In old cities, the buildings were packed in tightly so that more structures could be within the city walls for protection. (Culver Pictures)*

Figure 12.1   Europe in 1763

were significant for at least two reasons. First, they were usually capital cities that functioned as political centers of territorial states. As such, they gradually imposed administrative and social order throughout the states (for example, London dominated England and Paris ruled France). Second, the cities served as economic hubs of national markets. The large cities lived off the produce of the surrounding countryside, and national economic markets were gradually formed by the process of transporting goods to and from the cities. Often, the cities were centers of wealth and innovation. By the eighteenth century, London and Paris were competing to see which would be the first to have paved streets and street lights.

The Netherlands and England

The two wealthiest cities were Amsterdam in the Netherlands and London in England, for both were beneficiaries of a geographical shift in European and world commerce. Italy had been the commercial leader of Europe during the late Middle Ages and the Renaissance, but that leadership slowly disintegrated for several reasons. One was the growth of oceanic shipping, which fostered the prevalence of Atlantic over Mediterranean trade. Another was the slow emergence of territorial states (France and England, for example) that could foster larger-scale economic activity. Yet another reason was Italian population expansion, which outpaced food production and thereby created widespread poverty. In addition, the rise of Protestantism encouraged an increase in literacy and education in northern Europe because Protestantism encouraged believers to study the Bible. By the late sixteenth and seventeenth centuries, commercial power was passing first to Amsterdam and then to London.

London surpassed Amsterdam by the eighteenth century, largely because England had a greater population and more resources than the Netherlands. The English capital was at that time an exciting place to be (at least for the wealthier classes). The writer Samuel Johnson said: "When a man is tired of London he is tired of life, for there is in London all that life can afford."[4] Wealth was being created by large merchant companies—such as the Muscovy Company and the East India Company—that held government monopolies to carry products to and from various parts of the world. These companies helped to make England the wealthiest nation in Europe during the eighteenth century.

Another source of English and Dutch prosperity was an agricultural revolution that began in the Netherlands in the seventeenth century, spread to England, and then to much of the rest of Western Europe. The revolution consisted of three elements:

1. The old three-field system (in which one-third of farmland lay fallow and uncultivated each year) was gradually replaced by continual farming of all land, as new fodder crops could both replenish the nutrients in the soil and feed livestock.
2. Livestock thus increased in size and quality and supplied more manure that was, in turn, used to enrich the soil.
3. New and better farm implements such as hoes and plows were developed.

The agricultural revolution resulted in increased food production. Between 1730 and 1750, for example, England enjoyed an unusually long succession of good harvests. Greater food supply was one of the factors that allowed England to start an Industrial Revolution in the mid-eighteenth century (see Chapter 15).

France

Except for England and the Netherlands, most European states continued to gain their wealth from agriculture rather than from commerce. France was the most prestigious and powerful of the agricultural states during the late seventeenth and eighteenth centuries. French prestige was personified in Louis XIV, king of France from 1643 to 1715, one of the longest recorded reigns in history.

Louis XIV was often called the "Sun King," because just as the sun was the center of the universe he was the center of France. His primary goal was to gather all power into his hands. One way of doing this was to dazzle those who came near him, so Louis behaved and dressed ostentatiously. By doing so, he displayed his superiority over others. He also built a glamorous palace at Versailles (near Paris), from which he governed France. Versailles became a center of elaborate court ceremonials and parties and a symbol of French prestige. Despite the magnificence of Versailles, however, life there was often crude. Toilet facilities were virtually nonexistent, and people often urinated in corners of hallways. At meals, Louis sometimes amused himself by throwing food at the women. One woman, winged by a piece of fruit, retaliated by throwing a salad at the Sun King's head.

Louis also sought to enhance his power by increasing the wealth of France. The dominant economic theory of his time was *mercantilism,* which holds that the amount of wealth in the world remains constant and thus a nation's share can increase only at the expense of others. Like most other monarchs of his time, Louis was a mercantilist. He directed his government to subsidize those businesses most important to the national economy and to encourage French exports. He also engaged in wars designed to expand French boundaries and to increase national territory and wealth. Most of these wars were not particularly brutal or destructive, since armies were small and strategists preferred to win victories through skillful maneuvering of troops rather than through pitched battles. However, Louis's ambitions were so obvious that much of the rest of Europe, especially the English and the Dutch, eventually united to oppose him. By the end of his life, he had added very little land to France, and on his deathbed Louis conceded that he had liked war too much. The expense of Louis's wars would continue to haunt France, since the growth of the national debt was one of the underlying causes of the French Revolution that began late in the eighteenth century (see Chapter 15).

Russia

Among the other nations of Europe, Russia was potentially the most powerful and influential. The history of Russia is examined in detail in Chapter 13, but Peter the Great—one of Russia's greatest rulers—should be discussed at this point.

Peter (reigned 1682–1725) was an extraordinary character, a giant (nearly seven feet tall at a time when most European men averaged little

Louis XIV   (1638–1715) Known as the "Sun King," Louis the XIV's reign was characterized by absolute monarchical authority—his most famous phrase was "I am the
state." His instigation of numerous wars greatly increased the French national debt,
which was one of the causes of the French Revolution of the late eighteenth century
(see Chapter 15). (French Cultural Services)

over five feet) who was fond of orgies, drinking bouts, and deformed
people such as dwarfs and hunchbacks. He inherited a Russia that was
backward and isolated from Europe and began the process of forcing his
people to modernize. After capturing some land on the Baltic Sea, Peter
built the new city of St. Petersburg to serve as a Russian gateway to
Europe. Through that gateway, Russia slowly started to import European
engineering skills, scientific knowledge, and styles of behavior. Peter's

zeal to Europeanize Russia led him to do some extraordinary things. Once he ordered his nobles to eat European-style salads; when one noble refused, Peter stuffed lettuce and vinegar down the man's throat until the man's nose bled.

Russia was still a backward nation at the time of Peter's death in 1725, but the rest of Europe was becoming aware of a new great power rising in the east. That awareness would increase later in the eighteenth century, as Russia gained new territory around the Black Sea and took land from a disintegrating Poland.

The Enlightened Despots

Several eighteenth-century monarchs were known as the "enlightened despots," absolute rulers who were reputedly different from their predecessors in two important ways. First, in an increasingly secular age, they said that they governed in the name of the state or of the people as well as in the name of God. Second, they professed to be "enlightened," in that they tried to institute reforms and good government that would strengthen their countries.

One enlightened despot was Charles III of Spain (reigned 1759–1788). He sought to rejuvenate Spain by curbing the power of the Inquisition (the Catholic church court that punished heretics), encouraging the growth of industries, and removing restrictions on commerce. Another was Joseph II (reigned 1780–1790), ruler of the Hapsburg Empire. The Hapsburg Empire was a collection of peoples centered on the Danube River in southeastern Europe and united by being ruled by the Hapsburg family. Joseph II issued literally hundreds of reforming edicts in an attempt to modernize his domains, but few of them were effective. Perhaps the most famous of the enlightened despots was Frederick the Great of Prussia (1740–1786). Prussia (in northeastern Europe along the Baltic coast) was a state dominated by its army, and Frederick tried to encourage his subjects to serve the state in the same disciplined and efficient fashion as his army did. He claimed to be creating a well-ordered state, in which all people would be both disciplined and happy.

The enlightened despots were of only limited significance. Few of their reforms had any lasting impact, and although they sometimes said they were working for the people, they had no real intention of allowing the people to participate in government. The enlightened despots are significant because they represent a prominent example of a shift in thought—from a religiously oriented political theory (that monarchs serve God) to a more secular political theory (that monarchs serve the state or the people). This shift in thought is usually associated with the Enlightenment, as we will see later in the chapter.

The Common People

While some intellectuals created great ideas and some monarchs sought fame and glory, the common people continued to live as they had for centuries. Most were peasants trying to wrest a living from the land. Most of those in eastern Europe were serfs, under the control of their masters and legally obligated to remain on the land they tilled. In Western Europe, most peasants were legally free.

Peasants lived in the thousands of villages that dotted Europe. In these villages, there were some gradations of wealth, as a relatively few peasant families slowly accumulated some land and material well-being. Most peasants, however, were poor, usually malnourished, and lived in crude housing. Their clothing was always dirty, since they usually had only one change of dress. The peasants' greatest fear was running out of food. During times of famine, peasants rioted in a desperate effort to force the authorities to provide sustenance.

The lower classes in the cities were also characterized by some social gradations. Artisans (craftspeople who made clothing, for example) were sometimes relatively well-off. The unemployed or underemployed usually had to resort to begging to survive. Life was so harsh for some lower-class families that they abandoned their new born infants in the city streets. It was the job of some municipal workers to collect these abandoned babies each morning and take them to orphanages.

However, life for people in the cities and countryside did improve to a small degree. The agricultural revolution mentioned earlier enabled some peasants to become more prosperous, although others lost their land and fell into desperate poverty. More generally, economic conditions were slowly improving because of the absence of major wars and increased production of new crops, particularly the potato, originally brought to Europe from the Americas. Better economic conditions probably helped women more than men, since in bad times women usually suffered the most from lack of food and malnutrition. Another thing that helped women was the growing understanding of contraception, which enabled many women to assert some control over the number of children they bore.

THE ENLIGHTENMENT

"Light" was the most popular metaphor used by European intellectuals during the late seventeenth and eighteenth centuries—the English spoke of an age of *Enlightenment*, the French of *les lumières*, and the Italians of *illuminismo*. Many intellectuals believed that modern science and human reason were enlightening people by liberating them from the tyranny of ancient superstitions and myths.

The new enlightened way of thinking included at least two radically new assumptions:

1. A growing number of people began to believe that the chief goal of life is happiness on this earth rather than eternal bliss in heaven. They assumed that the new science was giving human beings greater control over nature and that nature could be used to make life better (for example, through increased food production).
2. Intellectuals argued that ideas and beliefs are relative to their time and place, that no beliefs are absolutely and eternally true for all people at all times.

One source of the new outlook was the growing knowledge of other cultures in the Americas and in Asia. The people of these cultures usually believed and thought differently from Europeans, and some intellectuals concluded that European ways of life were not always necessarily better than other ways of life. Another source was increasing knowledge of history, which revealed that ideas and beliefs change over the course of time. One effect of this growing relativization of ideas and beliefs was to create spiritual and intellectual discomfort for many people. After all, it is always easier and more comfortable to presume what is true and false, for there is no need to question or argue about things. But another effect was to produce greater creativity, since the questioning of old ideas led intellectuals to think new thoughts and ponder new beliefs.

A New Political Theory

One of the most influential creations of Enlightenment intellectuals was a new political theory. For over a thousand years, European political thought had rested on religious foundations. Most political theorists (with a few exceptions like the Renaissance writer, Niccolo Machiavelli) assumed that governments were ultimately established by God and that certain people—monarchs—were designated by God to rule. This assumption was known as the "divine right of kings." An accompanying belief was that the welfare of society—the common good—was more important than the well-being of any individual.

In the seventeenth and eighteenth centuries, the divine right theory was gradually replaced by a new *social contract* theory. In this theory, political thinkers used an imaginary experiment—the "state of nature"— to analyze human society. They asked, in effect, these questions: What were people like in a state of nature, the state of human existence before governments were formed? Why and how were governments established? Different thinkers gave somewhat different answers to these questions, but most agreed that governments were formed by some kind of social contract—an agreement among people to organize themselves into a society and a government. One conclusion from social contract theorizing was that individuals existed before governments, so the individual is in one sense more important and fundamental than society. Another was that individuals have certain natural rights (such as the right to property) derived from "natural laws"—laws established by God, the author of nature. A third was that governments are a human rather than a divine creation.

The social contract theory developed for several reasons. First, European intellectuals were increasingly inclined to explain things in human rather than divine terms. Second, in some countries, especially England, the aristocratic and business classes were gaining political influence, and the social contract theory was used by them to oppose monarchical claims that kings rule by divine right and should have absolute power. Third, the social contract theory responded to a new economic situation created by the discovery of North and South America. The existence of a vast array of natural resources (land, water, and so on) in the New World allowed Europeans to envision a future filled with greater economic prosperity. The social contract theorists were philosophers of prosperity, in that they recognized the new availability of natural resources and developed a theory that focused on the individual's pursuit of material well-being and happiness.

Hobbes   Thomas Hobbes (1588–1679) was the first major social contract theorist. Perhaps because he lived through the murderous chaos of the English civil war, Hobbes was skeptical about human nature and the existence of God. According to his political theory, presented in *Leviathan,* people are egoistic creatures who, when in a state of nature, struggled and fought with one another to gain wealth and power. Life was "nasty, brutish, and short." To gain social peace, people had to form a social contract that established a government—preferably an absolute monarchy—strong enough to control everyone. Thus, Hobbes used social contract theory to justify absolutism, but his argument was based on humanistic grounds rather than on the divine right of kings.

Locke   John Locke (1632–1704) was more optimistic than Hobbes. In *Two Treatises of Government,* Locke argues that, in a state of nature, humans were free and intelligent and possessed certain natural rights (such as the right to private property). Government was formed through a social contract intended to protect and preserve these rights.

The short-term effect of Locke's theory was to justify intellectually the Glorious Revolution of 1688, in which English people of property gained greater influence in the English government. The long-term effect of his theory was to foster the idea that people have rights and thus should be represented in government (an idea that would later influence the founders of the United States). Despite his innovative thinking, Locke

John Locke (1632–1704)   An English philosopher and physician, Locke spent more than 20 years developing his empirical theories of human understanding. Locke's ideas, expressed most classically in his treatise *An Essay Concerning Human Understanding*, became one of the foundations of contemporary philosophy. (Art Reference Bureau Inc.)

was no democrat; he believed that only those with property should have governmental representation.

Locke's optimism also underlay his theory of knowledge, contained in *An Essay Concerning Human Understanding*. He rejected the traditional assumption that humans are controlled by heredity. Knowledge, he said, originates with sensory impressions (what people see, feel, smell, taste) that are imprinted on the mind. The mind itself is a *tabula rasa* ("blank tablet") that receives sense impressions and organizes them into what we call "knowledge." Thus, humans learn from their environment, and since the environment is always changing, people can constantly learn more and become both more intelligent and free. Locke's idea that people can learn and grow intellectually influenced many people in the eighteenth century and encouraged the assumption that human society can continually improve.

Locke clearly thought of society as a collection of individuals who have some freedom and opportunity to compete with one another. That raised a question: How does a society that tolerates competition and even conflict achieve some degree of social peace and harmony? The answer was the essentially new idea that individual competition leads naturally to the good of the community. For example, individuals may engage in economic competition to gain greater wealth for themselves, but in the process they create greater prosperity for the entire community.

Mandeville   Bernard de Mandeville (1670–1733) was the first to elaborate on this theory that "private vices" lead to "public benefits." In *Fable of the Bees* (1714), he tells the story of a beehive in which vices like greed help the bees to thrive:

> The worst of all the multitude
> Did something for the common good. . . .
> Thus vice nursed ingenuity,
> Which join'd with time and industry,
> Had carry'd life's conveniences,
> It's real pleasures, comforts, ease,
> To such height, the very poor
> Lived better than the rich before.[5]

Mandeville's fable outraged many people because it implied that evil people could prosper and be happy and that "happiness" was not necessarily connected with "goodness." These ideas were completely foreign to the intellectual traditions of Christian thought and Greek philosophy, both of which assume that "goodness" is necessary for "happiness." But Mandeville's argument expressed an attitude that was increasingly popular in the eighteenth century and later. The economic philosopher Adam Smith would later use that attitude as a basic component of nineteenth-century capitalism.

Rousseau   Jean-Jacques Rousseau (1712–1778) was the most radical of the social contract theorists. His *Social Contract* begins with the ringing assertion: "All men are born free, yet everywhere they are in chains." Rousseau believed that in a state of nature *all* people (not just those with property) were equal and that the creation of civilized society caused social inequality. To restore equality, society had to be based on a new social contract that Rousseau called the "general will"—an agreement or consensus among all men (not women) on how society should be governed. Once a general will was formed, the community was, in Rousseau's view, a democratic force entitled to enforce its decisions on everyone. Thus, one thrust of Rousseau's thought was to encourage a kind of radical democracy that excluded women; another was to place great value on the will of the community and to oppose individualism, which he regarded as selfishness.

Rousseau and the other social contract theorists influenced many of the people who carried out the political revolutions—the American, the French, and the Latin American—of the late eighteenth and early nineteenth centuries. The social contract theorists helped create an intellectual climate favorable to political change. Their criticisms undermined old political beliefs about the divine right of kings and their proposals provided intellectual justification for a new political order.

France—The Center of the Enlightenment

By the eighteenth century, France, particularly Paris, was the center of the Enlightenment. Those who taught Enlightenment ideals were known as *philosophes*. The *philosophes*, unlike most formal philosophers, used rational thought to criticize existing social institutions and practices. Because Christianity was central to traditional eighteenth-century intellectual and social life, many of their criticisms were aimed at religious beliefs and customs. The *philosophes* argued, for example, that Christianity is largely a collection of superstitious stories and that Biblical accounts of miracles are hoaxes designed to induce ignorant people to accept Christian doctrine. They also argued that the Catholic priesthood deliberately propagated these hoaxes so to maintain the church's influence. Thus, the *philosophes* were staunchly anticlerical; that is, hostile to the organized priesthood.

Although some of the *philosophes* were atheists, most were *deists*. Deism portrays God as a supreme rational being who created the world and then left it alone. Deists believe that God is properly worshipped by those who live rationally, not by those who believe in miracles, mysteries, faith, or other vague notions. *Reason* was the watchword for the *philosophes*. They wanted a society that would cultivate the search for knowledge, be tolerant, and encourage human progress. They also wanted governments that would treat people humanely, so they argued against customs like witchcraft trials and torture for criminals. Although the *philosophes* did not believe in political democracy, they did foster the idea that all people are ultimately governed by the same rational God and are therefore equal in that sense. They claimed to be liberating the human spirit, but they usually accepted traditional assumptions about male superiority and therefore opposed the liberation of women. Ironically, though, the ideals of toleration and openness that the *philosophes* fostered helped a few women to become publicly influential. In England, for example, Jane Austen became one of the most prominent novelists of the early nineteenth century. In Paris, several aristocratic women had some impact on the Enlightenment because of their involvement in salons—combination dinner parties and discussion groups at which Enlightenment intellectuals met to exchange ideas. The salons were arranged and sponsored by wealthy women, such as Ninon de Lenclos and Julie de Lespinasse, who often attracted guests with their intelligence and wit.

Voltaire Of all the Enlightenment figures in France, Voltaire (1694–1778) was by far the most famous. He personified Enlightenment ideals, in that he was intellectual, rational, humane, witty, and sensible. Voltaire lived by writing plays, histories, essays, and letters in which he criticized wars, bigotry, and religious persecution. He hoped and campaigned for a more tolerant world. One ringing statement attributed to him was: "I disapprove of what you say, but I will defend to the death your right to say it."

Of all *philosophes* of the Enlightenment, Voltaire spoke most strongly for the ideal of toleration. Many *philosophes* argued that truth is unattainable, so those who hold divergent or heretical views should not be persecuted. That argument gradually helped make toleration an appealing ideal in the eyes of many. Another factor that encouraged the growth of toleration was the memory of the religious wars of the sixteenth and seventeenth centuries. In those wars, different religious groups often fought and persecuted one another until gradually a growing number of governments became more tolerant in order to end the constant hostility and fighting.

Voltaire was also influential in what later became known as *anticlericalism*, a hostile attitude toward the power and prerogatives of the clergy. In the nineteenth century, anticlericalism was especially strong in France, Italy, Spain, and Germany, where the Catholic church exercised considerable authority over education, marriage, divorce laws, and other aspects of a person's life.

Other Philosophes Another *philosophe*, the Baron de Montesquieu (1689–1755), greatly influenced political thought. His *The Spirit of the Laws* compares the legal institutions of many societies and celebrates the British constitution as the best form of government. Montesquieu believed that the British system, with its separation of powers between monarch and Parliament, was a good protection against tyranny. Two other *philosophes*, Denis Diderot (1713–1784) and Jean Le Rond d'Alembert (1717–1783), compiled an *Encyclopedia* that includes hundreds of articles that rationally analyzed religion, politics, economic activities, and many other subjects.

Most of the well-known *philosophes* came from the upper-middle classes. However, there were hundreds of obscure enlightened writers from the lower classes whose names have long since been forgotten. These lesser-known *philosophes* had acquired some education and were part of a "literary underground" that fought the French government's attempts to censor books and ideas. The literary underground consisted of publishing houses that produced books condemned by the government, book smugglers, and poverty-stricken writers. The writers usually survived by writing anything that would sell—pornographic novels, slanderous attacks on prominent people, and enlightened criticisms of French society and government. Thus, they helped popularize all sorts of unorthodox ideas.

Nations other than France also produced Enlightenment intellectuals. Some of these *philosophes* fostered the study of history. Giambattista Vico (1688–1744), a relatively unknown philosopher from Naples, proclaimed in *The New Science* that analyzing history is the supreme form of human learning. He believed that history is the story of human creativity, the story of all that humans have ever thought and done. Vico's thought had little impact in his own day, but he eventually influenced Rousseau, Karl Marx, and others. Much more famous was the English historian Edward Gibbon (1737–1794), whose *Decline and Fall of the Roman Empire* is an eloquent account of the end of ancient history. Consistent with Enlightenment hostility to Christianity, Gibbon contended that the rise of the Christian religion was one of the primary causes of the fall of Rome.

Another connection between religion and history was explained by the German writer Gotthold Ephraim Lessing (1729–1781). In the *Education of the Human Race,* Lessing argues that religion evolved historically, that human understanding of religious truth had increased over time and was continuing to increase. According to Lessing, no one can ever have final, absolute knowledge of God or God's laws because that knowledge is always growing and changing.

Religion and Music during the Enlightenment

Even though many Enlightenment intellectuals were sharply critical of organized religion, most people in Europe and the Americas were still Christians. A notable spokesman for traditional Christianity was the English minister and satirist Jonathan Swift (1667–1745). Swift argued that people can live decently and humanely if they follow the common sense given them by God. Most people are foolish, however, he thought, and in *Gulliver's Travels* Swift satirizes human stupidities. Gulliver is a European who visits various strange lands—one inhabited by giants, another by pygmies—in which the people point out the absurdity of many European ideas and customs.

Christianity also continued to appeal to most common people, and religious revivals occurred in some areas. *Pietism,* which stresses enthusiastic preaching and praying, swept through much of Germany in the second half of the eighteenth century. In England, John Wesley led a religious revival and helped strengthen the Methodist church. In the British colonies in North America, a movement known as the *Great Awakening*—an enthusiasm for emotional preaching and camp meetings—spread during the eighteenth century.

Religious impulses were also expressed through musical compositions. One of the greatest composers in European history was Johann Sebastian Bach (1685–1750). A devout Lutheran, Bach produced numerous organ and vocal works for performance during church services. Examples of the latter include the great oratorios, *St. John Passion* and *St. Matthew Passion.* He said once that music is "for the honor of God and the recreation of the spirit."

George Frederick Handel (1685–1759), a German composer who lived much of his life in England, created the *Messiah,* one of the most popular Christian musical compositions. The *Messiah* is an oratorio that uses the words of the Bible to tell the story of the coming of Jesus Christ. (Both Bach and Handel also composed many great secular works.)

Less overtly religious than Bach or Handel were Joseph Haydn (1732–1809) and Wolfgang Amadeus Mozart (1756–1791). Haydn said he was trying to express a "moral attitude" in his music. He was the "father" of both the string quartet and the symphony; during his long career Haydn wrote over one hundred symphonies. His younger colleague Mozart (an astounding prodigy as a child) also wrote in those forms and many others as well. Some of his operas express Enlightenment ideals of equality and benevolence.

The Significance of the Enlightenment

The philosophy of Immanuel Kant (1724–1804) reveals the ultimate significance of the Enlightenment. The most fundamental claim of the Enlightenment was that the world is a rational reality, that human reason can understand how nature operates and can also make human society more humane. Kant, more than anyone else, demonstrated philosophically just how important is the role of human reasoning abilities. In his *Critique of Pure Reason,* Kant postulates that all human knowledge begins with sensory experience but that this experience becomes knowledge only after it has been organized and ordered by the human mind. For example, when a person sees something, the eyes and nervous system transmit various sensory impressions to the mind. The mind quickly organizes these impressions according to certain categories inherent within it, two of which are space and time. The mind then "knows" that something exists in a particular space at a particular point in time. The mind, according to Kant, is an active, creative agent that organizes reality into what we call knowledge. It is, therefore, central to all of human experience.

CONCLUSION

The Scientific Revolution and the Enlightenment involved only a limited number of people, intellectuals who had little direct influence on the majority of people living in their day. But these few intellectuals defined many of the ideas that have dominated Western Civilization during the last three centuries. The belief in the importance of experimental science, the belief that humans can create their own governments, the belief in toleration and freedom of thought, the belief that humans can use their reasoning abilities to make the world better—all these ideas became prominent during the seventeenth and eighteenth centuries. Their influence would grow during the nineteenth and twentieth centuries.

THINGS YOU SHOULD KNOW

The Scientific Revolution
How modern science differs from
    earlier science
Copernicus
Brahe
Kepler
Galileo
Descartes
Bacon
Newton
The mechanical clock
The agricultural revolution of the
    seventeenth and eighteenth cen-
    turies
Louis XIV
Peter the Great
The enlightened despots
The Enlightenment

Social contract theory
Hobbes
Locke
Mandeville
Rousseau
The *philosophes*
Voltaire
Montesquieu
Vico
Gibbon
Lessing
Swift
J. S. Bach
Handel
Haydn
Mozart
Kant

SUGGESTED READINGS

Marie Boas, *The Scientific Renaissance, 1450–1630* (New York: Harper and Row, 1966) provides good historical background for the Scientific Revolution. Thomas Kuhn, *The Structure of Scientific Revolution* (Chicago: Univ. of Chicago Press,

1962) is a challenging but excellent analysis of how and why scientific revolutions occur. A standard introduction to the history of the Scientific Revolution is Herbert Butterfield, *The Origins of Modern Science, 1300–1800* (New York: Free Press, 1965). A more recent work is Margaret C. Jacob, *The Cultural Meaning of the Scientific Revolution* (Philadelphia: Temple Univ. Press, 1988). For the significance of clocks during the Scientific Revolution and later, see David Landes, *Revolution in Time* (Cambridge, Mass.: Belknap Press of Harvard Univ. Press, 1983) and Carlo M. Cipolla, *Clocks and Culture, 1300–1700* (New York: Norton, 1977).

For intellectual history in general, Franklin L. Baumer, *Modern European Thought: Continuity and Change in Ideas, 1600–1950* (New York: Macmillan, 1977) offers a stimulating synthesis. More specifically on the Enlightenment is Peter Gay, *The Enlightenment: An Interpretation* (New York: Norton, 1977) and Paul Hazard, *The European Mind, 1680–1715* (Cleveland: World Publishing Co., 1935). William Ophuls, *Ecology and the Politics of Scarcity: Prologue to a Political Theory of the Steady State* (San Francisco: W. H. Freeman, 1977) provides a unique analysis of modern European political thought from the perspective of twentieth-century ecological concerns. Robert Darnton, *The Literary Underground of the Old Regime* (Cambridge, Mass.: Harvard Univ. Press, 1982) is an interesting study of those lesser-known Enlightenment writers who helped spread the ideas of the era to the educated public.

NOTES

[1]Franklin L. Baumer, *Modern European Thought: Continuity and Change in Ideas, 1600–1950* (New York: Macmillan, 1977), pp. 26–27.

[2]Quoted in A. Lloyd Moote, *The Seventeenth Century: Europe in Ferment* (Lexington, Mass.: D. C. Heath, 1970), p. 91.

[3]John Herman Randall, Jr., *The Career of Philosophy*, from vol. 1 entitled *From the Middle Ages to the Enlightenment* (New York: Columbia Univ. Press, 1962), p. 224.

[4]Quoted in Carlo M. Cipolla, *Before the Industrial Revolution: European Society and Economy, 1000–1700*, 2nd ed. (New York: W. W. Norton, 1980), p. 293.

[5]Quoted in Otto Mayr, *Authority, Liberty, and Automatic Machinery in Early Modern Europe* (Baltimore: Johns Hopkins Univ. Press, 1986), pp. 185–86.

13

The Expansion of Western Civilization, 1300 to 1800

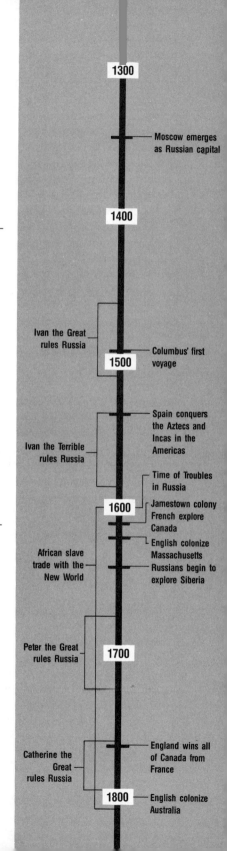

1300

Moscow emerges as Russian capital

1400

Ivan the Great rules Russia

1500

Columbus' first voyage

Spain conquers the Aztecs and Incas in the Americas

Ivan the Terrible rules Russia

Time of Troubles in Russia

1600

Jamestown colony

French explore Canada

English colonize Massachusetts

African slave trade with the New World

Russians begin to explore Siberia

Peter the Great rules Russia

1700

Catherine the Great rules Russia

England wins all of Canada from France

1800

English colonize Australia

For a thousand years after the fall of Rome, Western Civilization was centered in western and southern Europe. During the sixteenth to the eighteenth centuries, however, the influence of Western Civilization expanded. It expanded eastward as the Russians became more Europeanized and the Russian state conquered territory all the way to the Pacific Ocean. It expanded westward as the Spanish and Portuguese colonized much of South and Central America and the English and French competed for control of North America. It also expanded into the southern Pacific during the late eighteenth century, as Europeans settled in Australia and New Zealand. The result of this expansion, according to the contemporary historian Alfred W. Crosby, Jr., was to establish several "neo-Europes," areas far from mainland Europe where Western traditions and culture helped to define these new societies and nations.[1]

The growth of neo-Europes was made possible by an enormous migration of peoples from both inside and outside of Europe. Russians moved into Siberia, Swedes into Finland, and the English and Scottish into Ireland. Many Spanish migrated to South and Central America, many English and Germans came to North America, Africans were brought as slaves to both South and North America, and English convicts were among the first colonizers of Australia. Most of the migrants were seeking a better way of life and greater economic opportunity than was available in the European homes they left. Some of the migrants—African slaves and European convicts—were forced to emigrate.

In this chapter, we examine several important aspects of this great migration of peoples and the expansion of Western Civilization. These include the origins and expansion of Russia, the African slave trade, Spanish and Portuguese America, English and French America, and Europeans in Asia and the South Pacific.

RUSSIA

Much of Russia is a flat steppe, a vast prairie interrupted only by rivers and a few mountains and extending thousands of miles from central Europe into Siberia. That geographical reality had a profound impact on Russian history. The absence of natural obstacles like rugged mountain ranges made it easier for Asian nomads (Huns, Turks, Mongols) to invade and sometimes conquer parts of southern Russia. These nomadic invasions were frequent and eventually forced the Russians to create a strong and powerful military-based state in order to survive. Once this strong state was developed in Russia, the Russians took advantage of the flat landscape to expand their influence and to build a large empire across much of the Eurasian plain.

Kievan Russia

The first Russian state was formed in the ninth century A.D. in the city of Kiev. The Kievan state established its dominance over the eastern Slavic peoples who lived there (located in present-day western Soviet Russia). Kiev was a commercial city located on a trade route that connected Scandinavia and northern Russia to the Byzantine Empire. It thus introduced the East Slavs to the religious and cultural heritage of Byzantium. In A.D. 988–989, the Kievan Prince Vladimir renounced traditional paganism, converted to Byzantine Christianity, and began to encourage and force the people he ruled to do the same. By adhering to the Byzantine variant of Christianity, the Russians became religiously and culturally distinct, both from the Muslims to their south, and from the Roman Catholic Christians to their west. They also gained access to the artistic, architectural, and religious riches of Byzantium. As a result, Kiev became known as a city of religious beauty:

> a city glistening with the light of holy icons,
> 	fragrant with incense,
> ringing with praise and holy, heavenly songs.[2]

Kievan Russia prospered about three centuries until it eventually weakened. Recurring civil wars were caused by East Slavic princes fighting one another. Growing Italian commerce in the Mediterranean weakened the business economy in Kiev during the eleventh and twelfth centuries. In addition, foreigners attacked the Kievan state. Most important were the Mongols, who drove across Eurasia in the thirteenth century and eventually conquered Kievan Russia in 1237–1240. Beginning with Genghis Khan, Mongol rule continued well into the fifteenth century. In the late thirteenth century, the Mongols established the *Pax Mongolica* ("Mongolian peace"), a peaceful era in central Eurasia. Western Europeans benefited from the Mongol Empire, for it facilitated trade and cultural exchange between Europe and Asia.

The Rise of Moscow

The thirteenth and fourteenth centuries were a chaotic time in Russia; the Mongols controlled the south, the Lithuanians attacked and conquered much of what is today southwestern Soviet Russia, and the Swedes and Germans periodically invaded in the north and west. To escape these enemies, many Russians left their native lands in the south and sought refuge in the cold, dense forests of northern Russia (where they confronted the bear, a powerful and ferocious animal that became an integral part of Russian folklore as well as a symbol of Russia itself).

Here in the north, a previously obscure town—Moscow—slowly became the new center of Russian government and culture.

Moscow originated in the mid-twelfth century as a small fortress city. Located near the headwaters of several river trade routes (the Volga, the Don, the Dnieper) and ruled by a succession of able princes, Moscow gradually expanded as Muscovite rulers asserted their authority over nearby lands. Then, in the early fourteenth century, Moscow gained spiritual and cultural prestige when the chief bishop of the Russian church, Theognost, established his residence there and thus made Moscow the religious capital of Russia.

By the early fifteenth century, Muscovite princes were repudiating Mongol overlordship and thereby beginning to restore the independence of the Russian people. When the Turks captured Constantinople and destroyed the Byzantine Empire in 1453, the political and religious leaders of Moscow began to describe their city as the center of a new Christian empire—a "third Rome" succeeding the Christian Rome destroyed a thousand years earlier by German barbarians and the Byzantine Constantinople now in the hands of Muslims. Moscow thus acquired a sense of mission, as described by a fifteenth-century monk in addressing his prince: "But this third, new Rome, the Universal Apostolic Church under thy mighty rule radiates forth the Orthodox Christian faith to the ends of the earth more brightly than the sun."[3]

The reign of Ivan III (the Great, 1462–1505) was a significant juncture in Russian history. Ivan was the first Russian ruler to call himself a *tsar* or *czar* (derived from the Roman word *caesar*), thus indicating that he saw himself as the emperor of an independent and great empire. Ivan is most significant because he defeated the Mongols around 1480, ending Mongol domination of the Russians, and because he increased Muscovite territory by expanding westward toward the Baltic Sea.

By the sixteenth century, Muscovite Russia was an intensely religious society located in a harsh frontier area. Historian James H. Billington describes Muscovite society through two symbols—the "icon" and the "axe." Icons—paintings on wood of religious figures such as Christ or the Virgin Mary—exemplified the deeply religious side of Russian culture. They appeared almost everywhere and were used, for example, to lead political and religious processions or to guide Russian armies into battle. The axe represented the frontier conditions of Muscovite Russia. It was a tool used by peasants to clear the forests and to drive off wild animals; it was also used by the government to behead criminals and invading enemies.[4]

The Muscovite combination of religion and cruelty was most clearly manifested in Tsar Ivan IV (the Terrible, reigned 1533–1584). Ivan the Terrible was in some ways a devout man, for he often made extended pilgrimages to religious shrines. But he was also an extremely cruel

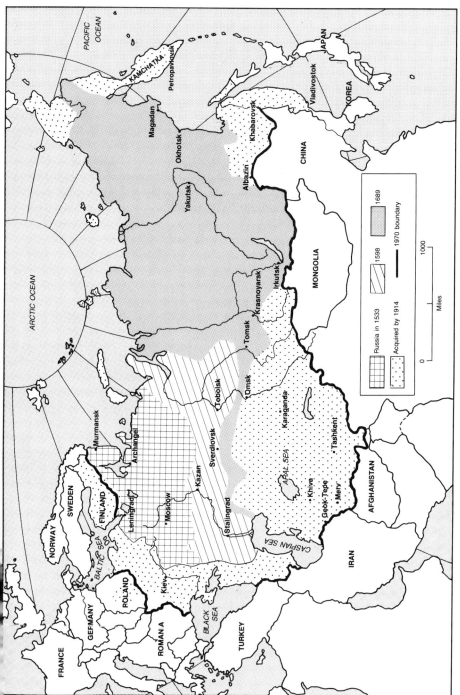

Figure 13.1 The Growth of Russia, 1533–1914

Legend:
- Russia in 1533 — 1598
- Acquired by 1914 — 1689
- 1970 boundary

Miles: 0 — 1000

emperor, torturing and killing those who opposed him. Ivan's cruelty was the product of both personal madness and a desire to increase his monarchical power. He believed, as one of his advisors told him, that "a Tsar [who] is feared and wise will see his realm enlarged and his name praised in all the corners of the earth. . . . A realm without dread is like a horse beneath a Tsar without a bridle."[5]

Ivan the Terrible, like many of his predecessors, expanded the territory under Muscovite control, pushing Russian boundaries southward toward the Caspian Sea. Also during his reign, Cossack explorers began to penetrate into Siberia. (The Cossacks were a people from southern Russia known as great warriors and skilled horsemen.) In 1533, when Ivan came to power, Russian territory included about 900,000 square miles; by the end of his rule in 1584, Russia extended over 3.3 million square miles.

The Time of Troubles

Shortly after Ivan's death, Russia entered into a chaotic period known as the *Time of Troubles* (1598–1613), during which the Russians faced political turmoil, war, and revolution. In particular, three great problems confronted Russia at this time—leadership, peasant rebellions, and foreign invasions—and their resolutions had profound, long-range effects.

Leadership   The first problem had to do with succession to the throne, and the ultimate result was an increase in monarchical power. The last direct heir of Ivan the Terrible was Theodore, a feeble-minded youth who ruled from 1584 to 1598. He was succeeded by the powerful aristocrat Boris Godunov (1598–1605), who, in turn, was succeeded by a succession of several powerful men who claimed a right to the throne. During the Time of Troubles, the Russian government was largely controlled by *boyars*, aristocrats who hoped to use the absence of a strong monarch to increase the influence of the aristocracy. Boyar power was traditionally asserted through the *duma*, an assembly that advised tsars. Another assembly—the *sobor*—sometimes represented clergy and townspeople as well as the aristocracy and also advised tsars. These assemblies had some potential to limit the power of tsars just as the English Parliament limited the power of English monarchs. But the potential ended in the seventeenth century, when a sobor appointed Michael Romanov to the Russian throne in 1613. The autocratic Romanov family would continue to rule Russia until 1917. Michael Romanov and his immediate successors together eliminated the influence of the duma and sobor and forced the aristocracy to become a service nobility obligated to serve the state. This meant, in practice, that aristocrats became leaders of the army and administrators of the government, but they remained under the command of the ruling tsar. Thus, the Time of Troubles led to a political victory by the tsars over the nobility.

The tsars gained another victory when they asserted power over the Russian Orthodox church. In 1667, a religious dispute known as the *Old Believer's controversy* produced a split within the church hierarchy. The resulting chaos gave the tsars the power to appoint and thereby control many church officials. Thus the monarchs dominated both the church and the nobility. By the late seventeenth century, with the elimination of the boyar assembly and an independent church hierarchy, nothing remained to limit tsarist power.

Peasant Rebellions The Time of Troubles was also a period of peasant rebellions that resulted in widespread enserfment of peasants. The rebel peasants, angered by their harsh living conditions, were led by Cossack warriors who detested tsarist absolutism. For a time, the peasant rebellions succeeded in frightening the Russian upper classes. Eventually, though, tsarist armies crushed the rebels and, in the aftermath, serfdom was imposed on many peasants. As serfs, the peasants lost all freedom; they were forced to remain on the land that they worked and to accept the discipline of the master to whom they were bound. Although the practice of serfdom had been slowly evolving for some time, it was during the seventeenth century that the enserfment process became dominant throughout Russia.

Foreign Invasions Foreign invasions also occurred during the Time of Troubles and resulted in the expansion of Russian power and territory. During the seventeenth century, the Russians constantly fought the Swedes in the north, the Poles in the west, and the Ottoman Turks in the south. At first, the foreigners were the aggressors, trying to take advantage of the Time of Troubles to seize land from the Russians. The fighting was often fierce and brutal; in one instance, Russian leaders became so angry that they punished suspected traitors by tearing their ribs out with hot irons. Eventually, though, the Russians defeated the Swedes, gained control of many Turks in the south, and took the Ukraine—a large agricultural region in southern Russia—from Poland. Indeed, the foreign invasions left Russia in control of much of eastern Europe.

Long-term Effects Russia emerged from the Time of Troubles with an autocratic tsarist government that dominated a service nobility, the church, and an enserfed peasantry. The Russian government continued to expand its territory, not only in eastern Europe but also in Siberia, a vast, unexplored wilderness stretching across northern Asia. The Russian drive into the Siberian wilderness was in many ways similar to the expansion of the United States across the prairies of North America. At first, the lure of riches from the fur trade brought explorers to Siberia, and then the desire for a free and independent way of life induced some colonists to settle in the area. But Siberia's climate was too harsh and cold to attract large numbers of people, so the wilderness remained underpopulated.

More importantly, Siberia became to Russia a passageway to the Pacific Ocean. In 1639, the Cossack explorer Ivan Moskvitianin led an expedition to the Pacific coast. Then, in 1648, Semen Dezhnev sailed through what would later be known as the Bering Strait (near present-day Alaska). By the eighteenth century, the Russians were building fur-trading posts that extended from Alaska almost to California and were beginning to establish their presence in the Pacific region.

European Influence

Until the seventeenth century, Russia had little contact with Western European civilization. As Russia expanded, however, Russian society was influenced by the outside world, particularly by Europe. The Russian upper classes adopted a few European customs such as eating salads and having their portraits painted, and the government allowed some foreigners to live in Moscow and work as merchants or technicians. Russia was beginning to break out of its isolation, especially during the dramatic reign of Peter the Great (reigned 1682–1725). Peter sought to Westernize Russia by adopting European technologies and administrative methods that would make his nation more modern, efficient, and powerful. To this end he invited foreigners to teach European technology to Russians, built canals to facilitate internal trade, reorganized and modernized the army, and created Russia's first large navy. Peter also sought to expand Russia's boundaries, particularly along the eastern shores of the Baltic Sea. In a long war with Sweden (1700–1721), the Russians conquered those Baltic lands. And there, on the coast, Peter built a "window" to the West—the new city of St. Petersburg, which replaced Moscow as the capital of Russia.

After Peter's death in 1725, Russia was governed by a succession of six rulers, several of whom were weak. Then came a strong monarch, Catherine II (the Great; reigned 1762–1796). Catherine increased tsarist authority by modernizing the state bureaucracy and encouraging the expansion of serfdom. Her greatest accomplishments, though, lay in foreign policy and wars, as Russia continued to expand to the south and west. A series of conflicts with the Ottoman Empire gave Russia control of the northern shores of the Black Sea. At the same time, Russia participated, along with Austria and Prussia, in the partitioning of a weakened Poland. Between 1772 and 1795, those three nations seized for themselves portions of Polish territory. By the end of the eighteenth

Peter the Great Peter I (1672–1725), one of the most influential Russian tsars, sought to modernize his country by bringing it into closer contact with Europe. (Charles Phelps Cushing)

century, Poland ceased to exist and Russia became the most powerful European state east of France.

Late eighteenth-century Russia was a massive empire, stretching from eastern Europe to the Pacific Ocean, and was increasingly influenced by Western ideas and technologies. Indeed, Russia was becoming an extension of Western Civilization. Some Russians feared the Western influence, believing that their homeland was losing its uniqueness. The Orthodox church, increasingly conservative and strongly supportive of tsarist power, resisted Westernizing influences. Furthermore, many Russian intellectuals were ambivalent about Russia's relationship with the West. The great nineteenth-century Russian novelist Fyodor Dostoyevski, who believed that Western culture was dead but still fascinating, commented on his studies of Western thought:

> I know that I am only going to a graveyard, but to a most precious graveyard. . . . Precious are the dead that lie buried there, every stone over them speaks of such burning life that once was there, of such passionate faith in their deeds, their truth, their struggle, and their learning, that I know I shall fall on the ground and shall kiss those stones and weep over them.[6]

AFRICA AND THE SLAVE TRADE

When the Europeans began to explore the Atlantic Ocean in the fifteenth century, they quickly came to the west coast of Africa. Africa was a "new world" to the Europeans, but unlike the Americas it was a new world they were unable to conquer at first. The African coastline lacked many natural harbors, so the Europeans found few landing bases from which they could explore inland. Furthermore, some African states (such as the Congo) were sufficiently powerful to defend themselves against European aggressors. Also, the swampy African coast nurtured tropical diseases (such as yellow fever and malaria) that killed many of the Europeans who came there.

Even though the Europeans failed to conquer Africa until the nineteenth century, they were successful in organizing a slave trade in the sixteenth century. Slavery and the slave trade had existed in Africa for centuries, as Muslim slavers sold Africans in Mediterranean and Indian Ocean slave markets. But the slave trade organized by the Europeans was significantly different from the traditional Muslim system, in that the white Europeans regarded the black Africans as racially inferior. The Europeans therefore mixed racism with slavery to a degree the Muslims never had.

The European slave trade was part of what became known as the *South Atlantic System*. The system had three elements:

1. European slavers brought various goods to Africa with which they purchased slaves from Africans who had kidnapped or bought other Africans.
2. In what was called the "middle passage," the African slaves were shipped across the Atlantic to work in the fields of sugar or cotton plantations in Brazil, the Caribbean islands, and southern North America.
3. The products of the plantations were shipped back across the Atlantic for European consumption.

The South Atlantic System lasted from the fifteenth to the nineteenth centuries, and during that time over ten million Africans were transported to the Americas as slaves. The Portuguese controlled the slave trade in the sixteenth century, the Dutch in the seventeenth, and the British in the eighteenth.

For many Africans, slavery was an ordeal that began sometime between the ages of fourteen and thirty-five, when they were kidnapped or captured in war by other Africans. Samuel Ajoyi Crowther, an enslaved African whose name was later Europeanized, described what it was like to become a slave:

Slave Traders This drawing depicts eighteenth-century Europeans negotiating to buy slaves on the West African coast. Note the European ships (*left*) and the fortress of the African slave traders (*right*). (Library of Congress)

> After my price had been counted before my own eyes, I was delivered up to my new owners, with great grief and dejection of spirit, not knowing where I was now to be led. . . . I renewed my attempt at strangling myself, several times at night; but could not effect my purpose. . . . However, it was not long before I was bartered, for tobacco, rum, and other articles.[7]

After being captured and enslaved, the Africans were marched to the coast where they were sold to Europeans. When the slaves were put on ships they were usually stripped naked, with the men chained together below deck and the women and children allowed to stay up on deck. One slave, Olaudah Equiano, later recorded his reaction to this experience:

> The first object which saluted my eyes when I arrived on the coast was the sea, and a slave ship which was then riding at anchor and waiting for its cargo. These filled me with astonishment, which was soon converted into terror when I was carried on board. I was immediately handled and tossed up to see if I were sound by some of

the crew, and I was now persuaded that I had gotten into a world of bad spirits and that they were going to kill me. . . . When I looked round the ship too and saw a large furnace of copper boiling, and a multitude of black people of every description chained together, every one of their countenances expressing dejection and sorrow, I no longer doubted of my fate; and quite overpowered with horror and anguish, I fell motionless on the deck and fainted.[8]

During the voyage across the Atlantic, many Africans died of smallpox or dysentery and others jumped overboard to end their agony by drowning. Those who survived the trip were sold directly to plantation owners or by public auction. Most became plantation fieldhands and had no legal rights or protections. Life for slaves was extremely harsh; at times, the average slave could be expected to live only seven years after arriving in the Americas.

The impact of slavery on North and South American history is discussed in greater detail in later chapters. However, three key points need to be made here:

1. The slave trade was one part of a larger population movement in which growing numbers of people came to the Americas. Much of the native Indian population in the Americas died in the sixteenth century, in part because of being enslaved and overworked by the Spanish and also from infectious diseases carried by the Spanish. As a result, Africans were needed as a source of labor on plantations and in mines. Most of the slaves, then, ended up where the plantation system dominated—Brazil, the Caribbean, the southern part of British North America. (A plantation is a large farm that produces one or two export crops and requires large numbers of low-paid or enslaved laborers.)
2. The South Atlantic System led to high death rates for several groups of people. Slaves died in large numbers, usually on the voyage across the Atlantic or within a few years after being brought to a plantation. Many Europeans also died, particularly slavers who worked in the disease-ridden environment of the African coast and supervisors who worked on Caribbean plantations.
3. The slave trade and the plantation system were profitable for at least some Europeans, so slavery was one of the sources of growing European wealth.

The impact of the slave trade on Africa itself is difficult to assess. Some African areas were hardly affected at all; in other areas, some ethnic groups were almost completely destroyed. A crucial point is that the slave trade produced great fear and insecurity among many Africans and thereby inhibited African political and economic development. The African historian Walter Rodney points out that:

The European slave trade was a direct block, in removing millions of youth and young adults who are the human agents from whom inventiveness springs. Those who remained in areas badly hit by slave capturing were preoccupied about their freedom rather than with improvements in production. Besides, even the busiest African in West, Central, or East Africa was concerned more with trade than with production, because of the nature of the contacts with Europe; and that situation was not conducive to the introduction of technological advances.[9]

SPANISH AND PORTUGUESE AMERICA

As noted in Chapter 10, Christopher Columbus first led the Spanish to the Americas in 1492, where they encountered millions of people who had lived in the Americas for centuries. Columbus called these people Indians because he believed he had landed near India. In two areas, the native Americans organized large-scale civilizations: the Aztecs dominated much of present-day Mexico and the Incas much of present-day Peru. (Previously, Mexico had been the site where the Olmecs established a civilization around 1200 B.C.) Spanish *conquistadores* ("conquerors") soon destroyed both the Aztec and Inca empires. Hernando Cortés defeated the Aztecs in 1521, and Francisco Pizarro defeated the Incas in the 1530s.

The first half of the sixteenth century was the age of the *conquistadores* in Spanish America. These romantic adventurers explored much of the New World, sometimes seeking to find such legendary places as the Fountain of Youth (allegedly in Florida), the city of El Dorado (a city of gold), and the city of the Amazons (a society of powerful women). The age of the *conquistadores* was soon over, however, as the Spanish government established a centralized administration staffed by bureaucrats to rule Spanish America.

Spanish administration was originally divided into a viceroyalty of New Spain headquartered in Mexico and a viceroyalty of Peru. As population grew over the centuries, a viceroyalty of New Granada (Venezuela and Colombia) was created in 1717, and a viceroyalty of La Plata (Argentina) in 1776. In theory, the viceroys were the senior Spanish officials in the colonies, and they reported directly to Spanish monarchs who established colonial policy. In practice though, the monarchs were too far away to understand colonial life, so local colonial officials usually had to reinterpret royal decrees to fit their local situations. The somewhat cynical motto of these officials was "I obey but do not fulfill."[10] Yet, even though they did not always carry out the exact wishes of the monarchs, the local officials still defended a highly centralized system that allowed little local self-government.

Figure 13.2   European Colonies in the New World, 1775–1800

Spanish America was characterized by plantations and ranches, with a great deal of uninhabited land interspersed among the settled areas. The plantation system originated when the Spanish crown established a policy of giving Spanish emigrants a grant of land—called an *encomienda*—that included a village of native Americans to work the fields. The plantations, a few of which contained over one million acres, were supposed to produce crops for export to Spain. The owners were directed to care for and Christianize their workers, so a church administration was organized to convert and help control the workers.

TECHNOLOGY
The Cross-Atlantic Exchange

Many useful ideas and techniques were exchanged between Europe and the Americas during the sixteenth to eighteenth centuries. One was the ranching culture, transmitted from southern Spain to the Americas. Spanish emigrants brought with them ranch animals—the horse and tough long-horned cattle—and ranching techniques—cattle roundups and the overland drive of cattle to markets. The horse, which had earlier died out in the Americas, was thus reintroduced to the New World.

The Europeans brought other techniques associated with living in frontier conditions. The log cabin, for example, came from Scandinavia. Swedes who migrated to the Delaware area in North America built log cabins, and that style of housing gradually became the typical frontier house. The stagecoach was a European invention, and the stirrup used by New World cowboys was also brought from Europe.

From the native Americans, the Europeans learned new agricultural techniques and transmitted them to Europe and eventually to much of the rest of the world. In particular, the Europeans learned how to cultivate new crops, including maize, several kinds of beans, peanuts, pumpkins, tomatoes, and potatoes. The potato was especially important, for it gradually became a staple food for common people in some parts of Europe.

The native Americans and Europeans also gave each other diseases to which each was unaccustomed, the native Americans getting smallpox from Europeans and the Europeans getting syphilis from native Americans.

Log Cabin *Using the timber available, settlers in forested areas carved out clearings and built log cabins in the wilderness. This drawing depicts a relatively well-off family that owned several animals. (The Granger Collection)*

The cattle ranches were one of the most distinctive features of Spanish America. They developed in three large grassland areas—the pampas of Argentina and Uruguay, the Ilanos of Venezuela, and the southern edges of the prairies that stretch from Mexico to Canada. The ranch culture did not extend far into the Plains area of North America, in part because the Plains Indians became formidable warriors and resisted the Spanish more effectively than did others.

By the seventeenth and eighteenth centuries, the upper classes in Spanish America were quite prosperous. They lived in grand plantation houses or townhouses, sent their sons to universities in Mexico City or Lima, and filled the higher offices of the military, the church, and the colonial administration. For them, life was pleasant, as the historian C. H. Haring points out:

> The Spanish colonies possessed vastly greater wealth than English America, and had achieved all the outward signs of opulence: imposing public buildings, universities, churches, hospitals, and populous cities which were centers of luxury, learning, and refinement. Mexico [City] and Lima were larger cities in 1790 than Philadelphia and New York.[11]

Life was much more harsh for the vast majority of the population—poor whites, native Americans, and African slaves. They were not only impoverished but were also constantly observed and controlled by a conservative colonial administration and a church that preached acceptance of one's lot in life.

One part of South America—Brazil—was colonized by Portugal. The first Portuguese emigrants received large blocks of land from the Portuguese crown and organized that land into sugar plantations. "In the beginning was sugar," comments one Brazilian historian.[12] The first workers on the plantations were native Americans, but as they died out Brazil became a major importer of African slaves. One distinctive feature of the Brazilian colony was that settlers usually remained near the coast, because the interior was dominated by thick forests and jungles. Another was that the Portuguese emigrants rarely included women, so the men usually married native Americans or blacks and thereby created a racially mixed society.

ENGLISH AND FRENCH AMERICA

Millions of native Americans were in North America before the Europeans came. Many lived in small villages and survived by farming and some hunting. Others, particularly in Florida and the Mississippi valley, lived in urban areas, where they not only farmed and hunted but also conducted commerce over relatively long distances. Native Americans in

Florida for example, sometimes traded with those on the Caribbean islands.

The Europeans began to impinge on the native American world in North America during the second half of the sixteenth century. Explorers from England, the Netherlands, and France began to seek wealth—particularly through precious metals and plantation crops—there.

English America

The English were the most aggressive and successful at developing a new source of wealth in North America because England contained many private individuals with both the money and energy necessary to conduct overseas ventures. The English government, unlike the Spanish government, was at first uninterested in establishing colonies, so the original English settlements were privately endowed operations uncontrolled by royal administration. Some English businesspeople financed Caribbean plantations, directed by European overseers and worked by African slaves. Others, hoping somehow to make a profit, supported colonies on the North American continent.

In 1585, a colony was established on Roanoke Island (North Carolina), but it failed because of inadequate capital, quarreling among the settlers, and Spanish refusal to trade with it. The Roanoke Island venture became known as the "Lost Colony" because the settlers eventually disappeared without a trace. A more successful colony was developed at Jamestown, Virginia (1606–1624), but it also collapsed because of settler quarrels, the harsh wilderness conditions, and the hostility of native Americans from whom the settlers had taken land. However, Jamestown lasted long enough to open the Virginia area to other English settlements.

In 1620, another settlement area was established, this one in Massachusetts. The Pilgrims, a radical religious sect seeking freedom from the church of England, came to Massachusetts. The Pilgrim death rate was high and the colony was in danger of disappearing, but in 1630, the Massachusetts Bay Company brought over the Puritans, another radical religious sect, who established a strong, permanent settlement there.

During the seventeenth century, a growing number of European emigrants came to various parts of the Atlantic coast. Catholic refugees from England settled in Maryland. The Dutch established a trading post at New Amsterdam (New York), which they soon lost to the English. The New York and New Jersey areas attracted English, German, Dutch, and Swedish colonists. In the south, the Carolinas contained two settlement areas, one around Albemarle Sound (North Carolina) and the other called Charles Town (South Carolina). The southern settlers began to import African slaves to work the tobacco plantations.

By the end of the seventeenth century, the native Americans had disappeared from most of the Atlantic coast. Many died from diseases transmitted by Europeans, and the rest were driven inland by settlers. A string of European coastal settlements was organized into eleven provinces loosely controlled by the English government. The northern settlements of New England survived on fishing and commerce, the middle area from New York to Maryland produced grain and timber, and the southern area along with the Caribbean islands had a plantation economy. The latter was most important to the English, because plantation products—sugar, coffee, tobacco—were in great demand in Europe.

In the eighteenth century, English North America had already become more prosperous than most other areas of the world. In the port cities—New York, Boston, Newport, Philadelphia, and Charleston—a growing merchant class became relatively wealthy. In the south, the planter class was economically well-off and politically influential. However, neither the merchants nor the planters ever became an exclusive aristocracy, at least not in the European sense of a privileged class entitled by birth to dominate politics and society.

Most of the settlement populations were common people—farmers, artisans, tradespeople—who came to the New World to seek a better standard of living. Many found a better way of life, for land was readily available and it was relatively easy to become a landowning farmer. The availability of land had both political and religious implications. Landownership entitled males to vote in elections for local colonial assemblies, which the English government allowed the settlers to establish. The result was a relatively large electorate. Widespread landownership also made it difficult to enforce any kind of religious orthodoxy, since settlers were scattered all over the Atlantic seaboard and were often out of reach of the established authorities.

Not all emigrants prospered. Many farmers lived in one- or two-room wooden houses and barely scratched a living from the soil. Furthermore, many in the lower classes were not legally free, having come to North America as indentured servants obligated to work several years for whomever paid their ship passage across the ocean. A typical story is that of John Harrower, an impoverished shopkeeper from Scotland. In 1773, he left his wife and three children to look for work, found nothing, and in London sold himself for four years of bonded servitude in exchange for ship passage to Virginia. He became a tutor for a Virginia planter's children but died in 1777 before he had saved enough money to bring over his family.

John Harrower's story demonstrates the danger and risk faced by those who came to the New World. English North America was a place where European civilization confronted the wilderness, where life was relatively precarious and the traditional rules of civilized behavior were not always maintained. The Moravians, Protestant refugees from eastern

Europe, responded to the wilderness by establishing utopian religious settlements in Pennsylvania and North Carolina, where they could live as they thought God wanted. Others, like Dr. Andrew Turnbull, became half-mad and brutalized in the wilderness. Turnbull led a band of settlers to Florida in an attempt to establish an ideal pioneering community, but heat and disease killed many and Turnbull became a petty tyrant who beat and severely disciplined the survivors. The doctor eventually returned to Charleston, South Carolina, and, once out of the wilderness, behaved so normally that he lived out his life as a respected citizen and physician.

Living in a wilderness with weak civilized restraints was one reason white settlers treated native Americans and African slaves so brutally. Another, of course, was their desire for the native American's land. Constant settler-Native American wars usually led to the natives being driven off their lands. The conflicts were characterized by savagery on both sides. One settler report claims that after defeating some native Americans in a battle, "we have now the pleasure, Sir, to fatten our dogs with their carcasses and to display their scalps neatly ornamented on the top of our bastions." The native Americans were often brutal, since in their eyes they were defending not only their land but their very existence. In one episode reported by a white settler, white women were "laid on their housefloors and great stakes [were] run up through their bodies. Others [who were] big with child, [had their] infants ripped out and hung upon trees."[13]

Slaves were often disciplined harshly. For example, the Virginia planter William Byrd II was an educated, sometimes genteel man who read the Bible daily, studied Greek and Hebrew, and built a Georgian mansion on his estate. He was also a strict disciplinarian, who repeatedly beat a black female slave and once forced another young slave, who habitually wet his bed, to "drink a pint of piss."[14]

William Byrd's life was in many ways a microcosm of the entire history of English North America. Byrd and millions of other Europeans were slowly building a new society on the edge of the wilderness, and this society was characterized by economic opportunity, some religious freedom, and local self-government. It was also characterized by white racism that led to the subjugation of black slaves and the strict separation of native Americans from white society.

A Comparison

Several notable differences distinguished English America from Spanish and Portuguese America:

1. The Spanish and Portuguese, although they often treated the native Americans harshly, were more willing than the English to intermarry, in part because few Spanish or Portuguese women

came to the New World. As a result, Spanish and Portuguese America contained more racially mixed societies in which some native culture was absorbed by the Europeans. The English colonists, on the other hand, tended to remain totally separate from the native culture and people.

2. Religious differences helped make Spanish and Portuguese America more conservative than English America. The Spanish and Portuguese emigrants were Catholic, many of them imbued with a Reformation-inspired zeal to defend and strengthen their church. Consequently, a well-organized Catholic hierarchy quickly became entrenched in Spanish and Portuguese America. This hierarchy converted many native Americans to a Catholicism that stressed social conservatism and obedience to authority. Emigrants to English America were more likely to be Protestant dissenters seeking religious freedom in the New World. The various Protestant sects were often intolerant of each other, but the diversity of religious groups meant that religious debate and differences of opinion would continue.

3. The Spanish colonial administration was much more centralized than either the Portuguese administration in Brazil or the English colonial government in North America. The English, unlike the Spanish, tolerated local colonial assemblies and some local political debate, so English settlers developed a limited tradition of local self-government.

French America

The English did not, of course, control all of North America, for the French claimed large sections of land. French America included several Caribbean islands—Martinique, Guadaloupe, Haiti—and Canada. In Canada, French territory theoretically extended from Quebec in the north to the Great Lakes and down the Mississippi River. In reality, however, there were few French settlers, so French America consisted mostly of scattered trading posts and forts.

In 1608, Samuel de Champlain built a small fort at Quebec in Canada. The fort was a trading center where French fishers and trappers brought cod and furs, especially beaver, to make fur hats for the European upper classes. The beaver trade had a major impact on native American populations, who were commissioned by the Europeans to capture and bring in beaver hides. As a result, many natives gradually gave up their traditional occupations as independent farmers and hunters and became employees of a trading post, dependent on Europeans for their livelihood.

By 1700, only about 20,000 Europeans lived in Canada, most of them male trappers and hunters. (At the same time, about 200,000 Europeans were in English America.) The French never emigrated in large numbers, so French North America looked large on a map but was really weak and vulnerable to attack. The ultimate result was that France lost Canada to England. In 1713, at the end of a long European war, England gained the Hudson Bay area from France. Then, in 1763, England took the rest of Canada after winning what the North Americans called the French and Indian War. (The French and Indian War was the North American part of the Seven Years' War, fought in Europe from 1756 to 1763.) One result was that the British forcibly deported the Acadians—French settlers in Nova Scotia, some of whom moved to Louisiana where their descendants became known as "Cajuns."

After 1763 Canada was under British rule, even after the United States became independent from Britain. The French still claimed the Mississippi valley, but it was sold to the United States in the Louisiana Purchase of 1803 (See Chapter 15). Thus, French America no longer existed by the early nineteenth century.

The English and French, much more than the Spanish and Portuguese, found or thought they found in the Americas a striking new political idea—*liberty*. Traditionally, the Europeans had thought of liberty as the privileges enjoyed by certain well-defined groups of people. Thus, nobles had certain liberties or privileges that monarchs could not abuse. But when English and French political thinkers studied the native American societies of the New World, they believed they saw a new conception of liberty. The native Americans seemed to them to be unhindered by rules and customs, to be "free" in the sense of not being controlled by government or other authority. Of course, native Americans did have their own social rules and forms of government, but to the Europeans they appeared to have a great deal of freedom to live as they chose. The notion of liberty as the absence of obstacles (or the absence of authority) became an important new idea in European political thought during the seventeenth and eighteenth centuries. In particular, it encouraged the political revolutions of the late eighteenth century (as we will see in Chapter 15). One important source of this new conception of liberty was European knowledge of native American societies.

EUROPEANS IN ASIA AND THE SOUTH PACIFIC

After the Portuguese sailed around Africa to Asia in the late fifteenth century, they established a large trading network to transport goods between Asia and Europe. Portuguese trading posts extended from Ormuz at the entrance to the Persian Gulf to Goa in India to Macao in China to Malacca in present-day Malaysia. But the Portuguese began to decline in the seventeenth century, as the Dutch replaced them as the primary carriers of Asian-European trade. Portuguese and Dutch power was limited to seagoing commerce, for neither was able to conquer large land areas in Asia. The Asian societies were, for a time, strong enough to resist the Europeans. It was not until the eighteenth century that Europeans began to conquer and dominate Asian lands (as we will see in Chapter 18).

In the South Pacific, however, Europeans were able to colonize Australia and New Zealand, mainly because both areas were sparsely inhabited by peoples unable to defend themselves against the invaders. The Dutch landed on various parts of the Australian coast during the seventeenth and eighteenth centuries, but the first European settlements came after the English Captain James Cook explored parts of Australia in 1770. In 1788, English courts punished over one thousand convicts by sentencing them to live for seven years in Australia. Those convicts established the first colony at Botany Bay (present-day Sydney). They were gradually joined by other English, including free emigrants. During the nineteenth century, Australia slowly became an English-dominated country, as the indigenous natives (the aborigines) were gradually outnumbered and overpowered. Much the same happened in New Zealand. Several English settlements were in place by the 1820s, and New Zealand gradually became an English country. European infectious diseases rapidly decimated the native Maori tribes in New Zealand.

CONCLUSION

The establishment of European colonies from the sixteenth to eighteenth centuries had far-reaching consequences:

1. "Europe" was much larger than before. In the fifteenth century, "Europe" meant the western-most part of the Eurasian continent. By the eighteenth century, an expanding Russia increasingly shared European culture and participated in European politics. Furthermore, "neo-Europes"—new societies that were political and cultural extensions of Europe—existed in South America, North America, Australia, and New Zealand.
2. The European colonization of North and South America led to a massive interchange between continents of people, diseases, animals, and plants. Interchange of peoples meant that North and South America were populated by mixtures of native Americans, Europeans, and Africans. Interchange of diseases meant that native Americans suffered from European diseases like smallpox, and Europeans who went to the African coast contracted tropical diseases like malaria and yellow fever. Syphilis may also have been contracted by Europeans in the New World and then brought back to Europe. Interchange of animals and plants meant that Europeans brought to the New World the horse, sheep, sugar, the banana, and many other things. It also meant that native Americans taught the Europeans how to cultivate crops previously unknown in Europe. These crops quickly spread to various parts of Europe,

Africa, and Asia, thereby greatly expanding the variety of products available throughout the world.

3. Many people suffered as a result of European expansion. Native Americans lost much of their lands and often died while mining gold and silver to be sent to Europe. African slaves were brought to the Americas to produce plantation crops such as sugar for Europeans. Serfdom was imposed on many peasants in Russia and eastern Europe, in part to facilitate production of cash crops such as wheat for European markets.

4. European expansion modified and sometimes undermined many of the traditional ideas and beliefs of Europeans. The discovery of new lands increased geographical knowledge, and the discovery of plants and animals previously unknown to Europeans expanded scientific knowledge. The growing awareness of non-European religions and societies led some Europeans to conclude that other peoples might have admirable customs and beliefs and that the European way of life was not necessarily the best. In particular, some European political theorists derived a new conception of liberty from their study of native American societies.

THINGS YOU SHOULD KNOW

Kievan Russia
Moscow
Ivan III (the Great)
Ivan IV (the Terrible)
Time of Troubles
Peter the Great
Catherine the Great
South Atlantic System
Impact of the African slave trade
Conquistadores
The interchange between Europe and the Americas

Differences between Spanish and Portuguese America and English America
First English colonizations in North America
Early history of Canada
Early history of Australia and New Zealand
Consequences of the establishment of European colonies

SUGGESTED READINGS

James H. Billington, *The Icon and the Axe: An Interpretive History of Russian Culture* (New York: Knopf, 1968) is an excellent interpretation of Russian intellectual and cultural history. On Africa and the slave trade, the works of Philip Curtin are fundamental, particularly *The Atlantic Slave Trade* (Madison: Univ. of Wisconsin Press, 1969). Edward Reynolds, *Stand the Storm: A History of the Atlantic Slave Trade* (London: Allison & Busby, 1985) is a good short history of the slave trade. A good introduction to Latin American history is E. Bradford Burns, *Latin America: A Concise Interpretive History*, 2nd ed. (Englewood Cliffs, N.J.: Prentice-Hall, 1977). Bernard Bailyn, *The Peopling of British North America* (New York: Knopf, 1986) provides an excellent and interesting analysis of the kinds of people who emigrated to North America and the types of problems they faced. Lynn White, Jr., "The Legacy of the Middle Ages in the American Wild West," *Medieval Religion and Technology* (Berkeley: Univ. of California Press, 1978) analyzes the ideas and techniques that medieval Europe contributed to the American "Wild West."

Two books by Alfred W. Crosby, Jr.—*The Columbian Exchange: Biological and Cultural Consequences of 1492* (Westport, Conn.: Greenwood Press, 1972) and *Ecological Imperialism: The Biological Expansion of Europe, 900–1900* (New York: Cambridge Univ. Press, 1986)—detail the ecological consequences of European expansion. Eric R. Wolf, *Europe and the People without History* (Berkeley: Univ. of California Press, 1982) examines the impact of the Europeans on some of the peoples they encountered. Immanuel Wallerstein, *The Modern World System I: Capitalist Agriculture and the Origins of the European World-Economy in the Sixteenth Century* (New York: Academic Press, 1974) is the first volume of a major synthesis in which the author argues that from the sixteenth to the nineteenth centuries most of the world became integrated into a world-economy dominated by Europe.

NOTES

[1]Alfred W. Crosby, Jr., *Ecological Imperialism: The Biological Expansion of Europe, 900–1900* (New York: Cambridge Univ. Press, 1986), p. 2.

[2]Quoted in James H. Billington, *The Icon and the Axe: An Interpretive History of Russian Culture* (New York: Knopf, 1968), p. 7.

[3]Quoted in ibid., p. 58.

[4]Ibid., pp. 26–35.

[5]Quoted in ibid., p. 76.

[6]Quoted in ibid., p. xii.

[7]S. A. Crowther, "Narrative of S. A. Crowther," in *Africa Remembered: Narratives by West Africans from the Era of the Slave Trade*, ed. Philip Curtin (Madison: Univ. of Wisconsin Press, 1967), p. 308.

[8]Quoted in Edward Reynolds, *Stand the Storm: A History of the Atlantic Slave Trade* (London: Allison & Busby, 1985), pp. 47–48.

[9]Walter Rodney, *How Europe Underdeveloped Africa* (Washington, D.C.: Howard Univ. Press, 1974), p. 105.

[10]E. Bradford Burns, *Latin America: A Concise Interpretive History*, 2nd ed. (Englewood Cliffs, N.J.: Prentice-Hall, 1977), pp. 39–41.

[11]C. H. Haring, quoted in George Pendle, *A History of Latin America* (New York: Penguin, 1963), p. 92.

[12]Germán Arciniegas, *Latin America: A Cultural History*, trans. Joan MacLean (London: Barrie & Rockliff, 1969), p. 98.

[13]Quoted in Bernard Bailyn, *The Peopling of British North America* (New York: Knopf, 1986), pp. 115–16.

[14]William Byrd II, quoted in ibid., p. 119.

14

The Rise of the West, 1500 to 1900

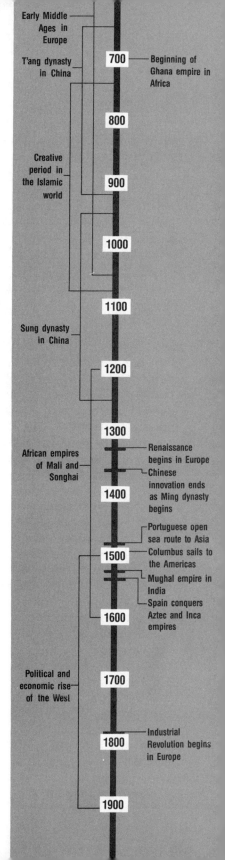

Early Middle Ages in Europe

700 — Beginning of Ghana empire in Africa

T'ang dynasty in China

800

Creative period in the Islamic world

900

1000

1100

Sung dynasty in China

1200

1300

African empires of Mali and Songhai

Renaissance begins in Europe

Chinese innovation ends as Ming dynasty begins

1400

Portuguese open sea route to Asia

Columbus sails to the Americas

1500

Mughal empire in India

Spain conquers Aztec and Inca empires

1600

Political and economic rise of the West

1700

Industrial Revolution begins in Europe

1800

1900

"**T**he Rise of the West" is the phrase used by historian William H. McNeill to designate one of the most significant developments in world history—the dominance of Western Civilization over much of the rest of the world in recent centuries.[1] Western dominance has taken two forms since its beginnings:

1. Over the course of about four hundred years, Western Civilization became far more powerful, politically and militarily, than any other civilization or society in world history. As a result, many Western nations were able to build colonial empires in parts of Asia, Africa, and Latin America.
2. At the same time, continuing industrialization has made Western Civilization the wealthiest society in history.

The political and military rise of the West occurred between 1500 and 1900. In 1500, the West was one of several large civilized areas scattered around the world. By 1900, it controlled most of the world. During that four-hundred year span, large parts of the world—Russia, North and South America, Australia, New Zealand—became extensions of Western Civilization, at least in the sense that Western ideas and institutions defined how people in those areas lived. In addition, most non-Western parts of the world—Asia, Africa, Islamic societies—were conquered and controlled by Western nations during this time, although non-Western peoples retained their own indigenous traditions and cultures (as we will see in Chapter 18).

The economic rise of the West also originated around 1500 but proceeded most rapidly after the Industrial Revolution of the eighteenth century (as we will see in Chapter 15). In *The Perspective of the World*, historian Fernand Braudel compares the average annual incomes of people living in various parts of the world during the 1700s and the 1970s.[2] His data reveal that the eighteenth-century standard of living in the West and in many other parts of the world was essentially similar; by the late twentieth century, however, the Western standard of living had increased dramatically (see Table 14.1).

Why was the West able to conquer so much of the world? Why was the West able to create experimental science and an Industrial Revolution and to become so much wealthier and more powerful than the rest of the world? In this chapter, we pause to consider these questions. First, in order to gain a better understanding of the similarities and differences between the West and non-West, we need to consider the important historical developments in several non-Western societies. These include the civilized areas of China, India, and the Islamic world, as well as Africa and the Americas. In addition, we need to review some of the major developments in Western history, as these help to explain why the West achieved its dominance.

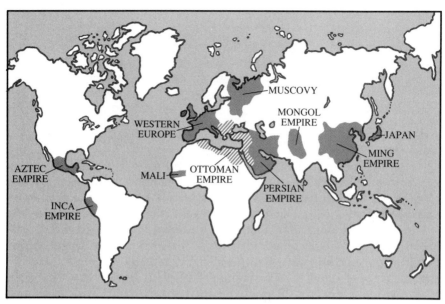

Figure 14.1 Major Civilizations in 1500

In comparing the West to non-Western societies, it is important to avoid the assumption that Western peoples are superior to or more advanced than people in other parts of the world. It is all too easy for the twentieth-century observer to place Western and non-Western societies into vague categories like "successful" or "unsuccessful," in terms of modern science or industrialization, for instance. This limited view wrongly assumes that non-Western societies both attempted and failed to accomplish the same things as the West. We must keep in mind that different ways of life and different goals and purposes caused non-Western societies to develop in different ways. (The Chinese culture, for

---

TABLE 14.1   ESTIMATED AVERAGE ANNUAL INCOME PER PERSON, 1700s AND 1970s (IN 1960 $U.S.)

Eighteenth Century (1700s)	Twentieth Century (1970s)
England $150–190	Western Europe $2300
France $170–200	
China $230	China $370
India $160–210	Third World nations $355

Source: Fernand Braudel, *The Perspective of the World,* vol. 3 of *Civilization and Capitalism, 15th–18th Century,* trans. Sian Reynolds (New York: Harper & Row, 1984), pp. 533–535.

example, valued social harmony far more than aggressive economic development.)

In the final analysis, the crucial question is not why other civilizations did not develop as the West did but why Western Civilization was so distinctively different from other civilizations.

CHINA

Chinese civilization began during the second millennium B.C. A succession of ruling dynasties—the Shang, the Chou, and the Han—controlled all or much of China until the third century A.D. During that long period, two developments of particular importance occurred. The first was the evolution of the Confucian moral tradition, which stressed the goal of social harmony and accepted the Chinese reality of a hierarchical society in which most people were poor peasants. Confucianism was founded by the great Chinese teacher Confucius in the sixth century B.C. The other major development was the gradual construction of the Great Wall along China's northern border. The construction of the Great Wall began during the third century B.C. and wasn't completed until the Ming dynasty of the fifteenth and sixteenth centuries A.D. The purpose of this nearly 1,500-mile-long wall was protection against invading nomadic tribes from the north. Symbolically, though, the wall represented the Chinese desire of isolation from the outside world.

For our analysis, an important period in Chinese history is the seventh to the tenth centuries A.D., when a new ruling dynasty—the T'ang (618-906)—assumed control of China and ruled for nearly three hundred years. A period of political disorder followed in China after the last T'ang emperor was deposed in 906, but a strong, centralized government was restored by the Sung dynasty (960–1279). In theory, the T'ang and Sung emperors were considered absolute rulers; in practice, though, much political authority was in the hands of the imperial civil service. The civil service was staffed by upper-class Chinese scholars who had successfully completed a series of examinations based on knowledge of Confucian tenets and texts. Thus, one of the unique features of Chinese history is that Confucian scholars helped govern China.

Chinese Innovations

The Chinese were technologically and economically advanced during the T'ang and Sung dynasties. Three important inventions—the compass, gunpowder, and the printing press—occurred at this time. The compass was developed by Chinese mariners who traveled and explored the Indian Ocean. Gunpowder was originally used to make firebombs, but by the thirteenth and fourteenth centuries Chinese technicians were putting

The Great Wall of China The Great Wall, originally constructed about two thousand years ago and later restored by the Ming dynasty (1368–1644), stretches fifteen hundred miles across the northern frontier of China. Designed to keep invaders out, the wall is symbolic of the Chinese desire (particularly that of the Ming and Manchu dynasties) to keep China separate from the rest of the world. (The Granger Collection)

gunpowder inside an iron barrel so that pellets could be shot out. Woodblock printing was an early form of the printing press. It was invented because Confucian scholars needed a large amount of written material to study for the civil service examinations. All three Chinese inventions were eventually disseminated to other peoples, including Western Europeans.

The inventions occurred during a time of economic growth in China. Traditionally, the center of Chinese government and society had been in northern China. But as the Chinese population grew rapidly, the search for more agricultural land led to expansion southward. The river valleys of South China led Chinese farmers to develop several innovations that stimulated wet-field rice cultivation, such as improved irrigation systems using sluice gates and new kinds of water pumps, greater use of fertilizers, and new strains of seeds. The result was increased agricultural productivity; by the thirteenth century, Chinese farmers were feeding a population of over 100 million.

Agricultural growth in China also helped to expand its business and commerce. Chinese peasants built small timber industries, refined sugar, raised fish in ponds, and produced large quantities of silk textiles. Both paper production (to supply the scholars with books) and iron production (to supply the warriors with firearms) increased. To distribute all these products, an elaborate system of road and water transport was organized. Chinese shipping quickly came to dominate much of the Pacific and Indian Oceans. In the early fifteenth century, the admiral Cheng Ho led a series of commercial voyages to Indian and east African ports. The Chinese economy was so vibrant that in the thirteenth century it amazed the Italian traveler Marco Polo, who wrote this about a city on the Yangtze River: "I give you my word that I have seen in this city fully five thousand ships at once, . . . the river flows through more than sixteen provinces, and there are on its banks more than two hundred cities, all having more ships than this."[3]

The Chinese also developed an impressive scientific tradition between the tenth and fourteenth centuries. In the field of astronomy, large observatories traced the movements of planetary bodies with increasingly greater precision. In the field of medicine, Chinese physicians began to understand and treat some diseases more successfully. They also began to dissect cadavers and learn more about human anatomy. One motivation for studying anatomy was the Chinese practice of acupuncture, by which needles are inserted into a person's body to relieve muscle and nerve injuries. To be effective, the therapist had to know where to insert the needles. By the fourteenth century, Chinese scientists had accumulated a great deal of scientific knowledge, and Chinese science constituted a sophisticated body of learning.

An End to Innovation

Beginning in the late fourteenth century, a succession of conservative imperial governments deliberately ended the period of technological, economic, and scientific innovations in China. The Sung dynasty, which had to some degree encouraged innovation, was destroyed when the Mongols invaded China in 1279. Mongol rulers then controlled the country until 1368, when the Ming dynasty (1368–1644) assumed power. The Ming dynasty was followed by the Manchu dynasty (1644–1911), which governed China until the early twentieth century.

The Ming and Manchu emperors were conservative rulers who sought to maintain social order and stability. To accomplish this goal, they needed the help of the nobility, who dominated Chinese agriculture and supplied the Confucian scholars to staff the civil service. Thus the Ming and Manchu emperors sought to strengthen the influence of the nobility and to weaken the power of all other groups, such as the merchants and entrepreneurs. Over a period of time, the Ming dynasty abolished the use of coinage and thereby undermined the commercial economy, restricted the use of mechanical contrivances, and halted the oceanic voyages across the Indian Ocean. Furthermore, the Ming decided to prohibit most contacts between Chinese and foreigners, and the Manchu emperors continued that policy when they came to power. Thus, an all-powerful imperial government deliberately inhibited scientific and technological curiosity and forced China to remain a traditional agricultural society.

Other factors also contributed to the conservative traditionalism that enveloped China. One was its large population. The Chinese farmed efficiently enough to feed large numbers of people, but they were never able to produce a continued agricultural surplus that would lead to a higher standard of living. Therefore, the Chinese economy always focused on basic food production and rarely stressed commercial or industrial activities. Another factor was the Chinese language, a nonalphabetic system using pictographs to express words in writing. Since thousands of pictographs were needed for an entire vocabulary, it took years of study to learn how to write and only a few Chinese—mostly upper-class Confucians—were literate. Most Chinese were illiterate and uneducated.

The cultural arrogance of the Chinese upper classes also contributed to conservatism in China. Chinese leaders assumed that their civilization was superior to all others and that they did not need to cooperate with or learn from other peoples. This attitude prevented Chinese from comprehending the strength and power of European nations. One eighteenth-century Chinese emperor, for example, rejected an English request for greater Chinese–English trade for this reason: "I do not forget the lonely remoteness of your island, cut off from the world by intervening wastes of sea, nor do I overlook your excusable ignorance of the usages of Our Celestial Empire."[4]

INDIA

The history of India is quite different from that of China. While China usually had a strong centralized government, India remained politically fragmented, the huge subcontinent divided into a patchwork of small provinces and independent states. One reason for this fragmentation was India's geography, as North India and South India were separated by dense jungles. Another reason was cultural, as India rarely had the strong, disciplined ruling class needed to develop political unity. The Mauryan empire of the fourth and third centuries B.C., the Gupta empire of northern India during the fourth and fifth centuries A.D., and the Mughal empire of the sixteenth and seventeenth centuries are the few exceptions when a ruling elite emerged to impose unity on all or most of India.

Even though it lacked strong political unification, India was bound together by a common culture based on religion and the caste system. Most Indians were Hindus and thus shared a common religious and moral attitude. Also, most Indians were members of a hereditary caste, so the caste system provided a social structure in the thousands of Indian villages. However, the caste system also hindered economic development in India. Members of the lower castes usually lived in abject poverty and were so malnourished that they often could not work productively. Members of the higher castes were restricted with regard to the types of occupations they could perform (some castes could not engage in business or commerce, for example), with the result that social movement and innovative practices were retarded. In general, the caste system was so rigid that Indian creativity was systematically discouraged.

Other factors also contributed to the lack of economic development in India. Many Indian rivers, for example, were not easily navigable, so long-distance commerce was difficult. In addition, the ruling princes and nobility often lived luxuriously, absorbing the wealth of India in conspicuous consumption rather than investing in productive enterprise. One eighteenth-century Indian prince owned 20 palaces, 100 private gardens, 1,200 elephants, 3,000 horses, and had 3,000 servants to manage all his possessions. Similarly, a seventeenth-century Mughal prince, Shah Jahan, built the Taj Mahal, a magnificent but very expensive tomb for his favorite wife.

Yet Indian society was never completely stagnant and backward. In the eighteenth century, India's textile industry exported cotton goods all over the world. Furthermore, Indian medical practices were relatively advanced. Doctors practiced plastic surgery, using skin grafts to help those whose bodies were disfigured. They also prevented smallpox by injecting a mild dose of the disease into people and thus producing immunity to the fatal form.

In general, though, by the eighteenth century India remained a relatively poor society, one that did not regard social change or sustained economic growth as desirable goals.

THE ISLAMIC SOCIETIES

The Islamic world stretched from the Arabian peninsula westward across northern Africa into Spain and eastward across central Asia to India. From the eighth through the twelfth centuries, much of the Islamic world was economically prosperous and intellectually vibrant. Muslim merchants transported goods to and from Asia, Europe, and Africa. Muslim scholars did much creative work, particularly in the areas of science, mathematics, and medicine.

This prosperous, vibrant period ended during the twelfth and thirteenth centuries, as several interplaying forces undermined the

Taj Mahal   A tomb completed in 1648 by an Indian prince, for his wife, who held the title "Crown of the Palace" or Taj Mahal, the elaborate construction of the structure shows the ostentation of, and luxury available to, the Indian ruling classes of the seventeenth century. (India Tourist Office)

strength and confidence of the Islamic societies. Foreign invaders— Christian Crusaders attacking the Holy Land, Mongols conquering central Asia, Berber tribespeople raiding in North Africa—weakened many Muslim states. The constant attacks helped produce a conservative revival within Islam, for political and social chaos encouraged Muslim religious leaders to argue for a return to Islamic fundamentalism and an expansion of religious authority over Islamic society. As a result, a growing spirit of conservatism and religious orthodoxy enveloped the Islamic world. In such an atmosphere, Muslim scholars and scientists were unable to continue their creative and innovative work. In addition, the Muslim merchant class was prevented from becoming strong enough to develop sustained economic growth.

Another blow struck the Islamic world in 1498, when the Portuguese opened the sea route from Europe around Africa to Asia. Transporting goods by sea was cheaper and safer than by land, so the new sea route outflanked the Muslim land routes across Asia and thereby undermined their commercial power. The effects of the new sea route were obscured for a time, because some Muslim states were expanding in the sixteenth century. The Muslim Mughal dynasty invaded northern India and

established a Muslim state there. Muslim colonists moved into parts of
Indonesia. The Ottoman Turks, converts to Islam, destroyed the last
remnants of the Byzantine Empire in 1453. The Ottoman Empire soon
extended northward almost to Vienna, westward across North Africa to
Morocco, and eastward to the Persian Gulf.

This new surge of Muslim power did not last, however. Mughal
strength in India ended early in the eighteenth century, as Hindus—the
overwhelming majority of the Indian population—rebelled against
Muslim government. The Ottomans, who dominated the Islamic world,
appeared huge and powerful on maps but began to deteriorate slowly
from within. Ottoman rulers were usually military leaders interested
more in wars and foreign conquests than in encouraging commerce or
economic growth. Furthermore, because they considered themselves
superior to the neighboring Europeans, they were not interested in
learning about the scientific and technological advances of Western
Civilization. By the eighteenth century, the Ottoman Empire was
militarily weak, economically backward, and intellectually sterile.

SUB-SAHARAN AFRICA

The history of sub-Saharan Africa is largely a story of people trying to
cope with a harsh natural environment. One element of that environment
was the prevalence of tropical diseases; Africans were constantly
vulnerable to debilitating diseases like malaria and the sleeping sickness
transmitted by the tsetse fly. Another was geography, which separates
sub-Saharan Africa from other areas of the world. The west African coast
has few natural harbors that could serve as centers of commercial
interchange, and the Sahara Desert in northern Africa remained for
centuries a gigantic barrier to communication with Mediterranean
societies. As a result, sub-Saharan Africa was for a long time isolated
from and unstimulated by contacts with other areas.

Nevertheless, Africans gradually created some well-organized and
sophisticated civilizations. In the eighth and ninth centuries, Muslim
merchants began to send camel caravans across the Sahara, and trade
between Africa and eastern Mediterranean lands increased rapidly. This
trade stimulated the growth of several commercial empires in the
western hump of Africa. First was the empire of Ghana (700–1200), then
the empire of Mali (1200–1500), and finally the empire of Songhai
(1464–1600) that included the famed trading city of Timbuktu. Some
cities within these empires were impressive, both in size and appearance.
For example, when the Dutch first came to Africa in the sixteenth century
one observer described the city of Benin (in present-day Nigeria) as
follows:

Timbuktu A major commercial city in western Africa from the fourteenth to the early sixteenth centuries, Timbuktu (part of which is shown here) at one time contained many large businesses, a university, and several large mosques. (The Granger Collection)

The king's palace is a collection of buildings which occupy as much space as the town of Haarlem. . . . The town is composed of thirty main streets, very straight and 120 feet wide, apart from an infinity of small intersecting streets. The houses are close to one another, arranged in good order. These people are in no way inferior to the Dutch as regards cleanliness; they wash and scrub their houses so well that they are polished and shining like a looking-glass.[5]

Political and economic development also occurred in several areas outside the western hump of Africa. The Ibo people of Nigeria, for example, were not only excellent farmers but also skilled ironworkers and brass manufacturers. Furthermore, on the east African coast there were several commercial empires that were part of a large Indian Ocean trading network.

Still, sub-Saharan Africa never achieved sustained economic growth or scientific and technological creativity to the extent that Western Europe did. The reasons for this include not only the disease-ridden climate and the geographical isolation of sub-Saharan Africa, but also low productivity in agriculture. Much of Africa has relatively poor soil, so Africans were rarely able to produce the large agricultural surpluses needed to raise the standard of living and stimulate economic and cultural innovations.

THE AMERICAS

The Aztecs of Mexico, the Incas of Peru, and the Maya of eastern Mexico and Guatemala developed complex civilizations in the Americas, but they were largely destroyed by the Spanish *conquistadores* in the 1520s and 1530s (though the last Maya stronghold was overrun only in 1697). Like the Africans, the Aztecs, Incas, and Maya were geographically isolated from the rest of the world, so they did not have the advantage of learning new ideas and techniques from Eurasian civilizations. Furthermore, their economic development was limited by a relatively low population base. (It is interesting to note here that China's overpopulation and the Americas' underpopulation both had the same negative effect on economic development.)

In addition, neither the Aztecs, Incas, nor Maya developed the large-scale system of water transport needed to encourage commerce and the evolution of a large merchant class. As a result, early American civilizations remained agricultural societies, living and working according to traditional agricultural patterns. These civilizations were highly developed in some respects, but the military power of the Spanish overwhelmed them.

WHY WESTERN CIVILIZATION CAME TO DOMINATE THE WORLD

Why did Western Civilization become so different from other civilizations and eventually capable of dominating much of the world? We cannot answer this question with absolute certainty for at least two reasons: (1) most Westerners have far more knowledge of Western history than the histories of non-Western societies, so some issues—such as why a technologically creative China did not produce an industrial revolution—are particularly difficult to explain; and (2) Western Civilization is so unique and the result of so many related factors and complex relationships that it is impossible for any analysis to take everything into account.

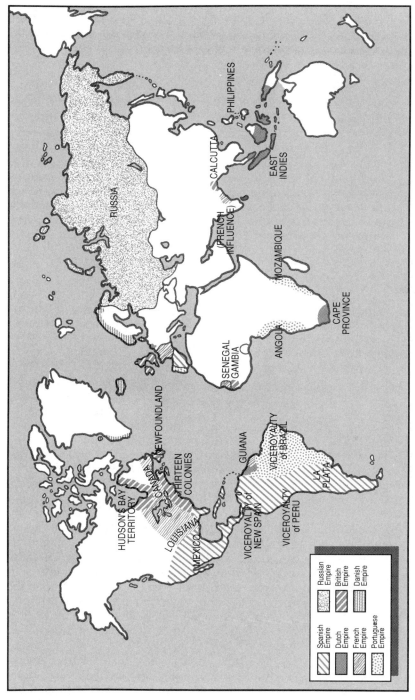

Figure 14.2 European Colonial Empires, 1750

However, it is possible to point to certain characteristics of Western Civilization that contributed to some degree to Western dominance. The following outlines these elements chronologically, from earliest to most recent:

1. *The Jewish-Greek-Christian heritage.* The Jewish and Christian conception of a transcendent God de-spiritualized nature and thereby encouraged Europeans to perceive the natural world as an inanimate thing to be used and exploited. This perception, in turn, encouraged Europeans to think technically and mechanically. The Greek conception of rational thought, particularly the assumption that all reality is rational and governed by universal laws, became a foundation of modern science. Certainly, non-Western civilizations also used technologies to exploit and understand the natural world, but they did not do so to the extent that the West did. They also did not stress rational, logical thought as much as the West.

2. *The European frontier of the early Middle Ages.* When the great Eurasian civilizations weakened during the third to sixth centuries A.D., the western half of the Roman Empire collapsed. For the people of Western Europe, the disappearance of Rome appeared to be a calamity but in the long term was an advantage. Europe became a frontier area where a new civilization, one that was culturally and technologically innovative, was created.

3. *The division of authority among European institutions.* No dynasty or ruling class was ever able to establish a centralized empire that dominated all of Europe, so the European continent was divided into nation-states. In addition, religious institutions—first the Roman Catholic church and later the various Protestant churches—usually remained separate from political institutions. These divisions helped prevent economic and technological stagnation, because nations competed with one another to achieve economic power and technological breakthroughs. (For example, Columbus, an Italian, went to Spain to find support for his oceanic voyages.) The divisions also encouraged freedom of thought, since a person harassed by one nation or church could often move to another area. Finally, during the Middle Ages, political and religious divisions encouraged the development of representative political institutions in some areas as well as the growth of free cities. Some of the cities made their own laws and controlled their own futures; some also became dynamic places where capitalism and a market economy developed. Thus, division of authority in the West left room for freedom, creativity, and dynamism. (It also left room for chronic warfare between different states and different religions.) In China, by contrast, the centralized political system sometimes hindered economic and technological innovations (for example, the fifteenth-century decision to halt Cheng Ho's sailing expeditions through the Indian Ocean). Furthermore, the strong imperial government never allowed any autonomy to

Chinese cities, and an independent, dynamic merchant class never emerged. Another contrast is with the Islamic societies, where the influence of fundamentalist religious leaders was often so pervasive that it stifled creative and scientific thought.

4. *Europe's geographical position on the western end of the Eurasian landmass.* Europe was at once far enough from Asia to have some protection against the nomad invaders who often devastated Asian societies and close enough to the Islamic world to borrow technologies developed by Muslims or transmitted by Muslims from China and India. Also important were the effects of the differing climates of Europe and Asia. India was particularly susceptible to drought-induced famines, and China often suffered from flood-induced famines. Western Europe, however, benefited from a more stable climate, fertile soils, thick forests for timber, and a good river system. Especially in northwestern Europe, the rivers provided an easy means of transport and encouraged the growth of river cities, where merchants built a commercial economy. Europeans also enjoyed a more reliable standard of living, whereas many Asians were constantly concerned about mere survival.

5. *The conquest of the oceans.* European shipping dominated the oceans from the fifteenth to the twentieth century. As a result, Europeans gained access to land and products that stimulated their economy and slowly improved their standard of living. In addition, the Europeans established control of world trade, both with the Americas and with Asia.

6. *The Scientific Revolution.* By creating modern science, Europeans acquired a new way of understanding and using nature. The Christian worldview that de-spiritualized nature and the Greek worldview that stressed the rationality of reality provided the philosophical bases for modern science. The European borrowing of knowledge from other civilizations (such as the knowledge of printing received from China) and the European propensity to create new technical instruments (such as the telescope) were also basic components of the Scientific Revolution. Furthermore, seemingly unrelated cultural developments fostered the growth of science. Late medieval philosophers like William of Occam stressed the importance of studying nature *empirically.* The Reformation led to divisions of religious authority that made it more difficult for religious institutions to inhibit the rise of the new science.

7. Underlying all other factors is the fact that *Europeans were more aggressive than other peoples.* They were more aggressive at borrowing technologies from others, at exploiting nature, and at conquering the oceans. They were also more critically minded, more inclined to question traditional beliefs and institutions. Other civilizations experienced periods of critical thought, but the questioning spirit prevailed longer and more pervasively in the West. In short, the West has been more dynamic, more focused on

change than other societies. The causes of this dynamism may be difficult to explain and the results may not always be desirable (for example, exploitation of the natural environment has caused pollution and other problems). But it is this dynamism that is the ultimate source of Western wealth and power.

CONCLUSION

From the eighteenth through the twentieth centuries, one major issue dominated much of world history: How should other civilizations and societies react to Western dominance? This issue is explored in later chapters, but at this point we should note that non-Westerners had basically two options: They could accept Western dominance, or they could learn Western ideas and techniques so they would have the knowledge and power to resist the West. One Chinese writer analyzes the situation this way:

> Since we were knocked out by cannon balls, naturally we became interested in them, thinking that by learning to make them we could strike back. . . . From studying cannon balls we came to mechanical inventions which in turn led us to political reforms, which led us again to the philosophies of the West. On the other hand, through mechanical inventions we saw science, from which we came to understand scientific method and the scientific mind. Step by step we were led farther and farther away from the cannon ball—yet we came nearer and nearer to it.[6]

THINGS YOU SHOULD KNOW

The technological and economic revolution during the T'ang and Sung dynasties in China

Why conservative traditionalism came to dominate China

Why India remained economically undeveloped and politically fragmented

Why Islamic societies became conservative after the twelfth to thirteenth centuries

Factors that hampered economic development in sub-Saharan Africa

Underlying weaknesses of the Aztec, Inca, and Mayan civilizations

Factors that help explain why Western Civilization came to dominate the world

SUGGESTED READINGS

William H. McNeill, *The Rise of the West: A History of the Human Community* (Chicago: Univ. of Chicago Press, 1963) is an award-winning interpretation of world history and an excellent introduction to the rise of the West. The best summary comparison of Western and Asian civilizations is E. L. Jones, *The European Miracle: Environments, Economies, and Geopolitics in the History of Europe and Asia* (Cambridge: Cambridge Univ. Press, 1981). John A. Hall, *Powers and Liberties: The Causes and Consequences of the Rise of the West* (Berkeley: Univ. of California Press, 1985) is insightful on the political developments that contributed to the uniqueness of Western Civilization.

Several works by Carlo Cipolla are also very good, particularly his *European Culture and Overseas Expansion* (New York: Penguin, 1970). Mark Elvin, *The Pattern of the Chinese Past* (Stanford: Stanford Univ. Press, 1973) provides an excellent analysis of key questions about Chinese history. Claude Alphonso Alvares, *Homo Faber: Technology and Culture in India, China and the West from 1500 to the Present Day* (The Hague: Martinus Nijhoff, 1980) is a pro-Asian comparison of technological developments in India, China, and the West. A Marxist, anti-Western analysis of the rise of the West is presented in Walter Rodney, *How Europe Underdeveloped Africa* (Washington, D.C.: Howard Univ. Press, 1974).

NOTES

[1] William H. McNeill, *The Rise of the West* (Chicago: Univ. of Chicago Press, 1963).

[2] Fernand Braudel, *The Perspective of the World*, vol. 3 of *Civilization and Capitalism, 15th–18th Century*, trans. Sian Reynolds (New York: Harper & Row, 1984 trans. of 1979 ed.), pp. 533–35.

[3] Quoted in Mark Elvin, *The Pattern of the Chinese Past* (Stanford: Stanford Univ. Press, 1973), p. 145.

[4] Quoted in John A. Hall, *Powers and Liberties: The Causes and Consequences of the Rise of the West* (Berkeley: Univ. of California Press, 1985), p. 56.

[5] Quoted in Walter Rodney, *How Europe Underdeveloped Africa* (Washington, D.C.: Howard Univ. Press, 1974), p. 69.

[6] Quoted in Carlo Cipolla, *European Culture and Overseas Expansion* (New York: Penguin, 1970), p. 109.

15

An Era
of Revolutions,
1750 to 1815

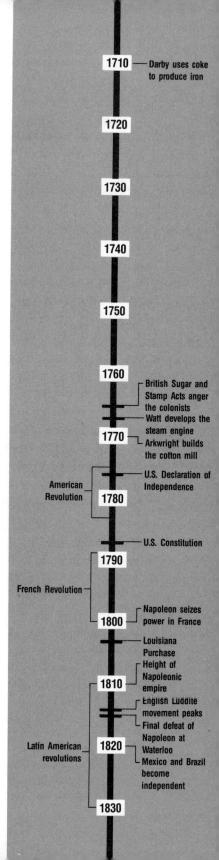

1710 — Darby uses coke to produce iron

1720

1730

1740

1750

1760

British Sugar and Stamp Acts anger the colonists

Watt develops the steam engine

1770 — Arkwright builds the cotton mill

U.S. Declaration of Independence

American Revolution

1780

U.S. Constitution

1790

French Revolution

Napoleon seizes power in France

1800

Louisiana Purchase

Height of Napoleonic empire

1810

English Luddite movement peaks

Final defeat of Napoleon at Waterloo

Latin American revolutions

1820

Mexico and Brazil become independent

1830

$\mathbf{T}$he term *revolution* refers to some fundamental transformation that produces something new. Although the word is sometimes overused, it accurately describes the period in Western history from 1750 to 1815. During this time, the Industrial Revolution in England created a new urban industrial economic system that gradually replaced the old agricultural way of life. At the same time, a series of political revolutions—the American, the French, the Latin American—established a host of new nations and also brought into being a new political principle, the belief that "the people" rather than monarchs are the ultimate source of political authority.

This era of revolutions initiated a long period of profound change in Western and world history. During the nineteenth and twentieth centuries, the Industrial Revolution spread throughout Western Civilization, producing unprecedented economic prosperity and slowly improving many people's standard of living. The political revolutions fostered the development of new political and social structures (both democratic and nondemocratic) as well as new political ideologies. Together, the industrial and political revolutions produced so much economic power and political energy that Western nations were able to conquer and dominate much of the rest of the world.

THE INDUSTRIAL REVOLUTION IN ENGLAND

For thousands of years, little significant change occurred in the material conditions of life—food, clothing, shelter, transportation, and communication. As historian C. H. Waddington put it,

> If a Roman of the Empire could be transported some eighteen centuries forward in time, he would have found himself in a society which he could, without too much difficulty, have learned to comprehend. Horace would have felt himself reasonably at home as a guest of Horace Walpole and Catullus would soon have learned his way among the sedan chairs . . . and the flaring torches of London streets at night.[1]

The eighteenth-century European economy was still overwhelmingly rural, with over 80 percent of the population working the land. The land workers differed in legal status; in Western Europe most peasants were legally free, in eastern Europe most were enserfed, and in the Americas many were slaves. But everyone who tilled the land shared a common burden—a life filled with hard work and fear of famine.

The traditional European economy included some small-scale industrial activities. There were craftspeople like weavers, bakers, and cobblers who made things by hand in family-run workshops located in every sizable town. Some of the people who worked in small workshops were part of a dispersed factory system. In the textile industry, for example, a merchant would take wool or cotton to a spinning workshop, then to a weaving workshop, and finally to a dyeing workshop. Thus, each workshop was one step in a sequence of operations. In addition, some industries—textiles, glass production, breweries—completed all stages of manufacture in one building. A textile merchant, for instance, instead of traveling among various workshops, might bring the spinners, weavers, and dyers under one roof. But the operations of these early industries were usually uncoordinated and essentially distinct from one another. And only a few small factories—such as some sawmills and the naval yard at Amsterdam—used machinery powered by running water or steam. However, these early factories were so few and so small that they had little impact on the European economy.

The Industrial Revolution that began in England in the 1770s significantly changed all earlier industrial activities. Industrialization resulted in greater use of machines propelled by nonhuman sources like steam. Other results were the formation of larger factories, in which workers were supervised and disciplined to work at the pace of machines, and a new emphasis on mass production.

Why did the Industrial Revolution begin in England? The answer to this question is complex, but certain characteristics of the English and European past help to explain some possible reasons:

1. For the Industrial Revolution to occur at all, a distinctive mentality was required. One aspect of this mentality, derived from the Scientific Revolution that began in the sixteenth century (see Chapter 12), was the tendency of philosophers and scientists to think mechanically and to perceive nature as something to be analyzed and exploited. Another aspect of this mentality was an entrepreneurial spirit, a desire to search for economic opportunity and make money.
2. The European technological tradition began among peasants and artisans in the early Middle Ages. That tradition encouraged the development and use of new techniques. The English, for example, used blast furnaces, paper mills, and underground mine pumps as early as the late sixteenth century. Although the European tradition of technology contributed to industrialization, technology itself did not cause the Industrial Revolution to occur; for example, the ancient Hellenistic Greeks and the thirteenth-century Chinese also had advanced technologies but they did not industrialize. Unlike the ancient Greeks and Chinese, the eighteenth-century English had incentives to use technology in practical ways. One incentive was the growing consumer demand in England, for the agricultural advances of the seventeenth to the eighteenth centuries produced larger food supplies and population growth (see Chapter 12). Another incentive was the expanding

English empire, which offered access to markets in North America and India.

3. Commerce made England a relatively wealthy nation even before the Industrial Revolution. English wealth, in turn, provided the capital needed to invest in the first industries and fueled consumer demand to buy products.

4. The English political and social tradition provided some freedom for the lower as well as the upper classes. Those in the laboring classes could move about in search of work opportunities and many of them were employed by the first factories. In addition, the wages they received became an important source of consumer demand. If the English laboring classes had been dominated by slaves and serfs, who were forced to remain on the land they worked and did not receive wages, England would have lacked the freedom to industrialize.

5. England possessed ample supplies of certain crucial natural resources, especially coal. Northern England had such an abundance of coal that it was called the "Black Country." It was here that the Industrial Revolution began.

Textiles

The first factories in England developed because of a need to increase the production of cotton clothing. English consumers greatly preferred cotton to wool; cotton was cheaper and lighter than wool and cotton undergarments were much more comfortable to wear than those made of wool. However, clothing production was a time-consuming process that required about eight spinners to produce enough thread to supply one weaver, who turned the thread into an article of clothing. Innovations in spinning techniques were needed to meet consumer demand for cotton clothing and several inventors developed new spinning devices that increased production. One of these devices—the spinning frame—led to the creation of the first cotton mill (see the Technology box).

The Iron Industry and the Steam Engine

New technical innovations in the iron industry and the invention of an improved steam engine also occurred in England. (See the Technology box.) High-quality iron was needed to build steam engines. The steam engines were used to pump water from coal mines, which, in turn, supplied the fuel needed to produce iron.

Steam engines were also brought into the new cotton mills, since they provided a virtually unlimited supply of energy and were superior to both the waterwheel and windmill (streams sometimes dried up, and the wind could stop blowing). With steam-powered textile machines, cotton mills could operate continuously. Thus, industrialists began to institute the

Spinning Machines and the Cotton Mill

For centuries, the process of spinning cotton or wool into thread had been done one thread at a time, usually on a spinning wheel located in the spinner's home. In 1764, however, James Hargreaves developed the "spinning jenny," a device that held eight spindles of thread vertically side by side. Because only one worker was required to operate the device, small-scale mass production was made possible. Gradually, the number of spindles was increased to 120. Hargreaves's neighbors in the town of Blackburn, many of whom were spinners, destroyed his first jennies because they thought the new machine would destroy their livelihoods.

Another innovation in clothing production was the spinning frame developed by Richard Arkwright in the late 1760s. Arkwright's frame was an elaborate arrangement of rollers and spindles that could spin a dozen threads at once. More important, the threads it produced were of a higher quality than those made by the spinning jenny. Because the frame was too large to be powered by human energy, Arkwright attached it to a waterwheel by a small stream near the village of Cromford in northern England. He then summoned workers to leave their workshops at home and come to work in his cotton mill. The first cotton mill appeared in 1770–1771, and within a few years many others sprang up in northern England.

There were still other innovations in textile machinery. Samuel Crompton's "mule" was an improved combination of Hargreaves's spinning jenny and Arkwright's spinning frame. The most fundamental breakthrough, however, was not in textile machinery but in the formation of the cotton mill.

Spinning Jenny *James Hargreaves's invention of the spinning jenny in 1764, a major step in the development of the textile industry, increased the production of threads used to make cloth from one to eight threads at a time. (The Bettmann Archive)*

three-shift system, employing different groups of workers to keep the machines running around the clock. The three-shift system was a new and somewhat shocking experience for workers, but it did have the effect of increasing textile production and thereby lowering the price of cotton goods. (The steam engine was also fundamental to the development of the railroad later on, as we will see in Chapter 16.)

Industrialization Transforms England

The cotton mill, the use of coal to fuel an expanding iron industry, and the steam engine were the most fundamental breakthroughs of the first Industrial Revolution in England. Together, they transformed life in England. One obvious change was the effect of the new industries on the natural environment. Arthur Young, an unsympathetic observer, wrote this about Coalbrookdale:

> Coalbrook Dale itself is a very romantic spot, it is a winding glen between two immense hills which break into various forms, and all thickly covered with wood, forming the most beautiful sheets of hanging wood. Indeed too beautiful to be much in unison with that variety of horrors art has spread at the bottom; the noise of the forges, mills, etc., with all their vast machinery, the flames bursting from the furnaces with the burning of the coal and the smoak of the lime kilns. . . .[2]

Another change brought by industrialization was the growth of industrial towns. The port of Liverpool had a population of almost 80,000 by 1801, and nearby was a cluster of cotton mill towns, including Wigan, Preston, Blackburn, and Manchester.

The Middle Class   The industrial towns contained two new and expanding social classes: a *middle class* made up of wealthy businesspeople and a large industrial *working class*. The middle class was a varied group. Some were former merchants who knew how to invest and expand their income, others were inventors who became rich because of the devices they created, and still others were former craftspeople who were fortunate enough to be able to start a business with only a small investment.

The new middle-class business people also shared certain characteristics. Most were ambitious people interested in little else but their work. For example, Richard Arkwright, the developer of the first cotton mill, was born into a poor family, had little formal education, and as a young man worked first as a barber and then as a clockmaker. But he was aggressive enough to try to invent new devices and had the good fortune to produce his spinning frame at the time it was most needed. As a

Coal and Steam

Before the eighteenth century, iron foundries produced only small quantities of low-quality iron. One of the difficulties was that charcoal derived from wood was the chief fuel used in the iron-smelting process. It was hard to control the temperature of the charcoal and the foundries were consuming so much timber that wood became increasingly scarce and expensive in England.

One solution to these problems was to use coal instead of charcoal for fuel. But coal contains sulphur, which can damage the iron being produced. By charring or burning the coal, however, the coal is turned into coke and the sulphur is removed. Around 1710, at Coalbrookdale in western England, the ironmaster Abraham Darby began systematically to turn coal into coke in this way, enabling him to produce higher-quality and less expensive iron. His son made further improvements, and by the second half of the eighteenth century, Coalbrookdale became the stimulus of a growing English iron industry. In 1779, the Coalbrookdale foundry produced a cast-iron bridge, the first of its kind, that still spans the Severn River.

The Darby family used a steam engine, originally built in 1708 by Thomas Newcomen, to pump water out of coal mines. Newcomen's engine was relatively inefficient, however, because it had to be continually cooled and then reheated. Around 1764, James Watt from Scotland discovered how to avoid the wasteful cooling process by building a separate cylinder (a condenser) where steam from the main cylinder of the engine could be collected. Watt produced his first improved steam engine in 1769.

James Watt *A Scottish inventor, James Watt (1736–1819) is depicted here examining Thomas Newcomen's steam engine in an effort to learn how to improve it. (Culver Pictures)*

businessman, Arkwright was notorious for his self-discipline and strict work habits. According to an observer,

> Arkwright commonly laboured in his multifarious concerns from five o'clock in the morning till nine at night; and when considerably more than fifty years of age . . . he encroached upon his sleep, in order to gain an hour each day to learn English grammar. . . . He was impatient of whatever interfered with his favorite pursuits; and . . . he separated from his wife not many years after their marriage. . . . Arkwright was a severe economist of time. . . . He generally managed in such a way, that, whoever lost, he himself was a gainer.[3]

Arkwright eventually accumulated a large fortune and was later knighted by the English government.

Many middle-class businesspeople shared a common religious heritage. About half of the first industrialists were members of dissenting religious sects that did not belong to the official church of England established during the Reformation; some examples of these religious sects include the Quakers, Baptists, and Presbyterians. As dissenters, these businesspeople were barred from attending universities and holding government offices, so they sought to channel their ambitions into the economic sphere. Most of them also shared a common attitude about their workers. They tended to believe that their workers required strict discipline in order to be productive, as this then-popular jingle indicates:

> In works of Labour or of Skill
>   I would be busy too:
> For Satan finds some Mischief still
>   for idle hands to do.[4]

The Working Class   The working class emerged as people from all over England came to work in the first factories. Some people moved to the industrial towns from the surrounding English countryside; others were emigrants from impoverished areas of Scotland and Ireland. Many women and children were employed in cotton mills, because they could be paid less than men and their smaller-sized hands could more easily mend broken threads in the machines. Since their hands were often caught in the machines, many had their fingers severed or mangled.

Working conditions were hard for the working class. The typical workday lasted fourteen to eighteen hours and included only a few minutes for lunch. The typical workweek included only a half-day off on Sunday. Discipline in the factories was strict, and workers who argued with supervisors were usually fired. At times workers were required to wear labels of different colors designating grades of good and bad behavior.

Some workers rebelled against industrialization. Traditional crafts-people—those who made things by hand—often feared that the new machines would destroy their livelihood and so tried to destroy their enemies. The destruction of machines began in England as early as the 1750s and peaked in the early nineteenth century with the Luddite movement, named after the fictitious character Ned Ludd. The Luddites began to destroy textile machinery around 1811. Their attacks continued for several years, until the English government eventually crushed the movement. Many Luddites were either hanged or transported to Australia, but their actions inspired others. In the 1820s, some French workers tried to kick machines to pieces; their actions were labeled "sabotage" because they wore wooden shoes called *sabots*.

Was early industrialization a blessing or a curse for the working class? Certainly, the first British industrial workers lived poorly, for they were usually clustered in urban slums where housing was scarce and sanitation facilities were inadequate. One result was the spread of diseases like typhus and cholera. Another was the prevalence of drunkenness, as many workers tried to escape their miseries by drinking themselves into oblivion. Many people were desperately poor; one report tells of a fifteen-year-old female orphan who supported herself, a brother, and a sister by selling flowers for a few pennies a day. At the same time, though, industrial wages rose in a few places and thus made life better for some workers. The Industrial Revolution offered the working class at least some hope that mass production would eventually lead to higher standards of living for everyone. Furthermore, the British government slowly adopted legislation designed to correct the worst employer abuses of early industrialization. The Factory Act of 1833 required a reduction in the number of work hours for children employed in textile mills, and another law of 1847 stipulated a ten-hour workday for both women and children. Thus, early industrialization both helped and hurt the economic well-being of the working class. The earliest workers probably suffered some decline in standard of living, but that decline was relatively small since most people's standard of living before industrialization was never very high.

In addition to physical hardships, the working class also experienced spiritual and psychological tensions associated with the Industrial Revolution in England. First among these was the new industrial sense of "time." In preindustrial days, most people worked at home at their own pace and in their own way. With industrialization, however, workers were expected to appear at their jobs at a certain time and to work at a pace set by the machine and the factory clock. The first factories may have seemed more like prisons to the workers, for many owners had great difficulty in getting workers to come to work "on time."

A further point is that many of the first British industrial workers lost access to traditional religion, the Christianity that for centuries had been the mainstay of rural village churches. Church organizations failed to build enough religious centers in the new industrial cities. By 1851, only 34 percent of the Sheffield working class had access to churches, in Liverpool and Manchester the figure was 31 percent, and in Birmingham 29 percent. Consequently, many workers became indifferent to religion and increasingly secular in their attitudes and beliefs. Others turned to emotional, revivalistic religions like the Methodist movement for spiritual comfort.

Industrialization at the End of the Eighteenth Century

By 1800, industrialization in the form of cotton mills and steam engines existed only in northern England and a few other scattered places such as northern France and Belgium. As we will see in later chapters, industrialization spread rapidly through much of Europe and North America during the nineteenth century.

THE AMERICAN REVOLUTION

The American Revolution erupted in the British colonies of North America at about the same time as the Industrial Revolution in England. The term *American Revolution* is somewhat of a misnomer, since only one group of Americans—those who lived in what became the United States of America—were involved. Everyone who lived in North and South America was "American" in geographical terms, but those in Canada and Latin America were not involved in the American Revolution.

Basic Causes

The British colonists in North America had more freedom than most other people of the eighteenth century. The British imperial administration governed leniently. Colonial administrators rarely interfered directly in the lives of people, and there was no state church to impose religious orthodoxy. Further, the variety of political and religious ideas encouraged thought and debate in British North America. There was greater diversity of religious beliefs than in most European countries, because many of the original colonists were religious dissenters who came to the New World in search of religious freedom. There was also great diversity of political ideas, since many of the educated colonists were familiar with the radical theories produced during the seventeenth-century English civil war and the innovative ideas created by Enlightenment intellectuals.

The North American wilderness also enhanced the growth of personal freedom. The availability of free land meant that a large number of people could own personal property. Also, land ownership gave male colonists the right to vote, so a large percentage of them voted in elections for local colonial legislatures. (Women, black slaves, and native Americans were not permitted to vote.) Other effects of the North American wilderness were to orient many of the colonists westward and to give them a sense of separation from Britain and Europe.

The fundamental problem that led to the conflict between Britain and the colonists was the British government's attempt to impose greater control over the colonies in the 1760s. The British government was neither tyrannical nor unreasonable compared to other governments of the time, but it was dealing with colonists accustomed to being left alone and therefore it seemed more tyrannical than it actually was. It was also remarkably unperceptive and insensitive to the attitudes and beliefs of the colonists.

The British quest for greater control over the North American colonies was precipitated by the Seven Years' War (1756–1763), known in the colonies as the French and Indian War. The war involved all the major European powers, but for our purposes in this discussion its most important feature was a global struggle between Britain and France. The British and French fought each other in Canada and in India, with the British winning and gaining control of Canada, most of the future United States east of the Mississippi River, and parts of India. Thus, the British empire grew enormously, and in the process incurred added expenses and responsibilities. The British had to administer and police vast new territories; they concluded that the North American colonists should help pay the expenses of the empire that provided peace and prosperity for them.

In 1764, the British government passed the Sugar Act, designed to halt colonial smuggling of sugar and to collect a tax on sugar imports. In 1765, the Stamp Act instituted a tax on legal documents and newspapers. The response in the colonies included riots in some cities and the calling of the Stamp Act Congress, which argued that the British Parliament had no right to impose taxes on colonists. Officials who tried to collect the stamp tax were abused. The following passage from a handbill expresses the hope that tax collectors would endure terrible torments:

> Grant Heaven that he may never go without
> The Rheumatism, Itch, the Pox, or Gout.
> May he be hamper'd with some ugly Witch,
> And dye at last in some curst foulsome Ditch.
> Without the Benefit of Psalms or Hymnes,
> And Crowds of Crows devour his rotten limbs.[5]

The Stamp Act was repealed in 1766, but the British continued to insist that Parliament had the right to tax the colonists.

The colonists saw it differently. To them, taxes on property were a fundamental political and human issue. Property ownership was a characteristic of freedom, and since high taxes could detract from or even destroy a person's property, they could also destroy personal freedom. Particularly vociferous in their protests were the merchants of Boston, who strongly opposed British efforts to regulate colonial shipping and trade. In 1768, British troops were stationed in Boston in an attempt to calm the situation, but their presence only inflamed tensions. Then, in 1773, Parliament passed the Tea Act, which included a tax on tea imports. In response, colonists disguised themselves as native Americans and dumped a shipload of tea into the Boston harbor in what was called the Boston Tea Party. In 1774, the British approved the so-called Coercive Acts, which closed the port of Boston and arranged for British troops to be quartered in private homes.

The Declaration of Independence

By 1775, many North American colonists were convinced that the British government was conspiring to destroy their traditional liberties, while the British were increasingly irritated by colonists who seemed excessively stubborn and unreasonable. This situation turned violent in April 1775, when British military units sought to confiscate colonial munitions stockpiled near Lexington and Concord, Massachusetts. Some colonial militia resisted, and the two sides fought briefly. Convinced that the British would continue to use force, the colonists sent delegates to a Continental Congress, which established a Continental army late in 1775 under the command of General George Washington. Then, in July 1776, the Congress approved the Declaration of Independence from Great Britain. The Declaration, among other things, affirmed such Enlightenment ideals as the existence of individual "rights" and the right of the people, rather than monarchs, to form governments.

The American War of Independence

The American War of Independence was, like most wars, a terrible affair for those involved. Battle reports tell of brains being knocked out, heads being cut off, and bowels gushing out. The British employed professional soldiers, who performed well according to the military standards of the time. Most of the American soldiers were volunteers inspired by the call to defend American liberties. The Americans had a major advantage in that they were fighting on home territory and enjoyed the support and aid of many private citizens.

Both sides of the revolutionary war confronted major problems. The British were handicapped by their inability to develop a coherent strategy

U.S. Declaration of Independence This handwritten version of the Declaration of
Independence—one of the most important documents in Western history—shows
some of the revisions made during the creation of the final draft. In the first line of
the second paragraph, the word *self-evident* was added to make the sentence read
"We hold these truths to be self-evident. . . ." (Culver Pictures)

against the colonists, by the 3,000-mile distance between Britain and
North America and the resulting communications difficulties, and by the
fact that some of the best British leaders opposed the war. Furthermore,
the British were fighting a dispersed enemy, one with no central authority
whose capture would end the rebellion. The Americans were hampered
by continual desertions from their army, often by men who simply
wanted to return home to their families. Also, the war was actively
supported by only about a third of the American population, for about
one-third remained loyal to Britain and another third did not seem to
care either way.

The turning point of the revolutionary war was the American victory
at Saratoga, New York, in October 1777. The victory encouraged France,
Britain's old enemy, to support the colonial rebellion. The American–
French alliance of 1778 frightened the British, for it suggested that
France might invade Britain. Furthermore, the French navy gave the

Americans some access to and control of the sea. It was French power combined with the strength of the Continental army that led to the defeat and surrender of British General Cornwallis at Yorktown in 1781.

Yorktown was the last major battle of the revolutionary war; the British were dispirited and more interested in increasing their industrial power than in continuing the war. The Americans were also tired of war, and the Continental Congress was virtually bankrupt. One delegate recalled what happened when Congress received the news of Yorktown:

> When the messenger brought the news of this capitulation to Congress, it was necessary to furnish him with hard money for expenses. There was not a sufficiency in the Treasury to do it, and the members of Congress, of which I was one, each paid a dollar to accomplish it.[6]

The Treaty of Paris of 1783 recognized the independence of a new nation—the United States of America. It was a new type of nation, one in which "the people" were considered sovereign. Many Americans believed that their country was divinely ordained to lead the rest of the world to a more enlightened and more democratic form of government. Some Europeans agreed, and the United States became a symbol of freedom and opportunity to those who hoped for political reform in Europe.

A New Constitution

At first, the new nation was governed under the Articles of Confederation, which centered political power in the various state legislatures. But the Articles left the central government so weak that it could not protect national boundaries from hostile powers. The British, for example, refused to evacuate some forts, and at one point Spain closed the Mississippi River to American commerce.

To establish a more effective government, a Constitutional Convention was held in Philadelphia in 1787. The delegates were a particularly creative group of political leaders. Among the most influential was James Madison of Virginia. He, more than anyone else, led the Convention in the writing of a new Constitution of the United States—one that created a strong central government in which power was divided among an executive, a legislature, and a judiciary. From the perspective of world history, the new Constitution was a unique document; it stipulated that "the people" were sovereign and provided for an elected president (the first being George Washington) rather than a monarch. In reality, however, most people were neither sovereign nor represented in government. Women were not allowed to vote, most blacks were enslaved, and native Americans were continually forced off their lands by white settlers with the support of the government. (The British writer Samuel Johnson once exclaimed: "How is it that we hear the loudest yelps for liberty from the drivers of negroes?")[7]

Growth of the United States

The new United States grew rapidly. In 1803, the government concluded the Louisiana Purchase, in which much of the Mississippi valley and the Great Plains were bought from France. The Louisiana Purchase doubled the size of the United States and opened the way for American expansion across the continent. That expansion was stimulated by the Lewis and Clark expedition of 1804–1806, during which Meriwether Lewis and William Clark led a group of explorers across the northern plains and the Rocky Mountains to the Pacific Ocean.

But the Americans still faced one more confrontation with their old enemy, the British. During the early nineteenth century, Britain was leading a prolonged war against France in an attempt to prevent Napoleon from dominating the European continent (as we will see later in the chapter). The British believed that the United States supported France, and in fact the Americans once tried to conquer parts of Canada. The friction led to the War of 1812–1814, during which British forces invaded the United States and burned much of the new capital at Washington, D.C. The United States was too large for Britain to reconquer, however, so British troops soon withdrew and never returned.

The British thus lost the long struggle with the Americans, but at the same time they won something else. During the last decades of the eighteenth century, the British were establishing their commercial and industrial leadership of the world economy, and they were more interested in that than in subduing a rebellious colony. In a sense, they let go of the United States to concentrate on their economic rivals—the Netherlands and France. In 1786, an obscure agreement named the Eden Treaty opened France to British imports, and the British iron and textiles industries quickly captured much of the French market. British economic power soon expanded to include the rest of Europe, the United States, Latin America, and Asia.

THE FRENCH REVOLUTION

The French Revolution had a far greater impact than the American. France was in the midst of Europe and thus in a position to have a significant influence on many other countries. The French Revolution was more radical and more violent as well, because deep social cleavages existed in France. Unlike Britain's American colonies, France had a privileged nobility that was fiercely hostile to revolution as well as a large and poor lower class that came to see revolution as a way of striking back at its aristocratic enemies.

Because the revolution in France had such a great effect on European and world history, it is important to examine its history in some detail. The revolution can be divided into five periods: (1) the aristocratic phase (1787–1789), (2) the National Assembly (1789–1791), (3) the Reign of Terror (1792–1794), (4) the Thermidorean Reaction and the Directory (1794–1799), and (5) the Napoleonic era (1799–1815).

The Aristocratic Phase (1787–1789)

The French Revolution was precipitated by a financial crisis in the French state. The expenses of numerous military campaigns—the wars of Louis XIV during the late seventeenth and early eighteenth centuries, the attempts to conquer an empire in North America and Asia, the support of the American Revolution—had greatly increased the French national debt. The underlying difficulty was that national taxes were not sufficient to meet these expenses, in part because the nobility and clergy were exempt from paying direct taxes. To remedy this situation, Louis XVI (reigned 1774–1793) and his ministers hoped to institute tax increases, and their first target was the aristocracy.

Leaders of the aristocracy sought to use the financial crisis to carry out a political transformation similar to the English Glorious Revolution of 1688. (The Glorious Revolution, in which King James II was driven out of England and replaced by William and Mary, marked the end of a long civil conflict in England. One result was that the English upper classes gained more political power and influence.) Specifically, they hoped to limit the power of the monarchy and increase the influence of the aristocracy. Toward that end, they refused to accept new taxes and demanded that Louis XVI call into session the Estates General, an ancient assembly that largely represented the wealthy and powerful and that had not met since 1614. Louis, having no real choice, summoned the Estates General to meet on 1 May 1789. The aristocrats appeared to have triumphed, but they did not realize how angry the middle classes and peasants were about the aristocratic ability to evade paying taxes. They also did not realize that Enlightenment ideals, such as toleration and the right of people to consent to government, had influenced many middle-class people.

The National Assembly (1789–1791)

The Estates General consisted of three estates, the first representing the clergy, the second the aristocracy, and the Third Estate theoretically representing everybody else but in practice being dominated by middle-class businesspeople and lawyers. The traditional rules stipulated that the three estates would meet separately, with each having one vote. Thus, the first two estates, representing only a small part of France, had two votes and the Third Estate had only one vote. The effect was to leave power in the hands of the upper classes.

The delegates of the Third Estate refused to accept the traditional voting system, and for six weeks (from early May to mid-June 1789) the Estates General was immobilized by quarrels over voting procedures. Then, on June 17, the members of the Third Estate, joined by a few aristocrats and clergy, voted to declare themselves the *National Assembly* of the French nation. That vote was the first clearly revolutionary act, for it was a repudiation of tradition and a demand for political reform.

But a few hundred lawyers calling themselves the National Assembly could not by themselves make a revolution, since Louis XVI could easily have used the army to disperse the Assembly. He did not do so, because in the summer of 1789 many of the French common people were rioting, and the army was busy trying to maintain basic social order. The initial cause of the riots was not politics but food shortages resulting from bad harvests. The chaos quickly assumed political overtones, however. In Paris, a mob of hungry workers focused its hatred on an ancient prison, the Bastille. The Bastille was a symbol of an increasingly discredited government, and its capture on July 14 was hailed as a great revolutionary action (though ironically it held only a few prisoners). At the same time, an extraordinary phenomenon—the "Great Fear"—was surging through the French countryside. The causes of the Great Fear remain largely mysterious, but it was obvious that many French peasants were frightened—perhaps by wild rumors of invading armies, by the aristocrats, and by the unknown. As a result, peasant mobs roamed country roads, sometimes killing innocent but unfortunate travelers and often attacking and burning aristocratic estates.

The rioting French populace unknowingly saved the National Assembly, because under the circumstances Louis XVI was unable to focus the army's attention on the middle-class lawyers who claimed to represent France. Thus, the immediate cause of the French Revolution was the simultaneous occurrence of two unconnected events—the financial crisis that led to the calling of the Estates General and the food shortages that produced fear and discontent among the lower classes.

The events of 1789 caused great excitement throughout Europe. G. W. F. Hegel, then a young philosopher in Germany, called 1789 "a glorious dawn." The English poet William Wordsworth wrote:

Bliss was it in that dawn to be alive,
But to be young was very Heaven![8]

In Paris, journalists and pamphleteers began to popularize a new political vocabulary. The slogan of the Revolution soon became: "Liberty,

Fraternity, Equality." Some words—*democracy, republic, nation*—acquired new revolutionary connotations, and others—*Socialist, Communist*—were being invented.

To achieve the ideals of the Revolution required abolishing the privileges of the aristocracy and the church. In August 1789, the National Assembly voted to eliminate aristocratic feudal rights—various judicial powers, exemptions from taxation, and the like. Later that same month, the Assembly passed the Declaration of the Rights of Man and Citizen, which declared that all people would "remain free and equal in rights." In 1790, the Civil Constitution of the Clergy brought the Catholic church under government control and confiscated much of the church's wealth. The next year, the Constitution of 1791 was approved. It sought to establish a constitutional monarchy in which Louis XVI would remain king and govern in cooperation with a legislature elected by the wealthier citizens. The goal of the National Assembly was a relatively moderate political system, similar to that maintained in England since 1688.

However, the Constitution of 1791 was quickly undermined by several factors. The Catholic church, deeply resentful of the Civil Constitution of the Clergy, became increasingly hostile to the Revolution. Many devout peasants supported the church, and the eventual result in some parts of France was civil war between supporters of the Revolution and supporters of the church. In addition, most aristocrats refused to accept the loss of their privileges. Many emigrated to other European countries (hence becoming known as *émigrés*) and began to persuade foreign governments to launch a counterrevolution against France. Finally, war broke out between revolutionary France and counterrevolutionary Austria and Prussia in 1792. Austria and Prussia planned to invade France and crush the Revolution; the French revolutionaries hoped that the war would increase national support for the Revolution. The fighting, eventually joined by other nations, continued for twenty-three years.

These factors thus helped to radicalize the French Revolution. The reality of civil war and foreign attack convinced most revolutionary leaders that no compromise was possible, that whatever was needed to save the Revolution was justified. Therefore, political power within France passed to the radicals who vowed to destroy the enemies of the Revolution and establish an egalitarian democracy.

The Reign of Terror (1792–1794)

The *Reign of Terror* was, depending on one's point of view, either the high or low point of the French Revolution. To those who supported the Revolution, it was a time of great idealism when revolutionaries began to establish a new political and social order that would make life better for most French. To those who feared and opposed the Revolution, the Reign of Terror was a period of extreme violence and bloodshed that tarnished forever the reputation of the Revolution.

The government during the Reign of Terror was the Convention, a new assembly elected in 1792 by universal manhood suffrage. The Convention was strongly influenced by the *sansculottes* ("without breeches"), Parisian lower-class people whose name came from the trousers they wore instead of the knee-breeches characteristic of nobles. The sansculottes were artisans and working people who were hostile to the privileged aristocracy and who wanted a government based on political and social equality. To meet their demands, the Convention declared France a "republic," meaning a nation governed by an elected assembly. And, Louis XVI, increasingly perceived as a traitor by the revolutionaries, was executed along with his wife early in 1793.

By 1793, the Jacobins were the dominant group within the Convention. Founded in 1789, the Jacobins were a political organization of the most radical revolutionaries, and their influence had gradually increased as their ideals—political democracy and equality—became more popular in France. The leader of the Jacobins early in 1793 was Georges-Jacques Danton (1759–1794), but he was soon supplanted by Maximilien Robespierre (1758–1794). Robespierre was the central figure on the Committee of Public Safety, the committee of twelve appointed in 1793 by the Convention to lead the Revolution. He was also a selfless idealist who personified both the best and the worst of the revolutionary movement. Robespierre wanted to build what he called a "Republic of Virtue," a society in which all people would be equal and devoted to the welfare of the nation. His desire for an egalitarian social order was manifested in a number of ways. Legal titles associated with the aristocracy (such as "duke" and "count") were abolished, and everyone was called a "citizen" (as in Citizen Jones, Citizen Smith). A new calendar was created to symbolize the birth of a new society and a new period of history. The year 1792 became year I, and the months were given new names derived from the various seasons of the year. (For example, *Thermidor,* "the hot month," extended from mid-July to mid-August; and *Brumaire,* "the foggy month," went from mid-October to mid-November.) In addition, plans were drawn up for a national educational system, and the Ventose decrees proposed to redistribute land confiscated from aristocrats to poor peasants. These last two ideas never truly went into effect. But a new military system did—the *levée en masse,* a patriotic conscription that called the French into the army to defend their country. This creation of a mass "democratic" army led to a transformation in military strategy. Previously, most armies had been small professional units often composed of men who were forcibly conscripted. But with patriotism becoming a motivating force, French armies became much larger and other nations soon began to build their own citizen armies. One result was larger battles, involving more soldiers and more casualties.

The *levée en masse* was instituted because France was at war. Civil war raged in several areas of the country where conservatives and Catholics mobilized opposition to the Revolution. Foreign war threatened the borders, as Austria, Prussia, and eventually Britain tried to crush the Revolution. Robespierre and the other revolutionaries concluded that extreme measures were necessary. The civil wars in the provinces were brutally suppressed whenever possible, and many died. In Paris, the guillotine was set up to execute traitors. The guillotine—a machine designed to behead people quickly and therefore be more humane than traditional methods of execution—became the focal point of a patriotic ritual, as large crowds came to witness executions and demonstrate support for the French Revolution. Between 15,000 and 20,000 were officially executed by the guillotine and other methods during the Reign of Terror. Many others died unofficially.

By the summer of 1794, charges of treason and executions were so common in Paris that virtually everyone was afraid of becoming a victim. In the Convention, Robespierre's opponents decided to get him before he got them, and in July he was arrested and then executed. More moderate forces quickly assumed control of the government, and the Reign of Terror ended soon thereafter.

The Thermidorean Reaction and the Directory (1794–1799)

The execution of Robespierre occurred during the month of Thermidor (according to the revolutionary calendar), so the period of relative calmness and moderation that followed the Reign of Terror is usually referred to as the *Thermidorean Reaction*. France was still controlled by revolutionaries, but they were moderate rather than radical. As a result, executions greatly decreased, the guillotine virtually disappeared, the Committee of Public Safety was soon abolished, and the influence of the Jacobins declined.

A new government was established to sustain a moderate revolution. This was called the *Directory*, a committee of five people elected indirectly by the wealthier citizens. The Directory thus represented the liberal middle classes rather than the more radical lower classes. It ruled France from 1795 to 1799.

The Napoleonic Era (1799–1815)

The last phase of the French Revolution was dominated by one man, Napoleon Bonaparte (1769–1821). As a young man, Napoleon trained for a military career; then, when the Revolution broke out, he joined a

Napoleon This painting of French Revolution commander Napoleon Bonaparte (1769–1821), by the artist Jacques-Louis David (1748–1825), portrays the French emperor as a heroic figure seeking new worlds to conquer. (Archives Photographiques, Caisse Nationale des Monuments Historiques)

Jacobin club and eventually won a number of important battles for France. Napoleon's victories made him a national hero and encouraged his political ambitions. Then, in November 1799, he and his troops overthrew the Directory and Napoleon became ruler of France.

Napoleon was a complex figure. Unlike most powerful leaders who usually came from the upper classes, he rose to the top from humble beginnings. He was a despot who crowned himself "Emperor of the French" in 1804 and a military conqueror who dreamed of ruling all of

Europe. Yet, Napoleon also thought of himself as a child of the French Revolution and thus responsible for implementing revolutionary ideals. Both in France and in other countries he conquered, Napoleon tried to carry out such revolutionary reforms as modernizing legal codes and establishing educational institutions.

Napoleon's enduring fame resulted ultimately from his military career. He sought to dominate all of Europe. He was successful at first, as he used the mass armies created by the *levée en masse* and a daring offensive strategy to win great victories. By 1808, his empire extended into Spain, the Low Countries, northern Italy, and much of western Germany. But Napoleon's ambitions were so great that a coalition of other powers gradually formed to block him. Austria and Prussia had fought against revolutionary France since the 1790s, and they continued to do so. Britain organized a sea blockade of the Napoleonic empire (which helped provoke the War of 1812–1814 between Britain and the United States). The Spanish never accepted Napoleonic domination and carried on what became known as "guerilla warfare" (surprise raids by irregular troops) against the French enemy. Russia was responsible for Napoleon's greatest defeat. In 1812, Napoleon assembled a huge army of over half a million troops and invaded Russia. He reached Moscow in the summer of 1812, but the Russians refused to surrender and waited for the winter weather to destroy their invaders. The retreat of the French army during the autumn and early winter of that year turned into a nightmare, as the sniping Russian army and the winter cold gradually destroyed around 80 percent of the French. Then, in 1813, Napoleon was decisively defeated at the battle of Leipzig. In 1814, another defeat by a coalition of European armies forced Napoleon into exile. He soon returned to launch one last campaign in 1815, but the Battle of Waterloo ended his military career.

The final defeat of Napoleon marked the end of the French Revolution. In 1815, the nations of Europe met in the Congress of Vienna to establish peace in Europe and to restore monarchical rule in France. But Europe, and indeed much of the rest of the world, could never return to pre-1789 institutions and beliefs. French revolutionary ideals—liberty, equality, fraternity (meaning a sense of nationalism)—would continue to reverberate through Europe and eventually much of the world during the nineteenth and twentieth centuries.

THE LATIN AMERICAN WARS FOR INDEPENDENCE

The same forces that fostered the American and French revolutions also stimulated demands for political independence in Latin America. Geog-

Figure 15.1   Independence of Latin American Nations

raphy encouraged among Latin Americans a sense of separation from
Europe. The taxes and political control imposed by the Spanish crown
drove inhabitants of the Spanish colonies to resent imperial government.
The ideas of the Enlightenment also created interest in the new political
ideals of liberty and equality. So, when the British colonists in North
America gained their independence and the French revolutionaries
overthrew the monarchy, it seemed that the time was ripe for Latin
Americans to accomplish the same things.

Haiti

But ironically, the first Latin American revolution was directed not against Spain but against the leader of revolution in Europe, France. Haiti, a French colony since the late seventeenth century, was a land of large plantations worked by African slaves. The slaves rebelled in 1791. Savage fighting continued for a decade until 1801, when the black leader Toussaint L'Ouverture controlled the entire country and declared the slaves free. But Napoleon sent out an army to reassert French control, and L'Ouverture was soon imprisoned. The rebellion continued, however, under the leadership of Jean-Jacques Dessalines, and Haitian independence was established in 1804. Haiti, governed by black leaders, was only the second independent country in the Americas, but its future was to be one of poverty and tyranny.

Mexico

A rebellion against Spanish rule began in Mexico around 1810. Father Miguel Hidalgo y Costilla, a rural priest, encouraged native American peasants to rise up against upper-class Spanish oppression. His words were striking: "My children, will you be free? Will you make the effort to recover from the hated Spaniards the lands stolen from your forefathers three hundred years ago?"[9] Hidalgo's call for social revolution frightened both the Spanish government and the Mexican upper classes, and he was quickly executed. The conservative upper classes soon seized control of the independence movement, because an 1820 revolt in Spain brought liberal forces to power there and the Mexican conservatives wanted to be independent of a liberal Spain. Spain was too weakened by European political conflicts to control Mexico, so Mexico's independence became a reality in 1821.

South America

The struggle for independence in South America went through three stages: (1) from 1810 to 1814, independence movements grew and began to attack Spanish power; (2) from 1814 to 1816, Spain strengthened its forces and defeated some of the independence movements; and (3) from 1817 to 1824, a series of wars led to the final defeat of Spain and the attainment of independence throughout virtually all of South America. The wars were fought and supported largely by the South American middle classes; the lower-class native Americans and blacks had little impact on political decisions. The armies were led by a small number of brilliant generals who became the heroes of the independence era. One was Simón Bolívar (1783–1830), an Enlightenment-educated idealist who believed that "the freedom of America is the hope of the universe."[10]

Simón Bolívar Simón Bolívar (1783–1830) is one of the heroes of the Latin American wars of independence. The country of Bolivia was named for him. (Culver Pictures)

In 1816, Bolívar launched an attack against Spanish forces in northern South America and soon gained control of the areas that became Venezuela and Colombia. He then moved south into Peru, where he met another independence army pushing northward from Argentina. This army was led by another great general, José de San Martín (1778–1850), who in 1817 directed an Argentine army over the Andes into Chile. After liberating Chile, San Martín drove into Peru, where he and Bolívar surrounded the remaining bastions of Spanish power. The last Spanish army in Peru was defeated in 1824. At that point, the only areas in the Western Hemisphere still controlled by Spain were Cuba and Puerto Rico. Most of what had been Spanish America was independent although not united (as we will see shortly).

Brazil, a Portuguese colony, was the only place in South America where independence came relatively quietly and peaccfully. When Napoleon conquered Portugal in 1807, the Portuguese royal family escaped to Brazil and made it the governing center of the Portuguese empire. After Napoleon's defeat, the Portuguese monarch returned to Europe in 1821. By that time the rest of South America was on the verge of attaining independence from Spain, so the Brazilian upper classes demanded independence for their country as well. The Portuguese rulers, familiar with and knowledgeable about their colony, knew they could not control Brazil. Thus, in 1822, independence was granted to Brazil, and the son of the Portuguese king became Pedro I, the first Brazilian emperor. Brazil's independence was accomplished with virtually no bloodshed.

Latin American history after the winning of independence was significantly different from the history of the United States. For one thing, Latin Americans divided into more than a dozen separate countries—Brazil, Argentina, Colombia, and others—rather than uniting into one nation. One reason for this was geography, as high mountains and dense jungles separated population centers from one another and fostered a sense of isolation from other areas. Another difference involved the degree of popular participation in government. The British colonists in North America had enjoyed some measure of local self-government even before independence, but the Spanish and Portuguese colonists had not. After independence, most free males in the United States either had or soon gained the right to vote and participate in government. In most Latin American countries, however, political power was held by relatively small upper classes. The great majority of the population—native American, *mestizos* (people of mixed European and native American ancestry), blacks—was so overwhelmed by poverty and illiteracy that they were excluded from the political process. Yet another difference lay in the economic sphere. While the United States enjoyed a continually expanding economy during the nineteenth century, most Latin American countries were relatively poor. Furthermore, Latin American trade and commerce were controlled by outsiders, most notably Great Britain, the result being that Latin America remained economically subservient to European powers.

CONCLUSION

The Industrial Revolution in England and the political revolutions in North America, France, and Latin America transformed virtually every aspect of Western societies in the nineteenth and twentieth centuries:

1. Industrialization gradually changed the West from a rural to an urban civilization. One result was to separate humans from nature more thoroughly than ever before. Another was to "rationalize" Western societies, in the sense that many human decisions—what businesses were formed, who got what jobs, where and how people lived—were increasingly determined by rational calculations about how best to make money. For many people, the separation from nature and the growing rationalization made industrial society seem like a cold, hard way of life that ignored human feelings. As a result, there evolved a number of ways to

reassert the importance of human emotions. Two were the keeping of household pets and the growing of flower gardens, both of which kept people in touch with the natural world. Another was the growing emphasis on "romantic love" as the basis for marriage, for love was thought to create a bond of affection and emotion in an otherwise rational, cold world.

2. The industrial and political revolutions slowly secularized Western societies. A growing number of people lost faith in traditional Christianity and became more interested in pursuing happiness on this earth rather than salvation in heaven. Those who remained committed Christians faced the problem of adapting Christianity, traditionally associated with a rural way of life, to the needs of an urban, industrialized society.

3. The process of industrialization produced mixed emotions among Europeans and North and South Americans. Some were pessimistic, arguing that industrialization would create massive environmental pollution, encourage base human desires like greed and materialism, and destroy a slower-paced and better way of life. Others were optimistic, believing that industrialization would produce greater human progress and a rising standard of living. The pessimists and optimists would continue to debate this issue throughout the nineteenth and twentieth centuries.,

4. Originally, the industrial and political revolutions were separate developments, but they quickly became intertwined and mutually supportive in a variety of ways. Industrialization encouraged the expansion of political rights and freedoms, because it created the wealth that gave people, especially in the lower classes, more time and energy to participate in political life. The political revolutions facilitated the expansion of industrialization, because the growth of political freedom gave businesspeople more opportunity to invest as they wished and workers more opportunity (at least in theory) to move around in search of better jobs. The political revolutions also aided industrialization by breaking down the social barriers between science and technology. Throughout most of Western history, science was an aristocratic enterprise and technology was the province of the artisanal lower classes. Social barriers therefore hindered communication and cooperation between scientists and technologists. During the nineteenth century, however, the political revolutions gradually democratized Western societies and destroyed many of these social barriers. One result was increased cooperation between the pure scientist and the practical technician and greater application of scientific knowledge to technical inventions.

5. The industrial and political revolutions provided the power and energy that enabled Western Civilization to dominate the world by the end of the nineteenth century. Industrialization created the economic and military bases for that domination, while the ideals propagated by the political revolutions supplied the intellectual and emotional energy that led Westerners to believe that their civilization was superior to all others.

6. The most stirring Western ideal was that of revolution itself, the belief that a political and social upheaval could transform a society and make human life better. The belief in revolution as a transforming process began in Western Civilization between 1770 and 1815, and had great influence in Europe throughout the nineteenth century. By the twentieth century, its impact was being felt over the entire world, as Russia, China, and many other nations were led by revolutionaries who wanted to transform their countries. The appeal of the idea of revolution is that it offers hope for a better future to the lower classes everywhere.

THINGS YOU SHOULD KNOW

The Industrial Revolution in England
Hargreaves
Arkwright
Darby
Watt
The new industrial middle class in England
The new working class
Luddites
Causes of the American Revolution
Battle of Saratoga
The Constitution of the United States
Louisiana Purchase

The phases of the French Revolution
The Reign of Terror
Robespierre
levée en masse
Napoleon Bonaparte
Toussaint L'Ouverture
Independence of Mexico
Simón Bolívar
José de San Martín
Independence of Brazil
Transformations produced by the Industrial and Political Revolutions

SUGGESTED READINGS

Two good general studies of the revolutionary era are John R. Gillis, *The Development of European Society, 1770–1870* (Boston: Houghton Mifflin, 1977) and E. J. Hobsbawm, *The Age of Revolution, 1789–1848* (New York: Mentor, 1962). An old but still stimulating comparison of the English, American, French, and Russian revolutions is Crane Brinton, *Anatomy of Revolution* (New York: Prentice-Hall, 1938).

David S. Landes, *The Unbound Prometheus: Technological Change and Industrial Development in Western Europe from 1750 to the Present* (Cambridge, Eng.: Cambridge Univ. Press, 1969) is a superb analysis of the Industrial Revolution from the eighteenth to the twentieth centuries. A shorter, very readable introduction to the Industrial Revolution in England is Peter Lane, *The Industrial Revolution: The Birth of the Modern Age* (New York: Harper and Row, 1978).

On the American Revolution, Bernard Bailyn's works are excellent, particularly his *The Ideological Origins of the American Revolution* (Cambridge, MA.:

Belknap Press of Harvard Univ. Press, 1967). A good introductory survey to the American struggle is Robert Middlekauff, *The Glorious Cause: The American Revolution, 1763–1789* (New York: Oxford Univ. Press, 1982).

There are dozens of good surveys of the history of the French Revolution by eminent historians such as Georges Lefebvre, Alfred Cobban, and Norman Hampson. One of the most recent is Simon Schama, *Citizens: A Chronicle of the French Revolution* (New York: Knopf, 1989). More specific studies on the French Revolution include R. R. Palmer, *Twelve Who Ruled* (Princeton: Princeton Univ. Press, 1941) on the Reign of Terror and F. H. M. Markham, *Napoleon* (New York: NAL, 1964), a biography of Napoleon. The wars against Napoleon are immortalized in several great artistic works, including a series of etchings entitled *The Disasters of War* by the Spanish artist Francisco Goya, the *1812 Overture* by the Russian composer Peter Tchaikovsky, and *War and Peace* by the Russian novelist Leo Tolstoy.

A good introduction to the Latin American wars for independence is E. Bradford Burns, *Latin America: A Concise Interpretive History* (Englewood Cliffs, N.J.: Prentice-Hall, 1977).

Finally, James H. Billington, *Fire in the Minds of Men: Origins of the Revolutionary Faith* (New York: Basic, 1980) is a perceptive and interesting examination of the growing belief that revolution can lead to a better future for humankind.

NOTES

[1] C. H. Waddington, quoted in Carlo M. Cipolla, *Before the Industrial Revolution: European Society and Economy, 1000–1700,* 2nd ed. (New York: Norton, 1980), p. 298.

[2] Arthur Young, *Annals of Agriculture,* quoted in Humphrey Jennings, *Pandaemonium, 1660–1886; The Coming of the Machine as Seen by Contemporary Observers,* ed. Mary-Lou Jennings and Charles Madge (New York: Free Press, 1985), p. 79.

[3] Quoted in Peter Lane, *The Industrial Revolution: The Birth of the Modern Age* (New York: Harper & Row, 1978), pp. 188–89.

[4] Quoted in John R. Gillis, *The Development of European Society, 1770–1870* (Boston: Houghton Mifflin, 1977), p. 161.

[5] Quoted in Norman Gelb, *Less Than Glory* (New York: Putnam's, 1984), p. 36.

[6] Elias Boudinot, quoted in Hugh F. Rankin, *The American Revolution* (New York: Capricorn, 1965), p. 346.

[7] Quoted in Gelb, *Less Than Glory,* p. 174.

[8] Quoted in Frederic Ewen, *Heroic Imagination: The Creative Genius of Europe from Waterloo to the Revolution of 1848* (Secaucus, N.J.: Citadel Press, 1984), p. 14.

[9] Quoted in George Pendle, *A History of Latin America* (New York: Penguin, 1963), p. 93.

[10] Quoted in Germán Arciniegas, *Latin America: A Cultural History,* trans. Joan MacLean (London: Barrie & Rockliff, 1969), p. 259.

16

The Evolution of Industrial Societies, 1815 to 1905

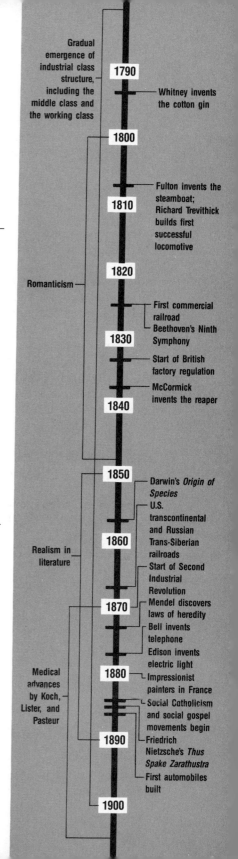

Gradual emergence of industrial class structure, including the middle class and the working class

1790

Whitney invents the cotton gin

1800

Fulton invents the steamboat; Richard Trevithick builds first successful locomotive

1810

1820

Romanticism

First commercial railroad
Beethoven's Ninth Symphony

1830

Start of British factory regulation

McCormick invents the reaper

1840

1850

Darwin's *Origin of Species*

U.S. transcontinental and Russian Trans-Siberian railroads

Realism in literature

1860

Start of Second Industrial Revolution

Mendel discovers laws of heredity

1870

Bell invents telephone

Edison invents electric light

Medical advances by Koch, Lister, and Pasteur

1880

Impressionist painters in France

Social Catholicism and social gospel movements begin

Friedrich Nietzsche's *Thus Spake Zarathustra*

1890

First automobiles built

1900

During the nineteenth century, Western Civilization slowly became an industrial civilization, the first of its kind in human history. Although industrialization occurred gradually and at first did not affect large areas of the Western world, the transition from a predominantly agricultural to an industrial way of life is a fundamental event in history. Indeed, it is comparable in scope and importance to the Neolithic Era of 12,000–10,000 B.C., when early humans first became farmers rather than hunters. Both events changed nearly every aspect of human life—how people worked and earned a living, where and how they lived, their political ideas, their religious and moral beliefs.

The history of Western Civilization in the nineteenth century is sufficiently important that two chapters are devoted to it. This one concentrates on the economic, social, and intellectual history of the West. The next, Chapter 17, focuses on the political history and political ideologies of the nineteenth century.

In this chapter, we examine three chief aspects of the nineteenth-century West. First is the acceleration of industrialization and the Second Industrial Revolution. Second is the gradual emergence of new social classes as a result of industrialization. Third is the effect of industrialization and political revolution on the ideas and beliefs held by Europeans and North Americans.

INDUSTRIALIZATION IN THE NINETEENTH CENTURY

It is important to remember that the industrialization of Western Civilization occurred slowly. Much of the West remained rural and agricultural throughout the nineteenth century. Most ordinary people were either peasants who worked the land or artisans who engaged in traditional craft work. In addition, most upper-class people were aristocrats, living on income derived from land ownership. But a new world of industrialization was simultaneously growing within the old, traditional society. During the first half of the nineteenth century, a growing number of cotton mills and other kinds of factories appeared in England, France, the United States, and some other areas of the Western world. The steam engine became more widely used and important, particularly in the new steamships and railroads (see the Technology box).

Expansion of Industrialization

Industrialization grew most rapidly in Britain, where the cotton mill towns produced so much clothing that Britain soon became known as the "workshop of the world." Profits from the cotton industry were so large

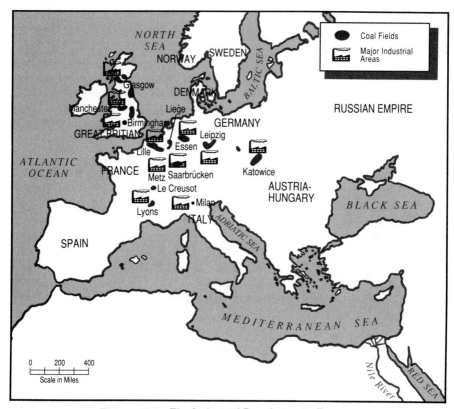

Figure 16.1 The Industrial Revolution in Europe

that British industrialists had huge sums available for investment. Many of them helped finance the new railroads, particularly in the United States, where the railroad was a major factor in opening the vast western areas of North America to human settlement and commerce.

In the 1820s and 1830s, industrialization was proceeding in other areas as well—parts of northern France, Belgium, western Germany, northern Italy, the northeastern United States, and elsewhere. First dozens and then hundreds of cotton mills were built in France. In western Germany in 1835, Alfred Krupp installed a steam engine at his armaments plant and began to develop what would soon be an enormous weapons industry. Two years later, in 1837, the first shaft was sunk in the Ruhr coal field, one of the sources of later German industrial power. At Vitkovice (present-day Czechoslovakia), a coke-fired furnace was set up to fuel an ironworks plant. Small textile mills appeared in northern Italy. In the United States, Eli Whitney's cotton gin (1793) and Cyrus McCormick's mechanical reaper (1834) began the process of mechanizing agriculture. Although these developments represent only the early stages of industrialization, it is interesting to note that it would be in these countries where full-scale industrial economies would develop later on.

By the mid-nineteenth century, an economic gulf was already beginning to develop between the industrializing countries (in Western Europe and North America) and the nonindustrializing countries (the rest of the world). Further, in the industrializing areas, an increasing number of people were optimistic about the future. For example, an English worker expressed his view of life in this way:

> There is a time coming when realities shall go beyond any dreams that have yet been told. . . . Nation exchanging with nation their products freely. . . . Universal enfranchisement, railways, electric telegraphs, public schools . . . these are some of the elements of a moral faith . . . which I daily hold, and never doubt upon.[2]

Similarly, an English noble who attended the first great industrial exhibition at London's Crystal Palace in 1851 (at which there were displayed such innovations as machine-made furniture, McCormick's reaper, and various kinds of false teeth), responded in this way:

> I made my way into the building; a most gorgeous sight; vast, graceful; beyond the dreams of the Arabian romances. I cannot think that the Caesars ever exhibited a more splendid spectacle. I was quite dazzled, and I felt as I did on entering St. Peter's [basilica in Rome].[3]

The Second Industrial Revolution

The industrialization process that began in the second half of the eighteenth century is often called the *First Industrial Revolution*. The *Second Industrial Revolution*, which began in Europe and North America in the latter half of the nineteenth century, involved a series of new technological and scientific developments. These developments included improved uses of steel and two important inventions, electricity and the internal-combustion engine.*

The development of high-quality steel allowed engineers to build new kinds of structures, including the tall buildings we know as skyscrapers. Steel is a derivative of iron that is very strong in proportion to its weight and size. Its combination of strength and compactness makes it a good construction material, and its resistance to abrasion makes it a good metal from which to make tools. Steel thus became the basic metal of the Second Industrial Revolution.

*The Third Industrial Revolution has been under way during the latter half of the twentieth century and includes developments in nuclear energy, the computer, and genetics (as we will see in Chapter 22).

The Steam Locomotive and the Steamship

The emergence of the railroad in the nineteenth century marked a revolution in land transportation. Previously, people moved about on land by walking, riding horses, or traveling in horse-driven coaches. Thus travel and communication were slow.

Before the nineteenth century, some coal miners had used wagons pulled by horses on wooden rails to drag coal from the mines to nearby rivers or ports. By the late eighteenth century, iron rails were in use, but the wagons were still pulled by horses. In the early nineteenth century, various experiments involving the steam engine led to the invention of the first steam-powered locomotive on rails by the English Richard Trevithick. In 1808, Trevithick advertised that his new machine, which he called "Catch me who can," could travel rapidly on rails. The *London Times* gave this account of the new engine:

> We are credibly informed that there is a Steam Engine now preparing to run against any mare, horse, or gelding that may be produced at the next October meeting at Newmarket; . . . the engine is the favorite. . . . Its greatest speed will be 20 miles in one hour, and its slowest rate will never be less than 15 miles.[1] (continued on page 372)

An Early Railroad   *An engraving of an 1837 train journey in Austria. Note the excitement among those participating in the event — the man on the train waving a flag* (above) *and the men on the ground waving their caps* (right). *(Culver Pictures)*

Trevithick's engine won the races, but it had no commercial application at this point.

A few years later, some businesspeople in northern England asked the inventor George Stephenson to build a railway that could transport people, coal, and other materials. In 1825, as a result of Stephenson's work, the 27-mile-long Stockton–Darlington line was opened. Forty thousand people came out to witness the new railroad locomotive and to celebrate the new line (one spectator was killed when he fell in front of the moving train). Between 1830 and 1850, miles of railroad were built—in 1830, only a few dozen miles existed; by 1840, there were over 4,500 miles; and by 1850, about 23,500 miles of railroad had been built. Most of the new railways were in Britain, but a few short lines were built in the United States, France, Germany, Belgium, and Russia.

Water transport also improved when the steam engine was applied to ships. The age of commercial steamships began in the United States in 1807, when Robert Fulton's *Clermont* traveled the Hudson River from New York to Albany. The steamship gradually replaced the sailing ship as the basic means of transportation on rivers and on the oceans.

The most important breakthrough in the field of energy was the development of electricity. Chemists such as Michael Faraday gradually came to understand electric energy. Then, in 1879, Thomas Edison invented the electric light. Soon cities and businesses were using electricity.

In the area of transportation, steamships increasingly replaced sailing ships on the oceans, for they could carry cargoes faster and more cheaply. Railroads also expanded rapidly and were particularly important in helping to unify two continental nations: the United States completed its first intercontinental railroad in 1869, and Russia completed its Trans-Siberian railway in 1905. The development of the internal-combustion engine created many new possibilities, and the first automobile was built late in the nineteenth century. In 1903, the Americans Orville and Wilbur Wright made the first flight by powered aircraft.

In the field of communication, telegraphy on land was already common by the 1850s and 1860s. After the laying of oceanic cables, rapid transoceanic communication became possible. Further innovations occurred when the American Alexander Graham Bell invented the telephone in 1876, and the Italian Guglielmo Marconi sent the first radio message in 1894.

An Early Textile Mill By the early nineteenth century, parts of Western Europe and North America were dotted with textile mills, many of which employed hundreds of people. Female workers (pictured here) were usually paid less than their male counterparts, though employment outside the home and in the mills was one step toward the gradual liberation of women. (Library of Congress)

Agricultural production also soared during the Second Industrial Revolution, with increased use of chemical fertilizers and the invention of new machines like the combination harvester-tractor. In addition, items such as the typewriter, the sewing machine, and the bicycle became available to consumers. Perhaps one of the most important developments of this period was the creation of modern medicine, which led to the successful treatment or elimination of diseases that had for centuries earlier been fatal (see the Technology box).

The innovations of the Second Industrial Revolution resulted in greatly increased production. Between the 1850s and the early 1900s, farm output rose 27 percent in France, 122 percent in Germany, and 77 percent in Italy. During that same period, industrial production increased ten times in Germany, eleven times in Russia, and seven times in Sweden. By 1913, Europe produced 47 percent of the world's total industrial output and the United States produced 35 percent.[4]

Some Results of Industrialization

Improved medical care, new medicines, and better food supplies led to a gradually improving standard of living for many Europeans and North

Figure 16.2   The Urbanization of Europe, 1850

Americans. Fewer infants died of childhood diseases and adults lived longer. As a result, population increased (see Table 16.1).

Some of the growing population in Europe migrated to the Americas, but even more moved from the European countryside to seek work in European cities (see Table 16.2). Some nations like Spain and Portugal remained largely rural countries with low urban populations but others were rapidly urbanizing. As people moved to cities, they adjusted to a new way of life. For example, the small, family-run enterprises that

TABLE 16.1   EUROPEAN POPULATION GROWTH, 1750–1900

1750	1800	1850	1900
140 million	188 million	266 million	401 million

Source: T. S. Hamerow, *The Birth of a New Europe* (Chapel Hill: Univ. of North Carolina Press, 1983), p. 61.

Modern Medicine

For ordinary people, one of the most beneficial developments of the Second Industrial Revolution was the creation of modern medicine. The most influential figures in the field of modern medicine were Louis Pasteur of France, Robert Koch of Germany, and Joseph Lister of England.

The chemist Louis Pasteur (1822–1895) demonstrated the germ theory of disease. Bacteria had first been seen under microscope in the seventeenth century, but it was Pasteur who discovered that bacteria carry diseases. His research became the basis of modern bacteriology and of modern medicine. Pasteur also invented vaccines to prevent rabies and anthrax.

Robert Koch (1843–1910), a bacteriologist, discovered the germs that cause cholera and tuberculosis. He also proved that cholera and typhoid are water-borne epidemics that can be controlled by water filtration. Koch's work was in large part responsible for the new emphasis on water sanitation in the nineteenth century.

The surgeon Joseph Lister (1827–1912) discovered that germs cause infections in surgical wounds. He sought to prevent infection through cleanliness in the operating room and antiseptic treatments (using carbolic acid) of wounds and surgical instruments. Lister's work became the basis of modern surgery. (He also lent his name, for a large fee, to the makers of a concoction that became known as Listerine.)

These three figures began the process of learning how to control deadly diseases—smallpox, malaria, rabies, cholera, tuberculosis—that had plagued people throughout history. By the middle of the twentieth century, many of these diseases were virtually eliminated in much of the world.

Louis Pasteur *A French chemist, Louis Pasteur (1822–1895) is considered one of the founders of modern medicine. (Culver Pictures)*

TABLE 16.2   PERCENTAGE OF EUROPEAN POPULATION IN
CITIES OVER 10,000, 1800–1890

	1800	1850	1890
England	21.3%	39.5%	61.7%
Prussia (Germany)	7.3	10.6	30.0
Belgium	13.5	20.8	34.8
France	9.5	14.4	25.9

Source: T. S. Hamerow, The Birth of a New Europe (Chapel Hill: University of North Carolina Press, 1983), p. 94.

typified the First Industrial Revolution were giving way to large businesses that sometimes employed tens of thousands of people. The Second Industrial Revolution also brought a new kind of economy, one increasingly oriented to the consumer. Previously, few people had ever "shopped" in the sense of going to a store and choosing the items they would purchase. Rather, people acquired material things by making them or by bartering for them with other people. But the Second Industrial Revolution produced so many consumer goods—clothing, furniture, kitchenware—that mass consumption was possible. The new mass-consumption economy, concentrated in the cities, was characterized by production of large volumes of standardized merchandise, selling of merchandise in large department stores and supermarkets, and constant advertising to ensure that consumers continued to purchase.

By the late nineteenth century, a growing number of Europeans and North Americans believed that modern technology had changed their lives for the better. As a result, monuments to that technology began to appear. The Eiffel Tower, for example, a tall iron structure built in 1889 and that still dominates the Paris skyline, is a symbol of technical power and ingenuity. Great urban railway stations were also built as gateways to travel and adventure. These and other monuments to the power of technology were built as symbolic celebrations of the profound transformation that had occurred in much of Europe and North America, particularly in the latter half of the nineteenth century. The contemporary historian Theodore S. Hamerow summarizes the transformation in this way:

In the course of a lifetime, they had seen the economy grow from the artisan shop to the mechanized factory; from the dray horse, the stagecoach, and the sailing vessel to the railroad, the automobile, and the steamship; from the semaphore and the carrier pigeon to the telegraph, the telephone, and the wireless; from the family firm to the joint-stock company; from the private money-lender to the giant investment bank.[5]

GRADUAL EMERGENCE OF NEW SOCIAL CLASSES

For centuries, the two social classes in Western Civilization were the nobility and the peasantry, both of which were defined by the roles they played in an agricultural society. A small middle class of businesspeople and professionals began to evolve in some towns during the late Middle Ages.

As discussed briefly in Chapter 15, two new classes—an enlarged, industrial middle class and a working class—began to emerge during the First Industrial Revolution. In those areas that were industrializing (Britain, Germany, Belgium, northern France, northern Italy, the northern United States, and a few others), these new classes at first existed side by side with the nobility and peasantry but gradually became larger and more influential than the older agricultural classes. Hence, a new industrial class structure was emerging. In those areas that were slow to industrialize (Russia, most of eastern Europe, southern France, southern Italy, Spain, Portugal, the southern United States), the traditional agricultural class structure remained dominant until well into the twentieth century.

The Upper Class

At the top of the new industrial class structure was an upper class of very wealthy big businesspeople who tended to merge with the old aristocracy. (No formal aristocracy existed in the United States, but in some areas "old families" regarded themselves as socially and economically superior to most other people.) Intermarriage between the two groups was encouraged by the desire of the business classes for aristocratic titles and prestige and the desire of the aristocrats for access to bourgeois wealth. Thus, it was not uncommon for the children of wealthy businesspeople to marry those of prestigious aristocratic families. The aristocracy also sought to retain its influence in other ways, such as filling the most important posts in governmental bureaucracies, the diplomatic service, and the military. By the beginning of the twentieth century, the upper class in many European countries was composed of a mixture of wealthy businesspeople who dominated economic affairs and aristocrats who still controlled politics and the armed forces.

The Middle Class

Below the upper class in wealth and social status was the middle class, composed of middle-level industrialists, independent businesspeople, and successful professionals like lawyers and doctors. The middle class

Luncheon on the Grass   Although the French painter Édouard Manet (1832–1883) refused to identify himself with the impressionists, his work actually helped initiate the impressionist movement. Manet's depiction of the nude woman in *Luncheon on the Grass* (1863) shocked many people of his time. (Caisse Nationale des Monuments Historiques)

was defined by its level of income; it was the second wealthiest group in industrial society but it was far less wealthy than the upper class. Many in the middle class were optimistic about the future, because industrialism was improving their standard of living. Some, however, were disgruntled, such as university professors who resented the materialism and greed that they associated with most businesspeople. Universities were largely middle-class institutions, since most workers and peasants could not qualify for admission and many aristocrats shunned formal higher education.

The Lower-Middle Class

The lower-middle class was comprised of those who were less wealthy than the middle class but who were not workers or peasants, such as small shopkeepers, schoolteachers, secretaries, and clerks of various kinds. The lower-middle class also included large numbers of people who held lower-level positions in large organizations, such as bureaucrats in government and accountants and salespeople in large businesses. Most members of the lower-middle class had acquired some education and used their training to improve their economic and social status. Sometimes they felt vulnerable, however, since an economic depression or business failure could threaten their livelihood and their class standing. They could easily "fall" into the working class.

The Working Class

By the late nineteenth century, the industrial working class comprised about 30–40 percent of the population in heavily industrialized countries like Britain, but a lesser percentage in those nations still industrializing. The working class included factory workers, urban craftspeople like printers and woodworkers, and many unskilled laborers in the cities. All of them worked directly with machinery in one capacity or another. (Nonindustrial workers included numerous domestic servants.)

Since workers tended to be clustered in cities, it was relatively easy for them to organize. Trade unions developed rapidly in many countries during the 1860s–1880s, and workers began to use the tactic of the strike to improve their working conditions and pay levels. Some strikes became violent, as employers often used armed "strike-breakers" to keep their factories open and strikers fought back with whatever weapons they had. In Europe, workers also tended to join Socialist political parties that represented them in elections, but for a variety of reasons the United States never developed a large Socialist party. The parties usually professed to believe in revolutionary overthrow of the capitalist order, but in reality most Socialist parties were relatively moderate organizations that used political pressure to procure gradual reforms for the benefit of workers.

The constant threat of strikes and the influence of Socialist parties gradually forced governments in some countries to approve social and economic legislation favoring the lower classes. Many governments eventually prohibited child labor and limited the number of hours that women could work. Some restricted the workday for men to ten or eleven hours. Other types of legislation sought to improve public sanitation and provide free elementary schooling for a growing number of people. Most innovative of all was social security legislation. Germany led the way in the 1880s with a governmental program that provided old-age pensions and monetary support for workers who became ill or were hurt in work-related accidents. Some other countries adopted similar programs.

In some areas, social legislation and general prosperity led to an unprecedented improvement in the standard of living of the lower classes. Many people remained quite poor, but others were much better off than their ancestors had ever been. In France, for example, real hourly wages rose 28 percent between 1850 and 1870, and in Britain the real wages of an average working-class family increased by over 50 percent between 1851 and 1881.

The Peasantry

Besides industrial workers, the other members of the lower class were the peasants. In those countries where industrialization grew rapidly, the number of people engaged in farming declined. In Britain, the percentage of people who farmed (out of the total population) decreased from 28 percent in 1831 to 21 percent in 1871; and in France from 63 percent in 1827 to 43 percent in 1866.[6] Other countries (like Russia) that were slow to industrialize had much higher percentages of farm workers. Yet, regardless of the differences among nations, it was generally true that agriculture was no longer as important as it once had been.

Most peasants remained quite poor, but some relatively prosperous farmers (mostly in Western Europe and the United States) were able to increase production by purchasing new tools like seed drills and threshing machines. However, even the prosperous peasants were hurt by a major agricultural depression that lasted in Europe from 1873 to 1896. Crop imports from Australia and the Americas drove European farm prices down and forced some peasants to sell their land and look for work elsewhere.

Politically, most farm workers were traditionalists who disliked the vast changes produced by industrialization. They usually voted conservatively in elections, except when they demanded agricultural reforms. Thus, the lower classes were politically divided—the workers usually supported reformist political parties and the peasants customarily supported conservative groups.

Mass Societies

Those areas where significant industrialization occurred experienced what some historians call the *rise of the masses,* meaning that the lower classes became more influential. (The word *mass* unfortunately implies a lack of individuality and personality, but it is nevertheless the commonly used term.) Because the lower classes were increasingly clustered in cities, they were better able to organize themselves in various ways and thus demand more power.

Mass participation in politics occurred in part because the upper classes feared the growing power of the working class; in particular, they feared the power of trade unions and Socialist political parties. Therefore, the upper classes began to "democratize" politics by expanding the right to vote, in the hope that the lower classes would support traditional, conservative rulers and policies. Universal manhood suffrage (the right of all men but not women to vote) became a reality in Great Britain, France, the United States, and several Scandinavian countries during the latter half of the nineteenth century. Italy and the Hapsburg Empire established universal manhood suffrage early in the twentieth century, and even Russia began to allow some people to vote in 1905. The short-term result was exactly what the upper classes wanted: the lower classes became more interested in earning a living than in political issues. So, they often voted for traditional leaders, politicians from the upper classes who were familiar. The long-term effect of universal manhood suffrage was political revolution, as elite politics gradually gave way to mass politics and the masses began to exert more influence in the political realm. In the twentieth century, the masses would often support new kinds of political leaders, often from the middle or lower classes, who preached new kinds of mass ideologies (democracy, fascism, communism).

With the advent of mass politics, political leaders had to seek loyalty and support for governmental actions from the lower classes. The need for lower-class support led in many countries to enactment of some social reforms, such as minimum-wage laws and legalization of trade unions. It also led to nationalism, the glorification of the nation and the fostering of patriotic emotions. Popular newspapers in most countries helped create enthusiasm for "national greatness." Patriotic celebrations, such as Bastille Day in France and the Fourth of July in the United States, stimulated allegiance to national flags and military heroes. The purpose of nationalist rituals and emotions was to create in people a sense of belonging to something greater than themselves—the "nation." Such a sense of belonging was appropriate to industrial societies, because industrialism forced people to move about in search of economic opportunity and it therefore broke down localistic loyalties in favor of a broader national loyalty. Traditionally, for example, people who lived their entire lives in the Provence area of France would have usually felt loyalty to Provence first and only secondarily to France. But upon leaving Provence to work in an urban factory elsewhere, a person would slowly become a part of a broader national culture and thus feel a part of France.

Educational opportunity for the lower classes grew rapidly during the nineteenth century. Throughout most of Western history, the great majority of people had little or no access to education and so remained ignorant and illiterate. Industrialization changed this, however. Technological progress necessitated an educated working class, because many jobs required the ability to read, write, and calculate. Also, the rise of mass politics meant that the masses had to be educated so they could help govern.

Prussia established a system of primary education early in the nineteenth century, its main purpose being to train better-educated soldiers for the Prussian army. Similar systems were created in Great Britain, Belgium, the Netherlands, France, and much of the United States during the second half of the century. The less prosperous nations— Portugal, Spain, Russia—were slower to expand educational opporttunity. But where primary education was available, the lower classes enjoyed the rewards of literacy. The newly literate could not only get better jobs but could also read newspapers and magazines. As a result, mass-circulation newspapers began to appear in several countries.

In addition to newspapers, the urban lower classes found new forms of entertainment. The music hall introduced new forms of music, such as ragtime and jazz in the United States, that became the basis of an urban folk music. Sports—soccer, American football, boxing, and many others—became more organized and began to attract large audiences. And, by the early twentieth century, the new artform of the film was becoming popular among the lower classes. Both jazz and films—each a major artistic innovation—were appreciated much more quickly by the urban lower classes than by the artistic elite.

IDEAS, BELIEFS, AND ART IN A RAPIDLY CHANGING WORLD

Industrialization and the political revolutions of the late eighteenth century stimulated a profound cultural debate, as philosophers and artists sought to understand and influence the enormous changes occurring in Western Civilization. Many welcomed both the industrial and political revolutions, believing that the former would bring material progress and the latter would foster liberty and equality. Others feared that the revolutions would encourage greed, materialism, environmental degradation, and political chaos.

Georg Wilhelm Friedrich Hegel

The German philosopher G. W. F. Hegel (1770–1831) defined the central idea of the age—the sense that change was the most fundamental reality. Hegel was an *idealist* who contended that ultimate reality is spiritual or ideal and that historical events constitute the working out of ideas in history. For Hegel, these ideas do not exist eternally and absolutely; rather, they are always changing and developing. The dominant idea at any time he called a *thesis;* because a thesis is always imperfect, it calls forth an opposing idea, an *antithesis*. The conflict between the thesis and antithesis leads to the formation of a new comprehensive idea, a *synthesis*, that is also a new thesis. The *dialectic* was Hegel's term for the thesis-antithesis-synthesis concept. An example of his dialectical approach to history is the evolution of Western Civilization. According to Hegel, the "Asian" societies that existed before the Christian era (ancient Egypt, for example) were organized by the idea of absolute monarchy; they were followed by their opposite, the Greek world where the idea of freedom was created; and the two ideas—absolute monarchy and freedom—were fused during the Middle Ages into a society where both freedom and energetic government were possible.

Hegel's philosophy, with its presumption that historical reality is dynamic, is a striking example of a new assumption in European thought. That assumption held that truth and reality are not eternal and static but are always changing and growing. Hegel's thought influenced a great many people, including Karl Marx (as we will see in Chapter 17).

Romanticism

Romanticism dominated European thought and art during the first half of the nineteenth century. It was more of an attitude than a fixed doctrine, so a definition of romanticism can only state some general characteristics shared by a large number of philosophers, poets, writers, and artists. One shared characteristic was opposition to Enlightenment thought. The romantics believed that the eighteenth-century Enlightenment was too rational and ignored the emotional side of human nature. They also contended that Enlightenment thinkers stressed order and harmony far too much and forgot that reality was dynamic. Also shared by romantics was a confidence in the creative abilities of the individual, of the artistic genius to explore his innermost feelings and find there a source of truth and knowledge. Since they admired the creative individual so much, the romantics were never a "school" of like-minded thinkers. They differed greatly in their ideas and beliefs, some supporting and others opposing the profound changes occurring in Western Civilization.

Goethe   The German writer Johann Wolfgang von Goethe (1749–1832) said explicitly that he was not a romantic, but he was nevertheless a precursor of romanticism. Goethe's *Faust* had an enormous impact on many romantics. It is the story of a legendary scientist-magician who agrees to give his soul to the devil in exchange for receiving the ability to comprehend all knowledge and reality. (The real Faust, a sixteenth-century astrologer, may have inspired the Faustian legend.) For the romantics, Faust was a symbol of the human desire to know and understand everything. The character also embodied the sense of human liberation produced by the industrial and political revolutions. The Faustian legend continued to inspire others during the late nineteenth and twentieth centuries, and a number of literary and artistic works are based on the legend.

Blake   Another early romantic was the English poet William Blake (1757–1827). Also a craftsman, painter, and printer, Blake was strongly opposed to Enlightenment rationalism because he believed that it wrongly imposed reason and order on everything. He argued that industrial factories were a concrete application of rationalism, in that the factories were used to discipline and dominate working people. In a memorable phrase, he castigated the first factories as "dark Satanic mills."

Wordsworth   The poet William Wordsworth (1770–1850) was another of the early English romantics. Like Blake, Wordsworth feared industrialization and an overly rational society. In "The World Is Too Much with Us," he contrasts the noisy chaos of modern society with the beauty and peace of nature:

> The world is too much with us; late and soon,
> Getting and spending, we lay waste our powers:
> Little we see in Nature that is ours;
> We have given our hearts away, a sordid boon!
> This sea that bares her bosom to the moon;
> The winds that will be howling at all hours,
> And are up-gathered now like sleeping flowers;
> For this, for everything, we are out of tune;
> It moves us not. . . .

Keats, Byron, and Shelley   After Wordsworth came another generation of English romantic poets—John Keats (1795–1821), George Gordon, Lord Byron (1788–1824), and Percy Bysshe Shelley (1792–1822)—who personified both the tragedy and the energy of the romantic movement. All three died young while still at the height of their powers—Keats of tuberculosis at the age of twenty-five, Shelley by drowning at the age of thirty, and Byron at the age of thirty-six as the result of a fever caught while fighting in a Greek war for independence. But in their short lives they composed some of the most powerful poetry in the English language.

Keats was a nonpolitical poet who wanted to create enduring images of beauty through his poems; he believed that "A thing of beauty is a joy forever." Byron and Shelley, however, celebrated through their work the human liberation that they believed would result from the revolutions of the late eighteenth century. In *Don Juan,* Byron wrote:

> For I will teach, if possible, the stones
>   To rise against earth's tyrants. Never let it
> Be said that we still truckle unto thrones.
>   But ye—our children's children! think how we
>   Show'd what things were before the world was free!

And Shelley, in *Prometheus Unbound,* retold the story of Prometheus, the Greek god who gave fire to humanity and was therefore a symbol of human power. Shelley portrayed Prometheus (Humanity) as master of the world.

> The tempest is his steed, he strides the air;
> And the abyss shouts from her depth laid bare,
> Heaven, hast thou secrets? Man unveils me; I have none.

Mary Shelley, wife of the poet (and daughter of the feminist writer Mary Wollstonecraft and the philosopher William Godwin), also dealt with the Promethean theme. In 1816–1817, she wrote *Frankenstein, or the Modern Prometheus,* the story of a student—Frankenstein—who creates an artificial human out of the remains of corpses. The creature becomes a monster that destroys its creator. In one sense, the novel warns that technology could get out of control and menace humanity.

French Romantics In France, one of the first romantics was François René Chateaubriand, whose *Genius of Christianity* (1802) contends that Christianity and the Christian mysteries are a source of beauty and humanity in the world. Chateaubriand encouraged other romantics to seek solace in religion, particularly Catholicism. A later romantic, the novelist Victor Hugo (1802–1885), was the author of such well-known works as *The Hunchback of Notre Dame* and *Les Misérables.* These novels reveal Hugo's belief in the ideals of the French Revolution, for he clearly sympathized with the common people. In his fiction, the common person is the hero, usually portrayed as a good, decent individual oppressed by bureaucrats or other members of the upper classes.

Living at the same time as Hugo was the major romantic artist Eugène Delacroix (1799–1863). For Delacroix, romanticism meant the free expression of his personal feelings. His *Liberty Leading the People* is a celebration of the French Revolution of 1830. (See the next chapter for a discussion of the 1830 revolution.)

German and Russian Romanticism In Germany, romanticism was both more heroic and more pessimistic than in England and France. The heroic aspect was exemplified in the music of Ludwig van Beethoven (1770–1827), who bridged the classical musical style of the eighteenth century and the romantic, more emotional style of the nineteenth century. Some of Beethoven's symphonies are joyful, expressive paeans to the heroes—both the common people and great individuals—of political revolutions. His Third Symphony was originally dedicated to Napoleon (although that dedication was eventually withdrawn), and his Ninth Symphony concludes with a mighty choral celebration of the ideal of human brotherhood.

The pessimistic aspect of German romanticism was the fear that

Ludwig van Beethoven
One of the greatest composers in Western history, Beethoven's (1770–1827) works include the *Third Symphony*, or *Eroica*, and the *Ninth Symphony*, also called the *Choral Symphony*. (Culver Pictures)

rationalistic modern society would destroy the human spirit and that the human soul was irrational and capable of great evil. The poet and essayist Novalis (1772–1801) hoped forlornly that Europe would re-create the spiritual unity that he believed had existed in the Catholic Middle Ages. An unknown writer called "Bonaventura" produced *Nightwatches*, a satire about a night watchman on the dark side—the fanaticism, arrogance, and greed—of a small village. The night watchman eventually goes to his father's tomb, finds nothing but dust in it, and yells "I fling this handful of dust into the air—and what remains is—NOTHINGNESS!"

The heroic aspect of German romanticism was reasserted by the composer Richard Wagner (1813–1883). Wagner created a new kind of opera, the music drama in which he sought to unify thought and feeling and combine music, poetry, and drama into a whole. Norse mythology was the subject of much of Wagner's work, including his four-opera cycle called *The Ring of the Nibelungen*. The "Ring" cycle focuses on a magic ring made from gold taken from the Rhine River and the curse that afflicts everyone who owns the ring.

Alexander Pushkin (1799–1837) was the greatest of the Russian romantics. His dramas, novels, and poems—such as *Eugene Onegin* and *Boris Godunov*—had immense influence on later Russian literature. In his works, he is sometimes pessimistic but also expresses a hope and exultation inspired by the ideals of the French Revolution. In "Ode to Freedom" he writes:

I will sing the freedom of the world,
And strike down iniquity sitting on the throne.
Tyrants of the world tremble!
And you, fallen slaves, take heart and hear.
Arise!

Growing Faith in the Power of Science

A number of major scientific achievements occurred during the first half of the nineteenth century. In chemistry, John Dalton defined the atomic theory, the idea that atoms are the basic particles of all chemical substances. (Dalton was not the originator of the atomic theory, for ancient Greek philosophers such as Democritus had theorized that all reality is composed of atoms.) Later, the Russian D. I. Mendeleyev worked out the periodic table of the elements. Also, A. M. Ampère began to delineate the basic laws of electric currents and, along with many others, to advance understanding of electricity. This work eventually enabled Thomas Edison to invent the electric light.

In physics, Hermann von Helmholtz used his and others' research to demonstrate the principle of the conservation of energy, one of the fundamental facts of modern science. In biology, Georges Cuvier published his major work on the study of fossils, and Charles Lyell wrote the highly influential *Principles of Geology*. These and many other works showed that the earth was much older than previously thought and thus prepared the way for Charles Darwin's theories about the evolution of life.

The many scientific discoveries encouraged a growing faith in the power of science. Auguste Comte (1798–1857) expressed that faith most unequivocally. In his *Cours de Philosophie Positive*, Comte argues that human history advanced through three stages: (1) the theological, when human thought was dominated by beliefs about God; (2) the metaphysical, when abstract ideas prevailed; and (3) the positive, when science replaced vague abstractions with accurate factual knowledge. Comte believed that *positivism*—his word for the scientific study of facts—would lead to the highest level of human advancement and that humans had no need for spiritual values or faith in God. He thus defined, perhaps unwittingly, one of the central dilemmas of the modern West: Does a scientific civilization inevitably undermine human belief in God and spiritual values, and can such a civilization endure without some means of defining spiritual goals and beliefs?

Charles Darwin

Charles Darwin (1809–1882) was the most famous and one of the most influential scientists of the nineteenth century. In 1859, Darwin published a momentous book, *On the Origin of Species*. His research provided a wealth of evidence to support the theory of evolution, the theory that all life-forms had slowly evolved to their existing state over millions of years. To explain how evolution occurred, Darwin developed his thesis of *natural selection*. In its simplest form, natural selection argues that there are more plants and animals in nature than there is food to support them, so living things have to compete for survival. Those with especially favorable physical characteristics are in effect "selected" by nature to survive. (For example, long-necked giraffes reach up into trees for food, whereas short-necked giraffes cannot and so did not survive.) Thus, some plants and animals endure by evolving certain useful characteristics, while other plants and animals do not.

There were two particularly unique features of Darwin's ideas. One was the time factor, for Darwin's work was based on the earlier work of geologists (such as Charles Lyell) who showed that the earth was millions of years old, long enough for evolution to occur. The other was natural selection, the idea that evolution occurrs through struggle rather than through some kind of natural harmony. And, there was one glaring weakness—the problem of heredity. Darwin never understood clearly how evolved characteristics passed from one generation to the next. Knowledge about the basic laws of heredity occurred only with the work of the Austrian monk Gregor Mendel (1822–1884); that work occurred around 1870 but was not publicized until early in the twentieth century.

Despite his lack of knowledge of heredity, Darwin's research was taken by many educated people as proof of the theory of evolution, and evolution became fundamental to the modern science of biology. Among the general public, however, Darwin's ideas produced an uproar. Most disconcerting for many were the implications of Darwinism for traditional religion. Many Christians believed that God created people in fully developed form only a few thousand years ago. That belief was obviously in conflict with the Darwinian thesis that humans evolved over millions of years. The result was what one writer called "the warfare of science and theology," a continuing and vociferous argument between supporters of Darwinian theory and supporters of traditional religious beliefs. Extremists often dominated the argument, with one side contending that Darwin had proved that humans were completely naturalistic creatures and that there was no God, and the other side insisting that Darwinism was an antireligious assault on Biblical truth. (Both sides ignored many

Charles Darwin The most famous and one of the most influential scientists of the nineteenth century, Charles Darwin's (1809–1882) theory of evolution is expostulated in his book *On the Origin of Species*, published in 1859. (Art Reference Bureau)

other possible conclusions, such as that God created life, which then evolved into existing life-forms.)

Another result of Darwin's ideas was *Social Darwinism*, the application of evolutionary ideas to human society. Darwin himself made little attempt to apply his ideas beyond the realm of biology, but others did. The English writer Herbert Spencer, for example, coined the phrase "survival of the fittest" to indicate his belief that human progress results when the best people or best societies win economic and political competitions. He contended that Darwinism supported capitalism, in that economic competition produces the success of the best businesspeople and the elimination of the weak and unfit. Other writers applied similar ideas in different ways, arguing that racism is good because competition among the races reveals which ones are superior, or that warfare is noble because it is a contest that shows which nation is "fittest." (As we will see in Chapter 20, Adolf Hitler advocated both racism and war, and in this sense may have been the purest Social Darwinist in the political world.) In general, Social Darwinism exalts strong and powerful individuals and nations. It had a great impact on political and social thought during the late nineteenth and early twentieth centuries. One effect was to encourage whites in Europe and North America to believe that they were the most intelligent and talented people on earth.

Christianity

Christianity was still a powerful spiritual force in the nineteenth century, but it was being sharply criticized or ignored by a growing number of people. Some scientists, particularly those influenced by Darwinism, disparaged Christianity as a collection of superstitions. Some political figures, particularly liberals and Socialists, were anticlerical, largely because most Christian organizations were politically conservative and opposed political reforms. Some philosophers and historians initiated a new era of biblical criticism, in which the Bible was treated with skepticism. D. F. Strauss, for example, argues in *Life of Jesus* (1836) that many of the stories about Jesus are simply unbelievable mythology. Finally, many in the urban working classes also lost contact with Christianity, because churches did not form enough new church organizations in urban areas.

Christianity was still vibrant, however. Some Catholic intellectuals such as the French romantic writer Chateaubriand argued effectively that Catholic Christianity provided a source of meaning and beauty in a rapidly changing world. Some Protestant intellectuals, particularly German theologians, engaged in a prolonged effort to rethink Christian teachings and make them more appealing to an industrial, secular age.

It was often difficult for Christian churches to adjust to the economic, social, and political changes engulfing nineteenth-century Europe. Pope Pius IX, for example, issued the *Syllabus of Errors* (1864) to condemn virtually all modern thought, including liberalism, Socialism, and Darwinism. Later in the century, however, Pope Leo XIII (1878–1903) succeeded in encouraging Catholics to support some political and social reforms. Also late in the nineteenth century, a movement known as *social Catholicism* sought with some success to bring Catholic priests into urban areas, where they could help workers with both their spiritual and economic problems. At about the same time, some Protestant theologians were starting the *social gospel* movement, which contended that Christians should help develop social reforms that would aid the working class. The social gospel movement was especially strong in the United States.

Amidst all the changes in the nineteenth century, most common people remained Christian believers. In many areas, the local church was still the hub of spiritual and community life. Clear evidence of the continuing strength of Christianity was the missionary movement, in which thousands of missionaries sought converts in parts of Africa and Asia. The missionary movement was part of the broader imperial movement, in which Europeans and North Americans conquered much of the world (as we will see in Chapter 18).

Realism and Impressionism

Romanticism dominated the art and literature of Europe during the first half of the nineteenth century. By the second half of the century, *realism* and then *impressionism* in art became dominant.

Nineteenth-century *realism* was a natural part of the industrial, scientific age that stressed production of material goods. The realists sought to portray life in an objective manner, with all the glamour and ideals left out. The French writer Honoré de Balzac (1799–1850) portrays in his novels (many known collectively as *The Human Comedy*) the materialism and greed of the French middle and upper classes. The English novelist Charles Dickens (1812–1870) exposes how the nineteenth-century poor in England were mistreated and abused in *Oliver Twist, Bleak House,* and other novels. Another French novelist, Émile Zola (1840–1902), describes in *Germinal* the hardships endured by French coal miners. Perhaps the greatest Russian realist was Count Leo Tolstoy (1828–1910), whose monumental *War and Peace* combines realistic descriptions of people and events with some moralizing about the results of human actions.

By the 1870s, a new school of art known as *impressionism* emerged in France. The impressionists—Edouard Manet, Camille Pissarro, Claude Monet, and others—wanted to paint immediate impressions derived from the direct observation of nature and people. They intended to portray life as it was at one precise moment, knowing that that moment would immediately end and that a new impression would replace the old. Particularly interested in how light affects objects, the impressionists often painted in the outdoors. As a result, impressionist paintings (for example, Monet's *Impression: Sunrise*) often present objects as shimmer-ing images without precise outlines because they were constantly changing. In a sense, impressionism was an artistic rendering of the phenomenon of change that was enveloping the Western world in an industrial age.

The Emergence of Sociological Thought

The gradual evolution of industrial society helped encourage the emergence of a new way of thinking about that society—*sociology*. One of the founders of the new sociology was Émile Durkheim (1858–1917), a profound thinker who was troubled by the social instability present during the transition from an agricultural to an industrial society. Durkheim argued that many people were losing their customary loyalty to traditional religion and morality. The result was *anomie* (absence of social norms and values), a condition in which people feel uneasy and anxious because traditional rules of behavior no longer seem important and new rules have not emerged to take their place. For example, many workers who migrated from the countryside to the industrial cities gradually ceased to be serious Christian believers and thus lost a traditional source of moral and religious instruction. In Durkheim's opinion, the industrial growth of the nineteenth century had produced economic improvements that were welcome, but it had also produced individuals who felt displaced, uprooted, and isolated from other people. (Another great sociologist, Max Weber, is discussed in Chapter 19.)

The Belief in Progress

Some Europeans and North Americans believed that economic prosper-ity, the slow development of democratic politics, and the growing influence of the masses were clear signs of progress in Western Civilization. The growing belief in progress marked a major change in Western thought, a change in which the age-old assumption that life is hard was being repudiated by many and replaced by confidence that life could be pleasant. Charles Frankel, a twentieth-century American philosopher, called this change the "revolution of modernity":

> the revolution of modernity has not been only a material revolution or an intellectual revolution. It has been a moral revolution of extraordinary scope, a radical alteration in what the human imagi-nation is prepared to envisage and demand. And it has changed the basic dimensions in which we measure happiness and unhappiness, success and failure. It has given us the sense that we make our own history; it has led us to impose new and more exciting demands on ourselves and our leaders; it has set loose the restless vision of a world in which men might be liberated from age-old burdens.[7]

A few intellectuals argued passionately, however, that what others called progress was actually degradation. The Danish theologian Søren Kierkegaard was sharply critical of rationalistic, middle-class culture, as was the Russian novelist Fyodor Dostoyevski. The most prominent critic of modernity was the German philosopher Friedrich Nietzsche (1844–1900). Nietzsche's most startling statement was his declaration that "God is dead." The death of God meant at least two things to Nietzsche: (1) most of those who claimed to believe in God did not take God seriously, so God was dead in their lives; and (2) God did not exist, so there was no intrinsic purpose or meaning in the world and no eternal truth such as reason. According to Nietzsche, then, Western Civilization was based on false beliefs that had led to a decadent, crassly materialistic way of life. To be more precise, it was based on Christian moral teachings that, according to Nietzsche, encouraged a slave morality. Christianity taught people to serve and help others, to be obedient to a nonexistent God, and to build a civilization characterized by weak, mediocre people. To replace Christian slave morality, Nietzsche wanted a "transvaluation of values" that would create a new ideal for a new kind of person. The new person would be a superior being who accepted the irrationality of human existence and who sought to attain a tragic wisdom beyond the reach of most mortals. Thus, Nietzsche repudiated not only rationalism but also the egalitarian democracy that professed to see all humans as equal. For him, the history of Western Civilization was a history of decline, not progress.

Nietzsche and those who believed in progress were absolutely opposed to each other, but ironically both may have been right in their opinions. In the twentieth century, the people of Western Civilization would enjoy continued technological progress and a gradually improving standard of living. But they would also endure degradation in the form of world wars, and, in some countries, concentration camps and mass murder campaigns by dictatorial governments.

CONCLUSION

The gradual evolution of industrialization brought many changes to large parts of Europe and North America. Some of the most important economic, social, and intellectual changes were (1) greater use of machinery and technology; (2) the imposition of factory discipline on many workers; (3) the expansion of urbanization, as many people migrated from countryside to city; (4) a slowly improving standard of living for many but not all people; (5) the evolution of two new social classes—the industrial middle class and the working class; and (6) a prolonged intellectual debate over the significance of the changes occurring in Western Civilization.

By the end of the nineteenth century, the industrial way of life dominated much of England, the Low Countries, northern France, western Germany, northern Italy, the northern United States, and a few other areas. The traditional rural, agricultural way of life still prevailed in Russia, most of eastern Europe, southern Italy, southern France, the southern United States, Spain, and Portugal. During the twentieth century, industrialization would spread into many of these rural areas and Western Civilization would become a predominantly industrial civilization.

THINGS YOU SHOULD KNOW

Growth of railroads
Second Industrial Revolution
Pasteur, Koch, and Lister
European population growth and
    urbanization in the nineteenth
    century
Social classes in European indus-
    trial societies
Mass society
Hegel
Romanticism
Goethe
Blake
Wordsworth
Byron, Keats, P. B. Shelley, and
    Mary Shelley
Hugo

Chateaubriand
Delacroix
Beethoven
Wagner
Pushkin
Comte
Darwin
The warfare of science and theology
Social Darwinism/Christianity in the
    nineteenth century
Realism
Impressionism
Sociology
Durkheim
Belief in progress
Nietzsche

SUGGESTED READINGS

David S. Landes, *The Unbound Prometheus* (Cambridge, Mass.: Belknap Press of Harvard Univ. Press, 1969) is good on industrialization during the nineteenth century. Theodore S. Hamerow, *The Birth of a New Europe: State and Society in the Nineteenth Century* (Chapel Hill: Univ. of North Carolina Press, 1983) provides a wealth of information on industrialization and its political and social effects. On the social structure of industrial societies, a good introduction is Peter Stearns, *European Society in Upheaval: European Social History Since 1750* (New York: Macmillan, 1975).

There are thousands of works that try to analyze the significance of industrialization. An insightful and critical study of the political and social effects of modern technology is Lewis Mumford, *The Myth of the Machine* (New York: Harcourt, Brace, & World, 1967–70). On some of the implications of the new mass-consumer economies, see Rosalind H. Williams, *Dream Worlds: Mass*

Consumption in Late Nineteenth-Century France (Berkeley: Univ. of California Press, 1982).

A very readable work on the age of romanticism is Frederic Ewen, *Heroic Imagination: The Creative Genius of Europe from Waterloo to the Revolution of 1848* (Secaucus, N.J.: Citadel Press, 1984). Jacques Barzun, *Darwin, Marx, Wagner* (Garden City, N.Y.: Doubleday, 1941) is a good introduction to three of the major intellectual figures of the nineteenth century. Loren Eiseley, *Darwin's Century: Evolution and the Men Who Discovered It* (Garden City, N.Y.: Anchor, 1961) is both fascinating and readable.

On science in the nineteenth century, see Charles C. Gillispie, *The Edge of Objectivity* (Princeton: Princeton Univ. Press, 1960); and on Christianity, see A. Vidler, *The Church in an Age of Revolution* (Baltimore: Penguin, 1961). Owen Chadwick, *The Secularization of the European Mind in the Nineteenth Century* (New York: Cambridge Univ. Press, 1975) shows how European thought and attitudes became less religious and more secular.

NOTES

[1] *The [London] Times*, 8 July 1808, quoted in Humphrey Jennings, *Pandaemonium, 1660–1886: The Coming of the Machine as Seen by Contemporary Observers*, ed. Mary-Lou Jennings and Charles Madge (New York: Free Press, 1985), p. 128.

[2] Alexander Somerville, quoted in Jennings, *Pandaemonium*, pp. 235–36.

[3] Lord Macauley, quoted in Jennings, *Pandaemonium*, pp. 257–58.

[4] Theodore S. Hamerow, *The Birth of a New Europe: State and Society in the Nineteenth Century* (Chapel Hill: Univ. of North Carolina Press, 1983), pp. 8, 12, 50.

[5] Ibid., p. 31.

[6] B. H. Slicher van Bath, *The Agrarian History of Western Europe*, A.D. *500–1850*, trans. Olive Ordish (London: Edward Arnold Publishers, 1963), pp. 238–39.

[7] Charles Frankel, *The Case for Modern Man* (New York: Harper & Brothers, 1955), pp. 208–209.

17

The Evolution of New Political Structures, 1815 to 1905

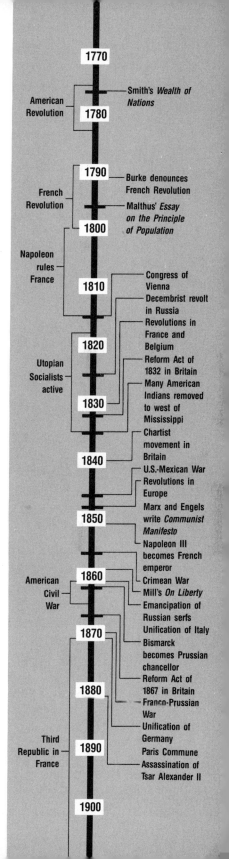

1770

American
Revolution

1780

Smith's *Wealth of Nations*

1790

French
Revolution

Burke denounces French Revolution

Malthus' *Essay on the Principle of Population*

1800

Napoleon
rules
France

1810

Congress of Vienna

Decembrist revolt in Russia

Revolutions in France and Belgium

1820

Utopian
Socialists
active

Reform Act of 1832 in Britain

Many American Indians removed to west of Mississippi

1830

Chartist movement in Britain

1840

U.S.-Mexican War

Revolutions in Europe

Marx and Engels write *Communist Manifesto*

1850

Napoleon III becomes French emperor

Crimean War

Mill's *On Liberty*

American
Civil
War

1860

Emancipation of Russian serfs

Unification of Italy

Bismarck becomes Prussian chancellor

1870

Reform Act of 1867 in Britain

Franco-Prussian War

Unification of Germany

1880

Paris Commune

Third
Republic in
France

1890

Assassination of Tsar Alexander II

1900

Most nineteenth-century European and North American nations experienced fundamental political change. Some countries—Britain, France, and the United States—gradually developed a more democratic political system, at least in the sense that most males were allowed to vote and government became more responsive to the electorate. Some nations—Germany and Italy—finally achieved national unification, while others—Russia, the Hapsburg Empire, and Spain—tried unsuccessfully to develop new political structures. Two primary factors helped produce the political changes of the nineteenth century: (1) industrialization created new social classes with new kinds of political demands, and (2) the continuing influence of the eighteenth-century political revolutions inspired many to believe that new and better kinds of political community could be created.

In this chapter, we examine the political ideologies that were defined in the late eighteenth and nineteenth centuries—nationalism, conservatism, liberalism, socialism, Marxism, feminism—as well as the major political developments in several European countries and the United States.

THE BIRTH OF POLITICAL IDEOLOGIES

Political ideologies did not exist before the late eighteenth century, because there was little room for political debate in societies where monarchs ruled in the name of God and made most political decisions. But the industrialization and political upheavals of the late eighteenth century undermined traditional institutions and beliefs, especially the assumption that government should be based on divine authority. Politics increasingly came to be viewed as a secular activity in which different groups, social classes, and nations competed for power and influence. Ideologies were the means by which these groups defined their goals.

Nationalism

Nationalism is the term used to refer to the ideal of loyalty to a nation or a state that is presumed to be the common fatherland or motherland of all those who are members of it. The loyalty of nationalism results from factors like a common language, history, and religion as well as emotions that make, for example, an American feel "American" and therefore different from people who belong to another nation. Modern nationalism began to develop during the late eighteenth century and became a more powerful and emotional force in the nineteenth century, motivating many different people in a variety of ways. It became powerful for several reasons: improved communications enabled people to feel that they were a part of a larger society rather than just their local communities; industrialization encouraged many to move to cities and thus break away from local communities and customs; and governments were increasingly based on the active participation of citizens, thus making them a part of a national community.

One of the intellectual founders of modern nationalism was Jean-Jacques Rousseau, who contended that a "general will" binds together the people of a nation (see Chapter 12). Politically, it was the French Revolution that stirred many nationalist ideals. The soldiers who fought in the French Revolution and the Napoleonic armies often felt that they were defending "their" country and "their" revolution. Conversely, many of those who fought against French armies came to feel that they were defending their countries against a foreign enemy. Some Germans, for example, first became conscious of being "German" when they fought against Napoleon.

During the nineteenth century, nationalism was manifested in many ways. Intellectuals encouraged the people of their nations to study the nation's history and culture. Political figures—such as Giuseppe Mazzini in Italy and Otto von Bismarck in Germany—used nationalist ideas to encourage politically disunified peoples to unify their country (as we will see later in the chapter). National groups like the Serbs and Czechs used nationalist ideas to justify seeking independence from the large empires that ruled them. Finally, in most countries, governments encouraged patriotism and patriotic rituals (celebrations of national holidays, for example), in an attempt to foster support for governmental policies, particularly when the policies led to conflicts with other nations.

Conservatism

Another political ideology, *conservatism*, was embraced by those who opposed political and social change. Conservatives—mostly monarchs and aristocrats as well as many peasants and others—feared that the Industrial Revolution would produce materialism and greed and that political revolution would lead to chaos. They tended to argue for continuity, for slow change consistent with tradition.

The original spokesperson for modern conservatism was the English statesman Edmund Burke (1729–1797). Burke favored the American War for Independence because he believed that American goals were properly inherited from the English political tradition. However, he opposed the turmoil caused by the French Revolution. In *Reflections on the Revolution in France* (1790), Burke argues that society is the product of a long, complex history and thus cannot be suddenly reformed or modified without causing great damage. Social change, according to Burke, must occur slowly and in pace with a society's past; therefore, revolutions are always harmful and destructive to society. Burke feared most those French revolutionaries who thought they could remake society quickly. He also feared the new industrializers—the "sophisters, economists, and calculators," as he called them—and predicted that they would subordinate everything to the pursuit of material gain. Further, Burke defended the traditional social order in which people of landed wealth dominated.

There were many other nineteenth-century conservative theorists. Joseph de Maistre (1753–1821) is particularly noteworthy because he vehemently defended the belief that God is the ultimate source of all political authority. Many ordinary people continued to hold that belief, even when most European governments were becoming secular.

Liberalism

Liberalism became the most influential political ideology of the nineteenth century, primarily because it expressed the beliefs of the industrial middle class that was steadily growing wealthier and more powerful. Liberals, mostly middle-class businesspeople and professionals, stressed the ideals of political and economic freedom. At first, they defined these ideals in such a way as to favor middle-class male interests, but gradually liberal theorists began to argue that the benefits of freedom should be extended to women and the lower classes.

Some of the principles of liberalism were first explored in the seventeenth and early eighteenth centuries by John Locke, Bernard de Mandeville, and others (see Chapter 12). However, it was not until the late eighteenth century that liberalism was fully defined by the Scottish economist Adam Smith (1723–1790). Smith was an eccentric who was several times admonished by ministers for mumbling aloud in church and once absentmindedly took a fifteen-minute walk through Edinburgh in his nightgown. He was also a brilliant economist and author of the classic text *Inquiry into the Nature and Causes of the Wealth of Nations* (1776). Smith contends in this work that governments should not interfere in a nation's economy, since an economy left alone will regulate itself. Further, the self-interest of individuals (that is, the desire to make money) induces them to produce whatever a nation needs, and competition among these individuals keeps the prices of products low. Thus, individual greed produces national wealth. In Smith's words, "it is not from the benevolence of the butcher, the brewer or baker, that we expect our dinner, but from their regard to their own self-interest."[1] Smith's doctrine, in justifying the economic freedom of individuals, soon became known as *laissez-faire* ("leave it alone") *liberalism*.

Smith's work was continued by the English economist Thomas Malthus (1766–1834). In his *Essay on the Principle of Population* (1798), Malthus argues that population tends to increase faster than food supplies, and that famines are nature's way of keeping population growth

Adam Smith (1723–1790)
A Scottish economist and
professor in Glasgow,
Smith lectured on theol-
ogy, ethics, jurisprudence,
and economics. His most
famous work, *Inquiry into
the Nature and Causes of
the Wealth of Nations*, became one of the most in-
fluential treatises in the dis-
ciplines of politics and
economics. (Culver Pic-
tures)

in balance. Malthus argues further that excess population should be
allowed to starve, since keeping the poor alive simply allows them to
produce more poor children and thus eventually make the situation
worse.

Unfortunately, the theories of Smith and Malthus were used in the
early nineteenth century to justify leaving the poor to suffer. Many
middle-class people believed that nothing—not even governmental aid to
the starving poor—should interfere with the freedom and well-being of
the marketplace. They opposed, for example, the legalization of trade
unions intended to help the working class earn higher wages. As a result,
many others came to view economic freedom as a harsh doctrine that
benefited only the most fortunate.

Gradually, liberal theorists began to expand the concept of liberalism
to include freedom and benefits for people not in the prosperous middle
class. This work was begun by the English philosopher Jeremy Bentham
(1748–1832) and was continued by John Stuart Mill (1806–1873), also
an English philosopher as well as an economist. In *On Liberty* (1859), Mill
elaborates his classic argument for freedom of speech and thought,
contending that the clash of opinions enables a healthy society to
distinguish the true from the false. In other works, he insists that the idea

of freedom must include freedom for the poor and for women. Mill favored the legalization of labor unions because workers would gain the right to bargain for higher wages and greater job security. He proposed that women be given the right to vote and therefore the opportunity to be as politically active as men. Mill in effect repudiated the old liberalism by stressing economic freedom for the working class and by defining a new, broader concept of liberalism—one that claimed to be a universal philosophy for all people. This new liberalism would influence some Western European and North American countries in the late nineteenth and early twentieth centuries.

Socialism

Despite Mill's arguments, liberalism remained a middle-class doctrine through much of the nineteenth century. The urban lower classes (mostly artisans and industrial workers) believed that economic freedom would lead to poverty and starvation. Most favored the dream of equality rather than the illusion (as it appeared to them) of liberty. That dream was defined by *socialism*, the belief that the collective ownership of property and the sharing of wealth produces a more humane and cooperative world.

Socialist ideas had been explored earlier by such writers as Plato and Thomas More. In the eighteenth century, the French agitator François Babeuf (1760–1797) argued for a social egalitarianism in which all men (not women) would share property equally. (Babeuf was later executed as a traitor by the revolutionary government in France.) The first to define the modern concept of socialism was a group of social reformers known as the *Utopian Socialists*—Robert Owen from England (1771–1858) and two social scientists from France, Charles Fourier (1772–1837) and Henri, Comte de Saint-Simon (1760–1825).

The Utopian Socialists were unusual characters. Owen was obsessed with his ideas on saving the world; Fourier once said that in some future golden age the oceans would turn to lemonade and the world would have thirty-seven million poets; and Saint-Simon sometimes claimed to be the second Christ. Nevertheless, the Utopian Socialists were shocked by the harsh living conditions endured by workers during the early Industrial Revolution and developed rational theories of how the world could be made better. Owen and Fourier argued for a decentralized form of socialism in which people would live in small communities, share labor and profits, and enjoy a spirit of communal cooperation instead of a selfish desire for individual wealth. Fourier also contended that socialism should include sexual liberation, so that men and women could change sexual partners at will. Saint-Simon proposed a more centralized form of socialism whereby an elite of social engineers (managers and economists) would govern industrial societies for the benefit of all. He argued for what would later be called *technocracy;* that is, government by experts and trained technicians.

The Utopian Socialists had little influence on the practical politics of their day and never received the support of the working classes. However, they are important because they were among the first to understand that industrialism could be used to improve dramatically the lot of the common people. They dreamed of a time when prosperity would eliminate poverty and cooperation would replace competition, a dream that inspired millions during the nineteenth and twentieth centuries. As the poet Pierre-Jean de Béranger wrote in the early nineteenth century:

> Fourier said to us: Rise from the slime,
> You who have been the slaves of lies![2]

Marxism

The work of the greatest socialist of the nineteenth century, Karl Marx (1818–1883), is known as *Marxism,* the political ideology that set the foundation for communism. Marx, assisted by his collaborator Friedrich Engels, produced a number of pamphlets and books, most notably *The Communist Manifesto* (1848) and *The Capital* (vol. 1 in 1867, vols. 2 and 3 published after Marx's death). He and Engels sought above all to emancipate humanity, to free people from the tyranny of nature and the tyranny of other people. Freedom from nature meant using technology to produce wealth and overcome poverty; freedom from others meant creating a communist society in which all people could share everything equally. According to Marx, these twin goals could be achieved only through an understanding of the deepest forces in human history. He thus sought to comprehend history through a philosophical framework that later became known as *dialectical materialism* (Marx never used this phrase, but Engels did). The word *dialectical* comes from the German philosopher Hegel (see Chapter 16) and refers to the idea that history operates through conflict between opposing forces. The word *materialism* refers to the assumption that economic and social circumstances condition how people think and behave. Specifically, it means that people are separated into classes according to the economic circumstances in which they live. (For example, all industrial workers are wage earners employed by others, so they are all members of a working class.) The term *dialectical materialism,* then, stipulates in Marx's theory that history is the story of class conflict, of continuing struggle between different socioeconomic groups.

According to Marx, the class struggles in nineteenth-century industrial nations were between *capitalists*—those who owned the factories and other means of production—and the *proletariat*—the wage-earning working class. Marx argued that capitalists "exploited" the proletariat by

Karl Marx (1818–1883) With his friend and lifelong collaborator, Friedrich Engels, Marx wrote and published *The Communist Manifesto,* which provided a foundation for the growth of socialism throughout the world. His other famous work, *Das Kapital,* is an analysis of capitalism. (Culver Pictures)

paying them wages much less than the value of the products they created and keeping most of the profit for themselves. According to his "labor theory of value," the value of a product depends on the amount of skill and time needed to produce it. (For instance, a shoemaker "makes" a pair of shoes and thus creates whatever value and price the shoes have.) Marx and other socialists believed that workers should receive the profits from a product since they create the value of the product.

Marx saw the conflict between capitalists and workers as short-lived. He predicted that the number of capitalists would decrease as the larger business firms absorbed the smaller ones. At the same time, the proletariat would continue to grow and eventually become the majority population in industrial countries. Marx believed that the workers would then launch a brief revolution, overthrow the capitalists, and operate the industries for the benefit of all people. Eventually, the working-class revolution would slowly lead to a world dominated by communism.

Of course, many of Marx's predictions about the future were never realized and some of his analyses have been disputed by economists and others. For example, economists often criticize Marx's labor theory of value because it fails to include factors other than labor that contribute to the value of a product. In addition, workers in many Western European and North American industrial nations have not been exploited to the extent that Marx thought they would be; rather, workers used labor unions and political influence to improve their working and living conditions. Another point often made is that twentieth-century Marxism has prevailed, not in industrial countries with large working classes, but in societies like Russia and China where industrialization occurred much more slowly. Furthermore, by the late 1980s, the Russian Communist conception of Marxism, in which the Communist Party dictated all political and economic decisions, was collapsing. In the Soviet Union (formerly Russia), the Communist government was trying to reform itself after decades of economic stagnation. In Eastern Europe, popular uprisings led to the overthrow of many Communist regimes (see Chapter 22).

Why, then, has Marxism remained so influential? In particular, why were Marxist groups able to gain the allegiance of millions and win control of Russia, China, and many smaller nations for much of the twentieth century? One reason is the comprehensiveness of Marx's thought; many people came to believe that Marxism explained all of human history and therefore discovered "truth." Another is the quasi-religious nature of Marx's predictions. He promised, for example, that a future Communist society would be a kind of heaven on earth, a promise that was enormously appealing to large numbers of poverty-stricken and oppressed people. And, as we will see in later chapters, Marxism gained influence as a result of certain political and economic events of the twentieth century.

Anarchism

Marxism came to dominate Socialist thought throughout most of Europe in the nineteenth century, but in a few areas workers turned to an extreme form of socialism called *anarchism*. Anarchists believed that all organization is evil and that the lower classes could live in freedom and justice only if the centralized state was abolished. The founder of modern anarchism, a French journalist named Pierre-Joseph Proudhon (1809– 1865), described the basic ideas of the ideology in this way:

> To be GOVERNED is to be . . . registered, recorded, docketed, stamped, measured, marked, assessed, licensed, authorized, recommended, admonished, hindered, reformed, rebuked, corrected. . . . Then—at the least resistance, at the first word of complaint—it is to be repressed, fined, vilified, annoyed, abused, beaten, disarmed, garrotted, imprisoned, shot, machine-gunned, judged, condemned, deported, sacrificed, sold, betrayed, and on top of everything, mocked, ridiculed, insulted, dishonored.[3]

The anarchists are most significant because they expressed in extreme form a growing fear of the bureaucratization that characterized industrial society. They had relatively little influence on the politics of their time, although some anarchists assassinated several prominent political figures, including Tsar Alexander II of Russia (1881), President Sadi Carnot of France (1894), Empress Elizabeth of Austria (1898), King Humbert I of Italy (1900), and President William McKinley of the United States (1901).

Feminism

Modern *feminism*, the struggle for liberation of women, originated from eighteenth-century French revolutionary ideals. In England, Mary Wollstonecraft argued for equality between men and women and greater educational opportunities for women in her *Vindication of the Rights of Women* (1791). In France, Olympe de Gouges wrote a *Declaration of the Rights of Women* (1793) to supplement the "Declaration of the Rights of Man and Citizen" proclaimed by the revolutionary National Assembly of 1789. She called for a social revolution based on profound cultural and sexual changes in European society. Neither of these early feminists had much influence in their own times, but their fame gradually increased as feminism gained influence.

Nineteenth-century women were still prohibited from voting and holding political office. In many places, women were not allowed to engage in business or to join a profession, and divorce was almost impossible for a married woman to initiate. To gain equality in these and other activities, a feminist movement made up of mostly middle-class women began to emerge in some countries. In the United States in 1848, a Women's Rights Convention at Seneca Falls, New York, endorsed the principle of female suffrage and protested against the economic subjugation of women. Other women's rights conventions followed and were led by such women as Elizabeth Cady Stanton and Susan B. Anthony. By the late nineteenth century, a few colleges made higher education available to women and some western territories—Wyoming and Utah, for example—granted women the right to vote. Active feminist movements also appeared in some European countries that were relatively liberal and dominated by Protestantism, such as Great Britain, Denmark, and the Netherlands. Finland and Norway gave women the right to vote in 1906 and 1913, respectively. Feminism did not thrive in countries where Catholicism was strong—France, Italy, Germany—because the Catholic church opposed the expansion of women's political and social rights. In Russia, women and men alike were subject to the autocratic tsarist system, so the few feminists often joined revolutionary movements hoping to overthrow tsarism.

Working-class women rarely participated in the feminist movement, as most of them were preoccupied with the economic survival of their families. The majority of working-class women were domestic servants or married with families and households to manage. Some worked at odd jobs to make extra money. Others worked in factories, but they were usually paid less than men and were often denied membership in trade unions. One major change for working-class women in the more prosperous countries was the increased use of birth-control techniques (rubber condoms, cervical caps), which gave couples some control over the size of their families. In addition, by the end of the nineteenth century, some Socialist parties (most notably the German Social Democrats) were beginning to support the suffrage for all women.

NINETEENTH-CENTURY POLITICAL DEVELOPMENTS

War was infrequent in nineteenth-century Europe; from 1815 to 1914, only a few short conflicts in the 1850s and 1860s interrupted this hundred-year period of relative peace. Most peaceful, on the international level, were the years 1815 to 1848. During this time, international diplomacy was dominated by five great powers—Great Britain, which until 1822 had a superb foreign secretary, Viscount Robert Stewart Castlereagh; the Hapsburg Empire, led throughout the period by a skillful diplomat, Clemens Prince Metternich; Prussia; Russia; and France. These five nations, guided initially by Metternich and Castlereagh, developed a "balance of power" diplomacy designed to guarantee that no one state became strong enough to dominate the others (as France had threatened to do during the Napoleonic era).

The specific goals of the balance of power system included preventing (1) the death and destruction that resulted from major wars; (2) the rise of another charismatic leader like Napoleon who might seek to dominate

Figure 17.1   Sites of Popular Uprisings, 1848

Europe; and (3) more revolutions against kings and princes. Thus, the balance of power system was built by conservatives to preserve the existing political and social order, but it also functioned as a successful peace system that fostered cooperation among the great powers and prevented major conflicts for several decades.

The diplomats were in part able to sustain peace because most European politicians were more concerned with maintaining social order and stability within their countries rather than competing for power on the international level. The early nineteenth century was a turbulent time in many countries, for revolts and occasionally full-scale revolutions resulted from the social tensions and conflicts produced by the ongoing Industrial Revolution, the memory of the French Revolution, and the ideas of the new political ideologies. Major revolutions that affected several nations occurred in 1830 and 1848, while smaller revolts in individual countries took place in 1819, 1820, 1821, 1822, 1825, 1831, 1834, 1839, and 1844. These revolts and revolutions were usually supported by various segments of the lower classes and revolutionaries who hoped to found a new political and social order in Europe. They were opposed by all those who feared radical social and political change—the upper classes, many in the middle class, and conservative peasants. Thus, the first half of the nineteenth century was dominated by a struggle between those who favored and those who opposed revolution.

Few revolutions occurred in the Western world during the latter nineteenth century, and a number of major political issues were resolved. In the 1860s, the American Civil War eliminated slavery but not the oppression of blacks in the United States; the liberation of serfs in Russia gave legal freedom to the lower classes there; the unifications of Italy and Germany were almost completed (final German unification came in 1871); and the Hapsburg Empire slowly began to disintegrate.

By the late nineteenth century, some countries—Britain, France, the United States, some Scandinavian nations—were developing more democratic political systems, as the right to vote was granted to larger numbers of the male population. This was also a time of relative peace, as there were no major wars in the Western world from the 1870s until the outbreak of World War I in 1914. One reason for the peaceful era was an alliance system engineered by the German Chancellor Otto von Bismarck. During the 1860s, Bismarck used military conflict to build a unified Germany (as we will see later in the chapter). After that, however, he furthered peace by helping to maintain an international stability in which Germany could prosper. To accomplish stability, he developed an alliance system that included Germany, the Hapsburg Empire, Russia, and Italy. The system served to bind many of the major nations together, so that no one nation could start a major war. If a nation outside the system threatened to start a conflict, the others would combine against it. In this way, France was isolated and prevented from gaining any military allies and so was too weak to consider initiating war. At the same time, Britain was preoccupied with conquering colonies around the world and therefore sought peace in Europe.

To explain how nations reacted in different ways to the new political and social forces unleashed by the industrial and political revolutions, we need to consider some elements of the political and social histories of several major Western nations in the nineteenth century.

GREAT BRITAIN

In 1815, the traditional upper classes in Great Britain still dominated British politics and society. However, the liberal middle class, growing in size and wealth because of expanding industrialization, was beginning to demand and achieve a greater share of political power. Three significant pieces of legislation—the Reform Act of 1832, the repeal of the Corn Laws, and the abolition of slavery in the British colonies—illustrated the increasing influence of the middle class in Great Britain.

The Reform Act of 1832 changed British politics. Prior to 1832, elections to the House of Commons, the lower house of Parliament, were dominated by rural electoral districts in which only a few landowners were entitled to vote. The new industrial towns were underrepresented. The Reform Act did primarily two things: (1) it redistributed parliamentary seats, so that the heavily populated industrial areas would get more representation; and (2) it expanded the suffrage to include all men with a certain level of wealth. The effect was to give more political influence to middle-class males.

The Corn Laws were repealed in 1846. They had placed tariffs on imported foreign grain, thus favoring British grain production and protecting the economic interests of the landowning aristocracy. Middle-class businesspeople opposed the Corn Laws because they raised grain and bread prices, which meant that urban workers had to be paid higher wages in order to survive. The Corn Laws thus became a major source of conflict between the aristocracy, trying to protect their incomes, and the middle class, seeking to keep prices and hence wages low. The repeal of the Corn Laws marked a significant victory for middle-class interests and laissez-faire liberalism favoring free trade. Many workers opposed the repeal because they predicted (correctly) that food prices would continue to rise while wages would be kept low.

Another important legislation was the 1833 abolition of slavery in the British colonies. (The Congress of Vienna had already condemned the slave trade in 1815.) Slavery was usually supported by agricultural interests, those who needed (or thought they needed) groups of unpaid laborers to work large plantations in various parts of the world. The British middle class opposed slavery, however, both for idealistic reasons—the belief in liberty and equality—and for economic reasons—the businessperson's need for free laborers who could move to wherever employment was available. The middle class won abolition of slavery in British-controlled areas in 1833, though British manufacturers continued to profit from cheap cotton imported from the slave plantations in the southern United States.

The British lower classes were at first much less successful at improving their economic and political status, as a series of lower-class demonstrations and movements were defeated. From 1815 to 1819, economic depression led to several large demonstrations by the unemployed and underpaid, the most notorious being at St. Peter's Field, Manchester, where soldiers killed eleven demonstrators. By the 1830s, some industrial workers were beginning to strike for higher pay and better working conditions, but they were largely ineffective. The largest lower-class movement was *Chartism*, named for a "People's Charter" drawn up in 1838. Over one million people signed the Charter, which demanded universal male suffrage. Chartism was thus a genuine mass movement of ordinary people who believed that greater democracy would give them a better life. Specifically, they believed that a democratic suffrage would give them greater control over the communities in which they lived and the factories and workshops in which they labored. But Parliament, controlled by the upper and middle classes, rejected the Chartist's demands and the movement died by the late 1840s.

At mid-century, the aristocracy continued to dominate British politics and society, but it increasingly had to share power with the middle class. Furthermore, pressure from the lower classes slowly impelled the British government to broaden the suffrage. The Reform Act of 1867 gave much of the urban working class the right to vote. Other acts in 1884 and 1885 established universal manhood suffrage.

During the late nineteenth century, Britain was the greatest political and economic power on earth. The British Empire extended across the globe (see Chapter 18), and British industry was still very productive. But British economic power—the basis of political power in the modern world—was beginning to decline. One reason was that very little had been invested in the technical and scientific education needed to foster industrial growth. British economic strength would continue to decline, relative to others, in the twentieth century.

FRANCE

Twenty-six years of revolution (1789–1815) and Napoleonic rule changed France greatly. The aristocrats lost many of their privileges, and many of them remained bitterly opposed to all that the French Revolution had done. The upper middle class—the great bankers and wealthy businesspeople—prospered during the revolutionary years and was eager to expand its political and economic power. The peasants, many of whom gained more land because of revolutionary reforms, were increasingly conservative. They had profited from the Revolution and wanted no more political upheavals. The urban lower classes were radically dissatisfied with their lot. The sansculottes feared that their traditional craft occupations would be lost to industrialization. The new industrial working class feared the long working hours and low pay in the early factories. The sansculottes increasingly demanded for men the right to vote—in the belief that political equality would give them the power to save their livelihoods. The workers wanted social and economic reforms that would improve their standard of living.

The revolutionary years left France divided, with some French supporting the revolutionary heritage, others opposing it, and still others wanting even more revolutionary changes. Consequently, as these various groups competed for power, the French experienced many political disputes and governmental changes during the nineteenth century. Several times, political change was accomplished through violent revolution.

The first change occurred in 1815. The nations that had defeated Napoleon sought to restore a conservative regime in France and installed a new monarch, Louis XVIII (reigned 1815–1824). Louis was not an absolute monarch, for he ruled in conjunction with a legislature representing the wealthy classes. He governed effectively for a time, but in 1824 he was succeeded by his brother Charles X (reigned 1824–1830), an extreme conservative determined to restore the prerevolutionary privileges of the aristocracy and the Catholic church. Charles antagonized so many people that in 1830 a revolution erupted in Paris. Workers, students, and tradespeople threw up barricades in Parisian streets, a few days of violence ensued, and the despised king was quickly forced into exile. In the aftermath, confusion about what type of new government ought to be established allowed a few powerful men to gain acceptance for a new monarch, Louis Philippe (reigned 1830–1848), a member of the royal family who was known to be more open-minded than Charles X. (The 1830 revolution in France stimulated radical activity in other parts of Europe, notably Belgium, which revolted against its union with the Netherlands and became an independent nation in 1831.)

Louis Philippe's regime was, in effect, government by the upper-middle class, since the right to vote was expanded just enough to allow wealthy bankers and businesspeople to control the legislature. This middle-class system quickly acquired a number of vociferous critics. One was Alexis de Tocqueville, the great political thinker who in *Democracy in America* analyzes the merits and defects of democratic societies. Tocqueville was particularly critical of the French middle class because of its greedy obsession with money and its lack of sympathy for the impoverished lower classes. Another critic was the radical female novelist whose pen name was George Sand. In many of her novels, Sand speaks out for greater justice and equality, particularly for women.

The lower classes were particularly hostile to Louis Philippe's government. The silk workers of Lyons rebelled in both 1831 and 1834, but they were bloodily suppressed. By the 1840s, economic depression produced growing unemployment and social unrest, which the government tried to repress by force. The situation deteriorated to the point that a revolution erupted in February 1848. Once again, workers and students threw up barricades, Louis Philippe was driven out, and for a few months there was great enthusiasm about establishing a more democratic government and a series of social reforms. (The 1848 revolution was so popular that it inspired other revolutions in various parts of central Europe. We discuss these later in the chapter.)

But the revolution of 1848 was a complete failure from the point of view of the lower classes and the revolutionaries who wanted a democratic society. In the late spring of 1848, the conservative middle class gained control of the government, which crushed a second workers' insurrection that erupted in June. Then, near the end of the year, a new president of France was elected—Louis Napoleon Bonaparte (reigned 1848–1870). Louis Napoleon was the nephew of Napoleon I and therefore the heir to the grandeur of the great name. He used his popularity first to become president and then to proclaim himself "emperor" late in 1851. Louis Napoleon governed France until 1870 and claimed that he was restoring the glory of the first Napoleonic years, but he was in reality a new kind of ruler. He was an emperor, a monarch, whose imperial name was Napoleon III. Yet, unlike traditional monarchs, he sought to derive his authority from his popularity with the masses rather than from the use of force or from claims about the divine right of kings. His approach was a new way of harnessing the political energies of the people to a nondemocratic, basically conservative system of government.

Napoleon III's regime collapsed in 1870, in the aftermath of France's defeat in the Franco-Prussian War (as we will see later in the chapter). The French once again became embroiled in a prolonged dispute about what kind of government France should have. Early in 1871, a national legislature dominated by conservatives was elected. The conservatives had the support of the peasants and small-town shopkeepers from all over France. But in Paris, much more radical than the rest of the country, the Paris Commune was set up, an urban insurrection intended to make French politics more democratic and revolutionary. The Commune was destroyed in deadly fighting in the summer of 1871, and only then did France begin to form a constitutional system that became known as the *Third Republic.* The Third Republic was a moderately conservative government controlled by the votes of businesspeople and peasants that endured from the 1870s to 1940. Although conservative, it was more democratic than anything the French had experienced since the 1790s, for one house of the legislature was elected by universal manhood suffrage.

France was not a leading industrial power in the late nineteenth century, mainly because of the political and cultural heritage of the French Revolution. The Revolution distributed much farmland to large numbers of peasant families, and as a result many peasants simply refused to leave their land and move to cities to become industrial workers. Thus, France remained more rural than other industrializing nations. The Revolution also protected the political and social positions of the lower middle class—shopkeepers and small businesspeople who practiced traditional crafts and maintained small stores. Many of these, just like many peasants, refused to be drawn into an industrial, mass-production economy. In consequence, France was a nation of peasants and shopkeepers, with a relatively small industrial base located in only a few areas. This resistance to industrialization meant that many French cities, Paris above all, were far more charming and delightful to live in than the industrial cities of Great Britain and Germany. But it also meant that France would gradually become less powerful than some other nations (such as Germany) and would be at a severe disadvantage when it had to fight two world wars in the twentieth century.

SPAIN

Spain endured a long decline after the heroic days of the Spanish Empire in the sixteenth century. During the seventeenth and eighteenth centuries, most Spanish monarchs were conservatives who stifled intellectual and cultural discussion. Furthermore, Spain lacked a large middle class that could provide the capital and develop the commerce needed to stimulate the economy. The agricultural system was dominated by a large, unproductive nobility who lived off the labors of a poor, uneducated peasantry.

By the beginning of the nineteenth century, however, revolutionary ideals of liberty and equality were filtering into Spain from France. A few educated Spanish in the professions and the army began to call themselves liberals and to argue for reforms that would reinvigorate the country. The liberals wrote and gained acceptance for a Constitution of 1812 designed to modernize Spanish politics, but King Ferdinand VII repudiated the document. In response, liberal elements in the army revolted against him. Even though the revolt was crushed fairly quickly, it helped to encourage the Latin American wars for independence from Spain (see Chapter 15).

For most of the rest of the nineteenth century, Spain was ruled by weak monarchs supported by conservative forces—the nobility, the Catholic church, and much of the military. Periodically, the liberal elements gained power briefly and tried to institute political and economic reforms, but they were largely unsuccessful. Thus, much of Spanish history in the nineteenth century is the story of a declining country unable to respond effectively to the industrial and political revolutions of the time.

GERMANY AND THE HAPSBURG EMPIRE

The area known today as Germany had been divided into several territorial states during the Middle Ages. By the early nineteenth century, the Germanic state of Prussia controlled much of northeastern Germany. In the southeast was the multinational Hapsburg Empire, a collection of both Germanic and non-Germanic peoples (Hungarians, Czechs, Slovaks, Poles, and others) held together by the power of a monarchy that had become hereditary in the Hapsburg family. (The Hapsburg Empire was sometimes known as the "Austrian Empire.") In central and western Germany there were about three dozen smaller states, such as Saxony, Bavaria, and Baden.

The Ideal of Nationalism

Most of the German states (with a few exceptions like Frederick the Great's Prussia) were politically quiescent and economically stagnant during the eighteenth century. At the end of the century, however, the French revolutionary ideals of liberty, equality, and fraternity began to inspire political discussions throughout the Germanies. For Germans, the most captivating ideal was fraternity, since it referred to something they lacked—the union of related peoples into a common nation. By the nineteenth century, the greatest political issue in the Germanies was nationalism. Would the Germans be able to unify and form a German nation? Who could or would accomplish such a task? Would a united Germany include the non-Germanic peoples of the Hapsburg Empire? What form of government should a unified Germany have? These were the major questions of the day.

After 1815, the Germanies—that is, all the German states as well as the German parts of the Hapsburg Empire—formed a German Confederation, a loosely organized body that enabled the states to cooperate while still retaining their sovereignty. The dominating force in Confederation politics was Prince Metternich of the Hapsburg Empire, a conservative who wanted to maintain the existing political and social order and prevent any growth of German nationalism. Metternich served an empire that was an uneasy collection of peoples—Germans, Magyars, Czechs, Slovaks, Serbs, and others—many of whom sought to assert their independence from the Hapsburg monarchy. For many peoples, nationalism was a promise to be fulfilled, since it meant that each people should have their own nation. For Metternich and the Hapsburg Empire, however, nationalism was a threat, because the empire would disintegrate and disappear if its various peoples became independent. Consequently, Metternich's German policy was to prevent any kind of political or social upheaval that might allow or encourage Hapsburg peoples to seek political change. For example, when some students held a festival in honor of freedom and nationalism at Hambach in 1832, the German Confederation led by Metternich approved legislation designed to repress political changes and impose censorship.

The German Confederation was thus a fundamentally conservative force, and by the 1840s the German people were little closer to national unity than they had been in 1815. In 1848, though, the revolution in

France sparked uprisings in many German states. New, more liberal governments came to power in several areas, and Metternich and other conservatives were driven into exile. Many of the new governments sent representatives to the Frankfurt Parliament, a meeting to establish a plan for the national unification of all Germans. The Parliament drafted a constitution for a united Germany based on liberal political principles, but the constitution never took effect. By late 1848, conservatives began to use military force to reassert control in the Germanies; the liberal governments quickly disappeared, and the Frankfurt dream of a liberal, united Germany died. Most Germans relapsed into a passive conservatism, as the poet Heinrich Heine describes:

> The wind's asleep, that howled so wild;
> At home it's quiet as could be;
> Germania, the great big child,
> Plays happily around his Christmas tree.[4]

Bismarck and German Unification

German unification was finally accomplished by the diplomatic and military strategems of Otto von Bismarck (1815–1898), chief minister of Prussia. Bismarck was unimpressed by the nationalist enthusiasms that inspired the Frankfurt Parliament. On becoming chief minister, he said that the great questions of the day would be settled by "blood and iron" rather than by resolutions and speeches. He was first and foremost a Prussian advocate dedicated to increasing Prussian power and only gradually became a German nationalist seeking the unification of Germany.

Bismarck's first goal was to eliminate Hapsburg power and competition for leadership in Germany. The first step was to get the Hapsburgs to join Prussia in a war against Denmark over the issue of who should control the provinces of Schleswig and Holstein (just south of Denmark). The 1864 war was a victory for the Prussians and Hapsburgs, but in the aftermath Schleswig and Holstein became a source of tension between the two German powers. The tension was one of the causes (along with the struggle for control of Germany) that led to the Austro-Prussian War of 1866. Although that war lasted only seven weeks, it resulted in a decisive Prussian victory and the removal of Hapsburg influence from Germany. Over the next two or three years, several small northern German territories were annexed to Prussia and a North German Confederation led by Prussia was formed.

By the late 1860s, Bismarck was thinking more about possible German unification and turned his attention to France. Most Germans considered France a traditional enemy, because the French systemati-

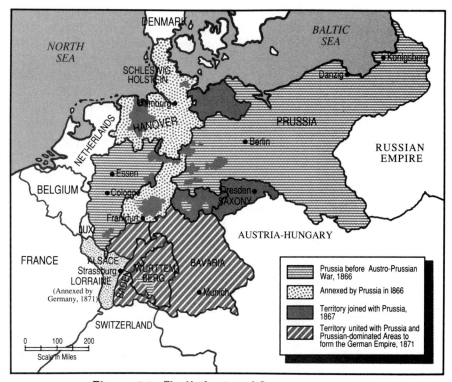

Figure 17.2 The Unification of Germany, 1866–1871

cally tried to keep Germany disunified and weak. A dispute with France would thus fan the flames of German nationalism. Dispute became war in 1870, after Prussia and France got into a diplomatic quarrel over the succession to the Spanish throne. The quarrel escalated into a major crisis, in part because of some behind-the-scenes trickery by Bismarck. Nationalist passions soon engulfed both sides, and France declared war on Germany. Unfortunately for the French, most of the German states rallied to the Prussian cause; furthermore, France was badly prepared for war, and the Germans won a complete victory. The aftermath of the war included the overthrow of Napoleon III and the Paris Commune in France. It also included the final unification of Germany. The rulers of several German states, impelled by nationalist enthusiasm as well as by Bismarck's urgings, invited King William I of Prussia to become emperor of a united Germany. The united German Empire was formed early in 1871.

The new Germany did not include those Germans who lived within the Hapsburg Empire. The empire, a polyglot of diverse people of diverse cultures, slowly began to disintegrate. In 1867, the empire was in effect divided into parts—an Austrian-German section and a Hungarian section—ruled by a common Hapsburg emperor. (Hence, it was often called "Austria-Hungary.") The division was intended to stabilize the empire by giving the Hungarians a degree of nationalist autonomy. However, it did not have the desired effect; rather, it only encouraged other national groups (Poles, Czechs, Serbs) to demand autonomy for themselves. By the end of the nineteenth century, the Hapsburg Empire was an increasingly ungovernable entity in which various nationalities competed for autonomy and even independence from the empire.

The Growth of German Power

The united Germany was characterized by strength and order. It was a politically conservative nation dominated by the traditional upper classes. However, some attention had to be given to the political wishes of the middle and lower classes, so one house of the federal legislature —the Reichstag—was elected by universal manhood suffrage. The Reichstag had some influence, but it lacked authority in foreign policy and the military.

After 1871, Germany industrialized rapidly. The sudden transformation of Germany from a quiet, rural area to a powerful industrial nation occurred for several reasons. First, the Germans had vast reserves of coal and iron, two basic elements of industrialization. Second, political unification created a national marketplace that stimulated economic growth. Finally, the German government actively encouraged and directed the industrialization process. The German practice of governmental support for industrialization was very different from the British and American approach of industrialization through private business-people. When Latin American, Asian, and African nations began to industrialize in the twentieth century, they were much more inclined to imitate the German and Russian model of governmentally directed industrialization than the British and American model. Usually, those nations lacked the technical skills and capital needed to industrialize, so governments had to assume the responsibility of fostering technical education and the accumulation of investment capital.

By 1900, Germany was the leading industrial power in Europe. German nationalism had also grown, as many Germans were intensely proud of their country's achievements. Nationalism would be one of the emotions that impelled Germany to fight two major wars in the twentieth century, for many Germans hoped to build a German-dominated Europe. In addition, many Germans felt uprooted from their rural way of life into a bustling, urban, industrial way of life. This led to their desire to belong to and believe in something—one of the reasons so many Germans embraced Adolf Hitler's Nazi ideology in the 1920s and 1930s.

ITALY

Politics in the Italian peninsula were also dominated by the issue of nationalism. Italy had been politically fragmented since the days of the Roman Empire, and by the nineteenth century the Italian peoples were divided into several territorial states, many of which were controlled by the Hapsburg Empire. The French Revolution stimulated the formation of several secret societies of Italian patriots, whose goal was to liberalize Italy and stop the intervention of foreign nations in Italian affairs. These societies helped initiate several insurrections against monarchs, one in Naples in 1820 and others in various other areas during 1830–1831. None of these insurrections produced any permanent changes, but by the 1830s a feeling of nationalism was growing among educated Italians. In 1831, Giuseppe Mazzini founded Young Italy, an organization intended to encourage the growth of Italian nationalism. Mazzini became the spokesperson and propagandist for the cause of Italian unification. In 1848, revolutions occurred in several Italian states. The revolutionaries wanted to drive out the Hapsburg armies that dominated so much of Italy, and some hoped that the revolutions would lead to national unity. But, just as in Germany, the 1848 revolutions were crushed and conservative forces returned to power.

Italian unification was finally accomplished largely through the efforts of Count Camillo Cavour (1810–1861), Prime Minister of the kingdom of Sardinia (which included the island of Sardinia and the north Italian area of Piedmont). Cavour was an Italian patriot, but he was also a conservative who believed that unification was possible only through skillful diplomacy and military might rather than popular uprisings. Accordingly, in 1858, Cavour negotiated an alliance between Piedmont and France that was directed against the Hapsburg Empire, still in control of much of Italy. (The French Emperor Napoleon III was hoping to replace the Hapsburgs as the dominant power in Italy, but he was unsuccessful.) The subsequent Franco-Piedmontese War against the Hapsburg Empire (1859) resulted in the Hapsburgs being driven out of much of Italy. Then, in 1860, several northern Italian areas were unified with Piedmont. Shortly afterward, Giuseppe Garibaldi (1807–1882), a flamboyant Italian nationalist, led his armies into southern Italy to conquer Sicily and Naples. Cavour, afraid that the popular Garibaldi would soon become recognized as the leader of all Italy, directed the Piedmontese armies south to the city of Rome, which was still controlled by the Catholic church. There, he and Garibaldi proclaimed the unification of Italy in 1861. (In 1861, two traditionally Italian areas— Venice and Rome—remained outside the new Italy. Venice, still occupied by the Hapsburgs, was added to Italy in 1866, and Rome was annexed in 1870, after French troops supporting the pope left the city.)

The new kingdom was a constitutional monarchy, Garibaldi having retired to his farm and the ruler of the kingdom of Sardinia becoming king of Italy. It was dominated by the aristocracy and the upper-middle class, so even though Italians had won national independence they had not gained political equality among themselves.

Italy also suffered fundamental economic divisions. For centuries, southern Italy had been an agricultural area, where aristocratic landowners and desperately poor peasants coexisted and periodically fought each other over control of the land. Northern Italy, however, was dominated by wealthy commercial cities. When industrialization came to Italy in the nineteenth century, it occurred primarily in the north. Thus, the north grew wealthier and the south remained rural and impoverished.

RUSSIA

Russia was deeply involved in European affairs during the Napoleonic wars; Russian armies helped defeat the French, and Tsar Alexander I (reigned 1801–1825) was an influential figure in the great power diplomacy after 1815. One effect of Russian involvement in Europe was to expose many Russians to French revolutionary ideals. For a time, Alexander was sufficiently enthusiastic to consider some constitutional reforms for Russia, but his conservative instincts eventually blocked any significant changes.

Another attempt to introduce revolutionary ideas into Russia was the Decembrist revolt of 1825. The Decembrists were army veterans who wanted to limit the powers of the tsars and establish a constitutional, rather than an absolute, monarchy in Russia. When Alexander died in December 1825, there was some confusion about who would succeed him, and during the chaos the Decembrists attempted a revolt against the tsarist system. They were unsuccessful, and several of the leaders were hanged. Some later Russians would remember the Decembrists as early martyrs to the cause of revolution.

Nicholas I

The new tsar, Nicholas I (reigned 1825–1855), was determined to prevent revolutionary ideas from changing Russia. Under his rule, Russia remained a bastion of conservatism characterized by autocratic government, secret police, an intolerant Orthodox church, and an enserfed peasantry. Nicholas sought to stamp out revolutions elsewhere as well. When the Poles (some of whom were conquered by Russia during the triple partition of Poland in the late eighteenth century) rebelled in 1830, Nicholas (who was king of Poland) sent Russian armies to destroy the revolt and drive thousands of Polish leaders into exile. In 1848, Russian troops helped the Hapsburg rulers defeat the revolutionaries who had briefly gained control over Hapsburg dominions. But Nicholas's attempt to rule Russia through secret police and military bureaucracies stifled Russian creativity and initiative. The shortcomings of his government were revealed in the Crimean War of 1853–1856.

The Crimean War originated in a religious dispute in the Holy Land, a quarrel between Western European Christians and Greek Orthodox Christians over their respective rights to use certain holy places in Palestine. The religious dispute quickly became a political struggle, with Russia supporting the Greek Orthodox position and the Ottoman Empire, Britain, and France on the other side. When the struggle erupted into the Crimean War, the major action centered on an Anglo-Franco-Ottoman siege of a Russian naval base at Sevastopol in the Crimea, a peninsula in the Black Sea. The siege began in 1854, and for several months both sides endured incompetent leadership and severe losses. The Russian military was particularly inept, for it suffered from an inadequate supply system, obsolete weapons, shortages of ammunition, and weak leaders. The conflict finally ended in 1856, with the defeated Russians having to surrender some territories to the Ottoman Empire and accept the neutralization (no warships, no fortifications) of the Black Sea.

Forces for Change

When Nicholas died in 1855, Russia was a relatively weak power unable to assert itself in international affairs. Many Russians believed that the bureaucratic conservatism practiced by Nicholas had to be stopped and that Russia had to find a way to modernize. In practice, modernization required resolving the problem of serfdom, since no society could modernize as long as most of its population consisted of unfree and uneducated laborers who were unable to move about in search of employment or to display any sort of personal initiative or creativity. The serf problem was similar to the slavery issue in the United States, in that it involved a large number of people who were legally unfree and economically downtrodden. Serfdom was different in that it was not a racial condition and the number of Russian serfs was much larger than the number of American slaves.

In 1861, Tsar Alexander II (reigned 1855–1881) decreed the emancipation of serfs and later established other reforms, such as the creation of *zemstvos* or local assemblies for limited local self-government. Emancipation was only a partial victory for serfs, however, since in order to get land they had to purchase it from their former masters. Most ex-serfs, now free peasants, were poor and unable to buy much land. Thus, the nobility continued to dominate Russian agriculture.

Although Alexander's reforms were intended to encourage the modernization of Russia, a growing number of Russian intellectuals argued that the tsarist regime was too backward and corrupt to accomplish modernization. Some of them became revolutionaries dedicated to overthrowing tsarism. The People's Will, a revolutionary terrorist group, was established in 1879, and in 1881 Alexander was mortally wounded by an assassin. By the late nineteenth century, two educated elites were competing for ultimate control of Russia: the revolutionary elite, some of whom were Marxists, sought to destroy tsarism; the official elite—the tsarist regime, the aristocracy, and government bureaucrats—was beginning to sponsor industrialization. Some industrialization occurred, particularly during the tenure of Sergei Witte as minister of finance (1892–1903). Under Witte's direction, the government invested in and encouraged the growth of the iron industry and railroad construction. The Trans-Siberian railway (completed in 1905) was intended to stimulate economic growth by tying western and eastern Russia together into one national market. And, growth did take place. Russia lagged behind other nations in absolute production, but its rate of growth surpassed the others. In the 1890s, Russian iron smelting increased by 190 percent and coal output expanded by 131 percent.

The drive for industrialization was not completely successful, however, for it intensified the political divisions that already existed in Russia. Some government officials and the expanding class of businesspeople favored more industrial growth, but many aristocrats and peasants feared the disruptive effects of industrialization. The dilemma faced by Russia at this time was a difficult one, for without industrialization the nation would remain backward, but the drive for industrialization would produce enough discontent to cause political turmoil. The end result was turmoil, as Russia experienced a series of revolutionary upheavals during the first decades of the twentieth century.

THE UNITED STATES

Unlike many European nations, the United States did not experience violent political or social revolution during the first half of the nineteenth century. One reason was that American politics was being gradually democratized, at least for white men. Some states expanded the right to vote to include all adult white males, and the presidency of Andrew Jackson (1829–1837), who professed to represent the common man, seemed to symbolize the advent of egalitarian political democracy. Another reason was that Americans were preoccupied by the issues of territorial expansion and slavery.

Manifest Destiny

The United States acquired the west bank of the Mississippi River and much of the Great Plains in the Louisiana Purchase (see Chapter 15). This was followed in 1819 by the acquisition of Florida from Spain. The Spanish, whose main concern was the Latin American wars for independence, could no longer control the growing number of American settlers in Florida and so gave up the peninsula without a struggle. By the 1820s, Americans were also migrating into Texas, then owned by Mexico. After several years and battles with the Mexican army, the American settlers declared Texas independent in 1836. In 1845, Texas became a part of the United States. These events produced considerable tension between the United States and Mexico, and a series of incidents led to the outbreak of what Americans called the Mexican War (1846–1848). American armies invaded Mexico and defeated the Mexicans relatively easily. In 1848, the Treaty of Guadalupe Hidalgo stipulated that Mexico would renounce claims to Texas and also cede New Mexico and California to the United States. (The areas ceded to the United States included what are today the states of Utah, Nevada, and Arizona in addition to California and New Mexico.) At mid-century, then, American boundaries extended from the Atlantic to the Pacific, and an American newspaper could speak of the nation's "manifest destiny to overspread the continent allotted by Providence for the free development of our yearly multiplying millions."[5]

Territorial expansion was a success story for the white settlers but a tragedy for the native Americans. Native American tribes often occupied the land that white settlers wanted to farm, particularly in the southern United States where numerous battles occurred during the early part of the nineteenth century. By the 1830s, the federal government decided to remove southern native Americans from their lands to west of the Mississippi. As President Jackson told them, "There your white brothers will not trouble you; they will have no claim to the land. . . . It will be yours forever."[6] Jackson was probably sincere, but for the native Americans the experience was far more harsh than the president described. The journey of the Cherokee to Oklahoma, for example, became known as the "Trail of Tears," as thousands died of starvation and the winter cold. By the 1850s, white settlers were pushing across the Mississippi, native Americans were again being pressured to leave their land, and the government was initiating a policy of forcing them to live on reservations. Native Americans, like many other peoples in other parts of the world, were confronting and losing to an expanding white civilization.

Slavery and the Civil War

The issue of slavery was far more volatile than the native American issue in the United States. Most black slaves worked on southern farms and

Battle of Gettysburg On July 1–3, 1863, at Gettysburg, Pennsylvania, there occurred one of the major battles of the American Civil War. The two sides suffered over forty thousand casualties in just three days. (Culver Pictures)

plantations. Thus the issue was divided geographically—those in the South believed that slavery was essential to their way of life, whereas a small but growing number of people in the North believed that slavery was both morally repugnant and economically inefficient. Territorial expansion exacerbated the conflict. As new areas were settled, southerners insisted that slaveholding should be allowed in those areas while northerners increasingly resisted the expansion of slavery. By the 1850s, radicals on both sides were overwhelming the voices of moderation. The stage was set for the American Civil War.

The most obvious source of antagonism between the North and the South was the slavery issue, but underlying that issue was another question: What kind of society would the United States become in the future? The South was a traditional agricultural area, and many southerners believed they were defending an ancient way of life that had prevailed in Western Civilization for centuries. The North, however, was increasingly a capitalistic, industrializing area that stressed economic production and an urban way of life. Southerners tended to think of northerners as materialistic and greedy, whereas northerners often portrayed southerners as economically backward slavers.

The election of Abraham Lincoln to the presidency in 1860 turned the antagonism between the North and South into war. Although Lincoln did not intend to abolish slavery, he did oppose the expansion of slavery into new territories. Many southern leaders believed that Lincoln's presidency would lead to the North imposing its will on the South. Thus, in late 1860 and early 1861, eleven southern states seceded from the United States to form the Confederate States of America. The North was determined to block the secession, and so the Civil War erupted late in the spring of 1861.

The Civil War was the first modern-day war, at least in the sense that machinery played a prominent role in the fighting. Railroads transported troops to the fronts, and the latest weapons, including Gatling machine guns, were used to fight them. Over 630,000 soldiers died in the war. At first, the Confederates had some advantages, such as a defensive strategy and better generals. The North, however, had the larger population and greater industrial capacity. The war ended in 1865 with the North's victory.

The Significance of the North's Victory

The victory of the North meant that the dominating political power shifted from the South to the North and that the northern vision of the future—a capitalist, industrial America—would triumph. It also meant the end of slavery but not the end of oppression of blacks. President Lincoln proclaimed the freedom of slaves in the Emancipation Proclamation (1863), and after the war the Fourteenth and Fifteenth Amendments to the Constitution were approved to protect the civil rights of blacks. Legal rights were relatively insignificant, however, for most blacks were ex-slaves who owned no property and had few employment skills. As one former slave said, "I'se free. Ain't wuf nuffin."[7] Many blacks ended up working as tenant farmers for their former masters.

Another difficulty confronting blacks was the attitude of whites, largely unchanged by the Civil War. Most whites disliked and feared blacks, and even in the North blacks were rarely allowed the right to vote. In the South, terrorist organizations like the Ku Klux Klan intimidated blacks and various kinds of state legislation legalized segregation of blacks.

The United States changed dramatically after the Civil War. An important development was the Atlantic Migration, when nearly fifty million emigrants came from Europe to North America. Another was the taming of the "Wild West." From the 1860s through the 1880s, the Wild West was a place—the Rocky Mountains and the great prairies west of the Mississippi—that produced an array of American legends. It was characterized by celebrated gunfighters like Billy the Kid and Butch Cassidy, famous lawmen like Wyatt Earp, cowboys driving cattle to railroad junctions for shipment east, native Americans hunting buffalo and resisting the spread of white civilization, and farmers settling the land. By the 1890s, the Wild West was gone. The buffalo herds were all

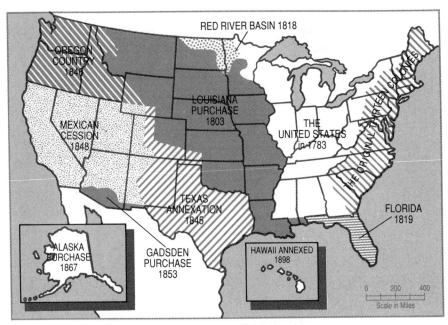

Figure 17.3 Growth of the United States, 1783–1898

but destroyed, the native Americans were defeated and forced to live on reservations, and much of the area was occupied by farmers and ranchers.

At the same time, industrialization was occurring in the northeastern and midwestern parts of the country. Cities like New York, Chicago, and Pittsburgh became major industrial centers where workers organized trade unions and "robber baron" businesspeople like Cornelius Vanderbilt and John D. Rockefeller became wealthy. The United States was transformed from an agricultural to an industrial nation almost as quickly as was Germany. By 1900, it was the most productive industrial power in the world.

CONCLUSION

By the end of the nineteenth century, political changes had transformed the major nations of Western Civilization. Great Britain and France were relatively stable, democratic nations, at least in the sense that most males could vote in national elections. Germany and Italy had achieved national unification but were restless to increase their influence in world politics. Germany, in particular, was a major industrial power and on its way to becoming a major military power. The Hapsburg Empire and Spain were powers in decline; the former was slowly being torn apart by nationalist tensions among its diverse peoples, and the latter was economically backward. Russia and the United States were huge continental powers that would become much more influential in European and world politics in the twentieth century. Each had partially resolved a major problem—serfdom in Russia, slavery in the United States—in the nineteenth century. Russia, however, had revolutionary movements bitterly opposed to the tsarist government, while the United States was generally stable and democratic.

THINGS YOU SHOULD KNOW

Ideologies—nationalism, conservatism, liberalism, socialism, Marxism, anarchism, feminism
Burke
Smith
Malthus
Mill
Utopian Socialists
Marx
Proudhon
Wollstonecraft
Balance of power diplomacy
Reform Act of 1832
Chartism
Reform Act of 1867
Revolution of 1830 (France)

Napoleon III
The Hapsburg Empire
Frankfurt Parliament
Bismarck
Mazzini
Cavour
Decembrist revolt
Crimean War
Emancipation of serfs in Russia
Witte
Mexican War
American Civil War
Slavery and the Emancipation Proclamation
Atlantic Migration

SUGGESTED READINGS

Robert Heilbroner, *The Worldly Philosophers* (New York: Simon and Schuster, 1987) is a delightful introduction to the great economists, including Smith, Malthus, and Mill. Guido de Ruggiero, *History of European Liberalism* (New York: Gordon, 1977) is more difficult to read but well worth the effort. Edmund Wilson, *To the Finland Station* (New York: Farrar, Strauss, & Giroux, 1972) is a very readable and interesting introduction to the history of socialism. On feminism, see Richard Evans, *The Feminists: Women's Emancipation Movements in Europe, America and Australia, 1840–1920* (Lanham, MD: Rowman, 1977).

A good trilogy, from a leftist viewpoint, on the political and social history of the nineteenth century is Eric Hobsbawn, *The Age of Revolution* (New York: New American Library, 1962), *The Age of Capital* (New York: New American Library, 1984), and *The Age of Empire* (New York: Pantheon, 1988).

Good introductions to the histories of the major nations include, for England, Robert K. Webb, *Modern England from the Eighteenth Century to the*

Present (New York: Harper & Row, 1980); for France, Gordon Wright, *France in Modern Times* (New York: Norton, 1987); for Italy, Dennis Mack Smith, *Italy: A Modern History* (Ann Arbor: Univ of Michigan, 1969); for Germany, Hajo Holborn, *History of Modern Germany, 1840–1945,* 3 vols. (New York: Knopf, 1959, 1963, 1969); for the Hapsburg Empire, A. J. P. Taylor, *The Hapsburg Monarchy, 1809–1918* (Chicago: Univ. of Chicago Press, 1976); for Spain, Raymond Carr, *Spain, 1808–1975* (New York: Oxford Univ. Press, 1982); for Russia, Michael T. Florinsky, *Russia: A History and Interpretation* (New York: Macmillan, 1953); and for the United States, Daniel Boorstin, *The Americans: The National Experience* (New York: Random House, 1965) and *The Americans: The Democratic Experience* (New York: Random House, 1973).

NOTES

[1] Adam Smith, quoted in Otto Mayr, *Authority, Liberty, and Automatic Machinery in Early Modern Europe* (Baltimore: Johns Hopkins Univ. Press, 1986), p. 174.

[2] Quoted in Frederic Ewen, *Heroic Imagination: The Creative Genius of Europe from Waterloo (1815) to the Revolution of 1848* (Secaucus, N.J.: Citadel Press, 1984), p. 168.

[3] Quoted in Theodore S. Hamerow, *The Birth of a New Europe: State and Society in the Nineteenth Century* (Chapel Hill: Univ. of North Carolina Press, 1983), pp. 219–20.

[4] Quoted in Ewen, *Heroic Imagination,* p. 595.

[5] Quoted in David Brion Davis, "Expanding the Republic, 1820–1860," in Bernard Bailyn, et al., *The Great Republic,* ed. Bernard Bailyn, et al. (Lexington, Mass.: D. C. Heath, 1977), p. 611.

[6] Ibid., p. 441.

[7] Quoted in James MacGregor Burns, *The Workshop of Democracy* (New York: Knopf, 1985), p. 70.

18

The West and the Non-Western World, 1800 to 1900

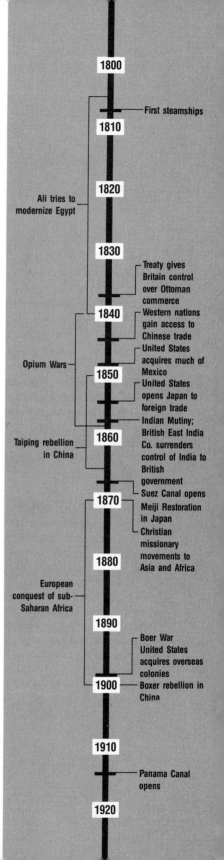

1800

First steamships

1810

1820

Ali tries to modernize Egypt

1830

Treaty gives Britain control over Ottoman commerce

1840

Western nations gain access to Chinese trade

Opium Wars

United States acquires much of Mexico

1850

United States opens Japan to foreign trade

Indian Mutiny; British East India Co. surrenders control of India to British government

Taiping rebellion in China

1860

Suez Canal opens

1870

Meiji Restoration in Japan

Christian missionary movements to Asia and Africa

1880

European conquest of sub-Saharan Africa

1890

Boer War United States acquires overseas colonies

1900

Boxer rebellion in China

1910

Panama Canal opens

1920

Since the end of the Middle Ages, Western nations increasingly began to dominate non-Western parts of the world. In the fifteenth and sixteenth centuries, Portugal and Spain used sea-power to develop new trade routes to Asia and to conquer much of North and South America. When Portuguese and Spanish power declined, the Dutch then dominated European trade with Asia and the English gradually acquired control of North America. In the seventeenth and eighteenth centuries, the West grew wealthier as European nations developed the African slave trade and brought laborers to the Americas. The power of the West to control other parts of the world reached its peak during the nineteenth century. This period is referred to as the *age of imperialism*, the age when the West ruled the world.

During the age of imperialism there was the European conquest of much of Asia and Africa. Several European nations built large empires composed of colonies scattered over much of the globe; the British, for example, ruled fifty-five colonies at one time. The integration of most of the world into a Western-controlled global economy also occurred during this period. Most of Latin America, Asia, and Africa became economically subservient to the West, forced to supply raw materials for use in Western factories and to buy finished products from the West.

Underlying the political and economic dominance of the West was a cultural and religious conflict between two very different ways of life. Westerners adhered to Christian religious and moral beliefs quite different from the beliefs held by non-Westerners. Furthermore, the West was an increasingly urban, industrial civilization accustomed to rapid change, whereas non-Western cultures were more traditional, agrarian, and unaccustomed to change.

In this chapter, we examine first the clash between Western and non-Western cultures during the age of imperialism. We then turn to that imperialism, particularly the causes of the imperial movement and the development of imperialism in certain parts of the world.

A CLASH BETWEEN CULTURES

Great Britain, France, Russia, Germany, Belgium, Italy, the Netherlands, and the United States were the most important imperialist Western nations in the nineteenth century. As they intruded into non-Western areas, they brought with them the mentality and technologies of their industrial culture. Specifically, they brought Western knowledge of modern science, the political ideals of liberty and equality, and new technologies like the railroad, steamship, telegraph, and modern weaponry. Most Western technologies were unknown in the non-Western world, and rural Asians and Africans were usually amazed at their first glimpse of a train or steamship.

Imperialism also provided a good opportunity for Christian missionaries to seek converts overseas. The Catholic church established the Society of Missionaries to convert Africans, the Germans sent members of the Society of the Divine Word to various parts of the world, and the Americans designed the Student Volunteer Movement in an attempt to evangelize the entire world. By 1900, over 60,000 Christian missionaries were in Asia and Africa, and about 40 million people outside of Europe and the Americas were Christians. In addition, the missionaries established schools and hospitals wherever they went, and these institutions helped spread Western ideas and customs throughout much of the world.

Many Western imperialists came to believe that they were part of a "civilizing mission," bringing the blessings of a superior way of life (modern technology and Christianity) to the backward peoples of the non-West. In 1885, Leopold II, king of the Belgians, described the benefits of this "mission" in these words:

> It is from here the light shines forth which for millions of men still plunged in barbarism will be the dawn of a better era. . . . The most intelligent of our youth demands wider horizons on which to expand their abounding energy.[1]

And, Rudyard Kipling, the greatest poet of the age of imperialism, wrote this in 1899:

> Take up the White Man's burden,
> Send forth the best ye breed. . . .
> To wait in heavy harness,
> On fluttering folk and wild—
> Your new-caught sullen peoples,
> Half devil and half child.[2]

However, not all Westerners were as idealistic about the benefits of imperialism. Some simply boasted about the power of Western technology, as a then well-known quip points out:

> Whatever happens we have got
> The Maxim gun and they have not.[3]

In addition, Social Darwinism (see Chapter 16) encouraged many Europeans and North Americans to believe that imperialism proved the superiority of the white races. Darwin's theory of the "survival of the fittest" was to some Westerners proof of their being the "fittest" people on earth. Some European racial theorists, such as Count Arthur de Gobineau and Houston Stewart Chamberlain, added to Western arrogance by arguing that the so-called "colored" races were inferior to the

The White Man's Burden Life magazine
published this cartoon on its cover in
1899. Intended as a satiric interpretation of
Rudyard Kipling's poetic reference to the
"white man's burden" of civilizing others,
the cartoon depicts Asians and Africans
with the burden of supporting (or giving
their wealth to) whites—the American
Uncle Sam *(front)* and the British John
Bull behind him. (Library of Congress)

white races. An 1899 *New York Times* parody of Kipling's poem mocked
the pretensions of the imperialists:

> Take up the White Man's burden,
> Send forth your sturdy sons,
> And load them down with whiskey
> And testaments and guns.
> Throw in a few diseases
> To spread in tropic climes,
> For there the healthy niggers
> Are quite behind the times.[4]

Many non-Westerners—especially those who were conquered and
colonized by the West—also believed in Western superiority because
they were the losers in the imperialism process. Many areas of Asia and
Africa lost both their political and economic independence. The Latin
American nations lost their economic independence but retained their
own governments. Most important, though, many Latin Americans,
Asians, and Africans lost their self-confidence as their ways of life were
made to seem inferior to that of the West. In this sense, Western
imperialism was a subversive force in many non-Western areas, for it
caused many non-Western peoples to view their traditional cultures as
weak and inadequate. Yet imperialism was also an invigorating force in
the non-Western world, for it brought Western ideas and technologies
that non-Westerners could use to fight back against the West.

The long-term effects of Western imperialism were to force non-
Western peoples to modernize and to spread Western technology,
science, and some political ideas throughout the world.

THE CAUSES OF IMPERIALISM

Historians and political writers have long debated the causes of Western imperialism in the nineteenth century. Writers like J. A. Hobson in *Imperialism: A Study* and the Communist leader V. I. Lenin in *Imperialism: The Highest Stage of Capitalism* contend that capitalism led to imperialism and that capitalists needed the colonies as places of investment and sources of raw materials.[5] Other writers argue that nationalism was a major cause of imperialism, in that European nations saw possession of colonies as evidence of national power and prestige.[6] Still others, such as the British historians John Gallagher and Ronald Robinson, maintain that imperial expansion resulted from commercial expansion. They point to the British Empire to support their argument. Originally a commercial empire intent on expanding trade, it became a territorial empire with colonies only after political problems in Asian and African areas forced the British to assume control of those areas. According to Gallagher and Robinson, the creation of the British Empire was to some degree unplanned.[7]

However, it is difficult to point conclusively to the causes of imperialism, partly because there were so many factors that played various roles in the imperial movement. Different imperialist nations had different motives at different times. During the early nineteenth century, for example, the British were primarily interested in economic expansion. They thus annexed relatively few territories and concentrated instead on forcing non-Western areas to sign free-trade treaties that favored British commerce. By the second half of the century, Britain and other Western nations became more interested in owning colonies. Growing nationalism, exemplified in the national unifications of Italy and Germany, impelled some Western nations to demonstrate their greatness by conquering colonies and building empires. Their desire for prestige was expressed by the German politician Bernhard von Bülow: "We do not want to put anyone in the shade, but we also demand our place in the sun."[8]

LATIN AMERICA

It is difficult to generalize about the impact of imperialism on all of Latin America in the nineteenth century, because the area was divided into many independent countries after the independence wars early in the century. Some countries—Mexico, Brazil, Argentina, and Chile—were relatively large, whereas others—Guatemala and Honduras—were quite small. However, we can point to three broad characteristics that applied to all or most Latin American nations.

First was the ambivalent nature of Latin America's relationship with

Western Civilization. In one sense, Latin American nations shared in the Western heritage, particularly the Spanish-Portuguese heritage, and thus were a frontier extension of Western Civilization. In another sense, however, they were not active participants in nineteenth-century Western Civilization, for they did not industrialize or experience the political and social changes associated with industrialization.

Second was the economic weakness of most Latin American nations. The fundamental cause of this weakness was the rigid social stratification of the Latin American plantation system. Most Latin American countries were dominated by a landholding aristocracy that controlled politics, society, and the economy. This aristocracy owned large plantations or estates, including cattle ranches and wheat farms in Argentina, sugar and coffee plantations in Brazil, banana plantations in Central America, and sugar plantations in the Caribbean. As a result, each Latin American nation focused on producing one or two major crops for export rather than on industrializing or growing food for its own people. In addition, since the native American–African lower classes that worked on the plantations received low wages and remained desperately poor and uneducated, they could not contribute to economic modernization. The result was Latin America's economic dependence on Europe, for most Latin American nations exported farm products to Europe in exchange for manufactured goods for the upper classes.

The third characteristic was the political system that prevailed in most Latin American nations following their independence. Politics was usually dominated by conservative forces: the plantation aristocracy, the army, and the Roman Catholic church. In practice, political power often fell into the hands of *caudillos*, strong military leaders who governed with the cooperation of conservatives and some liberals. Some caudillos were arrogant and acted more like dictators: "I neither want nor like ministers who think. I want only ministers who can write, because the only one who can think is I, and the only one who does think is I."[9] Others were reasonably effective rulers who carried out some improvements such as building railroads. In general, though, the caudillos fostered an authoritarian-style politics in which the vast majority of people were un-involved and power was in the hands of a small elite.

Despite these general characteristics of Latin America, individual nations excelled in various ways. Brazil and Argentina were exceptional in that they became relatively prosperous and stable by the late nineteenth century. As major traders on the world market, the Brazilians produced over half of the world's coffee and the Argentines exported large amounts of wheat and beef. Both nations also had large, vibrant cities—Rio de Janeiro in Brazil and Buenos Aires in Argentina. They also pursued economic modernization through the construction of railroads and a few small factories.

Also exceptional were Mexico and the Caribbean. These areas

suffered more direct foreign intervention than did the rest of Latin America, largely because they were close to the expanding United States. During the 1830s and 1840s, Mexico lost much of what became the western United States to the Americans (see Chapter 17). (In the 1860s, France intervened in Mexico and established the Austrian Archduke Maximilian on the Mexican throne. Maximilian was deposed by the late 1860s, and an indigenous Mexican government returned to power.) In 1898, the United States asserted its power in the Caribbean. After defeating the Spanish in the Spanish-American War, the Americans annexed Puerto Rico and established a protectorate over Cuba. That was followed in 1903 by American acquisition of a Canal Zone in Panama, where the United States constructed a canal linking the Atlantic and Pacific Oceans. The canal opened in 1914. The United States also intervened frequently in Cuba, Mexico, Nicaragua, Guatemala, and other countries during the first decades of the twentieth century to insure that governments friendly to the United States remained in power. The Caribbean became in effect an American lake (an American-controlled body of water), but Latin American resentment against American power—"Yankee imperialism"—was growing.

THE ISLAMIC WORLD

During the early nineteenth century, much of the Islamic world was nominally controlled by the Ottoman Empire centered in Turkey. Ottoman strength was declining, however, and European powers began to intervene in various Islamic lands. (The political turmoil that eventually resulted from the decline of the Ottoman Empire was known in the nineteenth century as the "Eastern Question.") France took control of Algeria in the 1830s and 1840s, and in the 1870s it began to dominate Tunisia. Italy conquered much of Libya early in the twentieth century. Persia, while remaining nominally independent, gradually came under the economic control of Russia and Great Britain—the Russians dominated commerce in northern Persia and the British in southern Persia. As for the Ottoman regime, it too remained nominally independent, but an Anglo-Ottoman free-trade treaty of 1838 effectively enabled Britain to control Ottoman commerce and economic investment.

Egypt was one of the few Muslim areas that did not easily submit to European power. (Another was Algeria, which resisted French colonization in the 1830s and 1840s.) Mohammed Ali, though technically subject to Ottoman control, effectively ruled Egypt from 1805 to the 1840s, at which time he tried to modernize the country so that it could resist European intervention. Mohammed Ali sent students to Europe to study industrial techniques, imported industrial machinery into Egypt, and built a number of factories. But he faced several obstacles, including an

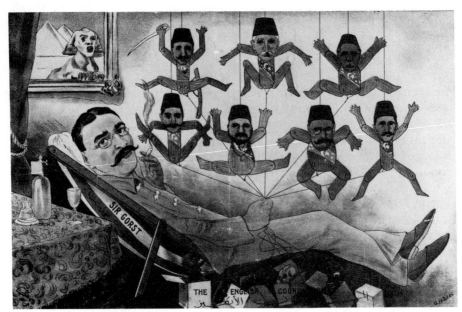

Indirect Imperialism   Imperialist nations often controlled colonies through indirect means, such as through commerce and business rather than direct political or military domination. This Egyptian cartoon depicts a British official pulling the strings of his puppets, the Egyptian political figures who nominally governed Egypt. (Library of Congress)

uneducated Egyptian populace that was ill-equipped to manage a modern industrial system and British opposition to Egyptian industrialization (the British feared Egyptian economic competition and wanted a weak Egypt that they could control). Mohammed Ali's plans for industrialization were unsuccessful, but his example would later inspire other Muslims to pursue economic modernization as a means of resisting the West.

Britain eventually won control of Egypt through its ownership of the Suez Canal. The British, who always sought to dominate sea routes, purchased a controlling share of the Canal Company in the 1870s and from that point on effectively owned the canal. Since profits from the canal were vital to the Egyptian economy, British domination of the Suez Canal meant British domination of Egypt.

ASIA

From Vasco da Gama's voyage in 1498 to the mid-eighteenth century, Europeans increasingly dominated the sea routes and oceangoing

TECHNOLOGY
The Suez and Panama Canals

One effect of imperialism and modern technology was to make the world seem smaller as communication and transportation between distant parts of the world became much quicker. The invention of the telegraph, for example, allowed messages to be sent around the world within a day or a few hours; previously, messages took months and even years to be transmitted. Similarly, the steamship made it possible to transport goods much more quickly.

In Egypt and Panama—Western nations built major canals to shorten shipping distances. In Egypt in 1859, a French company led by Ferdinand de Lesseps began to construct the Suez Canal to connect the Mediterranean Sea with the Red Sea. Upon its completion in 1869, the Suez Canal reduced the sea distance between Western Europe and India by about 5,000 miles; previously, the primary sea route between Europe and Asia went all the way around Africa. The French lost possession of the canal when the British purchased a controlling interest in the 1870s. The Egyptians, on whose land the canal was built, did not gain full control of the Suez Canal until 1956.

The Panama Canal was built by the United States in the early twentieth century to link the Atlantic and Pacific Oceans. Previously, ships going from the northern Atlantic to the Pacific had to face a 6,000-mile journey around South America. In the 1880s, de Lesseps, the builder of the Suez Canal, tried unsuccessfully to build a canal in Panama, but diseases like malaria and yellow fever killed many of his construction workers. By the early twentieth century, medical advances allowed physicians to control these diseases. The United States opened the Panama Canal in 1914, and has owned and controlled it through most of the twentieth century. In the late 1970s, the United States agreed to transfer ownership of the canal to Panama by the year 1999.

Dredging the Panama Canal *The technological advances of the Second Industrial Revolution made possible the construction of the Panama Canal (completed in 1914). (Culver Pictures)*

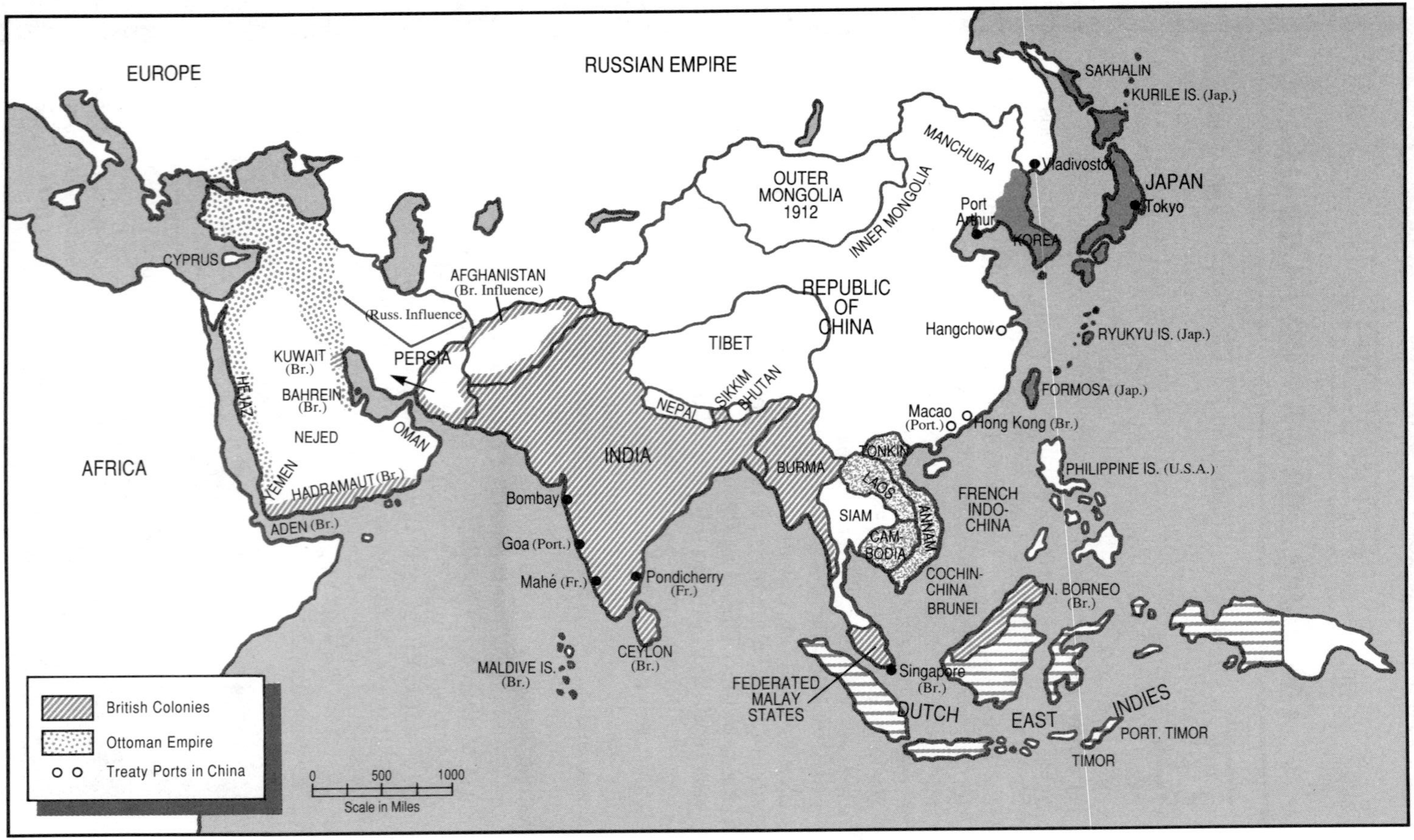

Figure 18.1 European Colonies in Asia, 1914

commerce of Asia. They did not control the land, however, for Asian countries were sufficiently well governed and so heavily populated that Europeans could not intervene effectively. But after the mid-eighteenth century, a combination of weak Asian governments and increased European military prowess enabled the Europeans to conquer large parts of the Asian landmass. The European impact on Asia was most significant in three countries—India, China, and Japan.

India

Much of India was ruled by a dynasty of Mogul emperors from the sixteenth to the early nineteenth centuries. The Moguls tolerated trade between Europeans and Indians, and gradually the British East India Company and others established a few commercial settlements along the coastline of India. Originally, the East India Company was a private business enterprise mainly interested in commerce. But as Mogul power slowly disintegrated during the eighteenth century, the Company gained control of more and more Indian land to protect its business. Its expansion led to conflict with France, which also had commercial interests in India. The Seven Years' War (1756–1763) between Britain and France was fought in North America and Europe as well as in India. The British won the war and effectively ended most French influence in India. The East India Company continued to conquer Indian territory until the early nineteenth century, when it dominated most of the Indian subcontinent.

Throughout the nineteenth and early twentieth centuries, hundreds of millions of Indians were ruled by only a few tens of thousands of British governors, soldiers, and administrators. Why could so few dominate so many for so long? One reason was that the Indians were politically and culturally fragmented and thus found it difficult to combine against the British. Another was British military power, sufficiently effective that British armies composed largely of Indian troops were usually able to defeat other armies in the area. A third reason was the British sense of superiority over the Indians, so well communicated that many Indians simply accepted British rule. This sense of superiority led to racist sentiments, as the British often referred to Indians as "niggers" and thought of them as children in need of discipline.

The Indian Mutiny of 1857 was the one major rebellion against the British. The rebellion was caused in part by a breakdown in discipline among Indian troops in the British army and in part by British offenses against the religious sensibilities of the Indians. The British gave the troops new rifles that used cartridges greased with either cow or pig fat. The use of cow fat ran counter to certain Hindu dietary customs, and the use of pig fat did the same to Muslim beliefs. When loading rifles, soldiers had to bite the cartridges and thus tasted the animal fats that they were forbidden to eat by their religions. The result was a rebellion that resembled a civil war.

Although the British crushed the Indian Mutiny in 1858, the rebellion changed the nature of British administration of India. The East India Company, which had ruled India for nearly a century, was discredited by the rebellion because it appeared to have lost control of the army in India. The British government thus assumed direct responsibility for the Indian subcontinent. By the late nineteenth century, many British thought of India as the most glamorous and exotic part of their empire, a land of intriguing religions, wealthy maharajahs, elephants, and monsoons. British entrepreneurs constructed railways and irrigation projects designed to produce greater wealth for the British. Economic development by Indians was not encouraged, however, and India was still a poor country at the beginning of the twentieth century. However, a harbinger of future change came in 1885 with the formation of the Indian National Congress, an organization that would later become the major source of Indian demands for independence from Great Britain.

China

European penetration into China was in some respects a direct outgrowth of British imperialism in India. The Manchu dynasty ruled China from the mid-seventeenth century on and at first kept most foreigners out of China. In the nineteenth century, though, the British East India Company began to seek greater profits by smuggling opium into China. When the Chinese resisted, the result was the Opium War of 1839, which the British easily won. The Treaty of Nanking in 1842 formally ended the war. It also gave the British the right to establish merchant settlements and conduct trade in five Chinese ports, including Canton and Shanghai. Within a few years, the Americans, the French, the Belgians, and the Russians forced similar agreements on the Chinese and also established merchant settlements. One outcome was that Chinese commerce and business quickly became dominated by foreigners. Another was growing Chinese resentment of foreigners. The foreign merchants had the right of *extra-territoriality*, meaning that they were not subject to Chinese laws and, in criminal cases involving a Chinese and a foreigner, the foreigner was tried in his own court of law where he was more likely to be acquitted. This foreign privilege offended many Chinese, as did the signs—"Dogs and Chinese not allowed"—that were posted in some parks used by Europeans.

The Manchu dynasty's inability to resist foreign intervention, together with its traditional exploitation of the Chinese peasantry, led to the Taiping rebellion of 1850–1866. (*Taiping*, meaning "great peace," refers to a future era of great peace on earth.) The rebellion was initiated by

Hung Hsui Chuan (1813–1864), a religious mystic who borrowed some ideas from Protestantism and preached that the Chinese could establish a paradise on earth through revolutionary principles (such as land reform and sexual equality). With an army of over two million peasants, the Taiping rebels gained control of much of south and east China by the mid-1850s. Evenutally, the Manchus crushed the rebellion, in which as many as twenty million people died.

However, the Taiping rebellion weakened the Manchu dynasty and made it easier for foreigners to exert even more control over China. The British, the Germans, and the Russians each forced the Chinese government to allow them to build railroads in various parts of the country, and the railways became means of extending foreign penetration into China. Still, China was too large and too densely populated for foreigners to control the entire country. In fact, foreigners often feared the Chinese; they spoke of the "yellow peril" and worried that someday hundreds of millions of "yellow" Chinese would overwhelm other peoples. To many Chinese it seemed that the foreigners were overwhelming them, and an uprising against the foreign menace occurred in 1900. The Boxer rebellion is so named because it involved young Chinese militia known as "Boxers" because of the physical exercises they performed. The rebellion resulted in the deaths of some Christian missionaries and other foreigners, but was soon crushed by foreign armies. The Boxers were forerunners of larger, more successful anti-foreign movements in China.

Japan

At the same time the Chinese succumbed to foreigners, the Japanese were learning how to resist them. Japan, being farther from Europe than India and China, was able to keep most European adventurers away until the mid-nineteenth century. But in 1853, the American Commodore Matthew Perry sailed into Tokyo and demanded trading privileges for American merchants. In 1854, the Treaty of Kanagawa gave American sailors and merchants limited rights in some Japanese ports. Within a few years, the British, the Russians, and the French forced similar treaties on the Japanese. These events created a sense of crisis among Japanese, since they opened the door to foreign economic domination of Japan.

Yet the Japanese had both the will and the ability to resist foreign domination. Unlike India and China, Japan was a compact island nation with a culturally united, well-organized population. Furthermore, it had a thriving merchant class that was able to compete with foreigners. And, since the Japanese traditionally borrowed many cultural ideas from the Chinese, they were psychologically prepared to borrow other ideas and techniques from the Europeans and Americans.

Most important, though, the Japanese possessed the political will to mobilize themselves against foreign intervention. When the last of the line of Tokugawa Shoguns (military leaders who ruled Japan) died in 1866, the Japanese upper classes seized the opportunity to create the Meiji Restoration of 1868. Although its main purpose was to designate a new emperor—Mutsuhito (reigned 1867–1912)—the Restoration also served to bring to power all the groups favoring the modernization of Japan. During the next few decades, these groups developed a new legal and administrative system to strengthen the power of Japan's central government, reorganized and modernized the armed forces, built railroads and telegraph lines to facilitate transportation and communication, imported foreign technicians and machinery, and encouraged industrial development. By the beginning of the twentieth century, Japan was strong, somewhat industrialized, and able to compete militarily and economically with Western nations.

The new Japan, like the Western nations, became ambitious and expansionistic once it gained economic strength. In the late nineteenth century, the Japanese began to assert their influence in Korea and other areas near China. In the process, they encountered the Russians, who were also seeking to expand in these areas. This encounter resulted in the Russo-Japanese War of 1904–1905 (as we will see in Chapter 19).

Other Asian Areas

Asian areas other than India, China, and Japan also felt the impact of Western imperialism. The Dutch controlled the island chain later known as Indonesia, the French conquered the area they called Indochina, and the British took Burma as well as other colonies. Particularly significant for the future was the growing American interest in Asia, the result of American expansion across the Pacific. The Americans purchased Alaska from the Russians in 1867, annexed Hawaii in 1898, and in the same year took the Philippines from Spain. The stage was thus set for American intervention in China and conflict with Japan in the twentieth century (as we will see in later chapters).

SUB-SAHARAN AFRICA

The Europeans were relatively slow to penetrate into sub-Saharan Africa. The lack of good ports on the African coast hindered European explorers, and the prevalence in Africa of deadly diseases like malaria and sleeping sickness made the continent uninviting to Europeans. During an exploring expedition of 1777–1779, 132 out of 152 Europeans died. Africa became known in Europe as the "white man's grave." Circum-

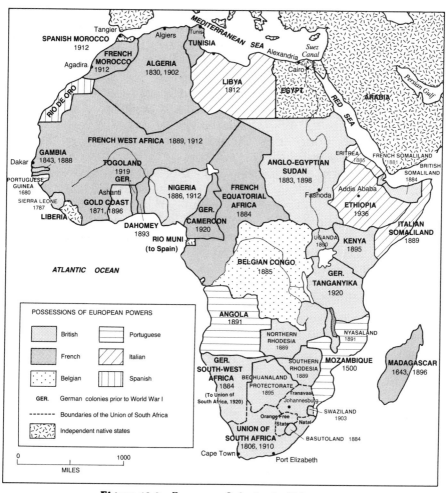

Figure 18.2 European Colonies in Africa, 1914

stances began to change in the nineteenth century, however, as Europeans learned how to avoid or treat some tropical diseases (quinine, for example, was used to treat malaria). In addition, technical breakthroughs like the river steamship and the repeating rifle made it easier for Europeans first to explore African rivers and then to conquer sub-Saharan Africa.

The Africa that the Europeans found was an area containing a variety of peoples, languages, and religions. Some Africans lived in small villages with little political organization; others lived in tribal states; and still others were organized into relatively large military confederations. However, none were able to resist the European intruders for long.

Between 1870 and 1900, almost all of sub-Saharan Africa was annexed by various European states. The Belgian king, Leopold II, placed the Congo area under his personal control and exploited it so thoroughly that the Congolese population decreased significantly. The British, who already controlled much of southern Africa, took Nigeria, the Gold Coast (Ghana), Rhodesia, and Kenya. The French seized several areas, including French Guinea and the Ivory Coast. The Germans conquered large parts of eastern Africa, and the Italians and the Portuguese each acquired a few African territories. By 1900, Ethiopia and Liberia were the only African areas not controlled by Europeans.

The effects of the European conquest of sub-Saharan Africa were manifold. The Europeans reorganized African peoples into political units designed to suit the convenience of colonial powers. The result was to create countries in name only, as they had little cultural unity and were populated by diverse ethnic groups unaccustomed to cooperating with one another. In addition, the boundary lines between countries were often vague and obscure. A British prime minister once commented:

> We have been engaged in drawing lines upon maps where no white man's foot has ever trod. We have been giving away mountains and rivers and lakes to each other, only hindered by the small impediment that we never knew exactly where the mountains and rivers and lakes were.[10]

The European reorganization of Africa caused great difficulties for Africans later on. When African states gained independence in the late twentieth century, they most often failed to maintain political unity in those countries without natural boundaries and without natural cultural loyalties among the national populations.

Another effect of the European conquest of sub-Saharan Africa was *cultural imperialism,* as Europeans encouraged and persuaded Africans to accept European values and ideas. Christian missionaries converted many Africans to Christianity, a religion quite different from traditional African religions. The missionaries also built schools with the good intention of educating Africans, but the schools often taught racism by portraying Africans as inferior to whites. One African, for example, wrote a doctoral thesis justifying slavery of Africans.[11]

In southern Africa, the European conquest led to continuing conflict. Dutch settlers, whose descendants became known as Afrikaners, came to southern Africa in the seventeenth century. But the British annexed the area in 1806, and British settlers began to arrive when gold and diamonds were discovered there in the late nineteenth century. The Afrikaners (then called "Boers") and the British began to struggle for control of what became the colony of South Africa, and the result was the Boer War

(1899–1902). The British won the war and retained South Africa as a colony during the first half of the twentieth century. However, the Afrikaners eventually prevailed and imposed a policy of *apartheid* or racial separation on the native Africans. By the late twentieth century (as we will see in Chapter 21), the conflict in South Africa was no longer between Afrikaners and British but between African blacks, protesting against apartheid, and Afrikaners, trying to maintain a racially segregated society.

SELF-GOVERNING BRITISH COLONIES

Three British colonies—Australia, New Zealand, and Canada—stand out from the others because they achieved a considerable degree of political and economic independence during the nineteenth century. All three colonies were frontier extensions of Western Civilization and were populated primarily by Caucasians of European descent. The British assumed they were capable of governing themselves.

In 1850, the British allowed the four Australian provinces to draft constitutions and form their own legislatures, thus granting them the power of self-government. Then, in 1900, the provinces were allowed to create a central government—the Commonwealth of Australia. The new Australia was loyal to British monarchs and coordinated its foreign policy with British policy, but in all other matters the Australians governed themselves.

Much the same happened in New Zealand. The British allowed New Zealanders to draft a constitution in 1852 and shortly after to develop their own local government. By the early twentieth century, New Zealand was a self-governing country but loyal to the British crown and British foreign policy.

The various Canadian provinces were united into the Dominion of Canada in 1867, and from then on Canada largely governed itself with little interference from Britain. Technically, Canada was still a colony subject to the British crown, but the Canadians tended to be more concerned with their own problems than with those of the British Empire. Three issues dominated the Canadians' attention. First was Canada's relative underpopulation, with many northern areas being virtually uninhabited and some prairie areas having only small clusters of people. The second concern focused on the existence of two distinct cultural groups—English-speaking British Canadians and French-speaking French Canadians—which made it difficult for Canada to achieve political and cultural unity. Finally, the proximity of a powerful neighbor—the United States—was viewed as a threat to Canada's economic and cultural independence.

CONCLUSION

By the end of the age of imperialism, European nations controlled approximately 84 percent of the land on earth. The British, with fifty-five colonies, had the largest of the European empires; in fact it was larger than any other empire in history. The French, with twenty-nine colonies, had the second largest empire at this time. Other nations had smaller empires: Germany controlled ten colonies, the Netherlands eight, Portugal eight, and Russia, the United States, Italy, and Belgium possessed fewer numbers.

The most enduring effect of imperialism was the Westernization of the world, as Western ideas and technologies spread to the non-Western world. Some non-Westerners, particularly in Africa and China, converted to Christianity. More pervasive was the influence of Western science and technology, as a growing number of Asians and Africans came to European and American universities to learn and then bring Western knowledge back to their native countries. As a result, many non-Western societies began to modernize and to confront the difficulty of adjusting their traditional beliefs and customs to a modern way of life.

The modernization of the non-Western world proceeded slowly, however, and Western nations remained far more wealthy and powerful than Asian, African, and Latin American nations. One estimate is that, in the early twentieth century, Europe's per-capita income was seven times higher than that of the non-Western world. This economic disparity would continue through the twentieth century, such that the world was divided into rich nations—the West—and poor nations—the non-West.

Many people in the non-Western world came to resent bitterly Western political and economic power. In the nineteenth century, there were several major reactions against Western power—Mohammed Ali's attempted reforms in Egypt, the Indian Mutiny of 1857, the Taiping rebellion, the Boxer rebellion, Japan's modernization, and the Boer War. In the twentieth century, nationalist movements emerged in many Asian, African, and Latin American areas, and after 1945 many of these areas regained their political independence. The nineteenth century poet Rudyard Kipling foresaw the disintegration of the Western world:

> Far-called, our navies melt away;
> On dune and headland sinks the fire:
> Lo, all our pomp of yesterday
> Is one with Nineveh and Tyre!*
> Judge of the Nations, spare us yet,
> Lest we forget, lest we forget.[12]

---

*Nineveh and Tyre, now ruins, were large, wealthy cities in ancient times. Nineveh was the capital of the Assyrian Empire and Tyre the most important Phoenician city.

THINGS YOU SHOULD KNOW

The clash between Western and
    non-Western cultures
The Christian missionary movement
The causes of imperialism
Characteristics of nineteenth-
    century Latin American nations
Western intervention in Mexico and
    the Caribbean
Mohammed Ali
Suez and Panama canals
East India Company

Indian Mutiny of 1857
Opium War of 1839 in China
Taiping rebellion in China
Boxer rebellion in China
Meiji Restoration of 1868 in Japan
European conquest of sub-Saharan
    Africa
Self-governing British colonies in
    Australia, New Zealand, and
    Canada

SUGGESTED READINGS

Raymond F. Betts, *Europe Overseas: Phases of Imperialism* (New York: Basic Books, 1968) is a good factual survey of nineteenth-century imperialism. John Gallagher and Ronald Robinson, *Africa and the Victorians* (Garden City, N.Y.: Anchor-Doubleday, 1968) is an authoritative analysis of the causes of imperialism. On the attitudes—idealistic, racist, and otherwise—that underlay the imperialist movement, see V. G. Kiernan, *The Lords of Human Kind: Black Man, Yellow Man, and White Man in an Age of Empire* (New York: Columbia Univ. Press, 1969). On the new technologies that allowed Europeans and Americans to dominate the world, a good source is Daniel R. Headrick, *The Tools of Empire: Technology and European Imperialism in the Nineteenth Century* (New York: Oxford Univ. Press, 1981). L. S. Stavrianos, *Global Rift: The Third World Comes of Age* (New York: William Morrow and Co., 1981) provides a detailed analysis of how imperialism affected non-Western nations. And, Walter Rodney, *How Europe Underdeveloped Africa* (Washington, D.C.: Howard Univ. Press, 1974) illustrates, from a native African's viewpoint, how imperialism harmed Africa.

NOTES

[1] Quoted in William Woodruff, *Impact of Western Man: A Study of Europe's Role in the World Economy, 1750–1960* (New York: St. Martin's, 1966), p. 5.

[2] Quoted in Sean Dennis Cashman, *America in the Gilded Age* (New York: New York Univ. Press, 1984), p. 323.

[3] Quoted in Raymond F. Betts, *Europe Overseas: Phases of Imperialism* (New York: Basic Books, 1968), p. 51.

[4] Quoted in Cashman, *America*, p. 324.

[5] J. A. Hobson, *Imperialism: A Study* (Ann Arbor: Univ. of Michigan, 1965); and V. I. Lenin, *Imperialism: The Highest Stage of Capitalism*, in *The Lenin Reader*, ed. Stefan Possony (Chicago: Henry Regnery, 1966).

[6]Raymond F. Betts. *Europe Overseas: Phases of Imperialism* (New York: Basic Books, 1968).

[7]John Gallagher and Ronald Robinson, *Africa and the Victorians* (Garden City, N.Y.: Anchor-Doubleday, 1968).

[8]Quoted in Theodore S. Hamerow, *The Birth of a New Europe: State and Society in the Nineteenth Century* (Chapel Hill: Univ. of North Carolina Press, 1983), p. 404.

[9]Quoted in James MacGregor Burns, *The Workshop of Democracy* (New York: Knopf, 1985), p. 97.

[10]Quoted in Hamerow, *The Birth,* pp. 391–92.

[11]Walter Rodney, *How Europe Underdeveloped Africa* (Washington, D.C.: Howard Univ. Press, 1974), p. 142.

[12]Quoted in E. J. Hobsbawn, *The Age of Empire, 1875–1914* (New York: Pantheon, 1987), p. 82.

19

Wars and Revolutions, 1905 to 1920

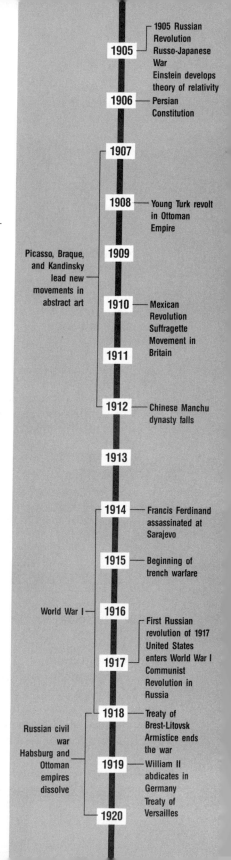

1905	1905 Russian Revolution Russo-Japanese War Einstein develops theory of relativity
1906	Persian Constitution
1907	
1908	Young Turk revolt in Ottoman Empire
1909	Picasso, Braque, and Kandinsky lead new movements in abstract art
1910	Mexican Revolution Suffragette Movement in Britain
1911	
1912	Chinese Manchu dynasty falls
1913	
1914	Francis Ferdinand assassinated at Sarajevo
1915	Beginning of trench warfare
1916	World War I
1917	First Russian revolution of 1917 United States enters World War I Communist Revolution in Russia
1918	Treaty of Brest-Litovsk Armistice ends the war
1919	Russian civil war Habsburg and Ottoman empires dissolve William II abdicates in Germany Treaty of Versailles
1920	

Our examination of the twentieth century begins with the period 1905–1920, for it was during these years that the West witnessed the birth of several trends that would continue throughout the century:

1. Between 1905 and 1911, revolutions in various parts of the world marked the beginning of the end of European imperialism.
2. Within the Western nations, an increasingly assertive working class and the suffragette movement demonstrated a new element in Western politics—a demand for political and economic power by people who had traditionally been excluded from power.
3. Also within the Western nations, an intellectual and artistic revolution began to transform the ideas, beliefs, and artistic expressions of Europeans and Americans in ways that would continue to the present day.
4. In 1914, World War I erupted and opened a new era of violence in Western and world history. As historian Jack J. Roth says, "The greatest tragedy of our time—its monstrous violence—begins in the trenches of World War I. Verdun and the Somme opened the way to Auschwitz and Hiroshima."[1]
5. The war was so cataclysmic that it led to a wave of revolutions that destroyed much of the old European order. Most important was the Russian Revolution of 1917, which for the first time brought a Communist movement to political power. There were also nationalist revolutions that destroyed the Hapsburg and Ottoman empires.

With World War I came revolution; just as in earlier times war and revolution were intertwined. The twentieth century has been in large part one of war and revolution.

THE BEGINNINGS OF GLOBAL REVOLUTION

The Russo-Japanese War

On 27 May 1905, the Japanese navy overwhelmingly defeated the Russian navy at the Battle of Tsushima, and the Russo-Japanese War of 1904–1905 came to an end soon thereafter. Japan and Russia had entered into war because both sought to expand into areas around China. The Japanese victory signaled the rise of a new power in Asia. It also caused a wave of excitement to surge throughout Asia, since for the first time in centuries the Asians had defeated the Europeans. According to the revolutionary Sun Yat-sen, most Chinese "regarded the Russian defeat by Japan as the defeat of the West by the East. We regarded the Japanese victory as our own victory."[2]

Russia

The conflict with Japan in part led to revolution in Russia. The country was at this time a traditional agricultural one just beginning to modernize. The disruptions of modernization—workers seeking higher wages, peasants migrating to cities in search of work—created social tension within Russia. Tsar Nicholas II (reigned 1894–1917) isolated himself from the Russian people and continued to believe in the divine right of monarchs. "Do you mean," he once asked, "that I am to regain the confidence of my people, Ambassador, or that they are to regain my confidence?"[3]

The social tension in Russia, together with Japan's victory in the Russo-Japanese War, led to the Russian Revolution of 1905. The revolution began on January 22 of that year—so-called "Bloody Sunday"—when the tsar's troops killed many peaceful demonstrators in St. Petersburg square. Over the next several months, sailors mutinied, workers went on strike, and peasants seized landed estates. Then, in October, the tsar promised a constitution and the election of a *duma*, a national assembly, and both became realities in 1906. Although in theory Russia became a constitutional monarchy, the *duma*'s power was greatly restricted and the tsar retained most of his authority in the decade after 1906. As we will see later in this chapter, the tsarist regime was overthrown in 1917.

Persia

The effects of the Russian Revolution spilled over into Persia (present-day Iran). The country had a corrupt monarchy and an economy largely controlled by two imperial powers—Russia and Great Britain. Late in 1905, a nationalist reform movement in Persia rebelled against the shah (*shah* is Persian for "king") and compelled him to issue a constitution in 1906, which included establishment of an elected parliament. The reform movement was not strong enough to establish an effective government, however. By 1911, Russian troops brought Persia under Russian control.

The Ottoman Empire

The next, and more successful, upheaval was the 1908 Young Turk revolt in the Ottoman Empire. The empire had slowly weakened throughout the nineteenth century, and the Young Turks were reform-minded military officers who wanted to restore its strength. The revolutionaries confronted a ruler (or sultan)—Abdul Hamid II—who was so isolated from his people that he lived in constant fear of assassination and several times shot to death people who startled him on his morning walk. The Young

Turks forced the sultan to restore a constitution in 1908 and then to abdicate in 1909. The revolutionaries controlled the empire until 1918, but World War I destroyed the Ottoman Empire and out of its ruins emerged modern-day Turkey (as we will see later in the chapter).

China

Another dynasty fell in China. During the nineteenth century, the Manchu rulers had slowly lost the confidence of the Chinese people because of their inability to protect China from Western imperialist intervention. In the early twentieth century, a reform movement known as the *Guomindong* was organized by Sun Yat-sen, a well-educated national patriot. The Guomindong easily overthrew the last of the Manchu rulers during 1911–1912, but was unable to establish a stable government. As a result, there followed a long civil war in China among warlord armies, the Guomindong, and eventually Chinese Communists. The Chinese civil war would last over three decades, involve hundreds of millions of people, and eventually result in a communist regime in China (see chapters 20 and 21).

Mexico

Revolution also broke out in Mexico. Many Mexicans feared the expanding power of the United States. The Americans had taken much of what became the western United States from Mexico in 1848, and then moved into the Caribbean in 1898. Mexico also resented the economic exploitation by foreigners, who controlled most Mexican commerce. In addition, the Mexican lower classes resented their own native rulers, who owned most of the land and kept the peasantry in landless poverty.

These factors combined in 1910 to produce the Mexican Revolution, in which a series of peasant rebellions and worker strikes forced out the old dictator, Porfirio Díaz. For the next few years, the revolutionaries Emiliano Zapata and Pancho Villa seemed poised to launch an agrarian revolution. But neither had the skills or the determination to organize an effective revolutionary government, and both were eventually assassinated, Zapata in 1919 and Villa in 1923. In 1920, a moderately liberal group of wealthy landowners and middle-class people won control of Mexico. By that time, over one million Mexicans had been killed during the years of revolution. After 1920, the new revolutionary government carried out some social reforms but did not fundamentally change Mexican society. The moderate liberals continue to rule Mexico today.

The various revolutions that occurred between 1905 and 1911 were similar in many respects. They all sought to overthrow ineffective governments that were unable to resist imperialist expansion by powerful Western nations. The revolutionaries also shared the common goal of modernizing their countries as a way to resist foreign exploitation. In addition, the various revolutions were largely unsuccessful because they were poorly organized and involved too few people to carry out a true radical restructuring of society. However, the revolutions opened a new era in world history—the revolt against the West.

SOCIAL UNREST IN THE WESTERN NATIONS

"The old world, in its sunset, was fair to see," said the young Winston Churchill.[4] For those in the European and American upper classes, Churchill's judgment proved true. The West continued to rule the world and the upper classes were still in control. In the European nations, some one thousand aristocratic and upper-middle class families dominated politics, society, and the economy. Even in the relatively democratic United States, a few men from the lower and middle classes gained wealth and political power but a small, male elite still prevailed. In no Western nations had workers, peasants or farmers, women, or blacks (in the United States) been able to enter the power structures and assume control of their own affairs. The Socialist working-class movement in France and Germany was no exception; there were no workers among the Socialist deputies in the French Chamber of Deputies and only two workers among the 110 Socialists in the German Reichstag.

Churchill's "old world" began to change early in the twentieth century, as those in the lower and middle classes found ways to assert themselves. Massive labor strikes took place in Germany, Italy, Sweden, Russia, and Great Britain as inflation threatened workers' standard of living. Some of the strikes took on a militant tone; one British strike manifesto proclaimed that "today the railwaymen are worse than slaves."[5] In the United States, a "nativist" movement feared the increasing number of immigrants, and in the South racial tensions led to a series of lynchings. In response, the NAACP (National Association for the Advancement of Colored People) was founded in 1909 to promote racial justice in the United States.

The suffragette movement was even more militant, especially in Great Britain. Led by Emmeline Pankhurst, the British suffragettes broke store windows, dug up golf courses, heckled politicians, and marched in the streets. These actions were the result of women's outrage and frustration over being excluded for so long from politics. In other countries, the women's movement was less militant. In the United States, Margaret Sanger was considered radical because she advocated birth control education for women and men. A clear sign of the growing power of the suffragette movement was the founding of the International Woman Suffrage Alliance in 1904.

Most of the social unrest of the early twentieth century was directly or indirectly related to rapid industrialization. In response, a few Western governments established reforms. From 1906 to 1911, the Russian

Suffragettes   Before World War I, British suffragettes campaigned in London for women's right to vote. Women finally won the vote in Britain and several other Western nations after World War I. (Culver Pictures)

Premier and Minister of the Interior Peter Stolypin pursued a policy intended to encourage prosperity and improve the lot of the peasants through industrialization. The British liberal government approved, in 1911, legislation that provided some social insurance for injured or unemployed workers. The progressive movement in the United States encouraged municipal reforms and social legislation to aid the working class. The most prominent progressive, President Theodore Roosevelt (in office 1901–1909), established regulatory commissions to control certain industries, presumably for the public good.

Many Western nations were torn by conflicting impulses in the first decade of the twentieth century. On the one hand, economic prosperity was slowly making life more secure and comfortable for greater numbers of people. On the other hand, many in the upper classes feared social upheaval. There was a concern about the possibility of war, either civil war within certain nations or international war between nations. As a result, many people, Europeans in particular, were at once optimistic about the future and concerned about social upheaval and war.

AN INTELLECTUAL REVOLUTION

While political revolution was erupting around the world and social unrest was troubling the Western nations, intellectuals and artists were redefining Western thought and culture. The first decade of the twentieth

Marie Curie During her distinguished career as a physical chemist, Curie (1867–1934) discovered and investigated radioactivity. Working with her husband Pierre—also a chemist—she identified alpha, beta, and gamma radiation, discovered polonium and radium, and won the Nobel Prize for physics in 1903. (Culver Pictures)

century was rich in cultural and scientific innovators—Albert Einstein, Sigmund Freud, Henri Bergson, Pablo Picasso, Max Weber, Georges Sorel, Henry Adams, to name only a few. Together, they created many of the ideas and beliefs that would continue to dominate Western Civilization throughout the twentieth century.

Science and Art

Einstein The work of the German physicist Albert Einstein (1879–1955) was among the most important of the age. For two centuries earlier, scientists had interpreted the physical world according to the precepts of Sir Isaac Newton. Newtonian physics portrayed the universe as a machine in which reality is composed of material bodies—atoms—that move in absolute space and time (that is, it was assumed that a unit of time never varies but always remains the same length). Einstein helped to define a new picture of the universe with his theory of relativity, which holds that space and time measurements are relative and only the speed of light is absolute. Furthermore, he showed that matter is in a sense not material. His famous equation, $E = mc^2$, demonstrated that matter and

Albert Einstein As a young man, Einstein's (1879–1955) theories about physical matter and energy helped to define a new conception of the physical universe. His thought laid a foundation for later developments in nuclear energy and laser research. (Library of Congress)

energy are two forms of the same thing, that matter is "frozen" energy. The implication that matter could become energy was later validated by research in atomic physics during the 1930s and 1940s.

Planck Another major component of the new physics was *quantum theory*, originally defined by Max Planck (1858–1947). Quantum theory attempts to understand the nature of energy in the universe, and Planck's work showed that energy is not continuous but rather occurs in small units, or quanta. Quantum theory, along with Einstein's work, deepened the theoretical understanding of the physical world and eventually supported development of such things as nuclear energy, lasers, and X-rays. (Newtonian physics was not completely displaced by Einsteinian physics, for it was still valid on the level of daily experience and is therefore studied as one part of modern physics.)

Freud At the same time that Einstein, Planck, and others were defining a new physics, Sigmund Freud (1856–1939) was defining *psychoanalysis,* a new form of psychology. Basing his theories on an examination and treatment of individual patients, Freud contended that there are two psychic realities within people—the unconscious and the conscious—and that the unconscious is the dominant force. More precisely, he described the human personality in terms of three forces: the *id* or the unconscious mind, the *ego* or the conscious mind, and the *superego* or the conscience and the connecting link between the two others. In Freud's great work *The Interpretation of Dreams*, he argues that it is possible to understand the unconscious through the analysis of dreams, as these are expressions of a person's unconscious desires (often sexual in nature). The impact of Freud's work was to change the way that many people thought about human nature. In arguing that human beings are basically irrational, Freudian theories seemed to point to at least one of the causes of the world wars of the twentieth century.

Picasso, Kandinsky, and Braque   The Spaniard Pablo Picasso (1881–1973), the Russian Wassily Kandinsky (1866–1944), and other artists helped create new kinds of abstract (nonrepresentational) art. Between 1907 and 1912, Picasso, Georges Braque (1882–1963), and other artists in Paris created *cubism*, painting in geometric patterns. At the same time, Kandinsky, working in Germany, helped develop *expressionism*, art that depicts the artist's emotions and inner visions through distorted forms and flamboyant colors. Picasso, Braque, and Kandinsky sought in their work to understand and express a spiritual realm underlying external reality, and so their art makes no attempt to represent external reality. Their search for the underlying reality was similar to that of the physicists, who sought to understand the underlying structure of the physical universe. In this sense, abstract art and the new physics inspired each other.

Political and Social Thought

Also in the early twentieth century important work occurred in the study of history and society.

Weber   The German sociologist Max Weber (1864–1920) wrote *The Protestant Ethic and the Spirit of Capitalism*, in which he seeks to explain why Western Civilization created capitalism and later the Industrial Revolution. One reason, he argues, is that Protestantism encouraged the belief that hard work is a duty (the *work ethic*) and this belief favored the pursuit of economic gain and hence capitalism. In other studies, Weber argues that the most fundamental characteristic of the modern age is *rationalization*, by which he means the tendency of people to organize and establish rules for virtually every aspect of life. For example, all modern governments, whether called capitalist or Socialist or Fascist, are basically bureaucracies in which "experts" apply rules to all situations.

Sigmund Freud   Austrian neurologist and founder of psychoanalysis, Dr. Freud's (1856–1939) theories about the nature of the unconscious caused great controversy when they were first introduced. Many of his teachings are still being disputed and reinterpreted today, yet most of his basic ideas about repression and the significance of sexual desires have formed the foundations of modern psychology. (Austrian Information Service)

Sorel   Georges Sorel (1847–1922) spoke for those who were disenchanted with the modern age. In *Reflections on Violence,* he calls for a revolutionary elite to destroy the materialistic, bourgeois civilization of his time and replace it with revolutionary socialism. At first, Sorel had hoped that trade unions (*syndicats* in French) using violence would carry out the revolution, so his doctrine was called *syndicalism.* Gradually, however, Sorel lost faith in the unions and hoped instead that one great leader would lead a revolution.

Max Weber argued that societies sometimes turn to charismatic individuals for leadership. His concept, together with Sorel's desire for a great leader, foreshadowed the rise of Benito Mussolini and Adolf Hitler after World War I.

Adams   Also disenchanted with the modern age was the American historian Henry Adams (1838–1918). In *The Education of Henry Adams,* he portrays himself as a typical modern man, unable to find any spiritual meaning in life. Adams greatly admired the medieval thirteenth century; he believed that in that earlier time Christianity had unified civilization and thereby bestowed spiritual significance on human existence. In his own time, Adams believed that spiritual values were being destroyed by human fascination with the mechanistic force of technology. His fear of technology was one shared by many in the modern world—that is, that technology would destroy rather than liberate humanity. World War I would give some credence to this fear.

WORLD WAR I, 1914–1918

Origins of the War

The origins of World War I are complex and thus difficult to point to conclusively. Yet human fears, tensions, and mistakes are among the factors that led to this cataclysm few wanted.

Fear existed in part because industrialization was changing the power relationships among the major European nations. As some countries became stronger, others grew weaker in comparison. Germany, for example, was the largest industrial power on the European continent, so both Britain and France feared German ambitions. The Germans, in turn, feared Russian power; though only beginning to industrialize, Russia's size was a threat. The Hapsburg Empire and Italy, both relatively poor countries, feared that they would lag in industrial competition with other nations.

One source of tension that led to war was national pride. Most European countries were so caught up in intense patriotism and nationalist emotions that each nation tended to see itself as great and noble and to view other nations as opponents. The Irish statesman Timothy Healy expressed his patriotism in these strong words: "I will tell the noble lord what nationality is. Nationality is a thing which man is ready to die for."[6] Indeed, many Europeans were so nationalistic and so heavily influenced by Social Darwinist ideas that they thought of war as something ennobling and even desirable. The Italian poet Filippo Tommaso Marinetti wrote in 1909: "We want to glorify war—the only hygiene of the world—militarism, patriotism, the destructive action of the anarchists, beautiful ideas which kill, and contempt for women."[7] Few people were as extreme as Marinetti, but most Europeans thought of war in a positive way. This attitude fueled an arms race; the defense expenditures of all European nations increased by 83 percent between 1883 and 1908, and they increased another 63 percent between 1908 and 1913.

Not everyone favored war, however, and especially not a major world war. Even those who did favor war usually meant some small heroic conflict that would end quickly and do little harm. Most Europeans

Trench Warfare   World War I soldiers engaged in trench warfare, in which they fought from wide ditches. This form of stationary battle was new to soldiers on both sides of the conflict. (National Archives)

believed that Western civilization was too enlightened to permit a major war. Even small wars were opposed by a strong antiwar movement; most Socialists opposed war because they thought it would benefit only the capitalists, and many businesspeople feared that war would undermine their prosperity. In short, then, European attitudes toward war were mixed—some favored it; others opposed it. And, since Europe had not experienced a major conflict since 1815, early twentieth-century Europeans had no real conception of what a major war would be like.

During the last few peaceful years before 1914, two blocs of allies engaged in a protracted power struggle that some called a "dry war." One alliance system included Germany, the Hapsburg Empire, and Italy; the other included France, Russia, and, to a lesser extent, Great Britain. Neither alliance was designed for aggressive purposes, though a series of international crises gradually led the alliances to regard each other as opponents and potential enemies. One such crisis occurred in 1911 in Agadir, a port in Morocco (northwestern Africa) and within the French sphere of influence. Germany sent a warship to Agadir, ostensibly to protect German mining interests but actually in an attempt to force the

French out of Morocco. When Britain supported France, Germany withdrew the warship and the crisis ceased. However, the affair served to increase tensions among the major European powers.

Sarajevo

Events in the Balkan town of Sarajevo turned the fears, tensions, and arms competition into the First World War. The Balkan peninsula was a hotbed of nationalist emotions, where for decades various peoples— Serbs, Croats, Bulgars, and others—had sought to establish their own national states. The Serbs had been most successful, for the independence of Serbia was established in 1878. Opposing the Balkan peoples was the Hapsburg Empire, which ruled many of these peoples and refused to allow them to establish national states. The reason, of course, was that the Hapsburg Empire was itself composed of several national groups, so if the Balkan groups were allowed to form their own nations the Hapsburg Empire would cease to exist. The turmoil in the Balkans led to increased hostility between the Hapsburg Empire and Serbia. The Hapsburgs feared the dissolution of the empire, and the Serbs resented Hapsburg opposition to the Balkan people's ambitions.

Relatively minor Balkan wars occurred in 1912 and 1913, but the decisive event came on 28 June 1914. On that day, Francis Ferdinand, heir to the Hapsburg throne, was assassinated by Serbian patriots in the Balkan town of Sarajevo. At first, the assassination caused little international concern, but the Hapsburg government soon decided that it would deal with Serbia decisively. On July 28, the Hapsburg Empire declared war, believing that it could destroy Serbia quickly in a small, localized conflict.

Russia supported Serbia because it had interests in the Balkan peninsula and didn't want the Hapsburgs to gain complete control there. Since the mobilization of Russian armies threatened Germany's eastern frontier, the Germans supported their ally, the Hapsburg Empire. In turn, German mobilization threatened France's eastern frontier, so the French supported their ally, Russia. The fighting began on August 3 with the German invasion of Belgium. The British objected to the violation of Belgian neutrality, in part because they feared it would lead to a German-dominated Europe. Great Britain thus declared war on Germany. Italy reneged on its alliance with Germany and, in 1915, entered the war on the other side. Hence, the two alliance systems had turned an isolated crisis—the assassination of Francis Ferdinand—into war. Like a row of dominoes falling, the Hapsburgs knocked Russia into the war, which knocked in Germany, which knocked in France and then Great Britain.

As the armies marched to the fronts, many Europeans rejoiced. A mood of national enthusiasm took hold throughout much of Europe as

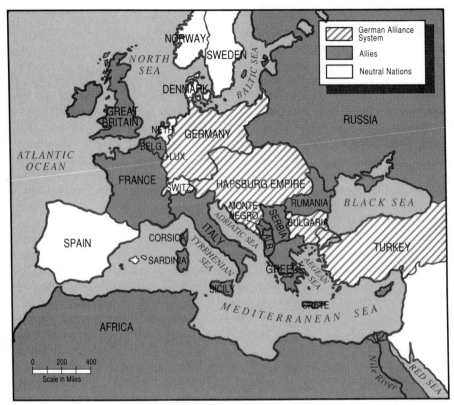

Figure 19.1   European Alliances in World War I

people came to view their particular nation's role in the war as something exciting and noble. A French writer proclaimed, "I believe in the might of our just cause, the crusade for civilization. I believe in . . . the spotless glory of the flag. . . . I believe in us, I believe in God."[8] A German professor wrote that "the world is divided into two camps—the merchants, the British, and the heroes, the Germans. The Germans will necessarily see their cause triumph, since it is the cause of civilization itself."[9] Only a few Europeans, such as the British Foreign Secretary Sir Edward Grey, foresaw what would follow: "The lamps are going out all over Europe. We shall not see them lit again in our time."[10]

The Western Front

The fighting began in Western Europe as the Germans moved through Belgium and into northern France. The German military followed the Schlieffen Plan, a strategy whereby Germans would attack and try to defeat France quickly and only then turn their full strength against

Russia in the east. In this way, the Germans believed that they could avoid having to fight both France and Russia at the same time. The Schlieffen Plan nearly worked, as the Germans drove into France almost to Paris. Early in September 1914, however, the French stopped the German advance at the Battle of the Marne.

At this point, the war changed from one of movement to one of trench warfare. Both sides on the western front—the Germans on one side versus the French and British on the other—were so evenly matched that neither could defeat the other. The armies quickly settled into trench warfare. The trenches were ditches, approximately six to eight feet deep and about five feet wide, in which soldiers huddled for protection. The British and French dug about 12,000 miles of trenches that stretched from the French-Belgian border across northern France to the Swiss border. In front of the trenches was barbed wire and beyond that was an area of one hundred yards to a mile wide called "No Man's Land." On the other side was the German line of trenches, also about 12,000 miles in total length (including the support trenches behind the front lines).

Periodically, one side would launch a massive attack in an attempt to break through the other. These attacks were preceded by massive artillery bombardments that lasted up to four days. The soldiers then charged across "No Man's Land" into machine-gun fire and barbed wire. Sometimes they got as far as the opposing trenches, but neither side was able to make a decisive breakthrough until 1918.

The Eastern Front

The war on the eastern front was equally indecisive at first, even though the two sides—the Germans and the Hapsburgs on one side versus the Russians on the other—engaged in a series of murderous offensives. The Russians were hopelessly unprepared for war. Not only was the Russian government inefficient but matters were made worse by the presence of Rasputin, a strange religious figure who, despite being a debauched drunkard, had acquired great influence in the government because of his claim that he could alleviate the hemophilia suffered by the heir to the Russian throne. One result of governmental incompetence was that Russian armies lacked enough artillery and rifles; in some instances, soldiers went into battle with only a bayonet tied to a stick. The Russian army resorted to "human wave" offensives in which the vast Russian population unsuccessfully attempted to overwhelm the enemy. In one German attack in 1915, 151,000 Russians were killed, 683,000 were wounded, and 895,000 were taken as prisoners. Despite such enormous losses, Russia's large armies prevented Germany from winning a decisive victory in the east (until 1918), even though the Germans gradually captured more and more Russian territory.

New Allies and New Weapons

Since neither side could defeat the other decisively, both sought to tip the balance with new allies or new fronts. Italy and Japan joined the western Allies, while the Ottoman Empire and Bulgaria signed on with the German alliance. The British and French tried to outflank the Germans by attacking Turkey in the disastrous Gallipoli campaign. None of these measures, however, were very successful.

World War I also encouraged the development of new and more deadly weapons, such as the machine gun and poison gas (see the Technology box).

Some Effects of the Prolonged Stalemate

What happens to peoples and nations embroiled in a conflict like World War I? A later discussion will show that the war led to revolution in Russia and to dissolution of the Hapsburg and Ottoman empires. Here we focus on the Western front, where the war slowly brutalized people and governments.

Governments became more authoritarian, as entire societies had to be organized and controlled to support the soldiers on the front. Propaganda whipped up enthusiasm by portraying the enemy as an evil force that had to be destroyed. At the front, the generals continued to use "cannon-fodder" tactics, in which large numbers of soldiers were sent to certain death in an attempt to defeat the enemy. The soldiers followed the generals' orders, in part because they would be shot if they did not and in part because they believed in their cause. The results were what one might expect. On 1 July 1916 at the Battle of the Somme, when 110,000 British soldiers attacked on a thirteen-mile front, 60,000 were killed or wounded on the first day alone. At Verdun, a series of battles in 1916 killed about half a million French soldiers and almost as many Germans.

Yet statistics tell only part of the story. The experiences of those who actually fought in the war tell the other part:

> The men slept in mud, washed in mud, ate mud, and dreamed mud. . . . Just try to sleep with a belt of ammunition around you, your rifle bolt biting into your ribs, with a tin hat for a pillow; and feeling very damp and cold, with "cooties" boring for oil in your arm pits.[11]

Other firsthand accounts tell of the prevalence of lice and rats. One British unit got a large cat to control the rats, but the rats ate it. Death intervened constantly: "Our gunner, the volunteer Mortullo, was killed by a shot through the head. Though his brain fell over his face to the chin, his mind was still clear when we took him to the nearest dugout."[12] After

Weapons Development

The search for an advantage in World War I stimulated new weapons development. The result was the rapid mechanization of warfare that has continued to the present day. During the war, several technologies transformed the nature of warfare: the machine gun, the tank, poison gas, aircraft, and the submarine.

Machine guns were the result of applying the principle of mass production to rifles. Because they could be fired continuously, they allowed a soldier to mass produce shots. They also allowed the mass production of casualties, since more people could be hit. The machine gun evolved slowly during the last half of the nineteenth century and became one of the basic infantry weapons of World War I.

The first tanks were little more than tractors with a kind of tub on top for protection. By 1916, however, the tank was a well-designed, maneuverable instrument. Tanks, along with the new armored cars, should have improved the mobility of armies, but most World War I commanders did not use mechanized transport effectively.

Military aircraft were first used for scouting the enemy. Gradually, the aircraft became fighter planes with machine guns, and the pilots fighting their lonely battles in the sky became some of the most heroic figures of the war. Aircraft were also used for bombing, though World War I planes were too small to carry large bombing loads.

The submarine changed the nature of war because it inhibited the use of battle fleets and made it possible to raid the commercial vessels of the enemy. It also turned the oceans into potential battlegrounds. During World War I, the Germans in particular used the submarine to disrupt British commerce.

World War I Tank *A World War I French tank sits in the midst of a barren landscape. (Culver Pictures)*

many battles, soldiers' corpses sometimes remained where they fell for days.

Despite the horrors, many World War I soldiers remained enthusiastic about what they saw as the noble cause of the war and their comrades. One American said that the soldier "finds relief in the fun and comradeship of the trenches and wins that best sort of happiness that comes with duty done."[13] A German soldier referred to his comrades as "princes of the trenches" and said of himself as an officer, "Honor and gallantry make the master of the hour. What is more sublime than to face death at the head of a hundred men?"[14]

Others, though, were overwhelmed by fear and the brutality of war: "Suddenly, bullets screamed; we dropped face-down on to the ground, in terror. . . . The men I could see were shaking and twitching, their mouths contracted in a hideous spasm, their teeth chattering." One corporal said, "if this is what it's like, I hope I'll be killed off now."[15] A British soldier recalled the attack on the first day of the Somme:

> I see men arising and walking forward; and I go forward with them, in a glassy delirium wherein some seem to pause, with bowed heads, and sink carefully to their knees, and roll slowly over, and lie still. Others roll and roll, and scream and grip my legs in uttermost fear.[16]

As the months of war turned into years, the armies on both sides reached a point when morale collapsed. In May 1917, several units of the French army mutinied and had to be pacified. In the summer of 1917, the Russian army began to disintegrate as many troops deserted, and late in 1917 the Italian Second Army simply quit. Then, early in 1918, units of the British army fell apart; later that year the German army in the west was unwilling to continue fighting.

The United States Enters the War

The British and French were saved only by American entry into the war. The United States had remained officially neutral at first, but the loss of American lives due to German submarine warfare gradually turned the United States in an anti-German direction. Then, the first Russian revolution of 1917 helped entice the United States to support the British-French-Russian side, because once the tsar abdicated it was easier for Americans to believe they were fighting for democracy. On 6 April 1917, the United States declared war on Germany. Eventually, American troops and supplies, combined with those of the British and French, were sufficient enough to overwhelm the Germans. The end of the war in the west was at last in sight.

THE RUSSIAN REVOLUTION OF 1917

On the eastern front, dramatic developments began to unfold in 1917. As mentioned earlier, the Russian army was starting to disintegrate. Within Russia, a growing number of people were tired of the war and increasingly critical of the tsarist government. The lower classes were suffering. A police report from early 1917 claimed that "the proletariat of the capital is on the edge of despair—it is generally believed that the slightest explosion will lead to uncontrollable riots."[17] The tsarist regime had proved too weak and inefficient to withstand the pressures of a long war, and so revolution in Russia was imminent.

Early in March 1917, a general worker strike in St. Petersburg was followed by a strike of many Russian soldiers at the eastern front. These were clearly movements led by the lower classes against the war and the tsarist government. The leaders of the *Duma* demanded that Tsar Nicholas II abdicate and, not having much if any support, he did so on March 15. (The tsar and his family were killed by the ruling Bolsheviks in 1918.) What followed was the so-called period of "dual government." Duma leaders formed an official provisional government, which was moderately liberal and reformist. The provisional government had to share power with *Soviets* (or councils) of workers', peasants', and soldiers' deputies, which were quickly established in the major cities. The Soviets tended to represent the urban working class and the ordinary soldier and to be more radical than the liberals in the provisional government.

The provisional government decided to keep Russia in the war. The Russian people were so war-weary, however, that the government became increasingly unpopular. Furthermore, it never had effective control of the countryside, where peasants were seizing land and killing some of the nobility. By the summer of 1917, three forces vied for power. The provisional government, now led by the young lawyer Alexander Kerensky, hoped to continue in the war and afterward establish a liberal democratic constitution in Russia. On the Left, radicals professing to represent the lower classes led the "July Days" riots in St. Petersburg in an attempt to overthrow the government, but Kerensky managed to suppress them. On the Right, military units led by General L. G. Kornilov launched a rebellion in August in an effort to restore a more conservative government, but it too was unsuccessful.

The Bolsheviks

The chaos in Russia at this time benefited the Bolsheviks, a Marxist party led by V. I. Lenin. Lenin was a seasoned revolutionary who had spent

V. I. Lenin Vladimir Ilyich
Lenin (1870–1924), as Bol-
shevik leader, directed the
Communist revolution in
Russia. He quickly became
the leading spokesman for
world revolution. (National
Archives)

many years in exile before returning to Russia in 1917. Under his
guidance, the Bolsheviks were one of the few revolutionary groups to
align themselves unreservedly with the lower classes. (The Social
Revolutionary party vigorously supported radical land reform.) The
Bolsheviks preached what the lower classes wanted to hear—immediate
peace, land to the peasants, bread and social justice for the oppressed. As
a result, the Bolsheviks quickly gained a mass following, especially
among workers and soldiers but not so much among peasants in the

countryside. In November, they carried out the second revolution of 1917, overthrowing the Kerensky government.

The Bolsheviks, who began to call themselves "Communists," were in a precarious position. At first, they controlled only the large cities of St. Petersburg and Moscow. It would be two or three years before they dominated all of Russia. Furthermore, the Germans were advancing rapidly against what was left of Russia's armies. The Bolsheviks decided that the only way to survive was to make immediate peace. Hence, in March 1918, they signed the treaty of Brest-Litovsk (a town in western Russia) with Germany. The treaty required Russia to cede huge amounts of land and population to the victors. Fortunately for the Bolsheviks, however, the subsequent German defeat in the west voided the treaty of Brest-Litovsk.

The Bolshevik Revolution shocked the world. Many in Western Europe and the United States feared the revolutionary threats of the new Communist power, and anticommunism quickly became a powerful political dogma among conservatives. For Russians and many others around the world, however, the revolution seemed to provide hope for the future. Lenin professed to be leading a revolution of the oppressed and held out Marxism as a revolutionary ideology that offered poor countries a new way to modernize. For a time, the new Marxist government would be an inspiration to those seeking a better life for the lower classes everywhere. The euphoria induced by the revolution was expressed well by an older Bolshevik, Maria Spiridonova:

> Before the workers of Russia open new horizons which history has never known. . . . There is no force in the world which can put out the fire of Revolution! The old world crumbles down, the new world begins.[18]

THE END OF WORLD WAR I

The war on the western front finally ended in 1918. The Germans tried one last major offensive in the spring, but by late summer they were defeated. Many ordinary German soldiers were on the verge of rebellion: "Our troops can simply not go on any longer. . . . Many of our younger men have had their heads turned by Bolshevik ideas."[19] German military commanders, realizing that the end of the war was near, insisted that the government seek an end to hostilities. An armistice went into effect on 11 November 1918. The end of World War I took on an ironic twist, as one German machine gunner compared it to the end of a theatrical production:

> On the Fourth Army front, at two minutes to eleven, a machine gun . . . fired off a complete belt without a pause. A single machine-

gunner was then seen to stand up beside his weapon, take off his helmet, bow, and turning about walk slowly to the rear.[20]

Just as the war ended, a brief revolution broke out in Germany. In October, many soldiers and sailors formed Soviets and appeared ready to launch a democratic, radically Socialist revolution. The situation forced Emperor William II, who was already being pressured to resign by the Allies, to abdicate early in November. Over the next few months, Germany teetered on the brink of radical revolution, but the moderate Socialists, supported by the army, gradually assumed control. In 1919, they helped establish a democratic government that became known as the *Weimar Republic* and that lasted until 1933. (It was so named because its constitutional convention was held in the city of Weimar.) But the change in German government was to some degree a surface phenomenon. German social structure remained unchanged, and many in the traditional upper classes were both powerful and hostile to the new democratic system.

A PEACE CONFERENCE AND A WAVE OF REVOLUTIONS

On 18 January 1919, hundreds of diplomats assembled in Paris to make peace. The Paris Peace Conference appeared to be led by the "Big Four"—President Woodrow Wilson of the United States, Prime Minister David Lloyd George of Great Britain, Premier Georges Clemenceau of France, and Premier Vittorio Orlando of Italy. Germany, the loser in the war, and Russia, increasingly thought of as a Communist and therefore an "outlaw" nation, were not allowed to participate in the conference.

The conference was dominated by the passions and emotions aroused during the war. Clemenceau spoke for those who were obsessed with punishing old enemies, an understandable reaction given the suffering that France had endured during the war. In particular, he wanted to ensure that Germany could never again threaten France. President Wilson and, to a lesser extent, Lloyd George tended to think in a broader, more global context. They hoped that liberalism, which to them meant national self-determination of peoples, could tame the Russian and other revolutions occurring around the world. In January 1918, Wilson had defined this liberalism in his Fourteen Points for peace, which included such things as covenants openly arrived at to replace secret diplomacy, freedom of commerce, disarmament, and self-determination of peoples. On his ocean voyage to Europe, Wilson said that "the conservatives do not realize what forces are loose in the world at the present time. Liberalism is the only thing that can save civilization from chaos—from a flood of ultra-radicalism that will swamp the world."[21]

Treaty of Versailles

The most immediate task confronting the peacemakers was concluding a treaty with Germany. After months of negotiations, the Treaty of Versailles was signed on 28 June 1919. Concerning Germany, the most important provisions of the treaty were (1) Germany lost all its colonies; (2) it also lost approximately 13 percent of its land (including Alsace-Lorraine, acquired after the Franco-Prussian War of 1870, which was returned to France), and a large strip of territory to Poland, now restored to statehood; (3) Germany was required to pay *reparations* (payments for damages done to the victors during the war), the total later set at $33 billion; (4) the German Rhineland was demilitarized to keep German troops farther from the French border; (5) the German army was reduced to 100,000 troops and the navy was dismantled; and (6) a so-called "war guilt" clause stipulated that Germany had to accept full responsibility for starting World War I.

From the perspective of the diplomats at Paris, the Treaty of Versailles was a compromise between Clemenceau's desire for revenge and the more moderate approach advocated by Wilson and Lloyd George. From the German perspective, it was an unduly harsh treaty, particularly since German territory had not been invaded during the war and therefore many Germans were not really reconciled to having lost. The Germans protested vehemently against the treaty but were finally forced to accept it. The German attitude was well expressed by Chancellor Philip Scheidemann: "May the hand wither which signs such a treaty."[22] Matthias Erzberger, one of the German politicians who did sign the treaty, was assassinated in 1921 by right-wingers who resented the treaty.

The Treaty of Versailles also included President Wilson's favorite project, the League of Nations. The League was to be an international organization that would represent all the nations of the world and work to prevent future wars. Although it failed in its quest for peace, the organization was significant in that it symbolized a new world politics in which peoples of all races and tongues met in a common assembly. (However, despite Wilson, the United States never did join, and Germany and Russia were not members at first.) For Wilson, the League was a concrete expression of liberalism on the international level, a liberalism that he hoped would blunt the Marxist message emanating from Lenin. In 1918–1919, Wilson and Lenin were rival prophets of a new postwar order, Wilson speaking for democracy and national self-determination and Lenin for world revolution and the Marxist classless society.

Civil War in Russia

Even though Russia was excluded from the Paris Peace Conference, events in that country were never far from the minds of those who were included. In 1919, some British, French, Japanese, and American troops were in Russia, engaged in a half-hearted attempt to overthrow the Bolsheviks. This foreign intervention naturally reinforced the Bolsheviks' fear and suspicion of the capitalist nations. The reason the foreigners could intervene was that from 1918 to 1920 Russia was enmeshed in a furious civil war. On one side were the Reds (Bolsheviks) trying to gain control of all of Russia, and on the other were the Whites representing conservative forces who wanted to overthrow the Red regime. (The color red was first associated with revolutionaries during the French Revolution, and in the nineteenth century the red flag became an emblem associated with Marxist radicalism. White, the color of the counter-revolutionaries, came from the white flag of the Bourbon dynasty, the French monarchs who opposed the French Revolution.)

The Russian civil war was a turbulent time. The fighting, coming on the heels of World War I, was a terrible blow to the Russian economy and the peasants. The Reds finally won the civil war in 1920, largely because the conservative Whites supported the former upper-class landowners and thus could not get the support of the peasantry. The result was to leave the Bolsheviks in full control of Russia.

In the cities, despite the turmoil, intellectual and artistic experimentation flourished at this time. Many young Communists demonstrated their contempt for bourgeois values by leaping naked onto crowded Moscow streetcars. The Bolsheviks proclaimed the emancipation of Russian women, with equal pay and more lenient divorce laws.

Two Empires Collapse

The Bolsheviks hoped to export Marxist revolution, but it was nationalist revolutions that destroyed the Hapsburg and Ottoman empires. The Hapsburg armies, with over six million casualties, suffered terribly during the war, and by 1918 the empire was thoroughly discredited. Even so, the diplomats at Paris negotiated peace treaties—the Treaty of St. Germain with Austria and the Treaty of Trianon with Hungary. But the treaties did not prevent rival national groups from proclaiming independence from the Hapsburg Empire. The Czechs and Slovaks organized the new nation of Czechoslovakia; the South Slavs seceded to join Serbia and form Yugoslavia; the Poles established Poland, which included large territories taken from Germany and Russia; and what was left of the Hapsburg Empire became the new countries of Austria and Hungary. The entire area was chaotic for a time, as the emerging nations fought among themselves to set national boundaries. As noted above, the diplomats at Paris concluded peace treaties with Austria and Hungary in 1919, but they had little control over events and could only watch the dissolution of the Hapsburg Empire.

The Ottoman Empire, already shaken by the 1908 Young Turk revolt, had joined the war on the German side, but the Arabs within the empire had fought on the Allied side because they wanted independence from the Ottomans. The Treaty of Sèvres (1920) recognized Arabic national liberation, although only the area that became Saudi Arabia was fully independent. Syria, Iraq, Lebanon, Transjordan, and Palestine became mandates of the League of Nations and were controlled by either Great Britain or France. The European powers also ruled many North African states, with Britain controlling Egypt and the Sudan, France governing Morocco and Tunis, and Italy dominating Libya. The Treaty of Sèvres was totally unacceptable, however, to the nationalist groups that succeeded the Young Turks in controlling what was left of the Ottoman Empire. These nationalist groups were led by Mustapha Kemal (later called Kemal Ataturk), and in 1920 he led a Turkish rebellion for recognition of a Turkish nation. After several years of fighting, a new agreement—the Treaty of Lausanne (1923)—acknowledged the independence of the new nation of Turkey.

Independence for Ireland

A national revolution in Ireland came to fruition at about the same time. The Irish had been seeking independence from Great Britain since the latter part of the eighteenth century, and the issue became so heated that before 1914 it almost precipitated civil war within Ireland and Britain. Many Irish supported the German side during the war, and in 1916 Irish radicals launched the Easter Rebellion in an attempt to drive out the British.

The rebellion was unsuccessful, but in 1922 Britain finally recognized the independence of Ireland. Because most Irish were Catholic, the conservative Protestants in northern Ireland insisted on remaining a part of Britain, so a small part of the Irish island became British Northern Ireland. Many Catholic Irish and Protestant Irish continue to fight each other, the Catholics wanting to unite the entire island under Catholic control and the Protestants seeking to remain a part of Britain.

CONCLUSION

The period 1905–1920 marks the beginning of the end of a long era when Europe dominated the world. During World War I, the United States surpassed all the European powers in industrial production and financial strength and quickly became a new superpower. Russia would soon become another. American world leadership developed slowly, however. Political conflicts between President Wilson and his republican opponents prevented the United States from ratifying the Treaty of Versailles or joining the League of Nations. Then, in the 1920s, the United States followed a policy of relative isolation from world affairs. The result was that for a time the most powerful world leader refused to lead.

In the non-Western world, the war had the effect of encouraging rebellion against European colonialism. The Chinese, for example, were incensed when the Paris Peace Conference refused to support China against Japanese aggression. The result was the May Fourth Movement of 1919, a surge of popular nationalism organized by Chinese students. The movement soon led to the formation of the Chinese Communist party, which eventually fought the Guomindong (the nationalists who had overthrown the Manchu dynasty in 1911) for control of China.

Within several Western nations, enfranchisement of women occurred soon after the war. Women got the right to vote in Great Britain (those over age 30 in 1918, those over age 21 in 1927), Canada (1918), Germany (1919), the United States (1920), and Sweden (1921). Enfranchisement was the result both of the suffragettes' campaigns and also of a desire to reward women for their participation in the war efforts. Even more important, though, was the general belief that women were basically conservative and that their votes would act as a stabilizing force in a tense, chaotic time.

By 1920, Europe and the United States had begun to calm down, and many people hoped for a brighter future. Woodrow Wilson, ever the optimist, said that "the world has been made safe for democracy." But, he quickly added, "democracy has not yet made the world safe against irrational revolution."[23] Wilson could not have known how prescient that remark was. The irrational revolution of which he spoke would soon grow out of the nationalistic passions that still inflamed Europe. An unrepentant German soldier gave words to these passions when he said: "We stand in the memory of the dead who are holy to us . . . so long as the blade of a sword will strike a spark in the night may it be said: Germany lives and Germany shall never go under!"[24]

THINGS YOU SHOULD KNOW

Russo-Japanese War	Freud
Russian Revolution of 1905	Picasso, Braque, and Kandinsky
Young Turk revolt	Weber
Overthrow of Manchu dynasty in China	Sorel
	Henry Adams
Mexican Revolution	Underlying causes of World War I
Suffragette movement	Sarajevo
Einstein	Schlieffen Plan
Planck	Trench warfare

New weapons development
The Russian Revolutions
Bolsheviks
Lenin
Wilson
Weimar Republic
Treaty of Versailles
League of Nations

Paris Peace Conference
Civil war in Russia (1918–1920)
Dissolution of Hapsburg and Otto-
  man empires
Independence of Ireland
Enfranchisement of women after
  World War I

SUGGESTED READINGS

Laurence Lafore, *The Long Fuse* (New York: Harper & Row, 1971) provides one of the more balanced interpretations of the origins of World War I. On the war itself, Marc Ferro, *The Great War, 1914–1918* (New York: Routledge, Chapman, & Hall, 1987) is a good introduction. Paul Fussell, *The Great War and Modern Memory* (New York: Oxford Univ. Press, 1975) examines the broad topic of how the war transformed attitudes and ideas (particularly among the British).

For the Russian Revolutions, Sheila Fitzpatrick, *The Russian Revolution, 1917–1932* (New York: Oxford Univ. Press, 1984) offers a good introduction. Arno J. Mayer, *Politics and Diplomacy of Peacemaking* (New York: Knopf, 1967) analyzes the peacemaking process in the context of global politics. A very readable, anecdotal survey of the collapse of the Russian, German, Hapsburg, and Ottoman ruling dynasties is Edmond Taylor, *The Fall of the Dynasties* (Garden City, N.Y.: Doubleday, 1963).

The period from 1905 to 1920 is rich in memoirs, diaries, and other firsthand accounts written by people who participated in or observed great events of the time. Three good memoirs are Arthur Guy Empey, *Over the Top* (New York: G. P. Putnam's Sons, 1917), the account of an American soldier who fought in the trenches; Ernst Jünger, *The Storm of Steel: From the Diary of a German Storm-Troop Officer on the Western Front* (New York: H. Fertig, 1975), the diary of a German soldier; and John Reed, *Ten Days That Shook the World* (New York: International Publishers, 1967), a description by a radical American journalist of some of the great events of the Bolshevik Revolution.

NOTES

[1]Jack J. Roth, "Introduction," in *World War I: A Turning Point in Modern History,* ed. Jack J. Roth (New York: Knopf, 1967), p. 6.

[2]Quoted in L. S. Stavrianos, *Global Rift: The Third World Comes of Age* (New York: Morrow, 1981), p. 389.

[3]Quoted in Edmond Taylor, *The Fall of the Dynasties: The Collapse of the Old Order, 1905–1922* (Garden City, N.Y.: Doubleday, 1963), p. 21.

[4]Ibid.

[5]Quoted in Geoffrey Barraclough, *From Agadir to Armageddon: Anatomy of a Crisis* (New York: Holmes and Meier, 1982), p. 27.

[6]Quoted in Élie Halévy, *The Era of Tyrannies*, trans. R. K. Webb (New York: New York Univ. Press, 1966), p. 246.

[7]Quoted in Theodore S. Hamerow, *The Birth of a New Europe: State and Society in the Nineteenth Century* (Chapel Hill: Univ. of North Carolina Press, 1983), p. 422–23.

[8]Quoted in Marc Ferro, *The Great War, 1914–1918*, trans. Nicole Stone (London: Routledge and Kegan Paul, 1973 trans. of 1969 ed.), p. 122.

[9]Ibid., p. 123.

[10]Quoted in Taylor, *The Fall*, p. 229.

[11]Arthur Guy Empey, *Over the Top* (New York: Putnam's, 1917), pp. 60, 64.

[12]Ernst Jünger, *The Storm of Steel: From the Diary of a German Storm-Troop Officer on the Western Front* (London: Chatto & Windus, 1975 rpt. of 1929 ed.), p. 231.

[13]Empey, *Over the Top*, p. 280.

[14]Jünger, *The Storm*, p. 27.

[15]Quoted in Ferro, *The Great War*, pp. 85–86.

[16]Quoted in Paul Fussell, *The Great War and Modern Memory* (New York: Oxford Univ. Press, 1975), pp. 29–30.

[17]Quoted in Ferro, *The Great War*, p. 177.

[18]Quoted in John Reed, *Ten Days That Shook the World* (New York: International Publishers, 1919), p. 311.

[19]Quoted in Richard Stumpf, *War, Mutiny and Revolution in the German Navy: The World War I Diary of Seaman Richard Stumpf*, ed. Daniel Horn (New Brunswick, N.J.: Rutgers Univ. Press, 1967), pp. 414, 410.

[20]Quoted in Fussell, *Modern Memory*, p. 196.

[21]Quoted in Lloyd C. Gardner, *Safe for Democracy: The Anglo-American Response to Revolution, 1913–1923* (New York: Oxford Univ. Press, 1984), p. 1.

[22]Quoted in Taylor, *The Fall*, p. 379.

[23]Quoted in Gardner, *Safe*, p. 346.

[24]Jünger, *The Storm*, pp. 318–19.

20

A Time of Passionate Intensity and Another World War, 1920 to 1945

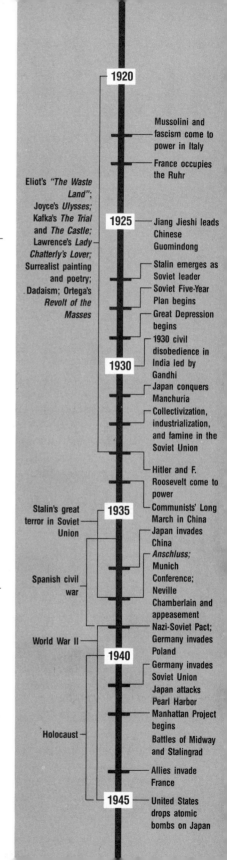

Eliot's *"The Waste Land"*; Joyce's *Ulysses*; Kafka's *The Trial* and *The Castle*; Lawrence's *Lady Chatterly's Lover*; Surrealist painting and poetry; Dadaism; Ortega's *Revolt of the Masses*

Stalin's great terror in Soviet Union

Spanish civil war

World War II

Holocaust

1920

1925

1930

1935

1940

1945

Mussolini and fascism come to power in Italy

France occupies the Ruhr

Jiang Jieshi leads Chinese Guomindong

Stalin emerges as Soviet leader

Soviet Five-Year Plan begins

Great Depression begins

1930 civil disobedience in India led by Gandhi

Japan conquers Manchuria

Collectivization, industrialization, and famine in the Soviet Union

Hitler and F. Roosevelt come to power

Communists' Long March in China

Japan invades China

Anschluss; Munich Conference; Neville Chamberlain and appeasement

Nazi-Soviet Pact; Germany invades Poland

Germany invades Soviet Union

Japan attacks Pearl Harbor

Manhattan Project begins

Battles of Midway and Stalingrad

Allies invade France

United States drops atomic bombs on Japan

In 1920, the Irish poet William Butler Yeats wrote in his famous poem "The Second Coming":

> Things fall apart; the centre cannot hold;
> Mere anarchy is loosed upon the world,
> The blood-dimmed tide is loosed, and everywhere
> The ceremony of innocence is drowned;
> The best lack all conviction, while the worst
> Are full of passionate intensity.[1]

Yeats's vision of the world was soon realized, for the period 1920–1945 was a time of "passionate intensity" full of ideological conflict and another world war.

Three ideological systems perpetuated the conflict in Europe: liberal democracy, communism, and fascism. Liberal democracy prevailed in North America and much of Western Europe but was relatively weak. World War I had undermined the power of several liberal states, most notably Britain and France, and the Great Depression of the 1930s (discussed later in this chapter) had the same effect. *Communism* was the official political ideology of Russia after 1917, and active Communist parties were present in most other European nations. Though communism appealed to some people inside and outside of Russia, it frightened many others, particularly during the 1930s when the regime of Joseph Stalin used terroristic methods to force the Russian people to industrialize rapidly. Fear of communism was one of the factors that led to the emergence of a new political ideology, *fascism*. Fascism appealed to the nationalist passions of those still angry about the outcomes of World War I. In 1922, Benito Mussolini initiated a Fascist government in Italy. A decade later, in 1933, Adolf Hitler began a National Socialist government in Germany (national socialism was the German variant of fascism).

Conflict was also common in other parts of the world. In Asia, the Japanese began to conquer and build an empire, and in China a long civil war continued. The hostilities in Asia and in Europe eventually led to the massive struggle known as World War II.

BENITO MUSSOLINI AND ITALIAN FASCISM

The memories of World War I—of those who had died, resentment of wartime enemies, intense patriotism—lingered long after the war's end, particularly among those who had fought in the war. Although many World War I veterans returned to a reasonably normal civilian life, many others were disillusioned and embittered by their wartime experiences. Some were unable to find work. Some found civilian life far less interesting or meaningful after the war. And most veterans resented those

Figure 20.1 Europe after World War I

who had found ways to avoid active participation in the war effort. The result in most countries, particularly in Italy and Germany, was the emergence of a strong nationalistic attitude that was often scornful of the routine of peacetime life.

In Italy, growing numbers of World War I veterans supported the new political movement of fascism led by Benito Mussolini (1883–1945).

Mussolini, a demagogic ex-Socialist newspaper editor and orator, had fought enthusiastically in World War I. He believed that Italy needed what he called a "government by men in the trenches." In 1919, Mussolini and fifty others formed the first Fascist group, a collection of young veterans who loved violence and were addicted to action. (The term *fascism* is derived from the Latin *fasces*, which refers to a bundle of rods symbolizing the power of ancient Rome.) The political program of this group was intentionally vague and often incoherent. Mussolini claimed that the essence of fascism was not in rational ideas or logical political programs but in a "military style," and that its goals were "to found an empire" and win "glory and honor."[2] To be more precise, Mussolini's fascism was a political movement that believed in anti-communism, nationalism, the individual serving the state, dictatorial government, and fascist control of all major social and economic activities.

Fascism appealed to Italians dissatisfied with the conditions in postwar Italy. It was particularly appealing to nationalists, who felt that Italy had not gained enough territory at the Paris Peace Conference; to conservatives, who feared Communist revolution; and to those who believed that the existing liberal government could not effectively deal with the postwar economic depression in Italy. Between 1919 and 1922, political violence increased in Italy as Fascist street gangs (known as the "black shirts" from the color of their uniforms) fought Socialist and Communist gangs. By 1922 the Fascists were a major political party supported directly or tacitly by several million Italians. In October of that year, Mussolini and ten thousand of his supporters staged the March on Rome to intimidate the government into giving power to the Fascists. The strategy was successful, for the government collapsed and King Victor Emmanuel III invited Mussolini to form a new Fascist government and to assume the premiership.

When Mussolini first came to power, he cooperated with the parliamentary government. However, he soon began to use terrorist tactics to intimidate his opponents. Fascist gangs killed some parliamentary leaders and abused others, forcing them to drink large doses of castor oil (which induces severe vomiting). By the late 1920s, the Fascists were in complete control of Italy and Mussolini was recognized as the *Duce* (or leader) of what he hoped would become a new Roman Empire. Early Fascist Italy and Mussolini's dictatorship were admired by many Europeans and Americans, for they believed that he had revived Italian pride and made the Italian government more efficient. Gradually, though, fascism and Mussolini lost the respect of Europeans and Americans. It became clear that Mussolini often claimed to have accomplished much more than he really had. Furthermore, his regime stifled intellectual dissent and sometimes murdered political opponents. In addition, some of Mussolini's attitudes and rules bordered on the ludicrous. He believed, for example, that fascism had to be portrayed as

THE LIBERAL DEMOCRATIC STATES

serious, so he prohibited photographs of himself in friendly portrayals and encouraged Italian children to adopt fierce poses whenever they encountered foreigners. The weaknesses and cruelties of the Fascist regime were not yet known in the 1920s, however, so for a time Mussolini was an imposing figure on the European scene.

THE LIBERAL DEMOCRATIC STATES

Mussolini's Fascist regime seemed so imposing in part because the major liberal democratic states—the United States, Great Britain, France, and Weimar Germany—were so unimpressive in comparison. Although these nations still enjoyed the appearance of being powerful and prosperous, they were actually suffering from ineffective political leadership. On the national level, basic social and economic problems often went unresolved; on the international level, the cooperation needed to maintain a stable peace was only occasionally successful. Political leadership failed for various reasons. One was the loss of many potentially strong leaders in World War I. Another was an almost paralyzing fear of communism. This fear induced many leaders to oppose social reforms that might change the existing order and to perceive fascism as a potentially positive force that would be a bulwark against communism.

The United States

The post-World War I United States deliberately isolated itself from European affairs and refused to join the League of Nations. Many Americans enjoyed a postwar prosperity and hoped to ignore the complicated world beyond the oceans. The American desire for a simpler, safer world led to Prohibition, a constitutional ban on the manufacture and sale of alcoholic drinks. It also led to a suspicion and fear of everything foreign. In 1919–1920, anticommunism swept the nation. Stricter immigration laws reduced the number of immigrants allowed to enter the United States, especially those from non-European parts of the world. Racism also grew, as the Ku Klux Klan, revived in 1915, spread hatred of Jews, Catholics, and blacks.

Great Britain

Great Britain, although one of the war's victors, lost in the sense that its economic strength was weakened. Many foreign markets had been lost during the war years, much shipping had been destroyed, and huge sums of money borrowed during the war were owed to the United States. The result was chronic unemployment, with many British malnourished and living in miserable slums. Political leaders in Britain were unable to solve the economic problems and feared that another war would destroy the nation completely. Most British leaders shared the view of their colleague Stanley Baldwin, the dominant political figure from 1923 to 1937: "Who in Europe does not know that one more war in the West, and the civilization of the ages will fall with as great a shock as that of Rome?"[3] Thus, British economic weakness was the soil in which the seeds of *appeasement* in foreign policy grew. The seeds would sprout in the 1930s.

France

France, another nominal victor in the war, was also weakened. So many French had been killed and so much property had been destroyed that the country faced serious economic problems. Furthermore, the French felt abandoned, for American isolation and British economic weakness left France to face Germany alone. The French government sought to keep Germany weak by enforcing strictly the Treaty of Versailles. The immediate issue in the 1920s was Germany's obligation to make reparations payments for World War I damage. When it became evident that Germany would avoid payment as long as possible, the French and Belgians in 1923 occupied the Ruhr, a major German industrial area, in an effort to extract reparations by coercion. The Ruhr occupation produced an international furor, and France was left diplomatically isolated since most of its Allies refused to support the occupation. One effect of the Ruhr occupation was to reveal French weakness, and the occupation was soon ended.

Germany

The 1923 Ruhr occupation harmed the German Weimar Republic as well. The Republic was already weak, in part because many Germans were right-wing conservatives opposed to democracy and in part because the government had to implement, and was therefore identified with, the hated Treaty of Versailles. Furthermore, postwar inflation undermined the German economy.

Germany opposed the Ruhr occupation through various forms of passive resistance. One of the methods used was to pay reparations in currency devalued by inflation. The result was a semideliberate inflationary spiral; for example, a product priced at 100 marks in July 1922 cost 74,787 marks in July 1923 and 944,041 marks in August 1923. The inflation destroyed the financial well-being of many in the middle and working classes of the Weimar Republic. One elderly writer, Maximilian Bern, "withdrew all his savings, more than 100,000 marks, and spent them on one subway ticket. He took a ride around Berlin and then locked himself in his apartment and starved to death."[4]

TECHNOLOGY
The Automobile and the Radio

During the 1920s and 1930s advances in mass transportation and mass communication in Western Europe and North America came with the automobile and the radio.

The development of the internal combustion engine in the late nineteenth century led to the automobile. By 1885, the German inventor Karl Benz was building a three-wheel vehicle that used the new engine. Over the next decade, several inventors produced automobiles of various kinds. Then, in 1908, the American Henry Ford began the mass production of automobiles with his Model T car. Ford's mass production turned the automobile into a popular consumer item. In the United States, the number of privately owned cars increased from 7 million in 1919 to 23 million in 1929. The automobile had a major impact on much of Western Civilization, for after World War II it allowed many middle-class people to move from urban centers into suburbs.

Radio also originated in the late nineteenth century, as scientists gradually learned how to transform sounds into electromagnetic, or radio, waves that can be transmitted through the air. No one person is credited with the invention of the radio, though the first radio signals were sent in 1894 by the Italian Guglielmo Marconi. During the first two decades of the twentieth century, a few experimental radio stations appeared. In the 1920s, broadcasting networks were established in some Western European and North American countries. Radio quickly became a medium by which political leaders could communicate their messages to a mass audience. Particularly effective at radio communication were President Franklin D. Roosevelt and Adolf Hitler. Radio also allowed the quick reporting of news events. In the 1930s, American news reporters began to broadcast, directly from Europe to the United States, the dramatic political events of the time.

Ford Model T *The Model T (first made in 1908), one of the earliest automobiles to be produced in large numbers, launched a new generation of Americans with unparalleled mobility. Henry Ford pioneered the assembly line method of production in the automobile industry. (Culver Pictures)*

The Ruhr occupation gradually produced a more conciliatory mood in Europe toward Germany. In 1924, the Dawes Plan established a less demanding reparations schedule for Germany. In 1925, the Locarno Agreements included a Franco-German promise to maintain peace along their common border. In 1928, the signatories (eventually numbering sixty-two nations) of the Kellogg-Briand Pact agreed to renounce war as a means of national policy. These well-intentioned treaties accomplished little in the long run, but they did provide the international framework for a brief period (1924–1929) of peace and stability in Europe.

THE WRITERS AND ARTISTS BETWEEN THE WORLD WARS

The horrors of World War I and the fear that modern technology would degrade humanity led many writers and artists to view early twentieth-century Western Civilization as decadent—"an old bitch gone in the teeth," as the poet Ezra Pound described it. T. S. Eliot, an American poet living in Britain, compares the spiritual stagnation of the time with the religious richness of other eras in his provocative poem "The Waste Land" (1922). In *The Trial* (1925) and *The Castle* (1926), the Czech novelist Franz Kafka portrays humans as victims, caught in an absurd world that they cannot understand. The Spanish philosopher Jose Ortega y Gasset argues in *The Revolt of the Masses* (1930) that Western Civilization is inundated by masses of uncreative people unable and unwilling to provide the political and cultural leadership necessary for civilized life.

Two new artistic movements, centered in France, stressed the irrationality of life. *Dadaism* was a kind of antiart revolt against established values and traditional art. Symbolic of the revolt was the name *dada*, which in French means "hobby-horse" and has nothing to do with art. The dadaists produced nonsense poems and deliberately shocking artistic works such as Marcel Duchamp's *Fountain*, a display of a urinal signed "R. Mutt." *Surrealism*, led by the French poet Andre Breton and the Spanish artist Salvador Dali, was partially inspired by dadaism. The surrealists believed that the irrational was far more powerful than the rational. Their writings and artistic works are thus free expressions of the bizarre and the unconscious mind.

Some intellectuals tried to find meaning in a chaotic world. The Swiss theologian Karl Barth argued with his crisis theology that the evils of the modern world are rooted in human sin and can be overcome only through the eternal salvation offered by God. A very different perspective was expressed by the British novelist D. H. Lawrence. In *Sons and Lovers* (1913) and *Lady Chatterley's Lover* (1928), for example, Lawrence denounces the emotional and aesthetic barrenness of industrial society and argues that sexual instinct is a source of spiritual health for modern humanity. In one of the most influential literary works of the time, *Ulysses* (1922), the Irish novelist James Joyce tells a story of decay that ends by affirming the goodness in life. The fact that *Ulysses* is patterned after Homer's *Odyssey* shows that for Joyce modern humanity is on a spiritual journey in search of truth.

The problems and possibilities of the early twentieth century were also explored in the new medium of film. Some of the most notable early films came from Germany, including *The Blue Angel* (1930) and *The Cabinet of Dr. Caligari* (1919), which expressed a fascination with the irrational. In Russia, revolutionary idealism inspired great films like Sergei Eisenstein's *Potemkin* (1925). In the United States, Hollywood was becoming the center of the American film industry. During the 1920s, many films featuring the prominent Hollywood actor Charlie Chaplin made comic but clever satirical comments on the modern world.

THE GREAT DEPRESSION

The Great Depression of 1929–1933 caused many people to doubt the future of liberal democratic nations. Agricultural overproduction and a slow decline in international trade weakened many Western economies even before 1929. But in that year a stock market crash (a sudden, precipitous decline in the value of stocks) in the United States initiated a major economic slowdown that spread to Europe in 1930 and 1931. Businesses failed and unemployment increased. By 1932, one out of four British workers required unemployment relief; two out of five German workers were unemployed; and fifteen million Americans—about 25 percent of the work force—were out of work.

For many ordinary people, the Great Depression meant despair. One American expressed his despair in a letter to President Franklin D. Roosevelt:

> I am faced with [the] proposition of being set out of my home because I cannot pay my rent. I have [ten days] to get another house, no job, no means of paying rent. Can you be so kind as to advise me as to which would [be] the most human way to dispose of my self and my family, as this is about the only thing I see left to do.[5]

Another letter received by the president came from a thirteen-year-old girl: "My mother can not read nor write and she have to take care of five in family. I have no shoe and we are suffin sometime we is with no fire and I am bare foot."[6] Yet not everyone suffered equally during the Depression, for those fortunate enough to have jobs lived fairly comfortably.

The Depression caused most Western economies to shrink, which not only left large numbers of people unemployed but also left them without the means to stimulate the economy or to create new jobs. The British economist John Maynard Keynes argued that governments should give money to the unemployed, thus enabling them not only to survive but also to buy products and thereby increase production and jobs. Few political leaders of the time understood Keynesian theories. However, a few reforms unintentionally accomplished some of what Keynes recommended: Roosevelt's New Deal program in the United States created some jobs and Adolf Hitler's rearmament program in Germany employed many Germans.

The overall effect of the Great Depression was to weaken the liberal democratic nations and lead many people to believe that either fascism or communism was the wave of the future. In addition, by undermining the already embattled Weimar Republic, the Depression was a major factor in enabling the dictator Adolf Hitler to come to power in Germany (as we will see later in the chapter).

JOSEPH STALIN AND THE SOVIET UNION

After the Russian civil war of 1920, the Communist rulers renamed Russia as the Union of Soviet Socialist Republics.

The Soviet Union was to some degree isolated from other nations during the 1920s. The United States and most European nations feared communism so much that they at first refused to grant diplomatic recognition to the Soviet government. Furthermore, the Soviet Union was not allowed into the League of Nations until 1934. The Soviets, disappointed that Communist revolutions had not occurred in other countries, turned their attention to their own political and economic problems. The Soviet Union's isolation from the world economy thus prevented it from being directly affected by the Great Depression.

By 1920, the Soviet Union was weary of war and revolution. Its industrial and agricultural production had also declined precipitously, and many Soviets had died of hunger or disease. Faced with this situation, the Communist regime acted pragmatically; from 1921 to 1928, it followed a semicapitalistic New Economic Policy that included allowing peasants to sell their grain on the open market. The Communist party, however, was embroiled in a leadership struggle. Lenin died early in 1924 and was soon virtually deified, his body placed on permanent display in a public shrine. At that point, the Communist party realized that it had no established means of selecting a successor to Lenin. For several years various claimants maneuvered for power, most notably Leon Trotsky and Joseph Stalin. As General Secretary of the party, Stalin used his position to appoint his followers to vital governmental posts throughout the Soviet Union. By the late 1920s, Stalin's patronage system enabled him to drive Trotsky into exile and consolidate his own power.

Stalin's Policies

Stalin (1879–1953) was a ruthless, harsh leader who sought to accomplish his goals through any means. He wanted most of all to industrialize the Soviet Union and make it a world superpower. He thus instituted a set of economic goals in 1928 called the Five-Year Plan. Through the Plan, Stalin focused on two things: collectivization of agriculture and the construction of large industrial enterprises (such as steelworks and tractor factories). These two goals were intertwined—industrialization required large numbers of urban workers and the creation of "collective" farms designed to furnish a reliable food supply to the cities would also force peasants to migrate to the cities in search of work.

Collectivization started in 1930, as officials of the Communist party intimidated wealthy peasants (called *kulaks*) into giving up their land. Once this was accomplished in a given area, the remaining peasants were forced to join collective farms, large state-controlled agricultural enterprises where (in theory) everyone worked "collectively." Many peasants resisted collectivization by any means at their disposal, such as slaughtering their cattle rather than turning them over to the state. As a result, the Soviet army intervened and about ten million peasants were executed or sent to labor camps. (Another five to six million peasants died in the famine of 1932–1933, caused largely by excessive confiscation of grain supplies by the Soviet government.) Stalin's collectivization plan was successful; by 1932, 62 percent of peasant households had been collectivized, and that figure rose to 93 percent by 1937. In addition, nineteen million Soviets moved from the countryside to the cities during the 1930s.

In Soviet cities, giant construction projects, such as steel mills and ironworks, were completed quickly. Factory managers, under intense pressure to fulfill production goals, sometimes resorted to ambushing trains in order to gain needed materials. The workers, many of them newly arrived from the countryside, often lived in ramshackle barracks. Despite the chaos, Soviet industrialization proceeded rapidly; by the end of the 1930s, the Soviet economy had a strong industrial base. The standard of living of the average citizen was still not high, but the Soviet Union was now an industrial nation. (Prerevolutionary Russia had industrialized rapidly before 1914, but World War I undermined much of that economic progress.)

The Great Terror

Stalin's government used armed force, mass executions, and labor camps to expedite its economic modernization program. Some historians refer to this period in Soviet history as Stalin's Great Terror.

The Communist party had since Lenin's regime used secret police and terrorist tactics to punish opponents, but Stalin expanded the scope

Churchill, Roosevelt, Stalin   Shown here are three wartime leaders at the Yalta Conference of February 1945: Winston Churchill (1874–1965) of Great Britain *(left),* Franklin D. Roosevelt (1882–1945) of the United States *(center),* and Joseph Stalin (1879–1953) of the Soviet Union *(right).* (AP/Wide World Photos)

of the terror to destroy all opposition to his authority. In 1936, he launched an attack against leading Communist party figures. Over the next three years, large numbers of once-powerful officials, some of them Stalin's former friends, went on public trial after being accused of and confessing to crimes (like treason) they had not committed. Most were only guilty of opposing Stalin in some way, yet were invariably convicted and executed. Why did so many prominent government and military leaders confess openly to crimes they had not committed? One reason may be that continual interrogation and torture over the course of several days made them weak. Some may have even hoped that their confessions would gain leniency for their families. Often, however, family members were arrested too. Further, many of the accused were long-time Communist party members psychologically incapable of opposing the movement that gave meaning to their lives.

Stalin's Great Terror affected ordinary people as well. Soviet citizens were encouraged to denounce anyone who lacked revolutionary vigilance, and as a result most people lived in constant fear and suspicion because arrest could come for anyone at any time. Those arrested were usually sent to labor camps, where they were forced to work in harsh conditions that in many cases led to death. By the early 1940s, there were about ten million Soviets in labor camps.

The Great Terror was a terrible time in Russian history. Even Stalin admitted that the 1930s in the Soviet Union was a worse time than World War II. It was similar in its destructiveness to other revolutionary periods—the Reign of Terror (1793–1794) of the French Revolution when tens of thousands of revolutionaries and aristocrats were killed and the Cultural Revolution in China (1960s) when millions of Chinese died or were sent to labor camps. These revolutionary "terrors" are always difficult to evaluate. Stalin could legitimately claim that he had carried out a "workers' revolution," in the sense that by the late 1930s most of the old managerial elite had been eliminated and the new elite was recruited from the working class. Also, the Soviet dictator claimed that the success of his industrialization campaign justified the violence, because only an industrially strong Soviet Union could survive in the modern world. The Soviet defeat of Hitler's Germany in World War II (as we will see later in the chapter) offered some support for this argument. Yet Stalin was clearly a cruel, harsh despot willing to destroy millions of people to achieve his goals. We do not know exactly how many died as a result of the Great Terror, but it was probably at least twenty million people.

Furthermore, one of the tragic ironies of the twentieth century is that the Stalinist industrial system proved to be counterproductive as well as cruel. Often, the quality of output was poor. And Stalin's tyrannical methods eliminated the originality and spontaneity necessary to sustain an industrial economy. The result was that the Soviet economy became increasingly rigid and uncreative. In the late 1980s, Soviet leader Mikhail Gorbachev began to try to reintroduce some spontaneity into the Soviet economic system, because the Soviet economy was simply not performing well. (See Chapter 22.)

THE NON-WESTERN WORLD

The Western nations still ruled much of the world in the 1920s and 1930s, but World War I had undermined European power. European prestige suffered because the spectacle of white men slaughtering white men seemed to destroy the claim of European cultural superiority. (Some Africans referred to World War I as the "war of the white tribes.") Furthermore, the Bolshevik Revolution offered colonial peoples an example to be followed. These factors, added to the resentments already felt in colonial nations, helped precipitate national struggles in three Asian countries—India, China, and Japan.

India

British rule in India was challenged by the Indian National Congress, an organization founded in 1885 to press the British for reforms. At first, the Congress represented only the moderate demands of the Indian middle

Mohandas Gandhi   Gandhi (1869–1948), Indian nationalist leader, is shown here addressing a crowd during the campaign for Indian national independence in the 1930s. Seeking to live simply, Gandhi preached nonviolence as a means for achieving social and political change. (AP/Wide World Photos)

class, but by the twentieth century the charismatic Mohandas Gandhi was transforming the Congress into a mass movement clamoring for national independence. Gandhi was unique among twentieth-century revolutionary leaders in that he was more a spiritual than a political leader. His Hindu followers eventually came to call him *Mahatma*, meaning "great soul." Gandhi's campaign against the British was based on nonviolent passive resistance, an effective strategy because the British (unlike Stalin, for example) were ultimately unwilling to enforce their will by slaughtering large numbers of people. In 1930, a massive civil disobedience campaign—strikes, boycotts of British goods, refusal to pay taxes—forced the British to arrest thousands of Indians. The British were on the defensive, for Indian nationalism had become too powerful to be stopped. Indian independence would finally occur after World War II.

China

The struggle in China was more complex. As noted in Chapter 19, the Manchu dynasty was overthrown in 1911, and a nationalist organization called the Guomindong (Kuomintang)* attempted unsuccessfully to assume control of China. From 1911 until the mid-1920s, real power remained in the hands of provincial warlords, but the Guomindong was reinvigorated when Jiang Jieshi (Chiang Kai-shek) assumed leadership of the organization in 1925. Jiang's goal was to build a government strong enough to rule all of China and to prevent Western imperialists from intervening in Chinese affairs.

In pursuing this goal, Jiang confronted several difficulties. One was the warlords (leaders of private armies), whom he gradually subdued. Another was the fact that the Guomindong was a largely middle-class organization of businesspeople and landlords that had little appeal to poor, landless peasants. A third problem was the existence of a small Chinese Communist party.

Founded in 1921, the Chinese Communist party was originally a part of the Guomindong. But the Communists became increasingly radical, demanding land reforms such as giving land to the poverty-stricken peasants. As a result, Jiang began to drive them out of the Guomindong by 1927. The Guomindong-Communist civil war eventually led to the famous Long March of 1934, in which 100,000 Communists led by Mao Zedong (Mao Tse-tung) and others retreated into the mountains to escape Jiang's armies. The Long March lasted a full year with only thirty thousand of the original marchers surviving; the memory of the Long March eventually assumed almost mythical proportions among Chinese Communists. After 1935, the Communists, even though subdued in the mountains, began to attract the loyalty of landless peasants and therefore to represent a viable political alternative to the Guomindong.

Japan

The Chinese civil war was eventually affected by the rise of Japanese military power. By the 1920s, Japan was the most powerful Asian nation, thanks to the industrialization program begun in the late nineteenth century. Nevertheless, the Japanese felt vulnerable. Their island lacked most of the natural resources necessary to sustain an industrial economy. Furthermore, they tended to see themselves as surrounded by much larger nations—China to the west, the Soviet Union to the northwest, and the United States far to the east.

Japanese came increasingly to believe that Japan could survive only by conquering an empire, in particular by seizing control of natural resources available in other Asian countries. So, in 1910, Japan annexed Korea, a small nation once dominated by China. Then, in 1931, the

---

*In recent years, the People's Republic of China has developed a new system for transliteration of Chinese words, so the new form of Chinese names is used in the text with the old form following in parentheses.

Japanese army conquered Manchuria, the northeastern province of China. A few years later, in 1937, Japan launched a full-scale invasion of China and soon controlled most of the Chinese coastline. Jiang Jieshi and the Guomindong, fearing the Chinese Communists more than the Japanese, offered only relatively minor resistance to the invasion. The main resistance to Japan would eventually come from the United States, which had long opposed Japanese expansion in China. By the late 1930s, Japan and the United States were increasingly perceiving each other as enemies.

ADOLF HITLER AND NATIONAL SOCIALISM IN GERMANY

Hitler's Worldview

By the 1930s, many Europeans and Americans were both fascinated and perturbed by Adolf Hitler's rise to power in Germany. Hitler (1889–1945) took to an extreme certain ideas that had long been circulating in Europe, particularly racism and Social Darwinism. He believed that races, embodied in nations, were the primary actors in history. The superior race was the "Aryan" (light-skinned Europeans), and the chief goal of Germany, the leading Aryan state, was in Hitler's words to "set race in the center of all life. . . . to keep it pure." Hitler saw the racial enemy of the Aryan as the Jew. He even feared that Jews would try to corrupt the Aryan race: "With satanic joy in his face, the black-haired Jewish youth lurks in wait for the unsuspecting girl whom he defiles with his blood, thus stealing her from her people."[7] Hitler's extremist ideas culminated in his belief that Aryans could only defend themselves against Jews by destroying the Jewish race.

Conflict, in Hitler's view, also prevailed on the international level. He supported the Social Darwinist philosophy that struggle and competition are the essence of life. Thus, the foreign policy goal of Aryan Germany was to acquire living space *(lebensraum)* for the superior race. To get this living space, Hitler believed that Germany, the superior nation, would have to dominate inferior nations through conquest and war. In particular, Hitler looked to the east, especially Poland and the Soviet Union, for additional *lebensraum* for Germany.

Hitler was born into a lower middle class German family and never developed a settled career before World War I. He fought in the German army during the war and came to share an ex-soldier's outlook similar to the one that supported the rise of Italian fascism. In 1919, he joined the National Socialist German Workers' party (*Nazi* was the shortened name of the party) and soon became its *führer* or leader.

Adolf Hitler Hitler (1889–1945), German Nazi leader, used the microphone to address large crowds at mass rallies and radio hookups to reach people in their homes. Hitler was one of the first to use radio effectively as a means of mass communication. (National Archives)

The Nazis Take Power

The Nazis tried to lead a national uprising against the German government in 1923, but they failed and Hitler received a short prison sentence. Until the late 1920s, the Nazi party remained a minor actor on the German political scene. With the Great Depression, though, that changed. By late 1930, the Nazi party had one million members and had won election of 107 seats (about one-fifth of the total) in the *Reichstag,* the lower house of the national legislature. Support for Hitler and the Nazi party gradually increased in Germany as many unemployed came to see Nazism as the only hope for the future. In addition, young idealists thought Nazism represented a revival of the national spirit, and conservatives believed it was a bulwark against communism.

The Weimar government had never been very popular in Germany, and the Depression destroyed what little strength it still had. Both the right-wing Nazis and conservatives and the left-wing Communists opposed the democratic system; together they had enough power to prevent democratic politicians from working effectively to end the Depression. Furthermore, the president of the Weimar Republic, Paul von Hindenburg, was an aging father figure who neither understood nor cared much about democratic politics. He also disliked Hitler, though was eventually persuaded that the Nazi leader was the only acceptable alternative to political chaos. Thus, on 30 January 1933, Hindenburg appointed Hitler to the office of Chancellor. Over the next few months, Nazi intimidation and terrorist tactics destroyed all significant opposition to Hitler. When Hindenburg died in 1934, Hitler assumed leadership and was proclaimed the führer of the German Empire.

For the next few years, Hitler's dictatorship was popular among Germans. The führer was a mesmerizing speaker who appealed to the emotions of the masses. One American observer described Hitler's audience in this way:

> They were swaying back and forth, like the Holy Rollers I had once seen . . . with the same crazed expression on their faces. . . . When he appeared on the balcony for a moment, they went mad. Several women swooned.[8]

Hitler's popularity was based on more than personal magnetism, however. The Nazi regime had accomplished two major goals in Germany during the 1930s: (1) it rearmed Germany and thereby recreated a sense of German power and pride, and (2) the rearmament drive helped spur Germany's economic recovery, so that unemployment quickly disappeared.

At the same time, Germany was being nazified. German universities began to teach what they called German physics and German mathematics. Young boys had to take an oath in which Hitler was hailed as the "savior" of Germany. Women were encouraged to remain at home, since the Nazis believed that politics and business were male bastions. (Many women continued to hold jobs, however, since they composed almost one-third of the work force and could not be dispensed with.) Political opponents of the Nazis along with some Jews, gypsies, and homosexuals were sent to concentration camps. Relatively few in the camps were killed during the 1930s, so many people outside Germany believed that Nazism would eventually become less violent and more reasonable.

THE SPANISH CIVIL WAR

Authoritarian governments seemed to be springing up throughout much of Europe in the mid-1930s. Fascist Italy and Nazi Germany were the

Guernica Pablo Picasso (1881–1973) painted *Guernica* in 1937. A small town in Spain, Guernica was bombed and machine-gunned that same year by German forces supporting General Francisco Franco during the Spanish civil war (see Chapter 20). The German military claimed the attack was intended to test the effects of terror bombing. Picasso's painting expresses a sense of rage and horror at the brutality of modern war. (Museum of Modern Art)

most prominent examples, but dictators also controlled the eastern European states, except for Czechoslovakia. In Portugal, Antonio Salazar, an economics professor supported by the military, ruled the country from 1932 to 1969. Even in France, quasi-Fascist forces threatened to seize power in the mid-1930s, but the Popular Front, an alliance of democrats and communists, won the 1936 elections.

It was Spain that for a time became the focus of the conflict among democracy, fascism, and communism in the Spanish civil war. Spain had long been controlled by a conservative upper class supported by the Catholic church and the military. Many in the lower classes—urban workers and the peasantry—were impoverished and rebellious. In 1931, lower-class discontent was so great that the Spanish monarch left the country and a republican, socialist government took power. That government implemented some reforms, such as removing church control over education, redistributing land to the poorest peasants, and granting women the right to vote. But Spanish society was deeply split by enduring resentments, and in 1936 a right-wing military revolt led by General Francisco Franco broke out. For the next three years, Spain endured a civil war that quickly became an international issue. Hitler and Mussolini sent military forces to support Franco, while the Soviet Union and a few democrats from Western Europe and the United States helped the Spanish republicans. Spain thus became a battleground for all the political forces dividing Western Civilization. In the end, it was the Spanish people who suffered. By 1939, over 500,000 Spaniards had been killed, and Franco's forces had reestablished clerical-military control in Spain.

AGGRESSION, APPEASEMENT, AND WAR

Both Mussolini and Hitler began to expand their power in the mid-1930s. The Italians attacked the African nation of Ethiopia in 1935 and soon thereafter controlled it. In March 1936, the Germans reoccupied the Rhineland—a strip of German land that had been de-militarized by the Treaty of Versailles. Shortly thereafter, Germany and Italy signed the Axis alliance, and near the end of 1936 Germany and Japan, soon joined by Italy, concluded a treaty of cooperation that was reaffirmed in 1940.

Germany, Italy, and Japan saw themselves as outsider nations, trying to win empires similar to those already established by others like Great Britain. The other nations, however, tended to believe that the "outsiders" were unacceptably aggressive. By 1937, the most prominent European figure dealing with Germany and Italy was Neville Chamberlain, the new British prime minister. Chamberlain pursued a policy known as *appeasement*, which sought to lessen friction and conflict. He believed that Europe could not survive another war, so international conflicts had to be settled through diplomacy. Unfortunately for Chamberlain, he faced Hitler and Mussolini almost alone. The United States was preoccupied with the Depression and France was weakened by internal political divisions as well as the Depression. Although the Soviet Union feared Hitler, it and the Western democracies distrusted each other; furthermore, the country was caught up in the turmoil of economic change and the Great Terror.

Chamberlain's primary opponent was Hitler, for he clearly did not believe in lessening conflict. In fact, Hitler thought that conflict, although not necessarily a major war, was inevitable. And, he was determined to build a German Empire in eastern Europe.

Hitler's methods included a war of nerves. Through propaganda and bellicose speeches, he created an international crisis over a piece of land that he claimed to be rightfully German, and then threatened war if German claims were not immediately satisfied. Hitler's first goal was *Anschluss*, the incorporation of German-speaking Austria into Germany. After a brief war scare, German troops occupied Austria relatively peacefully in March 1938. The next step was the Sudetenland, that part of Czechoslovakia nearest to Germany and containing many German-speaking people. Hitler claimed it for Germany, and another international crisis developed in September 1938. The most critical point of this crisis was the Munich Conference, at which Hitler, Chamberlain, Mussolini, and Edouard Daladier of France agreed to pressure Czechoslovakia into giving up the Sudetenland. War was thereby averted, and for a short time Chamberlain could believe that he had secured peace.

Until the end of 1938, Hitler's conquests seemed semilegitimate, since the territories involved were inhabited primarily by German-speaking people. But in March 1939, Germany occupied what was left of Czechoslovakia, clearly not a German-speaking area. The national mood in Britain began to shift, as much of the populace began to realize that appeasement had failed and that Hitler had to be stopped. Chamberlain offered military aid to Poland, Hitler's next likely target. The democratic nations were stunned, however, when on 23 August 1939, Germany and the Soviet Union, who loathed each other, signed the Nazi-Soviet Pact. The Pact was a treaty of convenience through which Hitler agreed not to invade the Soviet Union if the Soviets did not interfere with Germany's dealings with Poland. A week after the Nazi-Soviet Pact was signed Hitler was threatening the Poles. When no diplomatic compromises developed, German armies invaded Poland on 1 September 1939. (As provided for in the Nazi-Soviet Pact, the Soviets invaded eastern Poland two weeks later.) Within two days of the German invasion, Britain declared war on Germany and a reluctant France soon followed. Europeans went to war, not joyfully as in 1914, but with a sense of foreboding. The English poet W. H. Auden spoke for Europeans:

> In the nightmare of the dark
> All the dogs of Europe bark
> And the living nations wait,
> Each sequestered in its hate.[9]

WORLD WAR II, 1939–1945

World War II was not one but several conflicts—Japan versus China beginning in 1937; Germany and Italy versus Britain and France beginning in 1939; Germany versus Russia beginning in June 1941; and Japan, Germany, and Italy versus the United States beginning in December 1941. By the end of 1941, the countries were grouped as follows: on one side, the United States, Britain, France, the Soviet Union, and China were known as the Allies; on the other side, Germany, Italy, and Japan were called the Axis powers. (Note that a "Free French" government, headquartered in London, continued to fight against Germany even after France itself was conquered. Also, the Soviet Union did not enter the war against Japan until the summer of 1945.)

The War in Europe, 1939–1941

Germany destroyed Poland in just over two weeks. New *blitzkrieg* ("lightning war") tactics aided the Germans. These tactics included mechanized warfare, tanks, planes, and motorized transport. For thousands of years armies had moved slowly on foot; mechanization meant

Dachau   Dachau was one of the death camps where Nazis murdered those considered "inferior" peoples, mostly Jews. When Dachau was captured at the end of World War II, American and British soldiers found rows of corpses that had not yet been burned by camp guards. (National Archives)

that World War II would be more rapid and more likely to involve civilians. A poignant moment in the German-Polish battle was the last charge of the Polish horse cavalry against German tanks. As might be expected, the old way of battle was defeated by the new.

In the meantime, French and British troops marched to the front lines in Western Europe and did nothing, a tacit acknowledgment that neither side really wanted to fight. The French took shelter behind the Maginot line, a series of fortifications along France's eastern border. Germany used the lull in fighting to its advantage by conquering Denmark and Norway in the spring of 1940. Then, on 10 May 1940, Hitler launched his great invasion in the west. Just as in 1914, German armies poured through Belgium into northern France (bypassing the Maginot line), but this time they were more successful. French armies, which had fought the Germans to a standstill in World War I, crumbled in six weeks, in part because of ineffective commanders and in part because the French people were unwilling to endure another tragedy like in 1914–1918. Northern France and the French Atlantic coastline were then placed under a German occupation government, while southeastern France remained nominally independent with a government headquartered at Vichy, France. The British withdrew to their home island. Thus, by the summer of 1940, Germany and, to a lesser extent, Italy (which had belatedly attacked France in June) were masters of much of continental Europe.

The British now faced Hitler alone. But they did have a new leader—Winston Churchill replaced Neville Chamberlain as prime minister just before the German attack on France and quickly became a symbol of strong resistance to Hitler. Churchill's own words reveal his determination: "We shall fight on the beaches, we shall fight on the landing-grounds, we shall fight in the fields and in the streets, we shall fight in the hills; we shall never surrender."[10] Churchill's determination was needed, for Germany soon began a two-pronged attack against Britain. On the sea, German submarines blockaded Britain, thereby expanding the war to the entire Atlantic Ocean. One result was growing American assistance to the British, as President Roosevelt ordered American ships to assist British convoys and also developed the Lend-Lease program to provide American ships to replace British losses. In the air, the German air force tried to bomb the British into submission, perhaps the first time in history that one nation sought to terrorize and defeat another from the skies. The Battle of Britain raged throughout the summer and fall of 1940. The British survived for several reasons—the dogged courage of their air force and navy; the recently invented radar, which allowed them to locate German bombers more easily; the German decision at one point to bomb civilian targets rather than airfields, which eased the pressure on the British air force; and Hitler's decision to transfer his forces for an attack on the Soviet Union (despite the Nazi-Soviet Pact of 1939).

Hitler disliked many different peoples, including the Soviets. He saw the Soviets as racially inferior Slavs and politically inferior Communists whose western lands he considered Germany's *lebensraum*. By 1941, Hitler's hatred of the Soviets, plus his conviction that destroying the Soviet Union would weaken British resolve, caused him to ignore the Nazi-Soviet Pact and attack the Soviet Union. German armies of over four million troops invaded the Soviet Union on 22 June 1941. Soviet forces were surprised and overwhelmed, one unit plaintively asking its headquarters: "We are being fired on. What shall we do?"[11] The German-Soviet conflict continued as German armies drove deep into Soviet territory and huge numbers of Soviets were taken as prisoners. By December 1941, the Germans were close to Moscow, but the winter cold was taking a terrible toll on the invaders (just as it had done to Napoleon's armies 129 years earlier). German soldiers reported that it was so cold that soup froze if a man paused in getting it to his mouth; they thus nicknamed their battlefield medal the "Order of Frozen Flesh."

The Pacific War, 1941–1942

By the late 1930s, Japanese leaders were planning to initiate what they called the "Greater East Asia Co-Prosperity Sphere." In theory, the

500 A TIME OF INTENSITY AND ANOTHER WORLD WAR, 1920 TO 1945

Co-Prosperity Sphere would liberate Asia from Western colonial control and create prosperity for all Asians. In reality, though, the Japanese intended to replace Western domination with their own, for they believed they were racially superior to other Asians. (Racist attitudes were not limited to the Germans or Japanese. Americans often portrayed the Japanese as subhuman, picturing them as apes or vermin in cartoons and drawings.)

By 1940, Japan controlled Korea, Manchuria, and most of the Chinese coastline. In 1941, Japanese armies moved into Indochina (the peninsula extending south of China). The United States, which wanted to keep all Asian areas open to American trade and therefore did not want any one nation to dominate Asia, believed that its national interests were being threatened by Japan. The United States responded to Japanese expansion by proclaiming an embargo on Japanese-American trade in oil and steel. Negotiations between the two nations went on for several months, but the Japanese believed that their survival required the elimination of American power in the Pacific. Hence, on 7 December 1941, Japan launched a surprise attack on the American naval base at Pearl Harbor, Hawaii. Within a few hours, the Americans suffered major losses in ships and aircraft. Over the next hundred days, Japanese armies overran Hong Kong, the Philippines, Malaya, Singapore, and the Dutch East Indies (present-day Indonesia). The Japanese were exhilarated, their soldiers singing, "I shall die only for the Emperor, I shall never look back."[12]

The Japanese attack on Pearl Harbor transformed World War II by bringing the United States into the conflict. The Americans would henceforth fight Japan as well as Germany, for Hitler declared war on the United States a few days after the Pearl Harbor attack. By late 1941, World War II was a genuine global conflict. The war was fought primarily in two areas, Europe and Asia.

The War in Europe, 1942–1945

In Nazi-dominated Europe, a Germanic "New Order" was being carried out. One Nazi goal was to Germanize eastern Europe, and so large numbers of people were forcibly relocated—native "inferior" peoples were driven from their homes and replaced by "superior" Germans who moved in. Another goal was to force subject peoples to work in German war industries; this policy was at its extreme slave labor. Still a third Nazi goal was the most brutal of all—the extermination of "inferior" peoples.

Nazi mass murders occurred in a certain sequence. Starting in September 1939 over 100,000 German invalids, the physically handicapped as well as mentally disturbed and retarded people—the so-called "useless eaters"—were killed. At the same time began the extermination of gypsies, over 500,000 of whom were destroyed during the war. In the

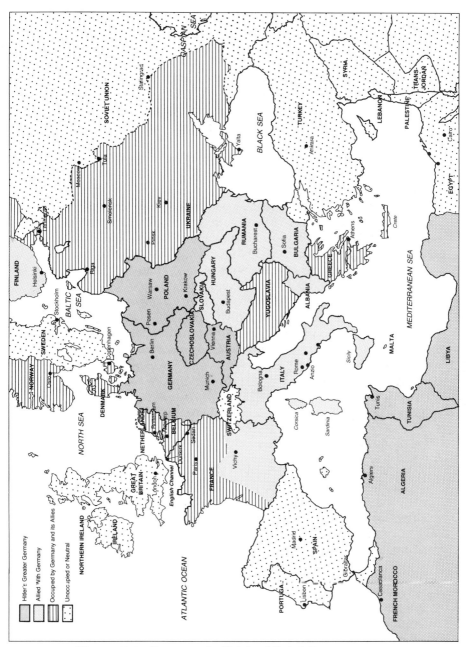

Figure 20.2 Europe at the Height of Hitler's Power, 1942

fall of 1939, the mass destruction of Polish intellectual and social leaders got underway; eventually over one million Poles were killed. Then, after the invasion of the Soviet Union, the Nazis began to kill Soviet prisoners. Several hundred thousand were executed, but over three million Soviets simply starved to death in POW (Prisoner of War) camps. The largest murder program was directed against the Jews; this was the "final solution to the Jewish problem" as the Nazis called it, or the Holocaust as the rest of the world would come to know it.

The Holocaust   The Holocaust began late in 1941, when four Nazi *Einsatzgruppen*—special murder squads that followed the invading armies—began to round up and murder the Jews of eastern Europe and the Soviet Union. In some cases, groups of Jews were sprayed with gasoline and burned alive. Most often, though, an *Einsatzgruppe* would march the Jews of a village out of town, force them to dig a mass grave, and then shoot them so that the bodies fell into the grave. The murder squads killed hundreds of thousands of Jews, but they proved to be too slow and inefficient for the Nazis and Hitler in particular. So, in 1942, "death camps"—concentration camps with gas chambers—were set up, two of the most infamous in Auschwitz and Treblinka. Jews from all over Europe were transported to the death camps. When they arrived, they were separated into two groups: those considered weak or unhealthy were sent directly to the gas chambers and those in relative good health became slave laborers for a time until they too were killed. Family members were often separated at this time and most never saw each other again. One death-camp survivor gave this account of arriving there:

> Grandfather and grandmother were thrown to the right and father and I to the left. . . . I don't think I'll ever forget their big helpless eyes. They kept turning to us with outstretched arms and their lips were moving but no words came out.[13]

At the gas chambers, men and women were separated and then forced to take off their clothes and have their heads shaved. As another survivor recounts:

> Several SS men [Nazi camp leaders] pushed the women with whips and bayonets to the building housing the chambers. . . . Those who did not want to enter were stabbed with bayonets and forced inside—there was blood everywhere. I heard the doors being locked, the moaning, shouting, and cries of despair. . . . Then came one last terrible shout . . . after which there was silence.[14]

Nearly eleven million people including six million Jews were killed by the Nazis by 1945.

Some people resisted the Nazis. The inhabitants of Jewish ghettoes sometimes fought pitched battles against Nazi forces, while some Jews within the death camps fought back or escaped to become guerilla fighters. Non-Jews also fought back. In Germany there was a small resistance movement, and Hitler was wounded in an assassination attempt in 1944. In France, the Resistance eventually became quite large. The Resistance included active measures such as publishing underground newspapers and blowing up railroad tracks as well as more passive acts like maintaining silence whenever a German was present. It also included hiding Jews from Nazis and in some cases smuggling Jewish children to relative safety in Spain.

The Resistance within Europe helped European morale but it was only through traditional military means that German nazism and Italian fascism were ultimately defeated. Germany and Italy were attacked from three directions—from the east by the Soviets, and from the south and west by the Americans and British.

The Soviet front was at once the most tragic and decisive. The turning point was the Battle of Stalingrad (November 1942–February 1943), when over half a million of Hitler's forces were killed, wounded, or captured. From there the Soviets began to push the Germans back. Their battles were, in the words of one historian, "the acme of (pre-nuclear) industrial warfare. The mechanized armies of tanks and workshops . . . churned up the countryside and at intervals blazed away at each other, leaving the land covered with warped steel, stinking oil and corpses."[15] By 1944, the Soviets began to enter and assume control of the eastern European countries, and by 1945 they were advancing into Germany itself.

The Soviets wanted their Allies to establish a major second front in Europe against Hitler, but the British and Americans could not accomplish that in 1942 or 1943. Instead, a British-American force attacked in the south, clearing North Africa of Axis forces by the spring of 1943. Then came an Allied attack on Italy, which was effectively knocked out of the war in 1943. Mussolini was forced out of office but then rescued by the Germans. He lived for two more years, only to be executed by Italian resistance fighters in April 1945. The Germans remained in control of northern Italy until the end of the war.

The major second front against Germany was established in 1944. In June of that year, Britain and the United States launched a massive seaborne invasion from Britain onto the Normandy coast (France). Once the Normandy invasion was successful, Hitler's defeat was certain. Pressed from both east and west, German armies fell back, and by 1945 Allied forces pushed into Germany. On 30 April 1945, Hitler committed suicide in Berlin. A few days later, Germany surrendered and the war in Europe came to an end.

The Pacific War, 1942–1945

In a sense, the war in Asia consisted of two theaters—a continental theater in which China and a few British forces from India fought against Japanese land armies, and a Pacific theater in which American forces fought both land and sea battles against the Japanese. But most of the fighting occurred in the Pacific.

A decisive battle in the Japanese-American conflict was the naval battle near Midway Island (June 1942) won by the Americans, who thereby blocked further Japanese expansion. Yet, Japan still occupied dozens of islands in the South Pacific. The American strategy against Japan became known as "island-hopping" because one island would be attacked and conquered, then one or two would be hopped over in favor of an attack on a fourth one. The Japanese on the hopped-over islands could then be blockaded into submission. The island battles—at places like Guadalcanal, Tarawa, Okinawa, and Iwo Jima—always started as American invasions from the sea and ended in ferocious face-to-face combat. Japanese troops usually refused to surrender, so the casualties were usually great. Atrocities such as killing the wounded or torturing prisoners occurred on both sides. Historian Guy Wint describes the island battles as "a war fought among tropical islands, with the same unreal beauty as a background, the same madness of non-surrender affecting the Japanese, the same monotony of desperate attack and desperate defence."[16]

The Japanese could not match the Americans in production of ships, aircraft, and the other requirements of war. Consequently, they were slowly pushed back, and by mid-1944 American bombers were attacking Japan. By 1945, American commanders were planning an invasion of the Japanese home islands, which was expected to produce at least one million casualties. That invasion never occurred, for American and British scientists had developed a new and more powerful weapon—the atomic bomb.

In 1942, a secret research effort called the Manhattan Project was instituted in the United States. Its goal was to discover how to use and control atomic energy so as to produce a massive explosion. The first atomic bomb was tested in July 1945. Then, on 6 August 1945, the United States dropped an atomic bomb on the Japanese city of Hiroshima, killing over 100,000 Japanese. Three days later, another bomb was dropped on Nagasaki and Japan surrendered soon thereafter. It was the end of the world war and the beginning of the nuclear age.

CONCLUSION

World War II was significant in several respects:

1. Approximately 60 million people died as a result of the war. The

Soviet Union suffered the most, with 20 million military and civilian deaths. The Nazis murdered 11 million people including nearly 6 million Jews. In Asia, the war was responsible for the deaths of 10 million Chinese, 2.5 million Japanese, and several million more in Indonesia and other countries.

2. Racism was a fundamental component of the war. The most obvious example is Hitler and the Holocaust. Another is the German-Russian conflict, which the Germans interpreted as a racial struggle. The Japanese considered other Asians to be racially inferior and often treated them brutally. American racism manifested itself in the wartime imprisonment of over 100,000 Japanese-Americans who were of Japanese descent.

3. The brutality of World War II, added to that of World War I, led to a significant change in European and American attitudes toward war. For much of Western history, war had been glorified as a noble activity wherein brave, courageous people performed heroic deeds. The industrialized warfare of the twentieth century undermined that old belief and replaced it with a general conviction that war is a horrible, frightful event that should be avoided.

4. On the political level, the two world wars hastened the decline of the traditional European powers. The United States and the Soviet Union probably would have become more powerful than the European powers anyway, but the wars speeded up the process. Furthermore, World War II left Europe divided, with Eastern Europe occupied by Russian forces and Western Europe dominated by American economic power.

5. World War II also hastened the revolt of colonial nations against Western imperialism. Even though most Asians disliked Japanese racism, they admired Japan's audacity in challenging the Western nations. The Japanese destroyed the old myths about Western superiority and shattered the colonial structure in Asia. As a result, Western political control of Asia (as well as Africa) would end in the years after the war.

THINGS YOU SHOULD KNOW

Mussolini
Fascism
Weaknesses of the liberal demo-
cratic states during the 1920s–
1930s
Origins of the automobile and the
radio
Dadaism
Surrealism
Joyce
The Great Depression
Stalin

Collectivization and industrialization
of the Soviet Union
The Great Terror
Gandhi
Jiang Jieshi (Chiang Kai-shek)
Japan in the 1920s–1930s
Hitler
Spanish civil war
Chamberlain and appeasement
Munich Conference
Nazi-Soviet Pact
World War II

blitzkrieg
Battle of Britain
Pearl Harbor
The Holocaust

Battle of Stalingrad
Island-hopping strategy
Manhattan Project and the atomic
bomb

SUGGESTED READINGS

Two good introductory surveys are published by Harper & Row in "The Rise of Modern Europe" series: Raymond J. Sontag, *A Broken World, 1919–1939* (New York: Harper & Row, 1971), and Gordon Wright, *The Ordeal of Total War: 1939–1945* (New York: Harper & Row, 1968).

On Mussolini and fascism, see Denis Mack Smith, *Mussolini* (New York: Knopf, 1982) and F. L. Carsten, *The Rise of Fascism* (Berkeley: Univ. of California Press, 1980). Two good biographies of Hitler are Alan Bullock, *Hitler: A Study in Tyranny* (New York: Harper & Row, 1971) and Joachim Fest, *Hitler* (New York: Random House, 1974). Of the many works on Nazism, one of the best is J. Bendersky, *A History of Nazi Germany* (Chicago: Nelson-Hall, 1984). A good introduction to Stalin and the necessity for modernizing the Soviet Union is Theodore H. von Laue, *Why Lenin? Why Stalin? A Reappraisal of the Russian Revolution, 1900–1930* (Philadelphia: Lippincott, 1971). On Stalin's Great Terror, see Robert Conquest, *The Great Terror: Stalin's Purge of the Thirties* (New York: Macmillan, 1968).

A good survey of World War II is Peter Calvocoressi and Guy Wint, *Total War* (New York: Penguin, 1972). Many works have been written on the Holocaust, one of the best being Martin Gilbert, *The Holocaust: A History of the Jews of Europe during the Second World War* (New York: Holt, Rinehart, & Winston, 1985). John W. Dower, *War without Mercy: Race and Power in the Pacific War* (New York: Pantheon, 1986) examines some of the underlying issues, including racism, of the war between the Americans and the Japanese.

There are many good memoirs on this period. Otto Friedrich, *Before the Deluge: A Portrait of Berlin in the 1920s* (New York: Harper & Row, 1972) gives a vivid description of life in Berlin, an exciting city in the 1920s, before the rise of Hitler. William L. Shirer, an American newspaper and radio correspondent during much of the twentieth century, captures the European atmosphere during the 1920s and 1930s in *20th Century Journey: A Memoir of a Life and the Times*, 2 vols. (Boston: Little, Brown, and Co., 1976 & 1984). And, William Manchester recounts his life as a young American marine in the Pacific war in *Goodbye Darkness: A Memoir of the Pacific War* (Boston: Little, Brown and Co. 1979).

NOTES

[1] William Butler Yeats, from "The Second Coming," lines 3–8, *The Variorum Edition of the Poems of W. B. Yeats*, ed. by Peter Allt and Russell Alspach (New York: Macmillan, 1940), p. 402.

[2] Quoted in Denis Mack Smith, *Mussolini* (New York: Knopf, 1982), pp. 30, 100.

[3] Quoted in Raymond J. Sontag, *A Broken World, 1919–1939* (New York: Harper & Row, 1971), p. 178.

[4]Otto Friedrich, *Before the Deluge: A Portrait of Berlin in the 1920's* (New York: Harper & Row, 1972), p. 127.

[5]Quoted in Robert S. McElvaine (ed.), *Down and Out in the Great Depression: Letters from the "Forgotten Man"* (Chapel Hill: Univ. of North Carolina Press, 1983), p. 159.

[6]Ibid., p. 118.

[7]The quotations in this paragraph are from Adolf Hitler, *Mein Kampf*, trans. Ralph Manheim (Boston: Houghton Mifflin, 1943 rpt. of 1927 ed.), pp. 403, 325.

[8]William L. Shirer, *20th Century Journey: A Memoir of a Life and the Times*, vol. 2, *The Nightmare Years, 1930–1940* (Boston: Little, Brown, 1984), p. 119.

[9]W. H. Auden, from "In Memory of W. B. Yeats," *The Collected Poetry of W. H. Auden* (New York: Random House, 1945), p. 51.

[10]Quoted in Peter Calvocoressi and Guy Wint, *Total War* (New York: Penguin, 1972), p. 327.

[11]Quoted in Gordon Wright, *The Ordeal of Total War: 1939–1945* (New York: Harper & Row, 1968), p. 38.

[12]Quoted in Calvocoressi and Wint, *Total War*, p. 740.

[13]Quoted in Martin Gilbert, *The Holocaust: A History of the Jews of Europe during the Second World War* (New York: Holt, Rinehart, and Winston, 1985), p. 225.

[14]Ibid., pp. 415–16.

[15]Calvocoressi and Wint, *Total War*, pp. 487–88.

[16]Ibid., pp. 775–76.

21

The

Postwar Era,

1945 to 1960

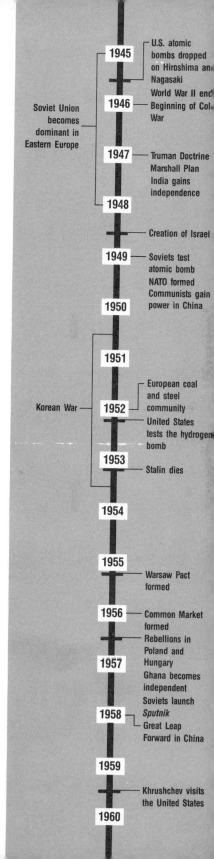

1945 — U.S. atomic bombs dropped on Hiroshima and Nagasaki

1946 — World War II ends Beginning of Cold War

Soviet Union becomes dominant in Eastern Europe

1947 — Truman Doctrine Marshall Plan India gains independence

1948

— Creation of Israel

1949 — Soviets test atomic bomb NATO formed Communists gain power in China

1950

1951

Korean War — 1952 — European coal and steel community United States tests the hydrogen bomb

1953 — Stalin dies

1954

1955 — Warsaw Pact formed

1956 — Common Market formed Rebellions in Poland and Hungary

1957 — Ghana becomes independent Soviets launch *Sputnik*

1958 — Great Leap Forward in China

1959

— Khrushchev visits the United States

1960

$\mathbf{D}$uring the postwar era 1945–1960, much of Western Civilization was trying to rebuild a stable world after the World Wars, civil wars, and revolutions of the first half of the twentieth century. But that attempt was only partially successful. A new conflict arose between the two super-powers—the United States and the Soviet Union—and a nuclear arms race accompanied it. At the same time, the political and economic recovery of Europe began and the colonized nations in the non-Western world rebelled against Western imperialism. In addition, major intellec-tual figures sought to understand and find meaning in the events of the twentieth century.

THE COLD WAR

In the years immediately following World War II, the United States and the Soviet Union engaged in a conflict known as the *Cold War*. The Cold War was not a military clash between the two superpowers; rather, it was a struggle for world power on all fronts—ideological, diplomatic, economic, and military.

The Cold War actually originated much earlier with the Bolshevik Revolution of 1917, when a Communist regime took control of Russia. The Communist revolutionaries rightly assumed that the United States and other capitalist nations would oppose them. Indeed, Americans had such fear of Communist totalitarianism that the United States refused to grant diplomatic recognition to the Soviet Union until 1933. During World War II, the United States and the Soviet Union were more concerned with Germany and Japan than with each other. So they, along with Great Britain and other nations, were allied in a common struggle against German and Japanese power. After the war ended, however, the Cold War struggle resurfaced. By 1947, the United States and the Soviet Union clearly perceived each other as enemies.

A series of events in Eastern Europe, particularly in Poland, strengthened the Cold War conflict. The Soviets were determined to control Poland. The country was to the Soviets an issue of vital national security, for in both world wars Germany had used Polish territory as an invasion route into Russian territory. Between 1944 and 1946, the Soviets gradually installed a new Communist regime in Poland as well as in other Eastern European countries. By 1947, Communist governments under Soviet domination ruled Poland, Rumania, Bulgaria, Hungary, and the Soviet zone of Germany. In 1948, as the result of a coup, Czechoslovakia also came under Communist control. Also in 1948, the Communist government in Yugoslavia, led by Josip Broz Tito, repudiated Soviet leadership. From that point on, Yugoslavia has remained Communist but independent of the Soviet bloc.

Figure 21.1   The Cold War in Europe

The Truman Doctrine

Soviet expansion in Eastern Europe was viewed as aggressive and undemocratic by the United States and Western Europe. The Soviet Union soon gained the reputation of being a hostile expansionist power. In 1946, the British wartime leader Winston Churchill declared that an "iron curtain" separated Eastern and Western Europe and proposed an Anglo-American Alliance against the Soviets. The next year, when Greece and Turkey were threatened by Communist takeover, President Harry S Truman (1884–1972) requested that the U.S. Congress grant economic aid to assist the non-Communist governments in these two countries. Congress approved the aid and thus established what became known as the *Truman Doctrine,* the practice of providing American support to foreign governments fighting communism. The Truman Doctrine marks the beginning of a new American foreign policy known as *containment;* from this point on the United States would take the lead in attempting to "contain" the expansion of communism.

The Marshall Plan

In 1947, the United States launched the *Marshall Plan,* named for Secretary of State (and former General) George C. Marshall (1880–1959). The Marshall Plan called for American aid in support of the economic recovery in Europe. The Western European nations accepted American aid, but the Soviet Union and Eastern European nations refused it. After the Soviets established a blockade in West Berlin designed to give them control of that city, the United States, Great Britain, and France organized the Berlin Airlift in 1948 to fly military and economic supplies into West Berlin (located in the middle of the Soviet-controlled part of Germany). In 1949, the United States and several other nations, mostly in Western Europe, created the North Atlantic Treaty Organization (NATO). Its purpose was the military defense of Western Europe in the event of a Soviet attack.

The Warsaw Pact

The Soviets tested their first atomic bomb in 1949. They also organized the Warsaw Pact in 1955, a military alliance between the Soviet Union and the Communist states of Eastern Europe. Thus, Europe was effectively divided into East and West—the Americans led the *Western bloc* and the Soviets dominated the *Eastern bloc.* Only a few countries—Finland, Austria, Switzerland—remained neutral. In addition, Germany was itself divided, with West Germany (the Federal Republic of Germany) allied to the United States, and East Germany (the German Democratic Republic) a part of the communist alliance. (Austria had been divided at the end of World War II but was reunified in 1955.)

Communist Victory in China and the Korean War

Two events extended the Cold War conflict to Asia: Communist victory in China in 1949, and the start of the Korean War in 1950.

The long civil war in China came to an end in 1949, as the Communist movement led by Mao Zedong won control of the country. The Communist victory frightened many Americans and Western Europeans because it strengthened the impression that communism was steadily gaining power in the world. In 1950, military conflict erupted in Korea. Pro-Soviet North Korea invaded pro-American South Korea, and the two sides fought each other for three years. American and other United Nations forces supported South Korea, and Chinese troops helped North Korea. An armistice was finally signed in 1953, and the Korean War came to an end. Yet North Korea and South Korea remained separated by essentially the same boundary that had existed in 1950. Hundreds of thousands of people—Koreans, Americans, Chinese, and others—died in the Korean War.

Mao Zedong One of the major leaders of the Communist revolution in China, Mao Zedong (1893–1976) was the primary instigator of the Great Proletarian Cultural Revolution of the late 1960s, during which millions of Chinese were killed or imprisoned. (National Archives)

Weapons and Talk

During the 1950s, the *nuclear arms race* between the United States and the Soviet Union intensified as each nation sought to be the leader in nuclear weapons development. The hydrogen bomb, which can be anywhere from twenty-five to a thousand times more destructive than the atomic bomb, was first tested by the United States in 1952 and by the Soviet Union in 1953. Then, on 4 October 1957, the Soviets launched *Sputnik*, the first space vehicle, and opened up the field of missile development. *Sputnik* was propelled into outer space by powerful rocket engines that could also be used to launch nuclear warheads. Shortly thereafter, both the Soviets and the Americans had missile-launched weapons in addition to the more cumbersome airplanes that carried atom and hydrogen bombs.

International crises and continued weapons development frightened people everywhere. Starting in the mid-1950s, following a change of leadership in both the United States and Soviet Union, the two superpowers sought ways to ease Cold War tensions. In the United States in 1953, President Harry S Truman was succeeded by the World War II hero General Dwight D. Eisenhower (1890–1969). In the Soviet Union,

Joseph Stalin died in March 1953, and Nikita Khrushchev (1894–1971) became the new Soviet leader.

Both Eisenhower and Khrushchev sought to moderate international tensions and Soviet-American relations gradually began to improve. The Geneva Conference of 1955, the first summit since World War II, accomplished little except to demonstrate that Eisenhower, Khrushchev, and other world leaders were at least willing to talk with each other. Then, in 1959, Khrushchev became the first Soviet leader ever to visit the United States. In addition to visiting Hollywood and attending a luncheon with several movie stars, Khrushchev met with Eisenhower at the presidential retreat at Camp David in Maryland. For a time the so-called "spirit of Camp David" seemed to signal a new era of Soviet-American cooperation, but that era would not effectively begin until the 1960s (as we will see in Chapter 22).

THE POLITICAL AND ECONOMIC RECOVERY OF WESTERN CIVILIZATION

The two world wars devastated many of the countries of Western Civilization, yet political and economic recovery developed fairly rapidly after 1945. In particular, the democratic, capitalist nations of Western Europe and North America began a rapid recovery, as did to a lesser extent the Soviet Union and the Communist countries of Eastern Europe.

At the end of World War II in 1945, the United States was the only major nation that was genuinely prosperous. The American industrial economy had grown so significantly during the first half of the twentieth century, that by 1945 the United States possessed roughly half of the world's total productive capacity. In that year, the average American diet included nearly 3,500 calories a day, whereas most Europeans lived on a daily intake of fewer than 1,500 calories and almost 400 million Asians faced starvation.[1] However, American economic dominance was so extreme that it could not possibly continue. Thus, over the decades after World War II, American economic power gradually declined in relation to that of other countries.

Western Europe and Japan

In Europe, the years immediately after the end of World War II were a time of great hardship. Anthony Sampson, then a British soldier, reported on what he saw in Germany in 1946:

> For the Germans that was the *schlechte Zeiten*, the terrible times, worse for many of them than the war itself. . . . There was no fuel, little work, little food; but their obsessive craving was for cigarettes.

TECHNOLOGY
The Environmental Threat

Technology has improved people's lives in many ways, such as through increased food production and advances in disease prevention. But it has also had less positive results like the destructiveness of military weapons. Yet the ultimate threat posed by technology is its harmful effects on the natural environment.

By the 1980s, three environmental problems related to technology and industry became major concerns—acid rain, depletion of the ozone layer, and global warming. Acid rain is a form of pollution that results when moisture in the air combines with chemicals emitted by factories and automobiles. It has damaged vegetation all over the world.

The ozone layer is that part of the earth's atmosphere that filters out much of the dangerous ultraviolet radiation from the sun. Researchers proved that the ozone layer is being depleted by synthetic chemicals such as chlorofluorocarbons (used as cooling agents in refrigerators and air conditioners). The depletion of the ozone layer may in the long term cause the destruction of vegetation and crops on our planet as well as increased instances of skin cancer.

A general buildup of gases in the earth's atmosphere, caused by the burning of fossil fuels, threatens to create the so-called greenhouse effect. The gases prevent heat from escaping from the atmosphere, causing the planet to warm to higher temperatures than ever before. Many scientists believe that global warming will cause sea levels to rise and coastlines to flood as glaciers melt, redefining the boundaries of land and oceans on the planet. A related factor is deforestation, occurring in many parts of the world. Trees absorb carbon dioxide, one of the gases contributing to the greenhouse effect, so the destruction of trees increases the danger.

The Earth from Outer Space *Photographs of the earth like this one heightened public awareness of our planet as the home of all humanity—a home that must be protected and preserved. That awareness helped create the environmental movement. (NASA)*

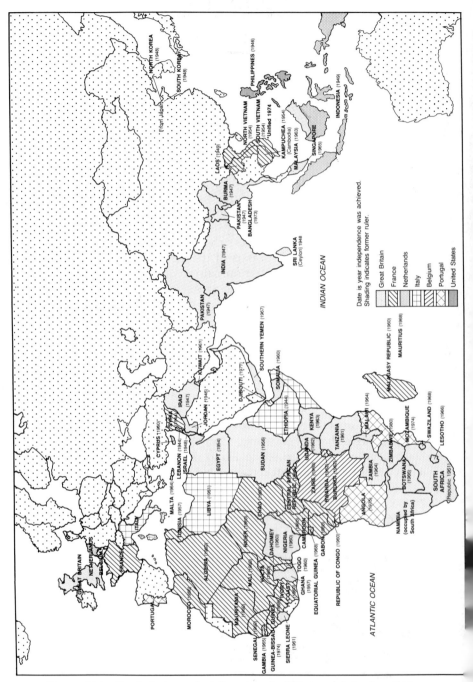

Figure 21.1 Newly Independent Countries in Africa and Asia after 1945

The country was governed by a cigarette economy, so that anything could be bought for packets of fags—cameras, food, binoculars, girls. When we drove into Hamburg it seemed not a city but a group of camps among the ruins; the rubble was flat, there was no shape. . . .[2]

Elsewhere, the situation was not much better. France and Great Britain endured food and coal shortages. Millions of refugees fled westward to escape the spreading power of the Soviet Union. And millions of prisoners were being liberated from prison camps and trying to find their homes and families.

In addition to the physical hardship, many Europeans were demoralized. Not only had they just ended three decades of war and economic depression, but they also had to confront what had happened in the Nazi death camps. It was a stunning revelation to discover what "civilized" Europeans had done to one another.

Under the circumstances, then, it was remarkable that political and economic recovery occurred as quickly as it did in Western Europe. Political renewal came first. Great Britain retained its democratic political system, and a Labour party government led by Clement Attlee enacted major social reforms between 1945 and 1951. After being occupied by the Nazis during the war, France restored a democratic polity and granted women the right to vote. West Germany, dominated by the Nazis since 1933, constructed a new democratic government under the leadership of Konrad Adenauer, who dominated German politics from 1949 to 1963. Italy, controlled by Fascist forces since 1922, also rebuilt a democratic system and extended the right to vote to women. Most of the smaller Western European nations also had democratic systems. The only significant exceptions were two dictatorships that were holdovers from the prewar period: General Francisco Franco ruled Spain, and Portugal was dominated by Antonio Salazar; both countries had remained neutral during World War II.

Closely allied to the Europeans and Americans was Japan, an enemy during World War II. During the American occupation of Japan (1945–1952), American authorities wrote a democratic constitution to govern Japan. Since 1952, the Japanese have adhered to this constitution and continue to govern themselves through the electoral process.

The European Community

Economic recovery accompanied the political renewal. One important factor in Western European recovery was the American aid channeled through the Marshall Plan. Another was the growth of international economic cooperation, the most innovative development being the evolution of the *European Community*. (The European Community was actually an umbrella organization, formed in 1967, that comprised the subsidiary organizations described in the next few paragraphs, but the entire movement for Western European cooperation is often referred to as the European Community.)

The European Community began in 1949, when the Council of Europe was founded to foster political unity among European nations. That unity has not been achieved, but the Council has served as a useful debating forum for over twenty European countries. Then, in 1952, the European Coal and Steel Community (ECSC) was created, in which six nations—France, West Germany, Italy, Belgium, the Netherlands, and Luxembourg—agreed to allow free circulation among themselves of workers, capital, and goods in the coal and steel industries. The effect was to pool the coal and steel resources of these countries.

The European Economic Community, usually referred to as the *Common Market*, was formed in 1957. The goal of the Common Market was to create one large economic market among the six nations of the ECSC by gradually eliminating all tariffs and other trade barriers. The tariffs were completely eliminated by 1968, and the result was a sustained economic boom throughout Western Europe. The Common Market was so successful that Great Britain, Denmark, and Ireland joined the organization in 1973, Greece in 1981, and Spain and Portugal in 1986.

Other steps were taken during the 1970s and 1980s. The European Parliament, a multinational legislative body elected by the citizens of European Community nations, became an advisory body for the Community. And, plans were underway to establish a completely open economic market in the European Community by 1992. The original Common Market abolished tariffs between countries, but the 1992 goal is to allow free movement of everything—capital, goods, people—across national boundaries.

The Welfare State

Another major innovation of the postwar era was the creation of the *welfare state* in most Western European and North American nations. The welfare state is a network of social reforms designed to ensure that all or at least most citizens enjoy the benefits of affluence. The essential idea is that government should provide social insurance against old age and disability, access to medical care, economic benefits for the poverty stricken, expanded educational opportunity, and greater worker participation in industry management. (The last provision was carried out only in some Western European countries.)

Creation of the welfare state began in many countries during World War II, when governments sought to control economies and ration the amount of goods available to citizens. After the war, welfare state reforms were enacted in Western Europe, North America, and Japan. In those

TABLE 21.1   PER-CAPITA INCOME, 1957 AND 1977 (IN $ U.S.)[a]

	1957	1977
France	$3,365	$7,177
West Germany	4,151	8,371
Japan	1,423	6,017
United States	5,593	8,715

[a]Data are given in 1977 U.S. dollars, adjusted to account for inflation.
Source: A. W. DePorte, *Europe between the Superpowers* (New Haven: Yale Univ. Press, 1979), p. 199.

countries, the welfare state constituted a peaceful social revolution. The democratic societies became more democratic because the lower classes enjoyed a better standard of living and greater educational opportunity. They also became more stable, because welfare state programs ameliorated political discontent by providing an economic cushion to carry people through hard times.

Economic cooperation, the welfare state, and many other measures produced sustained economic growth. Table 21.1 shows the increase in per-capita income between 1957 and 1977 in four countries. However, some people—the homeless, those without adequate job skills, and racial minorities—did not benefit from economic growth. And some entire areas—such as southern Italy, the Balkans, and the Appalachian area of the United States—remained mired in poverty. Yet the majority of people in Western Europe, North America, and Japan did prosper and benefit from such consumer items as the refrigerator, washing machine, television, automobile, and air conditioner.

The Communist World

The Communist nations of Eastern Europe were much less prosperous than Western Europe. At the end of World War II, the Soviet Union faced a mammoth job of reconstruction. Over twenty million Soviets had been killed during the war and numerous villages and industrial enterprises had been obliterated. In 1945, nearly twenty-five million Soviets were homeless. For years afterward, many Soviet families living in cities occupied a single room and shared cooking and toilet facilities with other families.

After 1945, the Soviet dictator Joseph Stalin concentrated on the economic reconstruction and redevelopment of heavy industries such as steel and iron as well as the production of armaments. Since Stalin believed that the Communist party should control every aspect of Soviet life, the nation's economic system was based on a "command economy." That is, government bureaucrats established prices and decided where and how to invest capital as well as how much of an item to produce. Monthly or yearly production quotas had to be met by all Soviet industrial enterprises and collective farms. The emphasis on heavy industry and armaments meant that production of consumer goods was de-emphasized. The Soviet Union, therefore, was a major world power whose citizens had a standard of living far lower than that of some less powerful nations.

The Soviet economic situation began to improve somewhat during the late 1950s, after Nikita Khrushchev came to power. The Soviets started to produce more consumer goods and the standard of living slowly improved. Food consumption increased, housing and food subsidies kept basic costs low for most people, and a growing number of consumers were able to purchase television sets, washing machines, and similar items. Yet, there were continuing serious problems in the Soviet economy, particularly in agricultural production.

The Eastern European nations also had mixed success in their pursuit of economic development, for they confronted at least two basic difficulties. The first was that at the end of the war most of these countries had backward peasant economies with little modern industry. The second was that the Soviet Union used the Eastern European area for its own benefit. Soviet-style command economies were imposed on each Eastern European country. Farmland was absorbed into state-owned collective farms, and trade patterns with Western Europe were broken. Furthermore, the Soviets dominated trade in Eastern Europe. By imposing low prices on Eastern European exports to the Soviet Union and high prices on Soviet exports to Eastern Europe, the Soviets in effect exacted forced contributions from Eastern Europe for Soviet reconstruction. As a result, economic development in Eastern Europe was very slow. Farmers' grievances, low industrial wages, and shortages of consumer goods—combined with resentment of the undemocratic political systems—gradually produced enormous discontent with Soviet domination. The discontent flared into open revolt with an East Berlin workers' strike in 1953 and the Polish and Hungarian rebellions of 1956. The rebellions were crushed, but afterward the economic situation slowly began to improve for many Eastern European consumers (as we will see in Chapter 22 in a discussion of the Communist world).

THE NON-WESTERN WORLD AND THE END OF EUROPEAN EMPIRES

The empires that the Europeans had built from the sixteenth to the nineteenth centuries began to disappear after 1945. A wave of decolonization swept the globe, and most former colonies gained their independence and became sovereign nations. The extent of the decolonization movement is demonstrated by the changes in the United Nations (UN) membership rolls. When the UN was founded in 1945 by the World War II victors, it had 51 members. As new nations became independent and joined the UN, the membership count rose to over 150.

To some degree, the Europeans inadvertently helped produce the decolonization movement. When they conquered and ruled colonies in earlier centuries, they often destroyed the existing traditional ways of life, and as a result the traditional rulers (such as Indian sultans or African tribal chiefs) began to lose their power. In their place came a new generation of leaders like Mohandas Gandhi in India and Kwame Nkrumah in Ghana, who were often Western educated and sufficiently aggressive to challenge the power of the colonial rulers. This new generation of leaders was able to appeal to people and lead national independence movements.

The two world wars also helped further the decolonization movement. The wars so weakened European nations that afterward most Europeans were unwilling to pay the taxes to maintain the military forces necessary to continue the colonial empires.

Asia

One of the first successful revolts against colonial rule occurred in India. The Indian National Congress, led by Mohandas Gandhi, had begun a campaign of nonviolent resistance against British colonialism during the 1920s and 1930s, and that campaign continued after World War II. The result was that Britain granted independence to India in 1947. But the Indian subcontinent immediately split into two parts, because of religious differences between Hindus and Muslims. India became a predominantly Hindu country, while Muslims formed the separate nation of Pakistan. (In 1948, Gandhi was assassinated by a Hindu fanatic who believed that Gandhi was too conciliatory toward Muslims.)

Other Asian states also won independence soon after World War II. The United States granted full sovereignty to the Philippines in 1946. In 1948, Burma and Ceylon (later named Sri Lanka) left the British Empire. The British granted independence to the Malaysian Federation in 1957. Indonesia won its freedom in 1949, after a brutal war against the Netherlands. And, four areas of Indochina—Laos, Cambodia, North Vietnam, and South Vietnam—became independent in 1954, after the French were driven out of the Indo-Chinese peninsula. (American involvement in Vietnam is discussed in Chapter 22.)

China

The most dramatic story of decolonization in Asia was that of the revolution in China. After the Communists won power in China in 1949, they faced many fundamental problems. One of the most important problems was achieving economic development in a chronically poor country. By the mid-1950s, a major policy dispute arose between two groups of Chinese leaders over how to achieve economic development. One group, led by Liu Shaoqi, wanted to emphasize urban industrialization and technological development. The other, dominated by Mao Zedong, preferred rural industrialization and agricultural development, based on the theory that peasants are the natural carriers of revolution. The two groups have alternated in determining policy in China since the 1950s. At first, urban industrialization was favored. Then, in 1958, Mao and his group announced the "Great Leap Forward" program, designed to produce rural industrialization and the organization of the Chinese population into communes. (The communes, where people worked collectively and owned little private property, usually contained about 30,000 people.)

When the Great Leap program was less successful than originally hoped, China returned in 1960–1965 to the urban industrialization model of Liu Shaoqi. In the late 1960s, though, Mao regained control and launched the Great Proletarian Cultural Revolution. The revolution was cultural in the sense that it attempted to transform Chinese civilization and to perpetuate revolutionary change. Rural industry was again encouraged, medical and educational facilities were built in rural areas, universities were sometimes closed, and students were sent to the countryside to be "re-educated" by working in the fields. Those who opposed the revolution were persecuted and many others died in street fighting or in labor camps. One estimate is that over one million Chinese perished as a result of the revolution. Mao and his policies dominated China until his death in 1976. After that, China became more tranquil for a time, as Deng Xiaoping revived the urban, industrial approach to modernization. (The events of the 1980s in China are discussed in Chapter 22.)

The Islamic World

The Islamic world also experienced an anticolonial movement after World War II. Lebanon and Syria became independent in 1944, Transjordan (later named Jordan) in 1946, and foreign troops left the nominally sovereign countries of Iraq and Iran in 1946. Egypt did not regain its independence completely until 1956, when the Egyptian leader Gamal Abdel Nasser asserted Egyptian control over the Suez Canal. In North Africa, independence came to Libya in 1951 and to Tunisia and Morocco in 1956. Algeria had to fight a long war to gain its freedom from France in 1962.

Several major issues have dominated the Islamic world since World War II;

1. The need for economic development in Islamic countries with large numbers of poverty-stricken people is an ongoing concern.

2. Some Islamic nations have vast reserves of oil and helped form the Organization of Petroleum Exporting Countries (OPEC) in an attempt to control world oil production and oil prices. The oil embargo of 1973, which hurt the economies of many nations, was a product of OPEC actions.
3. Some countries have embraced Islamic fundamentalism, which stresses strict adherence to the Koran and bitter resistance to Western culture. Fundamentalism was strongest in Libya after Mu'ammar Gaddafi came to power in 1969, and in Iran after the Ayatollah Khomeini became dominant in 1979. Even after Khomeini died in June 1989, fundamentalists still controlled Iran.
4. The warfare between Arabs and Israelis for control of the area traditionally known as Palestine is an ongoing struggle in the Islamic world. In the first half of the twentieth century, many Jews came to Palestine from Europe to escape persecution. In 1948, these Jewish immigrants proclaimed the independent Jewish state of Israel. Many Arabs resented what they considered to be the seizure of Arab land by the Jewish immigrants. Israel and neighboring Arab countries have fought five wars in recent decades—in 1948, 1956, 1967, 1973, and 1982. In the 1967 war, Israel conquered more territory from the Arabs, and the question of who should have ultimate control of that territory became a source of bitter dispute between the two sides. The 1982 war consisted of an Israeli invasion of Lebanon, which helped exacerbate a civil war that was being fought between Muslims and Lebanese Christians. Arab resistance movements, most notably the Palestine Liberation Organization (PLO), continue to oppose the Israelis, and the entire area remains in turmoil. Lebanon in particular continues to endure chronic violence.

Sub-Saharan Africa

Independence movements developed more slowly in sub-Saharan Africa than in Asia or the Islamic world, in part because relatively few Africans were well-educated or politically experienced. The first nation in the region to receive independence was Ghana (1957), led by Kwame Nkrumah. After that, new sovereign nations appeared almost every year—first Nigeria and the Belgian Congo, then Tanganyika, and then Kenya after a long colonial rebellion against the British. Numerous others became independent during the 1960s and 1970s, so that the old colonial empires gradually disappeared from the African continent. Table 21.2 lists some of the larger African states that gained their independence between 1957 and 1980.

Several problems continue to plague sub-Saharan Africa. One is South Africa, where black resistance forces oppose the apartheid policies of the white-dominated government. In 1989–1990, the South African government began to demonstrate some willingness to compromise and to consider negotiating with blacks in an attempt to end the long

TABLE 21.2 SUB-SAHARAN AFRICAN STATES IN ORDER OF INDEPENDENCE,
1957–1980

State Name	Colonial Ruler	Colonial Name	Date of Independence
Ghana	Britain	Gold Coast	1957
Guinea	France		1958
Cameroon	France	French Cameroun	1960
Central African Republic	France	French Equatorial Africa	1960
Chad	France	French Equatorial Africa	1960
Ivory Coast	France		1960
Malagasay	France	Madagascar	1960
Nigeria	Britain		1960
Senegal	France		1960
Zaire	Belgium	Belgian Congo	1960
Tanzania	Britain	Tanganyika and Zanzibar	1961
Uganda	Britain		1962
Kenya	Britain		1963
Zambia	Britain	Northern Rhodesia	1964
Angola	Portugal		1975
Mozambique	Portugal		1975
Zimbabwe	Britain	Southern Rhodesia	1980

black-white struggle. In that connection, the government released from prison several prominent black leaders, most notably Nelson Mandela. (See Chapter 18 for the background of the South African situation.) Another problem is the political turmoil that afflicts many of the newly independent African states. The boundaries of these states were established in the nineteenth century by the colonial powers, who often combined into single political entities groups that were accustomed to competing with or even fighting each other. In some cases, these groups continue to fight each other today, thus causing chronic political turmoil. Consequently, the army is often the only force that can maintain stability in some African states.

The most desperate difficulty, though, is the poverty of sub-Saharan Africa. In the 1980s, twenty-nine of the world's thirty-four poorest countries were African. The fundamental problem was that population grew faster than food production for several reasons:

1. Birth rates were higher than death rates because advances in modern medicine made it possible to treat some tropical diseases.
2. Droughts in the Sahel region and in east Africa slowed food production.

Apartheid This sign from a public park in South Africa illustrates some of the characteristics of *apartheid*, or "racial separation." Note that only so-called white "citizens" are permitted free use of the park, while black "natives" are not allowed to enter the park unless they are servants of whites. (United Nations)

3. Low food prices were paid to farmers, a result of government policies designed to provide cheap food for urban populations.

Latin America

Decolonization was not an issue for Latin American nations because they had gained their independence in the nineteenth century. Rather, the major issues in Latin America were, and still are, economic, social, and political. Population growth outpaced food production throughout the twentieth century because birth rates were higher than death rates, and the result was poverty for many Latin Americans. The population problem was exacerbated by the sharp class divisions, which allowed only the most fortunate to prosper and forced the majority of Latin Americans to remain poor.

Reactions to the economic problems have taken several forms. Many Latin American nations governed by military forces installed authoritarian-style governments to prevent social unrest in the poor classes (examples include Brazil during the 1960s and 1970s and Chile after 1973 through the 1980s). Some Latin American countries—Venezuela, Costa Rica, and Argentina after 1983—managed to develop civilian-managed governments that were democratic. A few Latin American nations turned to Marxist revolution. Under the leadership of Fidel Castro, Cuba became a Communist-dominated nation after 1959. In Nicaragua in the 1980s, the Sandinista revolutionaries established a vaguely Marxist regime, but in 1990 had to relinquish power to an elected non-Marxist government. And in the late 1980s, Marxist groups tried to gain control of El Salvador.

AN INTELLECTUAL DEBATE OVER MEANING

Human beings have always sought to understand the meaning of things—life, history, nature, the world. But questions about meaning became particularly significant during the period 1945–1960. Looking back at a half-century of war, upheaval, and mass murder, intellectuals tried to understand and find meaning in these events of their time. Some concluded that Western history and even human life are without meaning or purpose. Others found meaning in religious faith.

Several aspects of twentieth-century life led many writers and artists to view the world as without meaning:

1. The political events of the twentieth century—the wars, the concentration camps, the nuclear arms race—proved to some that people are basically irrational and inhumane.
2. Industrial civilization was viewed as a dehumanizing force because most large-scale organizations—governments, businesses, educational institutions—cause people to feel insignificant.
3. Many modern people have lost faith in God and live in a spiritual vacuum.

The French existentialist and philosopher Jean-Paul Sartre (1905–1980) argued that the world is without meaning. According to Sartre, human existence is absurd because people constantly search for a purpose to their existence but discover instead that only a silent universe, without God and without meaning, exists.

Albert Camus (1913–1960), a French essayist and novelist, also expressed the concept of the absurd. Sometimes called the "conscience of his generation," Camus was read by many in the United States and elsewhere during the 1950s and 1960s. His novel *The Plague* (1947) is one of the best explications of the absurdist view of the universe. On one level, the novel tells the story of a plague that besieges a city and kills innocent people. On another level, the plague is a symbol of the disease of war and totalitarianism that infected Europe in the 1930s and 1940s. It is also a symbol of an absurd universe in which innocent people are victims.

The twentieth-century idea of a meaningless universe was also portrayed by filmmakers. In *La Dolce Vita* (1960), the Italian filmmaker Federico Fellini (1920–) presents the "sweet life" of the leisure class in contemporary Rome. The film is about lonely, estranged people seeking excitement in an endless succession of wild parties, nightclubs, and orgies. Fellini said that he wanted the film to show modern people living "alongside each other without being aware of their solitude."[3]

Some Christian theologians responded to claims about the meaninglessness of the world by reinterpreting Christianity in light of twentieth-century events. Most prominent among the Protestant thinkers was the Swiss theologian Karl Barth (1886–1968). According to Barthian crisis theology, the evils of the twentieth century were caused by the sinfulness of people and their separation from God. Barth reaffirmed traditional Christian ideas by contending that people can only overcome sin through God's grace and his gift of eternal salvation.

One of the leading Catholic theologians was the French philosopher Jacques Maritain (1882–1973). Maritain argued that modern societies suffer from a cultural disease that he termed *anthropocentric humanism,* a kind of human egotism that falsely leads people to believe that they can live without God. Maritain called for a new Christian humanism based on the teachings of the great medieval theologian St. Thomas Aquinas. Christian humanism could inspire, Maritain argued, a new democratic political and social order based on principles of justice and Christian brotherhood.

Still another prominent Christian writer was the German novelist Heinrich Böll (1917–1985). In *The Train Was on Time* (1949), *Billiards at Half Past Nine* (1959), and other works, Böll emphasizes the healing power of Christian love in the modern world. His works are particularly critical of the mindless hedonism and overindulgent materialism of postwar Western societies.

CONCLUSION

During the postwar era 1945–1960, much of the world was recovering—politically, economically, and spiritually—from World War II. The superpower conflict between the United States and the Soviet Union dominated world politics. The United States and its allies in Western Europe (and Japan) were politically stable and increasingly prosperous economically. The Soviet Union and its Eastern European allies were less prosperous. Many non-Western nations attained national independence, as most of the European colonial empires disappeared. Intellectuals debated the meaning of life in the wake of the horrors of the first half of the twentieth century. The period after the early 1960s, however, would be dominated by different issues and problems.

THINGS YOU SHOULD KNOW

Cold War   Truman Doctrine
Bolsheviks   Marshall Plan
Soviet takeover of Eastern Europe   Warsaw Pact
  after World War II   Korean War

Nuclear weapons and missile development
Sputnik
The European Community
European Coal and Steel Community (ECSC)
Common Market
The welfare state
Soviet "command economy"
Eastern Europe after World War II
Khrushchev
Independence of India
Great Leap Forward program in China

Great Proletarian Cultural Revolution in China
Arab-Israeli conflict
Problems confronting sub-Saharan Africa
Political structures in Latin America
Sartre
Camus
Fellini
Barth
Maritain
Böll

SUGGESTED READINGS

Two good surveys of the Cold War are John Lukacs, *A New History of the Cold War*, 3rd ed. (Garden City, N.Y.: Doubleday, 1966), and Bernard A. Weisberger, *Cold War, Cold Peace: The United States and Russia since 1945* (New York: American Heritage, 1984). On the nuclear arms race, see Michael Mandelbaum, *The Nuclear Question: The United States and Nuclear Weapons, 1946–1976* (Cambridge, Eng.: Cambridge Univ. Press, 1979).

A good history of the United States is William E. Leuchtenburg, *A Troubled Feast: American Society since 1945* (Boston: Little, Brown, 1983). *Europe: Dream, Adventure, Reality*, ed. by Hendrik Brugmans (Westport, Conn.: Greenwood, 1987) provides a good introduction to the European Community. Hedrick Smith, *The Russians* (New York: Quadrangle, 1976) offers an interesting journalistic account of life in the contemporary Soviet Union.

Rupert Emerson, *From Empire to Nation: The Rise to Self-Assertion of Asian and African Peoples* (Cambridge, Mass.: Harvard Univ. Press, 1962) surveys the movement for national independence among Asian and African peoples. More specific works on the movement include Lowell Dittmer, *China's Continuous Revolution: The Postliberation Epoch, 1949–1981* (Berkeley: Univ. of California Press, 1987); Basil Davidson, *Let Freedom Come: Africa in Modern History* (Boston: Little, Brown, 1978); and John Obert Voll, *Islam: Continuity and Change in the Modern World* (Boulder, Co.: Westview, 1982). For intellectual history, see Warren Wagar (ed.), *European Intellectual History since Darwin and Marx* (New York: Harper & Row, 1966).

NOTES

[1]Godfrey Hodgson, *America in Our Time* (Garden City, N.Y.: Doubleday, 1976), p. 19.

[2]Anthony Sampson, *Anatomy of Europe* (New York: Harper & Row, 1968), p. vii.

[3]Federico Fellini, quoted in Georges Sadoul, *Dictionary of Film Makers*, trans. and ed. Peter Morris (Berkeley: Univ. of California Press, 1972), p. 81.

22

The Contemporary World, 1960 to the Present

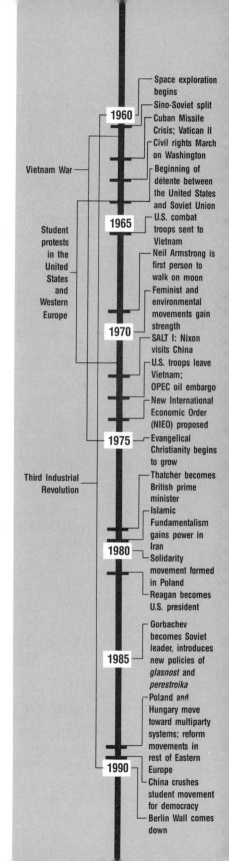

Vietnam War

Student protests in the United States and Western Europe

Third Industrial Revolution

1960 — Space exploration begins
— Sino-Soviet split
— Cuban Missile Crisis; Vatican II
— Civil rights March on Washington
— Beginning of détente between the United States and Soviet Union

1965 — U.S. combat troops sent to Vietnam
— Neil Armstrong is first person to walk on moon
— Feminist and environmental movements gain strength

1970 — SALT I: Nixon visits China
— U.S. troops leave Vietnam; OPEC oil embargo
— New International Economic Order (NIEO) proposed

1975 — Evangelical Christianity begins to grow
— Thatcher becomes British prime minister
— Islamic Fundamentalism gains power in Iran

1980 — Solidarity movement formed in Poland
— Reagan becomes U.S. president

1985 — Gorbachev becomes Soviet leader, introduces new policies of *glasnost* and *perestroika*
— Poland and Hungary move toward multiparty systems; reform movements in rest of Eastern Europe

1990 — China crushes student movement for democracy
— Berlin Wall comes down

Contemporary history is characterized by a tremendous variety of events occurring throughout the world. Most events of the 1960s to the present time have been directly or indirectly related to six major trends:

1. A gradual moderation of tensions in the Cold War superpower conflict.
2. Social upheaval in many Western nations during the 1960s and continued prosperity of the West.
3. Developments in the Communist world, including the Vietnam War and the upheavals of the late 1980s and early 1990s.
4. A quest for economic development by Third World nations.
5. A resurgence of religious beliefs in many parts of the world, alongside continued faith in the secular doctrine of progress.
6. The Third Industrial Revolution.

MODERATION OF THE SUPERPOWER CONFLICT

During the late 1960s and early 1970s, the French word *détente,* meaning "relaxation of tensions," was commonly used to describe a new era in Soviet-American relations. Détente occurred as world events encouraged the two superpowers to try to control the nuclear arms race and to resolve some of the conflicts of the Cold War.

Sino-Soviet Split

One important event was the Sino-Soviet split of the early 1960s. The Chinese and Soviet Communist governments had been allies since 1949, but that relationship had changed by 1960 for several reasons. One reason was a dispute over land located along the 4,500-mile Soviet-Chinese border. Another was competition between China and the Soviet Union as both sought to lead the world Communist movement. In addition, the Soviets feared that the Chinese would develop nuclear weapons. Thus, by the early 1960s, the two former allies were no longer friendly. And, since the Soviets saw China as a major threat to their national security, they became more willing to improve relations with the United States. In this way, the Soviet Union could avoid confronting two powerful enemies—the United States and China—at the same time.

Cuban Missile Crisis

The Cuban Missile Crisis of October 1962 encouraged Soviet-American cooperation. After Fidel Castro came to power in 1959, Cuba became a Communist nation allied to the Soviet Union. In 1962, American intelligence reports revealed that the Soviets were installing nuclear missile sites in Cuba. Seen as a direct threat to the United States,

President John F. Kennedy demanded that the missiles be removed and established a naval blockade around Cuba to prevent delivery of additional missiles or warheads by the Soviets. During the next few days, many people worried that a nuclear confrontation might result. But President Kennedy and Soviet Premier Nikita Khrushchev were able to defuse the issue. Eventually, the missiles were removed. The missile crisis thus encouraged cooperation between the superpowers. (Khrushchev did not have the opportunity to engage in further cooperation with the United States, for in 1964 he lost power in the Soviet Union and Leonid Brezhnev (1906–1982) became the dominant figure in Soviet government.)

The Vietnam War

American involvement in the Vietnam War also influenced relations between the United States and Communist nations. The Indo-Chinese peninsula—which includes Laos, Cambodia, and Vietnam—had been colonized by France from the nineteenth century until 1954, when the French were finally driven out by revolutionary forces. At that point, Laos, Cambodia, Communist North Vietnam, and pro-American South Vietnam became independent countries. South Vietnam refused to hold elections intended to unify Vietnam, so by the late 1950s North Vietnamese began to use guerilla warfare tactics against South Vietnamese in an attempt to unify a Communist Vietnam by force.

The United States, fearing a Communist victory, began to support South Vietnam, and in 1965 the first American combat troops went to Vietnam. The American government believed the North Vietnamese could be defeated quickly, but the fighting turned into a war of attrition, with each side trying to wear down the other and neither side able to win a decisive victory. American involvement in Vietnam gradually became very unpopular in the United States, and protest demonstrations erupted on many college campuses. Furthermore, the morale of American troops in Vietnam began to decline, since to many of them the conflict came to seem pointless and unwinnable. By the early 1970s, the United States wanted to withdraw from Vietnam but it needed the help of the Soviets and Chinese to get the North Vietnamese to agree to a negotiated settlement. American withdrawal finally came in 1973–1975, after the United States lost over 58,000 soldiers in the war. North Vietnam took over the South and a unified Vietnam came under Communist control. In the process, the Americans had to seek and gain improved relations with the major Communist nations.

Agreements between the Superpowers

Détente was above all else an attempt by the two superpowers to control the nuclear arms race. In 1972, the Strategic Arms Limitations Talks

The Vietnam War started as a conflict between Communist North Vietnam and pro-Democratic South Vietnam. Fearing a Communist victory, the United States entered the war in 1965. The war continued for nearly another decade, creating great social unrest in America and causing the loss of more than 58,000 American soldiers. (Dept. of Defense)

agreement—SALT I—was signed, in which the Soviet Union and United States agreed to freeze production of offensive strategic weapons (long-range nuclear weapons) for five years so as to slow down the nuclear arms race. The agreement also limited the development of antiballistic missiles (ABMs), which can in theory protect a nation from nuclear attack by destroying a weapon before it reaches its destination on land.

Other agreements intended to further détente followed. Although continued arms-control negotiations led to a SALT II agreement, it was not ratified by the U.S. Senate and never officially went into effect. A Conference on Security and Cooperation in Europe was held in 1975 in Helsinki, Finland. Agreements made at the Helsinki Conference helped stabilize Europe by demonstrating American acceptance of Soviet domination over Eastern Europe and by encouraging economic trade between Eastern and Western Europe.

Also important to détente was the development of improved diplomatic relations between the United States and China. When China came under Communist control in 1949, the United States refused to recognize it diplomatically. The U.S. government also refused to cooperate with the Chinese Communist regime on the basis that it was totalitarian and unjust. By the 1970s, however, a desire for more amicable relations by both nations had weakened the American and Chinese hostility toward each other. Then, in 1972, U.S. President Richard M. Nixon (1913–) made a historic visit to China that led to a growing cooperation among the two nations. By 1979, the United States and China had established normal diplomatic relations and thus moderated one of the major sources of political tension in the world.

New Problems and Opportunities

The era of détente ended during the late 1970s. The Soviets viewed the American rejection of SALT II as an undermining of the arms-control negotiations. Americans came to fear Soviet expansion in Africa (Ethiopia and Angola), Central America (Nicaragua), and Afghanistan. In 1979, Soviet troops were sent to Afghanistan to aid a Communist government there, but they were opposed by Afghan nationalists. After a long conflict, the Soviets withdrew their forces in 1988–1989.

Suspicion and distrust between the two superpowers increased during the early 1980s. In 1981, Ronald Reagan (1911–), a vociferous critic of Soviet communism, became president of the United States. The Reagan administration proposed the development of a Strategic Defense Initiative (SDI). Similar to the ABM idea, SDI was a defensive system intended to protect the United States from nuclear attack. Although the SDI proposal was hindered by insufficient technology and scientists' claims that a useful SDI system was impossible to create, the possibility of a new American weapon frightened the Soviets.

The Soviet Union also came under more aggressive leadership. Soon after Mikhail Gorbachev (1931–) became the Soviet leader in 1985, it became clear that he would be a dynamic new force within Soviet ruling circles. Gorbachev proposed major economic reforms inside the Soviet Union and also sought international cooperation. Although at first Americans feared Gorbachev's rejuvenation of the Soviet Union, he came to represent American-Soviet cooperation.

In the late 1980s, Reagan and Gorbachev began to renew efforts at superpower cooperation. In December 1987, the INF Treaty (Intermediate-Range Nuclear Forces) was signed by which the United States and Soviet Union agreed to dismantle all short- and medium-range missiles, most of which were deployed in Europe. Reagan and Gorbachev also tried to invigorate the ongoing negotiations for reducing the number of strategic missiles in their nuclear arsenals. A summit conference held at Malta late in 1989 and another at Washington, D.C. in 1990 indicated that Gorbachev and George Bush (who became U.S. president in 1989) would continue to encourage superpower cooperation.

A major problem in the 1990s is that weapons of all types—conventional, nuclear, chemical—are proliferating in many parts of the

Gorbachev and Bush   Soviet reform leader *(left)* Mikhail Gorbachev (1931–   ),
shown here with George Bush (1924–   ), who became president of the United States
in 1989. The two have met several times, notably at a Washington, D.C., summit conference in 1990. Gorbachev's policies of *glasnost* and *perestroika* have resulted in
major political and economic changes in the Soviet Union, the withdrawal of Soviet
military forces from Afghanistan, and the end of Communist domination of most
East European countries. (AP/Wide World Photos)

world. As the superpowers continue to expand their arsenals despite the
various treaties they signed, other nations (India, for example) are also
developing their own nuclear weapons. In addition, growing concern
exists over the possibility of nongovernmental forces, especially terror-
ists, acquiring small nuclear weapons. During the 1970s and 1980s, the
world had already witnessed several different types of terrorism, examples including the kidnapping of Americans and Europeans by Muslim
extremists in Lebanon, the hijacking of airplanes during which innocent
people were killed, and the torture of civilians by a communist guerilla
movement in Peru.

THE SOCIAL UPHEAVALS OF THE 1960s
AND CONTINUED PROSPERITY

During the 1960s and early 1970s, the democratic, prosperous nations of
North America and Western Europe experienced an extraordinary variety
of social upheavals. Millions of ordinary people participated in move-

ments that protested against what they considered to be the injustices and stupidities of arrogant governments.

The U.S. Civil Rights Movement

The civil rights movement in the United States sought to end a long history of racial discrimination against black Americans. In 1954, the U.S. Supreme Court declared racial segregation in public schools illegal. There followed an outburst of citizen activism—boycotts of segregated transportation facilities, "sit-ins" in segregated restaurants—designed to dramatize the injustice of racial segregation in the southern United States.

In 1963, the March on Washington led by the Reverend Dr. Martin Luther King, Jr. was a particularly dramatic event during which King and other civil rights activists demanded racial equality. Gradually, the U.S. government responded to the movement by enacting civil rights legislation. In 1964, racial discrimination in employment and public facilities was prohibited; in 1965, blacks in the South were guaranteed the right to vote; and in 1968, housing discrimination was outlawed.

The focus of the civil rights struggle then shifted to the northern United States, where many urban blacks lived in poverty-stricken ghettoes and endured chronic unemployment. A series of urban riots in the late 1960s dramatized the plight of these urban blacks but also frightened many whites. By the 1970s and 1980s, the civil rights struggle was more muted. The movement had succeeded in abolishing legalized racial discrimination and in creating some employment and educational opportunities, particularly for middle-class blacks. However, many other blacks remained poor and outside the mainstream of American life. Furthermore, many whites objected to "affirmative action" plans which appeared to them to give preference to blacks seeking, for example, certain types of employment.

Student Protests

The civil rights movement helped inspire the student rebellions of the 1960s. The student protests took two forms: one was a political revolt against large bureaucracies like universities and governments, and the other was a cultural protest against the materialism and consumerism thought to dominate Western Civilization.

In the United States, the political protests were usually directed against organizations that supported the Vietnam War. In some instances, universities that were thought to be engaged in war-related research were forced to close briefly because of student riots and demonstrations. In Western Europe, the political protests targeted large, overcrowded universities that seemed to have little personal concern for

Martin Luther King, Jr., and Malcolm X   These two civil rights leaders from the 1960s
advocated different approaches to the same problem. Dr. King (1929–1968) preached
nonviolence in his struggle to gain equal rights for blacks in America. Malcolm X
(1925–1965) took a less optimistic approach; he condoned the use of force by blacks
who were struggling for freedoms they rightfully deserved. Both men were assassinated; Dr. King in 1968 in Memphis, Tennessee, and Malcolm X in 1965 in Harlem,
New York City. (AP/Wide World Photos)

students. Many of the student protests of the 1960s were disorganized,
chaotic affairs. However, they did express the sense of outrage felt by
many ordinary people and had at least some influence in forcing the
United States to withdraw from the Vietnam War.

The cultural protests were led by young people called "hippies" who resented middle-class materialism and consumerism. In some cases, hippies in the United States and Western Europe withdrew from ordinary society to live in communes, where they experimented with drugs, wore clothes made of natural fibers, and celebrated the values of love, beauty, and peace.

The Feminist Movement

One of the most significant causes to emerge in the late 1960s and early 1970s was the feminist movement. As increasing numbers of women had to enter the work force to support their families, the political and economic strength of women grew. The feminist movement advocated reforms that would grant women equal pay for equal work, and legislation to that effect was approved in Great Britain and West Germany.

The most vigorous feminist movement has been in the United States. There Betty Friedan wrote the influential book *The Feminine Mystique* (1963), in which she argues that American society forced women into the predetermined roles of wife and mother by discouraging them from seeking other roles available in the job market. Friedan and others founded the National Organization for Women (NOW) in 1966 to advance the feminist cause.

The feminist movement helped encourage some significant changes during the 1970s and 1980s. In the United States, a growing number of women entered professions, such as law and business, that had previously employed few women in influential positions. In Sweden, a national daycare program provided facilities to care for small children during the day, so their mothers could pursue careers. However, the lives of many women did not change that much. Most women continued to fulfill subordinate roles within their families, and many of those who sought employment were often paid less than men in comparable positions.

One feminist issue, the liberalization of abortion laws, has been surrounded by controversy. Many people—probably a majority in most Western countries—believe that abortion is a matter of choice for the woman involved, while many others strongly feel that abortion is little different from murder.

The Environmental Movement

The environmental movement arose as the general public gradually became aware of the harmful effects of environmental pollution. In Europe, the Mediterranean Sea was shown to be dangerously polluted, and many ancient monuments of Western Civilization—the Parthenon and some Gothic cathedrals—began to crumble because of the vibrations and exhaust fumes of automobile traffic. In the United States, a form of air pollution from automobile exhausts known as smog blanketed some American cities.

By the late 1960s, movements protesting air, ground, and water pollution began to emerge in many countries. Governmental agencies designed to help protect the environment were established in the United States, Canada, and most Western European countries during the early 1970s. A conference in Stockholm in 1972 led to the United Nations Environment Program, which deals with environmental issues internationally.

During the 1980s, a number of developments increased public concern about the environment. For example, the 1986 accident at the Chernobyl nuclear plant in the Soviet Union killed a number of people and reminded people everywhere of the dangers of nuclear radiation. Several oil spills, in which wrecked or disabled oil tankers released large quantities of oil into the oceans, resulted in the destruction of much marine life and the pollution of ocean waters and shorelines. These and many other factors encouraged large numbers of people to be increasingly aware of the fragility of the natural environment. To what degree that awareness would be translated into active measures to protect the environment would be one of the major international issues of the 1990s.

Economic Developments

In the 1970s, and 1980s, economic issues preoccupied most governments and people in North America and Western Europe.

During the 1970s, a prolonged economic recession characterized by high inflation, high unemployment, and a slump in productivity plagued many nations. One cause was the oil embargo of 1973, when OPEC (the Organization of Petroleum Exporting Countries) drastically raised oil prices. The OPEC action followed the 1973 war between Arabs and Israelis. The Arabs used the oil embargo to pressure the United States to force concessions from the Israelis.

Economic recovery set in by the early 1980s, but the problems of the 1970s had already produced significant political changes. In some countries, the economic problems helped produce a trend toward conservative government. For example, in Great Britain, Margaret Thatcher became prime minister in 1979 and retained that office through the 1980s. In the United States, Ronald Reagan became president in 1981 and won reelection in 1984. In other areas the economic difficulties led to Socialist-oriented governments, as in France, where François Mitterrand was elected to the presidency in 1981 and reelected in 1988. Less clearly related to the 1970s recession were the new democratic governments in Portugal and Spain in which Socialist parties were influential. The Portuguese and Spanish movements toward democracy came after

TECHNOLOGY
Nuclear Weapons

T he superpower conflict was particularly dangerous because of the competition in nuclear weapons—the *arms race*—that accompanied it.

The field of nuclear energy emerged early in the twentieth century with Albert Einstein's theory of the interchangeability of matter and energy (see Chapter 19). In 1934, the Hungarian scientist Leo Szilard theorized about how to produce a nuclear chain reaction. In a nuclear chain reaction, a neutron escaping from an atomic nucleus strikes another atom, splitting it into lighter atoms. In the process, neutrons are released from the struck atom and, these neutrons split other atoms. Each splitting, or "fission," of atoms produces energy, such that a nuclear chain reaction generates a tremendous amount of energy.

During World War II, researchers sought ways to use nuclear energy militarily. On 2 December 1942, the first sustained nuclear chain reaction was carried out in a laboratory at the University of Chicago by a team of scientists led by Enrico Fermi (an anti-Fascist Italian scientist who had emigrated to the United States). This led to the creation of the Manhattan Project during the war, an American and British research effort that built the first atomic bomb (see Chapter 20). By the late 1940s, scientists were experimenting with nuclear "fusion," by which energy is released through the uniting of nuclei rather than through splitting. Fusion is used in the hydrogen bomb, a weapon so powerful that theoretically one could kill several million people.

Atomic Bomb Explosion *The atomic bombs dropped on Hiroshima and Nagasaki in 1945 killed about 200,000 people. The memory of those deaths has encouraged the superpowers to try to control the nuclear arms race, but the number of nuclear weapons in the world has grown enormously since 1945. (Smithsonian Institution)*

the deaths of two long-time dictators—the Portuguese Antonio Salazar in 1970, and the Spanish Francisco Franco in 1975.

Most of North America and Western Europe remained prosperous into the late 1980s. One sign of that prosperity was the large sums of money spent on spectator sports and other forms of entertainment like music and films. Another was the amount spent on illegal drugs, particularly in the urban areas of the United States. North Americans and Western Europeans hoped to sustain and even increase their prosperity. The members of the European Community planned to create a completely open Common Market among themselves in 1992 (see Chapter 21) and assumed that that action would strengthen their economies. Furthermore, Western Europe, the United States, and Canada were preparing to invest in and help rebuild the economies of the Eastern European countries that rebelled against communism in 1989 (as we will see later in the chapter).

THE COMMUNIST WORLD

The Soviet Union

The Communist nations also experienced significant economic and political changes during the 1970s and 1980s. For much of that time, the Soviet Union suffered from a stagnant economy, caused in part by the bureaucratic inefficiency of its centrally controlled economic system.

Glasnost and Perestroika   When Mikhail Gorbachev came to power in 1985, he sought to resolve the nation's economic problems and create an efficient, high-technology economy. His ongoing campaign for *glasnost* ("openness") and *perestroika* ("restructuring") is intended to open up the Soviet system, so that creativity and individual initiative can overcome bureaucratic lethargy and worker apathy. In practice, glasnost has meant more freedom for artists and writers and some choice for voters in elections. (The existence of some free elections, however, has not changed the fact that the Soviet Union is controlled by the Communist party.) Perestroika has meant imposing stricter discipline on factory workers in order to increase production while decreasing central control of the economy.

By the late 1980s, Gorbachev's campaign was being subjected to intense debate and questioning, particularly by some elements in the bureaucratic hierarchy who resisted his reforms. Furthermore, a coal miner's strike in 1989 and ethnic and nationalist tensions in the Baltic area and other regions of the Soviet Union threatened to create social upheaval. In 1990, three Baltic areas—Lithuania, Estonia, and Latvia—

Soviet Protests An estimated 170,000 people turned out for this pro-democracy demonstration in Moscow in 1989. Other demonstrations throughout the country followed, all indicative of the need for Soviet government reform. Subsequent to these protests, the politburo made significant changes in the Soviet constitution — including a statement that communism is no longer the official doctrine of the Soviet government. (AP/Wide World Photos)

began to seek independence from the Soviet Union. The Soviets are clearly engaged in a major political and economic experiment, the outcome of which may be unknown for some time.

Eastern Europe

The Eastern European nations were more prosperous in the 1960s and 1970s than in the years immediately after World War II. Hungary, for example, stressed production of consumer goods in pursuit of what was called "goulash communism." Czechoslovakia and East Germany enjoyed significant increases in per-capita income.

There were still problems, though. In 1968, a reformist group within the Czechoslovak Communist party tried to bring major political and economic changes to Czechoslovakia, but the Soviet Union sent in troops to quash what it saw as a rebellion against Soviet domination.

Then, economic difficulties in the late 1970s and early 1980s—high inflation and production declines—led to a political crisis in Poland. In 1980, the Solidarity trade union movement led by Lech Walesa engaged in a series of major strikes and protests against the Communist government. For a time, it seemed like the government would succeed in crushing Solidarity.

Events of 1989   By the late 1980s, economic difficulties and political repression produced popular unrest throughout Eastern Europe. Furthermore, Mikhail Gorbachev, the head of the Communist bloc, gradually made it clear that Soviet troops would no longer be used to destroy rebellions and reforms in Eastern Europe. The result was a series of extraordinary events throughout most of Eastern Europe in 1989.

In Poland in 1989, the Communist government collapsed, the Solidarity movement won parliamentary elections, and a non-Communist government was formed. In East Germany, reformers within the Communist party came to power and scheduled free elections for 1990. Furthermore, the Berlin Wall was torn down. It had been constructed by the communists in 1961 to separate East from West Berlin and thereby prevent East Germans from seeking a new home in West Germany. The opening of the Berlin Wall in 1989 not only allowed East Germans to travel freely but also led to much discussion about the possibility of future unification of East and West Germany. By 1990, unification seemed increasingly likely. In Czechoslovakia, popular protests led to the collapse of the Communist party there. A coalition government dominated by non-Communists developed, and playwright Vaclav Havel was elected president of Czechoslovakia. In addition, parliamentary elections were scheduled for 1990.

While Poland and Czechoslovakia were the only two Eastern European countries where non-Communist governments actually existed at the end of 1989, changes in other countries in that year signaled a general weakening of communism in Eastern Europe. In Hungary, the Communist party remained in power but only because it renounced Marxism as its official ideology and scheduled elections for 1990. In Bulgaria, the Communist party also continued in power but a growing pro-democracy popular movement encouraged the government to make some reforms and at least talk about holding elections. Finally, in Romania there occurred the most violent rebellion of 1989 in Eastern Europe. A popular uprising erupted against the tyrannical Communist dictator Nicolae Ceausescu, and he tried to crush it with force. Thousands died, but Ceausescu was overthrown and executed. The successor government scheduled elections for 1990.

The net effect of the extraordinary events of 1989 was that Communist control was disintegrating all over Eastern Europe. Eastern Europeans looked to the 1990s as a time of political, social, and economic

Lenin Statue Removed in Romania For over forty years, this statue of V. I. Lenin, the leader of the Communist revolution in Russia, dominated a public square in Bucharest, Romania. Removal of the statue in 1990 symbolized the end of Communist rule in Eastern Europe. (AP/ Wide World Photos)

reconstruction. A potential problem, though, was the possible resurgence of ethnic tensions, particularly anti-semitism, which have a long history in Eastern Europe.

China

Protests against the Communist regime were less successful in China. After Mao Zedong died in 1976, Deng Xiaoping became the dominant Chinese leader. He advocated an urban industrialization approach to modernization and encouraged economic development. The resulting economic changes gradually created political and social tensions in China.

In the spring of 1989, university students, particularly from Beijing University, launched massive demonstrations in which they demanded "democracy" in China. What they meant by "democracy" was unclear, but at a minimum it meant more freedom from the controls of the governmental bureaucracy. Deng Xiaoping and the uncompromising elements in the Communist party called out the army, and in June 1989 the Beijing protestors were crushed with many being killed. Deng and his supporters remained in control of China, but it was evident that there was significant opposition to them.

Thus, by the late 1980s, major reforms were being attempted in several Communist countries. It remains one of the most dramatic developments of the contemporary era.

THE THIRD WORLD

The nations of the world are often classified into three categories based on their prosperity. The *First World* includes the wealthy capitalist nations located mostly in North America and Western Europe but including Japan and Australia as well. The *Second World* covers the relatively prosperous Communist or ex-communist states—the Soviet Union and most of the Eastern European nations. The *Third World* designates virtually all the rest of the world—about one hundred countries in Asia, Africa, and Latin America that have roughly three-fourths of the world's population. Many Third World nations were a part of one of the European empires until after World War II, and most of them are poor.

In the mid-1980s, thirty-six Third World countries had an average annual Gross National Product (GNP) per person below $400, while about sixty others had a per-person GNP ranging up to $2,000. Table 22.1 gives the figures for some Third World countries as well as a few First World nations.

Life is a constant struggle for many people in Third World countries. In 1980, the World Bank reported:

**TABLE 22.1 AVERAGE ANNUAL GNP
PER PERSON 1986 ($U.S.)**

Ethiopia	$110
Zaire	140
China	310
Philippines	660
Nicaragua	860
Colombia	1,390
Brazil	1,720
Mexico	2,040
France	9,760
Japan	10,630
United States	15,390

Source: Data from *World Development Report, 1986* (New York: Oxford Univ. Press, 1986).

The [Third World] poor have other things in common, apart from their extremely low incomes. A disproportionate number of them— perhaps two in five—are children under ten, mainly in large families. More than three-quarters of them live in rural areas, the rest in urban slums—but almost all in very crowded conditions. . . .

As much as four-fifths of their income is consumed as food. The result is a monotonous, limited diet of cereals, yams or cassava— with a few vegetables and in some places a little fish or meat. Many of them are malnourished to the point where their ability to work hard is reduced, the physical and mental development of their children is impaired, and their resistance to infections is low. They are often sick—with tropical diseases, measles and diarrhea, and cuts and scratches that will not heal. Of every ten children born to poor parents, two die within a year; another dies before the age of five; only five survive to the age of 40.[1]

Chronic poverty exists in most Third World nations because of economic problems. The most important problem is food production. Although world food production per person has slowly increased in recent decades, the increase has not been distributed equitably. People in wealthy nations and the upper classes in poor nations consume a disproportionate amount of the world's food. The result is that large numbers of people in Third World nations suffer from malnutrition or protein deficiency. It is not known precisely how many people are chronically malnourished, but in 1986 the World Bank's estimation was between 340 and 730 million (excluding people in China). Most of these people live in two poverty belts—one extends across the middle of Africa, where droughts have caused famines; the other begins in Afghanistan and stretches eastward across South Asia (including Pakistan, India, and Bangladesh).

A fundamental reason for Third World poverty is the population explosion of the twentieth century. World population has grown as the death rate has declined, primarily because of advances in disease prevention. Malaria, for example, has been eradicated in many places through the use of insecticides that kill the disease-carrying mosquitoes. As a result total population growth has accelerated, as Table 22.2 shows.

In the mid-1980s, Asia was the most populous region in the world, while sub-Saharan Africa had the greatest difficulty feeding a growing

TABLE 22.2 WORLD POPULATION GROWTH, A.D. 1–1989

A.D. 1	250 million
1650	500 million
1850	1 billion
1930	2 billion
1986	4.8 billion
1989	5.2 billion (est.)

Woman and Starving Baby in Africa   While most Western nations became increasingly wealthier during the twentieth century, many people in Third World nations, particularly those in Africa, experienced desperate poverty and even famine. (United Nations)

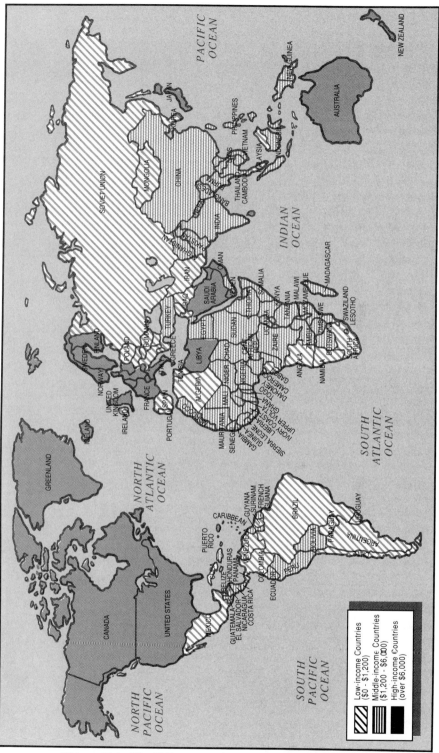

Figure 22.1 World Estimated Gross National Product and
Per Capita Income Levels, mid-1980s

population. A Third World nation with a large population faces several problems. One is sanitation, particularly providing clean water in urban slum areas. Another is housing. Many families, especially in large cities, live in ramshackle huts or even tents. A third problem is education. Many children are prevented from attending school because their families need them to earn supplementary income.

Third World nations have increasingly requested, and even demanded, that wealthy countries help them carry out economic development programs. And, to some degree, the wealthy nations have responded through international institutions such as the World Bank and the International Monetary Fund, which they finance so economic assistance can be given to the poor nations. In the 1970s, however, Third World nations demanded more. In 1974, at a special session of the United Nations General Assembly, a plan for a New International Economic Order (NIEO) was drawn. Designed to create economic equality among the nations of the world, NIEO would require wealthy nations to transfer technology to Third World countries so to allow them greater control over their own natural resources. However, NIEO was never implemented, in part because some wealthy nations refused to cooperate.

By the 1980s, some Third World countries—such as Singapore and South Korea—were achieving significant economic growth. Most remained mired in poverty. And, in some Third World nations, political conflict further hindered economic development and made life even more difficult for people. Civil wars brought chaos to Lebanon in the Middle East, to El Salvador in Central America, and to Angola in southern Africa. The Iran-Iraq War (1980–1988) caused much death and destruction in the Persian Gulf area. Perhaps most unfortunate of all was the conflict in Kampuchea (Cambodia), a nation in Southeast Asia dominated in the late 1970s by a Communist regime led by Pol Pot. Approximately one million Cambodians allegedly unsympathetic to Pol Pot's government were murdered by his forces. Although Pol Pot was overthrown when the Vietnamese invaded Cambodia in 1979, the nation's future has remained uncertain since the Vietnamese withdrew late in 1989.

One source of hope for some Third World countries was the Green Revolution that emerged in the 1960s. Agricultural advances resulting from discoveries in plant genetics enabled farmers to increase their production of tropical wheat, rice, and grains. In India, food production doubled from the 1960s to the 1980s, and in Java increased rice production led to a dramatic improvement in the standard of living. The Green Revolution was not a worldwide phenomenon, however. It was successful in only those areas with adequate soil moisture. Further, because it required some capital investment, only the wealthier farmers benefited.

RELIGION

Various religious beliefs continue to motivate large numbers of people in the contemporary world. Among those that gained influence during the recent decades are Protestant evangelicalism, Roman Catholicism, and Islam. In addition, the modern world continues to be influenced by a belief in the secular idea of progress.

In the United States and to a lesser degree in Western Europe, evangelical Christianity grew rapidly in the 1970s and 1980s. *Evangelicalism* is a theologically conservative form of Protestantism that emphasizes salvation through faith and preaching, or "evangelizing", rather than through more formal worship rituals. The appeal of evangelicalism is that it offers emotional comfort and spiritual security to people living in a turbulent world. In the United States, ministers like Pat Robertson and Jerry Falwell have popularized evangelicalism through the medium of television.

Another example of modern-day religious strength is the intellectual and spiritual renewal of Roman Catholicism. The process of renewal began with the papacy of John XXIII (1958–1963), who called the Second Vatican Council or Vatican II (1962–1965) into session. Vatican II gave Catholic intellectuals more freedom to debate intellectual matters, offered Catholic bishops and clergy a more active role in the governance of the church, and initiated a program of increased cooperation with other branches of Christianity as well as with non-Christian religions. One result of Vatican II was to reinvigorate the entire Roman Catholic church. Another result, particularly in Latin America, was the development of *liberation theology*—the idea that Christianity should aim to liberate people not only from spiritual sin but from economic poverty as well. Thus, in many parts of Latin America, Catholic priests have spoken out on behalf of the poor and oppressed.

Yet another example of religious vigor in the contemporary world is the revival of Islam in many parts of the world. Islamic fundamentalists in Iran, Libya, and elsewhere believe that the consumer-oriented societies of the West are excessively hedonistic and materialistic. The fundamentalists emphasize strict adherence to the rules and rituals upheld by Islam over the centuries. Some of them engage in terrorist acts against Western people, examples being the 1979 taking of American hostages in Iran and more recently the kidnapping of various people in Lebanon.

In addition to these and other traditional forms of religion, the secular idea of progress has also influenced many people of the contemporary world. Belief in progress includes, for example, faith in technological advancement, in that increased human knowledge will lead

Islamic Fundamentalism   After Islamic fundamentalists, led by the Ayatollah Khomeini, came to power in Iran in 1979, they applied highly conservative interpretations of Islamic doctrines to all aspects of Iranian society. Shown here are several blindfolded women being arrested for defying some Islamic law (perhaps for uncovering their faces in public). Many Iranians—men and women alike—were executed by the Islamic fundamentalists for similar reasons. (Abbas/Magnum)

to a better, happier future. The belief in progress is particularly appealing to the lower classes in many parts of the world. It provides hope for many Third World peoples and inspires revolutionary movements for change. It is also a basic belief of virtually every developed society, many of which idolize economic growth.

THE THIRD INDUSTRIAL REVOLUTION

During the latter half of the twentieth century, the Third Industrial Revolution emerged in Western Civilization and continues to develop today as a result of technological advances in three fields. In the physical sciences, there have been advances in nuclear energy and in space exploration. In the biological sciences, the most important discoveries have been in genetics and medicine. And in the communications and information spheres, major breakthroughs include the computer and mass telecommunications media.

Physical Science

The field of nuclear energy originated with the work of Albert Einstein, Max Planck, and others, who provided the groundwork that later scientists would use to learn how to create a nuclear chain reaction and the nuclear bomb. Nuclear physics also led to the development of laser technology. The word *laser* is an acronym for "light amplification by stimulated emission of radiation." Thus, a laser is intense, concentrated light derived from radiation energy that shines at a single wavelength. By the 1980s, lasers were being used in many applications, including conducting delicate eye surgery, cutting and welding steel, transmitting digital information and telephone conversations, and producing light shows at rock concerts.

The space age began in 1957 with the Soviet launch of *Sputnik*, the first satellite. By the 1960s, the Soviets and Americans were competing in space exploration. The United States sent men to the moon in 1969, and both used spy satellites for military purposes. In the 1970s, both nations put space stations and communications satellites in orbit, and the Western Europeans launched their own satellites. By the 1980s, however, economic problems hindered both the Soviet and American space programs.

Biological Science

In the biological sciences, the most important developments have occurred in genetics. Around 1865, Gregor Mendel discovered the basic principles of heredity, although his work remained essentially unknown until 1900. By the early twentieth century, scientists learned that *genes*, the basic units of inheritance, are located on long, microscopic bodies called *chromosomes*, present in every living cell. By the 1950s, continued research showed that chromosomes are composed primarily of deoxyribonucleic acid (DNA). In 1953, James D. Watson and Francis H. C. Crick, supported by the work of Rosalind Franklin, explained the structure of DNA.

This series of discoveries led to increased knowledge of genetics during the 1960s, and 1970s, and by the 1980s geneticists were beginning to understand the components of the genetic code, how genes "work." The new knowledge not only enabled scientists to start understanding how life begins but it also had many practical results. New drugs and chemicals were produced. The Green Revolution resulted from advances in plant genetics. And progress was made in the prevention and treatment of diseases caused by genetic disorders, such as sickle-cell anemia and Down's syndrome.

Advances in medicine also produced enormous benefits. The development of penicillin and other antibiotics helped control many infectious and previously fatal diseases. Vaccines were developed to prevent measles, smallpox, and polio. By the 1970s, some organ transplants were being carried out with limited success, and in a few instances babies were conceived outside the womb. By the late 1980s, an artificial heart had been created and used with some success, laser surgery was increasingly practical, and some types of cancer were being treated with some success.

The Computer and Telecommunications

The computer may well be the most significant development of the late twentieth century. The first real electronic computer, a very large machine, was produced in 1946 by Drs. John Mauchly and J. P. Eckert of the University of Pennsylvania. With the invention of the transistor, computer circuits could be miniaturized, and by the early 1970s hundreds of thousands of electronic circuits were being printed on a silicon chip the size of a child's fingernail. The result was the invention of the microcomputer, a small, inexpensive machine that can be programmed to perform a variety of tasks. By the 1980s, computers were being used to handle routine paperwork, to manage business inventories, to track down criminals, to guide humans into outer space, and to direct communications satellites. Computerized robots were also beginning to perform many routine jobs in factories.

Mass telecommunications media—television and radio—were also having a major impact on Western societies. The first experimental televisions were developed in the 1930s, and by the 1970s television was in use in most of the countries of the world. Communications satellites transmitted news and other live broadcasts from all over the world. In Western nations, television became a dominant form of leisure activity, and it also affected politics by dramatizing important political and social issues.

The Third Industrial Revolution has also made wealthy nations even more powerful and prosperous than ever before. Japan, in particular, has profited in this way as a result of the revolution. The Japanese became rich by trading with the United States and many Asian nations and by investing their profits in those areas as well as in Africa and Latin America. By the late 1980s, Japan was an economic superpower.

CONCLUSION

The Third Industrial Revolution is a reminder of a continuing theme in the history of Western Civilization—the influence of technology. More than any other civilization, the West has emphasized the importance of technological development. It has also used technology in ways both good and bad. As Western Civilization looks to the twenty-first century, technology is at the center of one of the most important issues in human history: Will we use technology to feed the hungry, to help the oppressed, and to create a better way of life for more people? Or, will we use technology in ways that may lead to nuclear war, environmental disaster, and the ultimate destruction of the world and ourselves?

THINGS YOU SHOULD KNOW

Détente
Sino-Soviet split
Cuban Missile Crisis
Vietnam War
SALT I
Reagan
Strategic Defense Initiative (SDI)
Civil rights movement
Student protests of the 1960s
Feminist movement
Environmental movement
Gorbachev
Glasnost and *perestroika*

Political changes in Eastern Europe
  in 1989
Deng Xiaoping
Student protests in China
Third World countries
World population explosion
NIEO
Evangelicalism
Vatican II
Islamic fundamentalism
The belief in progress
Third Industrial Revolution

SUGGESTED READINGS

For the reformist ideas proposed by the new Soviet leader, see Mikhail Gorbachev, *Perestroika: New Thinking for Our Country and the World* (New York: Harper & Row, 1987). H. Stuart Hughes, *Sophisticated Rebels: The Political Culture of European Dissent, 1968–1987* (Cambridge, Mass.: Harvard Univ. Press, 1988) is interesting on some of the European dissenting movements, such as the Solidarity trade union movement in Poland. Two memoirs by prominent Eastern European dissidents are Lech Walesa, *Way of Hope: An Autobiography* (New York: Henry Holt and Co., 1987) and Ludvik Vaculik, *Cup of Coffee with My Interrogator: The Prague Chronicles of Ludvik Vaculik* (Columbia, Louis.: Reader's International, 1987).

An entertaining, anecdotal work on the social upheavals of the 1960s is Godfrey Hodgson, *America in Our Time* (Garden City, N.Y.: Doubleday, 1976). For a good introduction to contemporary environmental problems, see Garrett Hardin, *Exploring New Ethics for Survival: The Voyage of the Spaceship Beagle* (Baltimore: Penguin, 1972). On the feminist movement, see Lynne B. Iglitzin and Ruth Ross, eds., *Women in the World: A Comparative Study* (Santa Barbara, Calif.: Clio, 1976).

A delightful, easy-to-read introduction to life in the Third World is Richard Critchfield, *Villages* (Garden City, N.Y.: Doubleday, 1981). More systematic but still good is Paul Harrison, *Inside the Third World* (New York: Penguin, 1979).

John T. Hardy, *Science, Technology and the Environment* (Philadelphia: Saunders, 1975) provides a comprehensible explanation of the major breakthroughs made by scientists in recent decades. Stephen W. Hawking, *A Brief History of Time* (New York: Bantam, 1988) is an impressive work by one of the most brilliant living physicists. (See also related works listed in the Suggested Readings for Chapter 21.)

NOTES

[1]World Bank, *World Development Report, 1980* (New York: Oxford Univ. Press, 1980), p. 33.

Index

Rodney, Walter, 306–7
Roman Catholic Church, 128, 168
  abuses in, leading to reformation,
    250–51
  anticlericalism in, 249, 289
  Avignon papacy, 248–49
  and Babylonian Captivity, 248
  for the common people, 170–71
  contributions of monks and nuns,
    141–44
  and Council of Trent, 255
  and Crusades, 128–29, 156, 174,
    176, 183–84, 327
  in England, 176
  establishment of Society of Mis-
    sionaries by, 431
  and French Revolution, 354
  and Great Schism, 249
  and inquisition, 169, 282
  and investiture controversy, 179–80
  and liberation theology, 549
  Monasticism, 170
  papacy, 168–69
  and the *Pax Ecclesiae*, 156–57
  and reactions to calamities, 224
  and the Reformation, 254–55
  Romanesque and Gothic architec-
    ture, 171–74
  significance of medieval political
    history, 182
  and social catholism, 390–91
  and status of women, 186
  Syllabus of Errors (Pius IX), 390
  and Vatican II, 549
Roman civilization
  Christianity in, 104–9, 1100
  conquest of Italy, 93–94
  decline of empire, 116
  early history of, 90–91
  empire, 98–100, 102–4
  end of the republic, 96–98
  first-century emperors, 102–3
  five good emperors, 103–4
  grandeur and degradation of Ro-
    man society, 100, 102
  impact of Roman conquests on,
    94–96
  laws in, 100, 102
  Pax Romana in, 98
  philosophy in, 94
  political transformation of Empire,
    109–10
  Punic Wars, 94
  religion in, 94

republic, 91–94
roads in, 101
slaves in, 102
spiritual transformation of the Em-
  pire, 111–12
teachings of Jesus in, 104
Western Europe after fall of, 121–
  23
women in, 100
Romania, changes in, 542
Romanov, Michael, 300–1
Romanticism, 383–87
Rome (city), 419–20
Romulus, 90
Romulus Augustus, 121
Rond, Jean Le, 289
Roosevelt, Franklin D., 483, 485, 486,
  499
Roosevelt, Theodore, 454
Roses, War of, 223, 257
Roundheads, 263
Rousseau, Jean-Jacques, 287-88, 290,
  399
Rubens, Peter Paul, 255
Ruhr occupation, 482, 484
Rumania, communism in, 510
Runnymede, 177
Russia. *See also* Soviet Union
  abdication of Nicholas II, 467
  under Alexander I, 420
  under Alexander II, 421–22
  under Boris Godunov, 300
  under Catherine II, 302–3
  civil war in, 471–72
  and Crimean War, 421
  European influence on, 302–3
  and expansion into Siberia, 300–2
  foreign invasions of, 296, 297, 301
  geography of, 296
  industrialization in, 373, 422
  influence on Byzantium on, 297,
    298
  under Ivan III, 298
  under Ivan IV, 298, 300
  Kievan Russia, 297
  under Lenin, 467–69
  literature in, 303
  under Michael Romanov, 300–1
  Napoleon in, 358
  under Nicholas II, 451
  under Nicholas I, 420–21
  1905 revolution in, 451
  1917 revolution in, 467–69
  and origins of World War I, 461